The Sleeter Group's

QuickBooks® Consultant's Reference Guide

How to Set Up, Troubleshoot and Support

QuickBooks and QuickBooks Enterprise Solutions

For QuickBooks Version 2015 and

QuickBooks Enterprise Solutions Version 15

Copyright © 2015

The Sleeter Group, Inc.

Website: www.sleeter.com

Email: info@sleeter.com

888-484-5484

| Printed Book | 978-1-942417-08-8 |

Developed and   Douglas Sleeter
Written By

Additional   Pat Carson, Esther Friedberg Karp, Bonnie Nagayama, Mario Nowogrodzki,
Contributors   Deborah Pembrook, Charlie Russell and Chuck Vigeant.

Thanks To   Nathan Fochler, Joy Prado, and especially Sherrill Sleeter.

Table of Contents

How to Use This Book

Thank you for purchasing this book and we hope you find it useful. It is intended for Accountants and Consultants who help clients with QuickBooks, and for power users who want to learn advanced topics to streamline the accounting processes.

Most of what you find in this book cannot be found in the QuickBooks manual or on-line help or anywhere else. All the recommendations are based on years of experience helping thousands of clients with QuickBooks. The book is not a tutorial on how to use QuickBooks, but rather it is intended as a reference guide for Consultants and Accountants who work with several different types of clients. Throughout the book, you'll find troubleshooting techniques designed to help you diagnose and fix problem situations. You'll also find instructions for how you can help your clients use QuickBooks, **completely**. That is, not just in utilizing the general ledger, but for detailed tracking of customers, vendors, sales items, job costs, and payroll. You'll be able to help your clients do proper bookkeeping **and** organize information that is required by management to make informed business decisions.

The 2015 edition of this book contains several significant changes. Of course, we have a chapter focusing on all the New Features with QuickBooks 2015 and have made significant updates throughout the book to make it as current as possible.

Intuit sells several **editions** of QuickBooks: the **Pro** edition; the **Premier** edition (sold in several different industry-specific editions); and the **Enterprise Solutions** edition. The information in this guide is relevant to *all* of these editions, but most of the examples are shown using QuickBooks Accountant since that is what most consultants use. Enterprise Accountant edition is covered in detail where it differs from Premier. Intuit also has a product called QuickBooks Online, which has many differences with the desktop version. Some of the material in this book is relevant to the Online edition.

In this guide, we refer to two different fictitious companies called Academy Glass, a window replacement company and Academy Photography, a photography studio. These sample companies might not be exactly like your clients' businesses, but you'll see how QuickBooks can work for several companies by seeing how it works for these sample companies.

WE NEED YOUR HELP! In order to produce an accurate and helpful reference book, we need your feedback and your bug reports. If you find anything in this book that needs clarification or fixing, please let us know. Please email helpdesk@sleeter.com with your specific suggestions.

Acknowledgements

I'd like to extend my heartfelt thanks to the co-authors, consultants, copy editors and contributors. The team includes my good friends Pat Carson, Esther Friedberg Karp, Bonnie Nagayama, Mario Nowogrodzki, Deborah Pembrook, Charlie Russell, and Chuck Vigeant

We hope the information in this book helps you succeed in your practice.

Douglas Sleeter

May 2015

Chapter 1
New Features for
QuickBooks 2015

QuickBooks 2015 and QuickBooks Enterprise Solutions 15.0 include a variety of new features, as well as a number of significant improvements to existing features. Some of these features will assist accounting professionals in managing their clients' files. Others will help your clients to be more efficient.

It is impossible to list EVERY change that Intuit has implemented, and even Intuit can't supply a list of all of the changes. We'll list the more noticeable changes, and go into detail on the ones that are significant.

Overview of New Features and Improvements

New and Improved in QuickBooks Pro, Premier & Enterprise

The following features have been added or improved in all of the Windows desktop versions of QuickBooks.

- Insights analytics is added
- QuickBooks Payments replaces Intuit PaymentNetwork
- Report presentation has been overhauled
- Income Tracker has a new time and expenses tab
- Pinned Notes has been added
- Flags are added to Billable Time and Costs
- Comments on Reports is a new feature
- Send Multiple Reports is a new option
- Send Portable Company File is an updated feature
- Accountant Toolbox has been added for use by accountant users
- And a variety of other smaller changes

New and Improved Features in QuickBooks Enterprise

These features have been added or improved in QuickBooks Enterprise edition.

- Hide Opening Balance fields is a new preference
- Don't Sell to Overdue Customers is a new preference
- Transaction form changes
  - Sorting columns on forms

- Total columns on forms
- Footer on last page
- Show *Cost* on sales forms
- Search on transactions
- Shaded lines on transaction forms
- Inventory changes
  - Don't Allow Negative Quantities preference
  - New report, Negative item listing
  - Shortage reports is a new feature
  - Several Inventory Stock Status Report improvements
- Advanced Reporting is a major new feature

New and Improved Features in Accountant and Enterprise Accountant

Intuit has created two special versions of QuickBooks for accountants, QuickBooks Accountant (equivalent to Premier) and Enterprise Accountant. This year there are no additional changes in these editions. However, there is an accountant-oriented feature in all versions, the Accountant Toolbox.

New and Improved Features in QuickBooks for Mac

A number of improvements have been added to QuickBooks for Mac 2015.

- Expense Tracker has been added
- A Budgets feature is added
- Batch import transactions has been added
- You can now attach documents

New and Improved in QuickBooks Pro, Premier & Enterprise

Insights

Insights is a new dashboard option that Intuit introduced in QuickBooks 2015. This is, to a degree, a replacement for the *Company Snapshot* feature (which is still available), based on research that Intuit did on what features of the *Company Snapshot* people were using the most. In addition, Intuit wanted a more up-to-date looking user interface. Note that this version is available in QuickBooks Pro, Premier, Accountant and Enterprise Solutions.

You can find this as a tab on the *Home Page*.

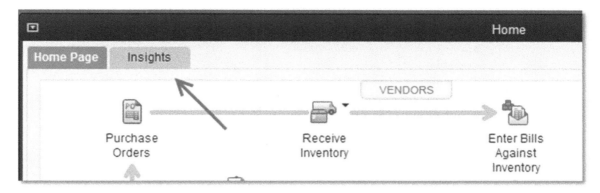

Figure 1-1 Insights Tab on Home Page

Here's what you see – note that this can be configured (somewhat) using the gear icon at the upper right. You also can add your company logo at the upper left.

Figure 1-2 Insights

The new *Insights* feature has fewer options than you have in the older *Company Snapshots* feature, but the appearance is cleaner and easier to read, you can print it all as one report, and you have more options to interact with the program. This is a more modern looking "dashboard" view of your company's financial picture.

In the upper right corner you have options to print the entire Insights dashboard, refresh the information, and configure the "carousel" of rotating graphs at the top. The carousel only has four optional graphs, you can choose which to include.

Figure 1-3 Insights options

The carousel is the top portion of the Insights page. You can rotate through them by clicking on the arrows on either edge. The next figure shows the *Profit & Loss* graph.

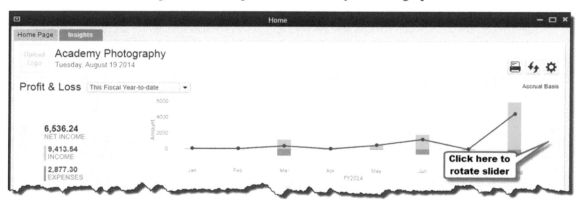

Figure 1-4 Insights Profit & Loss Graph

Here's the *Prev Year Income Comparison* graph.

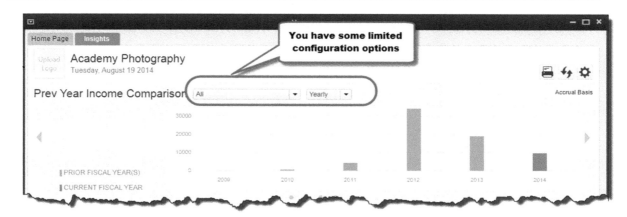

Figure 1-5 Insights Prev Year Income Comparison

Here's the *Top Customers by Sales* graph.

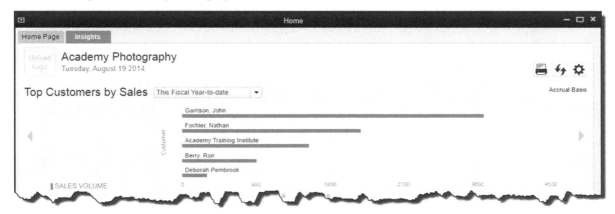

Figure 1-6 Insights Top Customers by Sales

And here's the *Income and Expense Trend* graph.

Figure 1-7 Insights Income and Expense Trend

Note that you can click on the graphs to see a supporting report, usually. You may get a customized *custom transaction detail* report, for example, or a *profit and loss detail* report. Each graph has an associated report, and in some cases even some details in a graph will have a report. For example, click on a particular customer in the *Top Customers by Sales* report and you get a *Sales by Customer Detail* report for that customer.

These are the only four graphs that you can show in the carousel area. Below this you see two additional charts, for *Income and Expenses.*

Figure 1-8 Additional Insights graphs for Income and Expenses

These graphs are interactive in several ways:

- Hover the mouse over a section of the expenses graph and you'll see a popup with details.
- There are links for *create invoice* and *create bill* that will open those transaction windows.
- If you click on a report element you will be taken to the *Income Tracker* (from the "Income" graph) or you will be shown a report, such as a customized *custom transaction detail* report.

QuickBooks Payments

For a number of years we've had multiple payment solutions from Intuit, which can be confusing: Intuit Merchant Services, Intuit Billing Solutions, Intuit PaymentNetwork, Intuit GoPayment, and more. It was difficult to know which one to use, and to manage them all. Intuit recognized this confusion and has created one consolidated payments account, which is called **QuickBooks Payments**. This encompasses many of the features of the prior accounts (but not all) and is the main payments system for QuickBooks.

Merchant rate fees will vary depending on your situation.

Note that this feature was introduced in the R5 revision of QuickBooks 2015, so you won't see it if you are running an older revision.

Also note that this feature is evolving rapidly as Intuit expands it and corrects problems based on customer feedback, so there may be differences between what is shown here and what you see in the product.

Connecting your QuickBooks company file to the new QuickBooks Payments account is done in several different ways depending on several factors:

- **If you already have a payment account and were using it in a prior version of QuickBooks,** then your account should automatically get converted to a QuickBooks Payments account when you open your file with QuickBooks 2015 with the R5 update.

In some cases it will be the same account you used before, if you only had an Intuit PaymentNetwork account then that will be converted to a new payments account. This should happen automatically and seamlessly – but if it can't be converted for some reason then a phone number is displayed to connect you with someone who can help.

- **If you already have a payment account with Intuit but have NOT used it in QuickBooks** then use the **Link Payment Service to Company File** option in the *Customers* menu. This will take you through a process that will connect your account to your company file.

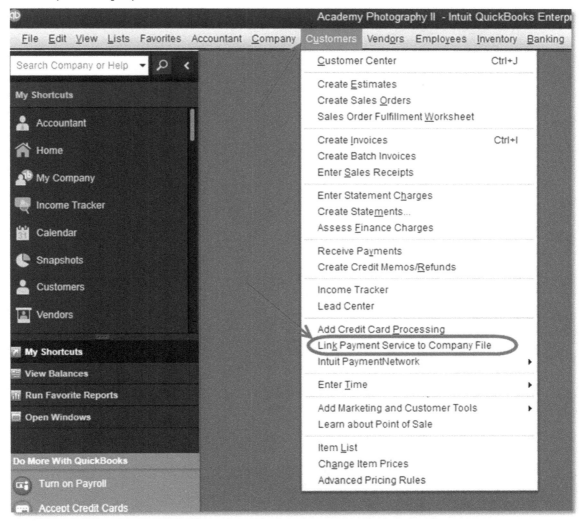

Figure 1-9 Linking QuickBooks Payments

You also can link your payment account if you try to check the *Process payment* box in a sales receipt.

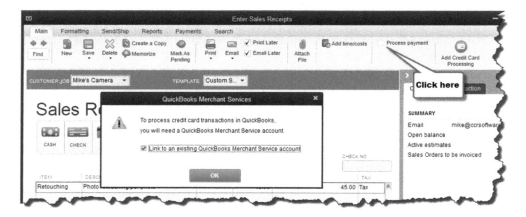

Figure 1-10 Linking from a Sales Receipt

- **If you don't have a payment account, and you are NOT a ProAdvisor** then you can turn this feature on through *Preferences*.

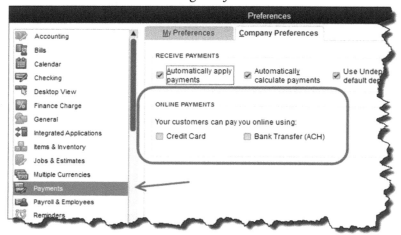

Figure 1-11 Online Payments Preferences

Click either of the check boxes in the *Payments* preferences and you will be taken to a website that lets you quickly set up a new QuickBooks Payments account.

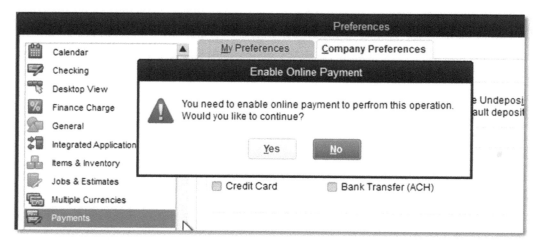

Figure 1-12 Enable Online Payment

- **If you don't have a payment account, and you ARE a ProAdvisor**, accessing this through your QuickBooks Accountant edition of the program, when you go to the *Preferences* window as shown above you will be directed to a page that shows you the rates, but doesn't let you sign up. Instead there is a phone number that you must call to set up your account. This is necessary to make sure that you get your special discounted rate.

E-invoicing with QuickBooks Payments

Let's take a quick look at how the new payment system works.

Here's an invoice, note that you now have a payments icon in the lower left.

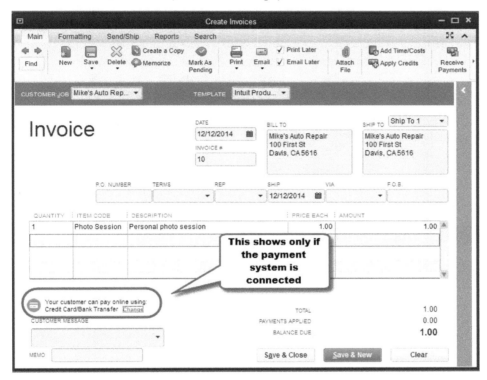

Figure 1-13 Invoice with QuickBooks Payments enabled

You can accept payments by credit card and bank ACH transaction. There are times when you want to restrict which method the customer uses. This can be controlled in three places:

- In the **Payments Preferences** – you have check boxes to choose which methods are allowed overall.
- In the **Payment Settings tab** of the customer record – you can restrict which method is available for an individual customer.
- In the **Invoice Options** window for the individual invoice, as shown below – you can restrict which method is available in an individual invoice.

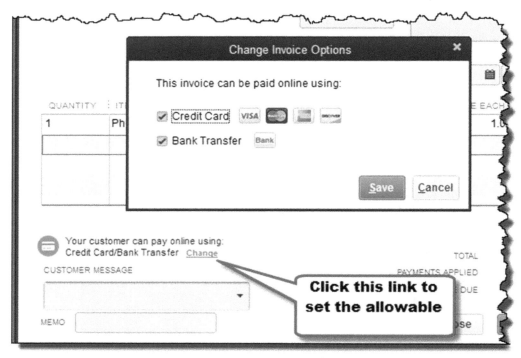

Figure 1-14 Changing payment options in an invoice

When you click the *Email* icon in the invoice to send it, the *Send Invoice* window opens (as before). The icons at the bottom show you which options are available to the customer.

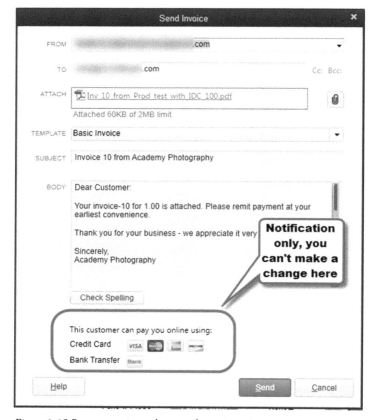

Figure 1-15 Payment options when emailing an invoice

Here is an example of the invoice that the customer receives.

Figure 1-16 Customer invoice notification

The invoice was attached to the email as a PDF, but there is no link information added to that form, unlike what we had with Intuit PaymentNetwork before. The only payment link is the button in the email.

When the customer clicks on the **View & Pay Invoice** button it takes them to a branded portal. They get to this very quickly, no sign in or credential entry is necessary.

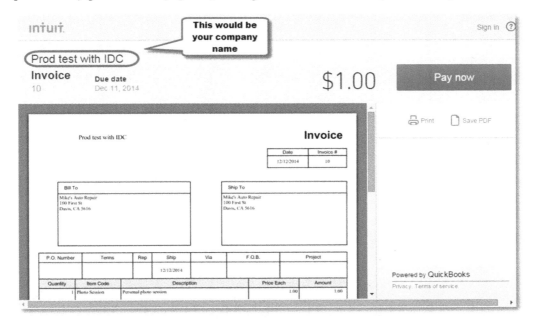

Figure 1-17 Invoice as viewed by customer online

Note the *Sign In* link in the upper right? If the user has an Intuit ID, or wishes to create one at this time, their payment information (credit card number, bank info, etc.) is recorded so that the next time they come to pay an invoice they don't have to retype all of the information.

Click **Pay Now** to enter the payment information.

Figure 1-18 Payment information entered by customer

Click *Next* to get a review and pay screen, which is not shown here.

After you approve the payment the *Payment sent* summary is displayed. Clicking *Print Receipt* will print just what you see here.

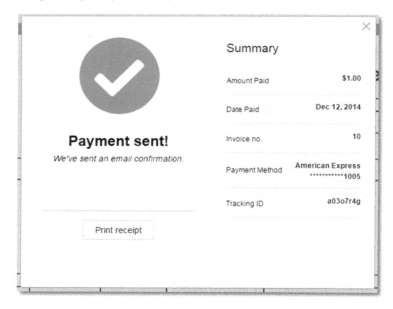

Figure 1-19 Payment summary

A copy of the receipt is emailed to the customer.

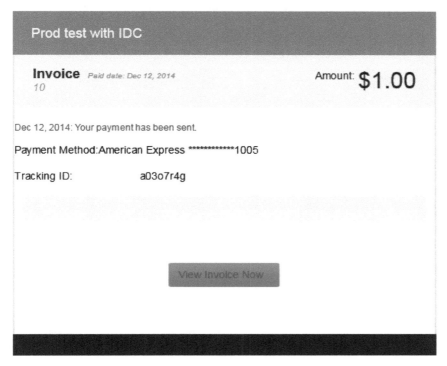

Figure 1-20 Payment receipt sent by email

If the customer clicks on the *View Invoice Now* button, they are taken to the payment website where they can see that the balance due is $0.00 and the invoice is marked as paid.

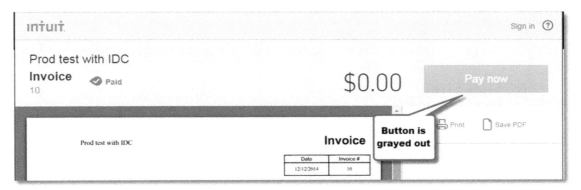

Figure 1-21 Fully paid invoice

Note that if you use a *sales receipt* instead of an invoice you have to check the *Process payment* box at the top, and then click on the appropriate payment icon. The workflow for processing a payment in a sales receipt is the same as for processing a payment that is being entered separately.

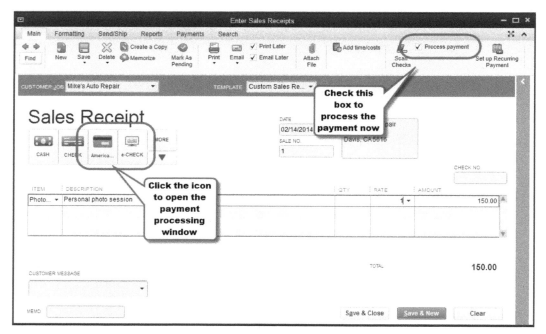

Figure 1-22 Payments in a Sales Receipt

Payments Entered Directly in QuickBooks

What if the customer doesn't want to enter a payment in the portal, but instead calls you with a credit card? No surprise, use the *Receive Payments* window in QuickBooks. However, to use the QuickBooks Payments system you must have the *Process payment* box checked.

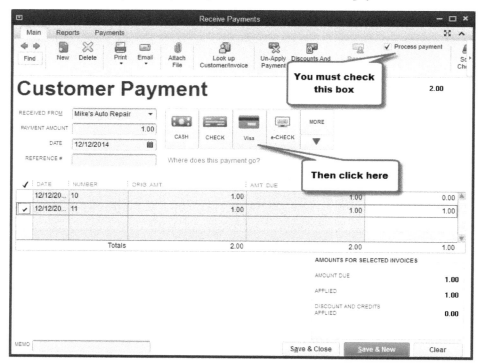

Figure 1-23 Receiving a Customer Payment

When you click the credit card icon the following window opens. You have options for commercial cards, voice authorization codes, and a credit card swiper.

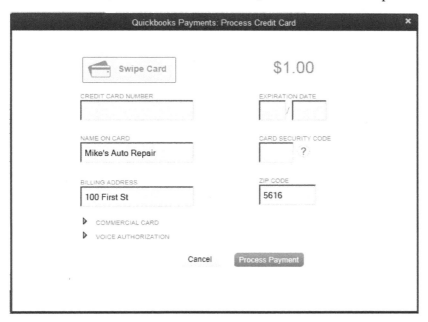

Figure 1-24 Processing a Credit Card payment

The *Swipe Card* button only fully works with card readers purchased from Intuit.

Once you click *Process Payment* the confirmation window opens to show you the transaction information.

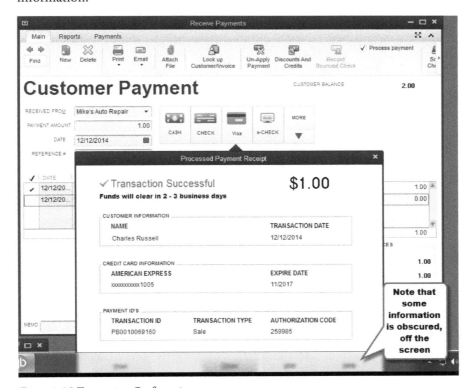

Figure 1-25 Transaction Confirmation

Merchant Account Reconciliation

Now that you have invoiced the customer and they have submitted payment, you have to reconcile the merchant account with QuickBooks.

To see your payments and reconcile with your account select the **Make Merchant Service Deposits** option in the *Banking* menu.

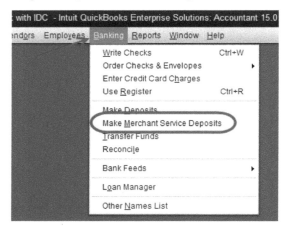

Figure 1-26 Merchant Deposits menu

This opens a window that shows you the bank activity for your merchant account.

Figure 1-27 Merchant Account bank activity

Note the colored bar, similar to what we've seen in the *Income Tracker*. You can use these to view different kinds of transactions.

- **Unmatched** are transactions that can't be automatically matched by QuickBooks.
- **Matched & Recorded** lists payments that were matched with QuickBooks transactions automatically. You hope to see most fall in that category. Note that if you manually match an "unmatched" transaction it is added to this tab.

- **Bank Activity** provides a view of the lump deposits indicated in your bank statement along with the applied fees.
- **Pending** shows transactions that are new but haven't been funded through the payments system.

Here's a look at the *Unmatched* transactions.

Figure 1-28 Unmatched Transactions

Clicking the **Apply Payment** button will open the *Customer Payment* window, and you can select the invoice to apply this payment to from the list of transactions for the specified customer. Note that once you click this button the payment is recorded, you **cannot back out from this window.** Once you click it something will be recorded, whether you have a match or not. If the customer listed in the deposits window doesn't exist in your customer file, **that customer will automatically be added** and an open payment record is saved. I'm not sure if I like this?

You can't drill down to the transactions from this window. It would be really nice to have the option to see the invoice, for example, in the *Matched & Recorded* tab.

Improvements to Reports

There are a number of changes that relate to Reports in QuickBooks.

Report Appearance Changes

When you look at a report *on the screen* in QuickBooks it can be difficult to interpret what you see. It is hard to follow a line of information horizontally, for example. Intuit has taken some time to review report appearance on screen and has come up with some improvements to make reports easier to understand.

To start, let's take a look at a typical report in **QuickBooks 2014:**

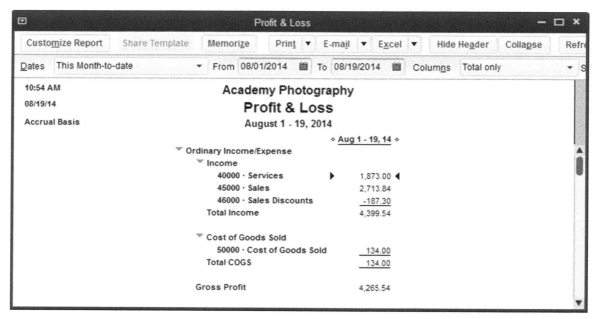

Figure 1-29 QuickBooks 2014 report example

Now let's look at the same report in **QuickBooks 2015**.

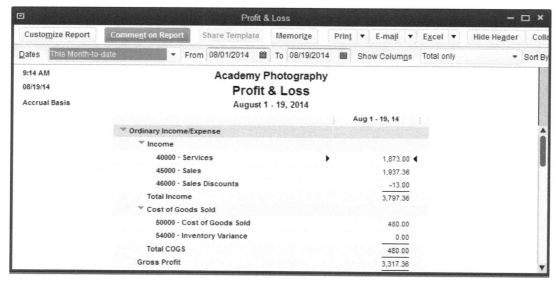

Figure 1-30 QuickBooks 2015 report example

The changes are:

- The use of background shading to highlight some levels of titles, when you have an indented report.

- The use of both vertical and horizontal lines to make detail lines and columns stand out better, and easier to follow.

- A slight increase in vertical spacing, so reports don't seem to be as crowded

- The "drag bars" that you use to adjust the horizontal spacing of columns have been changed to a symbol that is a bit easier to understand

Report Filters Sorted Alphabetically and are Searchable

When you *customize* a report, the fields in the *Filter* box are now sorted alphabetically, which is a really nice improvement. In addition, there is a *search filters* box, you can just start typing in the name of the filter and the list will show what you are looking for.

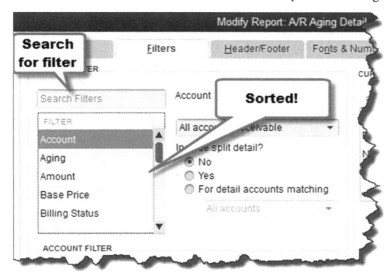

Figure 1-31 Improvements to Report Filters

Filter Inactive/Active Names on Name-Based Reports

Reports where a customer or vendor *name* is the primary key, like a *Customer Balance Detail* report, now have a filter where you can select all active or inactive names.

Select *Name* in the filter list, then the key name value for that report (such as "all customers/jobs" if it is a customer-oriented report) and you will see *Active Status* as a new option.

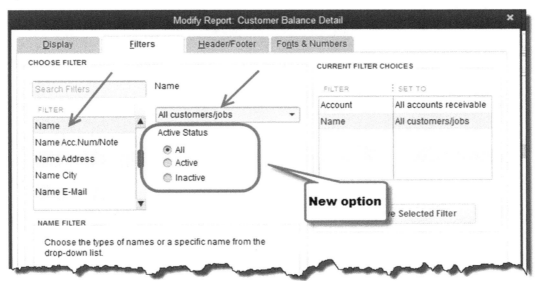

Figure 1-32 Name report option

Note that this isn't available in all reports. For example, while the *customer balance detail* report (as shown above) has this option, the *customer balance summary* does not. It looks like it is only found in "transaction detail" reports directly related to the customer and vendor lists.

Adding Other 1 and Other 2 to Reports

You can add two fields as columns in sales and purchasing transactions called "Other 1" and "Other 2". These were the only "user definable" fields that we had before Intuit added custom fields to QuickBooks. The drawback to these fields has always been that they cannot be added to reports. With this revision, Intuit has added these to the list of fields you can add in transaction detail reports, as well as allowing you to filter the report by these fields.

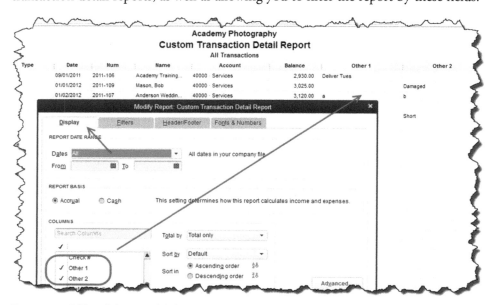

Figure 1-33 Adding Other 1 and Other 2 to transaction reports

Preferred Delivery Method

The *Preferred Delivery Method* is now available as a column on some reports.

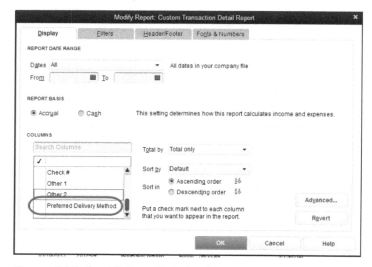

Figure 1-34 Preferred Delivery Method on Reports

Preferred Vendor

The *Preferred Vendor* has been added as a column to the "stock status" reports. It also can be used in a filter in those reports.

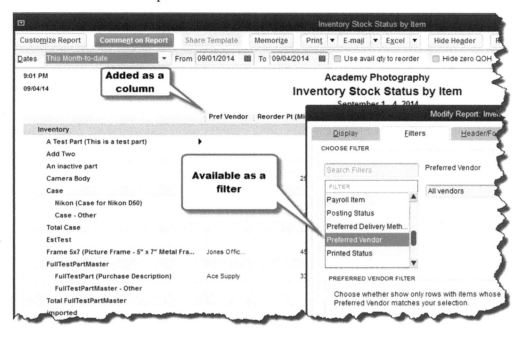

Figure 1-35 Preferred Vendor on reports

Income Tracker Time and Expenses Tab

Intuit added the **Income Tracker** in QuickBooks 2014, and in 2015 they implemented a few improvements.

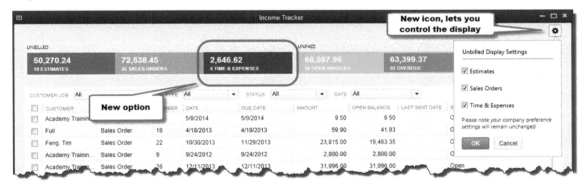

Figure 1-36 Income Tracker Time and Expenses Tab

There is a new option in the money bar, **Time & Expenses**. This lets you see any billable time & expenses records that haven't been billed to the customer. Note that there will be **only one line** for each customer – all of the outstanding billable time & expenses records for that customer are consolidated in one line.

In the upper right corner you'll find a gear icon, this gives you the option for hiding the bars for *Estimates, Sales Orders* and *Time & Expenses.*

In addition, with Time & Expenses records, if you right-click on the transaction the popup context menu has an option to *Create Invoice*. This will add *all* of the outstanding time & expenses for this customer to the invoice. If you want to pick and choose which to include on the invoice, select *Choose Billables*, the next option on the menu.

Figure 1-37 Additional menu options

Pinned Notes

The *Notes* tab was added to the customer, vendor, inventory and employee "Centers" in QuickBooks 2013. This year the feature has been enhanced to add the ability to "pin" a particular note, thereby making it the primary note that is viewed.

When you add a new note in QuickBooks 2015 you will see a new checkbox, **Pinned Note**. If you check this then this note becomes the "pinned" note, and it shows in the upper right corner of the Center.

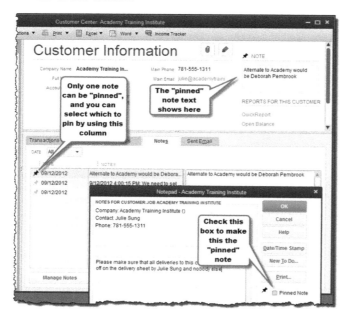

Figure 1-38 Pinned Notes

In prior versions none of the notes were displayed in the top display of the customer center. You had to select the *Notes* tab to see them.

Note the following:

- Only one note can be "pinned" per master record (Customer, Vendor, or Item).
- You cannot *un-check* the *pinned note* box when editing the note itself. Once you have at least one note for a record there has to be one that is pinned, so un-checking the selected one would leave you without one that is pinned. Can't do that! This was a bit frustrating at first. You *can* easily change which note is the pinned note by clicking on the pin icon by a note in the list in the notes tab.
- If you upgrade an existing file from a prior year, the top note on the list for each record (customer, vendor, etc.) will be marked as the pinned note, at least as far as any tests I ran showed.
- If a report lets you add a *Note* field, it will be the *pinned* note that is shown. Keep in mind that this is the *Note* field, not the *Notes* field, which (as you can see below) is very different.

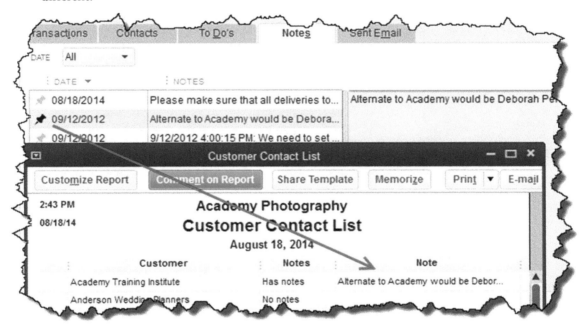

Figure 1-39 Pinned note on a report

Flags on Billable Time and Costs

When you elect to add "outstanding billable time and/or costs" to an invoice you will now see a number on each of the tabs in the *Choose Billable Time and Costs* window. These show you how many outstanding entries there are in each tab.

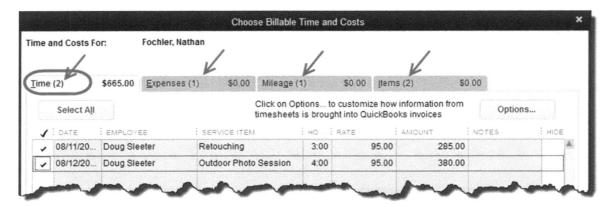

Figure 1-40 Numbers on the tabs are a new feature

This alerts you to the presence of costs on each tab, so you don't have to click on each one to see if there is something there (or, miss something because you didn't look).

Comments on Reports

At the top of the report window in QuickBooks 2015 you will see a *Comment on Report* button. When you click that you open the *comment view* of the report. At the end of each line of the report you will see a box that you can click to add a comment about that line.

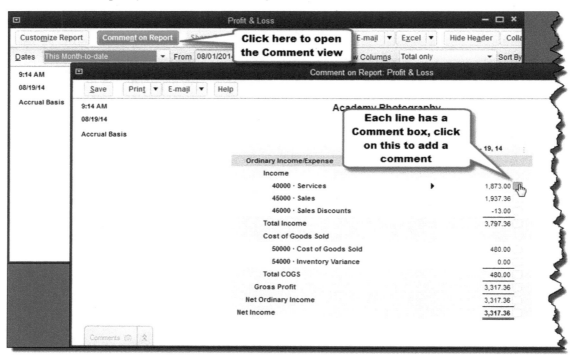

Figure 1-41 Comments on Reports

Click on that green icon will open the "Comments" box for that line of the report.

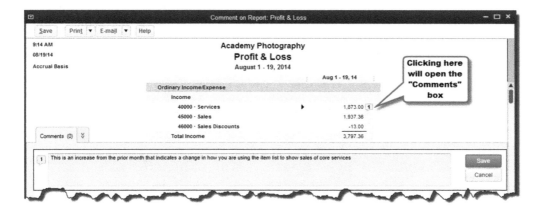

Figure 1-42 Comment box for Commented report

As you add comments to different lines, each is numbered sequentially. The number shows on the report as well. You can delete any comment, or edit it, using the icons at the left of the comment list.

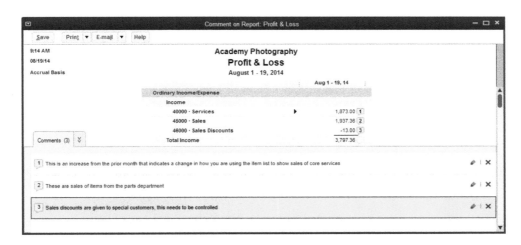

Figure 1-43 Comments are assigned numbers

Note that in multi-column reports there is a comment box by each column element as shown below.

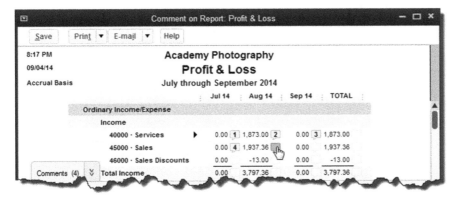

Figure 1-44 Comments in multi-column reports

At the top of the report there are several buttons:

- **Save:** This will let you save this report with a name. This will be a snapshot of the report along with the comments.
- **Print:** You can print the report or save as a PDF.
- **Email:** This will let you send the report as a PDF attachment. I'm not sure how good this is because email attachments aren't secure. Using a secure portal is a better way to handle this. Intuit notes this in a popup window, also.

Keep in mind that when you click that *Comment on Report* button, the snapshot freezes the report. If you have any customizations that you want to make to the report make them *before* you click the *comment* button.

If you print the report (or save to PDF) you get the report first, with the comment numbers, and a following page with the comments.

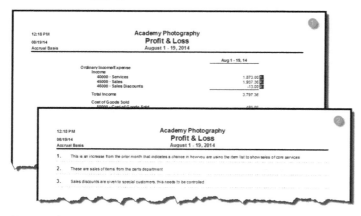

Figure 1-45 Comments print on last page

There is a *Commented Reports* option in the *Reports* menu, which opens a window listing your commented reports. You can display, email or print the reports, delete them, or change their name.

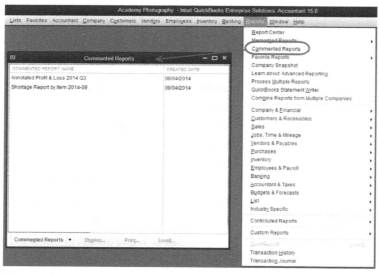

Figure 1-46 Commented Reports List

I think that this is a **great feature** that will be very useful for accounting professional.

Send Multiple Reports

Up until now if you were sending a PDF of a QuickBooks report via email you had to do so individually (one report per email), or you would have to save each PDF to your system separately and then attach them to a manually created email message. With QuickBooks 2015 you now have the ability to send multiple reports in one email attachment easily.

Select *Reports* and then **Process Multiple Reports**. There are two new options added to this window this year:

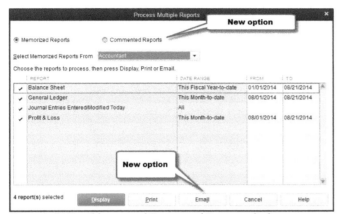

Figure 1-47 Email button and Commented Reports radio button

Note the *Commented Reports* option at the top. You can choose this to see a list of your saved commented reports to send in a group as an email attachment.

At the bottom is a new *Email* button. Click this and an email will be created (using the option set in your *Send Forms* preference) with all of the selected reports attached.

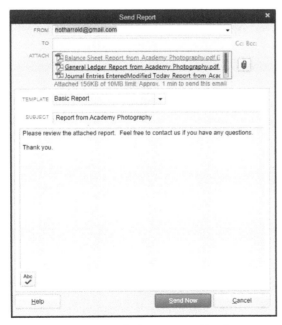

Figure 1-48 Sending Multiple Reports via Email

Send Portable Company File

Intuit has added a new option to make it easy for someone to send a *portable company file* via secure folder such as you might have when using SmartVault or DropBox. They've rearranged the options under the *File* menu to add an option, *Send Company File.* Under that you will find the *Accountant's Copy* option (which used to be directly under *File*) and the new option, **Portable Company File**.

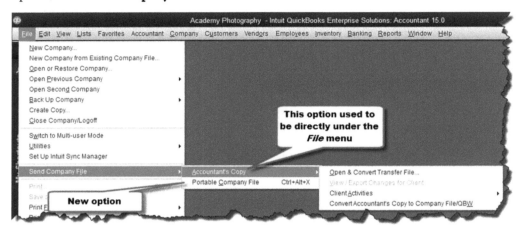

Figure 1-49 Send Portable Company File

When you select this new option a dialog will open as shown below. They are suggesting that if you use a secure "shared folder" in the cloud to transmit the portable company file that this is more secure than attaching the file to an email message.

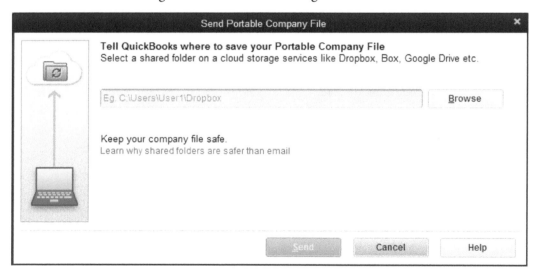

Figure 1-50 Select Location for the Portable Company File

QuickBooks will remember the setting here so that it will show as the default value the next time you use it.

The goal here is to try to make a seamless one-click file exchange between the accountant and the client (if you are transferring a complete file). The feature automatically selects the right format, remembers the folder name from the prior time.

Miscellaneous Small Changes

A variety of smaller changes that we'll outline here

- **Manufacturer's Part Number on sales transactions:** Now you can add the *Manufacturer's Part Number* as a column in invoices, sales receipts and sales orders. But not credit memos.

- **Customer Center can add Customer PO#:** You can now add a "P.O. Number" column to the *Transactions* tab in the Customer Center, when you are showing sales transactions ("all sales transactions" or individually estimates, sales orders or invoices). It is interesting to note that this customization is specific to each of the views – if you add the column to the "sales order" list, it won't show up in the "invoice" list automatically.

- **Admin user can end a session even if there is unsaved data:** In a multi-user QuickBooks environment there are times when you have to be in single user mode. The admin user has the ability to see what users are logged in, and those users can be shut down remotely by the admin. HOWEVER, if those users happen to have left an active transaction window open, the admin has not been able to kick them out. **Until now.** With QuickBooks 2015 there is an option to "Close even if users have unsaved data", for those times when the admin just has to close everyone else down regardless of what they are doing.

- **Estimates automatically close:** Now estimates are automatically marked as closed when they are fully invoiced.

- **Improved Selection of Sales Order Items:** If you create an invoice from a sales order and choose "Create invoice for selected items", the window that opens to let you select the quantities of items has been updated. A selection column is added on the left that lets you select the items to include in the invoice that is created.

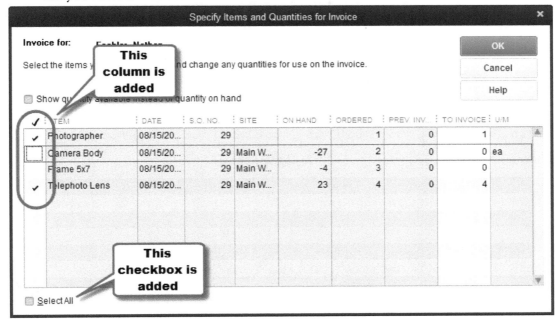

Figure 1-51 Option to easily select Sales Order details

- **Inventory Center filter "all inventory & assemblies":** In the *Inventory Center* we now have an option to list all of the inventory part and inventory assembly items (active and inactive), where before you were limited to just the active items (or, all items of just one type).

- **Warning on inactivating items with a quantity:** If you try to make an inventory part or inventory assembly item "inactive" when it has a non-zero quantity on hand, you get this warning:

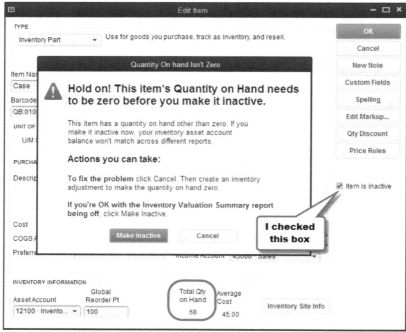

Figure 1-52 Warning when making item inactive

This is important, because if you have inactive items with a quantity on hand the value of these items won't be included in the inventory valuation reports, BUT the value *will* be included in your balance sheet. This is one of the first things that I check when working with a new client who manages inventory.

New and Improved Features in QuickBooks Enterprise

The following features are only found in QuickBooks Enterprise.

Hide Opening Balance fields

When you create a new customer, vendor or inventory part item (and assembly) you have the option to enter an "opening balance" (or initial value). We generally recommend that people don't do this, as it is one of the leading causes of having an incorrect initial value. You add a new record, enter the opening value, and then you enter your outstanding bills, invoices or item receipts. You have doubled up the initial value because that "opening balance" created an offsetting entry in the *Opening Balance Equity* account. Most people don't realize this, or know how to fix the problem.

Now we have a new preference that will let you **hide these opening balance/value fields**.

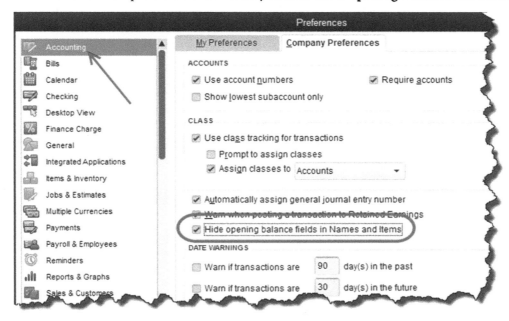

Figure 1-53 Preference to Hide Opening Balance fields

Here is what we normally would see:

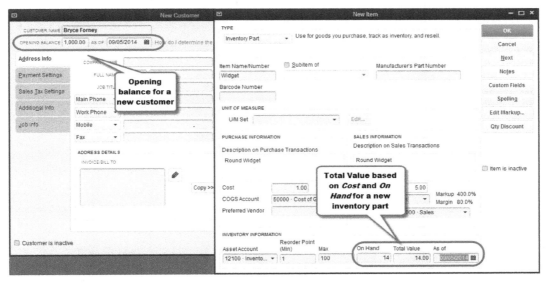

Figure 1-54 Opening Balance fields as they normally appear

Here is what you see if the new preference is checked.

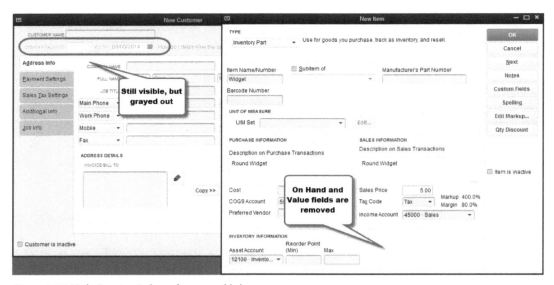

Figure 1-55 Hide Opening Balance feature enabled

Don't sell to overdue customers

Intuit has added a preference that will stop you from selling to someone if they have unpaid, overdue invoices.

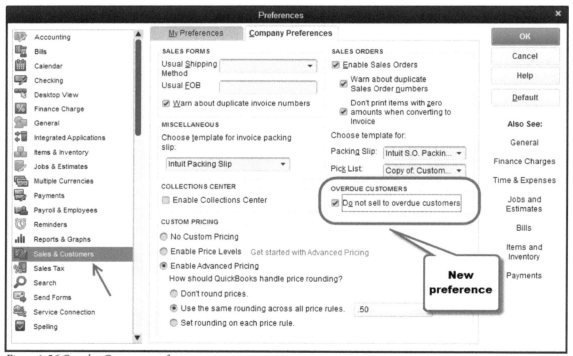

Figure 1-56 Overdue Customers preference

With this preference checked you are prevented from entering a sales transaction for any customer with an overdue balance.

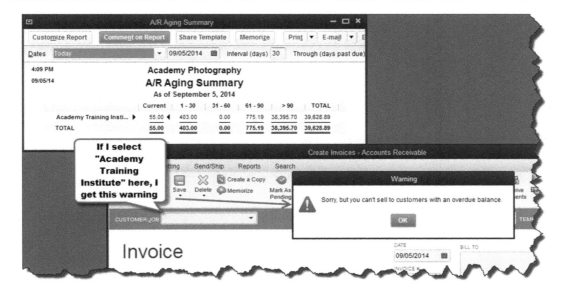

Figure 1-57 Overdue Customer Preference Enabled

This works for invoices, sales receipts and sales orders. Fortunately, a credit memo isn't restricted.

Note that if you have an existing sales order for this customer, you are allowed to click the *Create Invoice* button. The invoice is created, but if you try to save it you get the warning.

Transaction Form changes

There are a number of important and useful changes to transaction forms (invoices, purchase orders and so forth) in the Enterprise version this year.

Sorting Columns on Forms

An important change in transaction forms is the ability to **sort by column**. This is available in *Estimates, Sales Orders, Invoices, Build Assemblies, Checks, Credit Card Charges, Bills, Item Receipts, Credit Memos, Sales Receipts, Weekly Timesheets* and *Purchase Orders*.

Let's start with a sales order, with several items entered randomly (we entered an "ordered quantity" with sequential numbers so you can see the order that we started with).

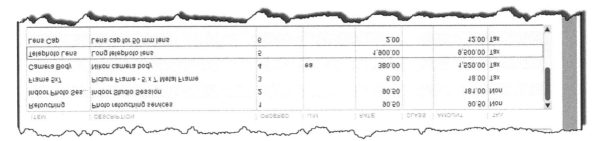

Figure 1-58 Starting order form, unsorted

By simply clicking on the column heading you can easily sort the order of the detail lines. For example, let's click on the "Item" heading:

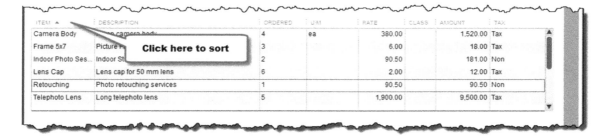

Figure 1-59 Order sorted by Item

You can sort by any column that you can display, even the "other" and custom fields.

It is interesting to note how this works with *Subtotal* items. Here's the sales order in the original sequence, but with a *subtotal* inserted in the middle.

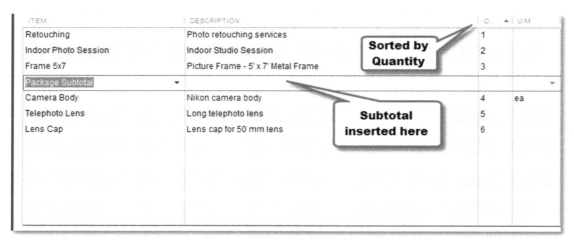

Figure 1-60 Starting order form, unsorted, with subtotal item

What happens if you sort by item? The subtotal remains in place and the program sorts in "groups", separated by the subtotal.

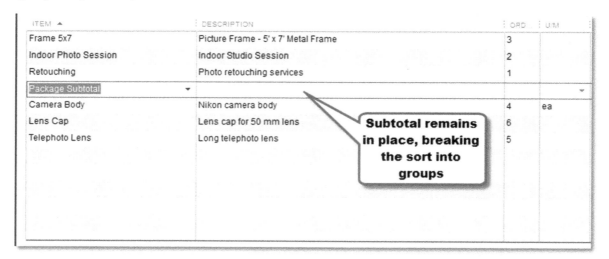

Figure 1-61 Sorted around subtotal

This is the proper behavior, and it is good that they caught this. You don't want the "groups" of items above the subtotal to be mixed in with other items, as that would change the value of the subtotal.

How about *Group Items*? Here's the same sales order, but with a *Group Item* inserted in the middle.

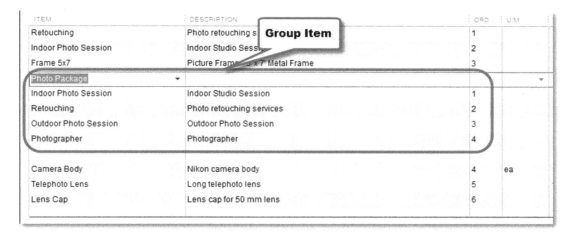

Figure 1-62 Starting order, with group item

If you sort this by *Item*, you get the following:

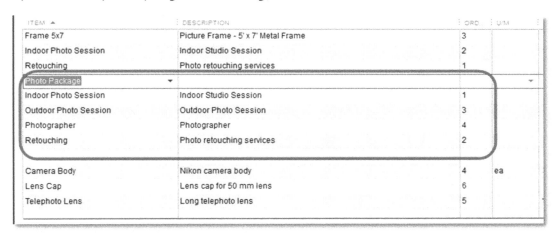

Figure 1-63 Sorted around Group Item

The *Group Item* is treated the same as a *Subtotal Item* and it stays in place, dividing the transaction into two separately sorted parts. The details *within* the group also is not sorted. Fortunately, the group was not split up and sorted with other items, which is good.

A few things to note:

- If you sort the transaction, and (before saving it) add a new line that is out of order, the transaction will not sort immediately, even though the "sorting pip" marker still shows at the top of the column. This can be misleading.

- If you save a sorted transaction it is saved in the sorted order, but the sorting indication is not saved, so adding more items later won't automatically cause the transaction to be sorted again.

- If you create a sales order and sort it, then change it into an invoice, the details remain in the sorted order. More importantly, if you re-sort the invoice to a different sequence this does *not* affect the relationship between the sales order and the invoice if there are backorders involved.

Total Columns on Forms

Transactions like invoices show the total of the *amount* column. Many businesses would like the ability to get a total value of other columns, such as the **total quantity** that you are shipping, or a total of a custom field such as the number of pallets, or total weight. You can do that now with QuickBooks 2015 Enterprise.

Here's the *edit item* window for a Subtotal item. You can see that an area has been added that lets you check a number of "columns to total".

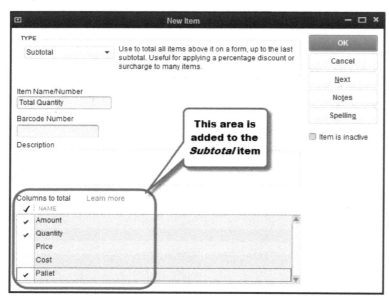

Figure 1-64 Additional options in Subtotal Item

If you use this *subtotal* item in an invoice you can see that it adds the "Quantity" column, as well as the "Pallet" custom field.

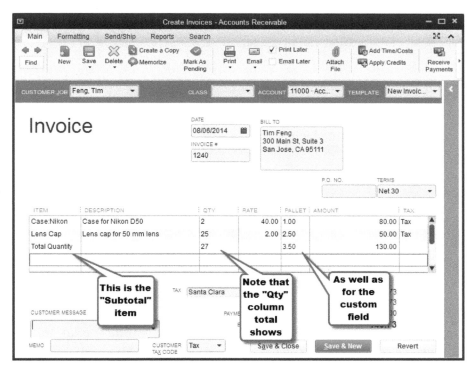

Figure 1-65 Totals on columns

Let's look at a few details:

- Certain kinds of items are not included in the totals.
    - Other-charge, payment, sales tax items are not included in the total.
    - Service and non-inventory items that have a *percentage* for a rate will not be included.
- Group items are not counted as a group, the program will count the values of the component items of the group. This works for most cases.
- This feature works in every kind of transaction that lets you add a *subtotal* item. This includes all the sales-oriented transactions, purchase orders, checks, bills, and credit card charges.
- Custom fields can only be subtotaled if they are set to be a numeric field. Text custom fields cannot be subtotaled.
- If a custom field has more than 5 values after the decimal the program will round the calculation to 5 places.
- The "Other 1" and "Other 2" fields cannot be subtotaled.
- You can "nest" subtotal items as before, and all the fields work as expected.
- If you add a *discount* item with a percentage under a subtotal it will only apply to the *amount* column, not to other subtotaled columns.
- If you have backorders in a *sales order*, and your *subtotal* item is totaling the quantity, this only applies to the *ordered* column, not to the *backordered* and *invoiced* columns.
- Subtotals print in the body of the transaction, not at the bottom of the form like the "amount", which will annoy some people.

If you have a sales order with a subtotal, and change it to an invoice while asking to select the items to include, you will see the subtotal item in the picking window *and* the subtotal will update to show the total of the *to invoice* column correctly.

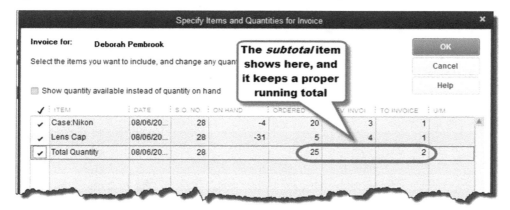

Figure 1-66 Column total on subtotal item

If you use the *unit of measure* feature you may find the subtotal feature to be limited. If you mix units of measure in a transaction then subtotals won't work. In some cases this makes sense – if you have 2 "each" and then 2 "dozen", what should the subtotal be? 4 (2 + 2)? 26 (2 plus 24 from the dozen)? It is hard to make a general rule that covers all situations.

Footer on Last Page

If you have a sales or purchasing transaction and the document is longer than one page, QuickBooks has always used the same page layout for each page. This means that the box for the "total" value shows on each page, even though it should normally only print on the last page. It doesn't look good to have the blank box show on the pages other than the last one. Here's an example:

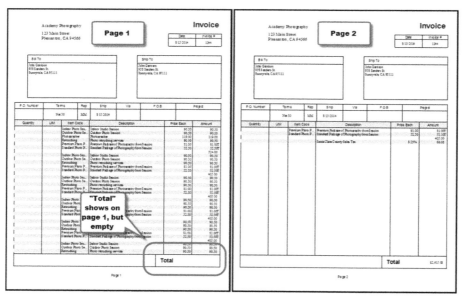

Figure 1-67 Footer shows on each page in versions prior to V15

With Enterprise Solutions V15 you now have the option of specifying that the total will only show on the last page. This affects invoices, sales orders, estimates and purchase orders (but not credit memos or sales receipts, for some reason).

Edit your transaction template and select *Additional Customization*. In the *Print* tab you will see a new option: **Only show Total on the last page.**

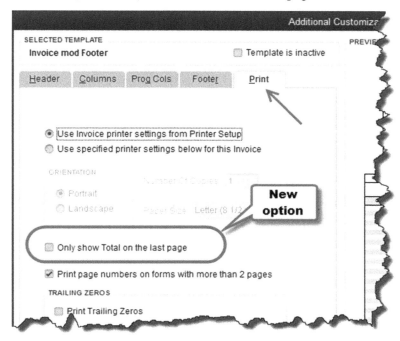

Figure 1-68 Preference for "Only show Total on the last page"

If you check this, you see the following:

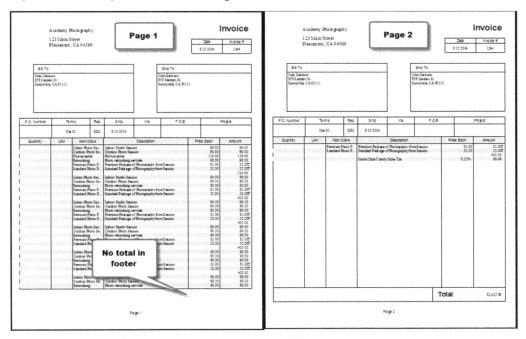

Figure 1-69 Totals only show on last page with preference enabled

Note that the "detail" section does *not* extend down into the space where the footer would have shown. That will bother some people, but it solves a lot of problems that can occur if you try to make the program extend down into that space. This is why you want to keep your footers as compact as possible.

As you can see, this doesn't just prevent the "total" field from printing on the first page (and any other page before the last), this affects the entire footer *other than* the page number.

Show Cost on Sales Forms

This is a feature that has been requested often: the ability to add the "cost" of an item on a sales transaction.

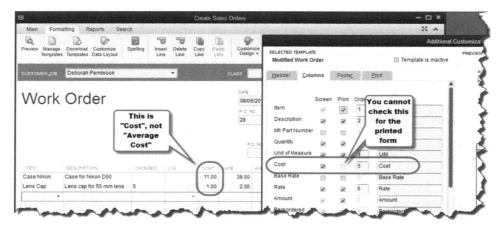

Figure 1-70 Cost column on a sales form

This is added to the invoice, sales order and sales receipt transactions. Note that this is "Cost", not "Average Cost", and that you can only add this to the screen view.

Search on transactions

If you have long transactions (many detail lines) it can be difficult to find a particular line if you want to update it or see if an item was included. The *Search on Transactions* feature helps with this.

In the transaction menu ribbon there is a *Search* tab. Enter the value you want to look for and click the **Search** button, and QuickBooks will highlight the matching lines in yellow. You can use the up/down arrows by the search box to rotate through the highlighted items.

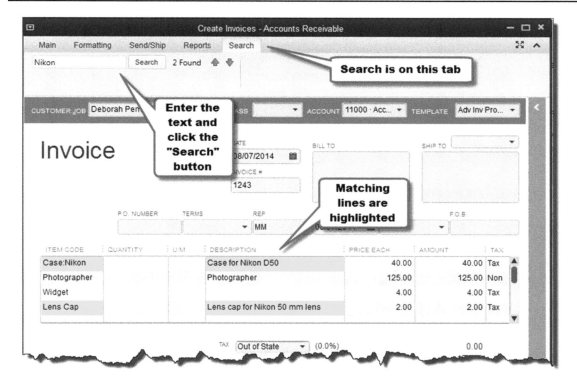

Figure 1-71 Searching within a transaction

This search works only within the current transaction (any sales transaction, purchase order, bill or item receipt), and only (at this time) searches the item code, description and QuickBooks barcode fields.

Shaded Lines on Transaction Forms

Another nice little update is the ability to set forms to have alternating shaded lines on printed transactions (and a couple of reports). This makes your forms easier to read when printed.

You will see the new option in the print dialog after you have chosen to print the form or report.

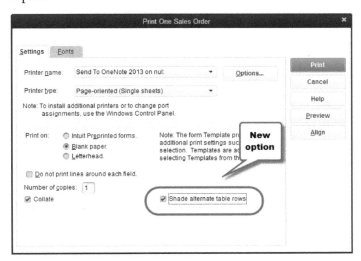

Figure 1-72 Option to shade alternate table rows in the printer dialog

Here's what you will see. Note that you don't have any control over the degree of shading.

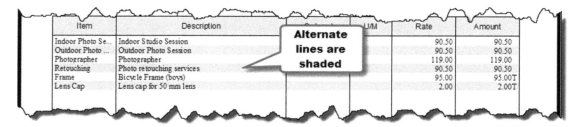

Figure 1-73 Alternate shaded lines in a form

This is available on estimates, sales orders, pick lists, packing slips, batch invoices, invoices, purchase orders, bills, item receipts, sales receipts, build assembly, physical inventory worksheet, and item price lists by item and by customer. Note that this is stored in the local printer preference file, so the setting is saved per form, per user.

Inventory

Intuit is placing an increasing emphasis on the development of the inventory features in Enterprise. This year there are several *very* interesting additions.

Don't Allow Negative Quantities

For *inventory part* and *inventory assembly* items, if you sell (or otherwise consume) more items than you have on hand, the "quantity on hand" will become negative. Unfortunately, having negative quantities on hand can cause major problems in QuickBooks with COGS calculations, it can introduce errors in various reports, and it can even lead to recurring data damage.

Intuit has finally given us an option to control this, something that people have been asking about for years. In your *Items & Inventory* preferences you will see a new option, **Don't allow negative quantities**.

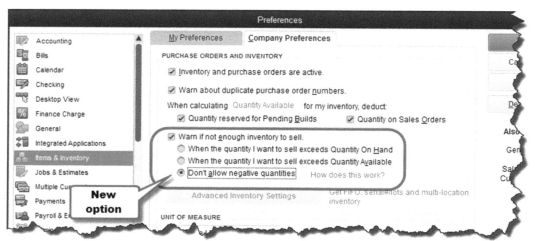

Figure 1-74 New option to not allow negative quantities

If you enable this preference, QuickBooks will prevent you from creating a transaction that will bring the *quantity on hand* for an *inventory part* or *inventory assembly* item below zero on the transaction date. As you can see below, in this invoice I have 13 on hand, and when you try to sell more than that a window opens that tells you that you can't do this (and why).

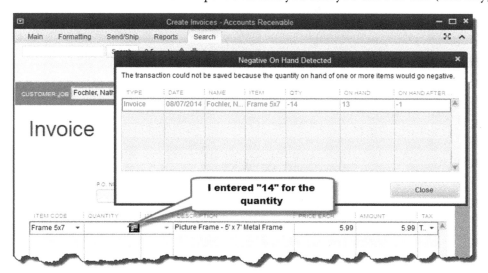

Figure 1-75 Trying to sell more items than you have available

After you turn on this preference, QuickBooks blocks any transaction that would make an item's quantity negative if it starts off with a quantity on hand that is zero or greater. However, QuickBooks doesn't prevent items that already have a negative quantity on hand from becoming more negative.

The program is smart enough to look at all detail lines in the transaction for that same item. Looking at the following example you can see that as above, the item has only 13 on hand. The first line sells one item, and then a second line is entered to sell 13 more, which brings the *accumulated* quantity in this transaction higher than what is on hand. The program catches it.

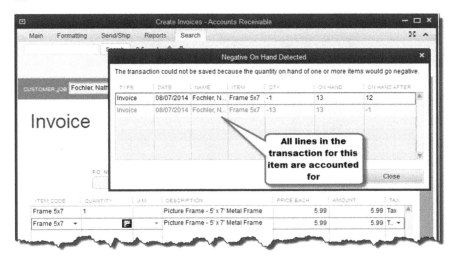

Figure 1-76 Each line is OK by itself, but the total exceeds available

A few things to point out:

- This only affects *posting* transactions. Non-posting transactions like sales orders are not affected.

- You **can** turn this feature on if you already have items with negative quantities. If you enter a transaction for an item that is already negative, you won't be blocked. You can make it "more negative" without any problem.

- *Inventory Adjustments* are handled in a slightly different way – the check for negative quantities is only performed when you click the *Save* button, rather than line-by-line as you enter the details.

If you are using the *Advanced Inventory* subscription and the *Multiple Inventory Locations* feature you have additional preferences:

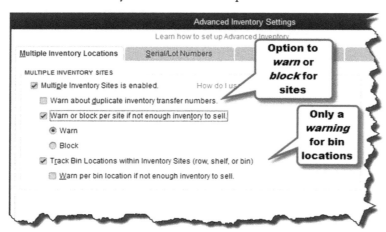

Figure 1-77 Additional preferences with Advanced Inventory

Note that you can set the program to just give you a *warning* if you don't have enough items at a particular site, or you can also *block* the transaction. If you set this to just warn you will still be blocked if the transaction requires more than you have on hand at all sites. You can take this even further and have it *warn* you per bin location.

There is one thing that is changed here that should be highlighted. This only works with *quantity on hand*. QuickBooks has an optional feature called *quantity available*, which can issue warnings if the quantity you sell is greater than the *quantity on hand* minus the quantity included in *sales orders* and/or *pending builds*. If you select the option to disallow negative quantity on hand you are no longer warned if the sale exceeds on hand minus the quantity promised to sales orders or builds. There are going to be situations where this is not good. Note that the quantity available calculation is still done (if you enable it) and you can see it if you click on the chart icon in the *quantity* column of a sales transaction.

Figure 1-78 Checking Quantity Available

Negative Item Listing

An interesting addition is the **Negative Item Listing**, found in *Reports/Inventory*. This lists all items that have a negative *quantity on hand*. Note that this report is available even if you haven't enabled the *don't allow negative quantities* preference enabled. If you are considering enabling this preference you can use this report to see which items are already negative, and then make corrections.

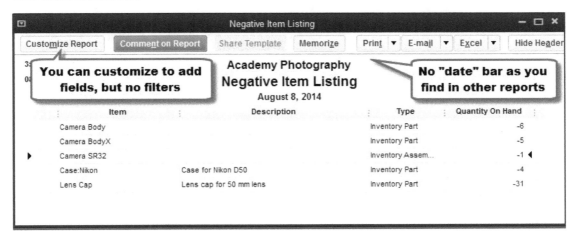

Figure 1-79 Negative Item Listing

Although you don't need to make these corrections *before* turning the preference on, It is recommended that you take the time to do it. If you aren't allowing negative balances, any item that *already* has a negative balance will continue to let you sell the item, driving it further negative. You won't be warned. So if you believe that you have this protective feature on, and you sell more of these items, you'll think that you are OK and that you have enough. That could be a problem.

Shortage reports

As a part of their inventory expansion in Enterprise, Intuit has added a **shortage report.** There are actually two ways you can obtain this report, and each serves a different purpose.

Enterprise Solutions is not a full "MRP" manufacturing planning system. To get that you need to use an add-on product such as MISys Manufacturing and others. However, barring a move to a more comprehensive system, there are things that you can do to get "shortage" information out of Enterprise. By "shortage" we mean that you want to build an assembly, and you don't have enough parts on hand, so what are you missing?

This can be looked at in several ways: what are you short to build this one assembly by itself, and what are you short for all of the assemblies you need to build. Intuit is providing some new tools that help with both of these questions this year.

Let's work with a very simple inventory assembly item in these examples. A more complicated assembly would make it too hard to follow. Here is a "Bicycle".

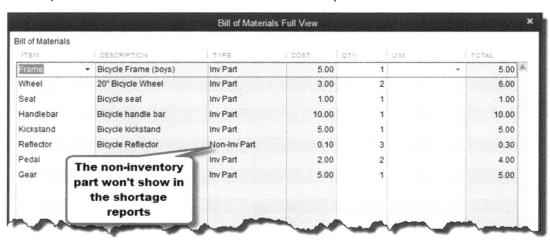

Figure 1-80 Example assembly - Bicycle

Shortage for One Assembly Build

You want to build an assembly. Here's a screenshot from Enterprise V14 (last year's product), where you want to build 8 of my "Bicycle" assembly, but you can't because you're short of some components. But, which components, and by how many are you short? You can't tell at this point because the "Qty Needed" column won't get filled in until you make this a *pending build*, and you might not want to do that now.

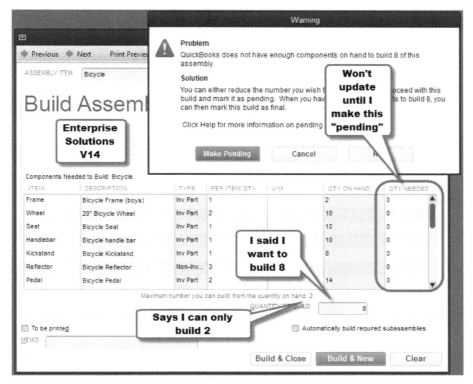

Figure 1-81 Canno issue a build, short of a part

In addition, even if you *do* make this pending, you still have to visually compare the *qty needed* vs. the *qty on hand* columns to determine where you have shortages. If you have a large BOM it can take quite a while to determine where the problems are in this one build.

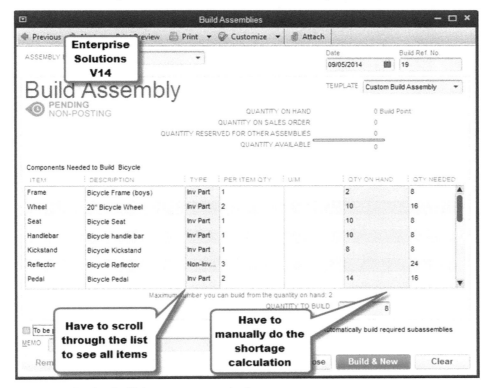

Figure 1-82 Pending build, how many are you short?

Now let's look at **Enterprise V15** for the same situation. Note that in the *Warning* dialog we have a new button, **Show Shortage.**

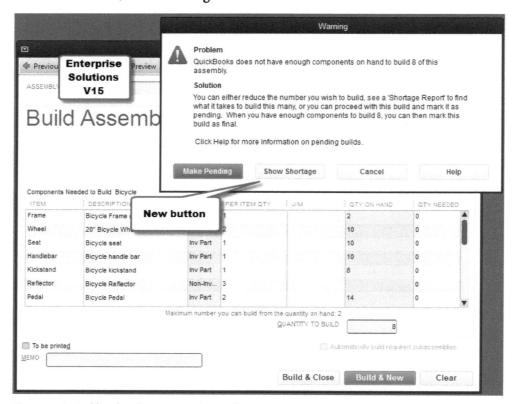

Figure 1-83 Build with a shortage, note the new button

When you click on **Show Shortage** Enterprise pops up a reminder that the values in this report reflect only the demand for this one build, which is an important point to keep in mind.

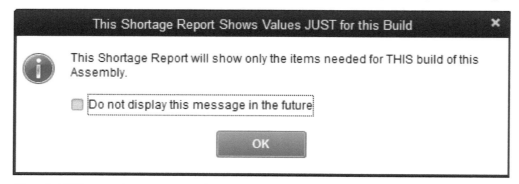

Figure 1-84 Warning when you request a shortage report

Here is the shortage report for this one build transaction.

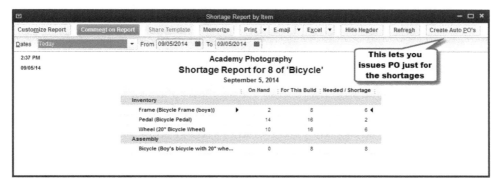

Figure 1-85 Shortage report for one build transaction

The report shows the component items that are needed, how many of the items you have on hand, and a calculation of what the shortage is. Only the items that are short are listed, which makes this very easy to work with.

This report is very useful, but you have to be careful when using this. Keep in mind that this is *only looking at this one assembly,* and making decisions based on just this information can be misleading. For instance, if you want to create purchase orders for these items, you don't see information about the needs for *other* builds that might be pending. You may order too few and not take advantage of a volume purchase point. Also, there is no information here about any *existing* purchase orders that might be coming in. This is a good report to show you what parts are preventing you from building this assembly, but we generally don't recommend making purchasing (or building) decisions from this particular form of the report.

When you have a *multiple level assembly,* where there is at least one component of the assembly that is itself an assembly, things get a bit more interesting. For example, you have a "Camera Kit" assembly that has a "Camera SR32" component that is an assembly. "Camera SR32" in turn has a "Telephoto Lens Kit" assembly as a component. You want to build a "Camera Kit", but you have a shortage of some of the assemblies. Here is the shortage report from the *build assembly* transaction:

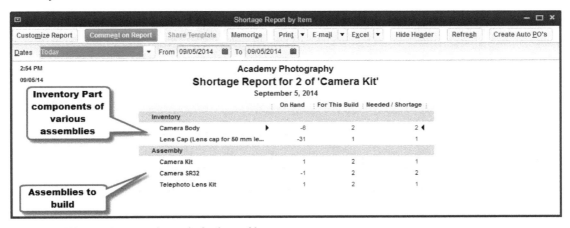

Figure 1-86 Shortage Report with a multi-level assembly

The shortage report lists the assemblies that have to be built (two are subassemblies of the higher level) and any shortage of inventory parts from any level. This is good, but note that **we didn't check the "automatically build subassemblies" box** in the *build* *assemblies* transaction. This report should reflect what we are asking the program to do in the transaction – the subassemblies should only be "exploded" if you say you want to issue a full level build.

A few notes:

- The report doesn't include any information about open purchase orders (supply transactions) or open sales orders (demand transactions).
- As is the unfortunate case with many inventory reports in QuickBooks, you can't make any significant customizations to this report (adding columns, etc.)
- Note that there is a **Create Auto PO's** button at the top of the report, similar to what we have in reports like the *Inventory Stock Status by Item report.* This isn't a good place for this feature, as this report doesn't take the entire business situation into account. Also, the shortage report **ignores reorder quantities.**
- Only inventory assembly and inventory part items are included in the report, which makes sense. Service items, non-inventory parts and so forth aren't included.

If you turn this into a *pending build* you can come back later and click the **Show Shortage** button that is added to the bottom of this window.

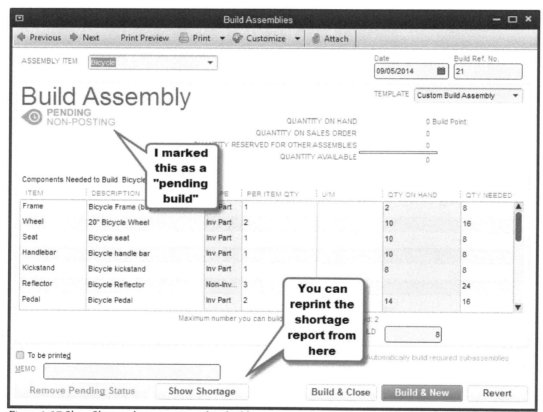

Figure 1-87 Show Shortage button on a pending build

Inventory Shortage Reports

In addition to being able to see the shortage report for a specific *build assembly* transaction, there are two new reports in the *Reports/Inventory* menu selection: **Inventory Shortage by Item** and **Inventory Shortage by Vendor**. These are going to be similar to the report shown above, but they will take into account all *pending builds* in the date range, not just a single build by itself.

In our example we have several *pending builds* for multiple assemblies. Here is the *Pending Build* report for the date range we are working with:

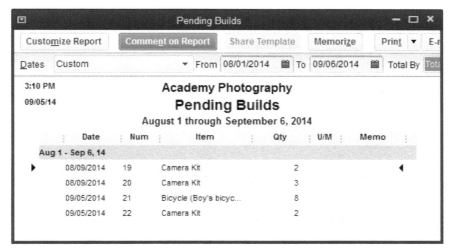

Figure 1-88 Pendig Builds report

We can select **Shortage Report by Item** from the *Reports/Inventory* menu, and see a report that shows the shortages from all of the *pending builds* in the date range.

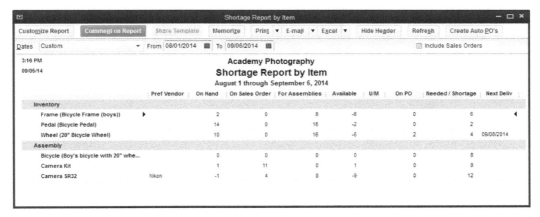

Figure 1-89 Shortage Report by Item

This is a similar concept to what we saw in the shortage report from the *build assembly* transaction but it contains more information (but *still* not a customizable report). Now we have information from other transactions, such as "supply" from open purchase orders and "demand" from open sales orders.

Some observations:

- Unlike the shortage report from the *build assemblies* transaction, this report does not explode subassemblies. It appears to ignore the "automatically build required subassemblies" checkbox in the pending build, but it reacts in the opposite way as the other shortage report.

- The "needed/shortage" column takes the quantity "On PO" into account. See the "Wheel" item? We need 6, but 2 are coming on a PO. There should be an option to not include this, or at least to have a column that shows the actual shortage without PO's. The "On PO" value is all open PO's, but only one PO will be the "next delivered" (the date that shows). We could have 20 items in "On PO", but only 2 of those in the next PO, with the other 18 not coming for 6 months. You can't trust the listed "On PO" values are going to be useful or not.

- Oddly, in our simple test, if our open PO's (regardless of date) fulfill the shortage, the item isn't listed in the report at all. Again an issue when the next PO may be 6 months or more out. You think that you are covered because the item isn't listed, but you might not be.

- Keep in mind that when looking at this report it ignores reorder quantities.

Inventory Stock Status Report Improvements

The *Inventory Stock Status* reports are key reports in the QuickBooks inventory system, and there have been several improvements in these reports in QuickBooks Enterprise V15.

Full Assembly Checkbox

This is an extension to the nested assemblies feature that was introduced with QuickBooks Enterprise Solutions V14. The concept is that if you have nested assemblies you might want the *Inventory Stock Status* reports to show the requirement for components of subassemblies show in the *For Assemblies* column. To enable this Intuit has added a "Full Assemblies" checkbox on the report.

If you have a *pending build* for a higher level assembly, this box should add the required components of the lower level subassembly. Unfortunately, this might not be working the way that is expected.

For a simple test, we have an assembly, "Low Assy" that has one component part, "Low Part". There is another assembly, "High Assy" that has two component parts, "High Part" and "Low Assy". We issue a *pending build* for one "High Assy" and get this shortage report (we don't have any parts on hand):

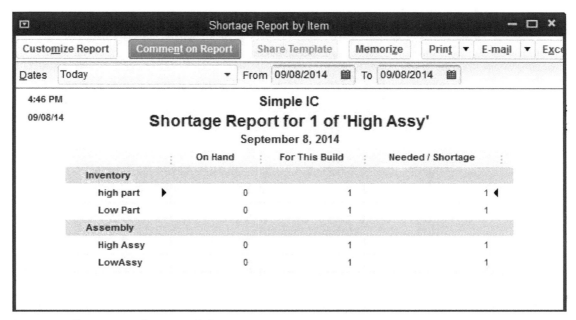

Figure 1-90 Shortage report for our sample data

Now let's take a look at the *Inventory Stock Status by Item* report, with the new option checked:

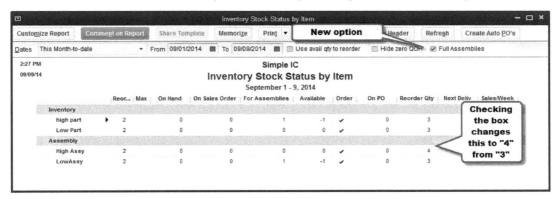

Figure 1-91 Inventory Stock Status by Item report with "Full Assemblies" checked

The only difference between checking that box and not is that the *Reorder Qty* for the "High Assy" assembly changes from 3 to 4. That isn't what weexpected at all. Shouldn't the change be that you see a reorder quantity for "Low Part" change?

Hide Zero Reorder Quantity

This is a helpful filter for the *Inventory Stock Status* reports – a way to hide items that have a "zero reorder quantity".

If you customize the report you will see the new "Zero Reorder Qty" filter.

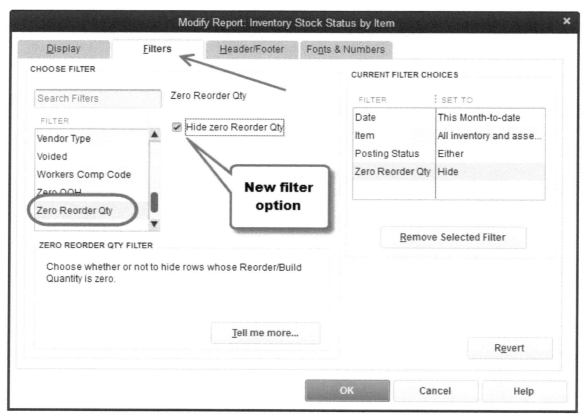

Figure 1-92 Zero Reorde Qty filter in report

This is very useful if you are using the *Inventory Stock Status* reports for reordering.

Advanced Reporting

Reporting hasn't really been the strong point in QuickBooks Desktop. While QuickBooks has advanced in other areas over the years, the capabilities of the reporting feature just aren't very well developed. To address this, Intuit is releasing an **Advanced Reporting** feature for QuickBooks Enterprise Solutions. This is a very flexible but somewhat complicated to use reporting function that will copy your database into a separate data store and let you generate all kinds of wonderful reports and graphs.

> *Note that Advanced Reporting is a new product with a rapid update schedule. It is very likely that by the time you are reading this, many of the screen shots will have changed. This section gives you a general overview of the product, the details may vary when you access the current release of the product.*

You will find the program under the *Reports* menu.

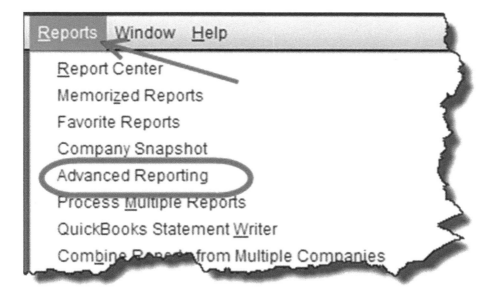

Figure 1-93 Advanced Reporting menu

The first time you select this option you have to be in multi-user mode. Then you will get this setup screen:

Figure 1-94 Advanced Reporting installation notice

Advanced Reporting creates its own separate database, outside of the QuickBooks database itself. All of the data in your current file is going to be copied over to the new separate reporting database as a part of the initial setup.

Some implications of this approach:

- You will need more space on your file system to hold this duplicate copy of the data.
- This is a "snapshot" of your data – that means that any changes you make (transactions added, lists changed, etc.) after this point will not show up in the reporting system *unless* you do an additional "sync" with the reporting database.
- By extracting the data Intuit can reorganize it and rename it so that it makes more sense. The internal structure of the QuickBooks database, and the names for fields, is crazy (as users of the "custom reporting" ODBC feature know).

- By having the reporting data in a separate database you don't impact the performance of QuickBooks itself (other than when syncing data), so you don't slow down other QuickBooks users when generating complicated reports.

- Note that since this is a read-only sync you don't have to worry about making a backup of this data.

- And, since it is in a separate database, it doesn't increase the size of your QBW file.

Working with Reports

Let's take a look at the "inventory stock status by item" built in report to see what options we have. Clicking on the report name in the template list will open that report in an editor window.

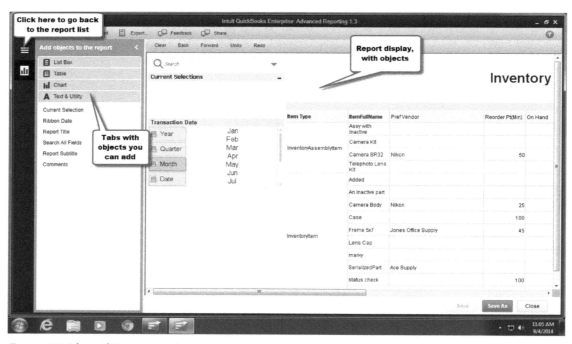

Figure 1-95 Advanced Reporting workspace

The report is a collection of "objects" that have been added to the report. The main report chart (or graph) itself, title objects, filter objects and more.

Every "object" in the report has a property list – you right-click on it and select *properties* from the popup menu. Here is a sample of the properties for the overall report:

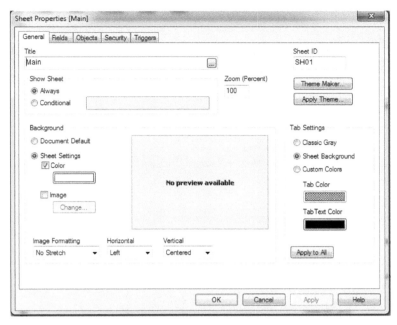

Figure 1-96 Advanced Reporting settings

And here are the properties for the main graph, or body, of the report:

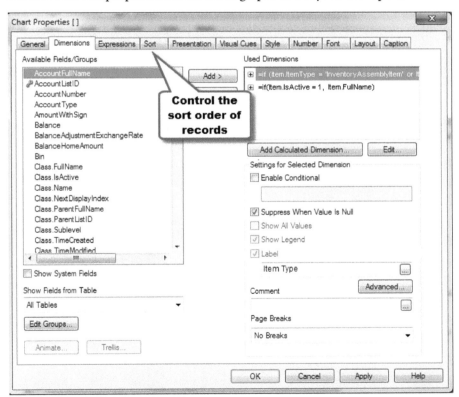

Figure 1-97 Advanced Reporting dimensions

In addition to the properties for each object you can modify the report by adding an object from the options in the left. For example, in the report below I've added an "Item Types" *List Box*, which gives me a list of all the possible item types. Click on one of them (such as

"InventoryAssemblyItem") and that adds a filter to the report. The filters that are enabled are shown in the *Current Selections* object.

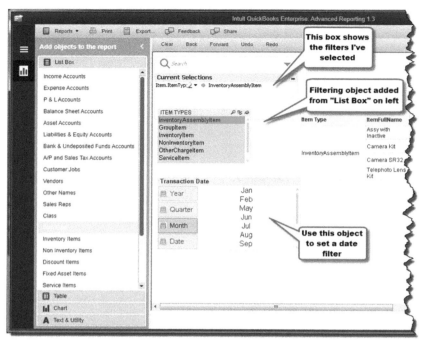

Figure 1-98 Filters in the workspace

Here's another example of how you can use objects to modify a report. I'm creating a report from scratch. I select the *Chart* objects from the left and add the "Sales (Last 12 Months)" chart.

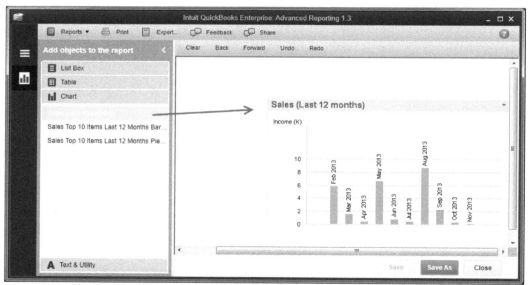

Figure 1-99 Adding an object to the report

I can add a *Current Selection* utility object and then a *Customer:Jobs* list box object, and then click on any customer to filter the report by that customer. This just takes a few moments to set up.

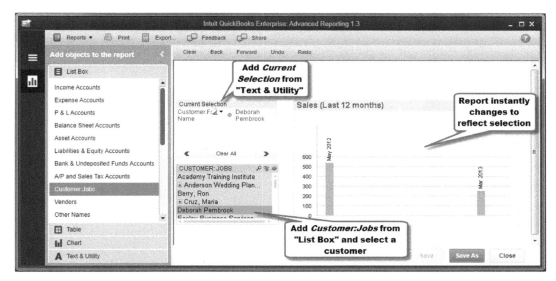

Figure 1-100 Adding a customer filter

Advanced Reporting Technical Information

The Advanced Reporting feature makes a copy of the QuickBooks database into a separate data store that is located in a folder that is relative to the location of the QuickBooks database itself. For example, I have a QuickBooks company file "Academy-14Enterprise", and you can see that there is a folder "Academy-14Enterprise Advanced Reporting" at that same location.

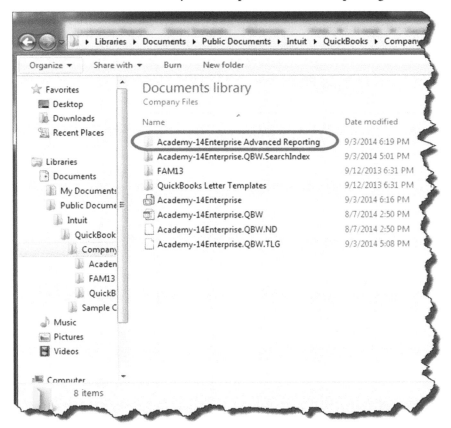

Figure 1-101 Location of folder for Advanced Reporting

Note that this is a Windows "hidden" folder, so you have to enable Windows Explorer to show hidden folders if you want to see it (there is no need to see this folder, though).

The data is encrypted and is not accessible through any other program.

Intuit has licensed an existing reporting product, **QlikView**, to be the engine that drives the analysis. Intuit's programmers are responsible for creating the data export, organizing the tables and views, creating the basic reports and objects.

Enterprise has a new user permission option to cover Advanced Reporting.

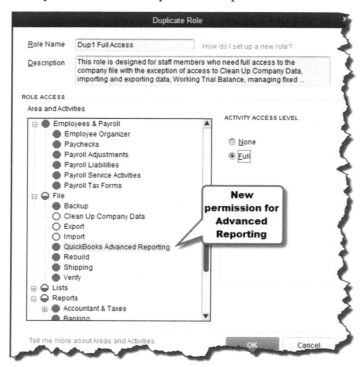

Figure 1-102 Advanced Reporting permissions

New and Improved Features in Accountant and Enterprise Accountant

Unlike prior years, there aren't any improvements that are found only in QuickBooks Accountant and QuickBooks Enterprise Accountant. However, there are several features that are beneficial to accountants, and one feature ("Accountants Toolbox") that, although it is found in QuickBooks Pro and Premier, is only accessible to accountants.

Here's some features that we've discussed earlier that should be of interest to accountants:

- **Comments on Reports:** The ability to annotate reports is going to be appreciated by accounting professionals. However, this feature is found in QuickBooks Pro, Premier and Enterprise, not just in QuickBooks Accountant.

- **Send Multiple Reports:** The ability to send *multiple* reports as attachments in one email message, rather than as separate emails, may be useful to accounting professionals.

However, this feature is found in QuickBooks Pro, Premier and Enterprise, not just in QuickBooks Accountant.

- **Send Portable Company File:** This is a simpler way for your client to send you a *portable company file* (or, for you to send one back to the client), simplifying the steps that it takes and making it less likely that an error will occur. However, this feature is found in QuickBooks Pro, Premier and Enterprise, not just in QuickBooks Accountant.

There is one additional feature for accounting professionals in the mix, called the **Accountant Toolbox**, which we will describe here. Note that at this time this feature is only available in QuickBooks Pro and Premier.

Accountant Toolbox

A few years ago Intuit added the "External Accountant User", a user that a client could add to the company file that the accountant could use when logging in to the file at the client's office. If you log in to QuickBooks Pro or Premier with this special user account then you have access to some of the features of the *Client Data Review*, which normally would only be available in QuickBooks Accountant versions. That would let the accountant perform a review while on site.

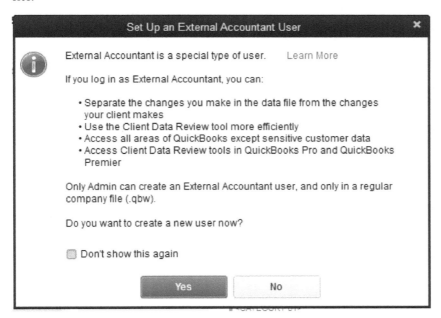

Figure 1-103 External Accountant setup

The problem is, when you did that, you didn't get *all* of the *Client Data Review* or other accountant features. With some options in the *Client Data Review* you would see a warning message:

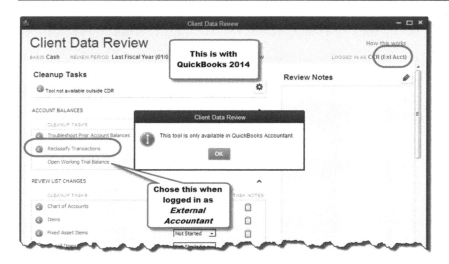

Figure 1-104 Client Data Review feature not accessible via the External Accountant

The features that you could not use when logged in as the external accountant are:

- Reclassify Transactions
- Write Off Invoices
- Troubleshoot Inventory
- Batch Enter Transactions (not in the CDR itself, but still not available to you in Pro or Premier)

This is changed in QuickBooks 2015 in the Pro and Premier products. If you are enrolled in the QuickBooks ProAdvisor Program or subscribe to the QuickBooks Accountant Plus program you now have the **Accountant Toolbox** available to you when you **log in to a client file as the "external accountant" user.**

To enable this feature you must be accessing a client's QuickBooks 2015 program (Pro or Premier, this isn't currently available in Enterprise) as the *external accountant* user. Select *Company,* and then *Accountant Toolbox,* and choose **Unlock Accountant Toolbox.**

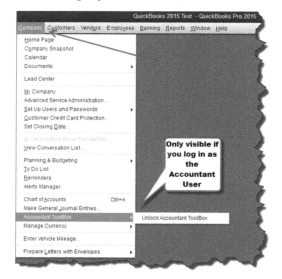

Figure 1-105 Unlock the Accountant Toolbox

You will need to log in with the Intuit Account email address and password that is associated with your ProAdvisor account or QuickBooks Accountant Plus subscription.

Figure 1-106 Log in to your Intuit account

Once you do this you can access the *Accountant Center*, the *Batch Enter Transactions* feature, and the entire *Client Data Review*. Here's the menu you will see after it is unlocked:

Figure 1-107 Accountant Toolbox menu after unlocking

Why do they do this? It makes *all* of these special features available to you if you are enrolled in one of the Intuit accountant subscription/membership plans, without giving all other users access to the features.

New and Improved Features in QuickBooks for Mac

This is a brief summary of the changes in QuickBooks for Mac in the 2015 release.

- **Expense Tracker:** Use this to see all expense related transactions in one place. You can get an instant overview of what's on order, what you owe, and what you've paid. Batch print or email transactions directly from the Expense Tracker list and filter by transaction or vendor.

- **Budgets enhancement:** Create budgets by fiscal year and gain business insights as you evaluate how you are doing against your plan. You can easily run reports and compare your actual performance to your goals.

- **Batch import transactions enhancement:** Save time by batch-importing invoices, payments and bills. No need to manually enter transactions, you can easily import them all in one spreadsheet directly into QuickBooks.

- **Attachments enhancement**: You can now attach any relevant files to: Chart of Accounts, Items List, My Company Preference, Employees and Other Names, Vehicles, Sales Reps, Make Deposits, Reconcile.

- **Additional improvements**
    - Customize e-mails: Customize the subject line and edit the reply to email address when you send an email within QuickBooks.
    - Sales Tax Liability Drill Down: Double click on any total in your Sales Tax Liability form to view the detail of the line items that make up this total.
    - Send to Accountant: Process to send files to your accountant has been streamlined. Additionally files are automatically verified before you export them.
    - Searchable and Sortable Registers: Filter line items and transactions in your registers.
    - Updated Deposits: Quickly access your deposits history with the improved and easy to use deposits window.
    - QuickMath: Complete simple math within all calculable fields.
    - Custom date formats: Now supports display and entry of dates in formats defined by Mac OS X system preferences.

Chapter 2
Special Setup Issues

Objectives

As a consultant, you'll often encounter complex company file setup issues, such as conversions from other accounting software packages or QuickBooks files that were improperly set up. In this chapter, we'll present several issues surrounding setup of company files, and we'll offer several remedies to improper setups. In addition, we'll present some special setup situations that occur infrequently.

After completing this chapter, you should fully understand the following:

- How to set up your Chart of Accounts (page 65)
- How to use Items in QuickBooks (page 66)
- How to use classes to track multiple departments, locations, or non-profit funds (page 71)
- How to enter partially paid Invoices and Bills during setup (page 75)
- Setting up Multi-currency (page 74)
- How to enter historical transactions to bring the file up to date (page 76)
- How to set up QuickBooks in the middle of a tax year (page 77)
- How to set up mid-year balances for 1099s (for mid-year setups) (page 80)
- How to set up a fiscal year company (i.e. non 12/31 year-end) (page 82)

Chart of Accounts

When creating a new company, QuickBooks prompts you to select an industry. Based on your selection, QuickBooks creates a default chart of accounts customized for that industry. Most of these accounts are income and expense accounts, but relevant balance sheet accounts are also included.

The name and numbers of these default accounts are set up to assist you in preparing an income tax return for a company in that specific industry. They are also set up with the features in QuickBooks in mind. For example, the default accounts include Opening Balance Equity, which is unique to QuickBooks and the way it works for setup entries. Also, there are predefined accounts for Inventory, Accounts Receivable, Sales Tax Payable, and several others that are used by transactions in QuickBooks.

Traditional accounting programs frequently used complex chart of accounts to provide details on items purchased and sold or to be able to create segmented reports for a division, department or project. Before duplicating a complex chart of accounts used in another system, consider how QuickBooks uses Items, Classes and Jobs to track more details with less complexity.

Accounts vs. Items

A very common misunderstanding among new users of QuickBooks is how Items differ from Accounts. Simply put, Items track each product or service you purchase or sell, while Accounts are general categories where you track income and expenses.

When designing your chart of accounts, keep in mind that Items can be used to track the details of products or services you sell. Accounts should have relatively high-level descriptions of the types of income and expenses in the company. By using items you will have access to many reports that show the details of what items were bought and sold.

Accounts vs. Classes

Another mistake that is made is using accounts to track income and expenses through departments or divisions. QuickBooks uses classes to track income and expenses to different segments of the company.

Think about using classes to track of the profitability of these different segments when designing your chart of accounts. By using classes, you will quickly generate Profit and Loss report by class to help you compare different segments of your company.

	Class 1	Class 2	Class 3
Account1			
Account2			
Account3			

Accounts vs. Jobs

Some businesses use accounts to track income and expenses to different projects or jobs that they manage. QuickBooks has very strong job costing abilities and can track income and expenses to a Customer:Job without requiring additional accounts.

Avoid creating accounts for projects or jobs when designing your chart of accounts. By utilizing customer:jobs instead, you can access a large number of reports specifically designed for analyzing and reporting on jobs.

	Job 1	Job 2	Job 3
Account1			
Account2			
Account3			

> **Tip** - It's best to keep the number of accounts in the Chart of Accounts to a minimum. If you need more detail, use **Items**, **Classes** or **Jobs**.

Adding New Accounts

After reviewing the default accounts set up in a new company, you will need to add accounts specific to that company. When adding these new accounts it is important that you use names and numbers that maintain consistency with the order and numbering guidelines of the default chart of accounts. This will help you to quickly find the accounts that you need when you are completing financial statements and tax returns, plus it allows for some level of comparison between companies.

Account Numbers

Account Numbers are turned off by default in QuickBooks, but they can be turned on in the Accounting Preferences window. When turned on, account numbers appear in the Chart of Accounts, drop down lists and reports. Account numbers are off by default because account names require less memorization.

> **Tip** – Turn on account numbers for yourself when setting up accounts or completing a year end, but keep them turned off for your clients.

Accounts are generated with a five digit number based on the following guidelines.

10000 - 19999	Assets
20000 - 29999	Liabilities
30000 - 39999	Equity
40000 - 49999	Income or Revenue
50000 - 59999	Cost of Goods Sold and Job Costs
60000 - 69999	Expenses and Overhead Costs
70000 - 79999	Other Income
80000 - 89999	Other Expense

Any accounts that you add should be well spaced to allow new accounts to be added at a later date without a change in account numbers. Sub-accounts should be created with numbers consistent with their parent accounts. For example, if Legal Fees were added as a sub-account of Professional Fees (66700), a consistent number would be 66710.

Within each type of account we recommend you add accounts as follows.

Assets are numbered from most liquid to least liquid as listed below.

10000 – 10999	Bank and short term investments
11000 – 11999	Accounts Receivable, Advances, etc.
12000 – 14999	Inventory and Other Current Assets
15000 – 17999	Fixed Assets and accumulated depreciation
18000 – 19999	Other Assets with the longest term assets listed last

Liabilities are also numbered in the order of liquidity as follows.

20000 - 21999	Accounts Payables
22000 - 23999	Credit Cards and short term loans
24000 - 26999	Other Current Liabilities
27000 - 29999	Long Term Liabilities

Equity should be numbered based on the reporting required in the balance sheet or retained earnings statement.

| 30000 – 39999 | Opening Balance Equity, Owners Draws, Retained Earnings, Other Equity |

Income accounts are normally set up based on the level of detail required on the profit and loss statement of the company. In QuickBooks it is **not** necessary to create income accounts for each item sold as there are more effective ways to see the details of your sales (see page 66).

| 40000 – 49999 | Income accounts |

Cost of Goods Sold accounts should be numbered consistently with your income accounts. Again, think about the level of detail necessary from the profit and loss statement.

| 50000 - 59999 | Job Costs/Cost of Goods Sold |

Expense accounts are generally numbered alphabetically with gaps between account numbers.

| 60000 – 69999 | Expenses |

Other income accounts are used for money received by the company that is not part of their normal business operations.

| 70000 – 79999 | Other Income |

Other Expenses are used for money spent by the company that is not part of their normal business operations.

| 80000 – 89999 | Other Expenses |

Account Names

A well designed chart of accounts uses account names that make sense for both the end user and the accountant. End users mostly select items in the sales transactions and expense accounts in some of their purchase transactions. Accountants need to be able to quickly understand the accounts to complete tax returns and prepare financial statements.

In order to meet the needs of both parties, profit and loss account names should have a high-level description of the types of income or expense that will be tracked to that account.

Some examples of **good income account names** are:

- Parts Sales
- Labor Income

These names describe the general category of sales and not the individual items that are sold. As the company grows and adds new items or services for sale, the accounts can remain the same.

Some examples of **bad income account names** are as follows:

- Widget Sales
- Gadget Sales
- Ken's Labor Income

These list very specific items or services that are sold which will force new accounts to be added as the company changes its product line or services offered.

Balance sheet accounts normally use names that are consistent across industries and companies. QuickBooks creates a select number of balance sheet accounts based on the features that are turned on by the user. Accounts Receivable and Accounts Payable accounts are normally set up in advance, but will be created automatically if you create invoices or enter bills. Other balance sheet accounts are created as follows:

- Payroll Liabilities created when payroll is turned on in the preferences
- Sales Tax Payable is created when sales tax is turned on in the preferences

In addition to these default accounts, you will need to add a few of your own.

Testing Your Account Setup

As you set up your accounts, review how they appear in your Balance Sheet and Profit and Loss reports. These reports are based on the account type and order of accounts as they are laid out in the Chart of Accounts. It is relatively easy to change the account types before opening balances have been entered. By reviewing accounts in reports before entering opening balances, you can easily identify and correct mistakes in account type.

By default these reports will only show accounts with amounts. In order to test the reports, you want to see all accounts including those with no balance. To do this you need to modify the report to display all rows.

To display all rows in a **Profit and Loss** report, follow the steps in this example:

1. Select the *Reports* menu, and then select *Company & Financial*.
2. Select *Profit & Loss* at the top of the list.
3. Click the **Modify Report** as shown in Figure 2-1.

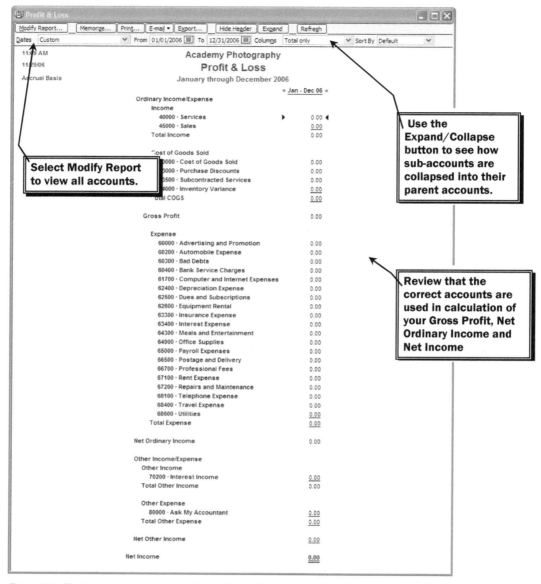

Figure 2-1- Testing your account setup in the profit and loss report

4. From the **Display** tab, click the **Advanced** button at the bottom right.

5. In the Advance Options window select Display Rows – All.

6. Click **OK** on the options and again on the **Modify Report** window.

The result is a Profit and Loss report that displays all accounts.

You can test Balance Sheet accounts as well by creating a Balance Sheet report and following 3 through 6 above.

Expanding and collapsing the reports helps to identify if you have consistently positioned your sub-accounts. Use this report feature to ensure that accounts that need to be compared are at the same sub-account level. When collapsed, these reports should be printed out to ensure they will print cleanly for a final set of financial statements. Even the largest businesses in the world can create a balance sheet or profit and loss report on one page, so if your reports cover multiple pages look for places to add sub-accounts to a parent account.

Setting up your accounts well at the beginning will save you and your clients lots of headaches and time later on down the road. So spending time here is well worth the effort.

Items

As mentioned above, items should be used to track each individual product or service you purchase or sell. Instead of creating accounts with these names, you could create **Items** called Widget, Gadget, and Ken. The Widget and Gadget Item could be associated with Product Sales Income, and the Ken Item could be associated with Services Income. Then when you sell Widgets and Gadgets, you fill out a sales form (Invoice or Cash Sale) using the Items on each line of the sales form. Because you associate these Items with Accounts, your Profit & Loss report shows the total sales of all Widgets and Gadgets in the Product Sales account.

But what if you need to see **detailed** reports about your Widgets or Gadgets? For detailed reports on Widget sales, for example how many you sold, the average price of a Widget sale, and the average cost of a Widget, you could create a **Sales by Item Report**.

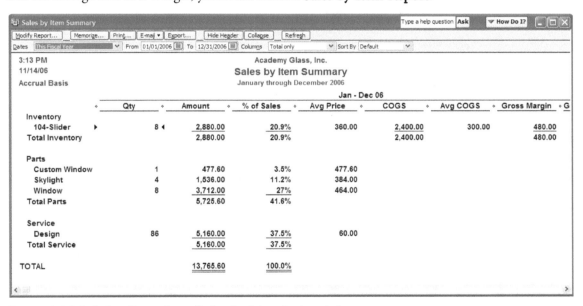

Figure 2-2 A Sales by Item Report shows all sales of each item for the period.

> **Tip** - It's best to keep the number of accounts in the Chart of Accounts to a minimum. If you need more detail, **use Items or Classes.**
>
> **Account Numbers –** To turn account numbers on or off, change the setting in the accounting preferences. Reports show account numbers only when account numbers are active.

Classes

You should use Classes to track separate departments or profit centers within a business.

In our sample company, Academy Glass uses classes to separate income and expenses for each of its two stores located in San Jose and Walnut Creek. You might use classes to separate departments within your company.

To activate Class Tracking in QuickBooks, follow the steps in this example:

1.   Select the *Edit* menu, and then select *Preferences*.

2.   Click *Accounting* at the top of the list.

3.   Check the box next to *Use class tracking* as shown in Figure 2-3.

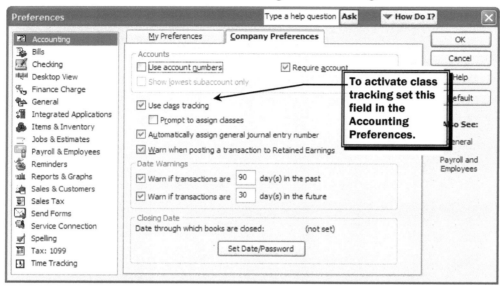

Figure 2-3 Use class tracking to track separate departments or locations.

When you use classes on each transaction (checks, bills, invoices, etc.), the Profit & Loss by Class report shows the profitability of each class.

On the bill in Figure 2-4, the Class field is tagged with *Walnut Creek*. This feeds this expense to the San Jose class (or store) so that the Profit & Loss by Class report shows the expense under the column for the San Jose class (see Figure 2-5).

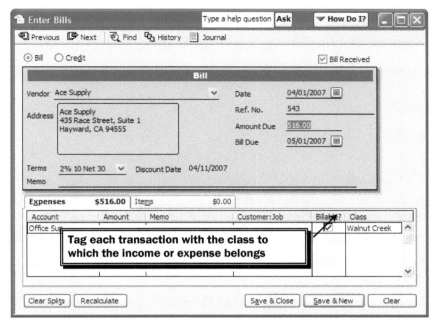

Figure 2-4 The Enter Bills window shows the class field.

Notice the report in Figure 2-5 above shows an *Unclassified* column. This happens when some of the transactions (or lines on transactions) did not get assigned to a class. QuickZoom on the balances in this column and assign the transactions to one or more Classes. It is best for the user to view this report daily to make sure all entries for that day include a Class. If there are numerous unclassified entries, you can move the balance from the *Unclassified* column to one or more Classes using a Journal Entry.

Profit & Loss by Class				
Academy Glass, Inc.				
Profit & Loss by Class				
January through March 2006				
	San Jose	Walnut Creek	Unclassified	TO
Ordinary Income/Expense				
Income				
Product Sales	28,960.00	34,194.00	0.00	
Services				
Design	0.00	12,032.40	0.00	12,032
Labor Income	7,032.00	0.00	0.00	7,032.00
Subcontracted La...	0.00	78,072.60	0.00	78,072.60
Total Services	7,032.00	90,105.00 ▸	0.00 ◂	97,137.00
Total Income	35,992.00	124,299.00	0.00	160,291.00
Cost of Goods Sold				
Cost of Goods Sold	0.00	0.00	24,000.00	24,000.00
Total COGS	0.00	0.00	24,000.00	24,000.00
Gross Profit	35,992.00	124,299.00	-24,000.00	136,291.00
Expense				
Office Supplies	0.00	1,468.00	0.00	1,468.00
Payroll Expenses				
Gross Wages	0.00	42,000.00	0.00	42,000.00
Payroll Taxes	0.00	8,000.00	0.00	8,000.00
Total Payroll Expen	0.00	50,000.00	0.00	50,000.00

9:19 PM
03/29/06
Accrual Basis

All income and expense transactions that are tagged with a Class show under their class column here.

Figure 2-5 Class tracking groups expenses on reports.

Use Classes to Separate

- Departments
- Profit Centers
- Lines-of-Business

Don't Use Classes for

- Customers, Vendors or Employees
- Worker's Compensation Categories

Multi-currency

QuickBooks supports all global currencies. Multi-currency tracking is available with sales, purchase, credit card and banking transactions in any currency your clients use.

> **Note:**
> QuickBooks multi-currency feature is enabled in a QuickBooks data file - but cannot be disabled once it is activated (see Figure 2-6).

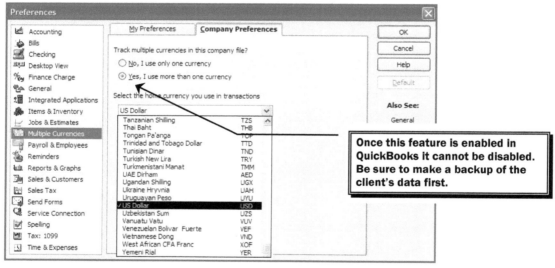

Figure 2-6 Enabling Multi-Currency

You can track sales and expenses in foreign currency just as you do for U.S. customers and vendors. QuickBooks automatically converts foreign transactions into the home currency. Current foreign exchange rates are downloaded either in QuickBooks or manually entered (see Figure 2-7). Any time you record a transaction that involves currency exchange, you can manually update the exchange rates as you're entering that transaction.

You can also process wire transfers and drafts from within QuickBooks.

QuickBooks records to the foreign A/R, A/P, Bank and Credit Card account the value at the time of the settlement. QuickBooks posts exchange rate fluctuations to an *Other Expense* account called *Exchange Gain or Loss*. You can track these fluctuations with the *Realized and*

Unrealized Gains & Losses Report. Balance Sheet financials are displayed in the home currency (U.S. Dollars). The home currency is in the country where your client pays taxes and processes payroll. Also, this selection determines the currency QuickBooks uses to present financial statements. Subsidiary ledgers such as Accounts Receivable or Accounts Payable can be displayed in either foreign currency or home currency.

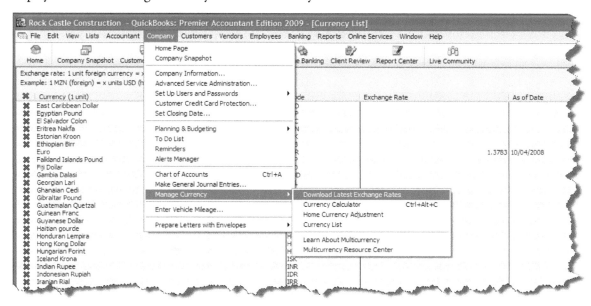

Figure 2-7 Downloading Latest Exchange Rates

Entering Partially Paid Invoices and Bills during Setup

As discussed in the setup process, when you set up a new QuickBooks file, you should enter each open Invoice and Bill into the file separately. In some cases, these open Invoices and Bills may be partially paid. If the company reports on a Cash Basis, you want to ensure that the income or expense is reported when the cash is received. For partially paid invoices, follow the steps in this example:

1. Enter each Invoice using its original detail (including the total dollar amount)

2. Enter a payment from the customer for the partial payment(s) and make sure the payment is deposited to Undeposited Funds.

3. Select Make Deposits to enter a zero-dollar deposit into the Journal Entries account. On the Select Payments to Deposit screen select the partial payments that were entered in the step above. In the Make Deposits screen you will select the Journal Entries account and enter an offsetting amount to Opening Balance Equity. See Figure 2-8.

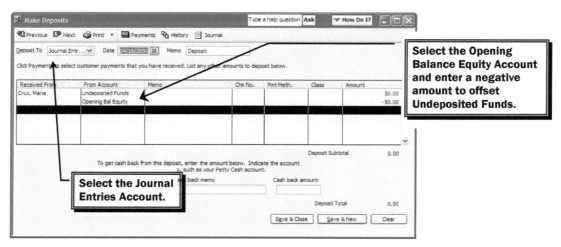

Figure 2-8 Entering a zero-dollar deposit

The result of these transactions will be an accurate Accounts Receivable account for the Start date, as well as accurate cash-basis Profit and Loss reports in the new year.

A similar process should be applied to partially-paid bills. When you create a Bill Payment for the partial payment of the bill, use the Journal Entries bank account to pay the bill. Then enter a Journal Entry to debit Journal Entries (to clear the balance) and credit Opening Balance Equity.

To understand this better, consider how QuickBooks calculates Cash Basis reports on partially paid Invoice and Bills. For a complete description of the cash basis topic, see page 580.

Entering Historical Transactions

If you're setting up sometime after the beginning of the year, you should enter every transaction from your *Start Date* through the current date.

Alternatively, you could enter monthly summaries of income and expenses using a journal entry for each month from the beginning of the year to your start date.

Make sure you enter your old transactions in the following order:

1. Purchase transactions (Purchase Orders, Item Receipts, Bills, Vendor Credits, Bill Payments, Checks, and Credit Card Charges).
    Entering the Purchase information first is essential if you track inventory in QuickBooks. Entering the Purchases/Expenses first is also essential if you use the time & billing feature, so any reimbursable expenses are in the database for you to use when recording Invoices.

2. Timesheets for each billable employee, if applicable.
    You need the timesheet detail for pass-throughs to Invoices and to create Paychecks.

3. Sales transactions (Estimates, Sales Orders, Invoices, Credit Memos, Sales Receipts, Payments from customers, and Deposits).

4. Sales Tax payments.

5. Payroll transactions (Paychecks, Liability Payments).

6.   Adjustments to your bank account (Transfers, Bank Charges, and Journal Entries).

> **Note:** You don't have to enter these historical transactions right away. You can start using QuickBooks before entering older transactions, however your balances won't be accurate and your reports will be wrong until you bring your file up to date.

Mid-Year Setup Issues

For calendar-year companies, it is preferable to choose a Start Date of December 31. However, if you must set up a company in the middle of the year, you must include a few additional steps in your setup.

Year-to-Date Adjustment for Income and Expenses

To record the total income and expenses so far during the year, use a journal entry like the one shown below.

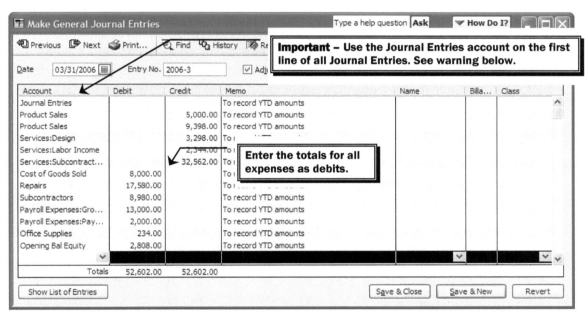

Figure 2-9 Year-to-Date adjustment for total income and expenses

Notice that the Journal Entry above does not record details of sales or expenses (by Customer, Vendor, or Item). It is not possible to affect Items with Journal Entries, but you can allocate income and expenses by Customer or Vendor if appropriate.

To adjust income by Item, see page 93.

To allocate the year-to-date income and expenses to individual Customers and Vendors, prepare the journal entry as shown below.

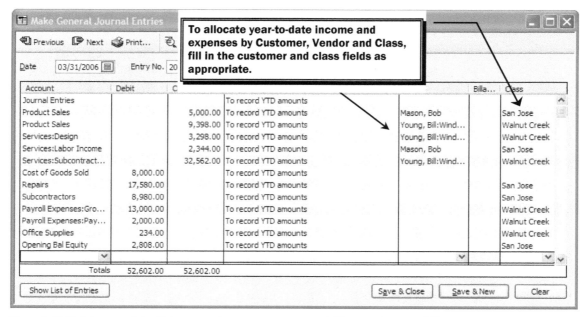

Figure 2-10 To job-cost and classify income and expenses, use names and Classes on the Journal Entry.

Important - Warning - Notice in the last two journal entries, the first line of the journal entries uses the special account called *Journal Entries*. This is a special *Bank* account in the Chart of Accounts, used as a clearing account for adjustments. See page 89.

Mid-Year Setup entry for Cash Basis clients

If the client files taxes on the cash basis, you'll need to do the following:

1. Using your previous accounting system, create a cash basis income statement for this year-to-date. Use those numbers for the journal entry that records the total year-to-date income and expenses in QuickBooks.

2. Enter all of your balance sheet account balances including your open invoices and unpaid bills (AR and AP) transactions (dated with their original transaction dates). Even though AR and AP are not relevant to the cash basis financial statements, you can still use invoices and bills in QuickBooks to manage your AR and AP. QuickBooks will calculate both the accrual and cash basis reports correctly.

3. Verify that the cash basis Trial Balance matches the Trial Balance from your previous accounting system.

Mid-Year Setup entry for Accrual Basis clients

If the client is on the accrual basis, you'll need to do the following:

1. Create an accrual basis income statement for this year-to-date. You can use your previous accounting system or whatever other source data to prepare the report.

2. Enter all of your Balance Sheet account balances including your open invoices and unpaid bills (AR and AP) transactions.

3. Create an accrual basis Profit & Loss report in QuickBooks and export this report to Excel.

4. Create a second column in your Excel spreadsheet and enter the numbers from your previous accounting system's accrual basis income statement.

5. Add a third column in your spreadsheet to calculate the difference between the second column and the first. The formulas in this column should calculate the difference by subtracting the first column of numbers from the second column. This subtracts the transactions entered in the opening AR and AP balances from all the transactions entered into the previous accounting system.

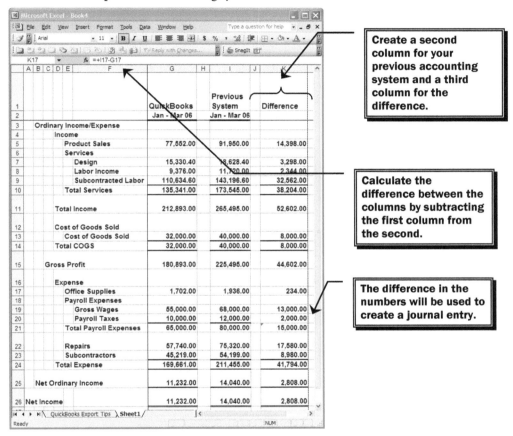

Figure 2-11 Exporting a Profit and Loss report to an Excel spreadsheet for comparison

6. Use the numbers in the third column for the journal entry that records the total year-to-date income and expenses. The offsetting account will be opening balance equity.

7. Create an accrual basis Profit & Loss report in QuickBooks and verify that it matches the one from your previous accounting system.

> **Note:** If the client received any money from invoices dated prior to the beginning of the year, this method will not provide accurate cash basis reports for the first fiscal year. If that is important to provide, enter the prior year invoices (dated in the prior year) and then enter the payments. Then, make a deposit, but zero out the deposit by adding a line that goes to Opening Bal Equity.

Allocating Year-to-Date Expenses to 1099 Vendors

When you enter year-to-date income and expenses, you'll need to allocate all relevant expenses to your 1099 vendors by creating a journal entry that separates the account balances to the individual 1099 vendors (as shown in Figure 2-10 above). This is necessary so that QuickBooks has the information it needs to print the correct amounts on the 1099s at the end of the year.

> **Note:** The setup shown above is the first step in making your 1099s work. You also need to set up the 1099 preferences and set the *Vendor eligible for 1099* field on each 1099 Vendor's record. For more information on 1099s, see the 1099 setup section starting on page **655**.

Setting up 1099 Balances in Mid-Year

When setting up a company in the middle of a calendar year you will need to take extra steps to ensure that 1099s are accurate. The following example assumes a March 31, 2006 start date.

Enter year-to-date income and expense amounts using Journal Entries and/or zero dollar forms. For the purposes of setting up year-to-date 1099 information, it makes no difference if you enter a single year-to-date entry or if you enter P&L summaries by month or quarter. See page 93 for more information about using zero dollar forms to adjust income.

Create a cash basis Profit & Loss report. Set the date range to **01/01/2006** through **03/31/2006**. Note the amount of year-to-date subcontractor's expense (see Figure 2-12).

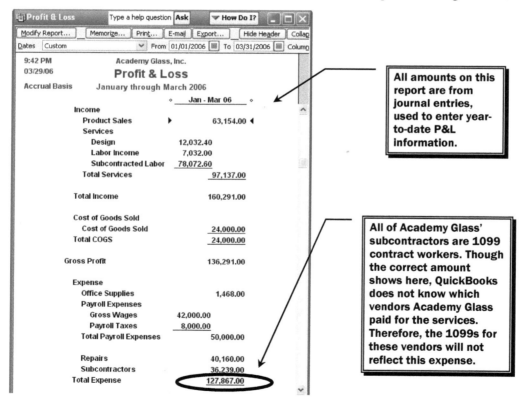

Figure 2-12 The Profit & Loss shows $36,239.00 in Subcontractors expense.

Using information from the client's records, or reports from their previous accounting software solution, determine how much of the $36,239.00 the company paid to each 1099 vendor. The records for Academy Glass show the following breakdown:

Boswell Insulation	$ 14,495.60
Wagner & Son Painting	$ 21,743.40
Total Subcontractor Exp	$ 36,239.00

Table 2-1 Subcontractor Expense by Vendor

To allocate the amounts shown in Table 2-1 to each 1099 Vendor, use a zero-dollar journal entry as shown in Figure 2-13.

Notice that Subcontractors Expense is debited and credited for the same amount. This makes it zero out. Enter the year-to-date total of payments to each 1099 vendor in the Debit column, and enter the Vendor in the Name column. Leave the Name column blank on the Credit line.

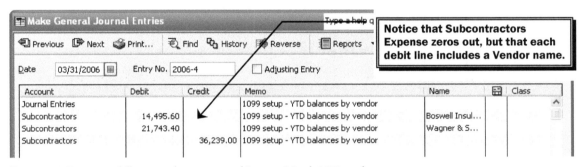

Figure 2-13 Enter zero-dollar journal entry to record January-March 1099 totals

Create a 1099 Summary report to confirm that it shows the correct year-to-date 1099 information for each Vendor (see Figure 2-14).

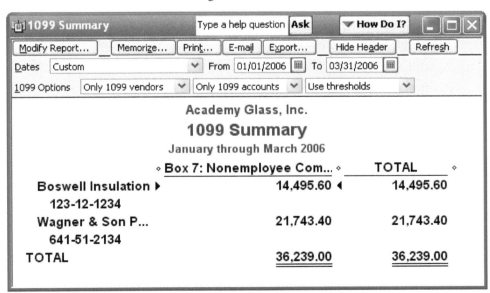

Figure 2-14 The 1099 Summary report now shows subcontractor expense for each vendor.

Mid-Year Payroll Setup

If you are setting up in the middle of a calendar year, you'll also need to set up payroll. For details on setting up payroll in the middle of a calendar year see page 413.

Checklists for Setting up a Fiscal-Year Company

This section includes three checklists for setting up a fiscal year company for different Start Dates. In this example, assume your fiscal year ends on April 30. The table below shows each step you must complete given three possible Start Dates.

Checklist for Setting up a Fiscal Year Company

If Start Date is:	Fiscal Year End	Mid-Fiscal Year	End of Calendar Year
Example Date	30-Apr	30-Sep	31-Dec
Balance Sheet Accounts Setup	Enter Account Opening Balances per 4/30 Trial Balance	Enter Account Opening Balances per 9/30 Trial Balance	Enter Account Opening Balances per 12/31 Trial Balance
Income and Expense Accounts Setup	No P&L adjustment necessary	May-Sept P&L Adjusting journal entry. Include totals for Payroll accounts. Use Splits to allocate 1099 vendors	May-Dec P&L Adjusting journal entry. Include totals for Payroll accounts
Payroll Setup	Setup YTD Amounts by Employee for Jan-Apr. Do not affect accounts	Setup YTD Amounts by Employee for Jan-Sept. Do not affect accounts	No Payroll detail necessary
1099 Setup	Zero Dollar 1099 Adjustment for Jan-Apr totals	Zero Dollar 1099 Adjustment for Jan-Apr totals	No 1099 detail necessary

Table 2-2 Checklist for setting up a fiscal year company

The following section covers each of these checklists in detail.

End of Fiscal Year Setup (Middle of Calendar Year)

If your fiscal year ends in the middle of the calendar year, and your Start Date is the end of your fiscal year (for example April 30), use this checklist for your setup.

Checklist for Setup - End of Fiscal Year

- Enter the opening balances in all Balance Sheet accounts using the amounts from the 4/30 Trial Balance.

- Enter Year-to-Date payroll information for each employee using Setup YTD Amounts. See the mid-year payroll setup section beginning on page 413.

- Enter a zero-dollar journal entry to "plug" the 1099s for the total payments made to 1099 vendors between January 1 and your fiscal year end. See page 80 for how to set up the 1099 balances.

Middle of Fiscal Year Setup (Middle of Calendar Year)

If your fiscal year ends in the middle of the calendar year, and your Start Date is in the middle of the fiscal year (for example, fiscal year ends April 30, but Start Date is June 30), use this checklist for your setup.

Checklist for Setup-Middle of Fiscal Year (not Dec. 31)

- Enter the opening balances in all Balance Sheet accounts using the amounts from the 6/30 Trial Balance.

- Year-to-Date adjusting journal entry for income and expense accounts using year-to-date totals through 6/30 (May 1-June 30) for each account. Use split lines to allocate any expenses that relate to 1099 Vendors.

- Enter Year-to-Date payroll information for each employee using *Payroll Setup Interview*. See the mid-year payroll setup section beginning on page 413.
  Enter a zero-dollar journal entry to "plug" the 1099s for the total payments made to 1099 vendors between January 1 and your fiscal year end (April 30). See page 80 for how to set up the 1099 balances.

Year-to-Date Adjusting Journal Entry for Income and Expenses

To record the total income and expenses so far during the fiscal year, use a journal entry like the one shown below. In this example, the Start Date is June 30 for a company whose fiscal year end is April 30. The amounts in the journal entry are totals of income and expenses for May and June.

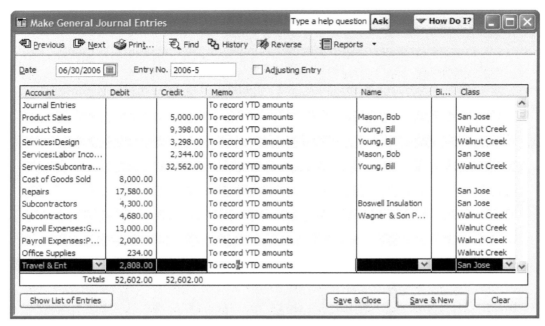

Figure 2-15 Use a journal entry to record fiscal year-to-date income and expenses.

Notice that the journal entry above does not record details of sales or expenses (by Item). It is not possible to affect Items with Journal Entries, but you can allocate income and expenses by Customer or Vendor.

To allocate the year-to-date income and expenses to individual Customers and Vendors, prepare the journal entry as shown below. Notice the Customer and Vendor names in the name field.

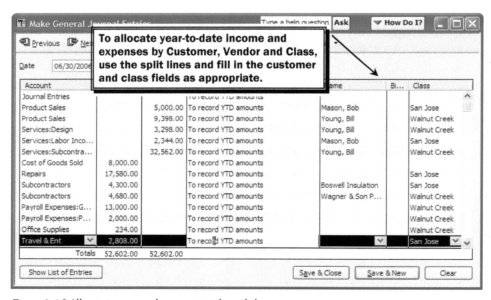

Figure 2-16 Allocate income and expenses to jobs and classes

1099 Setup - Middle of Fiscal Year (Middle of Calendar Year)

For a Mid-Fiscal Year setup, you'll do two things to set up your 1099s. Enter a zero-dollar journal entry to "plug" the 1099s for the period between January 1 and your fiscal year end

(April 30). Also, to record the 1099 amounts for this fiscal year-to-date, enter split lines on your Year-to-Date adjusting journal entry for each of your 1099 vendors.

To record the amounts for the January 1 through your fiscal year end, use a zero-dollar journal entry as shown in Figure 2-17. Notice that Subcontractors Expense is debited and credited for the same amount. This makes it zero out. Enter the year-to-date total of payments to each 1099 vendor in the Debit column, and enter the Vendor in the Name field. Leave the Name field blank on the Credit line.

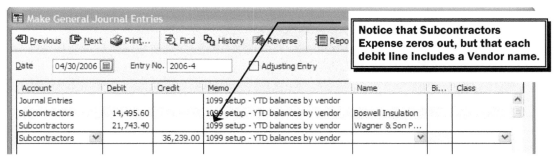

Figure 2-17 Enter another zero-dollar journal entry to record Jan-April (fiscal year-end) 1099 totals.

Middle of Fiscal Year Setup (December 31)

If your fiscal year ends in the middle of the calendar year, but you are setting up on December 31, use this checklist for your setup.

Checklist for Setup-Middle of Fiscal Year (Dec. 31)

- Enter the opening balances in all Balance Sheet accounts using the amounts from the 12/31 Trial Balance.
- Enter a year-to-date adjusting journal entry for income and expense accounts using year-to-date totals for each account.
- No payroll or 1099 detail is necessary.

Summary

In this chapter, you learned several special issues that can occur when you set up a client's QuickBooks file.

You should now fully understand the following:

- How to set up your Chart of Accounts (page 65)
- How to use Items in QuickBooks (page 66)
- How to use classes to track multiple departments, locations, or non-profit funds (page 71)
- How to enter partially paid Invoices and Bills during setup (page 75)
- Setting up Multi-currency (page 74)
- How to enter historical transactions to bring the file up to date (page 76)
- How to set up QuickBooks in the middle of a tax year (page 77)

- How to set up mid-year balances for 1099s (for mid-year setups) (page 80)
- How to set up a fiscal year company (i.e. non 12/31 year-end) (page 82)
-

Chapter 3 Things Accountants Must Know

Objectives

There are many aspects of QuickBooks that the average QuickBooks user may never understand. However, as the QuickBooks consultant or accountant, you must have a deeper understanding of QuickBooks in order to provide support services to your clients. In this section, we've gathered together several topics that are especially relevant to accountants.

After completing this chapter, you should be able to:

- Understand How and When to Adjust Account Balances in QuickBooks (page 88)
- Set up and Use a Special Bank Account to Track Journal Entries (page 89)
- Understand How to Use Forms to Adjust Income in QuickBooks, Preserving the Relationship between Items and Accounts (page 93)
- Use the Closing Date and Track Changes to Closed Periods (page 100)
- Understand How the Audit Trail Works in QuickBooks (page 103)
- Know what QuickBooks does automatically at year-end, and enter year-end adjustments as necessary (page 107)
- Understand QuickBooks Passwords (page 109)
- Understand How to Support Clients Remotely (page 110)
- Using the Toggle function to Toggle between QuickBooks Editions (page 117)
- Using Multi-instance (page 118)

Adjusting Account Balances in QuickBooks

In QuickBooks, every posting transaction directly impacts the General Ledger. The adjustments may also impact sub-ledgers (e.g. Accounts Receivable customer registers) and QuickBooks data management windows (like the *Bank Reconciliation* and *Payments to Deposit* windows). Also, QuickBooks uses both Item and Account information to build reports. In many cases it is important for you to affect both the Item and the Account to maintain integrity between these Account-based and Item-based reports.

Due to these issues, there are numerous considerations – and some workarounds – every Accountant must understand when adjusting account balances.

When to Use and Not Use Journal Entries

When first using QuickBooks, most accountants use far too many journal entries. This is probably because accountants are most comfortable using journal entries to enter data into other accounting programs.

However, you should use journal entries much more conservatively in QuickBooks because, among many reasons, they cause your item-based reports to be incorrect.

Here are two checklists for when you should and should not use journal entries.

When to Use Journal Entries

- Adjusting entries such as depreciation.
- *Closing* Partner's or Owner's Drawing and Investment Accounts to Retained Earnings or Owner's Equity.
- Accruing and reversing accruals of *prepaid* income or expenses.
- Adjusting *Sales Tax Payable*.
- Entering *bank charges* or *interest*.
- Entering *credit card service fees* or *interest*.
- *Reclassifying* transactions between accounts, classes, or jobs – when Items are not involved
- Adjusting Balance Sheet accounts (except A/R, A/P, Payroll, Inventory (if tracked perpetually), and Retained Earnings).

When Not to Use Journal Entries

- If you use QuickBooks Payroll, don't use Journal Entries when the transaction should affect a *Payroll Item*. See page 492 for more information on adjusting payroll.
- If you want your *Sales by Item* reports to match your financial (account-based) reports, don't use journal entries when the transaction affects (or should affect) an Item. See page 93 for more information on posting changes to Income accounts.
- Don't use Journal Entries when the transaction affects A/R, A/P. For example, don't use journal entries to write off bad debts. Instead, use a Credit Memo. The Credit Memo will affect the Account, the Item and the customer's balance.
- If you want QuickBooks to track *Sales Tax*, never use journal entries when adjusting revenue (sales or credits).
- To make corrections to *Retained Earnings*. There are some exceptions to this rule (e.g., distributing net income to partners), but if you need to make **corrections** to Retained Earnings it is best to adjust an income or expense account using one of QuickBooks' forms (Invoices, Bills, Credit Memos, etc.). Using the forms allows you to maintain the integrity of the management reports like Sales by Customer, while still achieving the adjustment to Retained Earnings. Using the forms also allows you maintain an accurate Retained Earnings balance when using the Accrual/Cash conversion. Essentially, the recommendation is to change last year's net income (using forms), which in turn impacts the Retained Earnings account. See *Adjusting Income Accounts that are Associated with Items* on page 93.

The checklists above are not all-inclusive. The two overall questions you must ask yourself before adjusting an account balance are:

1. Is the account you are adjusting linked to an Item, Sales Tax Item, Payroll Item or Fixed Asset Item?
    If so, you should not use a journal entry to adjust the account balance.

2. Does the adjustment to this account impact a sub-ledger or some data entry management window (like the *Bank Reconciliation* window or the *Payments to Deposit* window)?
    If so, you can use a Journal Entry most of the time, but you will have to massage the data to clear the journal entry from sub-ledgers and other QuickBooks reports and windows. For example, if you adjust a bank account and then reverse the entry on the first day of the following year, both the entry and the reversing entry will show in the *Bank Reconciliation* window. You will need to clear the entries from the Bank Reconciliation window (or tell the client how to remove the entries) before you give the file back to the client.

Using a Bank Account to Track Journal Entries

You can use a bank account called Journal Entries to keep track of the journal entries you make. This Journal Entries account is essential if you plan to adjust both the Item and Account detail in the client's file because you may need to use this account on forms as described on page 93. Perform the steps in this exampleto create and use the Journal Entries bank account on Journal Entry transactions:

1. Verify or create a bank account called *Journal Entries* in the *Chart of Accounts*.

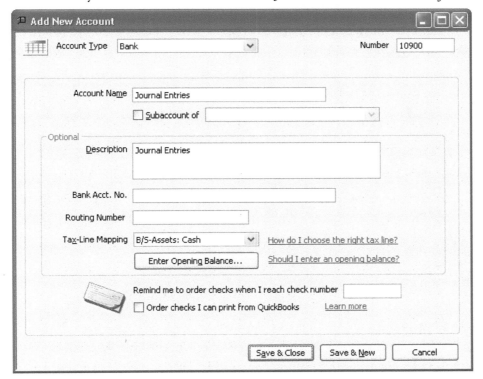

Figure 3-1 A bank account called Journal Entries to track all General Journal Entries.

2.   Use the *Journal Entries* account on the first line of each journal entry and enter a memo. Enter **only** the account and a memo on the first line.

> **Note:**
> If you use QuickBooks Premier or Enterprise Solutions, there is a preference to Autofill memo when you add lines to the Journal Entry.

Later, when you need to find or edit a journal entry, it will be very easy to find the entry by viewing the register for the Journal Entries account.

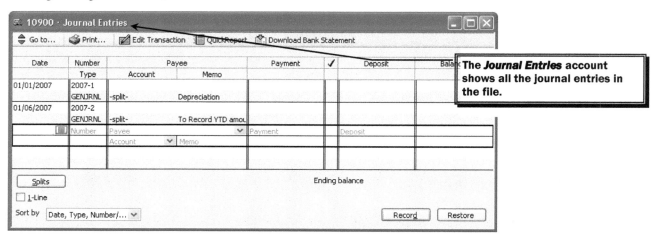

Figure 3-2 Use the Journal Entries account register as a list of all Journal Entries in the file.

Why Use the Journal Entries Bank Account?

There are a number of reasons why we recommend using a Journal Entries bank account, and adding this account to the top line of every journal entry.

1.   First, QuickBooks will use the memo and name fields from the top line in a journal entry as a default memo and name fields in the subsequent lines. As a result, if you enter a name or memo in the top line, but leave the subsequent lines blank, your reports will display the memo and name fields for all lines of the journal entry. This may be appropriate in some situations, but most of the time this default will result in incorrect memos and incorrect tracking for your jobs. (See Figure 3-3).

2.   Secondly, in order to make corrections to checks, sales receipts and other transactions that affect items, it may be necessary to enter a zero dollar transaction. We use the journal entry account to help us record these zero dollar transactions.

3.   Thirdly, the account is used as a place to store all journal entries made by the user. This allows you to open the register and quickly find and adjust journal entries made in the system.

4.   Fourth, there is a bug in the way QuickBooks treats the top line on journal entries. If there is a name entered on the top line of the journal entry, and there is NOT a name in any subsequent line of the journal entry, that blank entry will be treated as if the name on the top line had been used for that line. This results in assigning job costs (or income) to lines in journal entries, when that was not the intention of the user. So, to prevent this type of

problem, use the Journal Entries bank account on the top line, and always leave the name column blank on the top line.

5. Fifth, if the top line of a journal entry has Accounts Receivable or Accounts Payable, QuickBooks will consider the transaction open, and it will remove the journal entry from cash basis reports. So if your journal entry is meant to adjust A/R or A/P on the cash basis reports, the fact that the A/R or A/P account is on the top line will cause the cash basis reports to remove the transaction.

This Journal Entries account is also very useful for adjusting accounts by item, or if you need to record job costs for payroll when using an outside payroll service, or when making several other types of adjustments as shown throughout this book.

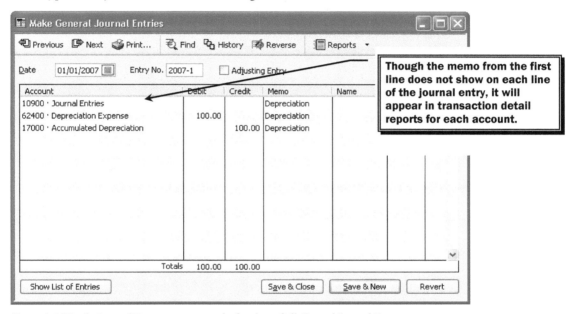

Figure 3-3 Use the Journal Entries account on the first line of all General Journal Entries.

Working with the Name Column on Journal Entries

Using the Journal Entries account on the first line of the Journal Entry protects the accuracy of job cost reports, reports for reimbursable expenses, and any other adjustment that requires a customer, vendor or employee name.

When a multi-line journal entry has a name entered on the top line, and not entered on a subsequent line, QuickBooks uses the name from the top line on every line that doesn't use these fields. In the example shown in Figure 3-4, Academy Photography is using a Journal Entry to enter summary Year-to-Date amounts as part of a mid-year setup. They are also using customer names so that job cost reports will be complete and accurate. However, because Bob Mason's name is on the top line, QuickBooks allocates all expenses without a name to his job on job cost reports.

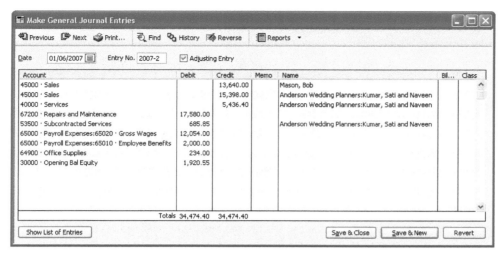

Figure 3-4 QuickBooks will use Bob Mason's name for each line that does not include a name.

Instead, use the Journal Entries account at the top of the entry so the name field on the first line will be empty. Enter the memo in the first line so that it will apply to all other lines of the Journal Entry when you create detail reports. See Figure 3-5.

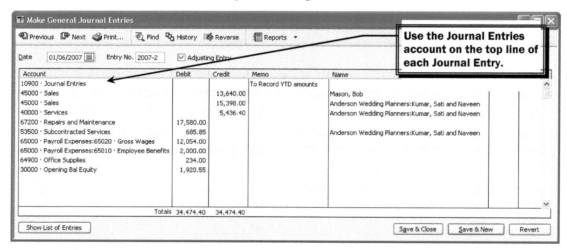

Figure 3-5 Bob Mason's name no longer affects the lines that do not include a name.

Adjusting Expense Accounts Associated with Items (Zero-Dollar Checks)

If you use Items to track the details of your expenses or costs, you may need to enter adjustments to the Items as well as the Accounts to which the Items are assigned.

The problem with using Journal Entries for this type of adjustment is that the Journal Entry screen has no provision for adjusting Items.

To solve the problem, use a transaction (such as a Check) that allows you to use Items. The Check will be a *Zero-Dollar Check* in that it will have an equal amount of debits and credits in the splits area of the transaction. You can use the Journal Entries bank account so you don't clutter the normal bank account with zero-dollar checks.

Follow the steps in this example to use zero-dollar Checks as Journal Entries:

1. Create a check using the Journal Entries bank account.

2. Enter the debits as Items with positive amounts and the credits as Items with negative amounts as shown in Figure 3-6 below. The total check amount should net to zero.

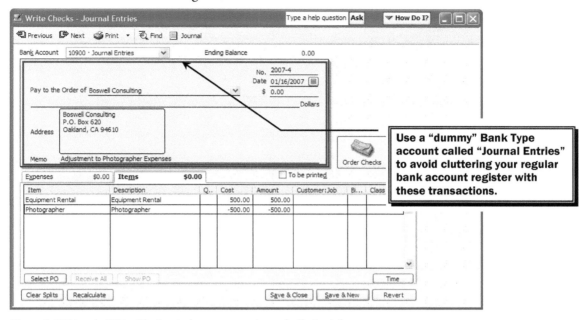

Figure 3-6 Using the Write Checks window to create a journal affecting job cost.

3. To review the adjustment to the General Ledger, save the Zero Dollar Check, select the **Reports** menu and then select **Transaction Journal**. QuickBooks displays the report shown in Figure 3-7 below. Notice that the report has the same columns as a Journal Entry – plus the Item column.

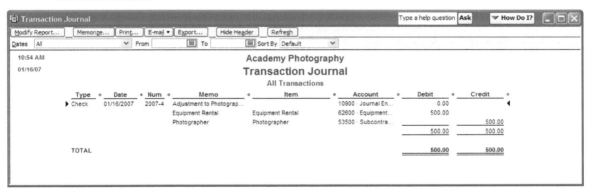

Figure 3-7 Transaction Journal from the Zero Dollar Check

Adjusting Income Accounts that are Associated with Items

As part of your period-end adjustments, you may find that income is overstated or understated in your client's financial statements. If your client uses sales forms, it is very important that you **not** use a Journal Entry to adjust income in QuickBooks because there is no way to link that adjustment to a sales Item. If you do use Journal Entries to adjust income, the Item-based reports such as the Sales by Item and Sales by Customer will not reflect the adjustment, and they won't reconcile to your Profit & Loss. To avoid this problem use a zero-dollar Sales Receipt instead of a Journal Entry to adjust income.

For example, assume a retailer decided to begin selling a new product line in January 2007, but didn't set up QuickBooks to properly track this new line of business. The owner opened up a new checking account for the new product line but did not enter any transactions into QuickBooks. The checkbook for the new checking account, used exclusively for the new line, shows the following summary information as of March 31, 2007.

Cash Balance	$3,000.00
Total Checks written for Equipment Rental	$2,000.00
Total Checks written for Repairs & Maintenance	$3,000.00
Total Deposits	$5,000.00

Table 3-1 Checkbook Summary - New Product Line Totals

Follow the steps in this example to enter the year-to-date activity shown in Table 3-1:

1. Create a customer called **Accounting Adjustments**.

2. Create an Other Current Asset account called **Adjustment Clearing**.

3. Create a Payment Item called **Adjustment Clearing** that posts to the *Adjustment Clearing* Other Current Asset account.

    Use a Payment Item so that the offset to your income account will not post to income on the Profit & Loss or to the Sales reports. Payment items do not affect sales reports. Do not point the Payment Item to Undeposited Funds. Instead, associate the Item with the new Adjustment Clearing account.

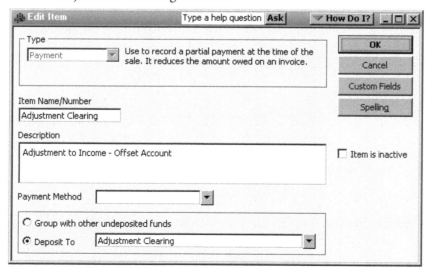

Figure 3-8 Payment Item for Adjusting Income on a Sales Receipt

4. Create an Other Charge Item called **Income Adjustment** that posts to an Income account on the Chart of Accounts.

Most of the time you will create an Item called *Income Adjustment* that posts to the main Sales account for the Company. Even though you do not refer to a specific business activity, the adjustment will still show on both the Profit & Loss and Sales reports, keeping the total income and total sales in agreement. However, if you know the specific area to adjust (e.g., product sales income) you can adjust the income using one or more of the existing Items on the Item list.

5. Create a Sales Receipt for the Accounting Adjustments customer. Enter the *Income Adjustment* Item on the first line and then enter the amount of your credit to Income in the Amount column.

6. Enter the *Adjustment Clearing* Item on the second line of the Invoice and enter a negative amount equal to the amount on the first line, to zero the balance of the Sales Receipt (see Figure 3-9).

7. Enter the *Journal Entries* bank account in the *Deposit To* field at the bottom of the Sales Receipt.

> **Note:** The **Deposit To** account will not appear if your Sales & Customers preference is set to Use Undeposited Funds as a default deposit to account.

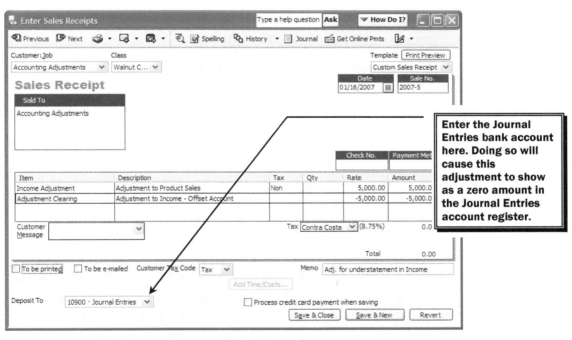

Figure 3-9 Using a Sales Receipt to adjust income by both Item and Account

> **Note:**
> You will use the Journal Entries bank account on zero dollar Sales Receipts, zero-dollar checks, and General Journal Entries. All adjustments will then show in the Journal Entries bank account register. This account will never carry a balance. See *Using a Bank Account to Track Journal Entries* on page 89 for more information. By using the Journal Entries bank account in all transactions you can also create a General Journal report that includes Zero Dollar Checks and Zero Dollar Sales Receipts. See page 96 for more information.

The Sales Receipt in Figure 3-9 creates the following *Journal Entry*. Notice that this adjustment to income affects both an Item and an income account, so your Sales reports will agree to your Profit & Loss. You cannot enter this transaction on the General Journal Entry window because Journal Entries do not affect Items.

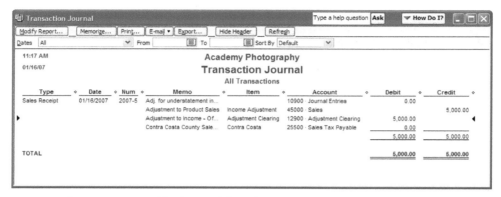

Figure 3-10 Transaction Journal for the zero dollar Sales Receipt

Also notice that the Sales Receipt debited a clearing account for $5,000.00. Since you may need to offset the income adjustment to several accounts, it is best to use a clearing account on the zero dollar Sales Receipt and then record a Journal Entry to clear the balance in the clearing account.

1. Create a Journal Entry to clear the balance in the Adjustment Clearing account, debiting the appropriate accounts as shown in Figure 3-11.

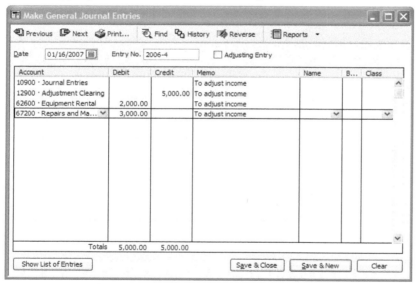

Figure 3-11 General Journal Entry to clear the balance in the Adjustment Clearing account

Creating a General Journal Report

Perform the steps in this exampleto create a General Journal report:

1. Select the **Reports** menu, select **Accountant & Taxes** and then select **Journal**.

2. Set the date range to the current fiscal year to date (or other preferred date range).

3. Filter the report by Account for the Journal Entries bank account and click Yes to include Split Detail, as shown in Figure 3-12 below. Since you used the Journal Entries bank account when you recorded adjustments on Journal Entries, Sales Receipts and Checks, all of your adjusting entries will show on the report.

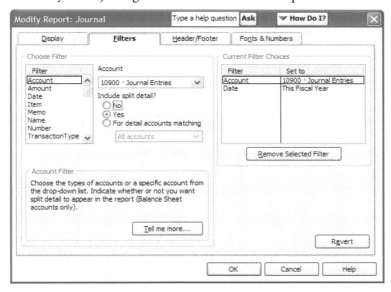

Figure 3-12 Modify the Journal Report to show Journal Entries only.

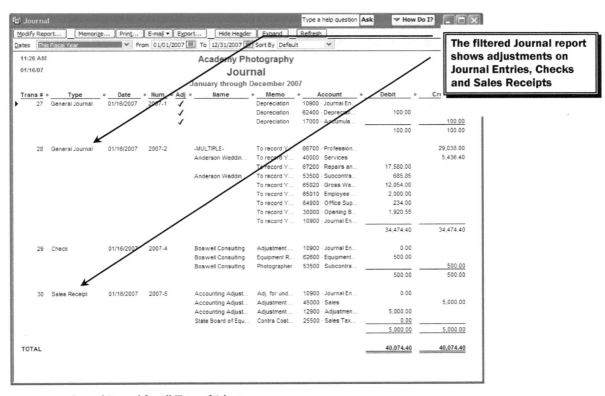

Figure 3-13 General Journal for All Types of Adjustments

4. Sort the report by **Num** so the Journal Entries will be in numerical order. Alternatively, you can sort the report by date or transaction type.

5. Change the title of the report to General Journal and memorize it for future use.

Creating Reversing Journal Entries

Note: This section applies to QuickBooks Premier and Enterprise Solutions only.

QuickBooks includes a **Reverse** button on the Journal Entry window.

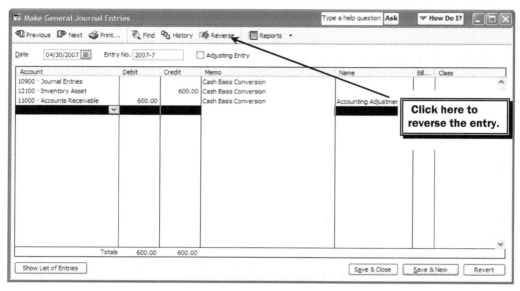

Figure 3-14 A General Journal Entry showing the Reverse button

The *Reverse* button creates a separate Journal Entry transaction with the debits and credits inverted. QuickBooks automatically dates the reversing entry on the first day of the following month. For example, if you enter a Journal Entry dated December 31, 2006 and click the *Reverse* button, QuickBooks creates a separate entry dated January 1, 2007 with inverted debits and credits. QuickBooks also creates the Journal Entry number automatically, using the number of the original entry followed by the letter "R." You have the option of viewing and making changes to the reversing entry before saving.

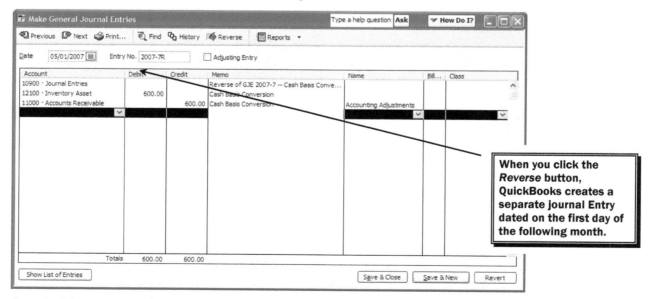

Figure 3-15 A reversing journal entry

Creating Adjusting Entries

QuickBooks: Accountant and QuickBooks Enterprise Solutions allow you to designate a Journal Entry as an Adjusting Entry. To do this you simply click the *Adjusting Entry* box at the top of the *Make General Journal Entries* window. See Figure 3-16 below.

Figure 3-16 Make General Journal Entry window with Adjusting Entry Checked

Designating a Journal Entry as an Adjusting Entry allows you to:

1. Filter reports by Adjusting Entry designation.

2. Segregate the Adjusting Entries on the **Adjusted Trial Balance** report (in the *Accountant & Taxes* section of the *Reports* menu).

3. Include the Journal Entry when printing the **Adjusted Journal Entries** report (in the *Accountant & Taxes* section of the *Reports* menu).

4. Segregate the Adjusting Entry on the Working Trial Balance.

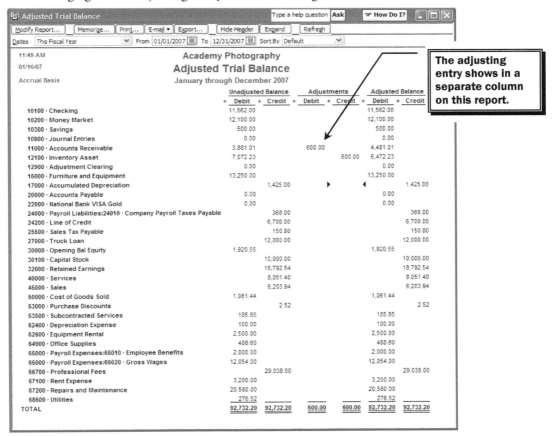

Figure 3-17 Adjusted Trial Balance Report

Adjusting Balances Using the Working Trial Balance Tool

The Working Trial Balance is available in QuickBooks Accountant and all editions of Enterprise Solutions (2005/5.0 and later).

The Working Trial Balance is similar to Trial Balance software you may already use. However, the data on this Working Trial Balance tool is dynamically linked to the General Ledger – allowing you to quickly research the detail behind any balance on the report.

To access the Working Trial Balance tool, select the **Accountant** menu, and then select **Working Trial Balance**. In Enterprise (non-accountant edition), open the Chart of Accounts window, click **Activities**, and then click **Working Trial Balance**.

Working with the QuickBooks Closing Date

QuickBooks allows you to set a Closing Date that effectively locks the file so that users cannot make changes to the file on or before a specified date. Even though this function is called the *Closing Date*, it is completely different from the Closing function in other accounting software solutions. These other programs will generate closing transactions at year-end to clear out profit and loss accounts and create an entry to Retained Earnings. The QuickBooks Closing Date feature does **not** create any entries, but only restricts users from making changes on or before the closing date.

Setting the Closing Date to Prevent Changes

Perform the steps in this exampleto set or modify the Closing Date and Closing Date Password:

1. Select **Preferences** from the *Edit* menu, select the **Accounting** icon and then select the **Company tab**.

2. In the **Closing Date** section, select **Set Date/Password**. A new window will appear.

3. In the **Date** section, enter the date in the *Closing Date* field (see Figure 3-18).

> **Note:** The date you enter specifies that users are restricted from making changes to transactions dated on or before that date.

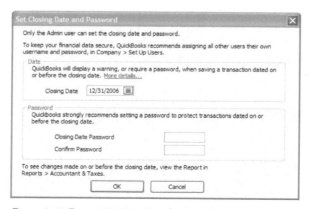

Figure 3-18 Enter 12/31/2006 in the Date through which books are closed section

> **Tip:**
> The user's setup affects his or her ability to add, change or delete transactions dated on or before the closing date. When setting up new users, always choose the setting that prevents them from making additions, changes, or deletions to transactions recorded on or before the Closing Date. However, unless the Closing Date Password is set, the Administrator of the file can always bypass the Closing Date with a simple warning window. To better protect the prior year data, require all users, including the Administrator, to enter a **Closing Date Password**.

4.   In the Password section, Enter a password in the *Password* and *Confirm Password* fields, and then click **OK** on the *Set Closing Date and Password* window. QuickBooks will now require all users, even the Administrator, to enter this password when attempting to add, change, or delete transactions dated on or before the Closing Date.

> **Tip:**
> If clients send you a data file at the end of each year for you to use when preparing the tax return, have the client close the year *before* they send you the file. If the client needs to enter any adjustments to their QuickBooks data, the user can use the Closing Date password as necessary to enter adjusting entries.

Tracking Changes Made to Closed Periods

> This section applies to QuickBooks Premier and Enterprise Solutions only.

The Closing Date Exception Report

Even if the file has a closing date set, the file administrator (and other users with certain privileges) can always use the password to make changes to a prior reporting period. The administrator can also remove the password protection or change the password. Since this could result in the changes to transactions the previous tax year's financial reports, QuickBooks (Premier and Enterprise Solutions) includes a Closing Date Exception Report that shows all changes, additions or deletions to transactions dated on or before the Closing Date.

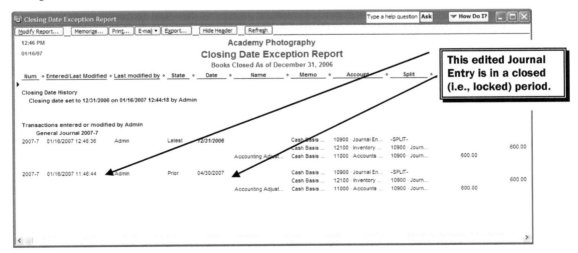

Figure 3-19 Closing Date Exception Report

> **Note:** The Closing Date Exception Report will show modified transaction by displaying the Latest transaction and the Prior transaction. New transactions will only be displayed with the State of Latest. Deleted transactions will be displayed with the type as Deleted.

Prior to QuickBooks 2007, there was one critical weakness of the Closing Date Exception report. QuickBooks would only populate this report if the Closing Date was set at the time the user changes, deleted, voids or adds the transactions. If the Administrator temporarily removed the Closing Date, QuickBooks would not track the change to the previous reporting period on this report.

In QuickBooks 2007 and later, if the Administrator did remove the Closing Date, QuickBooks will warn the user when they start up QuickBooks that a Closing Date has been removed and prompt them to set one up. The Closing Date Exception report will display transactions entered or modified prior to the last Closing Date that was set. Overall, this is an improvement but it is always best to enter a Closing Date and update it at year-end and as you complete sales or payroll tax filings throughout the year.

The Voided/Deleted Transaction Report

You cannot use the Closing Date Exception report if the Closing Date has never been set in QuickBooks. However, you may be able to use the Voided/Deleted Transaction Reports instead.

To view the Voided/Deleted Transaction Report select the **Reports** menu, select **Accountant & Taxes** and then select **Voided/Deleted Transaction Summary**. The summary report shows a single line for each transaction, while the Detail report shows all lines of the transaction. The summary report is shown in Figure 3-20 below.

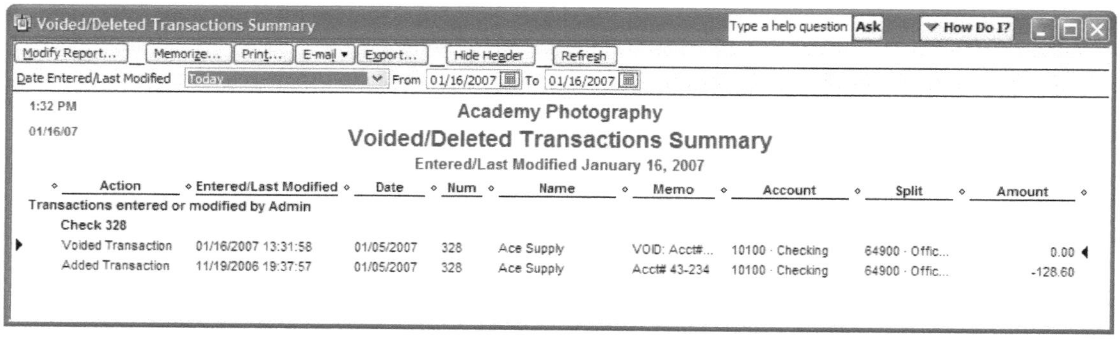

Figure 3-20 Voided/Deleted Transactions Report

The Voided/Deleted Transaction Reports are always on (if the client uses QuickBooks 2005 or later). Voided and Deleted transactions represent the majority of edits users make to the previous year's Trial Balance. And, most of the time the voided transaction is a Check. Voids to Invoices are also common.

QuickZoom on the Check to see the impact on the previous year's Trial Balance. QuickBooks displays the Voided/Deleted Transaction Detail report shown in Figure 3-21 below.

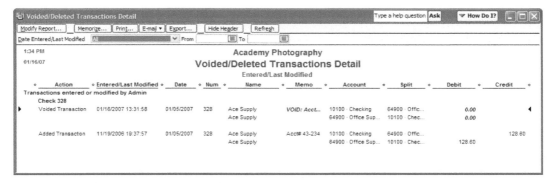

Figure 3-21 Voided/Deleted Transaction Detail report

To restore the previous period Trial Balance to its original condition, enter a Journal Entry that mirrors to original Check transaction (Credit Checking $128.60 and Debit Office Supplies). Then, reverse the Journal Entry in the current reporting period.

It is best to use a Journal Entry to restore the previous year's Trial Balance rather than editing the voided Check for three reasons:

1. If you click the Adjusting Entry box at the top of the Journal Entry, QuickBooks will include the Journal Entry on the Adjusting Journal Entries report. You can send this report to the client to enter into the live QuickBooks file.

2. If you create a Journal Entry you can reverse the entry in the current period by simply clicking the **Reverse** button at the top of the window.

3. You can use a single Journal Entry to replace numerous voided transactions, simplifying the data entry involved in restoring the prior year balances.

> **Note:**
> The always-on nature of the Voided/Deleted Transaction report is its greatest benefit. In QuickBooks 2006 and later the Audit Trail is also lways on, but the Audit Trail tracks all types of edits to existing transactions, not just voids and deletions. If you can't use the Closing Date Exception report, the Voided/Deleted Transaction report is a better tracking tool than the Audit Trail because *voided* or *deleted* Checks, Invoices and Bills are the most common types of changes clients make to the previous year's data.
>
> **Note:**
> QuickBooks 2006 and later versions offers a utility that will protect the prior year balances when you void a Check dated in the prior year. This utility creates the Journal Entry and reversing entry for you – at the moment that you void the Check. However, the utility only works with Checks (e.g., not with Bill Payments, Paychecks, etc.) and only if the Check is coded to Expense or Other Expense accounts. See page 260 for more information about this feature.

Batch Enter Transactions

Intuit recognizes that many accounting professionals need a simple way to quickly add certain kinds of transactions. This may be bulk entry of a number of transactions by key entry, or by pasting information from an Excel spreadsheet. To accommodate this they have added *Batch*

Enter Transactions. This feature is accessed from the *Accountant* menu (or the *Bookkeeper* menu in QuickBooks Professional Bookkeeper).

Currently the feature allows you to enter *Checks, Deposits, Credit Card Charges & Credits, Bills & Bill Credits,* and *Invoices & Credit Memos.*

If you are entering the transactions manually the program will automatically increment the transaction number (such as, the check number) for you.

If you paste information from Excel it is important to have the columns in your Excel document in the same order as is shown in this window. It is best to alter the order in your spreadsheet rather than trying to rearrange the *Batch Enter Transactions* window as it appears that this feature might not work correctly (at least in early revisions) if you change things there.

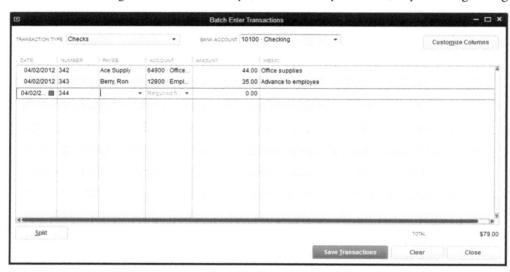

Figure 22 Batch Enter Transactions

When you paste information from Excel it is important that you spell names and accounts correctly. If you use a value that doesn't exist in QuickBooks then this window will highlight the information in red and not allow you to save the transactions.

As with the *Add/Edit Multiple List* feature, there are a number of functions available to aid entry. Right click on a cell to see a popup menu – you'll find the useful copy down, duplicate row and clear column functions (and more).

You can enter multiple lines (or splits) for the transaction by clicking on the **Split** button (or using ctrl-S).

Figure 23 Entering a Split

Audit Trail

QuickBooks provides an Audit Trail feature that allows you to see every change that is made to each transaction in the file.

Each time you edit, void or delete a transaction, QuickBooks posts the previous condition of the transaction to this report. As a result, QuickBooks retains both the old data and the new data for the transaction.

In QuickBooks 2005 and prior, this feature causes QuickBooks to run much slower, especially in a multi-user environment. The Audit Trail feature also causes the data file to grow faster. IN QuickBooks 2006, the Audit Trail is always on. However, QuickBooks 2006 and Enterprise Solutions 6.0 use a much more powerful database. This new database supports much larger files and allows you to track information on the Audit Trail without significant loss of performance.

In QuickBooks 2005 and earlier you turn on the QuickBooks Audit Trail in the Accounting Company Preferences window shown in Figure 3-24 below.

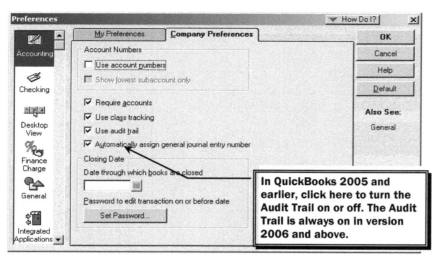

Figure 3-24 Turn on the Audit Trail using the Accounting Company Preferences.

The check shown in Figure 3-25 debits Cost of Goods Sold for $477.60. The Check formerly posted to Office Supplies, but a user edited the Check so the $477.60 charge for inventory would reduce Gross Profit, not just Net Income.

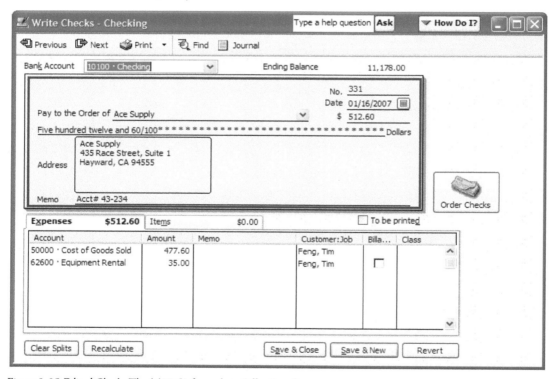

Figure 3-25 Edited Check. The $477.60 formerly to Office Supplies

To view the edits to this transaction in the Audit Trail report, select the **Reports** menu, select **Accountant & Taxes**, and then select **Audit Trail**. QuickBooks displays the window shown in Figure 3-26 below.

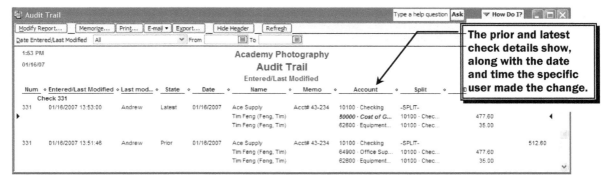

Figure 3-26 The Audit Trail report shows the details of the Prior and Latest Check transaction.

Consider the following about the Audit Trail:

- Filtering the Audit Trail produces limited results. In QuickBooks you filter for information *currently* recorded on *existing* transactions. The Audit Trail contains information about prior and deleted transactions that cannot be easily filtered. If you need to find specific information on the Audit Trail you can Export the report to Excel and use the Find command in Excel to locate the information.

- It is good practice for Accountants and Consultants to turn on the Audit Trail in QuickBooks 2005 and prior when setting up and editing the client's QuickBooks data. If the client wishes, turn the Audit Trail off when you finish.

- It is best to create a user name for yourself as the consultant/accountant so that QuickBooks will tag all your entries and edits with your name. After you work on the client's data, export the Audit Trail report to Excel and save the details in your files. This allows you to refer back to the work you do at any time in the future. Using the Audit Trail with your own user name will also protect you if the client accuses you of data entry errors.

- The Audit Trail tracks transaction data only. The Audit Trail does not track other changes to the file like edits to list items, memorized reports, edits to Memorized Transactions, edits to user access privileges, etc.

- The Audit Trail feature is a double-edged sword. On the positive side, using the Audit Trail allows you to determine *which transactions* the user changed or deleted, *which user* entered the change or deletion, and *when* the user entered the change or deletion. This information could help you determine the source of certain reporting or data management problems.

However, the Audit Trail feature cannot tell you *why* users changed or deleted transactions. The answer to why the user changed or deleted a transaction is very important when determining if the user had a legitimate reason for editing or deleting the transactions. Answering *why* is also important to prevent the user from creating reporting errors in the future.

What QuickBooks Does Automatically at Year-End

QuickBooks does not post any entries to the data file at the end of each fiscal year. When you create a Balance Sheet or Profit & Loss Report, QuickBooks looks at the date you set and depending on what fiscal year it is, QuickBooks calculates the Retained Earnings balance and the balances for Income, Cost and Expense accounts. There are three advantages to the QuickBooks auto-closing calculation:

- You don't have a complicated and irreversible year end process. Not only do most other accounting solutions require you to run a year-end process to close the fiscal year, many of these solutions allow you to enter data only through the first 2-3 months of the year before requiring you to close. Since the business tax return is due on March 31 (and for some companies April 15) at the earliest, you may not have solid year end balances for the previous fiscal year until months after other accounting solutions require you to close.

- You can always view transaction-level detail, regardless of how far into the past the transaction is dated. QuickBooks never removes the transaction-level detail from the file. This allows you to run very specific prior year comparative reports and highly detailed management reports (e.g., the three year sales trend for a particular customer or product).

- A Cash/Accrual conversion feature. Since QuickBooks calculates the Balance Sheet using transaction-level detail, the program has the ability to toggle this calculation between the Accrual and Cash Basis. If QuickBooks posted a year-end entry to Retained Earnings that was on the Accrual Basis, QuickBooks could only produce accrual basis Balance Sheets in future periods. The same limitation would apply to a Cash Basis closing entry, wedding the future reports to the Cash Basis.

Consider the following related to the QuickBooks year-end calculation:

- It is not possible to create a closed Balance Sheet on the last day of the fiscal year. QuickBooks does not recalculate Retained Earnings and Net Income on the Balance Sheet until you set the report date on the Balance Sheet to the first day of the *following* fiscal year (see page 670 for a full discussion).

> **Note:**
> You can produce a Closed Balance Sheet on the last day of the fiscal year using Financial Statement Designer. Simply create a year-end Balance Sheet and then use the Combine Account Rows feature in the *Format* menu to combine the Retained Earnings and Net Income rows. You can then name the combined row Retained Earnings or Owner's Equity.

- Even though QuickBooks does not post an entry to the General Ledger to close the year, QuickBooks displays a line entitled *Closing Entries* on detail reports for the Retained Earnings account (e.g., the General Ledger and Retained Earnings QuickReport), as shown in Figure 3-27 below. These lines show the debit or credit *impact* of the year-end calculation on the General Ledger.

Consider the following regarding this Closing Entry line on the General Ledger:

- Even though the line reads, *Closing Entry*, QuickBooks does not actually post an entry to the Retained Earnings account.

- Even though the entry shows a 12/31/2006 date, the Balance Sheet will not show the $473.80 increase in Retained Earnings until 01/01/2007.

- The Closing Entry (i.e., calculation) only shows in the General Ledger in QuickBooks 2005 and later.

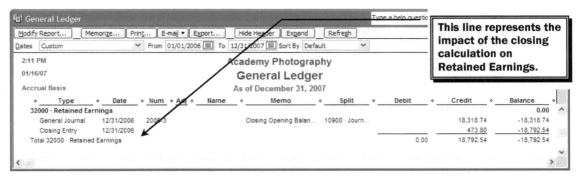

Figure 3-27 General Ledger for Retained Earnings

For a complete discussion of closing the year, see the section beginning on page 670.

QuickBooks Passwords

There are three password types in QuickBooks.

- The **Administrator password** is the password that allows you unlimited privileges. The person who is logged in as the Administrator can add, change, and delete Users of the file. The Administrator assigns a password to each new user when setting up the User account within QuickBooks.

- The **User password** is required to log in as a User of the file. Users can change their assigned password if they prefer, but they cannot change their user name or their level of access to the QuickBooks data.

- The **Closing Date password** locks the file so that users cannot add, edit, void or delete any transaction dated on or before a specified date – unless they enter the password. Only the Administrator of the file can set the Closing Date password and even the Administrator is required to enter this password to make a change to a closed period.

If your client loses the password for one of the **users** of the file, the Administrator can reset the password by logging in and modifying the User record in the Set up Users window.

If your client loses the **Closing Date** password, the Administrator can reset the password in the Accounting Company preferences window.

However, if your client loses the **Administrator password**, you will not be able to recover it without help. Intuit provides a password removal service that works with all versions of QuickBooks, but the fastest turnaround time is 1 business day. For more information, visit http://www.quickbooks.com/support/programs/password_removal.html.

> **Tip**
> Keep a record of your clients' Administrator passwords, perhaps as a custom field in your contact management software.
>
> **Note**
> It is best if no one, not even the owner, uses the file as the Administrator. Instead, setup a username and password for the Owner and give the owner full access to the file, except for the ability to affect closed periods. If the owner needs to perform an administrative task, he or she can always log off as themselves and login as the Administrator to perform this task. By setting up the owner with a separate log in, you will add another layer of protection to the closed financial periods.

Supporting Clients Remotely

Sending Data Files

Attaching a file to an email is one way to exchange files between consultant and client. However, QuickBooks files tend to get fairly large, often preventing them from being emailed due to server settings or email service provider restrictions. Some email service providers limit the size of attachments to as low as 2 MB and usually never more than 10 MB.

It is important to note that if the client gives the consultant a file in this manner, and the consultant intends to make changes to pass back to the client, the **client should not continue to update their copy**. If the client changes information, and the consultant hands an updated copy of the file back later, that copy will overwrite the client's file and the client's work will be lost. There is no way to merge the two copies from within QuickBooks.

You can send a data file, you can choose *Portable Company File* from the *Send Company File* option under the *File* menu.

File Sharing Portals

Exchanging files with clients through email attachments is not a secure way to handle confidential information. Rather than do this you should consider using a secure file sharing portal. There are many good options.

Using this approach you will have a website (which often can be branded with your company logo and information) that the client will log in to and use to upload a file to your account. You can also use this to send the file back to the client if you are making modifications (the same caution exists here as described in the *Sending Data Files* section, concerning not being able to merge copies of files). Often the website will send you an email notification that a file is available. These file sharing portals are generally much more secure than sending something via an email attachment.

One option is Sharefile. An account for this product is one of the benefits of membership to The Sleeter Group's Certified Consultant's Network. Visit www.sleeter.com for more information about this membership program.

Another excellent tool is SmartVault, which provides file and document management features as well as a file sharing portal.

Accountant's Copy

Another way to exchange information with your client is to use the Accountant's Copy feature, which is explained in more detail on page 291. This involves having the client send you a specially extracted version of their file that you can examine and make changes to, and then you sending just the changed information back to the client.

If you are a member of the Intuit ProAdvisor Program, or if you subscribe to QuickBooks Accountant Plus, you have access to the *Accountant's Copy File Transfer* service from Intuit. This is a secure way for you to exchange the accountant's copy (and accountant's changes) with your client.

Send General Journal Entries

Starting with the 2013 release, QuickBooks Accountant and QuickBooks Enterprise Accountant includes a feature that lets you send specific General Journal Entries to your client via email or a file download. You will use this in situations where you have a copy of a client file and you want to make a general journal entry in THEIR copy of the file, but you don't want to use the *accountant's copy* feature.

Sending General Journal Entries

To access this feature select *Accountant* and then **Send General Journal Entries**. It is also accessible from the *Send GJEs* icon in the ribbon for the *Make General Journal Entries* window.

Figure 3-28 Send General Journal Entries

The window will list all General Journal Entries for the date range selected. Choose the ones to send to your client by checking the box in the first column.

You can edit any General Journal Entry by clicking on the link for the transaction in the *Account* column.

There are two buttons at the bottom: *Email as Attachment* and *Save as File*. If you click *Save as File* the program saves a file with a file type of QBJ, which you can then send to your client via a safe method. Alternately, if you click *Email as Attachment* the program will create an email message for you that has the QBJ file as an attachment.

Note that at the bottom of the window is an option *Allow recipient to select which GJEs to post to file*. If you un-check this then all of the GJEs will be posted, otherwise the client can pick and choose which to post.

Receiving These General Journal Entries

On the receiving end the user will open the QBJ file by double clicking on it. This will start their copy of QuickBooks and present a window as shown below.

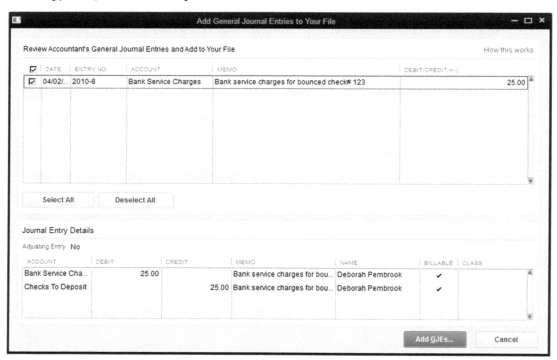

Figure 3-29 Receiving the General Journal Entry

If the *sender* has allowed the *recipient* to select the entries to apply then they can select the ones that they wish to use.

When you click on the **Add GJEs** button QuickBooks will post the general journal entries. You will see a summary of the actions, and you can get a report by clicking on **Show Details**.

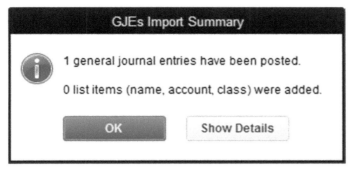

Figure 3-30 GJE Import Summary

If the general journal entry references a customer, vendor, item or account that doesn't exist in the receiving file then that list item will be added.

Figure 3-31 GJE Import Detail Report

If the user attempts to import the same GJEs a second time they will be warned.

Figure 3-32 Duplicate GJE Import warning

The program will also warn you if the receiving company file has a different company name than the sending file. You can proceed, however.

Client Collaborator

If you have exchanged a file with a client, you have the ability to create "conversations" that relate to specific transactions. This is only available if you have a file from the client that has been prepared properly, if the client also has the 2014 or later version of QuickBooks, and if you are using QuickBooks Accountant (and the client is NOT using that version). Setup is complicated, (see this article in the QuickBooks and Beyond blog: http://www.sleeter.com/blog/2013/10/installing-quickbooks-client-collaborator/). Once established, it allows you to exchange messages from within QuickBooks that relate to specific transactions.

Opening Data Files You Receive from the Client

When the client sends you a file it will be in one of four different formats:

> .QBW – QuickBooks Company File
>
> .QBB – QuickBooks Backup File
>
> .QBM – QuickBooks Portable Company File
>
> .QBX – QuickBooks Accountant's Copy Transfer File

In QuickBooks 2008 and later editions, all four file types can be opened by selecting the **File** menu, then selecting **Open or Restore Company**.

In QuickBooks 2007, Accountant's Copy Transfer File's must be converted to an Accountant's Copy Working before working on the file. To convert the file, select the File menu and then select Accountant's Copy, **Convert Accountant's Copy Transfer File**.

In QuickBooks 2006 and older, there are separate menu item for each of the file formats.

QuickBooks is upward but not downward compatible. By this we mean that you can use the most recent version of QuickBooks to open any older version of the file, but when you do, QuickBooks will convert the file format to the version you use. You cannot convert the file back to the format of the older version of QuickBooks. The upgrade is irreversible.

If you do not intend to return the file back to the client (for example, you intend to send the client just a list of Journal Entries to input into their copy of the file), it is best to convert the data file to the most recent version of QuickBooks. Doing so allows you to use the features from the most current version when working on the data file.

If you intend to work on the data file and then send the file back to the client, in many cases you will have to open the file using the same QuickBooks version the client uses (e.g., 2007, 2008, or 2009). This is typically an inefficient way to work in QuickBooks because the client cannot use QuickBooks until you complete your edits and send the file back to them. However, there are many situations where this method is the only practical way to work on and adjust the client's data.

Note that if you are using the Accountant's Copy method of exchanging the file, QuickBooks Accountant can work with a file from the same year as well as one older, and send back the accountant's changes. That is, if you have QuickBooks Accountant, you can work with a client file from recent editions of QuickBooks, and send back your changes. Again, only the accountant's changes, not a copy of the entire file.

Desktop Sharing Software

The ability to provide effective and efficient remote support to your clients is essential for any accountant or consultant. For remote support to be most effective you will need to view the client's screen – and in some cases you will need to use your computer to control the client's computer. This process is called desktop sharing. It allows you to work live on the client's computer.

Several software applications are available to help you do this. In order to provide support with remote access software, both the client and the consultant need a broadband Internet connection (e.g., Cable internet, DSL or T1) and the quality/speed of the remote support session is directly related to the quality/speed of both internet connections. Listed below are several examples of software applications or internet services to conduct desktop sharing (all tools work on Windows and Mac platform unless otherwise noted):

Tool	Company
Remote Desktop Connection / Remote Assistance / Terminal Server	Microsoft
GoToMyPC, GoToAssist, GoToMeeting	Citrix
LogMeIn	LogMeIn
Apple Remote Desktop (for Mac only)	Apple Computer
pcAnywhere	Symantec
TeamViewer	TeamViewer Inc.
VNC	RealVNC
Others: NTRglobal, Netop, CrossTec	Various

Table 3-2 Remote Support Tools

For remote support to be most effective, it is convenient to conduct an interactive session, where both you and the client can see their screen at the same time and you can pass control back and forth between you and the client. Microsoft Remote Desktop and Terminal Server options do not provide this type of connection. Instead, use Microsoft Remote Assistance or one of the other desktop sharing options for interactive remote support. Use Remote Desktop Connection or Terminal Server when you are working on the client's data without any interaction with the client (e.g., performing bank reconciliations, processing payroll or correcting setup/data entry errors).

The Microsoft options generally provide the fastest response time. Use these technologies – or obtain a backup of the file – if you intend work on the file for an extended period of time. Consider, though, that the client cannot work on the file if you are using it locally.

In addition, when you are accessing a client computer remotely in this fashion, the client cannot use that computer for any other kind of work at the same time.

Using Remote Desktop Server

When users run an application on Remote Desktop Server, the application execution takes place directly on the server. Only keyboard, mouse and display information is transmitted over the network.

This technology is better known as Terminal Server because that was its name until Windows Server 2008, when the service was renamed Remote Desktop Server. With Remote Desktop Servers, you store both the QuickBooks program and the data file on the server and users access the data and the program using any web-enabled computer. Remote Desktop Servers function similarly to remote desktop applications in that you control the server from a remote computer. However, unlike workstation-based remote desktop applications, more than one user can connect to a single Remote Desktop Server and run the same application simultaneously. In essence, it is like running multiple Windows sessions run from one server computer.

Online Applications

Online Applications are web hosted software solutions. You access these solutions using an Internet Browser. Another term commonly used to describe these applications is Software as a Service (SaaS), because software is provided as a service on demand on a subscription basis. Since SaaS is hosted on the Internet, any web-enabled computer (in most cases) can access the program and allow you to fully use the application. Many solutions are platform independent, allowing you to access the program for either a PC or Macintosh computer. Since the software and the data are as accessible as the Internet, there is no need for you to exchange data files with your clients or have your clients fax reports to your office. You simply log in to the web-based application and access their data file to enter, edit or print any information you need.

QuickBooks Online is Intuit's web-based version of QuickBooks Financial Software. It is a powerful and scalable (though not highly customizable) version of QuickBooks that you can access through any web-enabled computer. Instead of purchasing software, QuickBooks Online users purchase subscriptions that allow them access to the program – and to their data files. Subscription prices vary depending on the number of users and which features you wish to access.

QuickBooks Online is quite different than the desktop version of QuickBooks, with different capabilities and features. It currently is aimed primarily at service-oriented businesses. Note that Intuit is emphasizing that this is their primary product for future development.

Hosted QuickBooks

When we refer to *Hosted QuickBooks* we are talking about having your copy of **QuickBooks installed on a remote computer system that you access via the Internet.** This is a service that is provided by a company that is licensed to provide QuickBooks in this manner. The hosting provider handles all of the hardware management and software installation for you and the client.

If your client is using a Hosted QuickBooks system then you will be able to log in and use their system easily. You have the advantages of the remote login system, as there is just one copy of the database and you don't have to worry about transferring or syncing files. You aren't tying up a client's computer, and you don't have to worry about them letting you in or leaving the computer on. It is always available.

Due to licensing considerations there are a limited number of authorized Hosting services. For the most up-to-date list, see the Intuit Hosting Program website at
http://www.intuithostingprogram.com/.

Toggle Between Editions from QuickBooks Accountant

QuickBooks Accountant allows you to toggle between other editions of QuickBooks. This feature allows you to toggle (or switch) between *any* of the other editions (including Pro, Premier, or any of the vertical editions), to see the exact same features, reports, and navigators seen by clients who use those editions. This means the accountant only needs to install one edition (QuickBooks Accountant) whereas with earlier versions, accountants had to install every edition used by clients.

This tool offers four benefits to the accounting professional:

When offering telephone support to your clients, you can now make your QuickBooks appear like the edition of QuickBooks the client is using. You can now provide exact instructions when verbally guiding the client through the program.

You can open the client's data file using various editions of QuickBooks before recommending a certain product to your client (e.g., Premier: Manufacturing and Wholesale Edition). You can then experiment with the other edition (perhaps with the client present) to determine whether or not they should upgrade from Pro or Simple Start to an industry-specific edition of Premier.

If you write step-by-step procedures for a client, the toggle feature will allow you to provide procedures that will match the edition your client uses. This is especially useful when writing specific procedures for clients who use Simple Start.

If you teach QuickBooks (in a classroom or one-on-one), you can now use your computer to teach the client to use the specific edition of QuickBooks used by the client.

Perform the steps in this exampleto toggle from Accountant to another edition of QuickBooks.

Select the *File* menu, and then select Toggle to Another Edition. QuickBooks displays a window (see Figure 3-33) where you pick the edition you want to switch to.

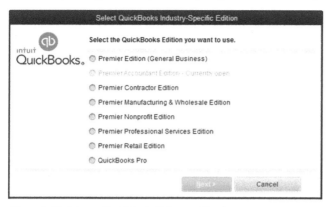

Figure 3-33 Select a QuickBooks Edition - Toggle

To toggle back to QuickBooks Accountant, close and re-open QuickBooks or click **Toggle** and select QuickBooks Accountant.

Multi-instance

QuickBooks 2011 and later editions provide a multi-launch feature, allowing two QuickBooks files to be open at the same time, but it has a number of pretty severe limitations.

> **Note:**
> This feature is found only in Enterprise (all editions) and Accountant.

Here's how it works.

If you have a QuickBooks company file open you can open a second QuickBooks company file at the same time. The first will be called your **Primary** file, the second your **Secondary** file.

Figure 3-34 Primary and Secondary Company File

The following is a partial list of restrictions on **both the primary and secondary file** (a full list is found in the Help file):

- You cannot <u>use</u> any application that uses the QuickBooks SDK.

- You cannot manage fixed assets.
- You cannot use the *QuickBooks Statement Writer*.
- You cannot install Intuit Workplace IPP applications.
- You cannot register QuickBooks or manage/change licenses.
- You cannot install a QuickBooks update.

The restriction that can be really tricky is the first – not being able to use applications that use the QuickBooks SDK. Many businesses rely on SDK based applications to provide vital features and functions, and you won't be able to use any of these if you have two company files open.

The following is a partial list of restrictions on **the secondary file** (a full list is found in the Help file):

- You cannot use the *Loan Manager*.
- You cannot manage currency.
- You cannot prepare letters with envelopes.
- You cannot us the planning and budgeting tools.
- You cannot use the *Collections Center*.
- You cannot perform many credit card processing activities found in the *Customer Center* (see the list in the QuickBooks help file for details).
- You cannot *Send Forms* from the File menu.
- You cannot use the Shipping Manager or do many shipping related functions).
- You cannot pay employees (Payroll).
- You cannot add, edit or delete payroll items.
- *QuickBooks Messenger* only works with the primary file.
- You cannot manage Templates in the Template List window.
- QuickBooks Help will only work with the primary file.

Consultants need to be very aware of these limitations. **We advise against recommending this feature to your clients until you are sure it will work in their situation.**

PCI Compliance

The Payment Card Industry (PCI) Security Standards Council has developed a rigorous set of data security standards (DSS) for how businesses must protect the security of customer credit card numbers. New compliance regulations are mandated by the credit card companies.

What is PCI DSS?

The PCI DSS is a set of comprehensive requirements for enhancing customer credit card data security. The standards were developed by the PCI (Payment Card Industry) Security Standards Council. This council includes representatives from dozens of credit card companies, including American Express, Discover Financial Services, JCB International, MasterCard Worldwide and Visa. The purpose of these standards is to help facilitate the broad adoption of consistent data security measures among merchants who store customer credit card data.

The PCI DSS is a group of six principles and twelve requirements. Here is the list of principles and requirements, taken directly from the PCI Security Standards Council web site (www.pcisecuritystandards.org):

Build and Maintain a Secure Network

Requirement 1: Install and maintain a firewall configuration to protect cardholder data

Requirement 2: Do not use vendor-supplied defaults for system passwords and other security parameters

Protect Cardholder Data

Requirement 3: Protect stored cardholder data

Requirement 4: Encrypt transmission of cardholder data across open, public networks

Maintain a Vulnerability Management Program

Requirement 5: Use and regularly update anti-virus software

Requirement 6: Develop and maintain secure systems and applications

Implement Strong Access Control Measures

Requirement 7: Restrict access to cardholder data by business need-to-know

Requirement 8: Assign a unique ID to each person with computer access

Requirement 9: Restrict physical access to cardholder data

Regularly Monitor and Test Networks

Requirement 10: Track and monitor all access to network resources and cardholder data

Requirement 11: Regularly test security systems and processes

Maintain an Information Security Policy

Requirement 12: Maintain a policy that addresses information security

Client Services for PCI DSS Compliance

As with all things in the compliance area, complex laws and/or standards that clients must adhere to are opportunities for accounting and consulting firms. While many accounting firms may choose to steer clear of this area completely, I strongly recommend that every firm at least assign a staff member to learn about the core principals and requirements of PCI DSS. Here are a few ways to get more information about the requirements, along with some information about where to get trained to provide client services to help them ensure compliance with PCI DSS.

The PCI Data Security Specification, authored by the PCI Security Standards Council is available on the council's web site at
https://www.pcisecuritystandards.org/security_standards/pci_dss.shtml

The PCI Security Standards Council operates an in-depth program for security companies seeking to become Qualified Security Assessors (QSAs), and to be re-certified each year. In order to become a QSA, you must first be an employee of a Qualified Security Assessor company. So there are many requirements both you and your company must satisfy before providing client services that are recognized by the council. For more information about becoming a QSA, see https://www.pcisecuritystandards.org/qsa_asv/become_qsa.shtml.

PCI Compliance in QuickBooks

Every business using QuickBooks should at the very minimum perform the steps here so as to ensure basic compliance with PCI DSS with respect to storing credit card numbers in QuickBooks. Keep in mind that these steps are just the QuickBooks part, so make sure you do this plus all the things in the list above.

To enable Customer Credit Card Protection in QuickBooks:

1.   Enable Customer Credit Card Protection.

Select Customer Credit Card Protection from the Company Menu. The button in the window (below) will either show **Enable Protection** (which means the protection is NOT enabled) or **Disable Protection** (which means the protection IS enabled).

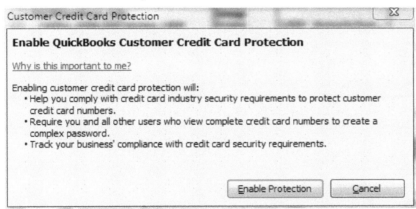

Figure 3-35 Customer Credit Card Protection

2.   Ensure that all users of QuickBooks store customer credit cards only in the Credit Card No. field on the Payment Info tab of customer records.

3.   Do not store sensitive authentication data such as card-validation codes (3-digit number near signature panel), personal identification numbers (PIN), or magnetic strip data.

4.   Limit access to credit card data by assigning or removing permission for users to view full customer credit card numbers.

5.   Set complex passwords and change them every 90 days for all users with access to credit card data.

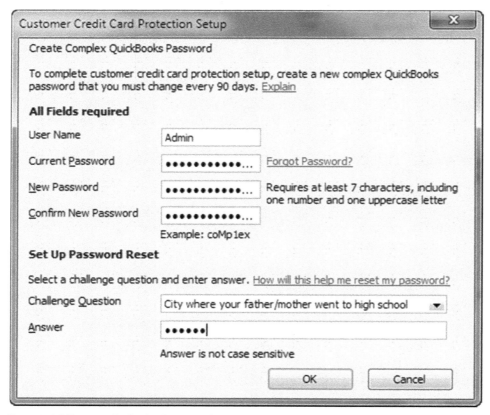

Figure 3-36 Customer Credit Car Protection Setup

6.   Keep QuickBooks updated by turning on automatic updates.

Summary

In this chapter, you learned several things about QuickBooks that accountants and consultants must know to support clients who use QuickBooks.

You should now be able to:

- Understand How and When to Adjust Account Balances in QuickBooks (page 88)
- Set up and Use a Special Bank Account to Track Journal Entries (page 89)
- Understand How to Use Forms to Adjust Income in QuickBooks, Preserving the Relationship between Items and Accounts (page 93)
- Use the Closing Date and Track Changes to Closed Periods (page 100)
- Understand How the Audit Trail Works in QuickBooks (page 103)
- Know what QuickBooks does automatically at year-end, and enter year-end adjustments as necessary (page 107)
- Understand QuickBooks Passwords (page 109)
- Understand How to Support Clients Remotely (page 110)
- Using the Toggle function to Toggle between QuickBooks Editions (page 117)
- Using Multi-instance (page 118)

Chapter 4
Tricky Transactions

Objectives

In this chapter, you'll learn about the following *tricky* transactions:

- Handle customer Deposits, Prepayments and Retainers (page 123)
- Process customer returns, credits, refunds, and overpayments (page 140)
- Handle prepayments to Vendors using Accounts Payable credits (page 148)
- Handle Refunds from Vendors (page 152)
- Handle *Barters* or *Trades* with customers and vendors (page 157)
- Handling 2-Party Checks Received (page 162)
- Handling Trust Funds (page 166)
- Handling Consignment Goods (page 171)

Customer Deposits, Prepayments and Retainers

When you receive money from a customer, but prepare an Invoice at a later time, you might want to set up an Other Current Liability account called *Unearned Income* (or similar name) to track all money received, but not earned. The following process can be accomplished using an Item, or a combination of Items and Liability accounts.

For this example, assume that Carl Nelson provides a prepayment of $5,000 for an estimated $7,500 in Window design and installation services. There are three ways to enter this prepayment into QuickBooks.

Option 1: The first option is to use the *Receive Payments* window to receive the initial deposit (see below for details), and

Option 2: The second option is to use the *Make Deposits* window receive the money and code a deposit to the Unearned Income account (see page 129).

Option 3: A variation on Option 2 is to create a Sales Receipt for the client using a service item called *Prepayment* linked to the *Unearned Income* account (see page 135)

The advantages of each method are as follows:

Advantages to Using Option 1:

You can create a printable form that shows the client's prepayment transaction, allowing you to provide a payment receipt for the customer. Simply press *Print*. Option 2 does not provide this receipt.

The prepayment shows on the customer's statement as of the date you record the prepayment. In Option 2 the prepayment does not show until after you provide the services/products and create an Invoice.

Option 1 requires no additional setup, data entry procedures or training. It therefore makes the most sense (intuitively) for the non-accountant QuickBooks user.

Since Option 1 uses receive prepayments, you can handle credit card payments easily if you use the QuickBooks Merchant Account Service. If you use Option 2 you'll have to manually process the credit card if you use the online Merchant Account Service.

Advantage to Using Option 2:

This method protects the integrity of QuickBooks financial statements. When you use Option 1, Accounts Receivable and Unearned Income will be understated until the company provides the services and/or products for which the customer prepaid. If the company consistently accepts prepayments or deposits for their services (e.g. a legal firm), you will need to enter an adjusting entry (with a reversing entry) when preparing financial statements or when using the Balance Sheet as a management tool.

Advantage to Using Option 3:

As is the case with Option 2, this method also protects the integrity of QuickBooks financial statements compared to Option 1. Unlike Option 2, however, this method allows you to provide the customer with a printed receipt.

> **Warning**
> The following method of accounting for customer prepayments may have serious tax consequences so you'll want to verify that you are handling prepayments correctly from the tax perspective. For example, if you are a cash basis taxpayer, you might have to treat customer prepayments as income for the year in which they were received. The accountant should provide guidance.

Option 1: Using Receive Payments to Record Prepayments

1. Click **Receive Payments** on the home page.

2. Enter a *Payment* for as shown in Figure 4-1. Do not save the payment transaction during this step. Also, if the customer has outstanding Invoices, do not apply this prepayment to those Invoices.

> **Note:**
> If you use the Auto Apply feature, QuickBooks will apply the prepayment to the outstanding Invoices automatically. You will need to clear all sections before proceeding to the next step.

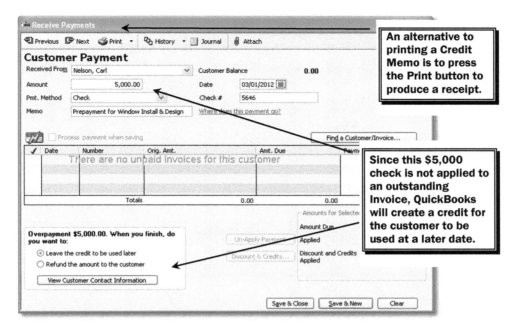

Figure 4-1 Use Receive Payments to record the prepayment

3.   Click Save & Close.

4.   Click **Print Credit Memo…** (see Figure 4-2).

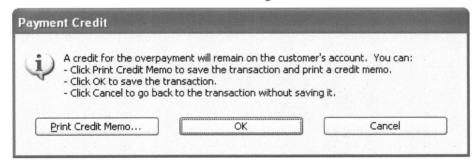

*Figure 4-2 Click **Print Credit Memo***

The Accounting Behind the Scenes:
The payment transaction show in Figure 4-1 debits Undeposited Funds and credits Accounts Receivable. The credit to Accounts Receivable will cause an understatement in Accounts Receivable until Academy Glass provides the services and products and creates an invoice for the customer.

5.   After the company provides products and services (including sales tax) the company creates the Invoice as in Figure 4-3. Save the Invoice with a *To-be-printed* status. Do not print the Invoice during this step.

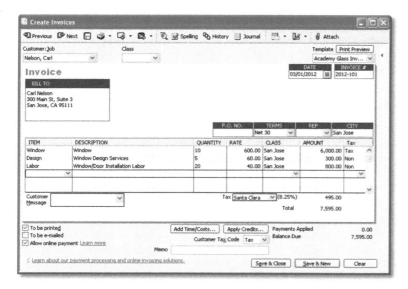

Figure 4-3 The Invoice without the prepayment applied

6.   When you save the invoice, QuickBooks displays the *Available Credits* screen as shown in Figure 4-5. Click **Yes** to apply the credit to this new invoice.

Figure 4-4 Available Credits screen.

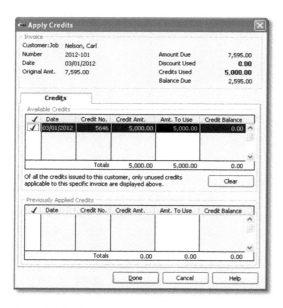

Figure 4-5 Apply the prepayment (credit) to Invoice 2014-101.

Note:
When you apply the $5,000 prepayment (credit) to Invoice 2014-101, QuickBooks links the two transactions so that the aging and opening invoices reports properly reflect the invoice and the receipt.

7.   Next print the invoice. Select the *File* menu, choose **Print Forms**, and then choose **Invoices**

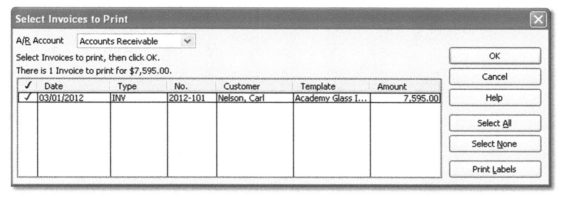

Figure 4-6 Select the Invoice.

8.   Select the Invoice and Click **OK** to print. The printed Invoice shows the Invoice total, the prepayment of $5,000 and the balance due (see Figure 4-7).

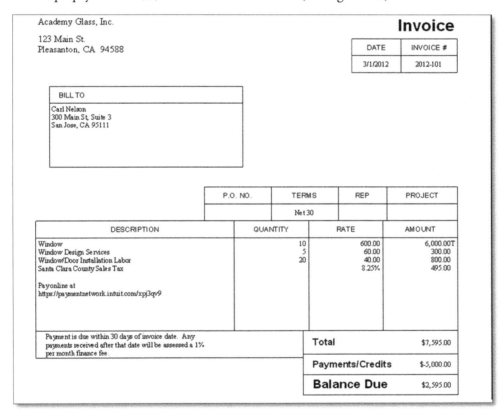

Figure 4-7 The Invoice shows the prepayment

Report for Tracking Customer Prepayments Using Option 1

Follow the steps in this example to create a report that tracks prepayments by customer:

1.   Select the *Reports* menu and choose Custom Summary Report.

2.   Enter **All** in the *Dates* field and *Customer* in the *Display rows by* field as shown in Figure 4-8.

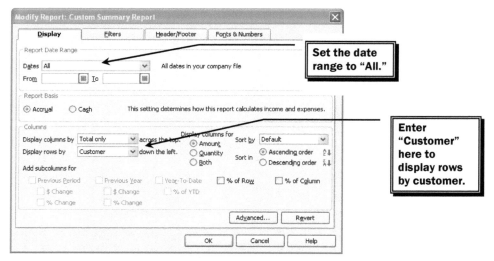

Figure 4-8 The Display tab of the Modify Report screen

3. Click the Filters tab and filter by **Account** for *All accounts receivable*, by **Transaction Type** for *Payment* and by **Paid Status** for *Open* (see Figure 4-9).

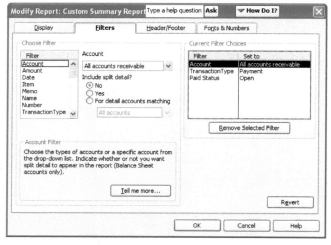

Figure 4-9 Filter by Account, Transaction Type and Paid Status.

4. Click the Header/Footer tab and enter *Customer Prepayments* in the *Report Title* field. Then unselect the *Subtitle, Date Prepared, Time Prepared* and *Report Basis* fields (see Figure 4-10).

Figure 4-10 Change the report title and remove additional header information.

5.   Click **OK** to save your changes. QuickBooks displays the report shown in Figure 4-11. Memorize the report for future use. Note that this report will zero out if you entered the invoice and applied the prepayment, but in the general case, this report will show the totals for each customer's prepayments.

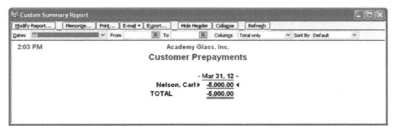

Figure 4-11 Report showing Customer prepayments

> **Note:**
> The total of this report reflects the understatement in A/R and Unearned Income. When using the Balance Sheet for reporting or tax preparation, create a Journal Entry to debit A/R and credit Unearned Income by the total amount on this report. Remember to enter a reversing entry as of the first day of the following period.

Option 2: Using Make Deposits to Record Prepayments

1.   Set up an Other Current Liability account called *Unearned Income* (or *Client Retainers*).

> **Tip For Cash Basis Taxpayers**
> If you need to treat customer prepayments as Income on your tax return, use an Other Current Liability account for management purposes and then change the account type to Income when preparing year-end financial reports or the company's tax return.

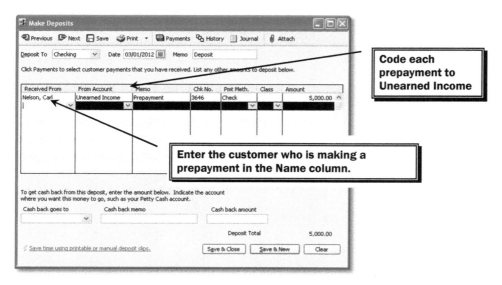

Figure 4-12 Deposit to record prepayment

2. Each time you receive a prepayment or retainer from a customer, create a Deposit transaction and use the *Unearned Income* account in the *Account* column. Also, enter the customer's name in the *Name* column (see Figure 4-12).

3. After the company provides products and services (including sales tax) the company creates the Invoice shown in Figure 4-13. Save the Invoice with a *To-be-printed* status. Do not print the Invoice during this step.

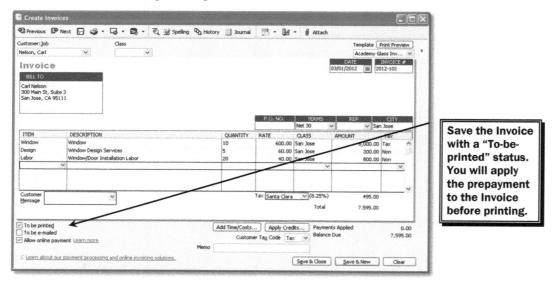

Figure 4-13 Invoice without the prepayment applied

4. Create a journal entry to credit Accounts Receivable for the amount of prepayment as shown in Figure 4-14. Enter name in the Name column for both the debit to Unearned Income and the credit to Accounts Receivable.

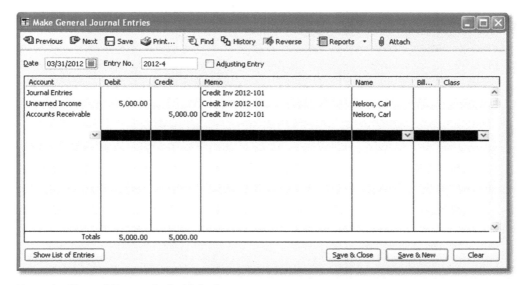

Figure 4-14 Journal Entry to Credit AR for Prepayment

5.   To apply the credit from the journal entry, display the *Invoice* (see Figure 4-15) and click **Apply Credits**.

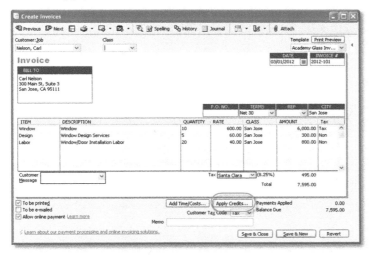

Figure 4-15 Click Apply credits to apply the credit to Invoice

6.   The credit from the journal entry is displayed in the Available Credits section of the Apply Credits window (see Figure 4-16) and click **Done**.

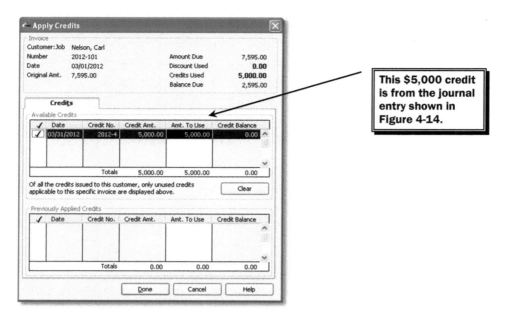

Figure 4-16 Click Done to apply the credit to Invoice

7.   Next print the invoice. Select the *File* menu, choose **Print Forms**, and then choose **Invoices**

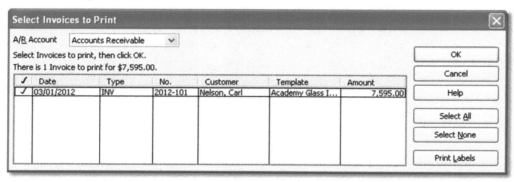

Figure 4-17 Select the Invoice.

8.   Select the Invoice and Click **OK** to print. The printed Invoice shows the Invoice total, the prepayment and the balance due (see Figure 4-18).

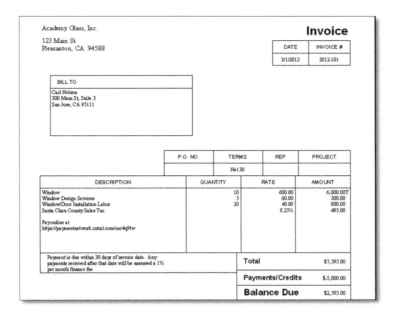

Figure 4-18 The Invoice shows the $5,000 prepayment.

Reports for Tracking Customer Prepayments for Option 2:

Follow the steps in this example to create a report that tracks prepayments by customer:

1.   Select the Reports menu and choose Customer Summary Report.

2.   Enter **All** in the *Dates* field and *Customer* in the *Display rows by* field as shown in Figure 4-19.

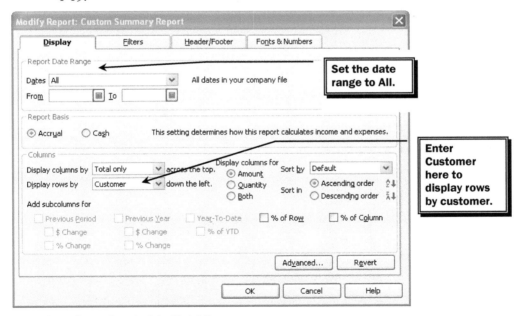

Figure 4-19 The Display tab of the Modify Report screen

3.   Click the **Advanced** button and set only **Non-zero** rows to display.

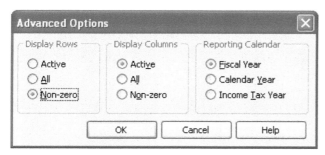

Figure 4-20 Show only rows with a balance.

4.   Click the Filters tab and filter by **Account** for the *Unearned Income* account (see Figure 4-21).

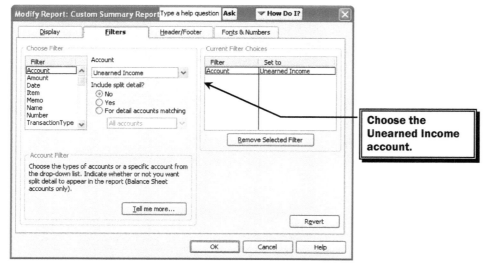

Figure 4-21 Filter the report to include only the Unearned income account.

5.   Click the Header/Footer tab and change enter *Customer Prepayments* in the *Report Title* field. Then unselect the *Subtitle, Date Prepared, Time Prepared* and *Report Basis* fields (see Figure 4-22).

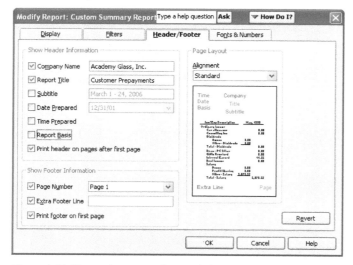

Figure 4-22 Change the report title to read Customer Prepayments.

6. Click **OK** to save your changes. QuickBooks displays the report shown below. Memorize the report for future use. Note that this report will zero out if you entered the invoice and applied the prepayment, but in the general case, this report will show the totals for each customer's prepayments.

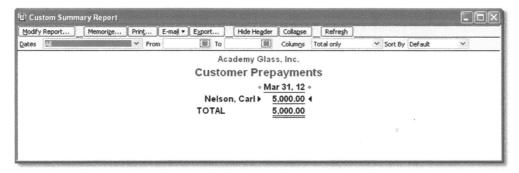

Figure 4-23 The report shows prepayments by customer.

Option 3: Using Sales Receipts to Record Prepayments

1. Set up an Other Current Liability account called Unearned Income (or Client Retainers).

2. Create a *Service* Item called *Prepayment* linked to this *Unearned Income* account.

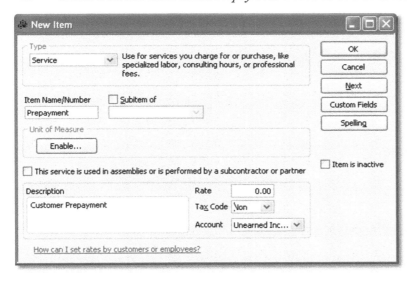

Figure 4-24 Create a new service Item called Prepayment linked to Unearned Income

> **Tip For Cash Basis Taxpayers**
> If you need to treat customer prepayments as Income on your tax return, use an Other Current Liability account for management purposes and then change the account type to Income when preparing year-end financial reports or the company's tax return.

3. Each time you receive a prepayment or retainer from a customer, create a *Sales Receipt* and use the *Prepayment* item in the *Account* column (see Figure 4-25). This will create a printable receipt that you can give or send to your customer.

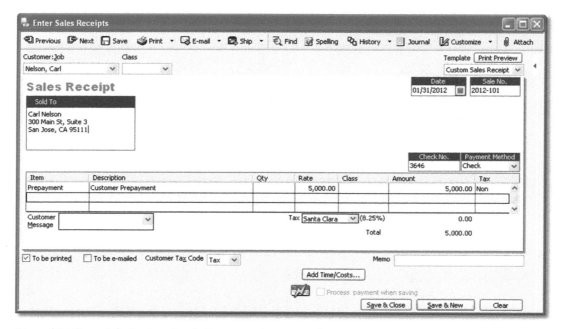

Figure 4-25 Create Sales Receipt using the Prepayment item to record prepayment

4.   After the company provides products and services (including sales tax) the company creates the Invoice shown in Figure 4-26. Save the Invoice with a *To be-printed* status. Do not print the Invoice during this step.

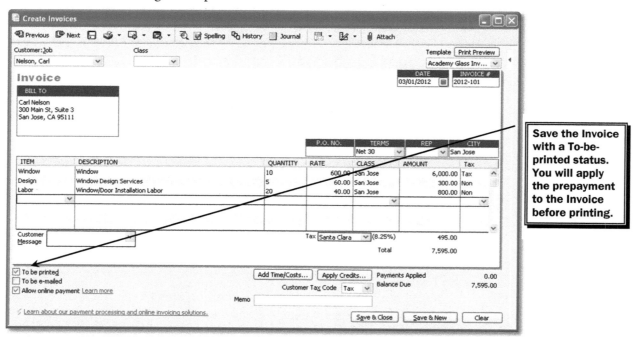

Figure 4-26 Invoice without the prepayment applied

5.   Create a journal entry to credit Accounts Receivable for the amount of prepayment as shown in Figure 4-27. Enter name in the Name column for both the debit to Unearned Income and the credit to Accounts Receivable.

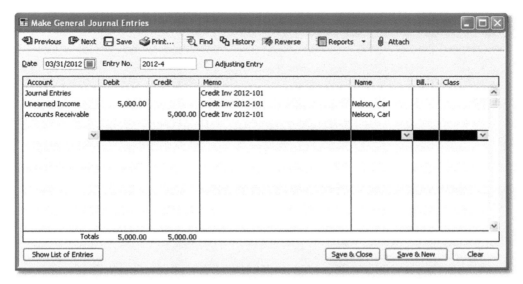

Figure 4-27 Journal Entry to Credit AR Prepayment

6.   To apply the credit from the journal entry, display the *Invoice* (see Figure 4-28) and click **Apply Credits**.

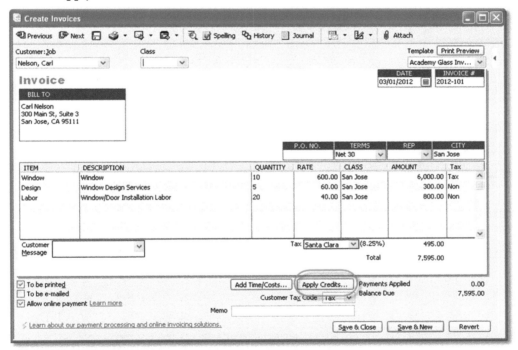

Figure 4-28 Click Apply credits to apply the credit to Invoice

7.   The $5,000 credit from the journal entry is displayed in the Available Credits section of the Apply Credits window (see Figure 4-29) and click **Done**.

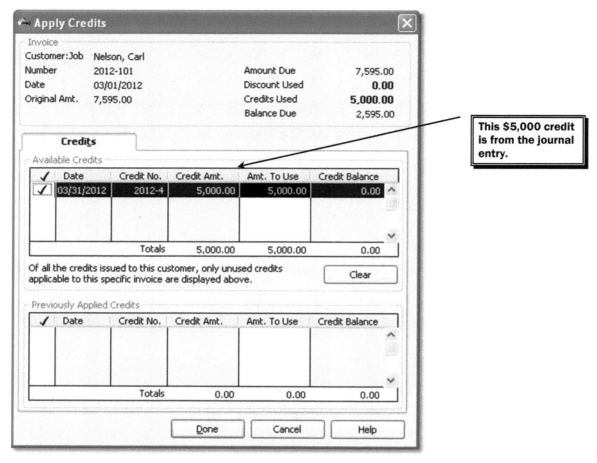

Figure 4-29 Click Done to apply the credit to Invoice

8.   Next print the invoice. Select the *File* menu, choose **Print Forms**, and then choose **Invoices**

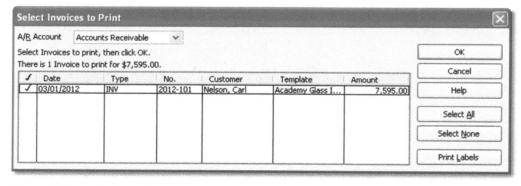

Figure 4-30 Select the Invoice for.

9.   Select the Invoice and Click **OK** to print. The printed Invoice shows the Invoice total, the prepayment and the balance due (see Figure 4-31).

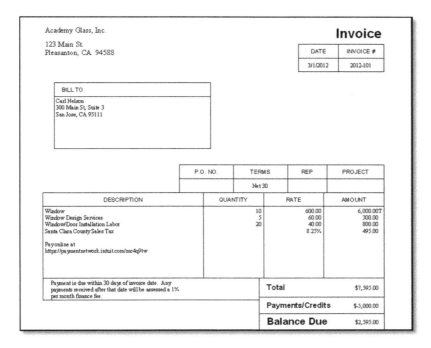

Figure 4-31 The Invoice shows the $5,000 prepayment.

Reports for Tracking Customer Prepayments for Option 3:

Follow the same methodology as the required for Option2.

If, however, you require a *detailed* listing of customer prepayments as opposed to summary totals of deposits by customer, here is something you can do.

1. Run a **Balance Sheet Standard** from the *Reports / Financial* menu.

2. In the *Modify Report* tab, click **Advanced** and then under Display Rows click **All**.

3. Click **OK**.

4. Double-click on the amount next to *Unearned Income*.

5. In the resulting *Transactions by Account* report, check *All Dates*.

6. Remove columns that are unnecessary such as the *Split* column.

7. In the *Total By* field, check *Customer*.

8. Check Modify Report.

9. In the *Filters* tab, click **Cleared** and then check **No**.

10. Check **Header/***Footer*.

11. *In the Report* Title field, enter **Customer Deposit Detail**.

12. Memorize this report.

13. On a regular basis, reconcile the Unearned Income account in the same way that you would reconcile a bank account. Ensure that the ending balance is $0.00, and check off increases and decreases to the account that would zero each other out. Ensure that the same customer is being chosen for each charge on the left side and each payment on the right side of the reconciliation window as in Figure 4-32 (choose to display an extra column on the right side

to show the name of the Payee). This will ensure that the memorized report created above will exclude all old transactions that add up to zero.

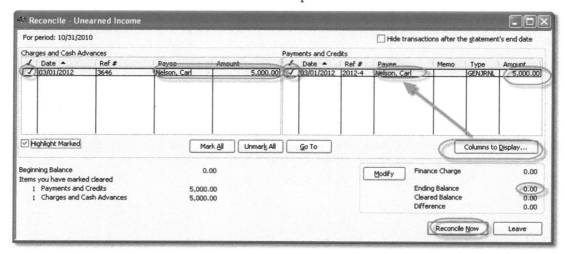

Figure 4-32 Reconcile the Unearned Income account with $0.00 ending balance

Recording Customer Returns and Credits

To record customer returns or credits, use QuickBooks Credit Memos. Credit Memos are used for the following situations:

- To record a return of merchandise from a customer.
- To record a credit-on-account for a customer.
- To issue a refund check to a customer.

In this example, Bill Young canceled an order that Academy Glass recorded on Invoice 2014-107. Since that Invoice shows in your books as unpaid, you could just void or delete the Invoice, but accounting conventions dictate that instead of deleting the Invoice, you should add a new transaction (a Credit Memo) to your books to record the cancellation. Then you'll need to apply the credit to the open Invoice.

> **Key Term**
> *Credit Memos* are sales forms that reduce the amount that a customer owes the company. They work exactly opposite to an Invoice in that they reduce (credit) Accounts Receivable and reduce (debit) income and sales tax. Use Credit Memos to record returns of merchandise, or courtesy discounts being applied to previously recorded Invoices.

1.   Click **Refunds & Credits** on the home page.

Credit Memos look similar to Invoices, but they perform the opposite function. That is, a Credit Memo reduces (credits) Accounts Receivable and reduces (debits) Sales. See Figure 4-33.

2.   Select Young, Bill:Window Replacement from the *Customer:Job* drop-down list and press **TAB**.

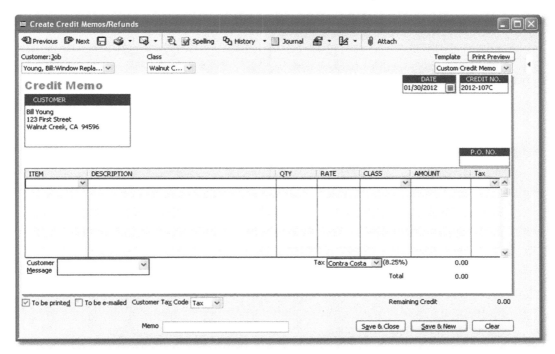

Figure 4-33 The Create Credit Memos/Refunds screen

3. Enter **Walnut Creek** in the *Class* field and press **TAB**.

4. *Custom Credit Memo* is preselected in the *Form Template* field. Press **TAB**.

5. Enter *1/30/2014* in the *DATE* field and press **TAB**.

6. Enter *2014-107C* in the *CREDIT NO.* field and press **TAB**.

   This credit transaction is included on statements and customer reports, so using the Invoice number followed by a *C* in the *CREDIT NO.* field helps your customers to connect this credit memo to the Invoice.

7. Enter the data shown in Figure 4-34 into the body of the Credit Memo.

ITEM	DESCRIPTION	QTY	RATE	CLASS	AMOUNT	Tax
Custom Window	Custom Window - Order #:7890	1	795.00	Walnut Creek	795.00	Tax
Labor	Window/Door Installation Labor	4	40.00	Walnut Creek	160.00	Non
Subtotal	Subtotal				955.00	
Disc 10%	10 % Discount		-10.0%	Walnut Creek	-95.50	Tax

Customer Message | Tax Contra Costa (8.25%) 59.03
Total 918.53

☑ To be printed ☐ To be e-mailed Customer Tax Code Tax   Remaining Credit 918.53

Figure 4-34 Enter this data in the body of the Credit Memo.

8. Enter Refund - Custom Window Order #7890 in the Memo field.

9. Verify that all of the data on your screen matches Figure 4-33 and Figure 4-34. Click **Save & Close** to record the Credit Memo.

10. The Available Credit window (Figure 4-35) gives you a choice of retaining the credit, giving a refund, or applying the credit to an invoice. To apply the credit, click *Apply to invoice* and press **OK**.

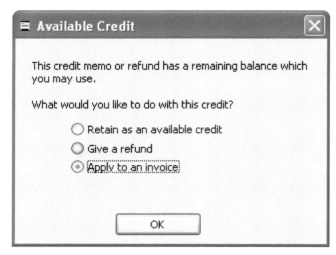

Figure 4-35 Available Credit window

11. Notice the credit is automatically matched with the open invoice for the same amount (see Figure 4-36). Click **Done**.

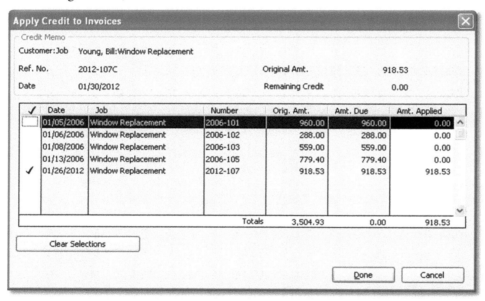

Figure 4-36 Applying the credit to an invoice

Applying a Credit Memo to an Invoice

To apply an existing credit memo to an existing invoice, follow the steps in this example:

1. Click **Refunds & Credits** on the home page.

2. Click Previous to display the existing Credit Memo (FC 5C) for Bob Mason.

3. Select the tiny drop-down arrow to the right of the hand icon at the top right of the credit memo, and then select **Apply to invoice** (see Figure 4-37). If the window on your screen doesn't say **Use Credit to**, it's because the credit memo needs to be stretched horizontally to make it wider.

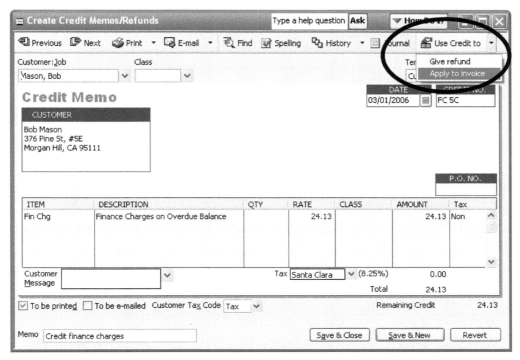

Figure 4-37 Applying a credit to an existing invoice

4. Similar to the last example, notice the credit is automatically matched with the open invoice for the same amount (see Figure 4-38). Click **Done**.

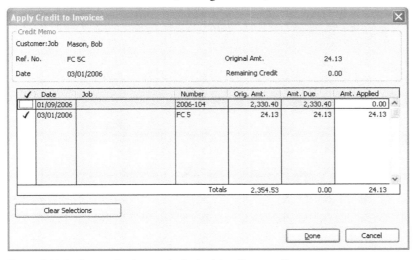

Figure 4-38 Preferences for Automatically Applying Customer Payments

Handling Customer Overpayments

When a customer overpays an invoice, follow the steps in this example to either apply the overpayment to a future invoice, or refund the customer.

1. Record the overpayment shown in Figure 4-39.

Figure 4-39 Customer overpayment - QuickBooks holds the overpayment as credit in A/R.

2.   When you receive more money than is due on invoices, QuickBooks allows you to issue a refund or hold a credit balance in Accounts Receivable. When you hold the credit as shown in Figure 4-39, QuickBooks displays the message shown in Figure 4-40. Click **OK** on this message screen.

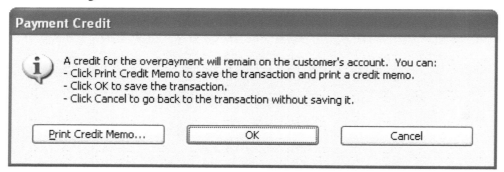

Figure 4-40 The overpayment will cause a credit to the customer's account.

Refunding Customer Overpayments

If a want to issue a **refund**, for overpayments or other existing credits, follow this procedure.

1.   Display the payment that "caused" the overpayment. In this case, it was the payment from Bob Mason on 1/30/06. See Figure 4-41.

2.   Click **Refund the amount to the customer** in the lower left of the payment screen (see Figure 4-41).Then click **Save & Close**.

Figure 4-41 Create a check coded to Accounts Receivable.

3. Click **Yes** on the *Recording Transaction* screen to confirm your changes.

4. On the *Issue a Refund* screen, enter **Refund of overpayment** in the memo field and then click **OK** (see Figure 4-42).

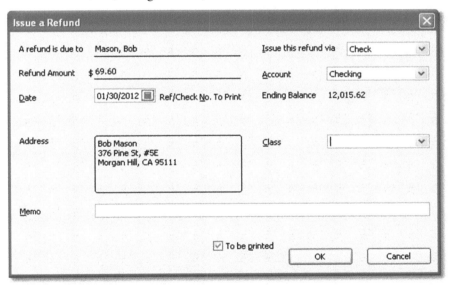

Figure 4-42 Issuing a refund for a customer overpayment

5. If you are crediting the customer's **credit card**, change the *Issue this refund via* field to **VISA** (or other card name) as shown in Figure 4-43.

6. Then click **OK** to record the refund.

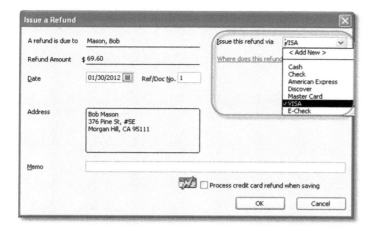

Figure 4-43 Refund created from a payment screen with an overpayment amount

7.   If you use the QuickBooks Merchant Account service, you should click *Process credit card refund when saving* before you save the refund transaction. This will process the actual credit to the customer's credit card.

8.   When you refund by credit card, QuickBooks will **credit** the *undeposited funds* account and tag the transaction with the payment type you selected on the refund. The next time you record a deposit, you'll see the negative amount in the Payments to Deposit screen (see Figure 4-44). Select this amount along with all the positive amounts for the day and the total "net" deposit will be recorded in your register.

9.   Click **Record Deposits** on the home page.

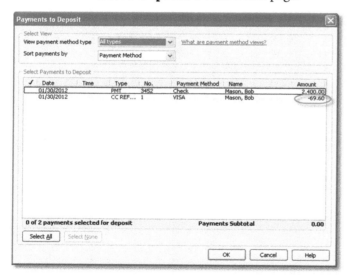

Figure 4-44 The credit card refund shows as a negative amount in the Payment to Deposit screen.

Negative Deposits

QuickBooks allows negative deposits as long as the Payment Method is a credit card. If you are using QuickBooks version 2006 or earlier and the total of a deposit is negative (as you see here because of the refund by credit card), use the following method to trick QuickBooks into making the "negative deposit."

1. On the *Payments to Deposit* screen, select all items (all positive and negative amounts) for whatever payment method you're working on. In this case, it's just the single negative amount for Bob Mason's VISA refund. Then click **OK**.

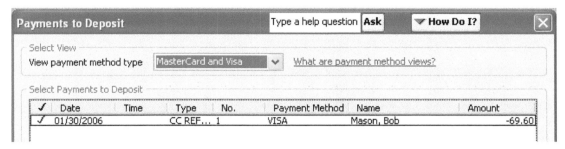

Figure 4-45 Selecting items to be deposited - In this case, negative amounts.

2. On the Make Deposits screen, change the Deposit To field to your *Journal Entries* bank account (or other bank account), and add an additional line at the bottom of your deposit, coded to your checking account with the amount necessary to zero out the deposit. See Figure 4-46. Then press **Save & Close** to record the "negative" deposit.

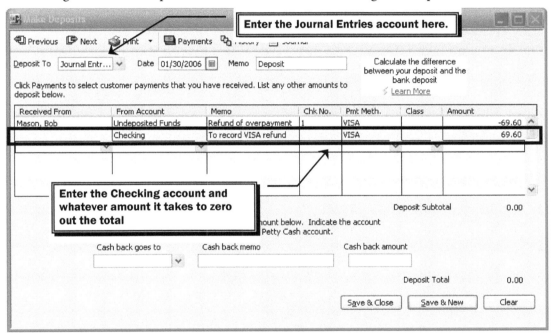

Figure 4-46 Recording a negative deposit when total credit card credits exceed sales for the day

3. The checking account register will show the "negative deposit."

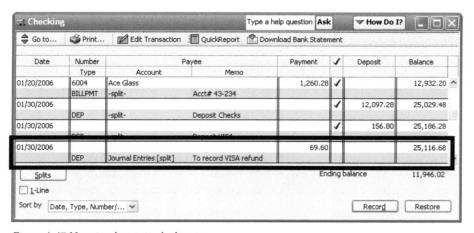

Figure 4-47 Negative deposit in check register

Vendor Credits

When a vendor credits your account, you'll need to record that transaction in QuickBooks and apply it to one of your unpaid bills.

There are two ways to record vendor credits.

Option 1:

One way to record vendor credits is to use the discount screen in the pay bills process. However, that method has a few serious limitations:

- Discounts don't allow you to allocate the credit to multiple accounts or jobs.
- Discounts don't allow you to track reference numbers and the specific credit date to match the vendor's records.
- You cannot enter a memo detailing the reasons for the credit when using discounts.
- Discounts don't allow you to create a report customized to show only the credits for a particular vendor or series of vendors.

Option 2:

The other, preferred way to record vendor credits is to use *Bill-Credit* transactions as shown here.

1.   First, enter a bill from Nellis Windows and Doors. Click **Enter Bills** on the *Vendors* section of the home page.

2.   Enter the bill for this example using the data in Figure 4-48.

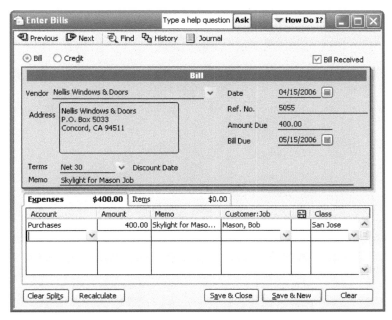

Figure 4-48 Enter a Bill from Nellis Windows & Doors.

3.   On the next (blank) Bill form, click the *Credit* radio button at the top left of the screen.

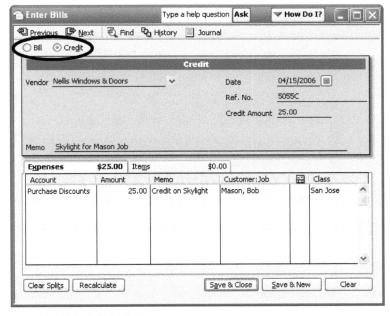

Figure 4-49 The Bill Credit form

4.   Fill out the Vendor Credit form as shown in Figure 4-49. Click ***Save & Close*** to record the credit.

> **The Accounting Behind the Scenes**
> When you record a Vendor Credit as shown in Figure 4-49, QuickBooks reduces Accounts Payable (with a debit) and reduces Expenses (with a credit). In this case it credits Purchase Discounts, a contra-Cost of Goods Sold account.

5.   To Apply the Vendor Credit to a bill for that vendor, click ***Pay Bills*** on the home page.

6.   In this example, select the open bill for Nellis Windows & Doors as shown in Figure 4-50.

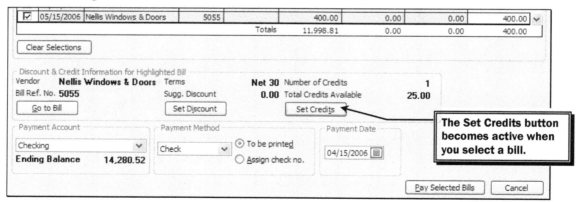

Figure 4-50 The Pay Bills screen with a bill selected for a vendor with an existing credit

7.   When an unapplied credit exists for a vendor, upon selecting a bill for that vendor in the Pay Bills screen, QuickBooks displays the total amount of credits for the vendor in the *Total Credits Available* field. Notice in Figure 4-50 that Nellis has a total available credit of $25.00.

8.   To apply some or all of the credits available, click the checkmark in the left column of the line for your bill. Notice that the *Set Credits* button becomes active when you select the bill (see Figure 4-51).

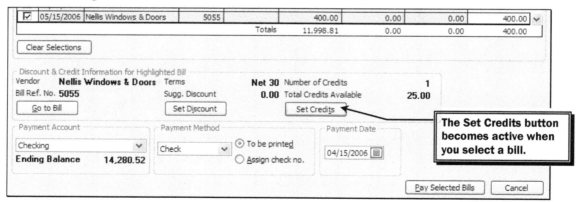

Figure 4-51 To apply the credit, click the checkmark in the left column of the bill and click Set Credits.

9.   Click Set Credits.

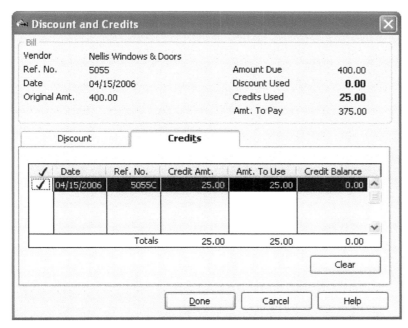

Figure 4-52 The Discounts and Credits Screen

10. On the *Discount and Credits* window, you can see that QuickBooks selects the credits to be applied to the bill. You can override what's shown by deselecting the credit (remove the checkmark), or by typing a new amount in the ***Amt. To Use*** field.

11. Leave the credit selected as shown in and click ***Done***.
     In Figure 4-53, you can see that the $25.00 credit has been applied to bill 5055 and the Amt. To Pay field has been reduced to $375.00.

12. To pay the bill now with the credit applied, click ***Pay Selected Bills***.
     If you just wanted to apply the credit without paying the bill, reduce the Amt. To Pay field to zero.

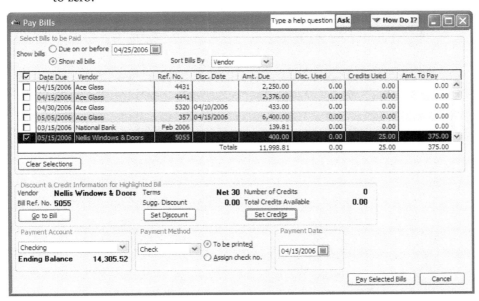

Figure 4-53 Pay Bills screen with credit applied

> **Important**
> In order to apply a credit, the vendor names must be the same on both the bill and the credit.

Handling Deposits To and Refunds From Vendors

There are several transactions between you and your vendors that need to be handled in a special way. This section covers how to handle deposits paid to vendors in advance of receiving the bill, refunds received from vendors for overpayment of a bill, and refunds received from vendors when Accounts Payable is not involved.

Vendor Deposits — When You Use Accounts Payable

Sometimes, vendors require that you give them a deposit before receiving service or product. If you have to pay a vendor before they send you a bill, create a check and code it to Accounts Payable. This creates a credit in QuickBooks for this vendor that you can use to apply to their bill when it arrives at a later date. In this example, there is a Vendor Deposit with Antigues Construction Rentals.

1.   Click **Write Checks** in the **Banking** section of the home page.

2.   Enter the data as shown in Figure 4-54. Notice that this check is coded to Accounts Payable. You only code checks to A/P when you're sending deposits to the vendor before receiving their bill. QuickBooks Bill Payments are also coded to A/P, but those are handled automatically by QuickBooks.

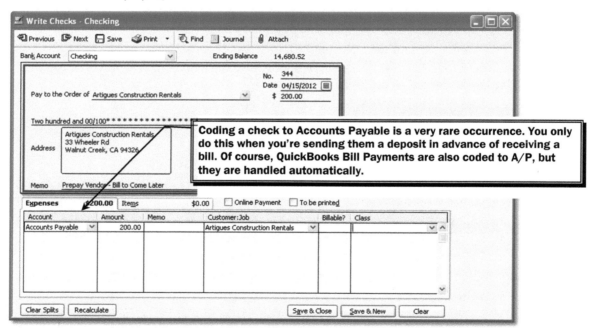

Figure 4-54 A check written to a vendor as a deposit before the bill comes.

Recording the Bill When You Prepaid With a Check Coded to A/P

When the bill arrives, enter it just like any other bill.

1.   Click *Enter **Bills*** on the home page.

2.   Enter the Bill to Artigues Construction Rentals as shown in Figure 4-55.

3.   Click ***Save & Close*** to record the bill.

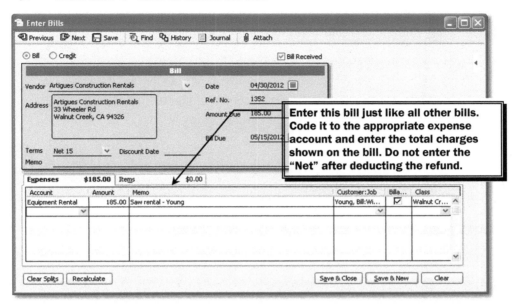

Figure 4-55 A bill from Artigues Construction Rentals

Depositing the Refund from the Vendor

Now record the deposit of your refund check directly onto your next deposit.

1.   Select the ***Banking*** menu and then select ***Make Deposits***.

2.   Click **Cancel** on the *Payments to Deposit* screen.

3.   Press the ***Tab*** key to skip the ***Deposit To*** field.

4.   Set the Date to 04/30/2014 and press the *Tab* key twice.

5.   Enter **Artigues Construction Rentals** in the **Received From** field and press the Tab key.

6.   Enter *Accounts Payable* in the ***From Account*** field and press the *Tab* key.

7.   Enter the rest of the data as shown in Figure 4-56.

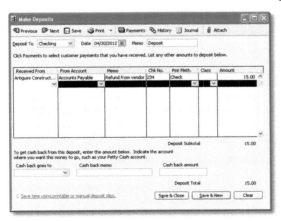

Figure 4-56 Recording a vendor refund deposit.

8.   Press **Save & Close** to save the deposit.

Applying the Refund and Credit to the Bill

1.   After you record the deposit shown in Figure 4-56, you'll need to "connect" the debit (the prepayment check) to the two credits (the bill and the deposit) so that your A/P aging reports are correct.

2.   Click *Pay Bills* on the home page.

3.   Select the first credit and then click *Set Credits* as shown in Figure 4-57.

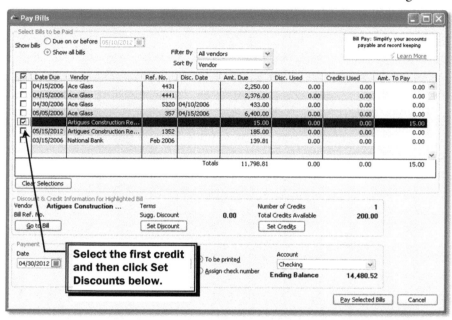

Figure 4-57 Selecting the credits before clicking Set Credits

4.   In the Discounts and Credits screen, click *Done*.

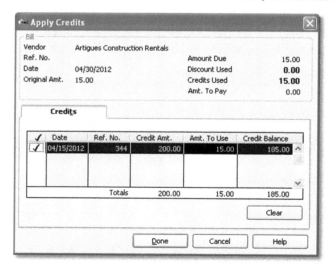

Figure 4-58 Setting the credit for the first line

5.   Then select the second credit and click *Set Credits* (Figure 4-59).

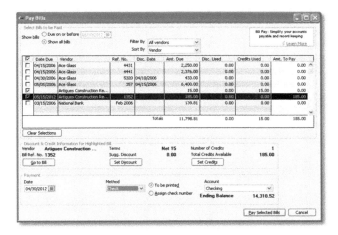

Figure 4-59 Selecting the second credit

6.   In the *Discounts and Credits* screen, click **Done**.

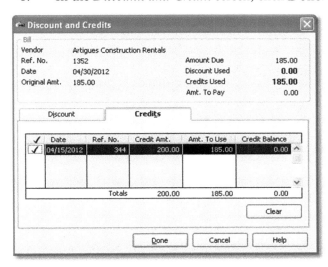

Figure 4-60 Setting the second credit

7.   As shown in Figure 4-61, applying the total debit ($200) to each credit ($15 and $185) has zeroed both credits out.

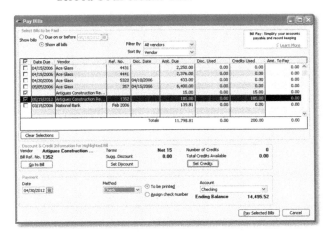

Figure 4-61 Both credits are zeroed out by the $200 debit.

8.   Click Pay Selected Bills.

9.   When you use the Pay Bills screen to connect credits to bills, you'll see the Payment Summary shown below. Read the message carefully and click **Done**.

Figure 4-62 Important message about Bills being paid by credits only

Vendor Refunds — When You Use Accounts Payable

When you receive a refund from a vendor, the transaction you enter in QuickBooks depends on how you paid the vendor originally.

If you prepaid the vendor using the method above and the amount of your prepayment was *more* than the bill, your Accounts Payable account will have a negative (debit) balance for that vendor and you'll need the refund to zero out this credit in A/P.

On the other hand, if you simply wrote a check to the vendor and coded the check to an expense account, you'll need to reduce the expense by the amount of the refund. Each of these situations is covered in the following two sections.

To deposit a refund from a vendor that you prepaid using the deposit transaction in Figure 4-54, create a deposit and code the deposit to Accounts Payable. In this example, assume you paid Artigues Construction Rentals $200.00 in advance of receiving the bill. Later, when the bill came, it was for only $185.00. Since you overpaid, the vendor sent you a refund of $15.00.

Vendor Refunds — When You Directly Expensed Payment

If you did not use the Accounts Payable features but instead wrote a check to the vendor and coded the check to an expense account, enter the expense account that should be credited for the vendor refund (see Figure 4-63).

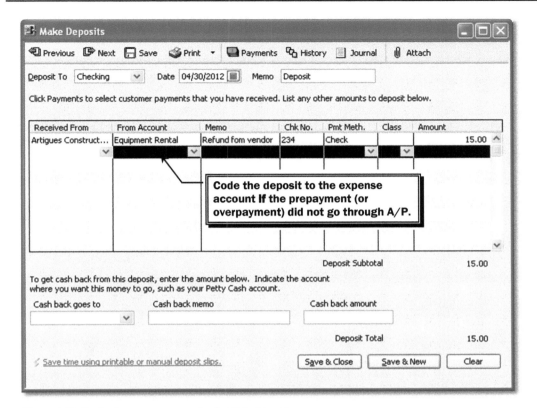

Figure 4-63 Credit the expense account in the Make Deposits screen.

Trading Services between Customers and Vendors

If you barter or buy services or products from your customers, you might want to "trade" instead of paying each other. If you don't exchange money, but instead exchange credits against what each other owes, you'll need to record a few special transactions in QuickBooks to ensure that all your reports are accurate.

For example, if you sell the customer taxable Items, or if you buy inventory Items in the trade, you want to make sure your accounting is accurate even though no cash changes hands.

Use the following method of accounting for trades when either of the following occurs:

You owe money to one of your customers and they owe money to you. You pay the customer by issuing a credit on their account. They, in turn, issue a credit for an equal amount on your account to pay you.

You owe money to one of your vendors and they owe money to you. You pay the vendor by issuing a credit to their account. They, in turn, issue a credit for an equal amount on your account to pay you.

For each customer you trade services with, set up a Customer record in the Customer Center, and a Vendor record in the Vendor Center. The Customer and the Vendor are actually the same company, but in order to track both purchases and sales in QuickBooks, you need a Customer and a Vendor for the same company. In this example, Smith and Smith is both a Customer and a Vendor.

Figure 4-64 Create a customer record and a vendor record for the same company.

1. Create a Bank account called *Trade Clearing* as shown in Figure 4-65. This account has already been created for this exercise, so you do not need to create it in this case.

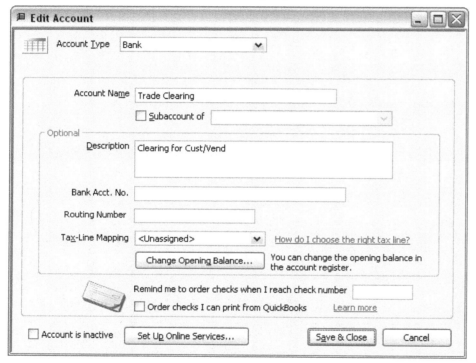

Figure 4-65 Trade Clearing account

2. When you buy from this customer/vendor, enter a Bill from the vendor Smith & Smith-V normally, and use whichever accounts or items to which the bill should apply. Enter a Bill recording the purchase of five 104 Sliders (an Inventory Part) from Smith & Smith as shown in Figure 4-66.

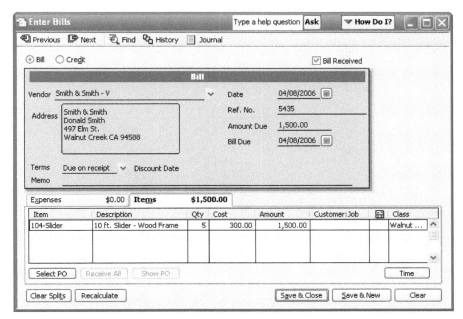

Figure 4-66 Enter a Bill from the Vendor when you purchase something from them.

3. When you sell products or services to this customer/vendor, create an Invoice to Smith & Smith-C. Enter the Items you sell just like on any other normal invoice. Enter an Invoice recording the sale of 20 hours of Design Services to Smith & Smith as shown in Figure 4-67.

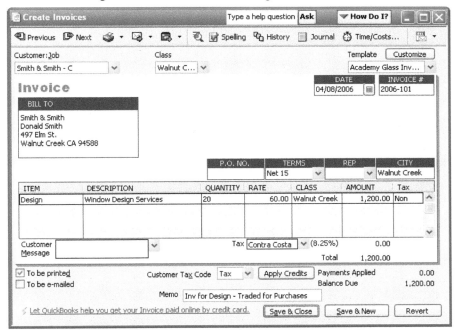

Figure 4-67 Create Invoices (not Sales Receipts) for the Customer

4. The next step is to clear the Customer invoice by receiving a payment for the amount of the trade using the *Trade Clearing Bank* account. Note that in order to see the Deposit to field on Figure 4-68, you need to uncheck the preference to *Use Undeposited Funds* in the *Sales & Customers Company* preferences. See Figure 4-69.

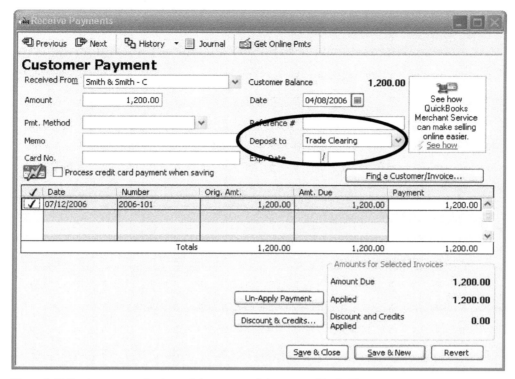

Figure 4-68 Receive payment for the traded amount and deposit it to Trade Clearing.

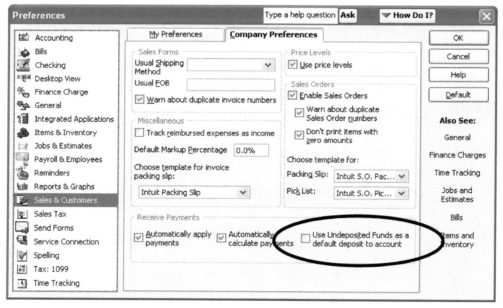

Figure 4-69 This setting allows you to select a bank account on the Receive Payments screen.

5.   Since you owe the vendor more than you invoiced him you want to Pay Bills and select to pay the amount of the bill in full, again using the Trade Clearing as your bank account.

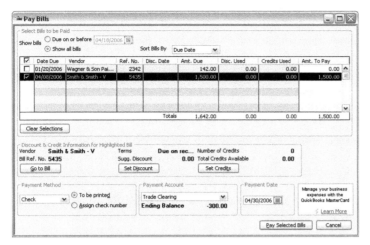

Figure 4-70 Pay bills for the full amount

6. The final step is to write a check to the Vendor for the $300.00 balance owed.

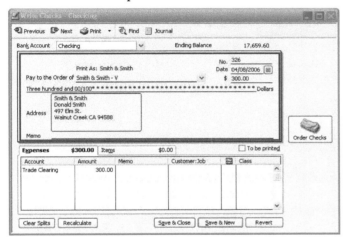

Figure 4-71 Create a check for the amount due your vendor

Below is a picture of your Trade Clearing register. Your balance in this account should be $-0- after each transaction. You can actually reconcile this like any other bank account and see which transaction is not in balance.

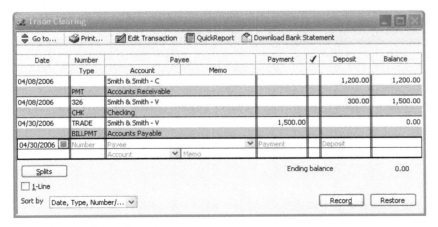

Figure 4-72 Trade Clearing register

If your Customer (Invoice) owes more than their Vendor bill to you, you would receive the excess payment into your deposit using Trade Clearing as the *From Account*.

Receiving 2-Party Checks

In the construction industry, the bookkeeper will occasionally have to handle receiving a "two-party check." A two-party check is payable to two companies, usually the prime contractor and a materials supplier, or other subcontractor. The reason is most often to ensure that the supplier is paid in a timely manner and that there is a direct link between the payment from the job and the payment to the supplier. It is also intended to prevent suppliers from attaching liens to the property by making it impossible for the prime contractor to fail to pay the supplier.

Here is our suggestion for how to handle two-party checks.

Start by sending the invoice to the customer just as you normally would. When you receive the payment (a two-party check), record the payment and deposit it to a *Trade Clearing* bank account. Next, record the bill from the supplier and pay the bill from the Trade Clearing account. Finally, send the endorsed check to the supplier and they should deposit the check into their bank account.

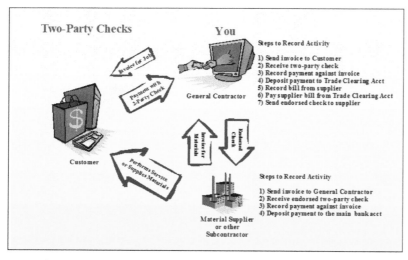

Figure 4-73 Handling Two-Party Checks in QuickBooks

The following pages show the detailed steps for how the general contractor in the graph above should handle the transactions in QuickBooks.

For our example Academy Glass does a job for a customer Bob Mason.

Figure 4-74 Create a customer record for Bob Mason.

Academy Glass charges $1,000 for a *Custom Window* plus sales tax on an invoice to Bob Mason.

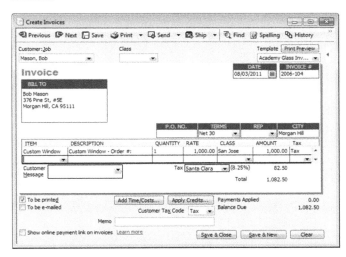

Figure 4-75 Create an invoice for the custom window in the amount of $1,082.50.

Academy Glass uses Ace Glass to provide the materials for the job.

Figure 4-76 Create a vendor record for Ace Glass.

Ace Glass submits an Invoice to Academy Glass who enters a Bill for $1,082.50.

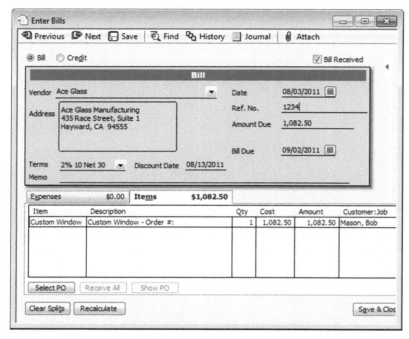

Figure 4-77 Create a bill in the amount of $1,082.50 for Ace Glass.

Bob Mason (customer) sends a check for $1082.50 to Academy Glass (General Contractor), payable to both Academy Glass (General) and Ace Glass (Supplier).

In QuickBooks, record the payment from the customer and deposit the payment into the Trade Clearing bank account. The result will be a debit balance in the Trade Clearing register in the amount of $1,082.50.

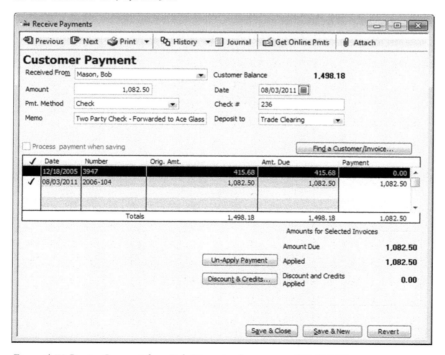

Figure 4-78 Receive Payment from Bob Mason in the amount of $1,082.50

Academy Glass endorses the check and sends it on to Ace Glass who will deposit it. Academy Glass then uses *Pay Bills* to record payment to Ace Glass for $1,082.50. This bill payment is recorded in the Trade Clearing bank account.

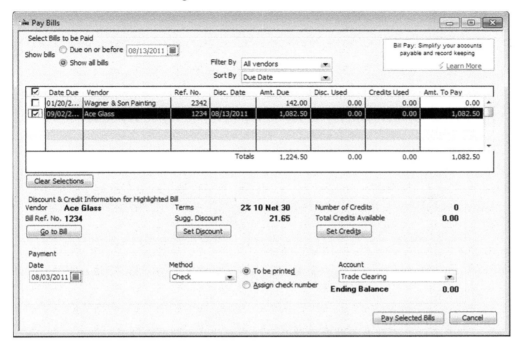

Figure 4-79 Bill Payment recorded in the Trade Clearing account.

After recording all of the transactions above, you now have a zero balance receivable from the customer (Bob Mason), and a zero balance due to the vendor (Ace Glass).

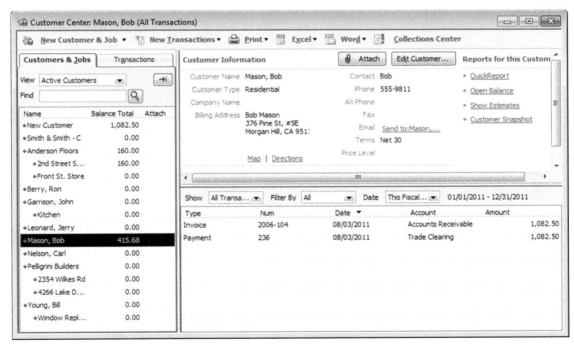

Figure 4-80 Transactions for Bob Mason showing the payment deposited to Trade Clearing

The vendor (Ace Glass) shows the bill was paid out of the Trade Clearing bank account.

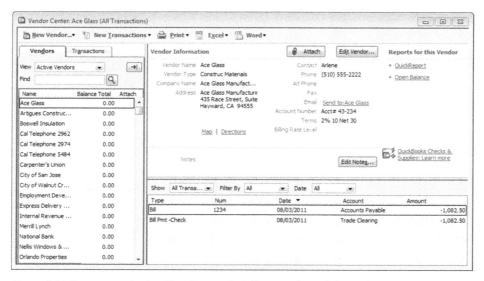

Figure 4-81 Transactions for Ace Glass showing the bill was paid out of the Trade Clearing account.

The Trade Clearing account shows the deposit from the customer, recording the receipt of the two-party check, and the bill payment to the vendor. These amounts zero out the balance of the Trade Clearing account.

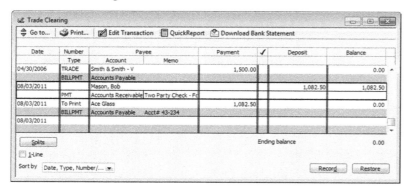

Figure 4-82 The Trade Clearing bank account register shows the deposit and the bill payment.

Trust Accounting

Trust accounting is necessary in many industries. These clients include, but are not limited to:

- Attorneys
- Paralegals
- Realtors
- Investment Advisors

Although specifics vary from industry to industry, there are two basic axioms in trusting accounting.

- Trust monies in the bank = Trust liabilities (in total and by customer or job)
- You must know *how much of each customer's* money you have in trust

Each state has its own rules for trust accounts in various industries, so be sure to know the rules in the appropriate jurisdiction and use QuickBooks to suit those rules.

Trust Accounting Setup

To set up trust accounting in a QuickBooks data file, create two new accounts in your chart of accounts: a *Mixed Trust Bank* (type: bank) and a *Funds Held in Trust* (type: other current liability) account.

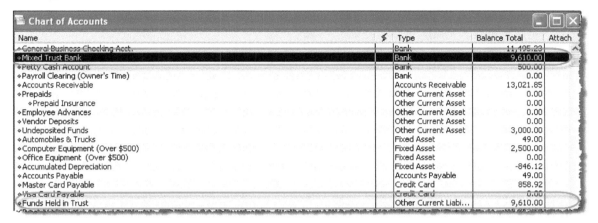

Figure 4-83 Create two new accounts in the chart of accounts

Create a new (one-sided) service item called *Trust Account Deposit* linked to the *Funds Held in Trust* account.

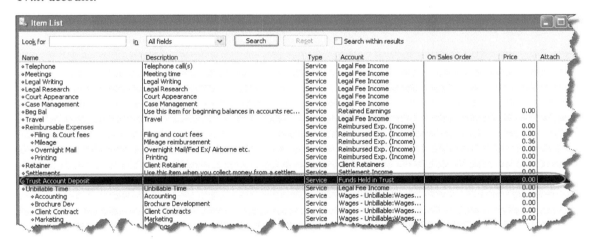

Figure 4-84 Create a Trust Account Deposit item

Trust Money Coming In

Any time monies go into the Mixed Trust Bank account on behalf of a matter or job, the other side of the entry is the liability account *Funds Held in Trust* (as is the case in the trust accounting firm being used).

Any time funds are drawn out of the Mixed Trust Bank account, regardless of the purpose of the funds, the other side of the withdrawal or check transaction is the Funds Held in Trust liability account. That keeps the Mixed Trust Bank total in "balance" with the Funds Held in Trust liability account. Monies going into the trust bank account are best recorded as sales receipts, very similar to Option 3 of receiving customer deposits (see page 135). This enables the professional to provide their client with a receipt. Remember to choose the job as well as the customer.

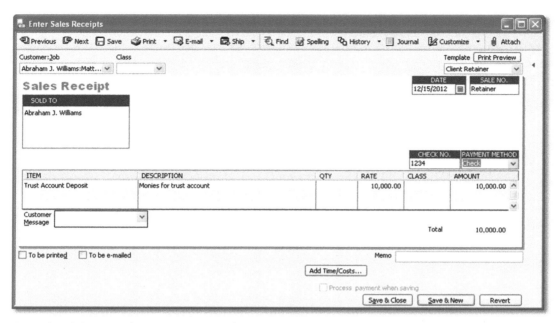

Figure 4-85 Sales Receipt for trust monies received

The Sales Receipt funds would be deposited either directly to the Mixed Trust Bank account or immediately after depositing it to Undeposited Funds (depending on your preferences), as all trust monies <u>must</u> be deposited into the Mixed Trust Bank account from Undeposited Funds in order for the Mixed Trust Bank and the Funds Held in Trust accounts to remain in balance with each other.

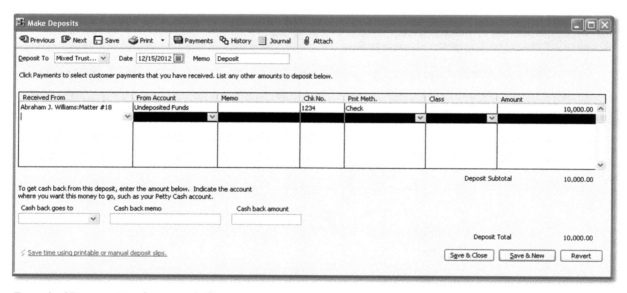

Figure 4-86 Deposit to Mixed Trust Bank if Sales Receipt for trust monies went into Undeposited Funds

Trust Money Going Out

When checks are issued for client disbursements out of the Mixed Trust Bank account, regardless of the name of the payee or what the purpose of the disbursement, the name of the matter or job must be specified in the Customer:Job field, and the expense account at the bottom of the check is always the Funds Held in Trust account.

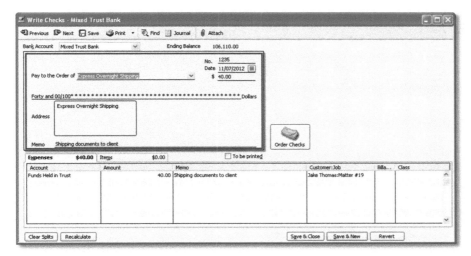

Figure 4-87 Disbursement out of Mixed Trust Bank account

Funds Held in Trust by Matter Report

As described on page 139, the Funds Held in Trust account should be reconciled on a regular basis.

Reconciling this account enables you to "clear out" any checks and deposits for a particular matter or job that add up to zero. If they are not cleared out, they will still appear on the Funds Held in Trust by Matter report.

Select **Reconcile** from the *Banking* menu and choose the *Funds Held in Trust* liability account. Enter the last date of the month and an ending balance of $0.00. Click **Continue**.

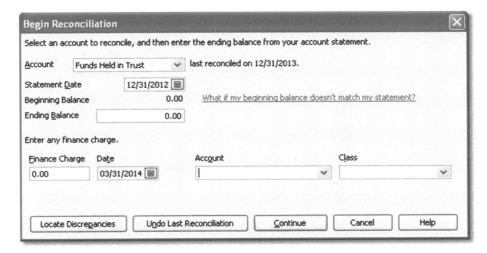

Figure 4-88 Reconcile Funds Held in Trust Account

Ensure that the Payee column is showing on each side of the reconciliation window. If it is not showing, click Customize Columns to add it. Next, check each charge (trust monies coming in) and payment (trust monies going out) that offset each other and add up to zero (make sure that the payee and the total amount are the same; in this case, two charges adding up to $13,500 were reconciled against one payment for $13,500). When finished and the difference is zero, click *Reconcile Now*.

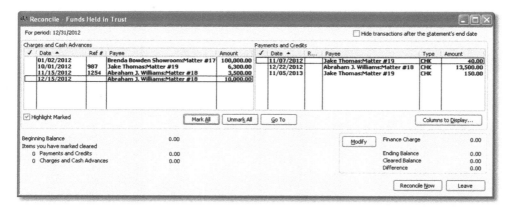

Figure 4-89 Checkmark all charges and payments relating to the same matter that offset each other

Once the Funds Held in Trust account is reconciled, run the Funds Held in Trust by Matter report:

1. Run a **Balance Sheet Standard** from the *Reports / Financial* menu.

2. In the *Modify Report* tab, click **Advanced** and then under Display Rows click **All**.

3. Click **OK**.

4. Double-click on the amount next to *Funds Held in Trust*.

5. In the resulting *Transactions by Account* report, check *All Dates*.

6. Remove columns that are unnecessary but retain the *Split* column.

7. In the *Total By* field, check *Customer*.

8. Check Modify Report.

9. In the *Filters* tab, click **Cleared** and then check **No**.

10. Check Header/Footer.

11. In the *Report Title* field, enter **Customer Deposit Detail**.

12. Memorize this report.

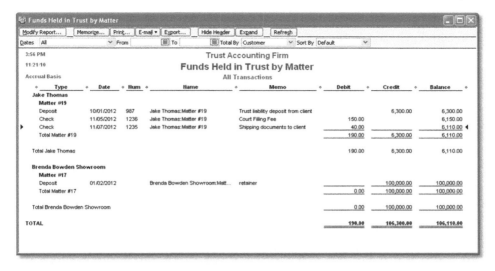

Figure 4-90 Funds Held in Trust by Matter report

Note how the balance in the Mixed Trust Bank account and the Funds Held in Trust are always equal, assuming that all trust funds have been deposited from any sitting in Undeposited Funds. Look at the balances in both accounts in the Chart of Accounts.

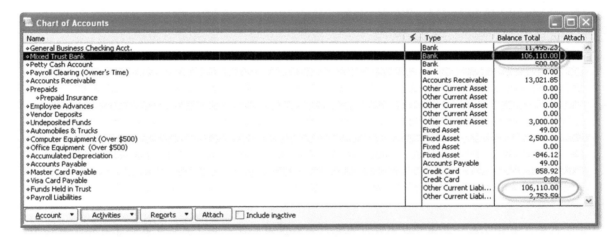

Figure 4-91 Mixed Trust Bank and Funds Held in Trust accounts must always equal

If these figures on the Chart of Accounts listing are *not* equal, check the following:

That no trust monies are sitting in Undeposited Funds – if so, make the appropriate deposits to move them into the Mixed Trust Bank account and out of Undeposited Funds.

Run the **Funds Held in Trust by Matter** memorized report and see if all the *Split* column contents show the Mixed Trust Bank account. If they don't, correct these entries.

Consignment Goods

There are two sides of consignment good tracking.

The first side of consignment good tracking is one in which you are the consignor: you have placed your goods in someone else's possession for them to sell. You must still track the goods even though they are no longer in the company's physical warehouse, because they are not actually sold yet.

The second side of consignment good tracking is one in which you are the consignee: a vendor has placed its goods in your possession for you to sell. You must know what you have on hand that belongs to the vendor (and segregate it from the goods you truly own), as the goods do not belong to you. Although these are not your goods, they must appear as being available for sale.

When you are the Consignor

This section addresses when you are the consignor, or when your goods are placed in another location for someone else to sell. To track goods placed in the hands of someone else, Sales Orders are required, and so you must use Premier or above.

Create a new Other Current Asset type of account called Consignment Inventory.

> Note:
> If QuickBooks Enterprise Solutions is being used, you can bypass this step if you have Multiple Warehousing activated, and you can create a new warehouse location called Consignment Inventory.

You will want to segregate items in your physical warehouse from similar items in your consignees' warehouses, so create an additional inventory item called *Consignment Items* and make sub-items for those items you send out to consignees. You may create these sub-items easily by first duplicating the items in your item list that typically go out on consignment and by editing the name (adding a suffix to indicate the Consignment status), the selling price (as the price paid by the consignee will generally be lower than the normal selling price), the asset account (change it to the new Consignment Inventory account unless Multiple Warehousing in QuickBooks Enterprise is being used, in which case you do not need to create these parallel items) and perhaps the description and the revenue account if desired (only the asset account and selling price have been edited in this example).

Figure 4-92 shows 3 consignment sub-items created by duplicating the regular stock.

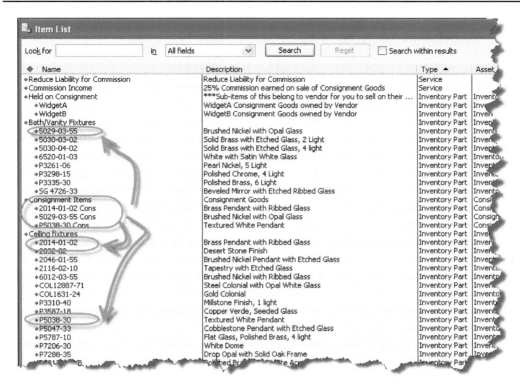

Figure 4-92 Consignment sub-items created as parallels to the items that are in the main warehouse

When consignees are shipped goods to sell, enter a Sales Order for each of the Consignment Item items being shipped. When the consignees sell some of the stock, they report to you how much of each item was sold, and so those sold items can be turned into an invoice straight from the Sales Order. When some goods from the regular stock go out on consignment, this method allows you to use the Inventory Adjustment function to *reduce* the number of *regular goods on hand* and correspondingly *increase* by the same quantity the number of *consignment* goods on hand. You still have the same overall number of items, but they are now readily identifiable as to which items are in your own warehouse, and which are out on consignment for sale at another vendor's shop. (If QuickBooks Enterprise Solutions is being used, then the Inventory Adjustment step is still required, but it would be used to transfer items from the main warehouse to a consignment warehouse.)

Therefore, record an inventory adjustment (see Figure 4-93: the total value of the adjustment is $0.00 but there still has to be an adjustment account specified – here the Supplies expense account is used) to reclassify items as consignment items ready to ship to consignees.

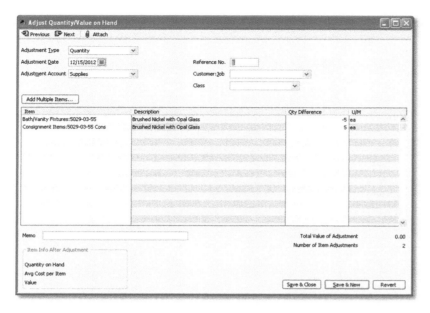

Figure 4-93 Inventory adjustment to move items into consignment

Every time Consignment sub-items go out to a consignee, there is now inventory of these items on hand (as a result of the inventory adjustment in Figure 4-93) and a *Sales Order to each consignee* (set up as a *customer*) must be created (see Figure 4-94).

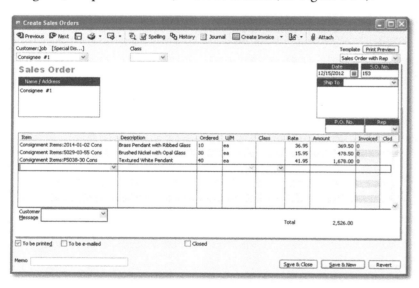

Figure 4-94 Consignment items ordered by consignee out of consignment inventory

When the consignee reports they have sold a specific quantity of each consignment item, simply produce an Invoice from the Sales Order for the quantity of each item reported sold. This will properly update the Stock Status by Item report and show how many unsold consignment items are still held by consignees as well as how much more consignment inventory can be ordered by consignees before another inventory adjustment must be made. (These are the *On Hand, On Sales Order*, and *Available* columns.) It will also properly deplete the number of consignment items reported sold by consignees from inventory on hand.

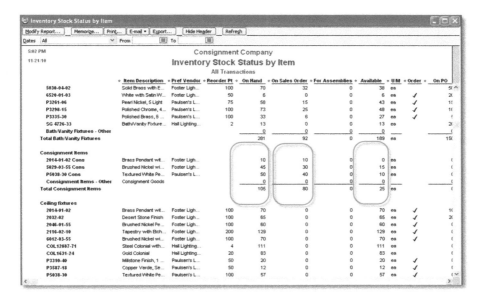

Figure 4-95 Inventory Stock Status by Item report showing Consignment Goods

In addition, the Sales by Customer Detail report, properly filtered for just consignee customer names, will show just how many of each consignment item were sold by each of the consignees.

When you are the Consignee

This section look sat when you are the consignee, or when goods are placed in your hands to sell on behalf of the owner. If you are the consignee, you have on hand goods for sale that belong to someone else.

Let's assume you get to keep 25% of the sales revenue on consignment items as commission.

Create an Other Current Liability account called *Consignment sales – liability*.

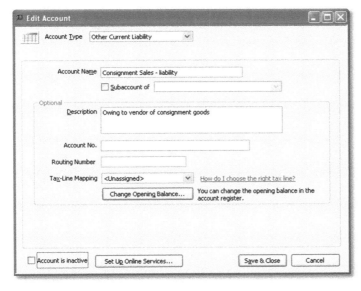

Figure 4-96 Consignment Sales - liability account

Next, create an Income account called *Commission Income*.

Figure 4-97 Commission Income account

Create a new one-sided service item, *Reduce Liability for Commission* and link it to the Consignment sales – liability account. Its rate is a percentage, not in dollars and cents. Give it a rate of -25% (negative 25%).

Figure 4-98 Reduce liability for commission item

Create a second one-sided service item, *Commission Income* and link it to the *Commission Income* account. Its rate is also not in dollars and cents. It is 25% (i.e. positive 25%).

Figure 4-99 Commission Income item

Create an inventory item called *Held on Consignment* and create sub-items for all items you bring in from vendors for you to sell on their behalf (in Figure 4-100, "A"). Each of these items (the parent item and all sub-items) is linked to the regular Cost of Goods sold and Inventory account. The Income account is the new *Consignment sales – liability* account.

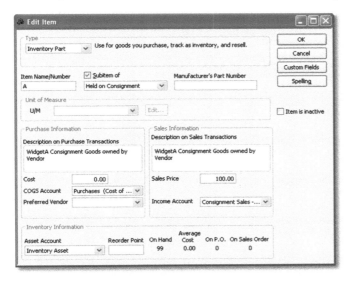

Figure 4-100 Setup of "A," a good held on consignment

Now create a group item for each Consignment item you might sell on the consignor's behalf. See Figure 4-101 for the setup for the group item for selling item A.

> **Note:**
> In the setup of this group item, we do *not* check the box next to *Print items in group*.

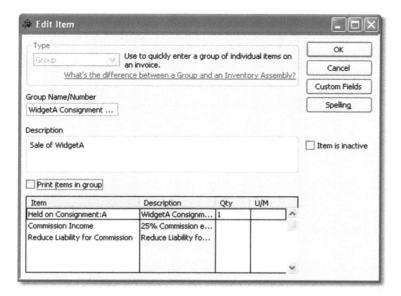

Figure 4-101 Group item for selling A

The consignor (set up as a vendor in QuickBooks) sells these items to you for $0 each so that you can enter the total on a bill for $0 as in Figure 4-102. That way you know exactly how many of the consignor's goods you have on consignment.

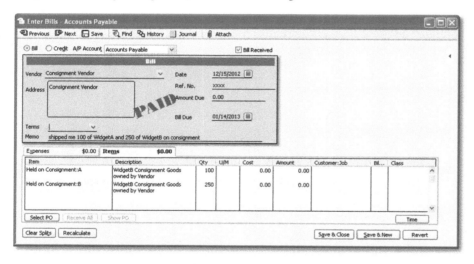

Figure 4-102 Buying consignment goods from consignor for $0

When you sell the consignor's goods, enter the invoice as usual but use the group items created for each consignment item. Remember, the items in the group will not appear on the printed invoice. That way, the commission is calculated behind the scenes.

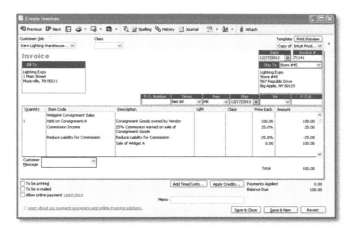

Figure 4-103 Create invoice for group item when selling goods on consignment

The customer sees this invoice without the group's individual lines appearing:

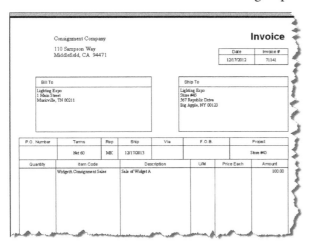

Figure 4-104 The invoice that the customer sees for consignment items

Figure 4-105 shows the debits and credits behind the scenes for this invoice:

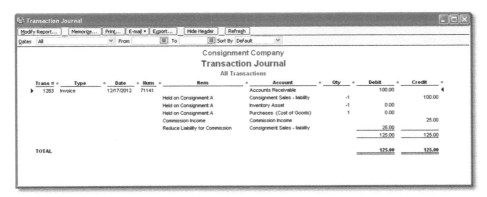

Figure 4-105 Behind-the-scenes posting of sale of group consignment item

Therefore, upon selling the group item, the quantity on hand of the consignment item goes down, and the income goes into the Consignment sales liability account. The Consignment sales liability account is reduced by the 25% commission you earned, and that goes into the Commission income account.

This method updates the liability to the consignor vendor upon each and every sale of a consignment item. It also updates the commission income earned immediately. The amount showing as the Commission sales liability ($100 sales less the $25 commission) shows accurately on the Balance Sheet:

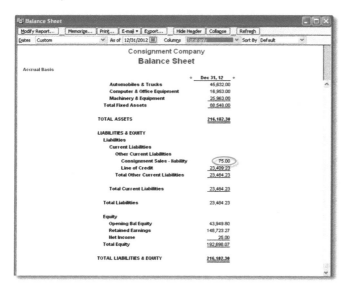

Figure 4-106 Consignment sales owing (shows net of commission earned)

Now write a check to the consignor for the net amount of the sales after deducting the commission you've earned:

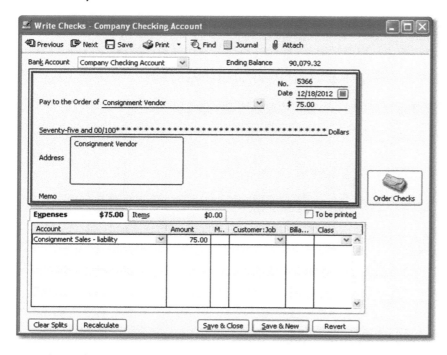

Figure 4-107 Check to consignor for sales revenue owing net of commissions earned

And the amount of commission earned shows accurately on the Profit & Loss:

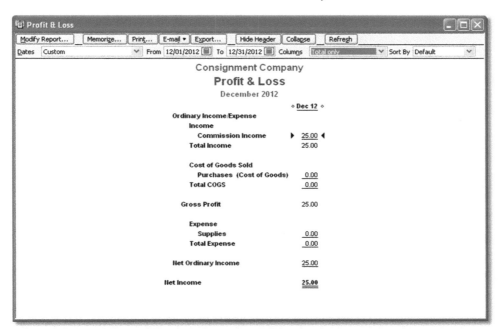

Figure 4-108 Commission earned shows on the Profit & Loss

The Sales by Item Summary report will be correct, and you can filter it for consignment items only, remove COGS columns and memorize it:

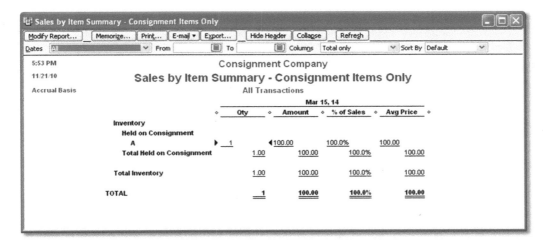

Figure 4-109 Sales by Item Summary report filtered for Consignment Items only

The Inventory Stock Status by Item report will also be correct, and you can filter the report for the Consignment Inventory asset account only, if you have assigned consignment goods to a separate inventory account as mentioned earlier:

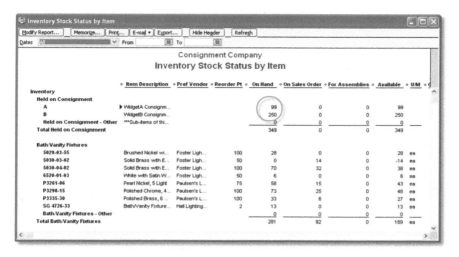

Figure 4-110 Inventory Stock Status by Item report

Summary

In this chapter, you learned about the following *tricky* transactions:

- Handle customer Deposits, Prepayments and Retainers (page 123)
- Process customer returns, credits, refunds, and overpayments (page 140)
- Handle prepayments to Vendors using Accounts Payable credits (page 148)
- Handle Refunds from Vendors (page 152)
- Handle *Barters* or *Trades* with customers and vendors (page 157)
- Handling 2-Party Checks Received (page 162)
- Handling Trust Funds (page 166)

Chapter 5 Troubleshooting QuickBooks Data Files

Objectives

After completing this chapter, you should be able to:

- Data File Analysis and Repair - Assessing the Health of Your Client's Data File (page 183).
- Troubleshoot Corrupted Data Files (page 210)
- Repair Out-of-Balance Balance Sheets (page 216)
- Fix Misapplied Customer Payments (page 220)
- Fix Misapplied Vendor Payments (page 231)
- Troubleshoot Non-zero Balances in Opening Balance Equity (page 238)
- Troubleshoot Account Names Beginning With * (page 239)
- Troubleshoot iif files (page 240)
- Troubleshoot Accountant's Review Importing (page 241)

Data File Analysis and Repair

Before you prepare the client's tax return or provide any type of assurances about the accuracy of the QuickBooks data, you must have confidence in the "health" of the QuickBooks data file. We use the word health to mean more than just the accuracy of the accounting data. In addition to accurate accounting entries, a healthy data file is free from data corruption and conforms to best practices in setup and usage of the software as discussed in this chapter.

Why You Should Provide Data File Analysis Services

At first glance the data file analysis engagement may appear to be quite lengthy and time consuming. Many consultants are accustomed to immediately diving right in to the client's books and fixing the problems, and of course this is typically the only thing clients want to pay for. However, the successful consultant will approach client engagements on a much broader and more professional manner. When you make data file analysis engagements a standard service for your clients, you provide a much higher level of service and you streamline your consulting practice to provide consistently high-quality service as you grow your client base.

The main goals of performing data file analysis services are:

- to ensure early identification of critical data errors

- to add value to the client's business (beyond fixing data entry errors) and improve the overall confidence in the business information,

- to improve the efficiency of compliance work, and

- to give the consultant a consistent methodology in which to approach every client file so as to provide consistency and reliability across your consulting practice.

Selling Data File Analysis Services

So if you like the idea, but you're having trouble with how to sell this engagement to your clients, here are a few thoughts.

First, regular, periodic data file analysis is best. We suggest monthly or quarterly analysis of every data file. If you regularly analyze the file you can locate data entry or setup problems while they are still relatively easy (and less expensive for the client) to troubleshoot and repair. Also, analyzing and troubleshooting the data file allows your clients to have confidence in their financial reporting throughout the year as opposed to just at the end of the year.

Ideally, you want your client to understand and appreciate the importance of this service, but quite often, he or she must be convinced that it is worth it, and not something that unnecessarily increases their costs. This is a real issue because in order for the client to understand the value, they must understand the technical underpinnings of their system and how it all fits together. It is a lot to understand, and usually clients don't really want the details. Issues such as file setup, list maintenance, proper coding of entries, proper backup procedures, and data file integrity are all critical to the overall health of the data, and for you to provide any assurances to the client about the accuracy of reports, you must verify that the data file is healthy.

The best approach is to be honest with the client and help them understand that your services are a two-way street. You can only provide top-quality service if you fully understand their data and have confidence that the information and reports are accurate. Assuming you are not the data entry person (the basic assumption that leads to the need for data file analysis), you cannot really be confident in the data without going through a methodical process designed to uncover errors that are quite often difficult if not impossible to spot by simply running a few reports.

How to Charge for Data File Analysis and Repair

Once you've convinced your client of the value of the data file analysis service, the next question is how to charge for the service.

A few things to consider here are how often you will perform the service, and how you will separate the components of the service into separate billable events. As for how often, we recommend monthly or quarterly, but **at least every 6 months** so that there is time to address the issues without the extra work being including during tax season. As for separating the components of the engagement, it's probably best to separate your billings for the analysis steps (looking at but not changing data) from the repair steps (troubleshooting and clean up). The reason for this is that QuickBooks troubleshooting and repair is a very time-consuming process, <u>no matter how knowledgeable or experienced the consultant is</u>.

Preparing a Report of the Analysis

The analysis steps are fairly predictable in terms of the amount of time it takes to perform, so it is probably best to charge a fixed fee for the analysis service, with the deliverable being a report on the results of your analysis.

After you deliver the report of your analysis, you can more accurately estimate the amount of work required to troubleshoot and repair any errors you found during the analysis. Since many errors are hidden behind other errors (for example one misapplied payment may be hiding another misapplied payment), it's very difficult to anticipate the full extent of the problems and therefore it is very risky for the consultant to perform troubleshooting and repair services at a fixed fee. Therefore, use your report from the analysis of the file to propose a troubleshooting and repair engagement at an hourly rate. Also, it's best to bill troubleshooting and repair services separately from other tax or accounting work because troubleshooting and repair is mostly focused on transactions and data entry as opposed to taxes or accounting. Of course everything in the QuickBooks data file affects tax and accounting, but the focus of troubleshooting and repair is very specialized, so it should be billed separately from all other services.

Consider billing your data file analysis services on a monthly schedule throughout the year so that it becomes one of your standard services that all clients receive.

Data File Analysis and Repair Phases

This section provides a list of engagement phases developed by The Sleeter Group to locate and repair data entry errors and other violations of best practices of the setup and usage of the QuickBooks data file.

The data file analysis and repair phases are:

1. Planning Phase
2. Understanding the business
3. Timing of the engagement
4. Location (i.e. where you perform the analysis)
5. Gathering information
6. Investigation Phase
7. Checking data integrity
8. Confirm that the lists are set up correctly
9. Confirm account balances
10. Comparing Reports
11. Troubleshooting and Repair Phase

12.   Editing transactions

13.   Repairing lists

14.   Starting a new file when necessary

15.   Recommending an alternative to QuickBooks

16.   Control Phase

17.   Documenting the system

18.   Test the system

19.   Train the staff

20.   Engagement closure and follow-up

Data File Analysis - Planning Phase

The planning phase helps you to understand the business, define the time required for this engagement and to ensure you have access to the right information. This phase is equally important for both existing clients and new clients, but typically it takes longer for new clients.

Understanding the Business

Before jumping into a new consulting engagement it is important to have a solid understanding of the business. At a high level this includes what the business sells or how they generate revenue, any industry idiosyncrasies, the roles within the organization, any owner "hot buttons" related to accounting issues, some of the workflows for completing tasks and the reporting requirements. For existing clients, this information should be available based on data from prior years.

For new clients this is an important step prior to making any modification in their data file. Typically, this involves sitting down with the right people in the organization and asking them to explain how the business works. New client checklists are helpful so that your discussions are complete and you don't miss any important details. Also, keep note of who you are gathering the information from, as there may be different opinions or knowledge within the organization about how things work or should work. Documenting this information will come in handy later in the engagement and in future years. Remember to think about who within the organization makes the decisions and who you are ultimately responsible to. You may find that an "improvement" based on the opinions of one employee may not be right for everyone in the organization.

Timing of the Engagement

For an **existing client** you can complete the procedures at the client's request at any point throughout the year, but the more regular the review, the greater the opportunity to prevent small problems from becoming large problems. By correcting a small error at the beginning of a year you can allow your clients to have confidence in their financial reporting throughout the year. With this confidence, they can make better business decisions and ideally become a more profitable and successful business.

For **new clients** it is best to perform a high level assessment of the QuickBooks data file before you begin working with them. If the client has been using QuickBooks without the support of an accounting professional – or perhaps with the support of an accounting professional who has limited QuickBooks experience – you will likely find problems with both the data entry and the data file setup. It is important to document these problems at the beginning of the relationship so you can recommend troubleshooting and repair, or starting over with a new data file. The objective of this high level assessment is not to identify every error or problem, but to identify the scope of the problems and to estimate the level of effort required to repair them.

Once you have a good understanding of the business and a high level assessment of the QuickBooks data file, take the time to prepare an estimate of the work involved and a plan to complete the work. Typically, this involves preparing an engagement letter that outlines what you are planning to do, when you are planning to do it and what it will cost the client.

Without completing this important step with a new client you are risking that your work will not be valued and potentially not wanted. Set the right expectations up front to avoid problems later in the engagement.

After you have agreed with your client that you will be checking their company file, you need to find a time and a process that is suitable for both parties. Completing the analysis as the first step helps to eliminate the potential issues when you both need to be working in the file. In addition, it clearly demonstrates to the client that the analysis is a specific task you are performing for them: separate and distinct from any troubleshooting and repair services that may be required. Armed with the report documenting your findings and an estimate and plan for addressing these issues, you appear more organized and professional.

Another argument against making changes while doing the analysis is that if you choose to use the working copy of the file, checking the accuracy of the file normally requires you to work in single user mode with the ability to make changes to list elements, transactions and reports without interfering with other users. Ideally, the client can afford to go without the accounting file for a few days which will allow you to work on the file without disrupting their business. If the client needs the accounting file to operate during the day, you may need to schedule time after hours to review and complete your work. A worst case scenario is you need to take a second copy of the data files to do your analysis. However, if you do take a copy, you will still need to repeat the necessary changes in the master copy of the file at the client site.

Either way, discuss the plan with your client so that they fully understand and agree with the timing of when you are taking the file and when you expect to return it. If you are going to make changes to the file, make sure that you have communicated to the client that they should not record any new data during this period, but that they are free to view their data if necessary.

Location

Before you attempt to work on your client's company file you will need to decide where you will perform the analysis. By working at the client's location you will have quick access to the records and the people who have the information you need. Frequently, the client site is short on space and you will probably have difficulty finding a suitable work space to set up. In your own office, you may be able to work more quickly while taking care of other business at the same time. Either way, discuss with your client where you will be working and what you need from them to complete the work. A checklist of required documents such as the most recent tax return, most recent bank statement, etc. will aid in getting the information you will require to do the analysis. If you are missing a piece of information, note that it is an open item. The majority of the analysis can be completed, and then you can either discuss the open items with the client prior to providing your report, or provide the client with the open items so they know what issues may still exist.

Gathering Information for the Analysis

If you decide to perform the analysis at your own office, make sure you gather all of the client's information necessary to complete the task off-site. Here is a list of information you should obtain from client.

- Note the Version, Edition, and Release of QuickBooks used by the Company.
- Create a backup copy of the QuickBooks data file. Make a copy of the backup on CD and leave it at the client's office. Label the backup CD with the date, and indicate that it is "before data file analysis." Verify that the backup file is restorable.
- Obtain the Administrator password for the data file. You will need to log in as the administrator in order to complete the data file analysis. You might suggest that the client change the password to a new temporary password for you to use while working on the file.
- A copy of the client's most recently reconciled bank statement.
- A copy of the client's most recent income tax return and financial statements for the previous year.
- A copy of the client's most recent sales tax return (if applicable).
- A copy of the reports provided by the client's payroll service or most recent payroll tax returns (if applicable).
- A copy of sales reports from the client's point of sale, inventory management, or billing system using the same date parameters as your analysis (if applicable).

In addition to the above list, take copies of any other critical information you need for your analysis. For example, you may need lists of fixed assets, ownership or stock information, inventory lists, etc.

Data File Analysis - Investigation Phase

In the investigation phase the goal is to identify errors but not change any data. By taking a structured approach, you ensure that your review is comprehensive and that all areas of the file are verified. As mentioned before, this can be a time consuming process but it is critical for assessing the health of the QuickBooks file and for the consultant to determine the issues to be addressed during the repair phase of the engagement. This section gives a step-by-step listing of areas for you to investigate.

Client Data Review

The Client Data Review tool has been designed to help streamline the Accountant's role when working with QuickBooks clients. The areas addressed by this tool are: Account Balances; Review List Changes; Unapplied Accounts Receivable and Accounts Payable payments; Undeposited Funds; Sales Tax Payments; and Payroll Tax Payments. The first year this tool is used, there is very limited analysis available. Once the initial review is marked as complete the information is "saved" for the starting point for the next review.

It is available in the Accountant pull down menu with QuickBooks Accountant products It is also accessible in non-Accountant edition products when logging in as an external accountant. These tools can serve as a jump start to locating (and potentially correcting) several issues within the file. For those clients who have upgraded to this latest edition, be sure to utilize this feature as a starting point, and then continue through the remainder of the analysis steps.

More information on the Client Data Review tool is on page 337.

Check Data Integrity

Before analyzing the QuickBooks data (lists, transactions, balances, etc.), you should first confirm that the data file itself is not corrupted at the database level. QuickBooks has a built-in tool that checks for database corruption. See page 210 for more information on using this tool, and for correcting corruption should you discover problems. After confirming the integrity of the database, continue with the rest of the steps in this section.

Confirm that Lists are Setup Correctly

Even before you review the balances in the accounts you should check to see that the lists being used by the client are setup well for their business. For existing clients, this may involve a quick review of any list items that appear new from previous engagements. In newer clients, you may discover a number of ways to improve how they use lists. As with all the other areas of analysis you will perform, take the time to document what you looked, what you saw, and what you recommend for future consideration.

Chart of Accounts

A good chart of accounts typically has 70 or fewer accounts with high level account names and a well thought out structure for sub-accounts. Perform the following analysis of the chart of accounts list.

Number of Accounts: How many accounts are in the file? Are there enough accounts to complete tax or information returns. Are there accounts that could be eliminated with the proper use of names, items, classes or jobs? Check the revenue accounts to ensure they have not created income accounts for every product, service or customer. Check expense accounts to ensure they have not been set up for individual vendors.

Account names and numbers: Is there a consistent method of naming accounts and the sub-accounts? Do the names make sense? Are they using capitalization appropriately? Do all accounts have numbers? Even if account numbers are normally turned off, all accounts should have account numbers. See page 67 for account numbering guidelines that conform to the default accounts included with QuickBooks 2008 and above.

Review Income Accounts: Ensure that the client has not created an income account for every product, service, or customer. This is a common problem stemming from misunderstanding about how QuickBooks tracks revenues by customer. Therefore, if you find income accounts named for customers, it is something you should discuss with the client, and most likely change to accounts with more general names such as Service Income or Product Sales.

Review Expense Accounts: Ensure that the client has not created an expense account for every vendor. The same issues apply to expense accounts as discussed above about income account naming. Make sure you scrutinize these account names and make the appropriate recommendations to your client about what changes should be made.

Check for duplicates: Frequently, a user may add accounts without realizing that an account with the same purpose already exists. If the client never reviews the account list or doesn't know how to edit accounts, entries start to get incorrectly entered. Review the accounts for names that are duplicated or that may be similar. Common examples of duplicate accounts include sales tax payable (liability) and sales tax expense and shipping expense as both a Cost of Goods Sold account and an expense account.

Check for account names that begin with an asterisk (*): QuickBooks creates several accounts automatically when users access certain windows, or turn on certain preferences for the first time. Examples of these accounts are: Retained Earnings, Inventory, Opening Bal Equity, Accounts Receivable, Accounts Payable, Cost of Goods Sold, Payroll Liabilities, Payroll Expenses, Undeposited Funds, Estimates (non-posting), Sales Orders (non-posting) and Purchase Orders (non-posting). If the user created an account with any of those names, then QuickBooks will add an asterisk (*) before the account it creates automatically. See page 239 for information on fixing this problem.

Check Account Types: If accounts are set up with the wrong account type the user may be able to enter transactions to that account, but it is unlikely the amounts will be reported correctly. Some common examples of accounts that frequently get set up with the wrong type include cost of goods sold accounts, accounts for intercompany transactions and unearned income accounts. In most cases, it is simple to change the account type (edit the account in the chart of accounts), but sometimes the fix could get more involved.

Item List

You can review the items list in a similar way to how the accounts were reviewed by checking the names for consistency and duplication (i.e. different names for the same item, or sub-items named the same as a master item). With items you have some additional checks you should perform:

Accounts attached: Use the Item Listing report to make sure that each item posts to the proper account(s) in the chart of accounts. Look for consistency and accuracy in how the items post to accounts in the chart of accounts.

Item types: Setting up the right item type can be confusing to new users of QuickBooks. Check the item type to ensure items are being used in the most effective manner. The following item types cannot be changed to any other item type: Service, Inventory, Inventory Assembly, Subtotal, Discount, Payment, Sales Tax Item, Sales Tax Group. In addition, it is not possible to merge items of different types. Therefore, if you find items that were set up with the wrong item type, it is quite likely that you'll need to set up a new data file to address the problem. Or, at a minimum, change the name of the incorrect item slightly and set up or import the items correctly to address the issue going forward.

> **Note:**
> While you can change a non-inventory part to inventory, you cannot switch it back and all the historical transactions are updated for the item type change which can have dramatic consequences.

Sales tax codes: By having sales tax codes associated with each sales item, QuickBooks tracks revenue by sales tax code. The Sales Tax Revenue summary report shows sales totals for each sales tax code for the specified date range. If sales tax codes were not set up correctly or if sales were recorded using the wrong sales tax codes, the repairs needed will be very time-consuming since each transaction may need to be modified. Depending on the number of transactions involved, errors in the sales tax codes setup or usage could necessitate a new data file setup or a decision to correct the issue from a specific point in time going forward.

Costs, Prices, And Unit of Measure: A quick review of the costs and prices may identify items that are not being consistently used in transactions. A review of the unit of measure from both a calculation perspective as well as usage as it relates to the costs and prices should also be completed.

Quantity: By looking for unusual quantities in the item list you may identify problems in how items are set up or problems with how transactions are entered (or not entered). A large number of negative quantities may indicate that items are being sold, but not purchased. Quantities that seem too high might indicate a problem with the units of measure.

> **Tip:** Some companies may use the Item list for purposes other than recording invoices and sales receipts. For example, construction companies often use the item list for job cost codes. If your client is using the item list for reasons other than the intended use, you should discuss this use with the client before you examine the list for correct account postings.

Payroll Items

Create a Payroll Item List Report to identify problems that may result in inaccurate payroll and accounting records.

> **Tip:** In the display tab of the Modify Report window of the Payroll Item Listing report, review all of the available columns and add new columns as necessary. Each available column represents a field or selection in at least one of the payroll item setup windows.

In addition to reviewing the names attached to payroll items check the following:

Accounts attached: Use the Payroll Item List report to make sure that each item posts to the proper account(s) in the chart of accounts. Look for consistency and accuracy in how the items post to accounts in the chart of accounts. By default QuickBooks uses one general account for each type of item; i.e. Payroll Expense; Payroll Liability, etc. Most Accountants and Clients find it more useful to split the expense account into gross wages and payroll taxes at a minimum. Detail reports are available for the liability type items so it may not be necessary to reclassify those. Note that when the account is changed for a payroll item, all of the historical transactions are updated to reflect this new account.

> **Tip:**
> It is required for tax withholding items that you choose one specific account. It is not possible to create multiple tax withholding items mapped to different types of accounts. For example, there is not a FICA employer for labor (COGS-type account) versus overhead (expense-type account). There is just one FICA employer item coded to one account. It is a manual process to reclassify a portion of the tax if required.

Amounts and limits: Frequently a client may complete payroll on their own and do not update rates and limits for a new year or quarter. Review the amounts to ensure they are up-to-date.

Gross or net calculations: Clients will often deduct items on a paycheck from the gross rather than from the net – like employee advance repayments.

Tax tracking: Having the correct tracking for tax purposes can save you time when it comes time to complete W-2's.

These errors may have a significant impact on the accuracy of the payroll information.

> **Tip:** Some changes to payroll items (e.g., name, tax status) do not affect prior period payroll information. However, changes to the expense and liability accounts do affect prior period financial reports. Consider the impact on prior period reports before editing the account fields on payroll items.

Confirm Account Balances

Once you have some confidence in the lists of the company file, you can move to confirming the account balances. Typically, we start with a review of the balance sheet accounts on both a cash and accrual basis. Within each account type you are looking for something slightly different to confirm that the balance is accurate and complete. Once the balance sheet is verified, income statement accounts are also reviewed.

Check Balance Sheet Account Balances. Before confirming closing account balances for the current year or period, it is a good idea to confirm that the opening balances for the accounts are correct.

Confirm individual account balances by doing a quick comparison between the account balance on the last day of the prior year to the account balance in the prior year's financial statements or tax return.

If there is a discrepancy between the year-end Balance Sheet and the prior year tax return, it may be due to one of the following reasons:

- The year-end adjustments from the tax preparer (e.g., depreciation expense and accumulated depreciation) may not have been recorded.

- The QuickBooks setup was either incomplete or incorrect. If this is the case, you must either complete or correct the QuickBooks setup before proceeding.

- The QuickBooks data file has uncorrected data entry and/or setup errors that affect the accuracy of financial reports. Many times QuickBooks users enter data into QuickBooks to track essential balances (e.g., Accounts Receivable, Accounts Payable, and Cash) but they do not perform bank reconciliations and do not attempt to maintain accurate financial information. The Company's tax preparer uses the QuickBooks data as a starting point when preparing the tax return but does not attempt to adjust QuickBooks balances to the tax return at year-end.

- A change was made to a transaction dated in the previous year after the tax return was prepared. To locate these discrepancies run a Closing Date Exception report. This report will show all changes to transactions dated on or before the closing date. Using QuickZoom, open each transaction and reverse the edits made by the client. Alternatively, enter an adjusting entry to reverse the impact of the client's changes on the General Ledger. If the client did not set a closing date in the data file, edit the Accounting Company Preferences to add the Closing Date so the previous period changes will be captured from this point forward. See page 260 for more information about troubleshooting changes to closed accounting periods.

Confirm that the Balance Sheet Balances by checking the totals at the bottom of the balance sheet. QuickBooks does not allow one-sided entries, so if the Balance Sheet does not balance; the data file is probably corrupted. Make sure to check the Balance Sheet on a cash and accrual basis. For more information on troubleshooting out-of-balance Balance Sheets, see page 216.

Once you have done a quick check on the opening balances you can begin a more detailed analysis of the different types of accounts.

Bank and Credit Card Accounts

Make sure the client accurately reconciled all cash and credit card accounts through the analysis date. Assist the client in completing bank reconciliations as necessary. See page 245 for more information on troubleshooting bank reconciliations. A more detailed analysis may include the following procedures.

Confirm when the client last performed a bank reconciliation. The client should be no more than 2 months behind on bank reconciliations for all accounts, including bank loans (if the financial institution sends monthly statements) and credit card accounts (if the company enters each credit card charge separately into QuickBooks).

Confirm that the Opening Balance field of the reconciliation window agrees to the ending balance of the last reconciled statement. If there is a discrepancy, the client has probably made changes to cleared bank transactions or the client deleted cleared transactions. To locate the changes and/or deletions, run a Reconcile Discrepancy Report. Then, QuickZoom from the report to each modified transaction and edit the transaction to reverse the client's edits. Doing so should correct the Beginning Balance field.

Check for excessive deposit detail on the bank reconciliation window or check register. If there is excessive deposit detail, the client is probably recording Sales Receipts and Payments received on Invoices directly to bank accounts instead of grouping them with Undeposited Funds. Advise the client to use Undeposited Funds beginning with the next Sales Receipt and/or Receive Payment transaction they record. Explain that doing so will greatly simplify their next bank reconciliation because the total on the reconciliation window will then agree to the statement without any additional calculations.

Check Undeposited Funds. If the Undeposited Funds account has a balance, the balance should represent receipts from customers that are applied to the customers' accounts but are not deposited in the bank. The transactions should all be current.

Accounts Receivable

Confirm the accuracy of the Accounts Receivable balance by performing the following procedures.

Review the Open Invoices Report for Zero Totals. Zero amounts will show as the total amount due for customers on the Open Invoices report when credit memos or payments are not applied to their respective Invoices or charges. Use the Receive Payments window or the Apply Credits button on invoices to link payments and Credit Memos to their respective Invoices and charges.

If Credit Memos or Payments are not applied to their respective Invoices, QuickBooks may show a balance (many times a negative balance) in Accounts Receivable on the Cash Basis Balance Sheet (see page 580). For example, if an invoice for services is open because the payment was not applied, the cash basis calculation (done behind the scenes by the software) removes the invoice (because it's open) but does not remove the payment (because the payment hits only Balance Sheet accounts). The result is that cash basis reports will show negative Accounts Receivable. Applying Credit Memos and/or Payments to the Invoices will eliminate this balance.

The Client Data Review tool is very effective in identifying and correcting this issue. To use the tool requires either an *External Accountant* user or QuickBooks Accountant. Choose Client Data Review from the Accountant pull down menu as shown in Figure 5-1 below.

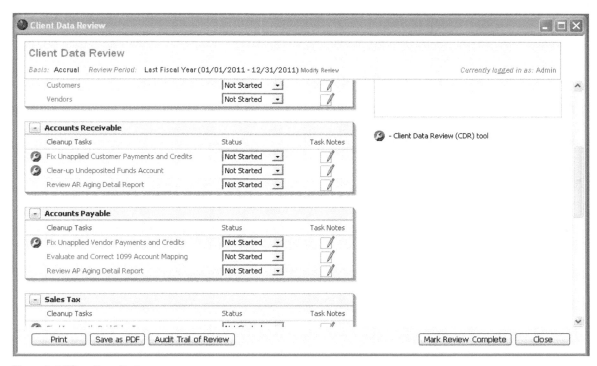

Figure 5-1 Client Data Review

Next, click on **Fix Unapplied Customer Payments and Credits** to see any unlinked transactions (Figure 5-2). The customer is listed to the left and the unlinked transactions to the right.

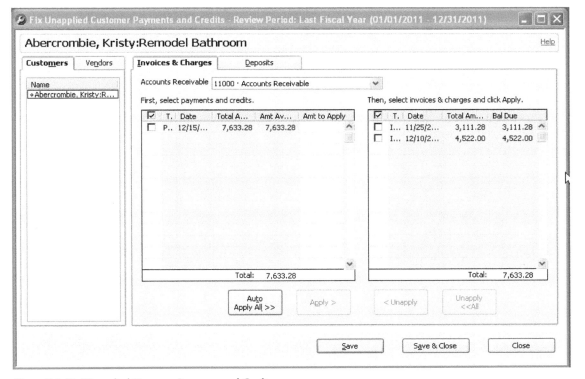

Figure 5-2 Fix Unapplied Customer Payments and Credits

Review the AR Aging Report for Old (over 90 days) Amounts. Work with the client to locate any invoices that should not appear on the report. In many cases, the client will tell you that the invoice is uncollectible (i.e. should be written off using a credit memo) or the invoice was paid already. If it is the later, the client may have made one of the following errors:

Recorded the deposit using the bank account register. If deposits were entered directly in the bank account register, locate each of the deposits and edit them to post to Accounts Receivable. Be sure that the customer is included in the name column. Then, use the Receive Payments window to link the Available Credits (the deposit(s) that credit Accounts Receivable) to their respective invoices. This will clear the invoices from the Accounts Receivable aging and Open Invoice reports.

Recorded the payment for the wrong customer. It could be that the wrong customer or job name was entered on a payment. In this case, break the link between the payment and deposit, edit the payment and change the customer and/or job name. After saving that change, apply the payment to the appropriate Invoice and re-link the payment to the deposit. Unfortunately, it is often quite difficult to find payments that were recorded for the wrong customer. See the section beginning on page 220 for more detailed troubleshooting steps for this situation.

Inventory

Confirm the accuracy of the **Inventory** balance by performing the following procedures.

Check Inventory for Negative Quantities on Hand. Using the Inventory Valuation Detail report, check for negative numbers in the on-hand column. If an inventory item ever drops below 0 units on hand, the stock status report contains errors. Advise the client to conduct a physical inventory as soon as possible and to enter an Inventory adjustment into QuickBooks to adjust the quantity on hand. Negative quantities on hand can cause problems with the calculation of average cost – resulting in incorrect Cost of Goods Sold on the Profit & Loss.

Confirm the Average Cost Calculation. Create a Sales by Item Summary report and review the margins for each inventory item. Compare each of the item-level margins with the company's margins as shown on the Profit & Loss. If the margins for an item are significantly higher or lower than gross profit on the Profit & Loss, there may be a problem with the calculation of average cost for that item. The average cost could be inaccurate because of an incomplete inventory item setup. If you enter quantities on hand during the setup of an inventory item but do not enter an amount in the *Cost* field, beginning inventory quantities will have an average cost value of $0.00. To modify the average cost for an inventory item, enter an inventory adjustment that adjusts the value of the item but not the quantity on hand. Consider the impact of the value adjustment on the Inventory balance on the Balance Sheet.

Using an inventory sample, reconcile stock status to the shelf. Using a representative sample of 5-10 inventory items, create a Stock Status by Item report in QuickBooks and confirm the quantities on the shelf. Even a single discrepancy between QuickBooks and the shelf indicates problems with the Inventory data.

Accounts Payable

Confirm the accuracy of the Accounts Payable balance by performing the following procedures.

Review the Unpaid Bills Report for Zero Total Due for any Vendor. The Unpaid Bills report will show a zero total due for a given vendor when Bill Credits or Checks coded to A/P are not applied to their respective Bills. Use the Pay Bills window to link the Bill Credits or Checks to their respective bills. If the client does not apply Bill Credits or Checks to their respective bills, QuickBooks may show a balance (many times a negative balance) in Accounts Payable on the Cash Basis Balance Sheet. Applying the Bill Credits and Checks to the Bills will eliminate this balance.

> **Note:**
> There is a feature included in the Client Data Review to aid in identifying and linking bills and bill payments. This feature works the same way for Accounts Payable as described above for Accounts Receivable.

Review the AP Aging Report for Payables with Aging of More Than 90 Days. If the Company pays its Bills on a timely basis, there are two reasons payables may be outstanding more than 90 days. First, it is possible that the client recorded the payment directly in the bank account register or used the Write Checks function. If this is the case, locate and edit each of the checks so that they post to Accounts Payable. Then, use the Pay Bills window to link the *Bill Payments* (the checks that debit Accounts Payable) to their respective bills. This will clear the bills from the Accounts Payable aging and Unpaid Bills reports. It is also possible that the client issued a Bill Credit to zero the vendor's balance but did not apply the Bill Credit to the Bill(s) from the vendor. In this case, both the Bill and Bill Credit will remain open and both will show on Accounts Payable Aging reports as Unpaid. To correct for this, use the Pay Bills window to link the Bill Credits to their respective bills.

Sales Tax Payable

If the client is required to collect sales tax, confirm the accuracy of the sales tax payable balance by performing the following procedures.

Confirm that Total Sales Tax Payable per the Sales Tax Liability Report Agrees to the Balance Sheet. There are three reasons why the balances will not agree. First, unlike the Balance Sheet balances, the Sales Tax Liability report balances are not as of a point in time. Change the *From* date to a period prior to any transactions being recorded in QuickBooks and confirm that the *Through* date agrees to the Balance Sheet. Also, the Sales Tax Liability Report may be accrual and the Balance Sheet may be cash basis. Change the two reports to the same basis and verify that the balances match. If the balances still do not agree, the data file may be corrupted.

Confirm that total sales per the Sales Tax Liability and Sales Tax Revenue Summary Reports agree to Total Income per the P&L. There are several possible causes for a discrepancy between these two reports. First, check for Journal Entries or Deposits that post directly to income accounts. Next, check for Sales Items that post to accounts other than income accounts. For example, the client may have an item called *Finance Charge* that posts to an Other Income account, so the total Ordinary Income (near the top of the P&L) will not include this account.. The amounts of your finance charges will show as sales (usually non-taxable sales) on the Sales Tax Liability report. Filter the sales tax reports to include *All Ordinary Income Accounts*. Then, compare total sales to total income on the Profit & Loss.

Review the Sales Tax Liability Report for negative numbers. If the report contains negative numbers, a user may have made corrective adjustments to Sales Tax Payable using a Sales Tax Adjustment, a Journal Entry or an entry in the Sales Tax Payable register.

Review the Sales Tax Liability Report for inappropriate vendors. If an inappropriate vendor exists on the Sales Tax Liability report, the probable causes include:

The use of non-sales tax related vendors when adjusting Sales Tax Payable on Sales Tax Adjustments, Journal Entries or through the Sales Tax Payable register. If this is the case, edit each entry to include the correct vendor.

The file contains multiple vendor records for the same sales tax agency, with variations in spelling. If this is the case, merge the vendor records together.

Someone may have merged the Sales Tax Payable account with another account. In some cases, this causes QuickBooks to create a vendor called *Rebuild Tax Vendor*. If you find this vendor in the list, merge *Rebuild Tax Vendor* with the correct vendor to whom the client pays sales tax.

Check for a balance in Sales Tax Payable for periods in which all Sales Tax was paid. If so, the client probably adjusted the amount due for sales tax directly on the Pay Sales Tax window instead of creating a proper sales tax adjustment. For example, the client may have reduced the amount of sales tax to pay due to a timely filing discount or rounding by reducing the amount of the sales tax payment, but did not record a sales tax adjustment. To correct this problem, enter a sales tax adjustment on the last day of that reporting period.

Payroll Liabilities

Confirm the accuracy of the payroll liabilities balance – See page 472 for more information about this analysis.

Opening Balance Equity

Check for a balance in the opening balance equity account – If there is a balance in the Opening Balance Equity account, see page 238.

Income Statement Accounts

The Profit & Loss report, also called the Income Statement, calculates the Net Income of the business by subtracting the expenses from the income. Normally, if your Balance Sheet accounts are correct it is safe to assume that the net income from the Profit & Loss report is also correct. Unfortunately, there may be coding errors on transactions that will cause the Profit & Loss accounts to be incorrect. Typically, the Income Statement can be reviewed for accuracy by performing the following procedures.

Comparing Reports

Reports are a fabulous way to quickly and easily determine if there are areas to be investigated in more detail. Entering the data accurately is obviously very important, but a significant part of the data analysis step is to determine if the date is being entered correctly, consistently, and completely.

Item-Based Reports

By comparing reports and identifying differences you can identify errors in how transactions are recorded. The following reports are all generated by filtering items. By comparing these item-based reports to the account-based reports you can identify transactions that may be impacting the balances of the accounts. We have listed a few select reports that you can use for comparison purposes.

Sales Reports

The Sales Reports can be displayed by customer, by item and by rep. By reviewing the sales reports you are trying to compare the total of the sales in the reports to the total of the sales in the Profit & Loss report. The sales reports are set to filter on *All sales items*, so entries that have been made to the income accounts without a sales item will not be included in the reports. In addition, items that have been coded to an account other than an income account will not appear as revenue on the Profit & Loss report. Some examples of entries that result in a variance between these two totals are:

- Journal Entries.
- Discounts on bill payments or customer payments.
- Deposits.
- Items that have been coded to non-Income accounts for sales transactions

If there is a large discrepancy between the sales reports and the Profit & Loss, the business may not be recording transactions in the best way or additional reconciliation steps may be required. Drill down from the Profit & Loss report to see what entries might be impacting the sales accounts without impacting the sales reports. Review the Item List report to determine the account used as sales transactions is recorded.

Purchase Reports

Purchase reports are designed to help you understand what items have been purchased, so they have also been set to filter on *All sales items*. Reviewing these reports will help to identify how the Cost of Goods Sold account is being calculated. As most operating expenses are entered without items, the purchase reports will not help to understand operating expenses. In addition, the purchase reports to not include transactions coded directly to Cost of Goods Sold accounts without the use of an item.

As was indicated for Sales Reports above, assuming all the items were coded to Cost of Goods Sold type accounts and all entries to the Cost of Goods Sold type accounts included an item, these reports can be used to reconcile the detail report to the total on the Profit and Loss report.

Payroll Reports

Most of the payroll reports are also set up based on items, which in this case are payroll items. So any entries made to the payroll accounts without payroll items will not display in these reports. By reviewing the payroll reports you may be able to identify data entry problems such as:

- Checks instead of paychecks being used to pay employees.
- Coding checks payable 1099 vendors to payroll expense accounts.
- Checks instead of Pay Payroll Liabilities being used to pay payroll liabilities
- Journal entries instead of Adjust Payroll to modify payroll

Profit & Loss Variance Analysis

One useful high-level analysis you can do is to compare the current period's Profit & Loss report with earlier periods. By simply comparing the current period numbers to previous periods, you will speed up the process of identifying and troubleshooting problems in the data. The following procedures are designed to quickly identify the most common issues.

A Profit & Loss report can be easily customized to compare the current year to previous years. In this comparison, you can quickly see how the accounts have changed on a dollar value basis as well as a percentage change basis. You are looking for large, out of the ordinary changes that are not consistent with changes in other accounts. From there, you should gather an understanding from the business owner or manager as to what took place in the business to result in these changes. The reports can only identify what is occurring in the accounting, the discussion with the client should help you to understand why.

Percentage Analysis

QuickBooks also allows you to create additional columns that calculate percentages. In Figure 5-3 below, you can modify the standard P&L report to include columns for percentage comparisons.

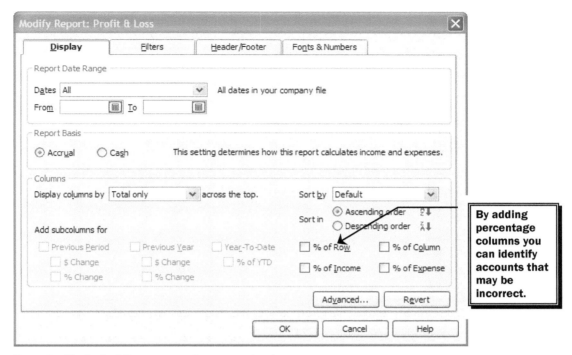

Figure 5-3 The Profit & Loss report can be customized to show percentages.

By adding the percentages and reviewing the results you may be able to identify trends in the business, or even errors in the accounting. The percentage of income is helpful in reviewing the sales, cost of sales and gross margins. By comparing these percentages across periods you may be able to spot trends in the margin. The percentage of Expense can help identify where money is spent in the business. Getting a comfort level in using these percentages and relating them back to changes in the business can help you provide valuable feedback to your client on how to improve their business.

Period Analysis

An easy method to identify errors in a relatively small business is to review the Profit & Loss report across different periods. By selecting different columns from the report heading you may be able to identify missing entries or timing differences in the accounts.

Figure 5-4 The Profit & Loss can be quickly modified to show different periods.

In the columns drop down list, select to display by month and you will see your Profit & Loss by month. You can quickly scan the accounts to see if there are large differences in the accounts. This can help on expense accounts that may have regularly scheduled payments that should show up each month. For example, you can quickly scan the rent account to see that 12 separate payments of rent have been recorded.

Account by Account Review

Normally the above procedures are used to identify accounts that may have problems. By adding columns, filtering and sorting you can get a good idea how the accounting looks. Once you identify potential errors in the accounts you may need to drill down to the accounts to see the details of transactions.

Data File Analysis - Repair Phase

In the investigation phase you identified file integrity errors, setup errors, and confirmed the accuracy (or inaccuracy) of the accounting data. In the repair phase you will correct those errors. It's very important that you complete the investigation phase before repairing any data. The main reason for this is because you must confirm that the file is not so "broken" that it would be impossible or impractical to repair. Also, by first accumulating <u>all</u> information about the file and analyzing <u>everything</u> that needs repair you are more likely to come up with the most efficient methods of repairing the file.

In the repair phase you have a number of options to consider before making any changes to the data. If the issues are relatively minor, transactions can be edited directly, but for problems with incorrect setup, it often gets much more involved.

Before making any changes you should make a permanent backup the file and copy the backup file onto a clearly labeled CD.

The rest of this section will help you think through the best methods of repairing errors in the QuickBooks file.

Editing Transactions

When the consultant comes across an error in how a transaction was recorded it is normally the easiest route to edit the transaction and correct the date, account, amount or item. Before doing this though, you need to consider the impact of your changes on financial statements that may already be in circulation. Even though there is an error in the accounting and you feel you should correct it, it may be more helpful to the readers of the financial statements to see this correction in the current period and separate from the day-to-day transactions. So prior to editing any incorrect transaction, consider creating a journal entry or other type of adjustment instead of changing the original transaction. If the transaction is in a current "open" period, it is probably best to edit the transaction but if the error is in a prior period, you should strongly consider how your change will impact the taxes that may have been filed or the financial statements that may have been produced and published.

Repairing Lists

Errors that occur because of mistakes (or poor practices) in the setup of list elements are relatively common. For example, the file might have a Shareholder Loan account set up as an expense account instead of a Liability account or an inventory item may have been set up to record the Cost of Sales entries to an expense account. These types of errors can be fixed by one or more of the following techniques.

Changing Account Types

QuickBooks allows the user to change the account types for most accounts. In some cases you can even change Balance Sheet accounts to Profit and Loss accounts. Before changing an account's type, consider how the change will impact the financial statements, and that changes to account types will affect all financial statements in all past periods, regardless of any closing date setting.

It is not possible to change to or from Accounts Receivable or Accounts Payable type accounts. In cases where an error was made for these accounts, you can reclassify the transactions to permit deleting the account (since it will no longer have any activity associated with it) or create journal entries to move the activity in total to the correct account and make the incorrect account inactive.

Changing Item Types

You also have some limited ability to change the type of an Item in the item list. A common mistake is to set up inventory, non-inventory, or service items with the wrong or inappropriate type. Unfortunately, the following item types cannot be changed to any other item type: Service, Inventory, Inventory Assembly, Subtotal, Discount, Payment, Sales Tax Item, Sales Tax Group. In addition, it is not possible to merge items of different types. Therefore, if you find an extensive number of items that were set up with the wrong item type, it is quite likely that you'll need to set up a new data file to address the problem. It is possible to use the functionality included with QuickBooks to export the lists, change the item type, and then import the list into the new file. The advantage to this approach is that the item names stay consistent if transactions are to be transferred using one of the tools available from third party developers.

Change Account References

In the setup of an item or a payroll item, you can modify the account(s) to which the item is linked. Before making this type of change you need to think through the impact. Payroll item account changes will reclassify all transactions, both historically and in the future. For items, making a change to the account will make future transactions use this new account, but you can optionally choose to make the account change retroactive as well. When you save the changes to an item after changing the account(s), QuickBooks will prompt you with a choice to also change existing (retroactive) transactions.

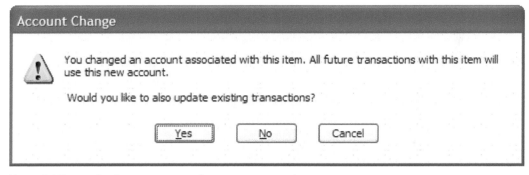

Figure 5-5 Prompt for changing account references on existing sales items.

If you do choose to update existing transaction this will most likely change prior year financial statements and information on which previous tax returns were based. Carefully, consider if this is the appropriate change because it is not something that can be undone. QuickBooks 2008 added the warning shown in Figure 5-6 if the account change will impact transactions dated prior to a closing date. Read these warnings carefully, before proceeding with the change.

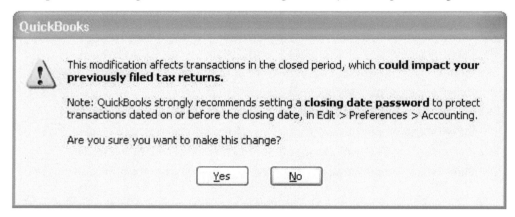

Figure 5-6 Prompt for account changes that impact prior year tax returns.

Changing accounts on payroll items can also impact prior periods. Unfortunately, with payroll items there are fewer warnings to prevent you from modifying prior periods.

If you just change the account to another account within the same account type (for example, payroll expenses to gross wages), the impact is relatively minor. However, if you change the account on a payroll item to a different account type, then you carefully consider the impact on your financial statements.

Merging List Elements

Using the merge capabilities in QuickBooks can help you fix the common problem of clients creating new accounts for every miscellaneous item that is bought or sold. For example, when the bookkeeper cannot find the Professional Fees account when paying a legal bill for a lease, he or she may set up a new account called Legal Fees Lease. Other users may see this setup and decide to set up new accounts for different types of Legal Fees. Before you can stop them, there are four accounts, set up across the chart of accounts to track Legal Fees, and several transactions are coded to each of the accounts involved. This is where the merge function is useful. You know that these accounts are redundant and they make for cluttered financial statements. To fix the problem, first confirm the account types are the same. Then edit the name (or account number if that preference has been turned on) for each of the accounts you want to remove to make their names match the account you want to keep. If the name matches exactly, then QuickBooks will prompt you to confirm the merge.

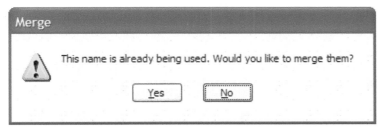

Figure 5-7 Confirming an account merge

Once confirmed, QuickBooks will combine all the entries made to the old account into the new account. The old account is then removed from the chart of accounts. All references to that account in items and transactions will be replaced with references to the new account. Merging is a very powerful function, and it allows you to make sweeping changes to the data file very quickly. However, this action cannot be reversed or undone so make sure you are aware of the risks before merging any accounts. It is wise to make a backup of your data file before each merge.

Deactivating List Elements

To clean up lists and reduce data entry errors, consider deactivating unused list elements. The longer the list of items, customers, vendors, and accounts, the more likely users are to select the wrong one. Make it a habit to review the lists with your client to determine which list items can be made inactive. Memorized transactions will continue to be recorded using the inactive items. Also note that even if you deactivate a list element, reports will still show the list element if there is data for that list element in the period covered by the report. The only exception is the inventory valuation summary report which only contains active inventory items, even if the inactive items have a quantity and value.

Starting a New File

Making a decision to start a new file is never an easy one, but in some situations it can be the right decision. If you uncover a large number of errors in a company file and/or the structure of file is not well designed, the best solution may be to set up a new file. In many cases you can probably complete the current year with the existing file, but then start a new file next year. As soon as you determine that a new file is the best course of action, you should begin planning for the new file setup.

One important factor to consider before starting a new file is the size of the current file. In a larger file, the time required to complete some of the list element changes recommended above will increase. Also, in a large file, edits to transactions may be painfully slow, making it economically unviable to repair the file. What may take a number of seconds in a small file may take minutes to process in a large file. So even if you are able to identify what needs to be done, it may be too time-consuming, thereby making the repair engagement an unviable option.

Another factor is how mission-critical the data file is to the business. Since many of the changes you will need to make require that QuickBooks be in single-user-mode, you won't be able make the repairs while other users are logged in. This means all the work will have to be done during non-business hours.

In many situations, you or the client's accountant can compile a list of the modifications or entries needed to complete a year end. These entries may be completed externally to QuickBooks, or entered as journal entries. Think about the legal and tax requirements for maintaining financial records. In some extremely rare situations, it may be necessary to re-enter historical transactions, for example when the bookkeeping has been performed so poorly that the accounting reports do not make sense.

Going forward with the existing file may be possible, but if you can set up accounts, items, classes, jobs, etc. in a way that would make the accounting and the business operate more effectively with a higher level of accuracy, then it is probably best to start a new file.

The time you spend thinking and talking with the client about what they would like from the system (and what would help them better manage their business) will save time and unnecessary aggravation later. Think especially about the information both you and the client will want to create reports. Now is the time to make the changes. Once you have completed the needs analysis, you will be prepared to determine what procedures will result in the best fit.

In addition, there are many alternatives as to how the various tasks can be accomplished. It is important to think about and discuss how the flow of information from the client to the bookkeeper, as well as from the bookkeeper to the client will occur. How, for example, is the client tracking day-to-day activity. How will that information be relayed to the bookkeeper (i.e. fax, scan and transfer the file, client to do some data entry into a shared file, transaction information will need to be imported and then manipulated)?

To take the process one step further, who is going to need access to the information? In what form is the information needed? Are there specific reports or spreadsheets they are currently using? The more information you can obtain about where the information comes from and in what format the more efficient the set up process will be.

When working through the process, don't forget to address any integrated applications that are currently set up to work with QuickBooks and how their existence may complicate the process: Assisted Payroll, QuickBooks Merchant Services, etc.

If you decide to create a new file, there are several ways to go about it.

Start from a Back Up

This is a great option if the problem is relatively recent (maybe a new bookkeeper has created some issues with the file) or if the new file is necessary due to data integrity issues that have been relatively recent. With this file, the data to get it to current can be entered or imported using one of the third party tools available.

Removing All Transactions to Start Fresh

Most often, the best approach to start a new file is to use the Clean Up Company Data function (File > Utilities > Clean Up Company Data) and then select Remove All Transactions. After removing the data you can clean up all the lists (add/change/delete whatever is necessary in all of the lists) before entering new opening balances as some new start date on which you will start the new file. For more detail on this process, see page 321.

Transferring Lists from the Old File to a New File

If for some reason you cannot use the Remove All Data function, then you will need to start a new data file from scratch. If you do this, you can streamline the new setup by first exporting any of several lists from your old file. Use the File > Utilities > Export > Lists to IIF function to select which lists from your old file you want to transfer into your new data file. For more information on exporting and importing lists, see page 298.

Recommending an Alternative to QuickBooks

Frequently, you will come across small businesses that are ineffective in maintaining accurate and complete accounting records. Of course there are several other accounting software applications that could be a better fit for the client, but quite often the problem is not so much about which accounting software they use, but how they are using it. So before you immediately jump to a different accounting application consider the big picture of the client's needs, and understand the true nature of the problems they are having.

Problems could be due to a number of reasons, including poorly designed workflows, a poor implementation of QuickBooks or inadequate training of staff. More specifically, it can be procedures that duplicate effort, have bottlenecks in the data entry or there is poor communication between employees. In these situations, you can provide great value to your clients by implementing a well-designed system and providing training to the staff. Remember, QuickBooks operates most effectively, if used in a real-time environment (i.e. transactions entered as they occur) with employees who are well trained.

If speed of the system is an issue, make sure that the client is running QuickBooks on current hardware. You can even test the company file on upgraded system to determine if that will increase the speed. In addition, make sure that you are using the latest version of QuickBooks.

Another area where you can add value is by recommending third party add-ons that may take the load off QuickBooks and spread it across other applications. Make sure to assess the needs of your client to determine if an integrated product could help the company. It may provide a few more years of life into a QuickBooks file.

It is important to realize that at some point, many businesses become so large and complex that it becomes difficult for QuickBooks and even QuickBooks Enterprise Solutions to handle. So after you have tried the add-on products, the updated hardware as well as a well-designed

QuickBooks system, it may be necessary to discuss with your client plans to upgrade beyond QuickBooks. This is also the time in a company's life-cycle where they start to hire a full-time accountant or controller to run the accounting. Some of the employees may go kicking and screaming away from QuickBooks, but it is might just be the necessary route for the company to grow and prosper. Which software you'll recommend is beyond the scope of this book, but you should make sure you get the appropriate knowledge or other consulting resources needed for your client to make the right choices as their needs grow.

Data File Analysis - Control Phase

After repairing the file, your work is still not quite done. When these issues are still fresh in your head, take the opportunity to document all procedures and train the staff so as to prevent the same issues from re-occurring. In some situations, this work can require as much time as the previous phases so you should first confirm that your client is willing to pay for this documentation. Your client may feel that they already have procedures in place or that documentation of the procedures is not important. Even experienced employees may have a different way of doing things that is not consistent with the manual. These inconsistencies can create problems in the long run. You'll need to convince them that a well-documented set of procedures will not only increase accuracy of the accounting data, it will save consulting, data repair, and tax preparation fees.

A procedural manual serves several purposes:

1. It forces the accounting activities to be examined and documented. This process alone will uncover many of the most obvious problems with the internal control system.

2. It provides a resource for activities that are not completed regularly.

3. It serves as a benchmark in determining employee performance.

4. During times of illness or vacation, it is possible for someone else to step in and help get the job done.

5. In the event of turnover, it expedites the training process.

Once you have convinced your client of the value of this phase, here are some general guidelines for completion.

Documenting the System

For any system or set of procedures to work consistently as people come and go, it must be documented. If it is not documented it is probably not a system or set of procedures, but a random occurrence that sometimes works and sometimes does not. The key is to document a system so that it works well all of the time. Some people refer to this as an Operating Manual. Others may call it a Policies and Procedures Manual.

In a small business, most of the systems and workflows are centered on QuickBooks and how to enter data into QuickBooks.

While there are many training books for QuickBooks, many developed by the authors of this book, it is best if each client has a customized document that specifies how each process for that client situation should be handled.

Your job is to document the steps involved in completing these workflows in the client's business. Many of the steps will be based on QuickBooks activities, but there will also be steps that are outside of QuickBooks, such as signing the checks or taking the money to the bank. For each of the steps, this document should identify **why** the task is done, **who** does the task (use job title, not a specific person's name), **when** it should be done, **where** any of the necessary tools or information can be found, and finally, **how** to complete the task. Don't forget to include information on what happens after the task is completed: Where is the paperwork filed; who does it need to go to for approval; etc. Consider a list in the front of the manual stating who is assigned the various titles to efficiently handle the challenge of knowing who is responsible for what: It is easier to update a single summary sheet than to find and replace someone's name throughout the manual. Look for ways to streamline the process by creating templates, memorizing transactions or reports, or setting preferences in QuickBooks. In addition, think broadly about the environment and make recommendations that will help improve the process. Sometimes even simple things like re-arranging furniture or filing cabinets can make a big difference.

The procedural manual should be step by step so that anyone can follow it without prior knowledge of the business or software. Screen shots are extremely helpful. For most versions of Windows, it is possible to have the software screen open and then press Ctrl+Prnt Scrn then open Microsoft Word and choose Edit > Paste to paste the screen shot into the Word document. There are also inexpensive tools to provide better quality and edit capabilities such as SnagIt. Keep in mind that different people learn in different ways. For some detailed instructions are sufficient, for others you need to "draw them a picture" so they can see exactly what they are to do. Including copies of the forms with references on how the information is transferred from the form to the software is also very helpful. Consider including blank forms in the procedural manual too as a backup for the electronic documents. Consider including the directory and file name in the footer of the document to make future updates and reprints more efficient.

Test the System

Once the system is documented, pass the documentation to the employee responsible for each area and confirm that the workflow makes sense. All businesses have staff turnover, so it may even be useful to have someone not experienced in this area to complete the tasks in the system. If possible, compare the new system to the old system to identify clear improvements in speed, accuracy and employee satisfaction with the process. This type of results documentation helps to further show the value of the services you provide to the client.

Train the Staff

Once the system is documented and tested, it is still necessary to train the staff to be able to complete the tasks. As time progresses and as each staff member learns their tasks, they may find ways to improve the process further. Keep in touch with this process and help your clients continually improve their processes.

Engagement Closure and Follow-up

Once you have completed the work for your client you need to make sure the client realizes the value that you have provided and they will be paying you promptly for this work. The clients want confirmation that their money was well spent. You need to provide a detailed breakdown of the work done and the improvements made.

Make sure to discuss payment for your services as well as book a time for follow-up. In future visits you can assess how the procedures were followed and how they can be improved. This is also the time to set expectations that data analysis is not a "one time only" type service but monitoring the file helps to ensure it remains healthy.

Troubleshooting Corrupted Data Files - Verify and Rebuild

Occasionally you may find that a data file fails the *verify data* test. This means the structure of the database on which QuickBooks is built is corrupted.

Several things can damage a QuickBooks file. Damage could occur when power is lost during QuickBooks data entry, when there is damage to your hard drive, or possibly, even when you import iif files that are improperly created.

> **Note:** QuickBooks releases periodic updates to each version of the program to correct problems or irregular behavior not detected during beta testing. Your clients should update QuickBooks regularly to avoid these problems.

Verify the Company File

To find out if your file is damaged follow the steps in this example.

1. If your company file is not open, open it and login as the Administrator. Also, verify that you are in single-user mode. (Note: With 2009 and later versions, this can be done in multi-user mode, although it is not recommended.)

2. Close all windows (reports, lists, registers, etc.) (Note: If you don't, QuickBooks will close them for you)

3. Select the **File** menu, choose **Utilities**, and then choose **Verify Data**.

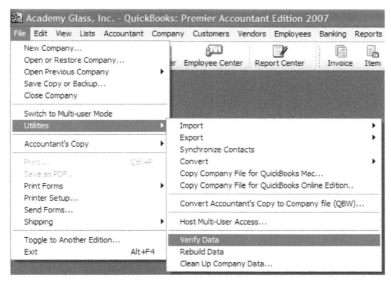

Figure 5-8 To verify your data, select the File menu, then select Utilities, and then select Verify Data.

4.   QuickBooks shows a progress bar while it's verifying your data. Don't interrupt your computer while QuickBooks is verifying your data.

5.   When QuickBooks finishes verifying your data file, a message shows whether your data has lost integrity. If your file is ok, you'll see this message.

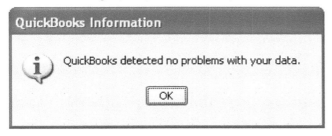

Figure 5-9 QuickBooks displays this message when the data file has no errors.

6.   If your file is damaged, you'll see this message. See the next section for how to troubleshoot and fix damaged files.

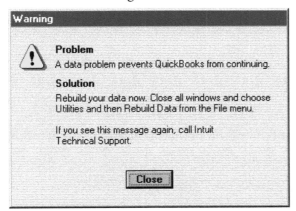

Figure 5-10 If your file is corrupted, you'll see this message. Try rebuilding the file.

Rebuild the Company File

If your data file is damaged, you might be able to fix it by using the Rebuild command in QuickBooks.

1.   If your company file is not open, open it and login as the Administrator in single user mode.

2.   Close all windows (Reports, Lists, Registers, etc.)

3.   Select the *File* menu, choose **Utilities**, and then choose **Rebuild Data**.

4.   QuickBooks forces you to back up your data before it rebuilds the file. Then it shows a progress bar while it's rebuilding your data. Don't interrupt your computer while QuickBooks is rebuilding your data.

> **Important:**
> Use a unique file name when backing up a corrupted data file or allow QuickBooks to add the date and time to the backup file name which makes it unique. If the corruption occurred since the client's last backup, you will replace the backup of the uncorrupted file with this backup of the corrupted file.

5.   QuickBooks displays a small message screen when the rebuild is complete.

6.   It is a good idea to re-verify the data file after rebuilding. If the rebuild did not correct the problem, refer to the section called *Determining Which Transactions are Damaged* below.

Determining Which Transactions are Damaged

Sometimes, even the Rebuild command doesn't fix the problem. In this case, try deleting the transactions that are causing the problem.

To determine which transactions are damaged, follow the steps in this example

1.   Choose **Ctrl+1**, then **Ctrl+2**. This opens the *Tech Help* application.

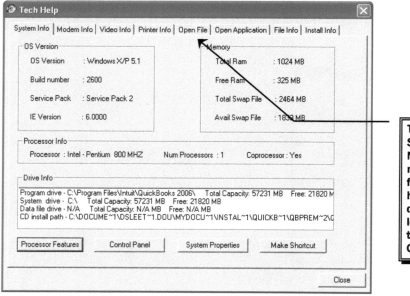

Figure 5-11 The Tech Help application helps troubleshoot problems with QuickBooks.

2.   Click the **Open File** tab on the Tech Help screen.

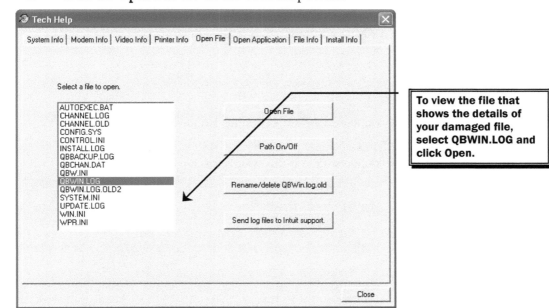

Figure 5-12 The Open File tab on the Tech Help screen. Click Path On/Off if you can't see the file names.

3.   Select the **QBWIN.LOG** file and click **Open File**.

If you cannot see the file names, you need to turn the path off so that only the filenames show in the *Select a file to open* section.

4.   When WordPad opens, you'll see your QBWIN.LOG file. Scroll to the very bottom of the file.

QBWIN.LOG

The QBWIN.LOG file contains details of all errors found in your file. Each time you verify or rebuild the file, or when the QuickBooks program crashes, a new section is added to this file.

A section of the QBWIN.LOG file is shown below. This section was added after verifying a file. There were no problems found during this verification.

```
===============* BEGIN VERIFY LOG *====================

verify.c (365) :  CHECKPOINT: Wed Mar 29 22:37:47 Verifying data, file
name: C:\Sleeter CRG 2006\ACADEMY Expert (corrupted).QBW

DBSQLFileManager.cpp (4444) :  CHECKPOINT: Wed Mar 29 22:38:01 Database
validation completed. No error detected

verify.c (468) :  CHECKPOINT: Wed Mar 29 22:38:03 Beginning Transaction
Verify/Rebuild

verify.c (531) :  CHECKPOINT: Wed Mar 29 22:38:05 Ending Transaction
Verify/Rebuild

prefuser.c (16995) :  CHECKPOINT: Wed Mar 29 22:38:06 Permissions
Analysis Starting...
```

```
prefuser.c (17027) :  CHECKPOINT: Wed Mar 29 22:38:06 Permissions
Analysis Finished.

verify.c (640) :  CHECKPOINT: Wed Mar 29 22:38:06

===============* END VERIFY LOG *========================
```

Figure 5-13 Sample Verify Log – No corruption found.

In the section of the QBWIN.LOG file shown below, the report below shows that some transactions are damaged. The doc# field shows the number of the transaction that was damaged. Since it is a Sales Receipt, the doc# field is the Sales Receipt number. If it were an Invoice, the doc# would refer to the Invoice number.

```
========================* BEGIN VERIFY LOG =========================

Verifying data, file name: C:\2002_QTW\ACADEMY Expert corrupted).QBW Mon
Apr 22 11:44:37 2002

Error: Verify Link 960: Error: Verify Links: T2 missing
    Type: sales receipt    txn#: 00052   date: 01/25/1999   doc#: 97002
PO#: 456       Source accnt: Undeposited Funds    $: 770.74    name: Leonard,
Jerry          --- has a history / link error to ---

!Link Error Code: 00010(HEX),        DEP-PMT, linkRecNum = 00960, sibling =
00961, key (m1) = 226, tOne = 227, mTwo = 286, tTwo = 457 Error: Verify
Link 961: Error: Verify Link: T1 missing      --- has a history / link
error to ---      Type: sales receipt    txn#: 00052   date: 01/25/1999
doc#: 97002    PO#: 456
    Source accnt: Unde]The doc# is the number (chk #, Inv#, Sale#, etc.) eonard, Jerry
                     of the corrupted transaction. Find this transaction,
!Link Error Code: 00( delete it and then re-add the transaction.     00961, sibling =
00960, key (m1) = 28                                                 7
=====================:                                          :=============
```

Figure 5-14 Sample Verify Log – Damaged transactions found.

Fixing the Damaged Transactions

To fix damaged transactions, delete the affected transactions and then reenter them. Follow the steps in this example:

1. Note the doc numbers of all damaged transactions shown in the QBWIN.LOG file. In the example above, Sales Receipt number 97002 is damaged. Don't worry about the exact error message; just find the transactions that are causing the problem.

2. Find the affected transactions using the Find command. Select the ***Edit*** menu, and choose **Find** (or press **Ctrl+F**).

3. Enter *Sales Receipt* in the *Transaction Type* field and 97002 in the *Sales No.* field. Then click **OK**.

    QuickBooks will display Sales Receipt #97002.

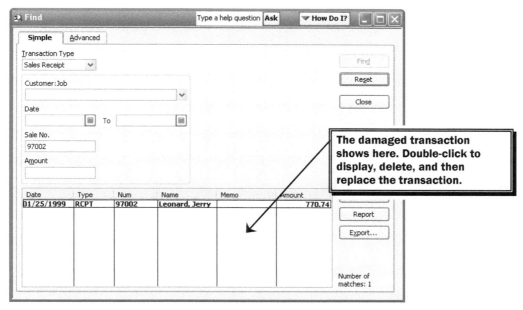

Figure 5-15 The Find command helps locate the corrupted transactions.

4. Double-click to display the transaction.

5. Take a note of everything about the transaction.

6. If possible, delete the transaction. Select the *Edit* menu, and choose **Delete** (or press **Ctrl+D**). In the example above, you won't be able to delete the Sales Receipt because it has been deposited. So you'll first have to delete the sale from the deposit and then you can delete the transaction.

7. Repeat this step for each damaged transaction

8. When all damaged transactions have been deleted, run the Verify Data utility again and confirm that the data file is no longer corrupted.

9. Add the deleted transactions back into the file, exactly as originally entered.

    In the first example transaction, you'll also need to re add the sale to the deposit so you put everything back the way it was.

> **Warning**
> Make sure to note all of the details of the transaction before you delete it. Simply printing the Sales Receipt may not show you all of the information you need to re-enter the transaction because the template designer lets you add fields to the screen display but then omit the same fields from the printed form.

10. When all damaged transactions have been reentered, run the Verify Data utility again to ensure that the file is no longer corrupted.

If you are unable to fix the file using the process described above, you should contact Intuit's Data Recovery department.

Intuit will provide data recovery and password removal services only for currently supported versions of QuickBooks, or if you are upgrading from a retired version of QuickBooks to a currently supported version.

Troubleshooting Out-of-Balance Balance Sheets

You may find that your client's balance sheet does not balance. Notice that the cash basis Balance Sheet in Figure 5-17 is out of balance by $4,068.00.

Follow the steps in this example to correct the problem:

1. Check the file for customer discount transactions coded to balance sheet accounts. For example, if an invoice was paid, or partially paid using a discount transaction and the other side (the Debit) was coded to a balance sheet account (e.g. Customer Prepayments or Retainers), it will cause the cash basis Balance Sheet to be out of balance. Unfortunately, QuickBooks doesn't provide an easy way to search for discount transactions, so you'll have to use the Search command, filtered for all Payment transactions. The resulting find report will show the transactions *Type* column, and you can look for Discount transactions in the report. If you see any coded to balance sheet accounts, those are the problem transactions.

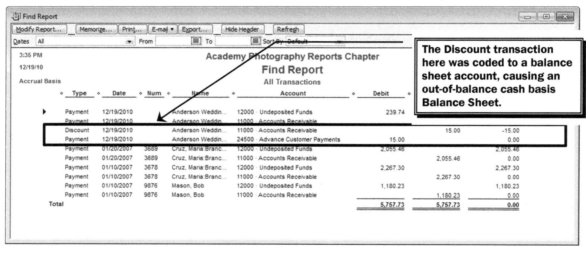

Figure 5-16 Find Report showing customer discount transactions

2. To fix the problem, delete the discount transaction(s) and create customer Credit Memo(s) instead. For more information about Cash Basis reports, see page 580.

If you did not find any discount transactions, or if your balance sheet is still out of balance, follow the steps in this example:

1. Run the Verify Data utility as described in the previous section. If the Verify Data utility detects problems with the file follow the steps in the previous section to correct the damaged transactions.
   If the Verify Data utility doesn't detect any problems with the data file, you will need to isolate the damaged transactions yourself.

2. Search for by amount for 4,068.00. If a transaction shows for that exact amount it may be the cause of the problem. Delete the transaction, rebuild the file, and re-enter it. Then

confirm that the Balance Sheet balances. For the Balance Sheet in Figure 5-17 the Search command shows no transaction in the data file for $4.068.00.

3.   Research to find the year in which the corrupted transaction is dated.
     Change the date range to all, and then change the columns to Year. This will provide a Balance Sheet with each year displayed as a column. Scroll across the report until you find where the change from in balance to out of balance occurs. (Note if the report is too long to effectively see the two totals, consider using the Balance Sheet Summary report instead. In the above example, the balance sheet does not balance until you enter 12/31/1999. This lets you know that the corrupted transaction is dated between January 1, 2000 and December 31, 2000.

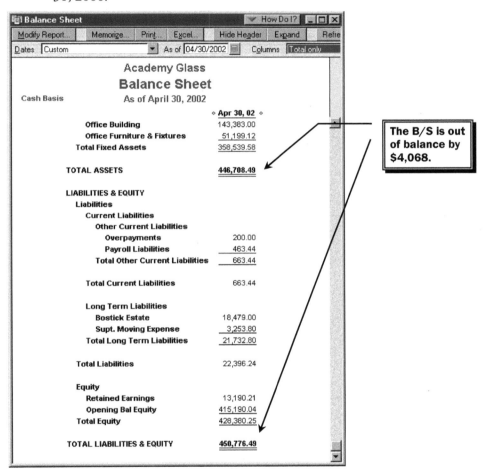

Figure 5-17 This Balance Sheet does not balance.

4.   Research to find the month in which the corrupted transaction is dated.
     From the same Balance Sheet report, you can modify the report so the date range in the year in question, and change the columns to by the month. You learn from doing this that the imbalance began as early as the end of January (01/31/2000). This lets you know that the corrupted transaction(s) is dated between 01/01/2000 and 01/31/2000.

5.   Research to find the day on which the corrupted transaction is dated.
     Change the date to each day of the month in which the corrupted transaction is dated. In this example you would begin with 01/01/2000, then 01/02/2000 and so forth.

Alternatively, you could select *Day* from the columns drop-down menu at the top of the balance sheet, and modify the date range on the balance sheet to include the month where you suspect the problem.

You learn from doing this that the balance sheet balances for each day of the month through, and including, 01/10/2000. The balance sheet for 01/11/2000 does not balance, so the corrupted transaction(s) must occur on that date.

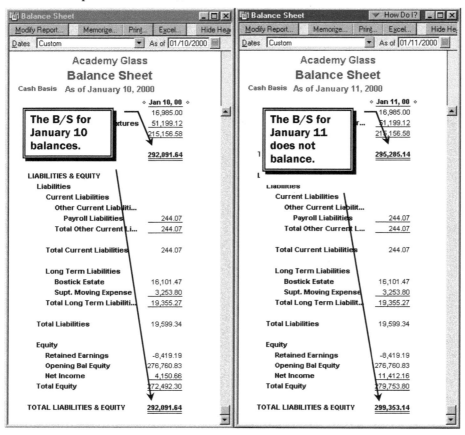

Figure 5-18 01/11/2000 is the first date the Balance Sheet did not balance.

6.   Since there may be several corrupted transactions in the data file, dated in various years, recalculate the amount of the imbalance on 01/11/2000. In this case, the imbalance in the Balance Sheet is still $4,068.00, so all of the corrupted transactions are dated 01/11/2000.

7.   Create a Custom Transaction Detail Report and set the date range to 01/11/2000 through 01/11/2000 (see Figure 5-19).

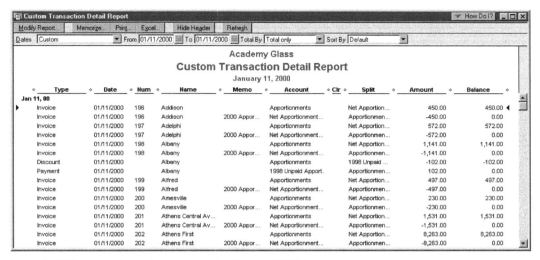

Figure 5-19 The report shows all transactions dated on 01/11/2000.

8. Scan the report for any amounts equal to $4,068.00 (or two or three amounts that may total $4,068.00). If you cannot find these transactions, or if the report is too lengthy, you will need to continue filtering the report.

9. Total the report by *Account List* to see if all transactions involving a particular account total $4,068.00. The subtotal for an account called *1999 Unpaid Apportionment* equals the amount of the discrepancy. It is safe to assume that each transaction in this section of the report is corrupted. Delete, rebuild, and re-enter each transaction.

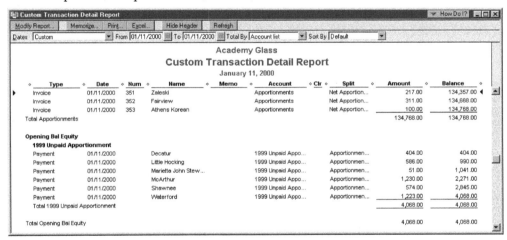

Figure 5-20 Custom Transaction Detail Report Totaled by the Account List

10. If totaling the report by account does not help you to detect the corrupted transactions, you may want to filter the report by transaction type for Payments and Bill Payments. Filter for both of these accounts together first, then separately. Continue to total the report by Account List when adding these filters.

Only the cash basis balance sheets are out of balance in the example above and both of these transaction types significantly affect the conversion from accrual to cash.

11.   Now that the 01/11/2000 Balance Sheet balances, create a Balance Sheet using the current date and confirm that it balances as well. If it does not, there are additional corrupted transactions dated between 01/12/2000 and the current date. Repeat Steps 3-10 to find any additional corrupted transactions in the file.

Since all corrupted transactions for this file were on a single date the Balance Sheet will balance.

Rules for Applying Customer Credits

A common area of confusion and mistakes in QuickBooks is the area of applying credits (or payments) to invoices. In this section, you'll learn how to fix problems caused by misapplying credits and payments, but to help you avoid problems altogether, here are a few general rules to teach your clients about applying credits to Accounts Receivable.

General Rules for Handling A/R Credits

- When receiving payments against Invoices, enter the application information in the Memo field of the Receive Payment screen. If payments are not applied correctly for some reason (e.g. blind dependence on the Auto Apply feature) you have a record from which to make corrections.

- When entering Credit Memos, enter the Invoice No. from the Invoice to which you intend to apply the credit followed by the letter C. For example, a credit memo to be applied to Invoice 2002-107 would have the number 2002-107C. This will help you to better match Credit Memos to the correct Invoices on the Receive Payment screen. Before doing this, make sure to note the reference number since QuickBooks sequentially assigns the number for the next transaction based on the last transaction entered. Consider making a note of the invoice number that should be linked to the credit memo in the memo section at the bottom of the transaction instead.

Misapplied Customer Payments

Occasionally, you'll discover customer payments that were applied to the wrong invoice. Fixing this is sometimes a little tricky, but it's not hard if you understand how payments are applied to invoices.

To illustrate, let's look at an example of a misapplied payment.

1.   First, create an Open Invoice report. From this report, you can see an open invoice for $1.36 (Invoice #FC 8 for Bill Young's Window Replacement job). Let's say that you know it was paid with a **previous** payment. We'll call this invoice our "target" invoice.

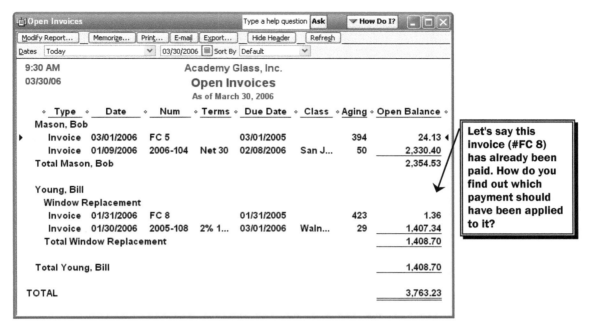

Figure 5-21 Open Invoices by Customer

2.   Since you know a previous payment from this customer must have been misapplied, look for that payment.

3.   To create a report of payments received from this customer, display the *Customer Center* and then select the job. See Figure 5-22.

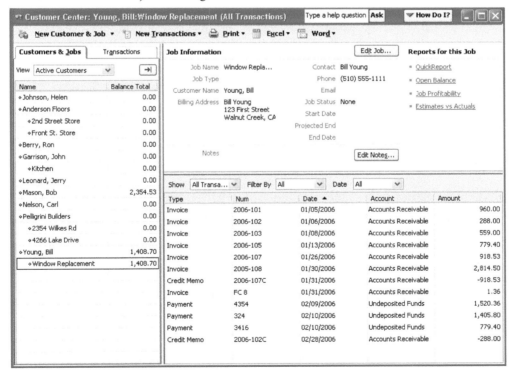

Figure 5-22 Select the job in the Customer Center.

4.   The *Customer Center* in Figure 5-22 shows a list of **all** transactions involving this job. To narrow this report down to include payments only, select **Received Payments** from the *Show* drop-down menu. See Figure 5-23.

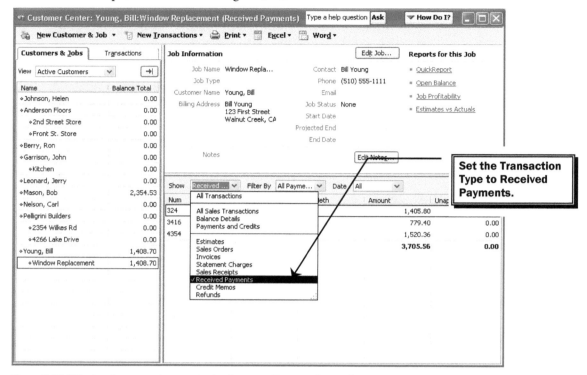

Figure 5-23 Filtering the transaction type in the Customer Center to Received Payments

5.   The filtered list of transactions in Figure 5-24 shows only the payments from this Customer:Job for the date range shown. Double-click on each payment until you find the payment that should have been applied to your target invoice.

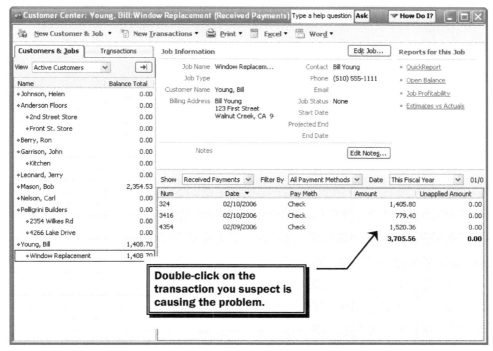

Figure 5-24 Now the report shows just the payments from this customer

6. Double-click on the payment you suspect was improperly applied. In this case, double-click on the first payment in the list (for 1,520.36). The Receive Payments screen (Figure 5-25) shows how the payment was originally misapplied.

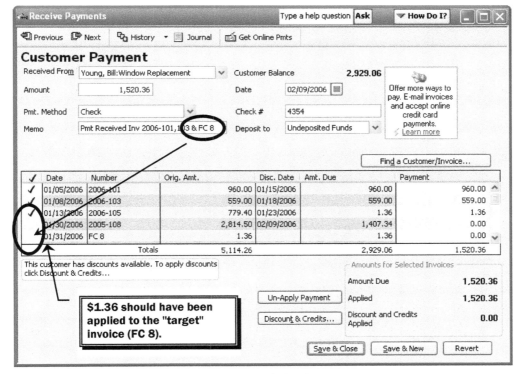

Figure 5-25 A misapplied payment. Notice the 1.36 is applied to the wrong invoice

7. In the example above, the payment was supposed to be applied to the first two invoices plus the finance charge (Inv. #FC 8) of $1.36.

    In this example, the fix is simple because the target invoice still shows in the payments screen.

8. Click the checkmark next to the wrong invoice. This removes the checkmark, making an *Unapplied Amount.*

9. Apply it to the correct invoice by clicking next to the target invoice as shown in Figure 5-26.

10. Then click **Save & Close** to save your change.

As long as you don't change the amount of the payment, this can be done whether or not the payment has been deposited to the bank.

> **Note** - If the payment has been deposited to the bank and you need to change the customer, payment amount, date, or payment method, you'll first need to delete the payment from the deposit. Then make your changes to the payment and add the payment back to the deposit. You can quickly locate the deposit to which this payment applies by clicking **History** at the top of the screen or by selecting the **Reports** menu and choosing **Transaction History** while Receive Payments screen is open.

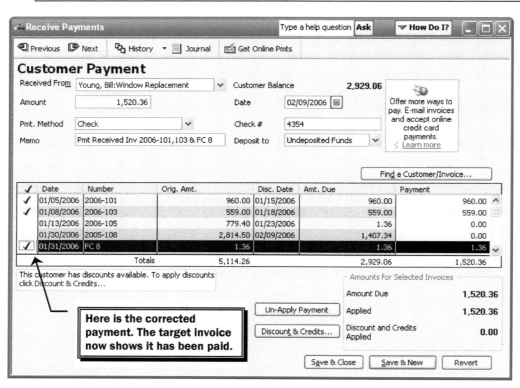

Figure 5-26 The corrected payment

1. Now that you've fixed the misapplied payment, look again at the *Open Invoices* report.

    Notice that Invoice #2006-105 is now open. That's because we just removed the 1.36 which had been misapplied from another payment. That caused this invoice to become open so now we need to find out what went wrong with this invoice.

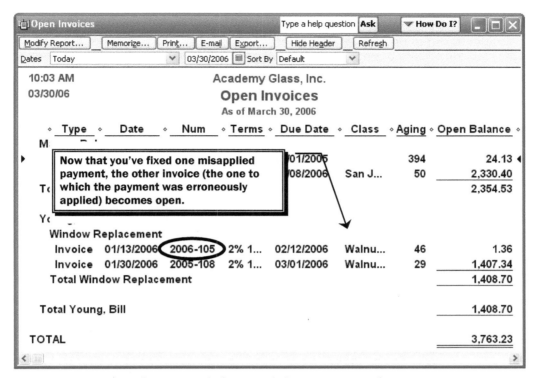

Figure 5-27 Open Invoices after correcting the first misapplied payment. Now another Invoice is open.

2.   To display the invoice, double-click Invoice #2006-105.

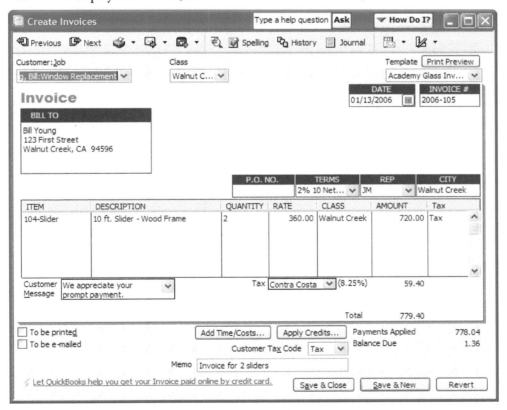

Figure 5-28 Invoice that is now open after fixing the misapplied payment

3.   To find out what payments were applied to this invoice, click **History**. This displays all transactions **linked to** the invoice.

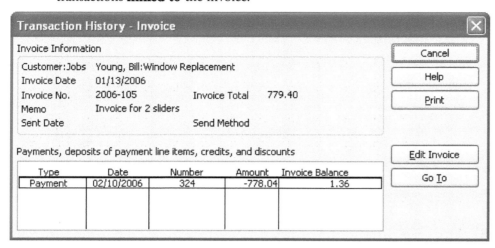

Figure 5-29 Transaction History for Invoice 2006-105 shows a payment applied to Invoice

4.   Figure 5-29 shows all transactions **linked to** invoice #2006-105 including payments or credit memos that were previously applied. If necessary, you can edit those payments or credits.

5.   To edit the linked transaction, click on the transaction and then click **Go To**.

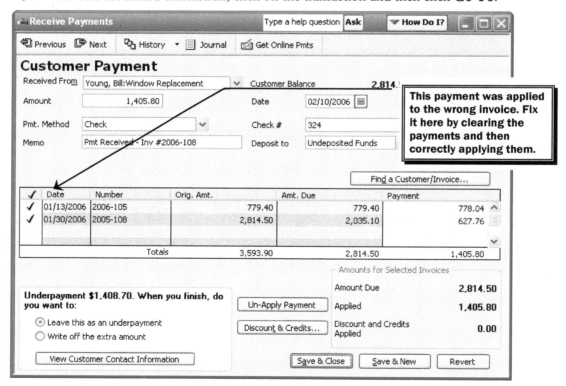

Figure 5-30 Payment showing another misapplied payment.

6.   This displays the original payment that was applied to invoice 2006-108. In this case, the payment was applied to two invoices (#2006-105 and #2006-108), but it should have only been applied to #2006-108.

7.   Click **Un-Apply Payment** to unapply all the payments. Then click on the left column of the line containing invoice #2006-108. Then click **Save & Close**.

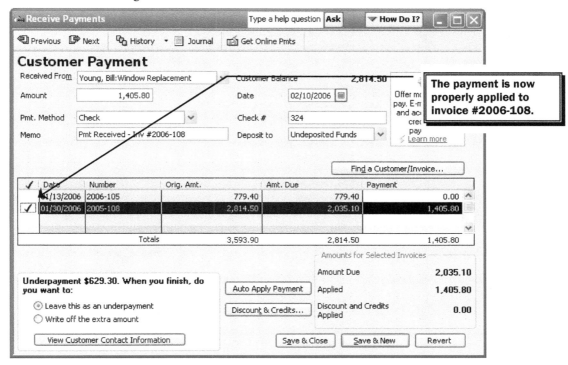

Figure 5-31 The Payment has now been properly applied to the correct invoice.

8.   Now that you've fixed the erroneously applied payment, Invoice #2006-105 is now open. See the *Open Invoices* report in Figure 5-32.

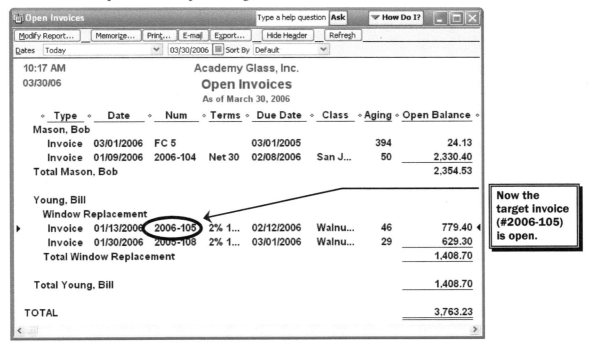

Figure 5-32 Open Invoices after fixing misapplied payment

9.   The next problem is to find the payment that should have been applied to Invoice 2006-105. Look at the Customer Center with the filtering you set earlier. See Figure 5-33.

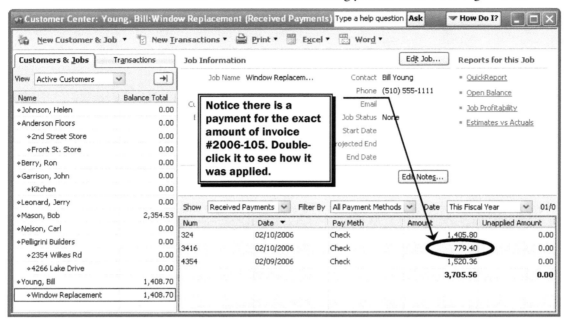

Figure 5-33 The Customer Payments report showing all payments for this customer

10.   Double-click on payment #3416 for $779.40.

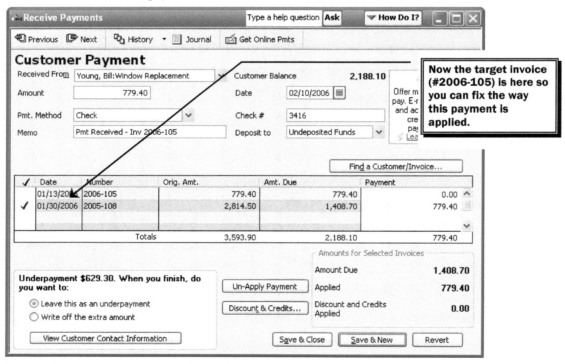

Figure 5-34 Customer Payment incorrectly applied to Invoice 2006-108.

11.   To correct this, first click **Un-Apply Payment** and then click on the line containing the target invoice. Then click **Save & Close**.

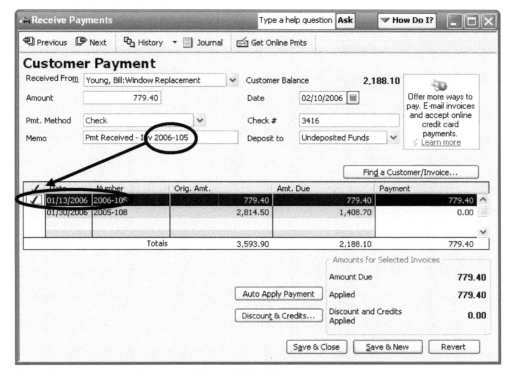

Figure 5-35 Payment properly applied to Invoice 2006-105.

12.   Now, the *Open Invoices* report (Figure 5-36) correctly shows that only one of the invoices
       from Bill Young is open.

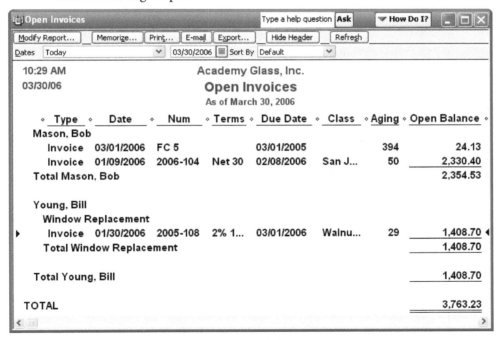

Figure 5-36 The Open Invoices Report after fixing misapplied payments.

When the Target Invoice Doesn't Show on A/R Reports

The last example is relatively simple. The seriousness of this type of problem is not the
complexity so much as the time involved in fixing it.

For a more difficult example, consider what would happen if you didn't see the target invoice on the payments screen. That is, what if you couldn't un-apply and re-apply all at the same time?

The target invoice won't show up in the *Open Invoices* report if either of the following occurs:

There are other payments or credits applied to the target invoice

The payment was applied to the wrong customer or job.

In either case, you must first find the payment or credit that got applied to your target invoice and correct that payment. Then the target invoice will show in the *Open Invoices* report and you can go through the process shown above to fix the problem.

Accounts Payable Issues

When you pay bills in QuickBooks, use the Pay Bills function. This function creates **Bill Payments** (checks) and applies them to **Bills**. Sometimes you also have **Bill Credits**, which are credits from vendors against what you owe them.

The correct way to pay bills in QuickBooks is to follow a three-step procedure.

Enter the Bill using **Enter Bills**. Do this when you receive the bill from the vendor. The date should be the date on the vendor's bill. Code the Bill to the appropriate expense account (or Item). If the Bill is the result of a Purchase Order you entered previously, QuickBooks will ask you if you want to match the Bill with a PO. This "accrues" the Bill by crediting the Accounts Payable account.

Pay the Bill using **Pay Bills**. Do this when you are ready to pay the bill. The date should be the date you want on the check. Click on the Bill or Bills you want to pay in the Pay Bills screen. This does three things. It reduces (Debits) A/P, changes the paid status on the Bill, and writes a check (Credits Cash).

As you use the Pay Bills function, QuickBooks creates checks in the checking register. When you're ready to print the checks, select the **File** menu, then select **Print Forms**, and then select **Print Checks**. Select which checks you want to print, load the checks in the printer and print the checks.

When Bills Are Not Paid Using Pay Bills

Clients often make the mistake of entering their bills into QuickBooks and then paying the vendor using **Write Checks** instead of **Pay Bills**. This causes two problems. First, the Bill never shows that it was paid (i.e. Accounts Payable is overstated), and second, the expense account used on both the Bill and the check is overstated. If the client coded the check to Accounts Payable, expenses and Accounts Payable will not be overstated, but the Bill will still show as unpaid.

To fix this type of problem, you have four options.

1. **Option 1 (most preferred)**: Use the Pay Bills function to create a bill payment (BILLPMT) that will replace the check (CHK) and then delete the check. Make sure that the check number and date match the one you deleted, and if the CHK has already cleared the bank, make sure you reconcile the BILLPMT using the Reconcile function.

2. **Option 2**: If the check was coded to *Accounts Payable*, use the *Pay Bills* function to apply the check to the *Bill* it paid. This "connects" the check to the Bill, thereby changing the paid status of the *Bill*. However, it does not change the check (CHK) into a bill payment (BILLPMT) transaction.

3. **Option 3**: If there are numerous checks involved, edit each check and code to *Accounts Payable*. To locate the checks easily, use the ***Find*** feature and filter for the vendor's name and the amount of the *Unpaid Bill*. Once all checks are coded to *Accounts Payable*, use *Pay Bills* to apply the checks to the *Unpaid Bills*. Depending on the specific situation and volume of transactions, there are two alternatives to the find option above. Choose Reports > Banking > Check Detail and filter the report for the transaction type of check then double click on the entry from the report to edit the account code. Or, from the Vendor Center, choose the appropriate vendor and double click on the check transactions.

4. **Option 4**: If the check was coded to the correct expense account (or Item), you *could* delete or *void* the Bill. Be careful with this one. You might change historical reports by deleting or voiding a transaction. In addition, you will no longer be able to run accrual basis reports for this time period.

> **Important:** Always Pay Bills using the **Pay Bills** function. The steps shown above shows you how to fix the problems caused by not using *Pay Bills*, but to avoid problems altogether, use Pay Bills or don't use Bills at all (if only cash basis reports will be required).

When Multiple Credits Are Applied to Multiple Bills

If you find misapplied vendor payments, it may be due to several causes.

The most probable cause is that multiple Bill Credits (or discounts) were applied to multiple Bills at the same time.

This often happens when the preferences are set to automatically use discounts and credits. See Figure 5-37.

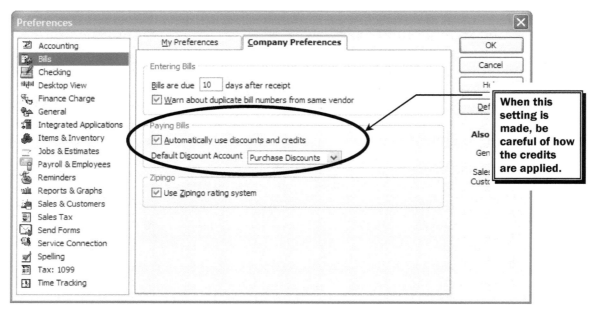

Figure 5-37 Preferences screen - Automatically use discounts and credits

With this setting, QuickBooks somewhat randomly determines which credits are applied to which Bills when you select all in the pay bills screen.

In this example, assume you have two credits and four bills as shown in Figure 5-38. Further, assume that you want to apply credit #5320 to bill #5320, and credit #357 to bill #357. After applying these credits, you want to create one bill payment for $4,659.00 to pay the rest of the balance on bill #5320 and the whole balance of the other two bills.

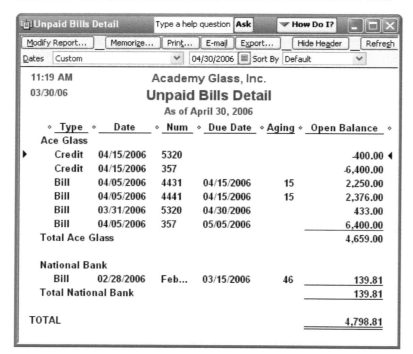

Figure 5-38 Unpaid Bills Detail report showing credits and bills

In Figure 5-39, you can see that only the last bill for Ace Glass (#357) is being paid by the BILL PMT check. The other bills were paid by credits. Assuming you want specific credits to apply to specific bills, don't ever click **Select all Bills** on the pay bills screen if your settings are set to automatically use discounts and credits.

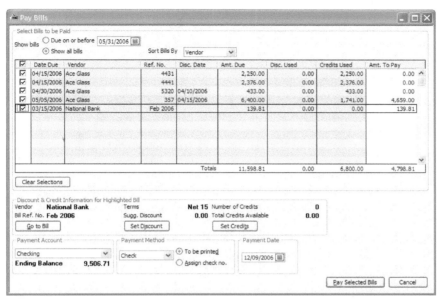

Figure 5-39 The Pay Bills screen with multiple credits and multiple bills

After incorrectly paying the bills as shown in Figure 5-39, follow the steps in this example to determine how the credits were applied and to reapply them correctly:

1. Display the *Vendor Center* and select Ace Glass. See Figure 5-40.

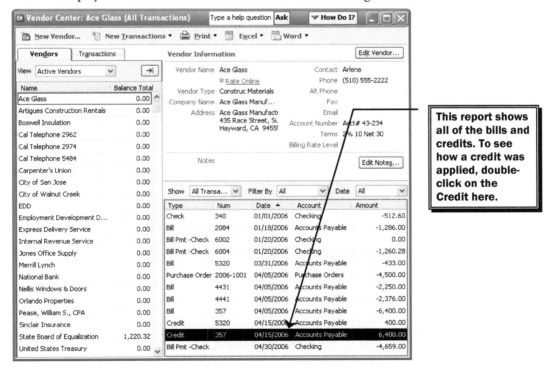

Figure 5-40 Vendor Center for Ace Glass

2.   Double-click on Bill Credit #357 to view it and see how it was applied.

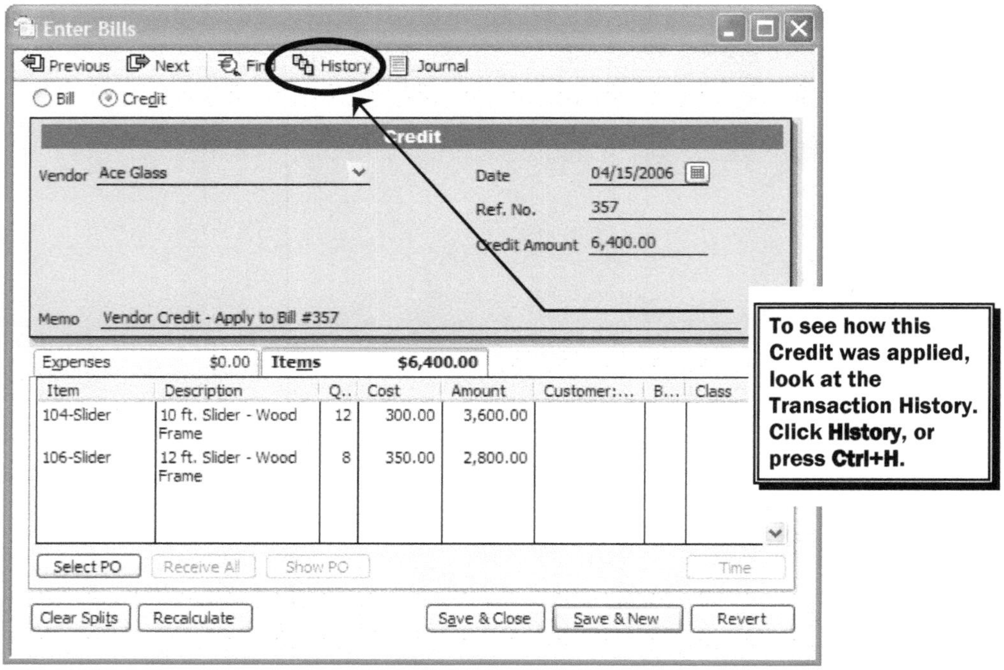

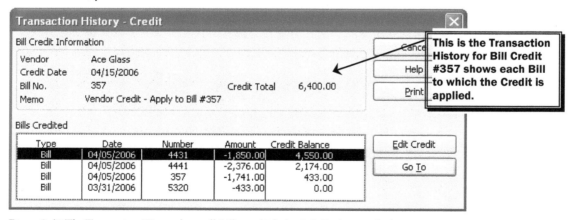

Figure 5-41 Display the Credit that was incorrectly applied in Pay Bills

3.   To view the Transaction History for the credit, click **History**, or press **Ctrl+H**.

The Transaction History shows the detail of how each transaction (in this case a Bill Credit) is connected to, or applied to other transactions (in this case several Bills). Notice from the transaction history report that the Credit was applied incorrectly. To fix this misapplied credit, you must **break the link** between the credit and the bill.

Figure 5-42 The Transaction History shows all Bills to which this Bill Credit is applied.

4.   Click **Cancel**.

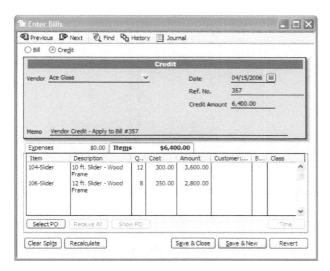

Figure 5-43 The Credit that was misapplied to several bills

5.   With the Credit displayed, change the name in the *Vendor* field to another vendor (just temporarily) and then save your change.

By changing the vendor name, you **break the link** between the credit and the bill to which it applies. See Figure 5-44 and Figure 5-45.

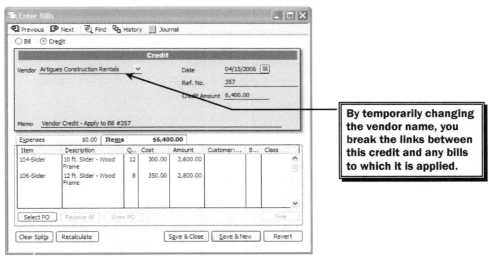

Figure 5-44 Temporarily change the vendor name to break the links between this credit and any bills

6.   The warning in Figure 5-45 shows that your change will affect other transactions. Click **Yes** to record the change. You're only changing the name on the bill temporarily so that it will break the links.

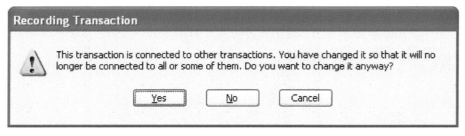

Figure 5-45 QuickBooks tells you that changing the vendor will break the connection to the Bills.

7.   Then, redisplay the credit and change the vendor name *back* to the original name. This credit is now ***unapplied*** to any bills.

8.   Repeat steps 2-7 above for Bill Credit #5320.

9.   To apply it to the correct bill, go to the *Pay Bills* screen and select one bill at a time and then apply the credits individually.

> **Note:** Another way to "disconnect" misapplied Credits (or any linked transactions) is to delete credits that are misapplied and then re-add them. This usually takes longer, and you'll have to be careful to write down everything about the credit before you delete it.

10.   The final step to undo the damage is to delete the bill payment check (BILLPMT) that was created when we clicked all the credits and all the bills in the Pay Bills screen. Go to the checking register and delete the bill payment. Pay close attention to the cleared status on this check. If the check is reconciled, you will need to clear it through the Bank Reconciliation feature after you re-pay the Bills.

Now that you've unapplied the misapplied credits and deleted the bill payment, the next step is to apply the credits correctly and pay the remaining amount due to the vendor in such a way that all the credits are correctly applied. These steps will illustrate how to correctly record the transaction, and can be used as a guide for paying bills with credits in the future.

1.   Select the *Vendors* menu and choose **Pay Bills**.

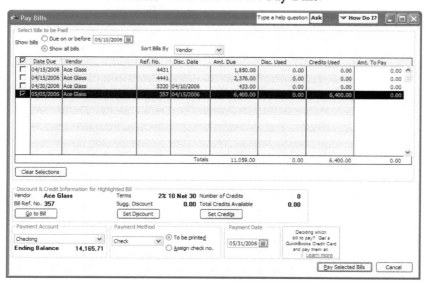

Figure 5-46 The Pay Bills screen.

Troubleshooting QuickBooks Data Files – Accounts Payable Issues   **237**

2.   Click on bill #357. This will apply credit #357 to the correct bill.

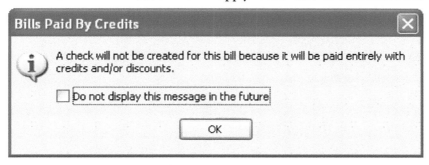

Figure 5-47 Message saying that the bill will be paid by credits instead of a check

3.   In Figure 5-47 you can see that QuickBooks automatically applies a credit to bill #357 and since the credit is large enough to pay the whole bill, QuickBooks informs you that a check will not be created. Click **OK**.

4.   Then click on bill #5320. This will apply credit #5320 to the correct bill (see Figure 5-48).

Figure 5-48 The Pay Bills screen shows Bill 5320 and 357 now have proper credits applied

5.   Next, click all of the other bills to be paid so that QuickBooks writes a check for the remainder of the open bills, after the credits are applied to the correct bills.

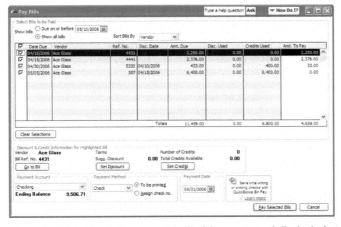

Figure 5-49 The Pay Bills screen with all of the remaining bills checked. A check will be created.

Troubleshooting QuickBooks Data Files – Accounts Payable Issues

6.   Click **Pay & Close**.

A BILL PMT check will be correctly applied to bill 5320 (partially), 4431, and 4441.

7.   Open the check register and confirm that the Check number, amount, and cleared status are the same as the Bill Payment you deleted in Step 10 above.

Non-Zero Balance in Opening Balance Equity

Opening Balance Equity is a very helpful account, **if used properly**. Although you might be tempted to delete this account, it's much better if you use it as it was intended. It will really help if you ever need to go back and look at the original setup balances.

A common problem is a non-zero balance in the Opening Balance Equity account. Normally, this account will always be zero after setup. However, certain errors made during data entry or reconciliation will cause this account to have a non-zero balance. The most common cause is a failed bank reconciliation in any QuickBooks version before 2006. That is, a bank reconciliation performed in one of these earlier versions did not completely balance, but the user clicked **Reconcile Now** anyway. When you do this, QuickBooks asks if you want to "adjust your records." However, you should **never** let QuickBooks adjust the bank account because QuickBooks creates a credit or debit to the bank account and an offsetting credit or debit to Opening Balance Equity, forcing the reconciliation.

To fix this problem, you first want to see exactly which transactions are in the account. Display the Opening Balance Equity Register to see the transactions in the account.

Review the account to identify the bank balance adjustment transaction. Once you have found the transaction you need to determine the best way to fix the problem. The entry was created by the client because they were not able to completely reconcile an account. If you can identify a single transaction that this adjustment was replacing you should be able to change the adjustment transaction from the Opening Balance Equity account to the correct account.

Unfortunately, it is pretty unlikely that the adjustment represents a single entry that the client did not correctly reconcile. The more likely scenario is that there are multiple transactions that have not been entered and reconciled properly. In this situation, it's usually best to undo the reconciliation and re-reconcile the account. For more information, see page 245.

After QuickBooks 2006, reconciliation adjustments are no longer posted to the Opening Balance Equity account but to a special QuickBooks account called Reconciliation Discrepancies Expense. Although entries to this account do not directly impact the Equity of the company it is still necessary to determine the cause of these entries and the appropriate solution. Hopefully, the amounts involved are immaterial and easily located.

There are two other situations which create a balance in Opening Balance Equity. The most common, if the balance in the account is relatively large, is that the Balance Sheet was not reconciled when the QuickBooks file was originally created. This is often the case when the client has done the set up themselves and only the accounts they deal with (bank accounts, credit cards, A/R and A/P, etc.) have been entered and reconciled but other Accountant accounts such as fixed assets, loan balances, etc. have not been handled appropriately. To solve this issue, create a Balance Sheet as of the conversion date and compare it to the tax return or financial statements prepared by the Accountant. This will provide the information as to which accounts need to be investigated and adjusted. The final reason for a balance is because the client has coded transactions to this account. Review the register and investigate the source of the transaction so that it can be correctly coded.

Accounts Beginning with *

If your Chart of Accounts has accounts that begin with an asterisk (*), it is probably due to QuickBooks automatically creating an account after the user had created one with the same name.

For example, if the following sequence occurs:

- The Inventory feature is turned off when you add a Cost of Goods Sold Account.
- You later turn on the Inventory feature and create an Inventory Part in the Item list.

QuickBooks automatically creates a Cost of Goods Sold Account as soon as the first Inventory Part is created. However, since there is already an account with that name, it adds an asterisk to the beginning of the account name to differentiate it from the one that is already there.

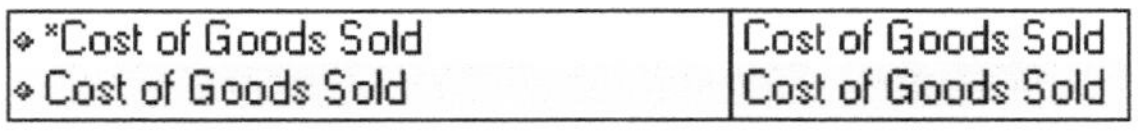

| *Cost of Goods Sold | Cost of Goods Sold |
| Cost of Goods Sold | Cost of Goods Sold |

Figure 5-50 Two Cost of Goods Sold Accounts.

To fix this, you'll need to merge the two accounts. Make sure you merge your account (the one without the *) into the automatically created Account (the one with the *). After the merge process has been completed, you can edit the account name to remove the *. The same process should be used to fix any account that begins with an asterisk: Accounts such as *Inventory Asset, *Accounts Receivable, *Accounts Payable, *Retained Earnings, *Estimates, *Sales Tax Payable and *Purchase Orders.

1.   Select the account (the one without the *) and press *Ctrl+E*.

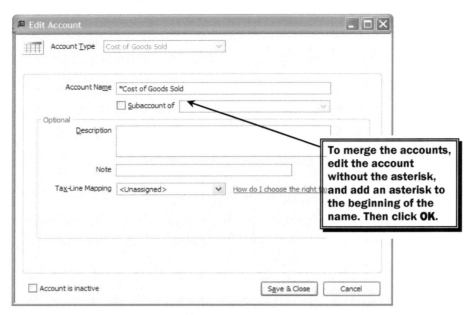

Figure 5-51 Edit the *Cost of Goods Sold account.

2.   Add an asterisk to the beginning of the account name and click *OK*. QuickBooks asks if you
      want to *merge* the accounts. Click *OK*.

3.   Then, with the two accounts merged, edit the account again to remove the asterisk.

Troubleshooting .iif Files

If QuickBooks gives an error message when importing from an **.iif** file like shown below, you
might have to edit the file to remove the problem.

In the figure below, there is a problem on line 29 of the .iif file. To fix the problem, you'll have
to edit the file using a spreadsheet program to see which fields need to be modified.

Figure 5-52 Error message during importing an iif file

To edit the .iif file, use Microsoft Excel or any spreadsheet program. Open the application and
find the error that was reported in the screenshot above.

Launch your spreadsheet application and open the .iif file.

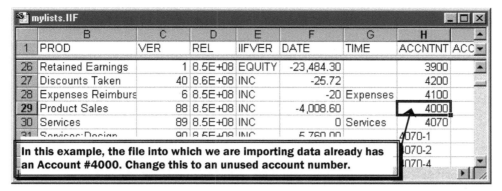

Figure 5-53 Editing the iif file directly in Microsoft Excel.

Notice the Account Number (column H) on line 29 is 4000. This account number is already in the current file. Since you can't have two accounts with the same number, you'll need to change the number of the account you are importing so that it doesn't conflict with any of your existing account numbers. You can change it here using Excel, or you can go back to the old company file, change the account number (and possibly other accounts), and then re-export the lists.

After you're finished changing all duplicate account numbers (and any other problems in the .iif file), you can try to import the iif file again.

Troubleshooting Accountant's Review Imports

QuickBooks 2006 and Prior Versions

Occasionally, you may have trouble with importing the accountant's changes into a client's data file. There are several scenarios that could cause the accountant's changes to not import and a few of them are shown below.

When Client Cancelled the Accountant's Review Copy

When the client who uses version 2006 or prior creates an accountant's review copy of their data file, it restricts them from performing certain tasks, for example modifying lists. Since this frustrates many clients, they often stumble upon the "cancel accountant's review copy" function.

If your client "cancels accountant's review copy", it will effectively "**orphan**" the changes you make and send back to them in the AIF file.

Background: When the accountant is working with the accountant's review copy and then "exports changes for client", QuickBooks creates a file (with an AIF extension) containing the journal entries that the accountant created and that are to be imported into the client's data file (their QBW file). This AIF file is nearly the same as an IIF file except that it contains some special information that specifies the company file into which it can be imported. This special information is stored on the **top two lines** of the AIF file. See Figure 5-54.

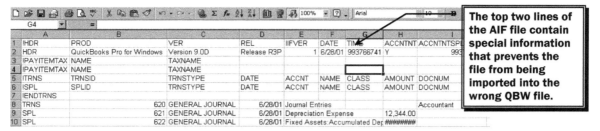

Figure 5-54 AIF file opened in Microsoft Excel.

When you try to "import accountant's changes," you'll see the message shown in Figure 5-55.

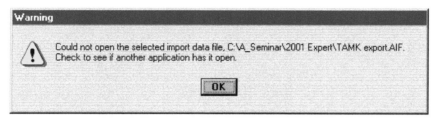

Figure 5-55 Warning shown when trying to import accountant's changes

To solve this problem and successfully import the accountant's changes into the client's file, follow the steps in this example.

1. Open the AIF file in a spreadsheet or word processing program.

2. Delete the top two lines from the AIF file and save the file.

3. Using the Windows Explorer, rename the AIF file, changing the extension to IIF. For example, change CHANGES.

4. Open QuickBooks and open the client's company file.

5. Import the IIF file that you just modified.

QuickBooks 2007 and later

In QuickBooks 2007, the Accountant's Copy process was completely re-written to take advantage of QuickBooks XML data exchange process. As a result, the accountant has the ability to make a larger number of changes directly in the Accountant's Copy. In prior versions of the Accountant's Copy the accountant was restricted to Journal Entries and other minor modifications to accounts. In QuickBooks 2007 and later, the account has the ability to add, edit and delete a much broader list of transactions.

Another change is that the file that is sent back to the client is no longer in an AIF format but instead is an encrypted XML file that can only be read by the company file that initially created the Accountant's Copy. The consultant has no ability to edit this file. If the client has made a decision to cancel the Accountant's Copy before the changes from the accountant have been imported, then the import file will not be imported. In this situation, you can print out the adjustments that you made and have the client manually input them back into their file.

Summary

In this chapter, we presented a data analysis process that will help you identify, repair and eliminate problems in a client's QuickBooks file. This can be a time consuming process that the client may or may not wish to pay for. Your job as the consultant is help the client understand the impact of these problems in their current file, but also in the future of their business. You must help the client weigh the cost of paying you to fix the problem today versus the cost of pushing the problem into the future. If the problems are left alone they are likely to continue to get worse.

As a consultant, you should be very clear with your client about how these problems will affect their reports, their taxes, and the integrity of the data in their QuickBooks file.

Troubleshooting can be challenging especially since the variety of errors the client can create can seem endless. Taking the time to correct the data entry discrepancies is critical for accurate and useful reports for making business decisions. In addition to correcting the errors, it is also the role of the consultant to train the client how to correctly enter the transactions to eliminate the same situations in the future.

The key lessons of this chapter were:

- Data File Analysis and Repair - Assessing the Health of Your Client's Data File (page 183)
- Troubleshoot Corrupted Data Files (page 210)
- Repair Out-of-Balance Balance Sheets (page 216)
- Fix Misapplied Customer Payments (page 220)
- Fix Misapplied Vendor Payments (page 231)
- Troubleshoot Non-zero Balances in Opening Balance Equity (page 238)
- Troubleshoot Account Names Beginning With * (page 239)
- Troubleshoot iif files (page 240)
- Troubleshoot Accountant's Review Importing (page 241)

Chapter 6
Banking and Credit Cards

Objectives

After completing this chapter, you should be able to:

- Troubleshooting Bank Reconciliations (page 245)
- Troubleshooting the Beginning Balance (page 245)
- Fixing Forced Bank Reconciliations (page 254)
- Clearing Bank Reconciliation History (page 259)
- Making Changes during Closed Accounting Periods (page 260)
- Handle bounced checks (page 263)
- Bank Feeds (page 268)

As a QuickBooks consultant, you know that reconciling is a very important step in the overall accounting process and ensures the accuracy of your accounting records.

In this chapter, you'll learn how to find and correct errors in the reconciliation process.

Troubleshooting Bank Reconciliations

Bank Reconciliations errors are common among QuickBooks users. Many users do not understand how the reconciliation works and have never performed a bank reconciliation outside of QuickBooks – including their own personal checkbook! Also, reconciliations of bank accounts with high transaction volume can be tedious and time consuming to perform. As a QuickBooks consultant, you need to understand some of the common mistakes that users make and how to correct those mistakes.

Troubleshooting the Beginning Balance

QuickBooks calculates the amount in the *Beginning Balance* field by adding all reconciled increases in the bank account (debits) and subtracting all of the reconciled disbursements from the bank account (credits).

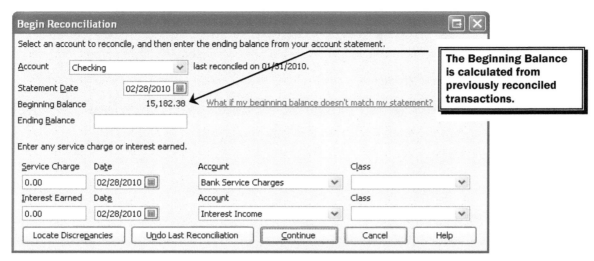

Figure 6-1 Begin Reconciliation Screen with calculated beginning balance

If the *Beginning Balance* field does not agree to the beginning balance on the bank statement, the client probably did one of the following:

- Edited the amount on a reconciled transaction
- Removed the cleared status of a reconciled transaction
- Deleted a reconciled transaction
- Changed the bank account on a reconciled transaction

Use a Reconciliation Discrepancy Report to locate and reverse the changes your client made to reconciled transactions.

The Reconcile Discrepancy Report shows all changes to reconciled transactions, including the transaction information before and after the change. This report allows you to see the net effect of the change on the *Beginning Balance* field.

The following section takes you through the process of creating several problems and then fixing them.

Four Causes of Incorrect Beginning Balances

If you'd like to practice these steps with the software, perform the steps in the this example:

In the example below, the client made changes to four reconciled transactions:

1. **Deleting a Reconciled Transaction.** The client deleted a reconciled Deposit for $1,060.69. The deletion caused the amount in the Beginning Balance field to go down by $1,060.69. Find and delete the transaction shown in Figure 6-2.

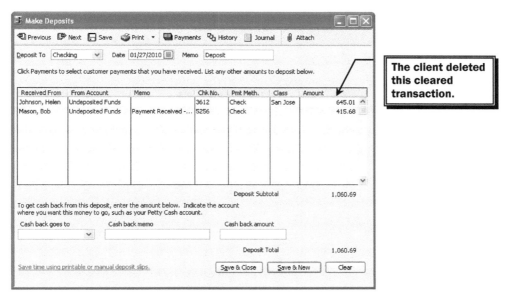

Figure 6-2 The client deleted a reconciled transaction.

2. **Removing the Cleared Status from a Reconciled Transaction.** Next, the client removed the cleared status of a reconciled Check by clicking the *Cleared* column. This action caused the Beginning Balance to go up by $276.52. Find and unclear the transaction shown in Figure 6-3.

Figure 6-3 The user removed the cleared status on a reconciled Check.

3. **Changing the Amount of a Reconciled Transaction.** Next, the user edited the amount of a reconciled Check to Orlando Properties. The original amount was $3,200.00. The user changed the amount to $3,000.00, causing the Beginning Balance to go up by $200.00. Find and change the amount of the transaction shown in Figure 6-4.

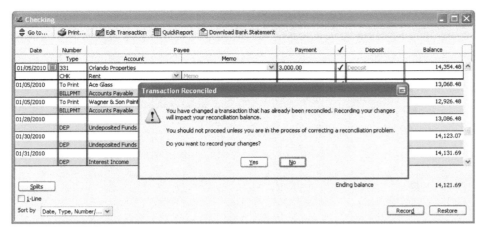

Figure 6-4 The user changed the amount of a reconciled transaction.

4.   **Changing the Bank Account on a Reconciled Transaction.** Next, the client changed the
      bank account of a reconciled transaction. Find and change the Bank Account on the
      transaction shown in Figure 6-5. When you change the bank account for a reconciled
      transaction, QuickBooks removes the cleared status. As a result, the change will not impact
      the Beginning Balance for the *new* bank account. In the example below, QuickBooks
      updates the Beginning Balance amount for the Checking account (original account), but not
      for the Checking 2 account (new account).

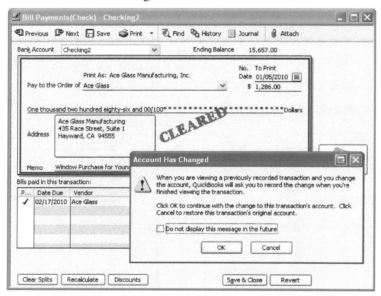

Figure 6-5 Payment with Edited Bank Account

The Beginning Balance in QuickBooks is now $701.83 less than the beginning balance on the
Bank Statement. Figure 6-6 below shows each transaction that affects this balance discrepancy.

Using the Reconciliation Discrepancy Report to Troubleshoot the Beginning Balance

The following is an example of the steps to correct the beginning balance for edits or voids to
reconciled transactions:

1.   Select the **Reports** menu, select **Banking,** and then select **Reconciliation Discrepancy.**

2.   QuickBooks displays the Reconciliation Discrepancy Report window prompting you to enter the bank account. Enter ***Checking*** in the *Specify Account* field and click **OK**. QuickBooks displays the Previous Reconciliation Discrepancy report shown in Figure 6-6.

QuickBooks shows changes to and deletions of reconciled transactions since your last reconciliation. Notice that QuickBooks shows both the type of the change and the effect the change has on the Beginning Balance. Changes only show on this report if they affect the Beginning Balance amount. Changes to the *Memo* field or the Expense account(s) of a Check will not show on the Reconciliation Discrepancy report because you do not need to troubleshoot these types of changes to correct the *Beginning Balance*.

> **Note**
> QuickBooks clears the Reconciliation Discrepancy Report as soon as you perform the next bank reconciliation. For that reason, it is important to research Beginning Balance discrepancies *before* performing the next bank reconciliation.
>
> **Tip**
> If the client cleared the detail from this report, you may be able to use a backup of the client's data file to research the changes. As a general rule, it is best to retain the files your clients send you for at least one year. Keeping multiple copies of the client data files will help you troubleshoot not only Bank Reconciliations, but also other areas of the file.

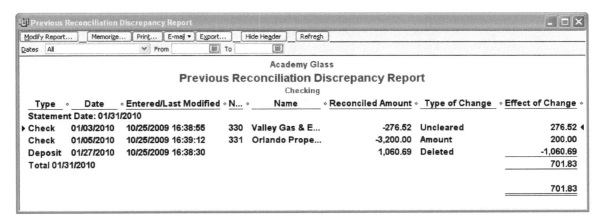

Figure 6-6 Previous Reconciliation Discrepancy Report

> **Note**
> On the report shown in Figure 6-6, the total amount in the *Effect of Change* column is $701.83. This amount is correct (the amount of the discrepancy), but it is not the sum of the three rows above. The *Effect of Change* column is off by $1,286.00 – the amount of the Bill Payment shown in Figure 6-5. When the bank account is changed on a reconciled transaction, QuickBooks does not show the change on the Previous Reconciliation Discrepancy Report.

3.   Using QuickZoom, open the Check to Valley Gas & Electric and restore the cleared status. See Figure 6-7.

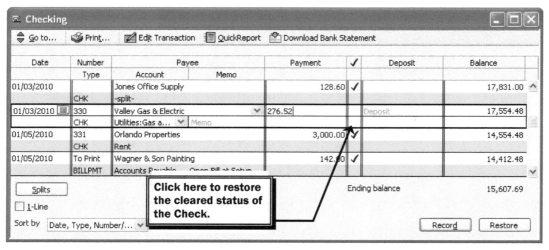

Figure 6-7 Click in the Check column to restore the cleared status of the check.

4. Review the Previous Reconciliation Report to make sure the check to Valley Gas & Electric no longer shows on the report.

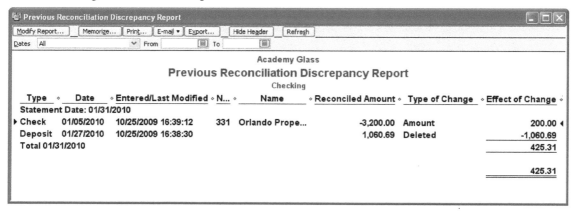

Figure 6-8 The Check with the changed cleared status no longer shows on the report.

> **Note**
> If a transaction was never reconciled, clearing the transaction in the account register will not impact the Beginning Balance. However, if a user previously reconciled the transaction, *re-clearing* the transaction will impact the Beginning Balance.

5. Refer to the *Reconciled Amount* column of the report and note the amount of the Check at the time it was reconciled. Then, use QuickZoom to open the Check to Orlando Properties and restore the reconciled amount.

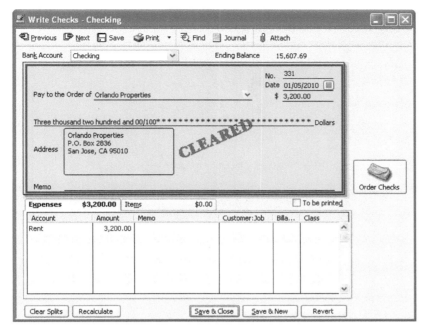

Figure 6-9 Enter the reconciled amount (original amount) for this Check.

6. Notice that QuickBooks removes the check to Orlando Properties from the Previous Reconciliation Discrepancy report. You've fixed the changed amount problem.

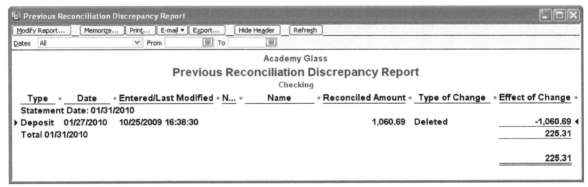

Figure 6-10 The Check to Orlando Properties no longer shows on this report.

Using Voided/Deleted Transactions Reports to Troubleshoot the Beginning Balance

Next, you need to address the problem of the deleted transaction. Since you cannot QuickZoom on deleted or voided transactions from the Discrepancy report (because the transactions don't exist), you will need use another method to find the transactions.

To find and fix voided or deleted transactions, use the Voided/Deleted Transactions Detail report. You can access this report from the Accountant & Taxes Reports menu.

Once you identify which transaction(s) were voided or deleted, you must re-enter them and then re-reconcile them. See page 252 for instructions on re-reconciling these re-entered transactions.

Using Audit Trail Reports to Troubleshoot the Beginning Balance

Finally, you need to address the problem of the transaction that was assigned to a different bank account after it had been reconciled. Although this will rarely happen, it could be quite difficult to find the transaction(s) involved. You may find it by comparing a static Previous Reconciliation Detail report with a dynamic report (as we did in the example above), but another approach to finding this type of problem is to use the Audit Trail report, if the report is available (Figure 6-11).

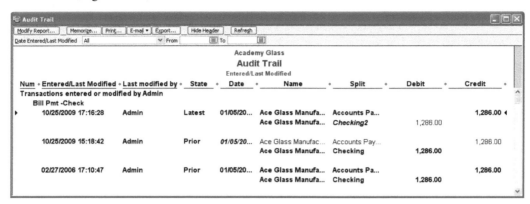

Figure 6-11 Audit Trail showing Bill Payment with Changed Bank Account

1. After you locate the edited transaction(s) using the audit trail or previous reconciliation detail report, edit the transaction(s) to return them to their original state as they were when they were reconciled.

Re-reconciling After Fixing the Beginning Balance

After you've fixed the transactions, you're ready to re-reconcile them, as in this example.

1. Open the Bank Reconciliation window.

2. Enter 1/31/2010 into the Statement Date field. You must do this because you are redoing the reconciliation for January.

3. Note that the Beginning Balance (15,407.69) is still off by $225.31. See Figure 6-12. This amount represents the deleted Deposit (decrease of $1,060.69) and the amount of the Bill Payment with the edited bank account (increase of $1,286.00).
    With these types of changes to the Beginning Balance, you have to re-reconcile the transaction using the Bank Reconciliation window.

4. Enter the date of the previous bank reconciliation in the *Statement Date* field. See Figure 6-12.

5. Enter the correct ending balance ($15,182.38) in the *Ending Balance* field. See Figure 6-12.

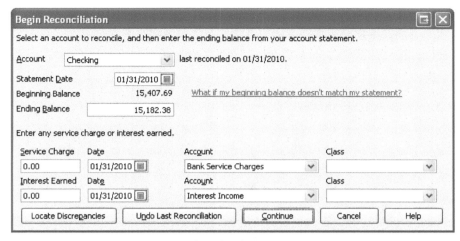

Figure 6-12 Change the dates and enter the ending balance.

6.   On the Reconcile – Checking window, locate the deleted transaction and clear it. Then, locate the Bill Payment with the edited Bank account. Confirm that the difference field shows *0.00* and click **Reconcile Now**.

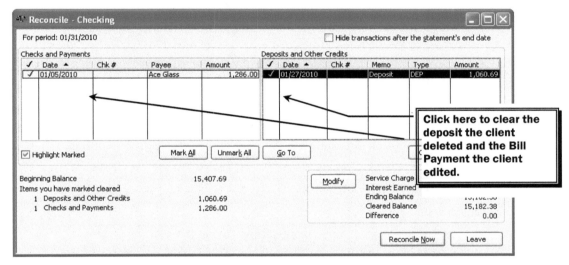

Figure 6-13 Locate the deleted transaction and mark it cleared.

7.   Re-open the *Bank Reconciliation* window and confirm that the *Beginning Balance* field now shows the correct amount ($15,182.38). See Figure 6-14.

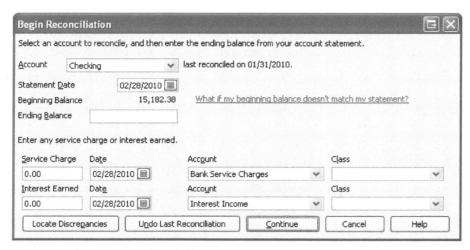

Figure 6-14 The Beginning Balance field now shows the correct amount.

8.   Click Cancel to cancel out of the bank reconciliation. You've completed the repairs and are
      ready to proceed with further reconciliations.

> **Note**
> When you re-perform the bank reconciliation(s) for the same date as we just did above,
> QuickBooks creates a single, consolidated bank reconciliation report for 01/31/2010. In
> effect, you insert the re-reconciled transactions back into their original Bank
> Reconciliation detail report.

Troubleshooting "Forced" Bank Reconciliations

QuickBooks allows you to "complete" the bank reconciliation even if the *Difference* amount is
not "0.00."

Notice in the Checking2 account (Figure 6-15) that the difference between the bank balance
and the cleared balance is $93.00.

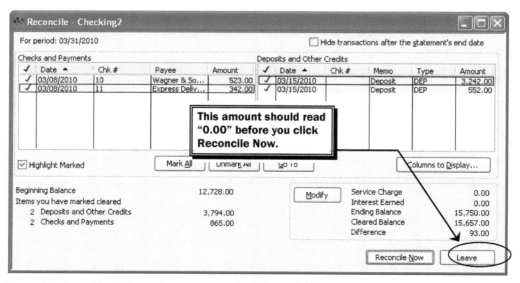

Figure 6-15 Reconcile window with an amount in the difference field

If you click **Reconcile Now** with this amount in the *Difference* field, QuickBooks displays the *Reconcile Adjustment* window shown in Figure 6-16.

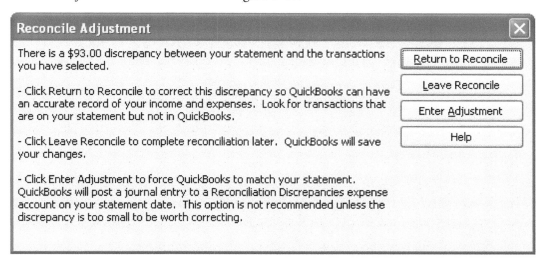

Figure 6-16 Reconcile Adjustment window

The *Reconcile Adjustment* window suggests that you return to the reconciliation and locate the reason for the discrepancy. The window also suggests that you can leave the reconciliation and finish it later.

However, you <u>can</u> simply give up and have QuickBooks enter an adjustment to the bank balance – an amount calculated by QuickBooks to force the cleared balance to agree with the ending balance on the statement from the bank. On this adjustment, QuickBooks uses the Statement Date you entered on the bank reconciliation. The offset account for the adjustment is Reconciliation Discrepancies – an expense account created by QuickBooks. See Figure 6-17.

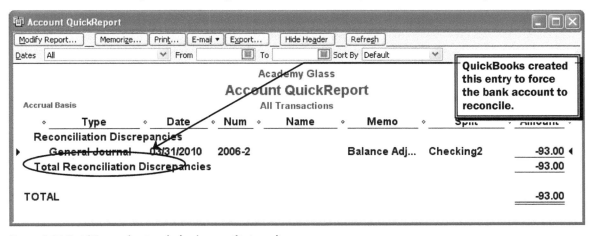

Figure 6-17 QuickReport showing the bank reconciliation adjustment

Perform the steps in this example to remove the balance in Reconciliation Discrepancies and to re-reconcile the account accurately.

1. Create a QuickReport for the Reconciliation Discrepancies account and locate the adjustment created by QuickBooks to force the account to reconcile. The adjustment will

have the same date as the bank statement and will have a memo that reads, "Balance Adjustment." See Figure 6-18.

2. Double-click on the transaction to QuickZoom to the balance adjustment entry and then delete the entry.

    When you delete the entry you will zero out the balance in Reconciliation Discrepancies and the offsetting over statement or understatement in the bank account. Also, there will now be a $93.00 discrepancy between the Beginning Balance on the Bank Reconciliation window and the ending balance of the 03/31/06 bank statement.

> **Tip**
> Consider the materiality of the Balance Adjustments. If the amounts are clearly immaterial, consider creating an adjusting entry in the current period to clear the balance in Reconciliation Discrepancies. Offset the adjustment to another expense account. If you prefer, you can simply edit the Balance Adjustment entry so that it posts to another expense account.

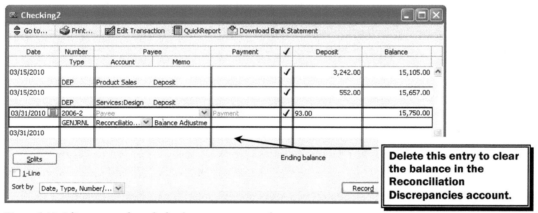

Figure 6-18 Adjustment to force the bank account to reconcile

> **Note**
> QuickBooks allows you to undo the most recent bank reconciliation only. If the client forced a bank reconciliation seven months ago (or if the client forced all seven bank reconciliations), you will have to undo seven bank reconciliations one month at a time and then re-perform all seven bank reconciliations.
>
> **Note**
> If the client "forced" numerous bank reconciliations, you may need to delete multiple Balance Adjustment entries from the Reconciliation Discrepancies account.
>
> **Note**
> Before you undo and re-perform numerous bank reconciliations, consider how many banking transactions the company records each month. If you have to re-perform several months of bank reconciliations – with numerous banking transactions each month – it may be best to delete the Balance Adjustment entries in the Reconciliation Discrepancies account, clear the bank reconciliation history and re-set the Beginning Balance manually. See page 259 for more information.

3. Open the *Bank Reconciliation* window and select the bank account (e.g., Checking 2). Then, click **Locate Discrepancies**.

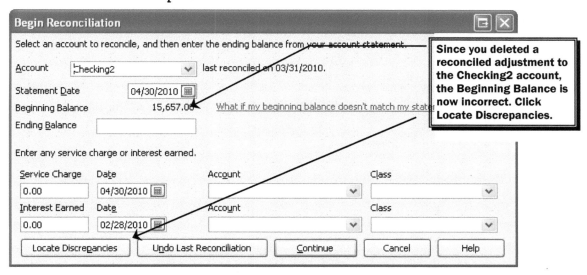

Figure 6-19 The Beginning Balance is now off by $93.00.

4. QuickBooks displays the *Locate Discrepancies* window. See Figure 6-20.

5. Click **Undo Last Reconciliation**.

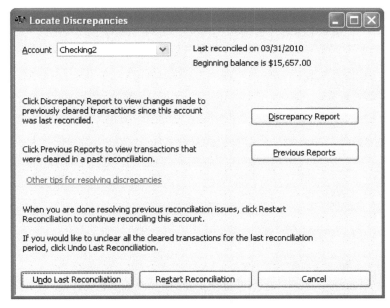

Figure 6-20 The Locate Discrepancies window

6. QuickBooks displays the *Undo Previous Reconciliation* window shown in Figure 6-21. Notice that QuickBooks provides you with the current Beginning Balance (that is $93.00 off) and the Beginning Balance from the previous reconciliation.

Figure 6-21 Undo Previous Reconciliation window

    7.   Click **Continue**.

Note
Pay special attention to the Beginning Balance amount for the previous reconciliation. If the previous reconciliation has a correct Beginning Balance, you only need to undo one month's reconciliation. If the Beginning Balance in the previous reconciliation is not correct, you will need to undo the bank reconciliation for as many months as necessary to fine a correct Beginning Balance.

Tip
Create a backup copy of the data file before you undo the bank reconciliations. If you have to undo several months of bank reconciliations you may need to restore the backup file, clear the bank reconciliation history, and reset the beginning balance manually. See page 259 for more information.

    8.   QuickBooks displays the *Undo Previous Reconcile Complete* window. See Figure 6-22. Click **OK**.

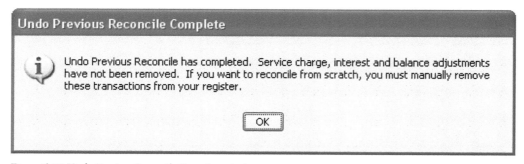

Figure 6-22 Undo Previous Reconcile Complete window

    9.   On the Locate Discrepancies window, click **Restart Reconciliation**.

10.   Now you can go and fix whichever transaction was off by $93.00 and then re-perform the reconciliation correctly.

Resetting the Default Statement Date on Bank Reconciliations

After you perform each bank reconciliation, the *Statement Date* field on the Begin Reconciliation window automatically advances by one month.

Therefore, if the user erroneously enters a future date in the *Statement Date* field (e.g. if he or she enters 01/31/2016 instead of 01/31/2015), QuickBooks will assume the next bank reconciliation is one month after the *erroneous* date (02/28/2016).

Though you can manually reset the date in the *Statement Date* field of the Begin Reconciliation window, the next bank reconciliation will still default to 30 days after the future, *erroneous* date rather than 30 days after the corrected date.

This behavior causes the following problems:

- It increases the likelihood of more date errors because the user will need to reset the date in the *Statement Date* field manually for months, or perhaps years.
- If the user does not manually adjust the statement date each time, QuickBooks will assign the wrong reconciled date to each transaction, distorting certain information on bank reconciliation reports.

To fix this problem, undo the Bank Reconciliation. When you undo the bank reconciliation on which the future date was entered, QuickBooks will reset the default date. However, consider the following before deciding to undo the Bank Reconciliations:

- The number of transactions you will have to reconcile to re-perform the bank reconciliation.
- The number of bank reconciliations the client performed since they entered the wrong date. If you have to undo multiple bank reconciliations the process may be too time consuming.

If undoing the bank reconciliation and re-reconciling the account is too time consuming, make sure the client understands importance of correct Statement Dates on Bank Reconciliations. Make sure they know to override the default statement date until they reconcile enough months to catch up with the future-dated default.

Clearing Bank Reconciliation History

At times clients will perform an erroneous bank reconciliation. If the client has performed only one erroneous bank reconciliation, you may want to undo the reconciliation and re-perform the bank reconciliation correctly. However, if the bank reconciliation feature is hopelessly distorted, or taking the time to re-reconcile each month is not cost effective, use the following steps to "reset" the bank reconciliation feature so that it agrees to the current period:

1.   Create a bank reconciliation manually for the current period, independent of QuickBooks.

2.   If the bank reconciliation reveals transactions that the client did not enter into QuickBooks, enter each transaction in the check register.

By the end of step 2, the cash balance in QuickBooks should agree to the *book* balance on the reconciliation performed in Step 1.

> **Tip:** To save time, summarize the unrecorded, cleared transactions using a journal entry. Record a single credit or debit to checking for the net amount of all unrecorded, cleared transactions and post to the appropriate offset accounts (e.g. Interest Income or Bank Charges).

3.   Using the Bank Reconciliation feature, clear all existing transactions (including those entered in Step 2) and enter whatever amount necessary in the Ending Balance field to force the difference to zero. Then click **Reconcile Now**. Print a Bank Reconciliation report for your records.

4.   Using a journal entry, enter a separate credit to checking for each outstanding check and a separate debit for each deposit in transit per the manual bank reconciliation performed in Step 1. Enter the applicable check number in the *Memo* field of each credit line. Enter an offset amount to the "Checking" account to balance the entry. Since all credits and debits are posted to the "Checking" account, this journal entry will not change the balance in the checking account.

5.   Clear the offsetting entry from Step 4 through the Bank Reconciliation feature. Open the Bank Reconciliation window for the account. Using the bank statement from your manual bank reconciliation (Step 1) enter the bank statement ending balance in the *Ending Balance* field. Enter the bank statement date in the *Statement Date* field. Then click **Continue**. Locate and clear the offsetting entry. The difference field should show 0.00. Click **Reconcile Now** and print a Reconciliation Detail report for your records.

Open the Bank Reconciliation window to confirm that the opening balance agrees to the bank. Also confirm that the list of outstanding checks and deposits in transit agrees to the manual bank reconciliation from Step 1

Correcting or Voiding Transactions in Closed Accounting Periods

When you find a check dated in the **current accounting period** that you know will not clear the bank (e.g., if you stop payment on a check) you will need to void the check. Double-click the check from the *Reconcile* window. Select the **Edit** menu and then select **Void Check**. Click **Save & Close** to return to the *Reconcile* window.

A *closed accounting period* is the period prior to and including the date on which a company officially "closes" its books (for example, 12/31/2009), creates its final financial reports, and presents its finalized reports to external stakeholders such as the IRS and investors. You do not want to change transactions dated in a closed accounting period because doing so will change financial reports during a period for which you have already issued financial statements or filed tax returns.

In QuickBooks, you can use the *closing date* to indicate the date on which you last closed the accounting period. For example, if you issued financial statements on 12/31/2009, you can set the closing date in QuickBooks to 12/31/2009. This will essentially "lock" your QuickBooks file so that only the administrator (or other authorized users) will be able to modify transactions before 12/31/2009. For more information on setting the closing date, see page 100.

To correct or void a check that is dated in a **closed accounting period**, follow the procedure described below.

1.   Display the check in the register as shown in Figure 6-23 and click on it to select it.

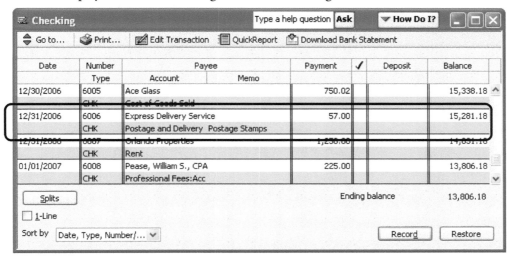

Figure 6-23 Uncleared Check #6006 from Previous Reporting Period

2.   From the **Edit** menu, select **Void Check**. QuickBooks zeros all dollar amounts and adds a "VOID" note in the Memo field as shown in Figure 6-24. Click **Record**.

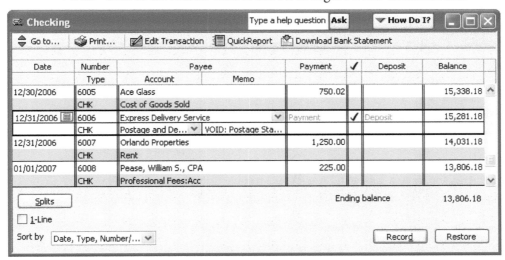

Figure 6-24 Voided Check - #6006

3.   QuickBooks prompts you that the transaction you are voiding is cleared and that it is dated in a closed accounting period. QuickBooks then displays the window shown in Figure 6-25. Click **Yes (Recommended).** This is the default response.

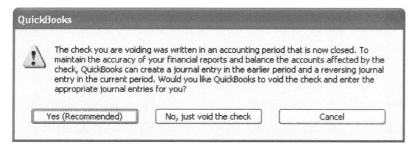

Figure 6-25 Voided Check Adjustment Prompt

4. QuickBooks performs three actions when you click **Yes (Recommended)** on the window shown in Figure 6-25 above.

5. QuickBooks adds wording to the Memo field of the check showing that the program reversed the impact of the void on the General Ledger

Figure 6-26 Voided Check - Additional Memo Text

6. QuickBooks posts a Journal Entry dated the same date that reverses the impact on the General Ledger caused by the voided check.

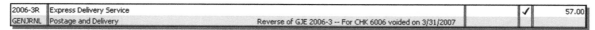

Figure 6-27 Journal Entry - Reverses GL Changes from Voiding the Check

7. QuickBooks then enters a reversing Journal Entry in the current period. The default date for the reversing entry is "today."

| 2006-3R | Express Delivery Service | | | ✓ | 57.00 |
| GENJRNL | Postage and Delivery | Reverse of GJE 2006-3 -- For CHK 6006 voided on 3/31/2007 | | | |

Figure 6-28 Journal Entry that "moves" the GL Change to the Current Reporting Period

> **Note**
> QuickBooks clears all entries. However, the entries will appear in the Bank Reconciliation window until the client reconciles them using the Bank Reconciliation feature.
>
> **Important:**
> The Void Checks tool only works with *Check(CHK)* transactions that are coded to one or more *Expense* and/or *Other Expense* accounts. The following transactions are not protected with the Void Checks tool:
> 1. Checks coded to accounts other than Expense/Other Expense
> 2. Checks that include Items
> 3. Checks that are not "Check" transaction types (e.g., Bill Payment, Payroll Liability Payment, Sales Tax Payment, Paycheck)

8. Next, enter the correct amount in a new transaction. Use the date of the current bank statement for the new transaction.

Handling Bounced Checks

Banks and accountants often refer to bounced checks as NSF (non-sufficient funds) transactions. This means there are insufficient funds in the account to cover the check.

When Your Customer's Check Bounces

If your bank returns a check from one of your customers, enter an NSF transaction in the banking account register.

For example, Bob Mason bounced the check #2526 for $1,180.23 and the bank charged the Company $10.00. Complete the steps below to complete the NSF transaction.

1.   Open the **Checking** check register.

2.   Enter two transactions, both dated 2/6/2007, as shown in Figure 6-29 – one for the amount of the check that bounced, and one for the fee charged by the bank.

   Notice that the bounced check is coded to Accounts Receivable. This transaction creates a receivable from the customer that will show in your A/R reports and customer statements until the customer repays you.

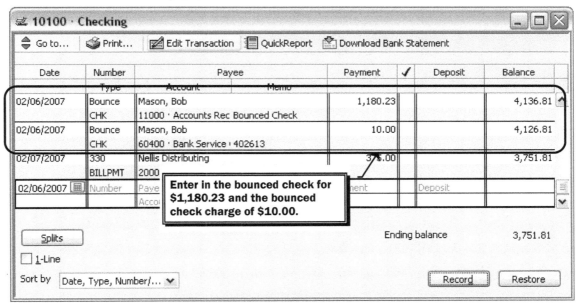

Figure 6-29 Add two transactions to your Checking register

> **Note:**
> If the bounced check was *not* a payment for one of your invoices (i.e. not recorded to Accounts Receivable), skip 3 through 8.

3.   After you enter the Bounced Check, select the **Reports** menu, select **Customers and Receivables,** and then select **Customer Balance Detail** (see Figure 6-30).

4.   Double-click the payment transaction (#2526 on 01/30/2007) in the **Customer Balance Detail** report to view the *Receive Payments* window you used to record the check from your customer (see Figure 6-30).

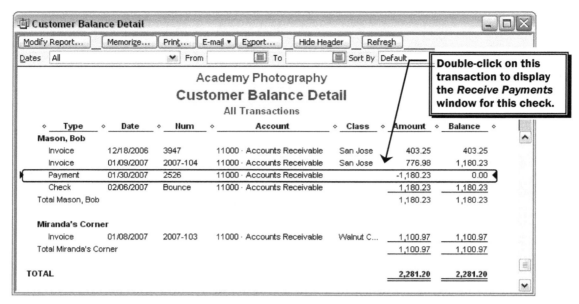

Figure 6-30 Customer Balance Detail report

5.   In the *Receive Payments* window click in the check column (✓) next to the original invoices, both 3947 on 12/18/2006 and 2007-104 on 1/9/2007 to un-apply the payments (see Figure 6-31).

6.   Next, click in the checkmark column (✓) next to the bounced check transaction you recorded in 2 above. You'll see this transaction in the *Receive Payments* window.

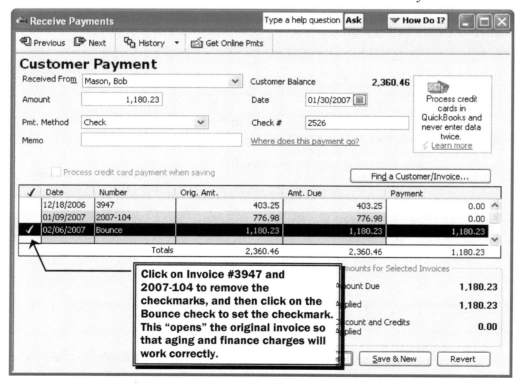

Figure 6-31 Select *the Bounced Check to apply to the original payment*

7.   Click **Save & Close** and then click **Yes** in the *Recording Transaction* dialog box.

8.   Close the Customer Balance Detail report.

> **Note:**
> The payment is reapplied to the bounced check so that the aging and finance charge calculations of the original invoice are restored. If you did not edit the *Receive Payment* window in this way, the Accounts Receivable aging would be incorrect because QuickBooks would still think the original check (the one that bounced) had paid the invoice. Since that check bounced, we want the original invoice to show as unpaid until the customer actually makes payment.

Next, if you charge your customers a service fee for processing their NSF check, create an Invoice for the customer as follows:

9.   Create an **Other Charge** Item called *NSF Charges,* as shown in Figure 6-32.

      Click the **Item & Services** icon on the Home Page.

      Press **Crtl+N** to display the *New Item* window.

      Verify your screen matches Figure 6-32. Click **OK** to create the new item.

      Close the *Item List*.

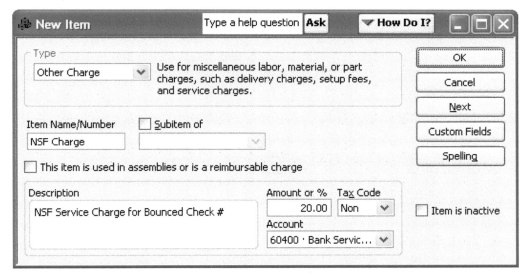

Figure 6-32 Use an Other Charge Item to charge your customers an NSF fee

10.   Create an Invoice for the amount for the NSF charge as shown in Figure 6-33. Change the Invoice number to *5256Bounce* and the terms to **Due Upon Receipt**.

11.   Fill out the rest of the fields on the Invoice to match Figure 6-33.

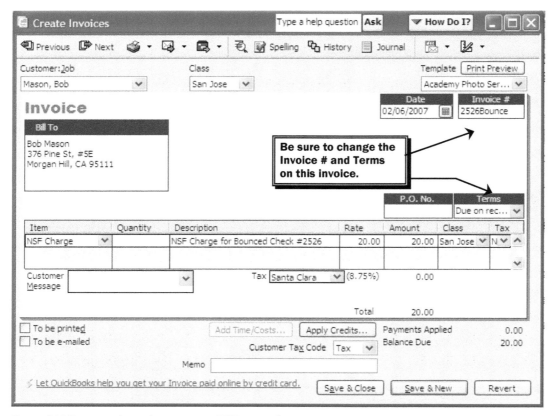

Figure 6-33 Invoice to charge the customer an NSF service charge

12.   When you add the **NSF Charge** Item to the Invoice, QuickBooks displays a warning that
       says the Item is associated with an expense account. Click **OK**.

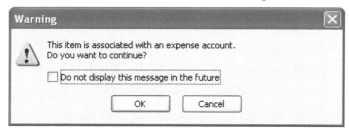

Figure 6-34 Warning dialog box

13.   Click **Save & Close** to record the Invoice.

14.   Since you changed the terms on this Invoice to **Due Upon Receipt** QuickBooks asks if you
       want to make the Due Upon Receipt terms the default for Bob Mason. Click **No** on this
       window since you will use the Net 30 terms on future Invoices for this customer.

The accounting behind the scenes:
The bounced check you entered in the register increases (debits) Accounts Receivable
and it reduces (credits) the Checking account for the amount of the original check that
bounced. The Invoice increases (debits) Accounts Receivable and decreases (credits)
Bank Service Charges for the amount of NSF fees you are charging the customer.

Receiving and Depositing the Replacement Check

To record the transactions for receiving and depositing a replacement check, follow the steps in this example:

1. Select the **Customers** menu, and then select **Receive Payments**.

2. In this example, Bob Mason sent a replacement check #2538 for $1,200.23 that includes the amount of the check plus the NSF service charge of $20.00. Fill in the customer payment information as shown in Figure 6-35.

    Make sure you apply the payment against the original invoices and the service charge invoice you just created in Figure 6-33.

3. Click Save & Close.

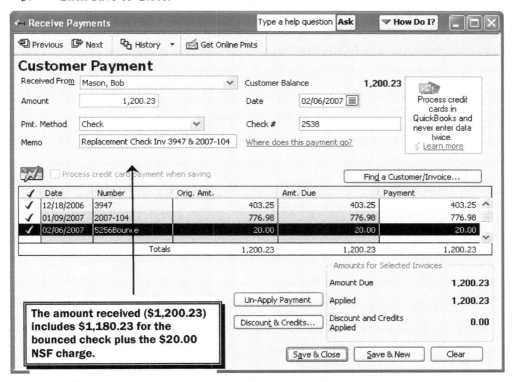

Figure 6-35 The Receive Payments window showing the replacement check

Next, add the replacement check to your next deposit just as you would any other check.

4. Select the **Banking** menu and then select **Make Deposits** (see Figure 6-36).

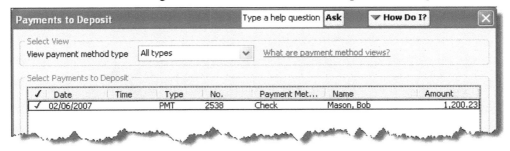

Figure 6-36 Add the replacement check to your deposit

5.   In the *Payments to Deposit* window, select check #2538 as shown in Figure 6-36 and then click **OK** at the bottom of the window.

6.   In the *Make Deposits* window, confirm that **Checking** in the *Deposit to* field is selected and that 02/08/2007 displays in the date field (see Figure 6-37). Then, click **Save & Close** at the bottom of the window.

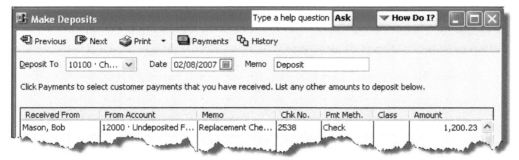

Figure 6-37 Make Deposits window

7.   Close the Checking register.

When Your Check Bounces

If you write a check that overdraws your account and your bank returns the check, follow the steps in this example:

1.   Decide with your vendor how you will handle the NSF Check. (e.g., send a new check, redeposit the same check, or pay by credit card).

2.   When the bank sends you the notice that your check was returned, there will be a charge from your bank. Enter a transaction in the bank account register. Code the transaction to Bank Service Charges and use the actual date that the bank charged your account.

3.   If your balance is sufficient for the check to clear, tell the vendor to redeposit the check.

4.   If your balance is not sufficient, consider other ways of paying the vendor, such as paying with a credit card. Alternatively, negotiate delayed payment terms with your vendor.

5.   If your vendor charges an extra fee for bouncing a check, enter a Bill (or use Write Checks) and code the charge to the Bank Service Charge account.

6.   If you bounce a payroll check, use the same process as described. Offer to reimburse your employee for any bank fees incurred as a result of your mistake.

Bank Feeds

The QuickBooks Bank Feeds feature allows you to process online transactions, such as payments and transfers, and download bank transactions into your QuickBooks file. Downloaded transactions save you time by decreasing manual entry and increasing accuracy. It is important to review each downloaded transaction to avoid bringing errors into your company file.

Online banking is secure. QuickBooks uses a secure Internet connection and a high level of encryption when transferring information from your financial institution.

Bank Feed Setup

To begin to use Bank Feeds, you will need to set up the appropriate accounts to communicate with the bank. Steps vary by institution. To complete this process, refer to the QuickBooks help files or the video tutorial.

Processing Online Transactions

You may have the option to enter online transactions, such as online payments, bill payments, or transfers (depending on your financial institution). Figure 6-38 displays an example of an online payment. You can create an online payment by opening the **Write Checks** window and checking **Pay Online**. Notice that there are several differences between a standard check form and an online payment form. For example, the check number field displays the word *SEND*.

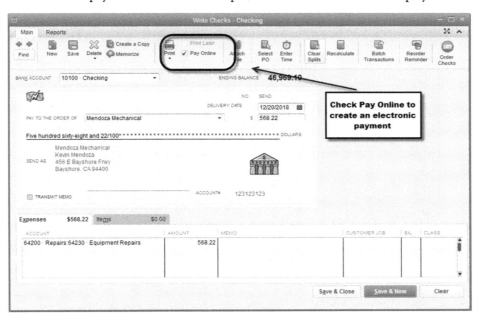

Figure 6-38 Check to be sent as an Online Payment

After saving an online payment, the transaction is queued up in the *Bank Feeds Center*. By clicking the *Send Items* button in the *Bank Feeds Center*, you can send the online payments and other online transactions to, as well as download transactions from, your financial institution.

Your financial institution may require additional steps. Follow any guidelines given after clicking the *Send Items* button. Do not click the *Send Items* button now.

Figure 6-39 Bank Feeds Center – your screen may vary

Opening the Sample File

With Bank Feeds, transactions are processed and downloaded directly from your financial institution through your internet connection. For this section, we will open a sample QuickBooks file for *Sample Rock Castle Construction*. This file contains downloaded transactions pre-loaded in the file.

We will not be able to use this file to set up an online banking connection or to send or receive transactions, since this would require a live account at a financial institution and cannot be simulated in an educational environment. We will use this sample file to process downloaded transactions that have already been loaded into the sample file.

Downloaded Transactions

When you click the *Download Transactions* button in the *Bank Feeds Center*, you download all the new transactions from your financial institution. After downloading, the transactions are ready for review. (Do not click the *Download Transactions* button now.)

As the transactions are downloaded, QuickBooks searches for similar transactions that have previously been entered. If an existing transaction is similar to the downloaded transaction, such as by having the same date and amount, QuickBooks *matches* the downloaded transaction with this entry. Any downloaded transaction that is unpaired with an existing entry is *unmatched*.

> **Note:**
> Some transactions will be downloaded with payee names that do not match the names in the *Vendor Center*. Downloaded transactions often include names appended with a numerical code. It is important to avoid creating duplicate vendors. QuickBooks allows you to create **renaming rules** so that these downloaded transactions are linked to the appropriate existing vendor. You can access the renaming rules by clicking the Rules button in the upper left of the *Bank Feeds Center*; however, the renaming rules window is not accessible in the sample file.

1.   Select Bank Feeds Center from the Bank Feeds option under the Banking menu.

2.   The *Bank Feeds* window opens (see Figure 6-40).

     A list of your Bank and Credit Card accounts that have been set up to receive downloaded transactions appears on the left. Information about the selected account, including a button for downloading transactions appears on the right.

3.   Click on the desired account. In this example, choose **ANYTIME Financial account** ending in *1235*. This account has 7 transactions downloaded and waiting to be added to QuickBooks.

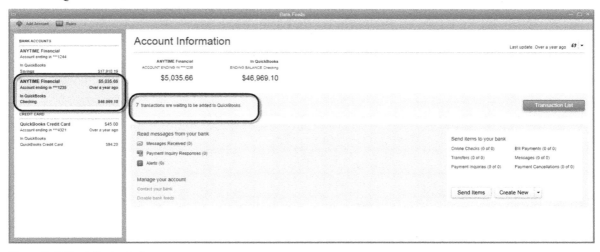

Figure 6-40 Bank Feeds window

4.   Click the **Transaction List** button on the right side of the window.

Figure 6-41 Transaction List

5.   The Transaction List window opens (see Figure 6-41). After reviewing each transaction, you can either select individual transactions for approval or for adding further detail, or approve all transactions in one batch action.

6.   Close the Transaction List.

7.   Close the *Bank Feeds* window

Troubleshooting Bank Feed Problems

Rejected Transactions

If your downloaded transactions are "rejected", or if you receive error messages when trying to import a download, it may be due to the fact that your financial institution needs to update their software for the latest versions of the required file format. For example, there have been several versions of the QBO file format, as well as the OFX format. Call QuickBooks technical support for help in determining the cause of rejected transactions.

Connection Problems

If you have trouble connecting to your financial institution, check your Internet connection and check to see that you can go to your financial institution's web site using a browser. Also, in some cases, pop-up blockers or other virus protection or firewalls could create a problem with your connections.

Error Messages and Software Problems

If you receive error messages from within QuickBooks, you can search the QuickBooks technical support web site for solutions to most problems at www.quickbooks.com/helpcenter. In some cases, it may be necessary to call Intuit Technical support to resolve the problems.

Summary

In this chapter, you learned how to do the following:

- Troubleshooting Bank Reconciliations (page 245)
- Troubleshooting the Beginning Balance (page 245)
- Fixing Forced Bank Reconciliations (page 254)
- Clearing Bank Reconciliation History (page 259)
- Making Changes during Closed Accounting Periods (page 260)
- Handle bounced checks (page 263)
- Online Banking (page 268)

Chapter 7
Data File Management

Objectives

In this chapter, you'll learn about managing QuickBooks data files to ensure that they are kept in good condition. Here are the topics covered:

- About QuickBooks files and file extensions in Windows (page 273)
- How to backup QuickBooks data files (page 281)
- How to restore QuickBooks backup files (page 285)
- Portable company files, and how to work with them (page 289)
- Using the Accountant's Copy (page 291)
- Importing and exporting data in QuickBooks (page 297)
- Using the Clean Up Data utility in QuickBooks (page 317)
- Cleaning up your Data with Excel (page 322)
- When and how to start a new data file (page 321)

About QuickBooks Files

When you create a new company in QuickBooks you are creating what is normally referred to as a **company file**. This company file is the primary file for entering data and creating reports. A company file is identified with the .QBW file extension. The term *file extension* refers to the letters after the dot (.) in a file name. These extensions are used by Microsoft Windows to associate files with the application program that uses them.

There are five main QuickBooks file extensions used for holding transactions and data for a company.

The table below describes these file extensions.

Extension	File Type	Description
.QBW	QuickBooks for Windows company file	This is the main file type for a QuickBooks company file. All of your data is entered into this file.

Extension	File Type	Description
.QBB	QuickBooks backup file	A backup file is a compressed file containing everything you need to recreate your company file and QuickBooks environment. Use a backup file to safeguard your QuickBooks files against accidental data loss. When you create a backup, QuickBooks starts a log of transactions that you've entered since the last time you backed up. In case of accidental loss of data, Intuit Technical Support can use your most recent backup in conjunction with the transaction log file to recover your data.
.QBM	QuickBooks Portable Company File	This file contains all the data of a QuickBooks company file, but not the database indexing, so it's much smaller than the QBW or QBB file. It is useful for transferring the data file through the Internet because the data size is much smaller than any of the other file types, but can be restored to the full QBW on the receiving end.
.QBX	Accountant's copy (Export File)	This is also a compressed file format, but it is used specifically for transferring a file from an end user to an accountant.
.QBA	Accountant's copy (working copy)	When the accountant opens a QBX file they must convert it to a QBA file to enter transactions and run reports.

Table 7-1 QuickBooks File Extensions

For QuickBooks 2008 and later, you can open or create Portable, Backup and Accountant's copy files from the **File** menu options **Open or Restore Company** or **Save Copy or Backup**.

For QuickBooks 2007 and later, the end-user will create an Accountant's Copy transfer file (QBX) which includes a **Dividing Date**. The Dividing Date prevents the end-user from creating transactions on or before this date. The accountant must convert the transfer file to an Accountant's Copy working copy, but can then enter transactions and make changes at the same time as the end-user. When the accountant has completed their changes, they can create an Accountant's Copy Import File (QBY) that is sent back to the client for import into their normal company file. The QBY file only includes the changes made by the accountant and not all of the transactions of the company.

In this chapter we will review the steps to create, open, convert and restore the different QuickBooks file formats.

Other File Types Associated with QuickBooks

QuickBooks also uses many other file extensions to access or store other types of data associated with QuickBooks.

These other file types associated with QuickBooks for Windows files are:

Extension	File Type	Description
.ADR	Auto Data Recovery	In QuickBooks 2011 R6 and QuickBooks 210 R12 and later of Pro and Premier editions. This is a backup copy of your QuickBooks company file, and a matching transaction log, that QuickBooks makes for you automatically.
.AIF	Accountant's review copy (import file)	In QuickBooks 2006 and earlier this is the Accountant's copy Import File. Created when Accountant's copy is exported; to be used for importing into user's company file.
.BDB	Timer backup file	A backup file created when the user backs up time data in the QuickBooks Pro Timer.
.BMP	Windows Bitmap file	These files contain bitmapped images used by QuickBooks.
.BPW	Business Planner file	QuickBooks Business Planner data file. Not backed up with the company file, so must be separately copied to backups.
.DES	Form design template file	This file type is created when you export a form design from the templates list.
.DOC	Word Documents	Word documents for the *write letters* function.
.FSM	Financial Statement Designer Tag File	The FSM file contains information about were the financial statement designer files are stored. This file is stored in C:\Documents and Settings\All Users\Application Data\Intuit\QuickBooks 2008\Components\FSD\data.
.FSD	Financial Statement Designer	The FSD is a supporting file for the Financial Statement Designer that contains the templates for reports. Normally, this is stored in: C:\Documents and Settings\All Users\Application Data\Intuit\QuickBooks 2008\Components\FSD\data

Extension	File Type	Description
.FSR	Financial Statement Designer	The FSR file contains all customized Financial Statement Designer data for each client. Financial Statement Designer creates this file and names it to match "company name" field inside the data file (e.g. Academy_Photography.fsr). To use the restored version of the FSR file, copy it to C:\Documents and Settings\All Users\Documents\Intuit\QuickBooks\Company Files\FSD\Clients.
.IIF	Intuit Interchange Format file	You can import and export lists and/or transactions using text files with an .IIF extension. Using IIF files is no longer recommended. Instead, the QuickBooks SDK is used by applications to read and write data between QuickBooks and other applications. See http://marketplace.intuit.com.
.INI	Configuration file	Configuration files that support online banking and bank feeds.
.LDB	MS Access file for Timer data	A Microsoft Access file needed for the *.TDB file.
.LGB	Little Green Box	This file contains encrypted information about user names and passwords. It is used when an SDK application connects to the company file and needs to open it in the unattended mode. The user name and password is needed to open the connection with the Sybase server.
.LMR	Loan Manager Data	This file is created by the Loan Manager, and keeps information about loans. Not backed up with the company file, so must be separately copied to backups.
.ND	QuickBooks Network Data File	A configuration file that allows access to the QuickBooks company file. Do not delete this configuration file.
.NPC	Online Banking File (obsolete)	An online banking format used by previous versions of QuickBooks. It was superseded by OFX and is no longer supported by financial institutions.
.QBA.TLG	Transaction log file (for accountant's review copy)	When you back up an accountant's review copy, QuickBooks starts a log of transactions that you've entered since the last time you backed up. In case of accidental loss of data, Intuit Technical Support can use your most recent backup in conjunction with the transaction log file to recover your data.

Extension	File Type	Description
.QBI	QuickBooks image file	Image file, "holds" transactions that have been written until they are posted to the hard drive. This file keeps the memory-resident changes to the data file while QuickBooks has the file open. When you close the company file, the .QBI file will be deleted automatically by QuickBooks. If you see QBI files when QuickBooks is not running, it probably means QuickBooks crashed while you had a file open. Do not delete a QBI file when the QBW file is open in QuickBooks.
.QBO	Web Connect file.	Web Connect online banking download file. This file is downloaded from the bank when you use the Web Connect method for online banking.
.QBR	QuickBooks Report	Memorized report format which can be exported and imported. This is feature must contain only generic filters, not filters based on specific list entries.
.QBW.TLG	Transaction log file (for QuickBooks company file)	When you back up your company file, QuickBooks starts a log of transactions that you've entered since the last time you backed up. In case of accidental loss of data, Intuit Technical Support can use your most recent backup in conjunction with the transaction log file to recover your data.
.QBW.TLG .ADR	Auto Data Recovery for TGL file	This is the Auto Data Recovery file for the Transaction log file.
.QBW192.1 68.X.XXmta	Temporary Database File	A temporary file created by the Database Manager while opening a company file. As soon as the file is opened successfully, the temporary file is deleted.
.QBY	Accountant's review copy (import file)	In QuickBooks 2007 and later, the changes that are created in an Accountant's Copy file (QBA) are tracked and can be exported to a file that is then sent to the client for import into their records. The file that contains these changes is a QBY file. This replaces the AIF file used in QuickBooks 2006 and earlier products.
.TDB	QuickBooks Pro Timer files.	By default found in the QBTIMER directory. Contains the time tracking data from the QuickBooks Timer.

Extension	File Type	Description
Archive Copy XX/XX/200X ABC.QBW	Archive copy of data file	When you condense a data file, QuickBooks creates a separate QBW file with the name Archive Copy XX/XX/200X followed by the name of the QBW file. This file is an exact copy of the company file before condensing, and can be used to look up information that was later removed during the condense process. In addition to this archive file, the condense process forces you to create a backup (QBB) copy of the file.
CONNLOG.TXT	Connection Log file	Online Banking connection log file that contains a log of each connection for online banking.
DownloadQBXX folder	Download folder	This folder is created by QuickBooks to store the updates that are downloaded when you use the Update QuickBooks function.
Images Folder	Images folder	A folder storing temporary copies of images used by QuickBooks.
INET Folder	INET	No longer used. Was used to store license information for QuickBooks.
QBInstance Finder	Instance Finder file	This empty file is no longer used by QuickBooks. You can delete the file, but it may get created again by some versions of QuickBooks.
QBrestor.TMP	Temp restore file	This file is created when restoring a QBB file deleted automatically when restore completes successfully.
QBWIN.LOG	QuickBooks Log file	This file is created/updated when a user runs verify and/or rebuild. Logs problems found/situations corrected. Located in the QuickBooks installation directory.
QuickBooks Letters Templates folder	Letters Folder	This folder contains the Word document templates for the QuickBooks write letters function.
Temp1234.qbt	Temp rebuild file	This file created during pass 1 of rebuild, and deleted automatically when rebuild is completed.

Table 7-2 QuickBooks File Extensions

QuickBooks File Manager

> This feature is found only in Enterprise Accountant and Accountant.

QuickBooks File Manager is a tool that can be used to manage multiple client files. It will help open client files in the correct version of QuickBooks, save login and password information, help you upgrade multiple files, and more. If you are an accountant, bookkeeper, ProAdvisor, or someone who works with multiple versions of QuickBooks with multiple files, this will be a helpful tool.

This feature is accessed through the **QuickBooks File Manager** option in the *Accountant* menu, as well as through an icon that is installed on your desktop.

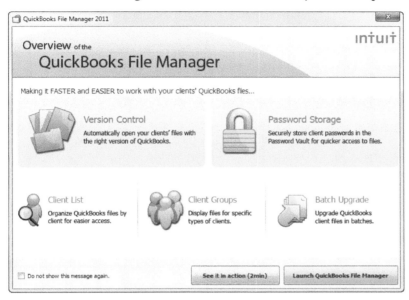

Figure 7-1 QuickBooks File Manager

The first time you use it, there is a "wizard" that will help you locate your client files stored on your computer or server. You can locate company files by folder name and structure, or from individual files.

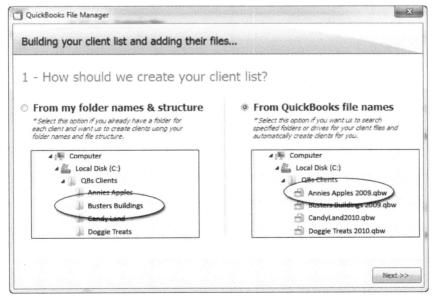

Figure 7-2 Adding Files with File Manager

You can also drag files from Windows Explorer and drop them onto the File Manager.

Clients and Groups

File Manager lets you organize the files by **Client**, and you can organize the clients into **Groups**.

A **Client** is one business entity that you will be working with. You can view all of the company files, accountant's copies, backups and portable files that you are managing for this particular business entity.

A **Group** is a collection of clients that share a common trait. *File Manager* will create several *Groups* for you – *QB2011 Clients, QB2010 Clients* and so forth. You could, for example, create a group of all clients that are manufacturers, or all clients that use Intuit Payroll.

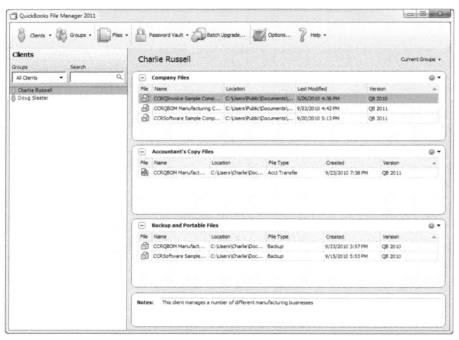

Figure 7-3 File Manager and Client Files

Note that **File Manager** identifies the **year** of QuickBooks that is to be used with each file. It will also identify those that are associated with QuickBooks Enterprise Solutions.

You can open any client file by double-clicking on it in the *File Manager*.

Password Vault

The **Password Vault** is an important feature of the *File Manager*. It allows you to store the login and password information for each client file in a secure list. This allows you to easily access your client files without having to write login information in an unsecured file on your computer or a notepad on your desk. The *Password Vault* will itself have a master user account and password.

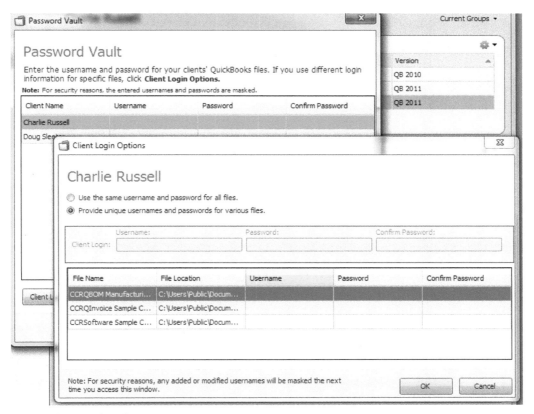

Figure 7-4 Password Vault

If you open a client file with the *File Manager* the program will use the user name and password from the *Password Vault*.

Backing Up Your Data

Backing up your data is a very important part of ensuring the safety of your data. If your computer stops working, your hard disk crashes, or you find a corruption in your data file, you'll be glad you have a backup of your data.

You can use any of the media in Table 7-3 to store your backed up data.

Media	Data Integrity	Size of Storage	Comments
CD-R Drive	Fair	700MB	CD-R drives allow you to create CD disks. The data integrity of CD-Rs is excellent, meaning your data is safest on this medium. Typically, a CD has enough space for large QuickBooks files. Double check that the file is on the CD after completing the process. Writing files to CD is an additional required step.
DVD-R Drive	Good	4.7GB	DVD's are similar to CD's, but with additional storage capacity. DVD's may allow you to back up more than just your QuickBooks data.

External Hard Drive	Good	Unlimited	A secondary hard drive connected through a USB or FireWire port is an excellent option for backing up either QuickBooks files or for an entire system. Unlike CDs or tape backups, you can save backup files directly to an external drive.
Internet	Excellent	Unlimited	You can use the Internet to back up your data off site. Businesses in hurricane or other disaster prone areas should consider remote options since physical media such as CDs and drives can be lost in a natural disaster. Talk to your Internet service provider to see what services are available or consider Intuit's Online Backup Service.

Table 7-3 Media to store data backups

To back up your data, follow the steps in this example:

1.   If you're backing up to removable media, insert the media. This step is not necessary if you plan to back up to your hard drive.

2.   Select the **File** menu and then choose **Save Copy or Backup....**

3.   Select **Backup copy** as the type of file you want to save. A backup file is used for recovery from lost or destroyed files. A portable company file is used to move files to another location. Click **Next** to continue.

4.   Select to save a **Local Backup.** QuickBooks also offers an Online Backup Service which provides an offsite, secure and convenient method of backup. This method is described following this step-by-step process. Click **Next** to continue.

5.   Select the folder and additional backup options. If your options have been set up previously you will skip this screen. If you are changing your options, select the **Options** buttons to access these options. On the Options window, notice also that you can verify the data integrity as part of the backup process (Figure 7-5). Verifying the data as part of the backup process will take more time.

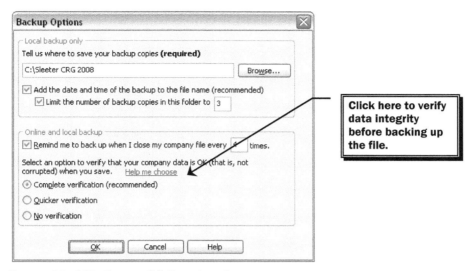

Figure 7-5 Back Up Company File Options window

6.   Click OK to continue.

7.   You may see a warning message if you are saving to the same hard drive as your data file. It is much more secure to choose a location that is not on the same drive. Click *Change this location* to save to another drive or *Use this location*.

8.   On the next window, select *Only schedule future backups*. Click **Next** to continue.

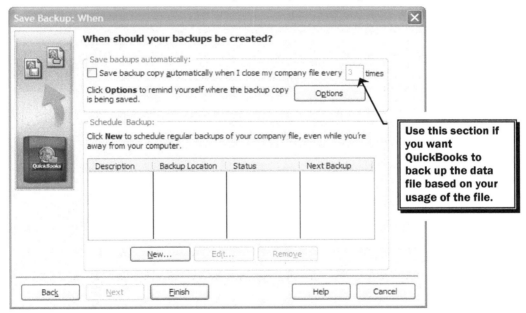

Figure 7-6 Save Backup: When screen of the QuickBooks Backup wizard

9.   In the Save **Backup: When** screen (Figure 7-6) you can set QuickBooks to automatically back up the data file based on file usage.

10.   Use the **Schedule Backup** section if you want QuickBooks to back up your data on pre-established times and days of the week, regardless of how often you have used the file. Click **New** to schedule a backup.

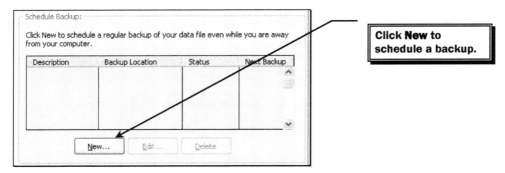

Figure 7-7 Schedule backup section

11.   Enter a **description** of your backup and choose a **location** where you want QuickBooks to
        save the backup (.QBB) files. It is best to keep your data for a period of at least one week.
        Since we are backing up the file at 1:00 a.m. every day of the week, we are keeping 7
        backups. With each backup QuickBooks will delete the file created on the same day of the
        previous week.

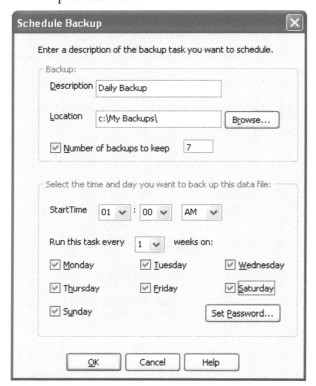

Figure 7-8 Use this window to schedule automatic backups

12.   Click **Set Password**. Enter your Windows username and password as shown in Figure 7-9.
        QuickBooks needs your Windows login information so it can run the scheduled back up. If
        you don't enter login information for the backup location selected, the backup fails due to a
        Windows permission failure.

13.   Click **OK**.

Figure 7-9 Enter your Windows username and password.

14.   Click the **Finish** button.

15.   QuickBooks displays the message shown in Figure 7-10 confirming that the backup is scheduled as specified.

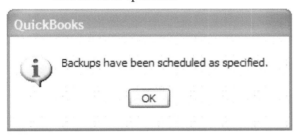

Figure 7-10 QuickBooks informs you that the backup is scheduled.

Intuit QuickBooks Online Backup Service

QuickBooks Online Backup is a service that enables you to automatically back up your critical files to a secure, remote location using the Internet. You select the files then set the frequency. Subsequently you can easily retrieve your data from any PC with an internet connection.

To begin the set up process requires single user access because you start through the Backup wizard. The most efficient way to begin the set up process is to start the backup process as detailed above, except in Step 4 choose **Online** rather than **Local**.

Restoring Backup Files

The process of turning a backup file to a company file is called restoring. When data is lost or damaged, restoring a recent backup file created before the data loss recovers most of the information in the company files. For example, if your computer's hard drive fails, you can restore your backup onto another computer and continue to work. QuickBooks keeps a transaction log file that keeps track of any transactions entered after the backup was made, which helps with recreating the transactions and changes to the files since the backup.

Before QuickBooks 2006, backup files were used to transfer data between computers. QuickBooks 2006 introduced Portable Company Files, which are now the recommended file format for transferring data (see the *Portable Company Files* section on page 289).

> **Important:** When restoring files it is important to take your time. If you restore a file over an existing company file, only the information in the restored file will be maintained. QuickBooks will prompt you to confirm that you are overwriting a file, but there is no way to recover a file that is overwritten. If you have doubts about whether you should overwrite an existing file, rename the file.

To restore a QuickBooks backup file, follow the steps in this example:

1.   Launch the QuickBooks program.

2.   Select the **File** menu and then select **Open or Restore** (see Figure 7-11).

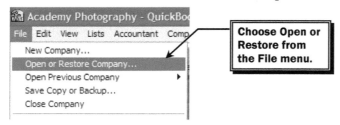

Figure 7-11 QuickBooks File menu

3.   Select to **Restore a backup copy (.QBB)** on the Open Company: Type window. Click **Next** to continue.

Figure 7-12 Open Company Window.

4.   Select to **Restore from a Local backup**. (If you will be restoring from an **Online** back up, you will need to Launch Main Application by right clicking on the Online Backup Icon in the Windows System Tray and follow the procedures detailed there.) Click **Next** to continue.

5.   Select the backup file that you want to restore from the **Open** window. If you're not sure of the exact location and name of your backup file, click the **Look in:** drop down field in the top half of the window in Figure 7-13.

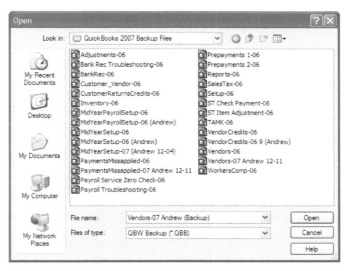

Figure 7-13 Open Company Backup window

6.   Click **Open** to continue.

7.   Click **Next** to continue.

8.   In the Restore To window (Figure 7-14), select the location that you wish to create the restored file. If necessary, change the name of the file that will be created.

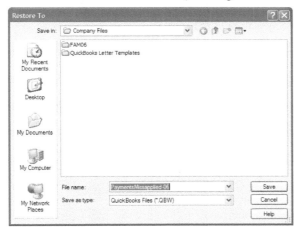

Figure 7-14 Restore to window

9.   Click **Save** to continue. QuickBooks will then restore your backup file onto your hard disk in the folder you specified. When QuickBooks restores the file, it creates a ".QBW" file in the directory you specified.

10.   If you receive the warning message shown in Figure 7-15, it means that QuickBooks is attempting to overwrite an existing file on your computer. If this is your intention, click **OK**. If you do not intend to replace an existing file, click **Cancel** and change the name of the restored file.

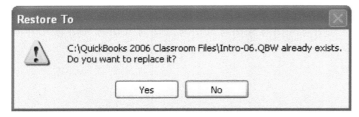

Figure 7-15 Restore/Replace file warning

Backing up Supporting Files

Prior to QuickBooks 2007, the QuickBooks Backup files only backed up the QuickBooks data file (QBW). In QuickBooks version 2007 and later, much more data is included in the QBB file. See Table 7-4 for a listing of all of the supporting files that are included in the QBB files.

QuickBooks Backup Files (QBBs) Contain the following:		
File Extension or Type	File Description	File Location (where XX is the name of the company file)
QBW	Company file	The main company data file is backed up into the QBB and restored to its original location (path) on the hard disk.
BPW	Business Planner	If present, this file is backed up into the QBB file and then restored into a folder called "Restored_XX_Files\Miscellaneous_Files" in the same directory as the restored company file. To use this restored version of the BPW file, copy it to the directory where the QBW file is stored.
CFP	Cash Flow Projector	If present, this file is backed up into the QBB file and then restored into a folder called "Restored_XX_Files\Miscellaneous_Files" in the same directory as the restored company file. To use this restored version of the CFP file, copy it to the directory where the QBW file is stored.
FSM	Financial Statement Designer Tag File	The FSM file contains information about were the financial statement designer files are stored. Note, the financial statement designer is only available with QuickBooks 2008 or earlier. This file is stored in C:\Documents and Settings\All Users\Application Data\Intuit\QuickBooks 2008\Components\FSD\data.
FSD	Financial Statement Designer	The FSD is a supporting file for the Financial Statement Designer. Note, the financial statement designer is only available with QuickBooks 2008 or earlier. Normally, this is stored in: C:\Documents and Settings\All Users\Application Data\Intuit\QuickBooks 2008\Components\FSD\data
FSR	Financial Statement Designer	Although the FSR file was intended to be included in the QBB, it is not there as of this writing. This is a known issue with Intuit. Check updates to see if it's fixed. To use this restored version of

		the FSR file, copy it to C:\Documents and Settings\All Users\Documents\Intuit\QuickBooks\Company Files\FSD\Clients.
Letters and Templates	QuickBooks Letters and Templates	To begin using the letters and templates included with the backup, copy them from the folder contained in the Restored_XX_Files\ Letters_Templates folder to Documents and Settings\All Users\Documents (or possibly shared documents)\Intuit\QuickBooks Letter Templates.
LMR	Loan Manager	If present, this file is backed up into the QBB file and then restored into a folder called "Restored_XX_Files\Miscellaneous_Files" in the same directory as the restored company file. To use this restored version of the LMR file, copy it to the directory where the QBW file is stored.
JPG, GIF, PNG, WMF, BMP	Logo and Images	To restore this file type, it should be copied from the Restored_XX_Files\Images folder to the same directory as the restored company file in a "XX – Images" sub-folder.
PrintEng.ini, wpr.ini, QB Print.qbp	Printer Settings	To restore this file type, it should be copied from the Restored_XX_Files\Printer_Settings folder to the Documents and Settings\All Users\Application Data\Intuit\QuickBooks 2009
Spell.ini, User Dictionary.tlx	Spell Checker	To restore this file type, it should be copied from the Restored_XX_Files\Spell_Checker folder to the Documents and Settings\All Users\Application Data\Intuit\QuickBooks 2009

Table 7-4 QBB files in 2007 and later contain all of these files

When a 2007 or later QBB file is restored, the QBW file plus all the other files shown in Table 7-4 are created. Just as with previous version, if the QBW file exists in the folder where the backup file is to be restored, a warning will appear asking the user to confirm that the existing data file will be overwritten. This warning specifically addresses the QBW file, i.e. the working QuickBooks data file. The additional information does not automatically overwrite the files, but instead a new folder called "Restored_XX_Files" is created to store the additional information. In order to use these additional files, you will need to copy them to the proper location as detailed in Table 7-4.

Portable Company Files

Transferring files between different computers and between different people is a common need for consultants and their clients. For example, a user might want to work at home by sending the file to herself as an email attachment and then opening the file at her home computer. Or, the user might provide her accountant with a copy of the data file for year-end tax preparation work. With previous versions of QuickBooks the user typically created a QuickBooks backup (QBB file) for this type of electronic transfer because the backup file is so much smaller than the data file. However, in QuickBooks 2006 and later, backup files (QBBs) are not that much smaller than the corresponding QBW file. The Portable Company File (.QBM file) is a highly compressed version of the data file that contains only the raw data from the QBW file without the database indexing, and without any supporting files (e.g. Loan Manager files). This new file type was created to allow faster transfers of data files over the Internet.

Another difference with the Portable Company file is that it does not "remember" the path where it should restore to. When you restore a normal backup file (QBB file), QuickBooks will remember which directory the QBB was backed up from so as to assist the user in putting it the same place on the hard drive or network.

> **Note:** Intuit does not recommend using the Portable Company file for the Company's daily backup. You should continue to use Backup files (QBBs) for the daily backups. If there is a problem restoring the QuickBooks backup file, Intuit Technical Support can often resolve the problem. However, they cannot provide as much help if you have trouble opening a Portable Company File.
>
> Depending on the size of the file, the Portable Company file could be as small as one sixth of the size of the QBW file.

Creating Portable Files

Portable files are created and restored in a similar way to creating and restoring a backup. When created, a portable file has a file extension .QBM.

> **Important:**
> When you move a data file from one computer (computer A) to another (computer B), any data you enter on computer B will cause the file on the computer A to become "obsolete." That is, the file on computer B has new data and there is no way to transfer that new data into the file on computer A, except by manually entering the data or by replacing the whole file on computer A with the new file. Therefore, when you copy data files from one computer to another, you cannot continue to work on the file in both places.

To create portable files follow the steps shown below.

1.   Select the **Create Copy** option from the *File* menu.

Figure 7-16 Creating Portable Files

2.   On the *Save Copy or Backup* window select **Portable** company file. Click **Next** to continue.

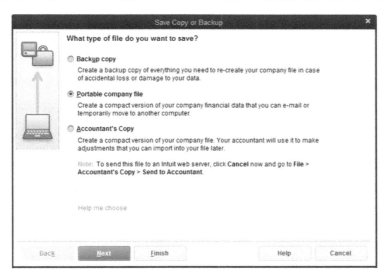

Figure 7-17 Portable File Type

3. The **Save Portable Company File As** window will appear. Set the file name and select the location of the file. If necessary, click **Save in** to select the location where portable file is to be stored. Click **Save** to continue.

4. A **Close and re-open** message will appear telling you that your company file must be closed (Figure 7-18).

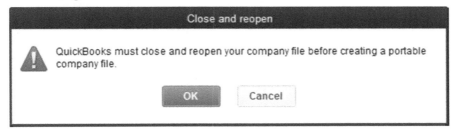

Figure 7-18 Close company file message

5. Once the portable file is created a message will appear telling you the file name and location of the file.

Restoring a portable file follows the same process as restoring a backup file, except that you have to specify the directory where you want to restore the portable file.

Using the Accountant's Copy

Accountants and their clients frequently exchange QuickBooks information. For example, when an accountant does a year-end tax return, the accountant needs access to the QuickBooks data for the year. If the accountant uses a backup or portable file, any changes the accountant makes won't be available to the client unless the original file is replaced with the new accountant file or all changes are manually entered.

The Accountant's Copy is intended to address this problem. The accountant can work on a copy of the client's file while the client continues to work in their original file. These two files can then be merged.

However, in QuickBooks 2006 and earlier versions, the Accountant's Copy was restrictive and difficult to import. Accountants could only add journal entries, and make some minor modifications to the chart of accounts. The changes made by the accountant were sent back in an .AIF format that could be imported in the same process as an .IIF. In practice, there were many problems with importing the .AIF into the client's file.

In QuickBooks 2007 and later, the Accountant's Copy feature has been dramatically improved. The client creates an Accountant's Copy transfer file and sets a *Dividing Date*. The dividing date allows the client to continue working in the company file on transactions dated after the dividing date, while the accountant can add or modify transactions on or before the dividing date. The accountant has access to a large number of transactions and can also modify the chart of accounts. All the changes made by the accountant are listed and can be exported back to the client.

Although this is a much more robust solution, there are still restrictions on what the accountant can do with an Accountant's Copy. Some of the restrictions include:

1.   Adding or adjusting any payroll transactions

2.   Reconciling accounts

3.   Merging and deleting list items

In QuickBooks 2009 and later, you can import changes to 1099 account mapping within the Preferences. When you make changes to accounting fields mapped in the Tax:1099 preference settings in a client's Accountant's Copy data, these changes will be imported back into the client's working file. In Figure 7-19, the shaded fields in the Accountant's Copy indicate that the data entered in these fields will be imported back into the client's file.

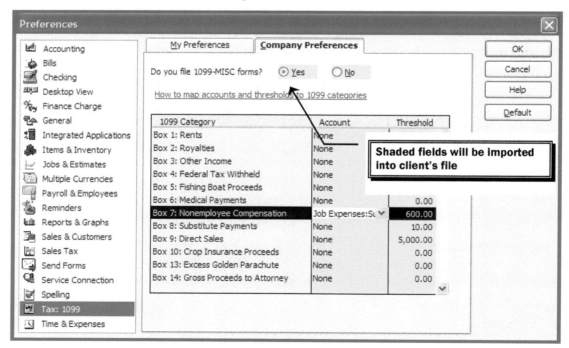

Figure 7-19 Account's mapped in 1099 Preferences will be imported into Client's File when using Accountant's Copy

> **Important:** The ability to open and make changes to an Accountant's Copy file is only available in the Accountant's Edition of the QuickBooks product. If you receive an Accountant's File and you are only using Pro or Premier you will need to convert the Accountant's Copy file to a regular working copy.

When deciding to use an Accountant's Copy, consider the changes the file will need. If you are preparing an income tax return for a client and the changes required will be relatively straight forward, then the Accountant's Copy is a good solution. If you will need to do a significant amount of error correction and clean up, then it is best to use a portable file. While you have the portable file, the client will need to refrain from making changes to their file until you have completed your work so that your file will replace their original file. If the client is unable to stop working on the file, it may be necessary for you to go to their office to do your work or schedule a time work on the client's data file remotely.

Creating an Accountant's Copy

The client can initiate and send you an Accountant's Copy directly from their installation of QuickBooks. In many cases, the consultant will perform these steps to ensure the process is done correctly.

To create an Accountant's Copy, follow the steps in this example:

1. Launch the client's QuickBooks program.

> **Note:** QuickBooks Pro and Premier only have the options to create, import changes and cancel an Accountant's Copy. QuickBooks Accountant has the additional functions of opening the Accountant's Copy and viewing the changes made.

2. Select the **File** menu and then select **Accountant's Copy, Send to Accountant** (Figure 7-20).

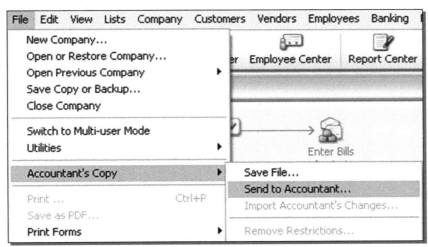

Figure 7-20 Creating an Accountant's Copy

3. The Accountant's Copy wizard appears which provides information about the Accountant's Copy and walks you through the process. The first screen provides a good **overview** of how the Accountant's Copy works. Click **Next** to continue.

4.   On the **Dividing Date** screen you must enter a date that separates what the client and accountant can work on (Figure 7-21). You can select a date from the drop down list.

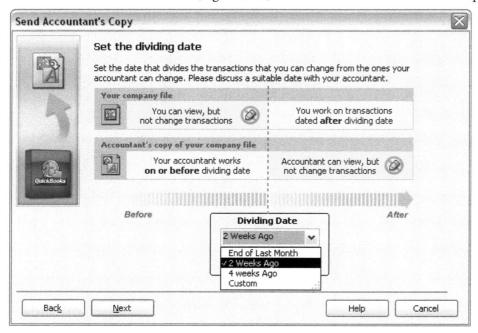

Figure 7-21 Selecting a Dividing Date

5.   Once the Dividing Date is entered, click **Next** to continue.

6.   The user is then prompted to enter the consultant's or accountant's email address (Figure 7-22).

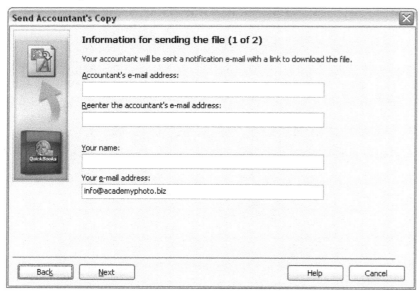

Figure 7-22 Send Accountant's Copy, enter email contact

7.   Next, enter a password. This password needs to include at least one number and one upper case letter, and be at least seven characters long (Figure 7-23). When finished click the **Send** button.

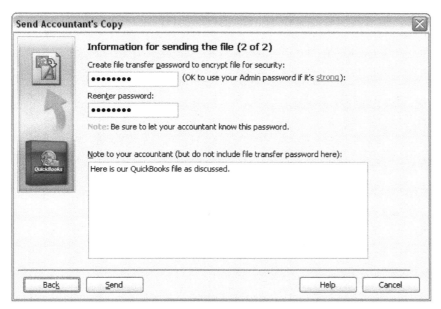

Figure 7-23 Send Accountant's Copy, enter password

8. Once the file is created you will receive a message that the Accountant's Copy Transfer File (.QBX) has been successfully created and the location of the file.

The file is sent to a secure server administered through Intuit. The consultant will receive an email with a link to download the file. The consultant will need the password to open the file. For more information about the Accountant's Copy, see page 292.

> **Note:** The Accountant's Copy Transfer File (.QBX) is a condensed file format and will be the same size as a portable file.

Working in an Accountant's Copy

Once the accountant downloads the Accountant's Copy Transfer File (.QBX) they can convert the file to an Accountant's Copy Working File (.QBA).

> **Note:** Only QuickBooks Accountant can convert an Accountant's Copy Transfer File (.QBX) to an Accountant's Copy Working File (.QBA).

To start working in an Accountant's Copy, follow the steps in this example:

1. Select the **File** menu and then select **Open or Restore Company.**

2. Select Convert an Accountant's Copy Transfer File and click Next.

3. The Convert wizard appears which provides an overview of the process and assists in converting the file. On the **Overview** Screen, click **Next** to continue.

4. Review the restrictions when dealing with an Accountant's Copy, click **Next** to continue.

5. The **Open** window appears which prompts you to select an Accountant's Copy Transfer File (.QBX). Once the file is selected click **Open** to continue.

6. Enter the password for the Accountant's Copy.

7. The next step is to **name** the Accountant's Copy file. Click **Save** to continue.

8.   QuickBooks will convert the file to the .QBA format. When complete you will receive a message with the Dividing Date. Click **OK** to continue.

In the Accountant's Copy, you are able to add, edit and delete a large number of transactions, but not all transactions. You can add and edit the Chart of Accounts, but cannot delete accounts or other list elements. For a complete list of what you can do in the Accountant's Copy, press F1 and search the QuickBooks Help.

Exporting Changes Back to your Client

While you are working in the Accountant's Copy, QuickBooks will track the changes you make. These changes can be viewed from the File menu, Accountant's Copy, **View/Export Changes for Client** (Figure 7-24).

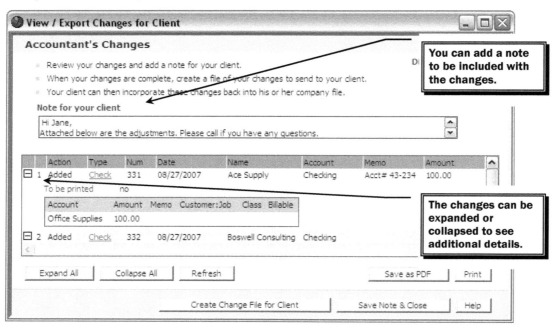

Figure 7-24 Viewing changes made in the Accountant's Copy

To send these changes back to your client, complete the following steps.

1.   From the Accountant's Changes window you can add a note and review the changes that you made. When you are complete, click **Create Change File for Client**.

2.   The **Save Accountant Change File** window will appear. Select a name and location of the file. Click **Save** to continue.

3.   QuickBooks will provide a confirmation dialog that the file was saved. Click **OK** to continue.

> **Note:** The changes are saved in an Accountant's Copy Import File (.QBY). This file contains only the incremental changes made in the Accountant's Copy and not the entire company file.

4.   The QBY file must be sent back to your client for them to import into their normal working copy of the company file (.QBW).

> **Note:** The Accountant's Copy Import File (.QBY) is encrypted so only the QuickBooks file that originally created the Accountant's Copy can read the file.

Importing Accountant's Copy Changes

Once the client receives the Accountant Changes File, he or she should import the changes back into the working copy of the file. While the Accountant's Copy was outstanding, the client was able to continue to add transactions after the dividing date and modify list elements. The changes made by the Accountant's Copy will be imported back into their company file.

To import the Accountant's Changes, complete the following steps.

1. From the File menu, select Accountant's Copy, **Import Accountant's Changes**.

2. Browse to the .QBY file and click **Open**.

3. The **Accountant's Changes** window appears and the client can review the note and the changes.

4. When the client is comfortable with the changes they will click **Incorporate Accountant's Changes**.

5. QuickBooks will close all windows and prompt the user to complete a **Backup**.

6. Once the backup is complete, the changes are imported. The results of the Import are presented in the Accountant's Changes window.

After the import process has been completed, the **Dividing Date** will be removed from the file and the client is free to make changes. This is a good time to set the closing date preference and prevent any changes to a period that has been completed.

> **Note:** If the client has cancelled the Accountant's Changes while you were working in the Accountant's Copy, there is no way for you to electronically import the changes back into their company file. You will need to print out the changes and manually re-enter them into the company file.

Importing and Exporting

In the **Reports** chapter you learned how to export reports to spreadsheets for further analysis on report data. In addition to exporting reports, you can export the following data:

*   **Lists** such as the Chart of Accounts, Customer list, Item list, Vendor list, and other lists. However, you **cannot** export the **Payroll Item** list.

*   **Report templates** that define the filtering, layout, and date range of reports. However, you cannot export reports that have filtering for specific names or accounts.

*   **Form templates** that define the layout of forms such as invoices. You can export templates for Invoices, Credit Memos, Sales Receipts, Purchase Orders, Customer Statements, Estimates, and Sales Orders. These form templates can then be imported into a different QuickBooks data file.

*   **Transaction data.** QuickBooks cannot export **transactions** to an iif file. You can export transactions by creating transaction detail reports, and then exporting the **report** to an excel file, but the transactions themselves are not exported.

> **Tip:** For the situation where you want to start a new file, an alternative to exporting and importing lists and transactions is to use the **Clean Up Company Data** utility with the *Remove All Transactions* option. See page 321. Then, you could use software created by independent developers that will transfer some transactions from your old data file (e.g., open Invoices, unpaid Bills and account balances) into the new data file. Visit www.marketplace.intuit.com for utilities developed by third parties

The exported list information can then be used other applications such as Word or Excel, or the lists can be imported into another QuickBooks data file.

Why Export?

Exporting lists is especially useful if it becomes necessary to rebuild your data file from scratch. For example, if fixing the setup issues and/or cleaning up incorrect data is more timing consuming than is economically viable (i.e., it would cost more to fix it that it's worth), it's probably better to start over with a new data file. In this section, you'll see how you can start by exporting your lists, and then importing them into a new data file which will save time and effort when rebuilding from scratch.

Another time when exporting and importing lists is useful is when your file grows too large, and you decide to start over from scratch. For recommended data file size maximums, see page 678.

Starting a new file does not have to include setting up lists all over again. Lists can be exported to a special file (called an "IIF" file) and then imported into a new, blank QuickBooks company file.

Exporting Lists in IIF Format

To export your lists to an IIF file, follow the steps in this example:

1. Select **Utilities** from the *File* menu, and then select **Export,** and then **Lists to IIF Files**.
2. Click the boxes next to **Customer List** and **Vendor List** and then click **OK** (see Figure 7-25).

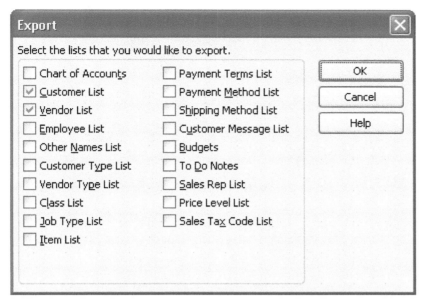

Figure 7-25 Click next to the lists to export.

3.   In the *Export* window, browse to locate the desired folder on your computer.

4.   Enter ***My Lists.IIF*** in the *File name* field (you may need to replace the contents in the field).

> **Note:** QuickBooks saves exported lists with an .IIF extension. The folder in which you save the .IIF file is not important though it is best to choose a folder that you can find easily (e.g. My Documents or the Windows Desktop).

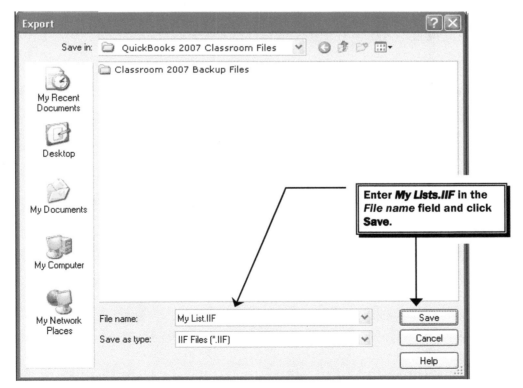

Figure 7-26 Name the export file.

5.   Click **Save** (see Figure 7-26).

6.   Click **OK** when the *QuickBooks Information* dialog box displays (see Figure 7-27).

Figure 7-27 Confirmation that the file has been exported

Exporting Addresses to Text File Format

To export your *addresses* to a text file, use the Export *Addresses to Text File* command.

> **Note:**
> QuickBooks Pro (and above) allows you to synchronize your contacts with Microsoft Outlook or ACT! See the onscreen Help for details.

To export Customers, Vendors, Employees, and Other Names lists for use with another program such as a database or word processor, follow the steps in this example:

1.   Select **Utilities** from the *File* menu, and then select **Export,** and then **Addresses to Text File.**

2.   QuickBooks displays the *Select Names for Export Addresses* window (see Figure 7-28).

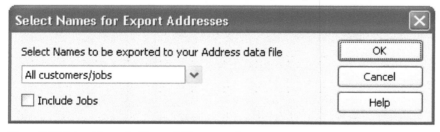

Figure 7-28 Select Names for Export Addresses window

3.   Select **All customers/jobs** from the *Select Names to be exported to your Address* data file drop-down list.

4.   Click **OK** to create a text export file.

5.   On the *Save Address Data File* window, browse to locate the desired folder and enter **Customer Addresses.TXT** in the *File name* field (see Figure 7-29).

6.   Click **Save.**

7.   Click **OK** on the message that warns you about empty fields in some of the customer records, and then click **OK** on the confirmation screen.

This tab-delimited .TXT file contains name and address information for the Customer and Job records in your QuickBooks file. You can now import this file into a word processing program (for mail merging), a spreadsheet program, or a database program. The fields exported into the export file are listed in Table 7-5 shown below.

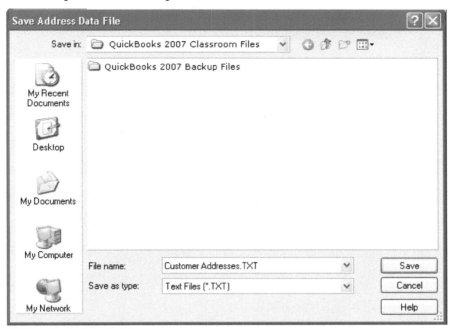

Figure 7-29 Name the export file

Fields Exported in the Address List	
Salutation	The person's title (Mr., Ms., Dr., etc.)
First Name	The person's first name
M.I.	The person's middle initial
Last Name	The person's last name
Company Name	The name of the company
City	The city name in the address. For a customer, the city name comes from the customer's billing address
State	The state in the address. For a customer, the state comes from the customer's billing address
Zip	The Zip Code in the address. For a customer, the zip code comes from the customer's billing address
Country	The name of the country where the customer's business is located
Contact	The name of your main contact person at a company
Alt Contact	The name of an alternate contact person at a company

Address 1 through Address 4	A line in the person's or company's address. QuickBooks exports a separate field for Address 1 through Address 5. For a customer, the address lines come from the customer's billing address
Shipping Address 1 through Shipping Address 4	A line in the customer's shipping address. QuickBooks exports a separate field for Shipping Address 1 through Shipping Address 5 for each line in the address
Shipping City	The city in the customer's shipping address
Shipping State	The state in the customer's shipping address
Shipping Zip	The zip code in the customer's shipping address
Shipping Country	If applicable, the country in the customer's shipping address

Table 7-5 Fields of the exported file

Exporting Form Templates

You can also export your custom form templates for Invoices, Sales Orders, Estimates, Credit Memos, Sales Receipts, Purchase Orders, and Statements.

To export a form template, follow the steps in this example:

1. Select **Lists** and then select **Templates**.

2. With the **Academy Glass Invoice** selected, choose **Export** from the *Templates* button drop-down list (see Figure 7-30).

Figure 7-30 Select Export from the Templates menu

3. The file name, *Academy Glass Invoice.DES,* is already entered into the **File name** section. Browse to locate the desired folder. Click **Save** (see Figure 7-31).

QuickBooks saves exported templates in a special file format with a .DES extension.

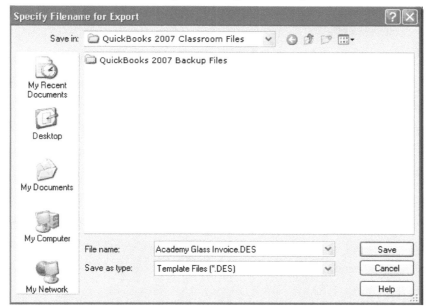

Figure 7-31 Select the folder in which you will save the exported template

Exporting Report Templates (Premier and Enterprise Only)

QuickBooks Premier and Enterprise allows you to transfer memorized reports from one QuickBooks file to another. You may wish to export your memorized reports when starting over with a new data file, or when coordinating reporting efforts with your accountant.

To export a memorized report, or a group of memorized reports, follow the steps in this example:

1. Select **Memorized Reports** from the *Reports* menu, and then select **Memorized Report List**.

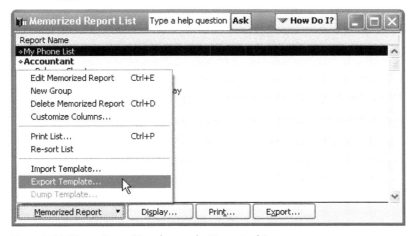

Figure 7-32 Choose Export Template on the Memorized Report menu

2. With the *My Phone List* selected, choose the **Export Template** command from the Memorized Report drop-down list at the bottom of the *Memorized Report List* window (See

Figure 7-32).

To export a whole group of reports, select the report group name in the list. You will be able to export several reports in one step.

3.   QuickBooks automatically creates the filename with a QBR extension. Browse to locate the desired folder and click **Save** (see Figure 7-33).

Figure 7-33 Specify Filename for Export window

> **Note:** You cannot export reports that contain non-generic filters. Generic filter options exist in every QuickBooks data file. Non-generic filter options are specific to one data file, like a specific customer, vendor, or service item. For example, you can export a report filtered by Item for "All Service (Item type) Items," but you cannot export a report filtered for a *specific* service Item like "Labor." "Labor" is specific to the Academy Glass data file and is therefore non-generic.

Importing Data

What Can I Import?

Importing data is especially useful if you want to enter data from outside sources into your QuickBooks data file.

For example, if you want to enter ecommerce transactions from your web store, invoices from your billing software, or transaction data from a spreadsheet, it would be much faster, easier, and more accurate to "import" as opposed to manually entering the data.

Here is a list of **data types** you can import along with recommendations for how to go about it:

- **Lists** such as the Chart of Accounts, Customer list, Item list, Vendor list, and other lists. You can import virtually any list except the payroll item list. Use IIF files (see below), Excel files (see page 310), or a QuickBooks add-on to import list information.

- **Report templates** that define the filtering, layout, and date range of "generic" reports. See page 316.

- **Form templates** that define the layout of forms such as invoices. See page 308.

- **Transaction data** can should be entered using the *Enter Batch Transaction* feature (see 103) or using an add-on applications from several vendors which provide a variety of ways to import and export transaction data from QuickBooks.

Here is a list of **applications** from which you can import data along with recommendations for how to go about it:

- **IIF Files (.IIF)** – Although there is no application that specifically creates IIF files, this format was defined by QuickBooks to facilitate data importing before the invention of the QuickBooks programming interface (SDK) used by add-on developers. Although IIF files still "work", and are fine for transferring list information to and from QuickBooks, it is much better practice to use an add-on application to transfer transactions to and from QuickBooks. Some of the reasons for this are (a) with IIF there is no way to prevent a user from importing data twice, (b) there is limited error checking with IIF imports, and (c) Intuit is no longer updating the functionality of IIF and is instead urging users to use add-ons.

- **Excel files (.XLS)** – QuickBooks can directly import lists (Customers, Vendors, Items, or Accounts) from Excel files. In addition, there are some add-ons that allow you to use Excel to send transaction data to QuickBooks.

- **Word, CSV, or Text Files (.DOC, .CSV., .TXT)** – If you have list data in Microsoft Word (.DOC) , CSV, or Text (.txt) files, you can format it into columns, separated by commas, and save it as a text file with a ".csv" extension. Then you can use the Excel import wizard to import the list information. If you have *transaction* data in Word, although it is possible to format it into an IIF format, and then import the file using IIF, most experts would consider this a daunting task and would advise against it. Instead, use an add-on application that can handle transaction data.

- **WebConnect Data (.OBO or .OFX)** – WebConnect files contain downloaded banking or credit card information including checks, deposits, credit card charges and payments that have cleared the bank. You can import this information via the Bank Feeds Center, or by using the File, Utilities, Import, Web Connect files.

- **QB Timer Activities** – If you use the QuickBooks Pro Timer utility to have employees enter timesheets, you can import the file from each timekeeper using the File, Utilities, Import, Timer Activities function. The file you're importing will be an IIF file, so all of the IIF importing rules apply.

Add/Edit Multiple List

Add/Edit Multiple List Entries is a way to easily update list information. It is available on the *List* pull down menu or from the bottom of the Customer, Vendor and Item lists. There are five list types that are available:

- Customers
- Vendors
- Service Items
- Inventory Items

- Non-inventory Items

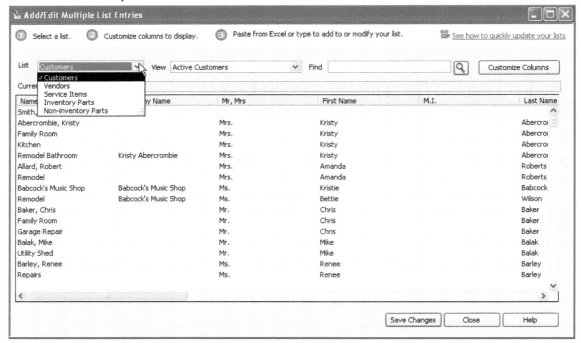

Figure 7-34 Add/Edit Multiple List Entries

Once the list has been chosen, the next step is to customize the columns to display. If this feature will be used for editing list information, the order of the columns is not as important. If the feature will be used to add data from Excel, the columns should be in exactly the same order as the Excel spreadsheet. To edit the columns that will be displayed, click on the **Customize Columns** button. Once the changes have been made, click on **OK**.

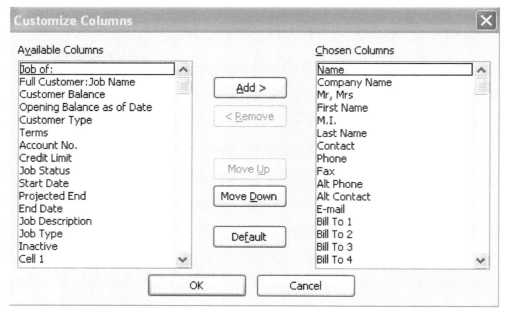

Figure 7-35 Customize Columns

Now you can edit the data. Click in a specific cell and then right click to display the menu of options. You can choose to duplicate a row, copy the data in that cell down for the rest of the entries, clear a column, and more.

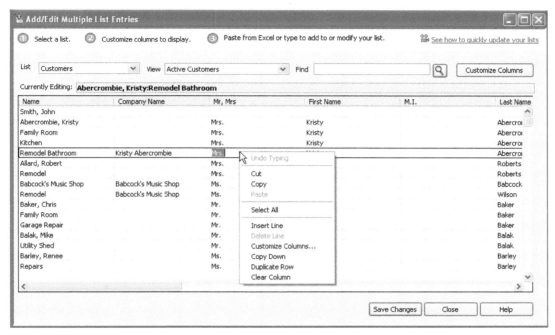

Figure 7-36 Add/Edit Multiple List Entries

To add data for the list, scroll to the bottom to the first blank row. In Excel, highlight the data to be added to QuickBooks and Copy it, click on the bottom row and then paste the data. Once the data appears (if copying a large amount of data it might take a little time to refresh the screen) click the **Save Changes** button. If there are any errors, they will be highlighted in red so they can be corrected and saved.

Importing IIF Files

To import an IIF file, follow the steps in this example:

1.   From the *File* menu select **Utilities**, then **Import**, and then **IIF Files**.

2.   In the *Import* window, browse to locate the desired folder and select the **My Lists.IIF** file. Click **Open** (see Figure 7-37).

3.   QuickBooks displays a dialog box that says, "Your data has been imported." Click **OK**.

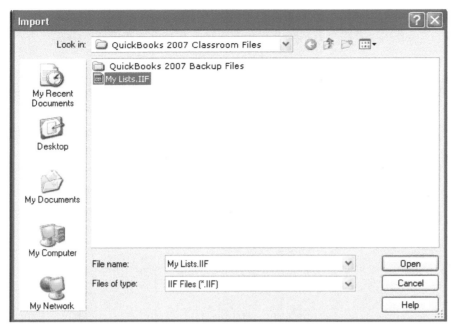

Figure 7-37 Select the file to import

Importing Form Templates

To import a form template (DES file), follow the steps in this example:

1.   Select **Lists** and then select **Templates**.

2.   Select **Import** from the *Templates* button drop-down list (See Figure 7-38).

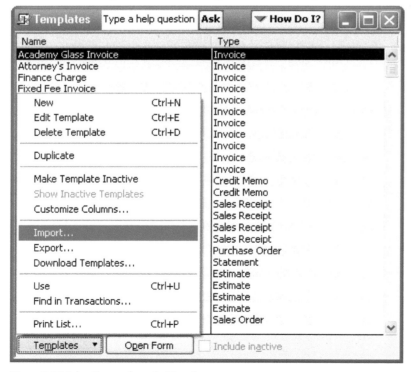

Figure 7-38 Select Import from the Templates menu

3. In the *Select File to Import* window, browse to locate the desired folder and select the **Academy Glass Invoice.DES** file. Click **Open** (see Figure 7-39).

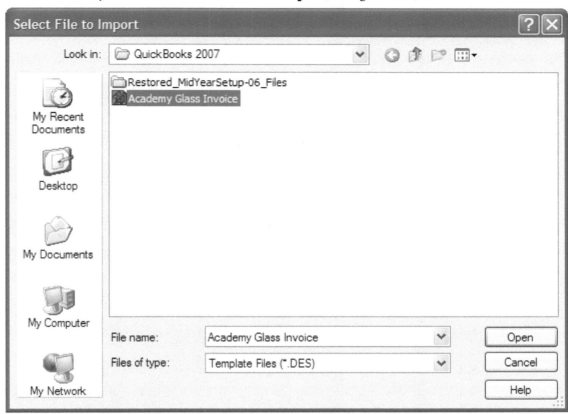

Figure 7-39 Select the file to import

4. QuickBooks opens the *Customize Invoice* window. The Template Name would normally display in the *Template Name* field. Since **Academy Glass Invoice** already exists in the data file, the *Template Name* field is blank, prompting you to enter a new Template Name. Type in *Academy Glass Invoice 2* in the Template Name field (see Figure 7-40).

Figure 7-40 Customize Invoice window

5. Click **OK** to close the *Customize Invoice* window.

6. **Academy Glass Invoice 2** now appears in the template list (see Figure 7-41).

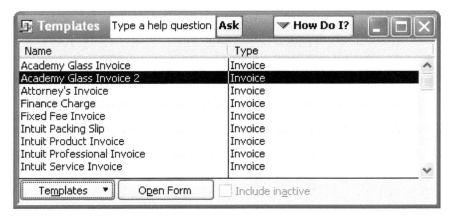

Figure 7-41 The Templates window now shows Academy Glass Invoice 2

7.   Close the *Templates* window.

Importing Excel Files

QuickBooks can import list data (Customers, Vendors, Items, or Accounts) from an Excel spreadsheet file. The process involves mapping the columns in the spreadsheet file to fields in the QuickBooks list and then importing the data.

To import an Excel file that contains your customer list, follow the steps in this example:

1.   Select **Utilities** from the *File* menu, select **Import** and then select **Excel Files**.

2.   The *Import a File* window displays (see Figure 7-42). Click the **Browse** button to locate the desired folder.

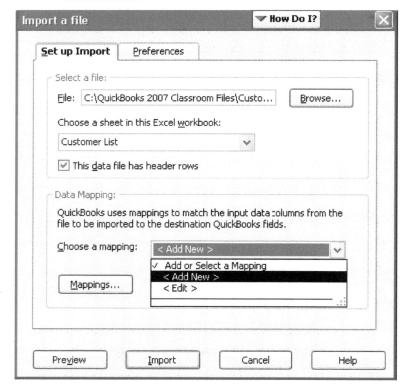

Figure 7-42 Importing an Excel File

3. Select the **Customer Lists.xls** file and click **Open** (see Figure 7-43).

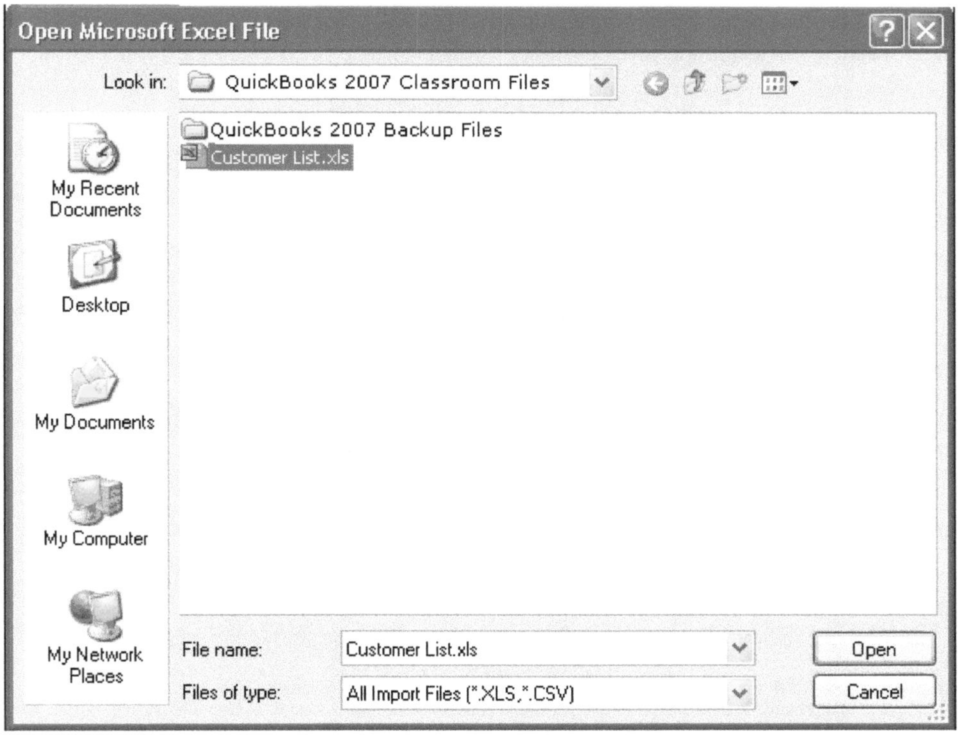

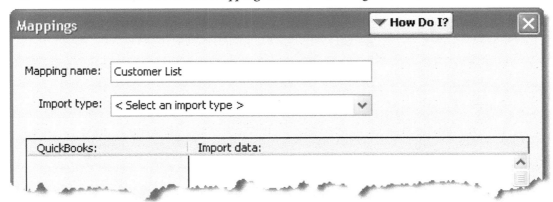

Figure 7-43 Select the Customer List.xls file.

4. Select the **Customer List** worksheet from the *Choose a sheet in this Excel workbook* drop-down list. The check box, **This data file has header rows** should already be checked (see Figure 7-42).

> **Note:** If there are multiple worksheets in your Excel file, select the sheet to import. If there is only one worksheet without a custom name, select "Sheet 1."

5. To map the header rows to fields in QuickBooks, choose **Add New** from the *Choose a mapping* drop-down list (see Figure 7-42).

6. Enter ***Customer List*** in the *Mapping name* field (see Figure 7-44).

Figure 7-44 Mappings window

7.   Select **Customer** from the *Import Type* drop-down list. When you select **Customer**, a list of fields will populate the *QuickBooks* column (see Figure 7-45). These fields correspond to the fields in QuickBooks customer records.

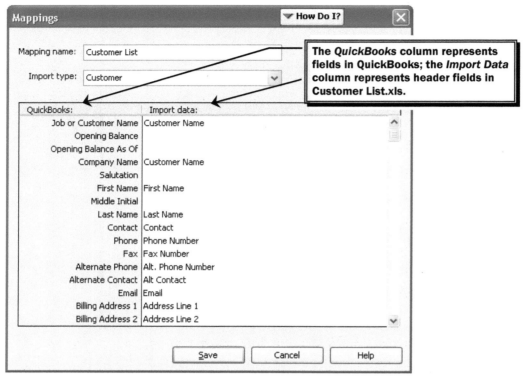

Figure 7-45 Completed Mappings tab using Table 7-6

8.   For each **QuickBooks** field listed in Table 7-6, select the corresponding name in the **Import Data** column shown in the *Mappings* window.

QuickBooks	Import Data
Job or Customer Name	Customer Name
Company Name	Customer Name
First Name	First Name
Last Name	Last Name
Contact	Contact
Phone	Phone Number
Fax	Fax Number
Alternate Phone	Alt. Phone Number
Alternate Contact	Alt Contact
Email	Email

Billing Address 1	Address Line 1
Billing Address 2	Address Line 2
Billing Address 3	Address Line 3
Shipping Address 1	Address Line 1
Shipping Address 2	Address Line 2
Shipping Address 3	Address Line 3
Terms	Terms
Tax Code	Sales Tax Code
Tax Item	Tax County

Table 7-6 Corresponding fields between QuickBooks and Excel Spreadsheet

9.   As you click in the Import data column, a dropdown list will appear from which you should select the appropriate header name. This assigns the data in the column in the import file to the appropriate QuickBooks field.

10.   When you are finished with the *Mappings* window, click **Save**.

11.   Select the **Preferences** tab on the *Import a file* window that appears to review your options on data importing.

12.   Keep the default settings on the **Preferences** tab (see Figure 7-46).

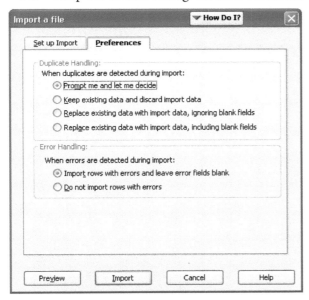

Figure 7-46 Choosing preferences for data import

13.   Click **Preview** to review whether there are any errors (see Figure 7-47). Once you have verified that there are no errors, select **Import**.

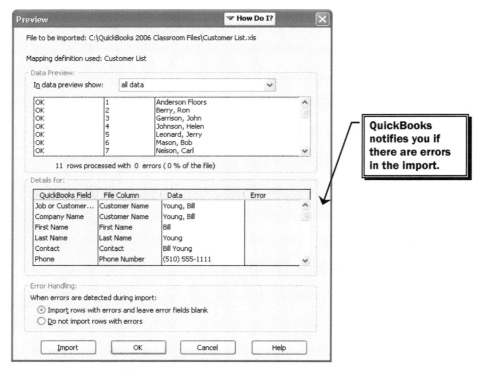

Figure 7-47 Preview window to catch any errors

14. Select **Import** and you will get a warning that importing is not reversible (see Figure 7-48). Click **Yes** to continue.

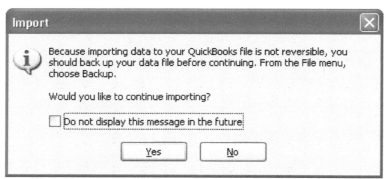

Figure 7-48 Import Warning

Tip: Backup your data before you import information. Then, if you have problems with the import, you can restore the backup to "reverse" the import.

15. If there is a match in the *Job or Customer name* field between the imported data and your QuickBooks customer list, QuickBooks flags that record as a duplicate. When duplicate records are found, the message in Figure 7-49 appears. For this practice, click **Keep existing data and discard import data** and then click **Apply to All**.

     This window allows you to control how QuickBooks handles duplicate records. Sometimes you may want to discard any data in the import file that matches a record in QuickBooks. In this case, select *Keep existing data and discard import data*. This ensures that nothing in the import file will overwrite any data in QuickBooks.

At other times, you may want to update your QuickBooks lists with new information in the import file. For example, you might want to update the addresses or phone numbers for your customers. The *Replace existing data with import data* options allow you to do this type of updating.

Figure 7-49 Duplicate Record Found warning

16. When the data has finished importing, the message in Figure 7-50 appears. Click **Don't Save** for this lesson.

Figure 7-50 Error Log Message from Importing

17. When the import of the **Customer List.xls** file is complete, one new record is added to the *Customer & Job List* for **The Sleeter Group, Inc.** (see Figure 7-51).

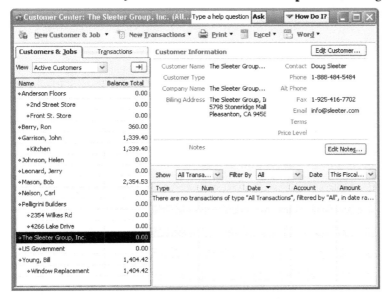

Figure 7-51 Customer & Job List updated with a new record

18. Double-click on the new or changed records to see what data has been added or changed.

Importing Report Templates

To import a report template (QBR file), follow the steps in this example:

1. Select the **Reports** menu, then select **Memorized Reports**, and then select **Memorized Report List**.

2. Select the **Memorized Report** menu, and then select **Import Template** (See Figure 7-52).

Figure 7-52 Select Import Template on the Memorized Report menu

3. Browse to locate the desired folder and then select the My Phone List.QBR file. Click **Open** (see Figure 7-53).

Figure 7-53 Select the QBR file and click Open.

4. The Memorized Report window will display unless another reports exists with the same name. Since **My Phone List** already exists as a Memorized Report, the message in Figure 7-54 appears. Click **OK**.

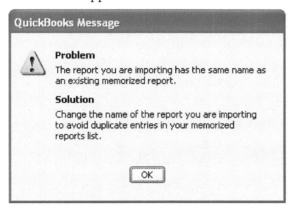

Figure 7-54 QuickBooks message regarding duplicate report name

5. In the *Memorize Report* window, type in **My Phone List 2** and click **OK** (see Figure 7-55).

Figure 7-55 Save the memorized report in the Customers group

6. **My Phone List 2** appears in the Memorized Report list (see Figure 7-56). Close the Memorized Report List window.

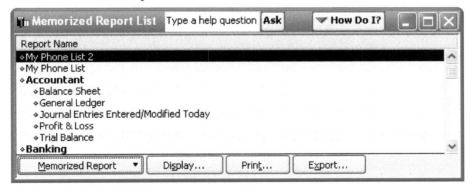

Figure 7-56 The updated Memorized Report list

Using the Clean Up Company Data Utility in QuickBooks

When you use the Clean Up Data Utility data, QuickBooks "condenses" the data file by delete all the transactions you no longer need and replacing them with monthly summary entries. At the same time, this utility will create two files, one is an archive of the data file (in QBW format), and the other is a backup of the file (QBB).

Using the Clean Up Data Utility

You access the Clean Up Data utility by selecting the **File** menu, selecting **Utilities**, and then selecting **Clean Up Company Data**. When you use the Clean Up Company Data utility, you can choose to remove some or all of the transactions in the file. If you want to remove ALL of the transactions, see page 321. If you're removing only some of the data, select Remove transactions as of a specific date (see Figure 7-57). Then specify a date through which QuickBooks will remove transactions from the file. The utility has no effect on transactions dated **after** the ending date. For example, if the ending date is 12/31/2005, all transactions dated 01/01/2006 and later remain unchanged in your company file.

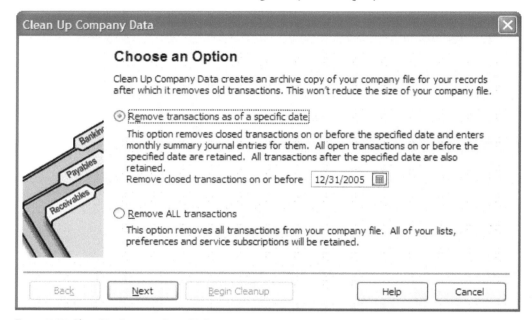

Figure 7-57 Clean Up Company Data Utility

Although the option reads "Remove transactions as of a specific date," QuickBooks does not remove <u>all</u> of the transactions. See below for information about which transactions do not get removed.

Also, QuickBooks enters additional transactions that summarize deleted entries, reducing the size of your file and increasing the overall performance of the program when you are using this file.

There are several rules that QuickBooks uses to decide whether to delete a transaction during the cleanup process. By default, QuickBooks will **not** delete transactions that meet these criteria:

- Uncleared transactions – for example, uncleared Checks in any account.
- Open transactions – for example, open Invoices, unpaid Bills.
- Most transactions involving inventory. QuickBooks removes all inventory transactions until it finds one that the utility is not supposed to remove. For example, if an unpaid Bill includes an inventory item, QuickBooks will not delete the Bill – because it is Unpaid. QuickBooks will retain *all* transactions that include inventory from the date of this Bill forward. Even if you allow the utility to delete open transactions, like the

Unpaid Bill, QuickBooks will not delete any transaction that impacts the *current* average cost of inventory. As soon as it finds one transaction that affects the current average value, it stops deleting any inventory transactions from that point forward. There is no way to override this setting. As a result, clients using inventory will usually see little or no significant file size reduction after using the Clean Up Data utility.

- To be Printed transactions.
- Time, mileage, and expenses marked as "billable."
- Transactions "linked" to other transactions that cannot be removed – for example, when a deposit includes a payment that is linked to an open Invoice, the deposit and the payment cannot be removed because they are "linked" to the open (and therefore un-removable) invoice.

Note: As shown in Figure 7-58, you can choose to **override** the defaults to remove the following transactions during the condense process:

- Uncleared bank and credit card transactions.
- Transactions marked "To be Printed".
- Invoices and Estimates marked "To be Sent".
- Transactions containing unbilled (i.e., un-reimbursed) costs.

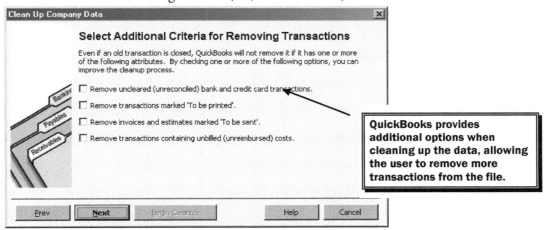

Figure 7-58 Clean Up Company Data – Additional Options

> **Warning:** Consider the effect that removing transactions will have on the usability of your data file. For example, removing and summarizing uncleared transactions could have a significant impact on your next bank reconciliation.

You then select the unused list entries you want QuickBooks to remove from the data file. For example, if you no longer do business with a Customer named John Maxwell and the Clean Up Data Utility deletes all transactions that include John Maxwell's name (e.g., Invoices, Customer Payments, etc.), you can remove his customer record by telling the utility to remove unused customers.

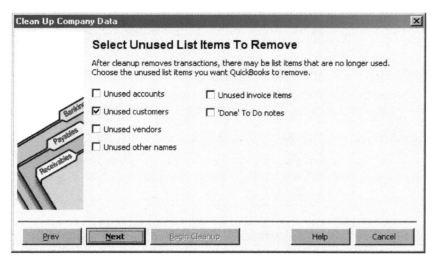

Figure 7-59 Clean Up Company Data Utility - Unused List Item Removal

Transactions Created by the Clean Up Data Utility

During the "clean up" process, QuickBooks creates summary transactions (Journal Entries) for the transactions it deletes from your file. There is usually one summary transaction per month representing the deleted transactions. For example, there will be one journal each month with the total of the Checks written for that month, along with the total amount in each account used on the deleted Checks.

You cannot edit any transactions created by the Clean Up Data Utility. In this example, you cannot edit or delete any summary Journal Entries dated 12/31/2005 or prior.

> **Note:** QuickBooks requires you to create a backup of your data file before using the Clean Up Data File utility.
>
> **Note:** QuickBooks creates an "Archived" copy of your data file. You can refer to this archived copy to view the transactions the utility removed from your primary file. However, you should not use this Archive copy as your working copy of the file.

Understanding the Clean Up Data Utility

The Clean Up Data Utility is not quite as simple as it seems on the surface. After cleaning up a file, you may discover that QuickBooks retained numerous cleared Checks, paid Bills, or closed Invoices. At first, it might seem that the cleanup utility didn't work correctly, however the more likely explanation has to do with the transactions involved.

Use the following checklist to determine why QuickBooks retained a transaction while cleaning up the data file:

- Is the transaction "uncleared," "open," or does it include an unbilled cost?
- Does the transaction include an Inventory Part Item? In many cases, inventory transactions will not be deleted.
- Is the transaction "connected to" or "linked to" a transaction matching one of the conditions above?

For example: If a Deposit transaction in the Checking account includes five Checks, but one of the Checks was for partial payment on an Invoice, the whole chain from the originating Invoice (Invoice, Payment, and Deposit) will not be deleted during the cleanup process. Also, since the other Checks on that same Deposit are associated with the open Invoice (because they are on the same Deposit), the rest of the five deposited Checks and their chains will not be removed. To fix this rather simple example, close the Invoice that still has an outstanding balance by issuing a Credit Memo (if appropriate). Then, apply the Credit Memo to the Invoice. Alternatively, you can change the original Invoice to match the amount received against it. However, it is usually better to create the Credit Memo since doing so will provide a better audit trail.

Consider the following before you use the **Clean Up Data File Utility**:

- If you have a large file, the utility usually runs for several hours.
- Quite often, the actual shrinkage in the file is small, especially if the client uses inventory or has numerous open or uncleared transactions.
- Investigating the cause for why transactions were not deleted is tedious and may take more time to troubleshoot than is economically viable.
- If you want to remove prior period information from the data file, starting over with a new file is a much cleaner way to accomplish the goal of shrinking the file, though doing so requires more effort. In any case, starting over allows you to significantly streamline the data file and allows you to correct problems with the setup of the data file, if applicable. If you decide to start over with a new file, open the Clean Up Company Data window and select **Remove All Transactions**. See the section entitled, "Knowing When to Start Over with a New Data File" below for more information.

Important: The option to *Remove Transactions as of a Specific Date* removes some, but not all, of the transactions dated on or before that date, and then replaces the deleted entries with summary entries. In QuickBooks 2005 and prior this option is called "condensing" the data. The *Remove All Transactions* option removes every transaction from the data file, while retaining Budgets and Timesheet detail.

Tip: When using the Clean Up Company Data utility with versions 2006 and higher, to achieve the maximum reduction in file size, create a portable company file and then open the portable company file to be used as the working copy going forward. This process will remove the "empty" spaces left in the data file from the condense process.

Tip: The Clean Up Company Data utility runs faster if the data file is on the same hard drive as the QuickBooks program. It is best to run the tool using the computer at your office or the client's office that has the most RAM and the fastest processor.

Period Copy

Period Copy allows you to remove ALL transactions from outside a range of dates.

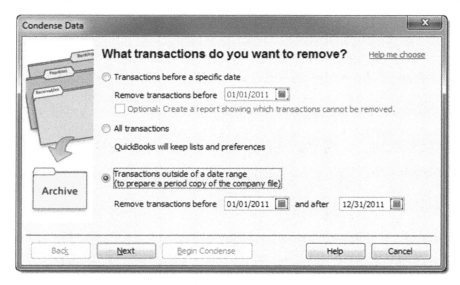

Figure 7-60 Period Copy option in Condense Data

This is useful if you wish to prepare a file for an audit that has only transactions from the year being addressed, or if you are providing detailed accounting information to a potential purchaser. Note, however, that will not provide you with a complete, balanced company file – you will need to make appropriate adjustments to set up the proper balance forward.

Using Excel to Clean up Your QuickBooks Customer Lists

Lists are one of the most important building blocks of QuickBooks. Lists store information which is used again and again to fill out forms. For example, when you set up a customer in the customer list, the customer's name, address, tax code, tax item, price level, etc. is used to automatically fill out an invoice, sales receipt, or customer letter. Similarly, when you set up an Item in the Item list, QuickBooks uses the Item's description, price, and associated account information to fill in details on the invoice, and record the appropriate debits and credits in the general ledger. Properly maintained lists help speed up data entry and maintain accuracy and consistency in the data file.

The problem is, as time passes, lists tend to get "dirty" in one way or another. For example, the customer list tends to have incomplete or inconsistent data. Perhaps some email addresses are missing, or customer types are not set correctly, or the sales tax codes or items are incorrect on several customer records.

These types of problems seem somewhat innocuous on the surface, but as lists get dirty, data entry tends to get inefficient and inaccurate. This leads to problems with reports, tax returns, and the overall quality of the QuickBooks data.

Consider the difficulties of filing a sales tax return from QuickBooks data. If you discover that the sales tax reports in QuickBooks are either wrong or do not give you enough data to properly fill out the sales tax return, you'll have a big project in front of you. Most likely, you'll have to modify every invoice and sales receipt for the whole quarter in order to make the reports give you the accurate and complete information for the tax return. The good news is that proper list maintenance can help you avoid this type of headache at tax time.

To avoid these problems, and provide a great service to your clients during the "slow" time of year, here is a simple, billable service you can provide for all of your clients. For some type of edits, standardizing accounts for items, or removing information from a specific field, the Add/Edit Multiple List Entries is a more efficient option. For editing specific data, however, the iif procedures detailed below are much more efficient.

To clean a customer list (or any of the lists) in QuickBooks use the following steps to export the list to an IIF file, then manipulate the list in Excel, and then import the list back into QuickBooks.

List Clean Up Step-by-Step

1.   Back up your file first
       You should always backup a data file before working on the data. It's a good "best practice" for all your consulting engagements because it allows you to completely undo all of the changes you plan to make. If for whatever reason you do need to restore the file to the point before you worked on it, you should use the "Restore" command in QuickBooks.

2.   Export the customer list to an IIF file
       Follow the steps below to export your customer list (or any other list you need to clean).

3.   Open IIF in Excel and use the flexibility of Excel filtering to select, sort, and modify the list as needed.
       Our example below will show how to change the area codes for a group of phone numbers.

4.   Import the list back into QuickBooks. This "overwrites" the list in the QuickBooks file with any changes you've made to the list. Note that you cannot delete list entries using this method, only add or change existing list items.

Exporting Lists in IIF Format

To export your lists to an IIF file, follow the steps in this example:

1.   Select Utilities from the File menu, and then select Export, and then Lists to IIF Files.

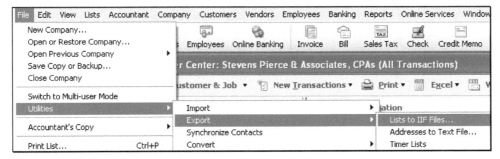

Figure 7-61 Export to IIF menu

2.   Click the boxes next to Customer List and Vendor List and then click OK (see Figure 7-25).

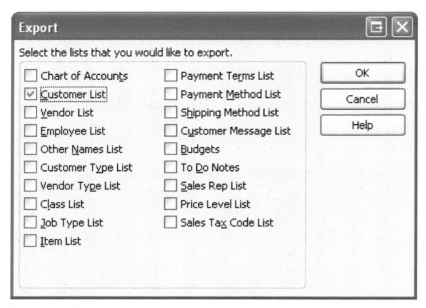

Figure 7-62 Click to select which lists to export.

3.   In the Export window, browse to locate the desired folder on your computer.

4.   Enter Customers.IIF in the File name field (you may need to replace the contents in the field).

Note: QuickBooks saves exported lists with an .IIF extension. The folder in which you save the .IIF file is not important though it is best to choose a folder that you can find easily (e.g. My Documents or the Windows Desktop).

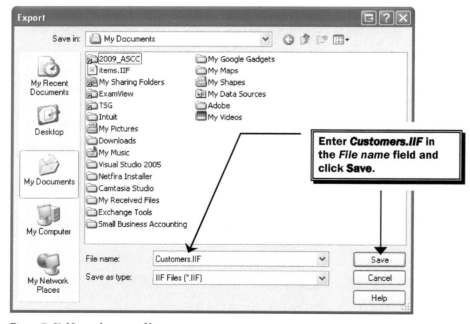

Figure 7-63 Name the export file.

5.   Click Save (see Figure 7-26).

6.   Click OK when the QuickBooks Information dialog box displays (see Figure 7-27).

Figure 7-64 Confirmation that the file has been exported

Cleaning the List in Excel

After you've exported the IIF file, open it in Microsoft Excel:

1.   Launch the Windows Explorer and browse to the My Documents folder.

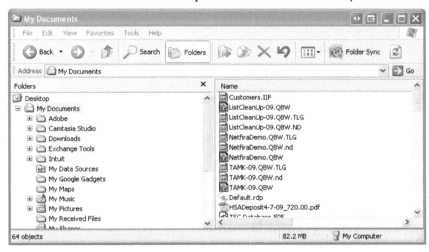

Figure 7-65 The My Documents folder

2.   Right-click on Customers.IIF file and select Open With and then select "Microsoft Office Excel", or if it's not one of the choices, then select "Choose Program."

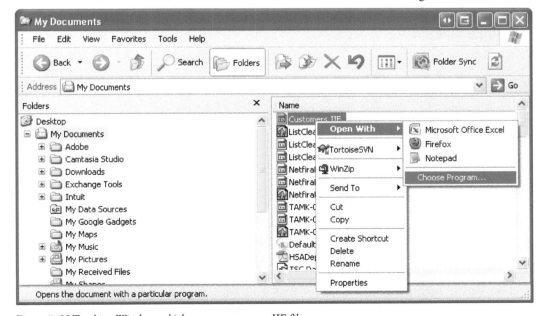

Figure 7-66 Teaching Windows which program can open IIF files

3.   The next screen lets you have windows use a "web service" to find the appropriate program to open your file, or to have you manually select the program yourself. Since the web service won't work for IIF files, select "Select the program from a list" (Figure 7-67) and click OK.

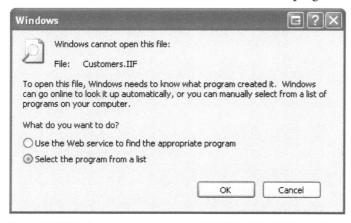

Figure 7-67 Windows cannot recognize the IIF file by default. You need to "teach it".

4.   Scroll through the list of your programs and select Microsoft Office Excel, and click "Always Use the selected program to open this kind of file" (Figure 7-68) and then click OK.

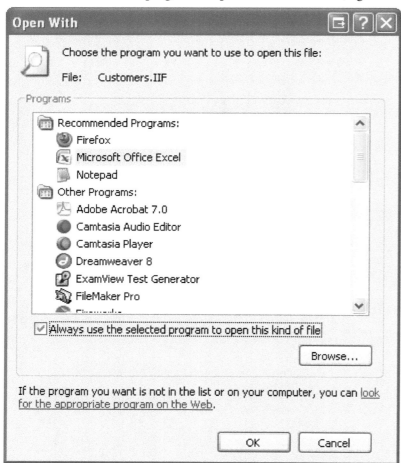

Figure 7-68 Selecting Microsoft Excel as the program to open IIF files

As you can see from the Excel screen below, the IIF file has several rows and columns that contain the various fields of the IIF file. Note that row 21 in this table is a "header" row that shows you the name of each of the columns.

From here on, the process of cleaning the list will be greatly aided by your Excel skills. A very useful feature of Excel for this type of thing is the "Filters."

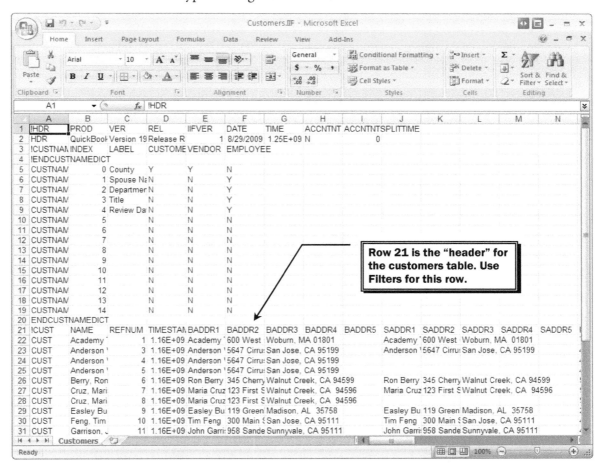

Figure 7-69 The IIF file opened in Excel

Since we're going to work on all the data in the rows below row 21, it really makes the task easier if we create a "filter" on row 21.

5.   Select row 21 in the IIF table above and then select Filter from the Sort and Filter icon in the ribbon.

Figure 7-70 After selecting row 21 in the IIF file, select Filter from the Sort & Filter icon in the Ribbon bar

The Filter command makes each of the columns in the "Header Row" into special

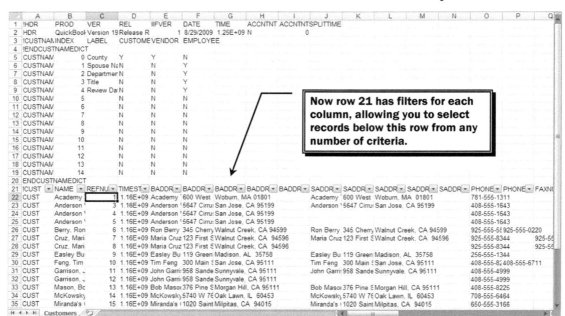

Figure 7-71 Row 21 now has been set as the filter header row

Filtered data displays only the rows that meet criteria that you specify and hides rows that you do not want displayed. After you filter data, you can copy, find, edit, format, chart, and print the subset of filtered data without rearranging or moving it.

You can also filter by more than one column. Filters are additive, which means that each additional filter is based on the current filter and further reduces the subset of data.

6. For our example, we'll set a filter on the "Phone" column to select only those customers who have a phone that begins with Area Code 408, and contains the prefix -555-. Notice that by clicking on the down-arrow in each column, you see a menu with all the options for setting filters on that column. You could click in the boxes to the left of each of the data elements shown, or you can create a "custom filter" to have Excel calculate which records to show.

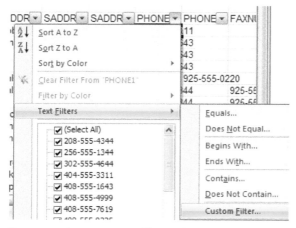

Figure 7-72 Setting a custom filter on the rows in the table

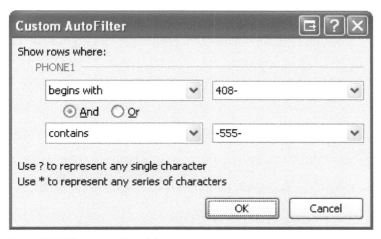

Figure 7-73 The custom filter definition

7. After setting the filter on the Phone column to the criteria shown in Figure 7-73, the list now will only display a subset of the records.

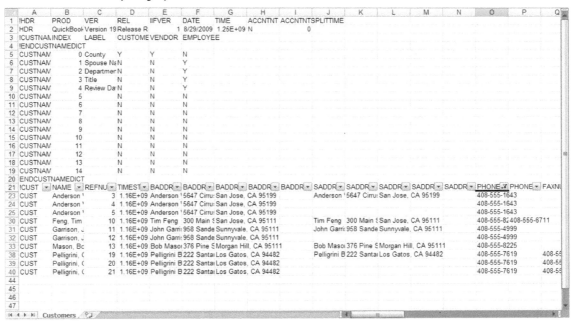

Figure 7-74 The filtered list

With this filtered list, it's easy to do mass updating. For example, if all of those phone numbers have a new area code, you could use the Find/Replace command in Excel to change all of them with one command.

8. In Excel select Replace from the Find & Select icon.

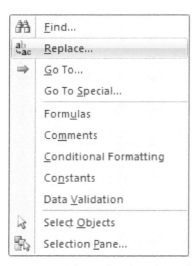

Figure 7-75 Select Replace from the Find & Select icon on the Home ribbon

9.   For example, if the area code changes from 408 to 346, enter these numbers into the replace
      command and click Replace All.

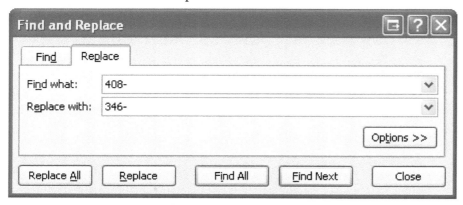

Figure 7-76 Replace command to change 408- to 346-

Figure 7-77 Confirmation of the replacements

Now all of the phone numbers for the filtered list have been changed.

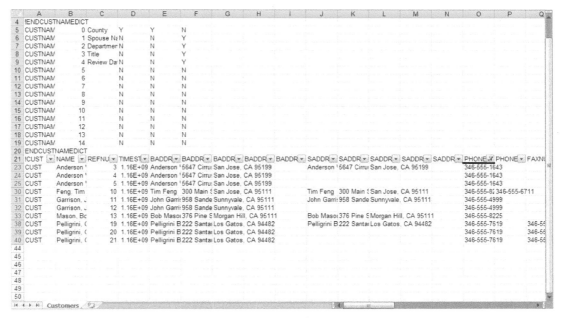

Figure 7-78 The filtered list with all of the phone numbers changed.

At this point, you can continue filtering the list in different ways, making similar modifications until you get all the changes made. When you're finished, save the file in the same format as it was (i.e. do not save it as an excel file).

10. Click the save icon, or press Ctrl=S. On the warning screen below, click Yes to continue saving the IIF file in the text (Tab delimited) format.

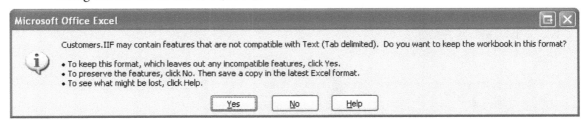

Figure 7-79 Tab delimited file warning. Click Yes.

11. After the file is saved, close it from Excel. Excel will ask you if you want to save it *again*, but this time just click No. You already saved it in the format you want in the previous step.

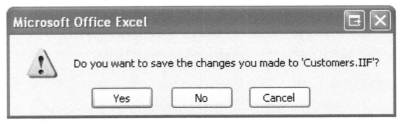

Figure 7-80 File close warning. Click No on this screen.

Now you're ready to import the modified IIF back into QuickBooks.

Importing IIF Files

To import an IIF file, follow the steps in this example:

1. From the *File* menu select **Utilities**, then **Import**, and then **IIF Files**.

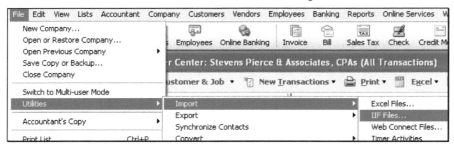

Figure 7-81 Select Import from IIF files in QuickBooks

2. In the *Import* window, browse to locate the desired folder and select the **Customers.IIF** file. Click **Open** (see Figure 7-37).

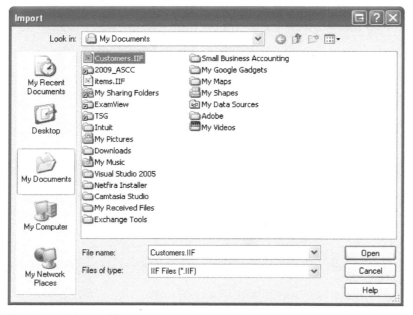

Figure 7-82 Select the file to import

3. QuickBooks displays a dialog box that says, "Your data has been imported." Click **OK**.

Now you've completed the process of exporting the list, making all the needed changes in Excel, and then importing the list back into QuickBooks. All your changes can be viewed in the QuickBooks list.

Warnings:

1. Note that in general the IIF file format is not recommended. However, for this specific example of doing list exports, cleanup, and imports, the IIF format works great.

2. Also, you cannot use this method to modify the "Name" field on any of the lists. The name field is the "primary key" for each of the lists, and it uses that field to match up the records you import and then update the fields with the new data in the IIF file. So if you modify the

name field in the list, there will be new records added to the list when you import the IIF file.

3. You cannot use this method to delete names from any list. You can add new ones, and modify existing ones only.

The slow season is a great time to approach your clients and propose a "clean up" engagement. It's a great billable service to help your consulting business, and the clients will benefit from more efficient data entry (e.g., all the invoices will populate with complete, accurate information), plus you'll be able to reduce the likelihood of big problems at tax time.

Starting Over with a New Data File (or Removing All Data)

If fixing the setup issues and/or cleaning up incorrect data is more timing consuming than is economically viable (i.e., it would cost more to fix it that it's worth), it's probably better to start over.

Salvaging As Much Data as Possible When Starting Over

When you start over with a new file, you will want to salvage as much data as possible. In particular, you probably want to salvage:

- User and Company Preferences.
- The user-level customizations of the Icon Bar.
- All lists in the data file, including Items, Payroll Items, Accounts, Customers, Vendors, Employees, etc.
- All open transactions, including Open Invoices, Open Estimates, Open Sales Orders and Unapplied Credit Memos, Open Purchase Orders, Item Receipts, Unpaid Bills and Unapplied Bill Credits.
- Customized Form Templates.
- Memorized Reports.
- Memorized Transactions.

Perform the steps in this exampleavoid re-entering this information:

1. Select the **File** menu, select **Utilities,** and then select **Clean Up Company Data.**

2. On the *Clean Up Company Data* window, select **Remove ALL transactions** (see Figure 7-83).

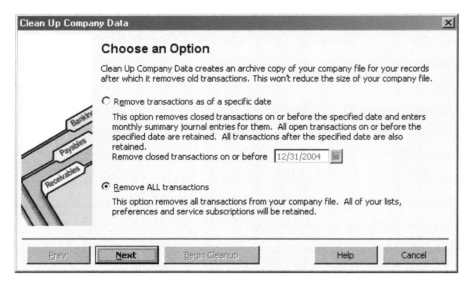

Figure 7-83 Clean Up Company Data window

3.   QuickBooks displays a dialogue window warning you that continuing with this process will remove all data from the data file. Click **Yes**. See Figure 7-84.

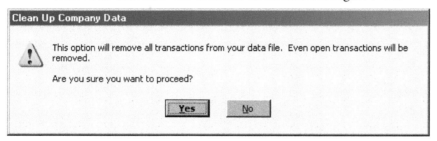

Figure 7-84 Clean Up Company Data warning message

4.   If you have payroll transactions in the current year, QuickBooks will not allow you to remove all data from the file. Instead, QuickBooks displays the window shown in Figure 7-85. If you do receive this message and are using the Standard or Enhanced Payroll Processing, proceed to the next step. If you do not receive this warning message, proceed to 11. Note: If you do receive this warning and the Assisted Payroll Processing from Intuit is used, you MUST start by creating a new file with the Assisted Payroll technical support department and they will walk you through the steps for creating a disaster recovery file.

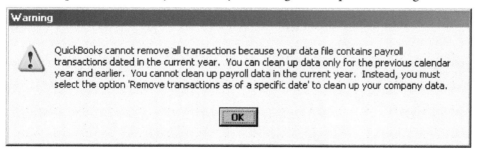

Figure 7-85 Clean Up Company Data warning regarding payroll transactions in the current year

5.   To bypass this restriction, close all of the programs on the computer, including QuickBooks.

6. In Windows, double-click the time in the bottom right corner of the screen. Windows will display the Date and Time Properties window shown in Figure 7-86.

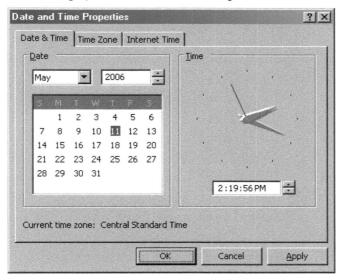

Figure 7-86 Windows Date and Time Properties window

7. Change the Windows system date to the first day of the following year (e.g. **January** 1, 20XX).

8. Re-open QuickBooks and click **No** if you are prompted to enter any memorized transactions. You may have to click **No** several times to bypass all of the memorized transactions.

9. Click **No** if QuickBooks prompts you to update payroll tax tables, to mark Reminders as *Done*, or to respond to any other date-sensitive messages.

10. Perform 1 through 3 above to re-run the Clean Up Company Data utility.

11. QuickBooks displays the window shown in Figure 7-87. Click **Begin Cleanup** to remove all data from the file.

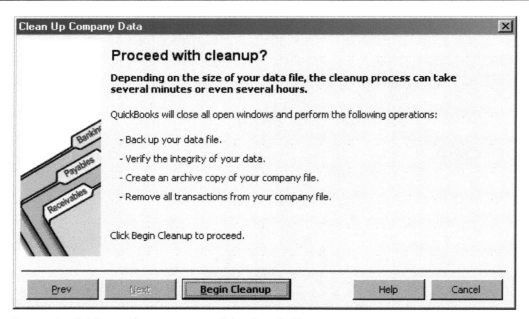

*Figure 7-87 Click **Begin Cleanup** to remove all data from the file*

12.   QuickBooks will prompt you to create a backup of the data file. Give this backup a special name to indicate that it's the last backup before condensing the file.

13.   QuickBooks will back up the data file, create an "archive copy" of the data file, verify data integrity, and then remove all transactions from the file. QuickBooks does not require any user action to complete all of these processes.

> **Note:** Removing all of the data from the file can be a very time consuming process. With large data files, QuickBooks may temporarily go into a "Not Responding" mode. It is best to schedule the *Remove All Transactions* activity so that you can give it several hours to complete. It is also best to close all programs on your computer, including any programs that start up automatically – located in the task bar on the bottom right of the screen.

14.   After the *Remove All Transactions* process is finished, perform a Data File Setup using the "stripped" data file. There is no need to perform the preliminary steps since you already have all of the list entries you need. However, you may need to edit the lists before you begin entering opening balances.

> **Tip:** There are software utilities available that allow you to transfer transactions between QuickBooks files. Here is a list of three utilities that can be used to copy data from your old file to your new (blank) data file.
>
> Data File Transfer Utility by Karl Irvin www.q2q.us/dtuoverview.htm
> Data Flow Manager from Atandra Systems, www.atandra.com/Prod_DFM.htm
> DataMover from Personable, Inc. www.personable.com/datamover/overview.asp
>
> You can find these and other solutions at www.marketplace.intuit.com. However, when you import transactions from the old file into the new, empty file, partially open transactions will import as fully open. If the client's file contains partially paid, partially received and partially billed transactions you will need to modify each of those transactions after you transfer them into the new file.

> **Note:**
> Timesheet data is not removed during the **Remove All Transactions** process.
>
> **Tip:**
> If you are starting a client over with a new file, you may want to create prior year comparison reports in your new file. Enter a journal entry for each month or quarter of the previous reporting year that summarizes P&L and Balance Sheet balances.

Client Data Review Tool

Overview of Features

The Client Data Review (CDR) tool was first included with the QuickBooks Accountant 2009 and QuickBooks Enterprise Solutions Accountant 9.0 versions. The CDR tool allows the accountant to review, detect, and correct errors in the client's data file. In a nutshell, the tool consists of the following features:

- A customizable master control screen with a checklist-style view that provides access to tools and reports used by the reviewing accountant. This master control screen tracks the "status" of each review task (not started, in progress, completed or not applicable) and allows you to keep "task notes" as you perform the data review.

- A printable "status" of your review progress that includes the status of each review task along with notes about each task.

- A "freeze" feature that takes a snapshot of your prior period reviewed balances. The next time you review the client's file your stored balances are compared to current QuickBooks balances for that review period. If CDR finds a difference, it recommends a journal entry to restore your original balances.

- Several tools are provided that allow you to detect problems (or verify accuracy) of transactions in the client data file. These tools provide review at the account level for any account in the general ledger, as well as tools to verify sales tax, inventory, payroll, and "links" between transactions. Incorrect links are often the cause of inaccurate financial statement reports. For example, when a payment is applied to an invoice, QuickBooks creates a link between the two transactions. If for example you find an incorrect "link" between a payment and an invoice (e.g. if the payment is applied to the wrong invoice), this could cause big problems in the reports, especially the cash basis financial statements.

- In addition to tracking changes to transactions, as is provided by the Audit Trail, the CDR tool tracks changes to the QuickBooks lists including additions, deletions, merges and edits to list items. This includes the Chart of Accounts, the Item list, the Fixed Asset Item list and the Payroll Item list.

Starting a Client Data Review

The CDR tool (shown in Figure 7-88) is launched from the Accountant menu in both QuickBooks Accountant and QuickBooks Enterprise Solutions Accountant.

> Note:
> You can also access the CDR in any QuickBooks Pro or Premier or QuickBooks Enterprise
> Solutions by using an External Accountant User. For more information on the External
> Accountant User, see page 355.

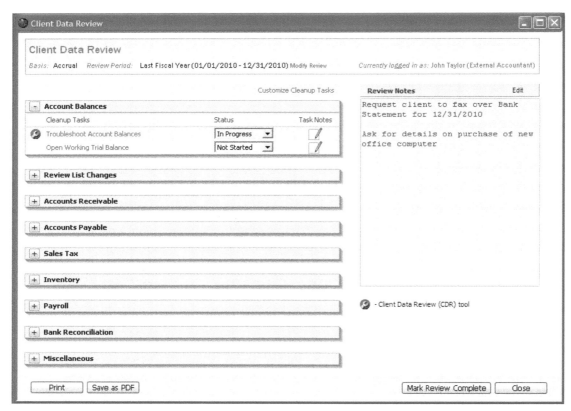

Figure 7-88 Client Data Review

The header at the top of Client Data Review control screen displays the review basis (accrual or cash) and the review period (specific date range). Also, the CDR will indicate when you are logged into the data file with the new External Accountant User type (see Figure 7-88). Although the CDR tool only works in single-user mode, it is possible for multiple reviewers (users) to work on the same file and perform review tasks. This allows the audit trail to report on the activities of each reviewer separately and it also allows reviewers to document their work using the task notes.

Customizing the Client Data Review

You can customize the view you have in the CDR center to make it unique for each client's QuickBooks file. To customize the task list, click **Customize Cleanup Tasks** at the top center of the CDR feature as shown in Figure 7-89.

Figure 7-89 Customize Cleanup Tasks

You can select the categories or tasks you want displayed in the Client Data Review tool to customize the review tasks for each QuickBooks data file (see Figure 7-90).

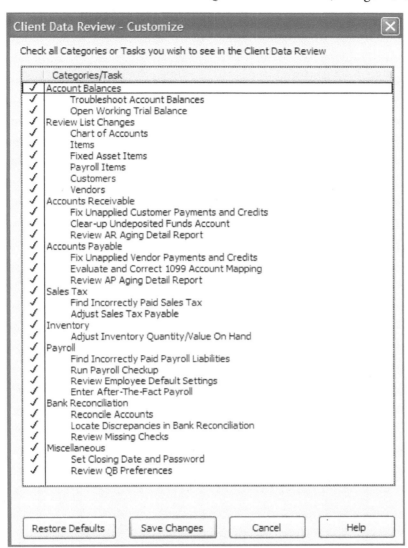

Figure 7-90 Customize the tasks you want to display. These settings are specific to each QuickBooks data file.

Client Data Review Tasks and Reports

The following sections provide general information about each of the Client Data Review tasks and reports.

Troubleshooting Account Balances

The Troubleshooting Account Balances (as shown in Figure 7-91) displays the current account balances and the "frozen" balances from the last review. Any differences are highlighted in the *Difference* column. You can set the view to *Only show accounts with different balances*.

You can create a new *Transaction Change Report*, listing those changes since the last review period, allowing you to drill down to the specific transaction(s) creating the difference.

If CDR finds a difference, a recommended journal entry to restore your original balances is prepared for your review. The journal entry can be modified if needed prior to saving so that you remain in control. Some re-work of the journal entry may be needed if both Accounts Receivable and Accounts Payable had differences. This is due to the limitation with a QuickBooks journal entry not allowing and adjustment to both Accounts Receivable and Accounts Payable in the same journal entry.

The *Last Review Balances* are updated after the completion of each review. These balances cannot be changed by clients.

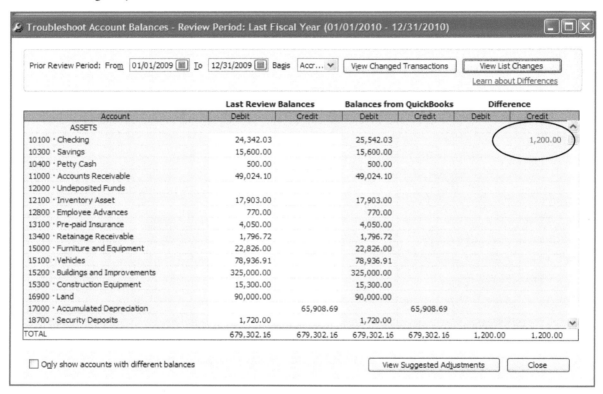

Figure 7-91 QuickBooks identifies differences between your reviewed balances and current data

Tracking Changes to QuickBooks Lists

QuickBooks 2009 and later tracks changes to list elements. The *Chart of Accounts, Items, Fixed Asset Items*, and *Payroll Items* lists are tracked when list elements are added, deleted, merged or edited.

To access the Review List Changes dialog as shown below in Figure 7-92, click on the + sign in front of the Review List Changes task in the CDR tool (as shown previously in Figure 7-88) to expand the menu options.

Once expanded, you can click the CDR Review List Changes link for Chart of Accounts, Items, Fixed Asset Items and Payroll Items. Optionally, once a Review List Changes menu is opened, you can also move between the lists by clicking on the tabs at the top of the Review List Changes dialog as shown in Figure 7-92 below.

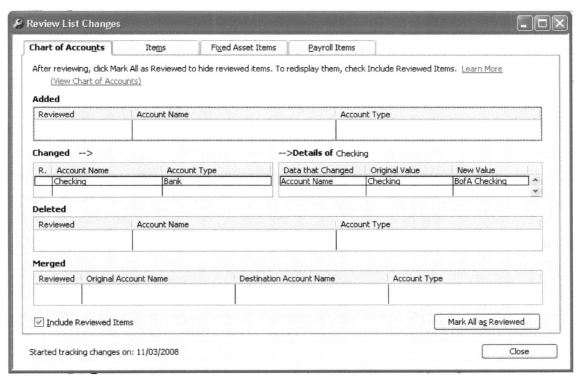

Figure 7-92 Review List Changes

Fix Unapplied Customer Payments and Credits

Often your clients will create a credit memo or receive a payment from a customer but not apply it to the original open invoice. The net total on the Aging Summary report is correct, but when looking at the Open Invoices report, both the credit memo or unapplied payment and open invoice amount are still listed.

To access the Fix Unapplied Customer Payments and Credits dialog as shown below in Figure 7-93, click on the + sign in front of the Accounts Receivable task in the CDR tool (as shown previously in Figure 7-88) to expand the menu options including a link to open this tool.

Use the new CDR clean-up feature to apply the open credit or unapplied payment to the open invoice as shown in Figure 7-93.

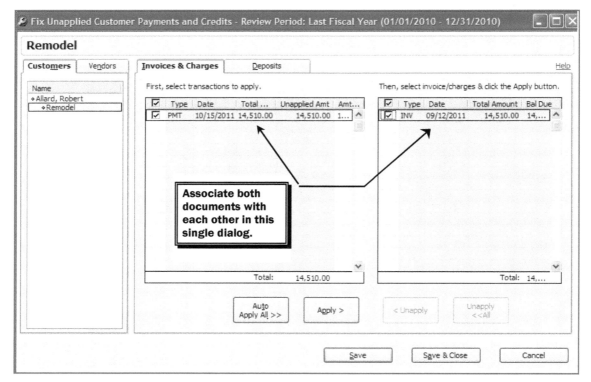

Figure 7-93 Apply open customer credits with open invoices

The window will only show those customers with open credits or payments that need to be applied. You can apply them one at a time, or select a customer on the left and auto apply to all transactions.

> **Note:**
> This feature is only available when you are working in a client's working file (.QBW file extension). The feature described here is not available when working with the Accountant's Copy of the client's data file.

Batch Write-Off

The *Batch Write-Off* tool does exactly what it says, it allows you to write-off uncollectable invoices in one step. From the *Accountant* menu, select **Client Data Review**. In the *Accounts Receivable* section of this window, select **Write Off Invoices** (see Figure 7-94).

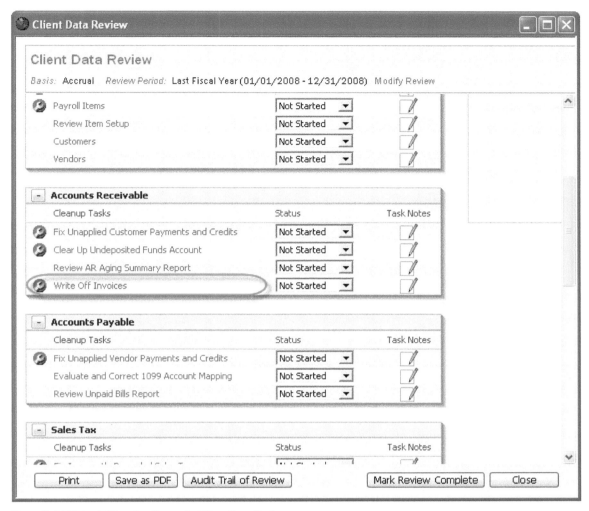

Figure 7-94 Write Off Invoices feature in Client Data Review

The *Write Off Invoices* window (see Figure 7-95) will appear, indicating all invoices that are aged beyond a certain number of days, which can be specified as greater than 120 days, 180 days, a custom period, or for a certain review period. In addition, the list can be refined for smaller balances that are not worth pursuing to collection. The transaction type can be filtered for invoices, finance charges, and statement charges or all three. The date of the write-off, the write-off account (shown in Figure 7-95 as *60300 Bad Debts*) and (if desired) the class are specified in this window.

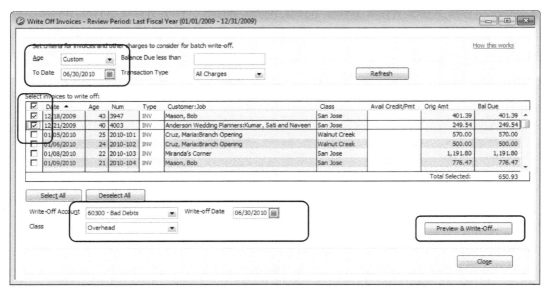

Figure 7-95 Choose the open receivables to write off

As with many lists in QuickBooks, this list of outstanding transactions can be sorted by many parameters by clicking on the appropriate column header. In Figure 7-95, the column header *Age* has been selected (twice) so that the outstanding transactions appear in descending order by age.

Select *Preview & Write-Off* to get to the confirmation screen and write off the outstanding receivables chosen.

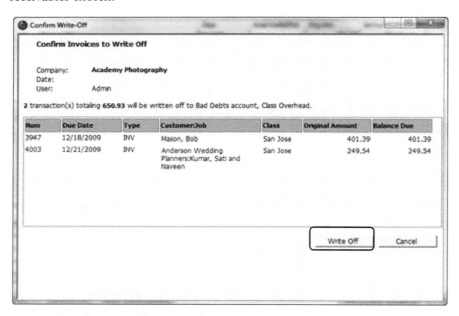

Figure 7-96 Confirm receivables to write off

Select **Write Off** in *Confirm Write-Off* window (see Figure 7-96). A window will appear detailing which invoices have been written off (see Figure 7-97), the date of the write-off, the account, and the class (if applicable). This window can be saved to a PDF if desired.

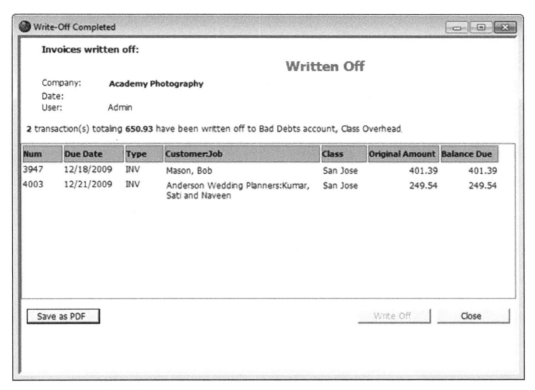

Figure 7-97 Write-Off Completed

Batch Reclassify

Very often an accountant will have to reclassify a number of transactions posted by his or her client. These reclassifications can be done by editing each entry and correcting the posting, or, in days gone by, by creating a journal entry to move the balance from one account to another for the period in question. If the client has created an erroneous general ledger account for one vendor, it would be easy to merge that account with the correct account where all that vendor's entries should have been posted. However, that is not always the situation. Sometimes the two general ledger accounts should not be merged. Other times it's not all transactions that were posted for a certain vendor but only *some* of them.

To remedy this problem, the Batch Write-off tool has been introduced. From the *Accountant* menu, select **Client Data Review**. In the *Account Balances* section of this window, select **Reclassify Transactions** (see Figure 7-98).

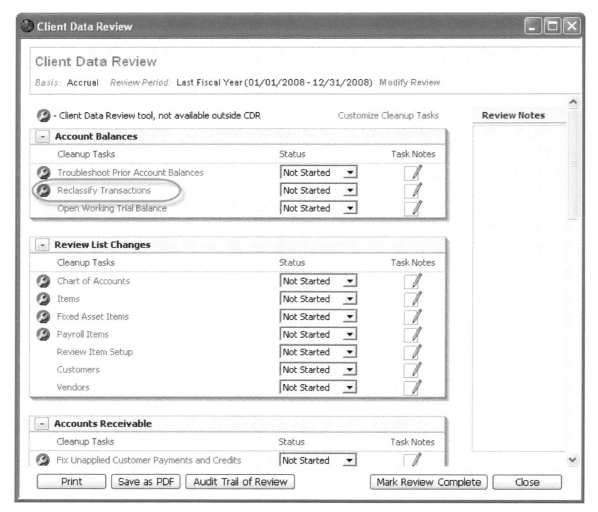

Figure 7-98 Reclassify Transactions feature in Client Data Review

Once the *Reclassify Transactions* window opens (see Figure 7-99), select the vendor, the date range, the range of transactions (including those that can be reclassified and those which cannot, such as item-based transactions), and whether or not journal entries can be included. The reclassification account and class (if applicable) are chosen as well. Note that one can select each transaction to be reclassified with a checkmark, and that each transaction is displayed with its current posting account and class for reference. Also, the *Profit & Loss Standard*, *Profit & Loss Detail*, *Balance Sheet*, and *Item Setup* screens can be reviewed from this window in order to determine what needs to be corrected.

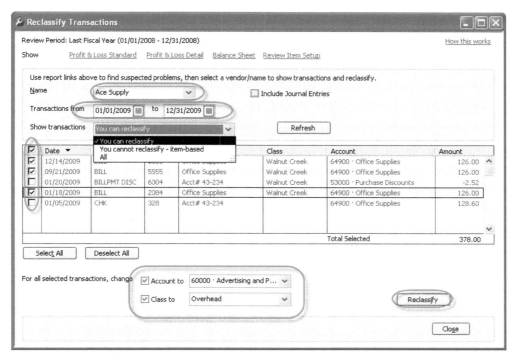

Figure 7-99 Reclassify Transactions options

Select the appropriate vendor, the transactions in question, the reclassification account and class, and then select **Reclassify**. The list of transactions for the vendor in question will be refreshed in the prior window with the transactions in question for that vendor showing the desired posting account and class (see Figure 7-100).

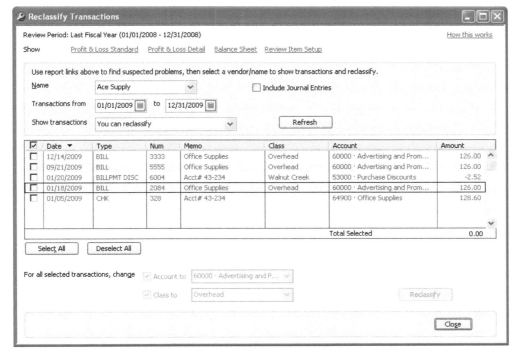

Figure 7-100 Transactions have been reclassified

Clear-up Undeposited Funds Account

When a client creates a customer receive payment but does not properly include that customer payment in a Make Deposit form, the result is a growing balance in the Undeposited Funds account on the balance sheet.

To access the Clear-up Undeposited Funds Account dialog as shown below in Figure 7-101, click on the + sign in front of the Accounts Receivable task in the CDR tool (as shown previously in Figure 7-88) to expand the menu options including a link to open this tool.

The Client Data Review provides a one-screen view (see Figure 7-101) of all customer payments that are included in the Undeposited Funds balance and any Make Deposit forms that were recorded and assigned to that customer.

You can associate the customer receive payment transaction to the make deposit form. The result is that the customer payment is no longer included in the Undeposited Funds account balance and the overstatement in the account used in the make deposit form is reversed. Note, you will have a credit in the accounts receivable account if the customer payment was not applied to an invoice.

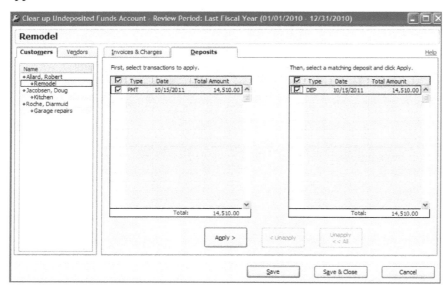

Figure 7-101 Fix client data when payments were not included on a Make Deposit

Fix Unapplied Vendor Payments and Credits

Some clients may create a vendor bill and create a vendor credit without applying the credit to the original open vendor bill.

To access the Fix Unapplied Vendor Payments and Credits feature click on the + sign in front of the Accounts Payable task in the CDR tool (as shown previously in Figure 7-88) to expand the menu options including a link to open this tool.

The options available with this feature are very similar in design to those in Figure 7-93 showing open customer credits.

Quick access is provided to assigning open vendor credits while working in the dialog shown in Figure 7-93by clicking on the Vendors tab to the right of the Customers tab. With the Fix Unapplied Vendor Payments and Credits, you have easy access to one window to apply the credit to the bill.

> Note:
> This feature is only available when you are working in a client's working file (.QBW file extension). The feature described here is not available when working with a client's Accountant's Copy file.

Fix Incorrectly Paid Sales Tax

Many of us have clients who do not use the sales tax utility properly, issuing regular checks to the tax agency in question. Although the general ledger may be fine, the records of what taxes have been filed in QuickBooks are not. That is the reason why the tool *Fix Incorrectly Recorded Sales Tax* was added to the *Client Data Review*.

From the *Accountant* menu, select **Client Data Review**. In the *Sales Tax* section of this window, select **Fix Incorrectly Recorded Sales Tax** (see Figure 7-102).

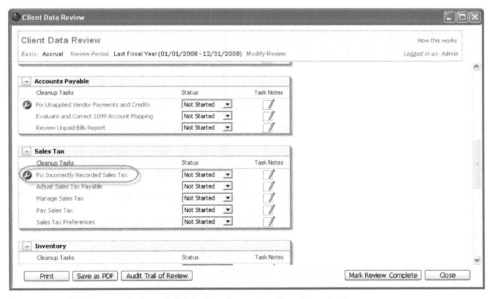

Figure 7-102 Fix Incorrectly Recorded Sales Tax feature in Client Data Review

By selecting **Fix Incorrectly Recorded Sales Tax**, one can see in the review period chosen that a regular check was written to the tax agency State Board of Equalization, rather than the proper procedure for filing taxes. Place a checkmark in the box beside the incorrectly recorded transaction(s) and select **Void & Replace** (see Figure 7-103).

Figure 7-103 Choose to Void & Replace incorrectly recorded sales tax transactions

A *Fix Sales Tax* window will pop up indicating what will be done. Select **Proceed** (see Figure 7-104).

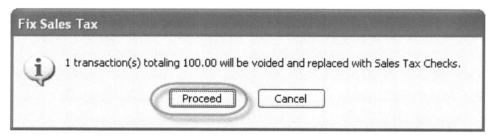

Figure 7-104 Fix Sales Tax window

A new window pops up indicating that the transaction(s) was/were fixed (see Figure 7-105).

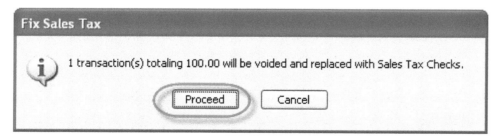

Figure 7-105 The transaction was fixed by QuickBooks

The check number, date and reconciliation status of the replaced check are unchanged. A memo indicating what was done appears on the replacement sales tax check (see Figure 7-106).

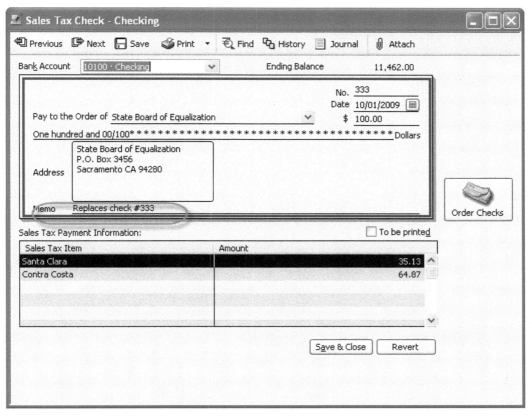

Figure 7-106 Replacement sales tax check

Find Incorrectly Paid Payroll Liabilities

The *Payroll Liabilities Paid by Regular Check* report provides details of transaction that were incorrectly recorded when paying payroll liabilities (Figure 7-107).This report eliminates the need to search through reports and the payroll liabilities register for payments made with the wrong QuickBooks form. If your client assigned an account *other* than the QuickBooks created Payroll Liabilities on a check form, CDR will list those transactions on the report. This Client Data Review custom report helps identify checks paying payroll liabilities but not using the proper payroll liabilities payment form.

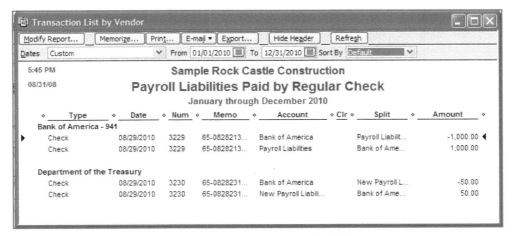

Figure 7-107 Review your client's data file for incorrectly paid payroll liabilities

While the CDR and the *Payroll Liabilities Paid by Regular Check* report help you identify payroll liability payment errors, you will need to take further steps to address any problems, including voiding the original check and re-creating the payment through the Pay Scheduled Liabilities screen or by using the Adjust Payroll Liabilities screen.

New Client Data Review Inventory Tools

You can use the Client Data Review to correct incorrectly posted inventory. This feature will enable the accountant or ProAdvisor to detect inactive items which have a quantity on hand, negative quantities on any item or items with a markup percentage that is less than a threshold specified by you. It will also detect a mismatch between the balance sheet inventory figure and the inventory valuation (the sub-ledger), which can happen any time the client posts transactions to an inventory asset account rather than using items.

To access this feature, From the *Accountant* menu, select **Client Data Review**. In the *Inventory* section of this window, select any of the following: **Review Inventory Setup, Compare Balance Sheet and Inventory Valuation, or Troubleshoot Inventory** (see Figure 7-108).

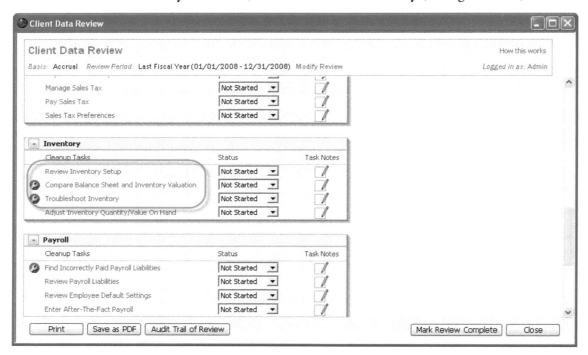

Figure 7-108 Inventory features in Client Data Review

Review Inventory Setup makes use of the new Add/Edit Multiple List Entries feature, enabling the user to make corrections to how items are linked to accounts, as well as many other corrections, all in one screen (see Figure 7-109). The columns can be customized in this window so that the user can review and correct any of the chosen parameters that refer to items such as name, price, description, tax code, and links to inventory, cost of goods sold, and sales accounts on the chart of accounts. In fact, new values and links can be copied and pasted as a block from an Excel spreadsheet if desired, minimizing the work.

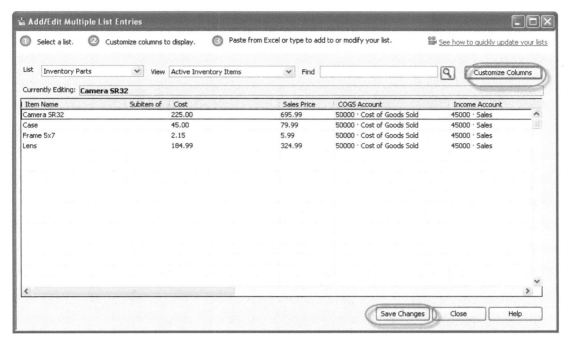

Figure 7-109 Review Inventory Setup feature in Client Data Review makes use of Add/Edit Multiple List Entries feature

Once changing an account link, the familiar QuickBooks message appears asking if all prior transactions using this changed item should have the same link, thereby changing the posting of those transactions (see Figure 7-110). It is up to the user how to answer this question.

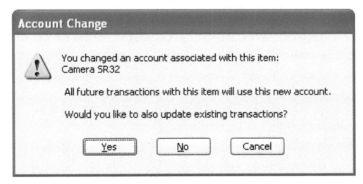

Figure 7-110 Once an item's link has been changed, this familiar window pops up

Compare Balance Sheet and Inventory Valuation compares the value of inventory on the *Balance Sheet* to the total in the *Inventory Valuation Summary* report (see Figure 7-111). A green circle indicates that they match.

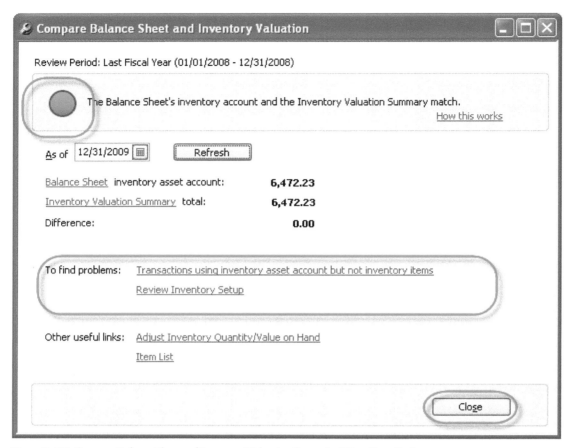

Figure 7-111 Compare Balance Sheet and Inventory Valuation feature in Client Data Review

Troubleshoot Inventory looks for negative quantities, items with lower than a chosen percentage markup, or inactive items with a quantity on hand (see Figure 7-112).

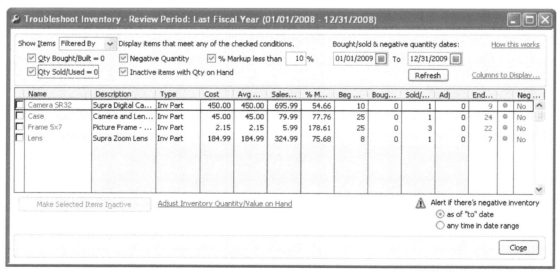

Figure 7-112 Troubleshoot Inventory feature in Client Data Review

This allows the user to change prices, inactivate certain items, and adjust the quantity/value on hand directly from this screen.

Marking a Review as Complete

After reviewing your client's data for a specific accounting period, you can finalize the review by clicking **Mark Review Complete**. Marking a review complete will transfer your reviewed balances to the Last Review Balances column in the Troubleshooting Account Balances task (see Figure 7-91) and it will prompt you to print a report of the review (see Figure 7-113).

When starting a new review, you can open the prior review or continue to a new review period.

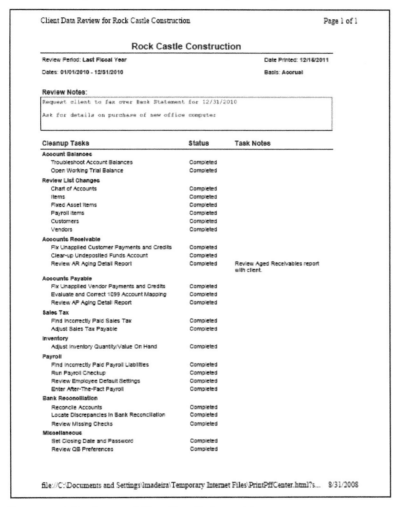

Figure 7-113 Final report of Client Data Review activity

External Accountant User Designation

With the user type External Accountant (Figure 7-114) allows complete Admin access (with the exception that you cannot create or edit users or view sensitive customer credit card numbers) and access to the CDR feature.

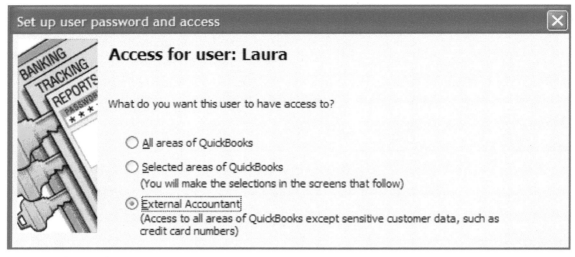

Figure 7-114 External Accountant user type

As an accounting professional using the Client Data Review tool, you will want to request that your client create a user name for you and assign the new External Accountant Type. If you have the Admin login, then you can create a new External Accountant user type for yourself.

Summary

In this chapter, you learned about managing QuickBooks data files to ensure that they are kept in good condition. Here are the topics covered:

- About QuickBooks files and file extensions in Windows (page 273)
- How to backup QuickBooks data files (page 281)
- How to restore QuickBooks backup files (page 285)
- Portable company files, and how to work with them (page 289)
- Using the Accountant's Copy (page 291)
- Importing and exporting data in QuickBooks (page 297)
- Using the Clean Up Data utility in QuickBooks (page 317)
- Cleaning up your Data with Excel (page 322)
- When and how to start a new data file (page 321)

Chapter 8
Versions and Conversions

Objectives

In this chapter, you'll learn about the different versions and editions of QuickBooks and how to update and convert files from version to version. You'll learn:

- How to upgrade QuickBooks as new versions are released by Intuit (page 357)
- How to install several versions of QuickBooks on the same computer (page 357)
- How patches can be downloaded and installed to update QuickBooks (page 358)
- How to upgrade data files from one version to the next (page 361)
- When you should consider upgrading to QuickBooks Enterprise Solutions (page 362)
- Converting data files from the Macintosh version to the Windows version (page 363)
- Converting data files from the Windows version to the Macintosh version (page 365)
- Converting data files from Quicken (page 368)
- Converting data files from QuickBooks for Windows to QuickBooks Online (page 369)
- Converting data files from QuickBooks Online to QuickBooks for Windows (page 373)

Upgrading QuickBooks

Every year or so, Intuit releases a new version of QuickBooks. It is best to have your clients upgrade to the most recent version each year, but many clients will be reluctant to do so. Therefore, as a consultant you will need to support more than one version of QuickBooks. The process of upgrading to the new version is usually uneventful: Install the new software and the first time the data file is opened a warning will appear stating that the data file is from an older version, would you like to convert it. If you say yes, it will prompt you for creating a backup of the data file, and then will proceed with the conversion.

Installing Several QuickBooks Versions on Your Hard Disk

When you run the installation program, it allows you to specify the directory where you want to install the new version of QuickBooks. By default, the installer wants to overwrite the old version by installing into the same directory where the previous version was installed. For your clients, this is usually fine since they will not need to access the older version of the software once the conversion has been completed.

However, if you need to work with clients who have older versions, you should keep the older versions on your hard disk. To install a new version and keep the older version, create a new directory for each new version of QuickBooks you install. For example, when you're upgrading to QuickBooks 200X, override the directory in the installation screens to place the program in a new folder called c:\Program Files\Intuit\QuickBooks\QuickBooks 200X. See Figure 8-1.

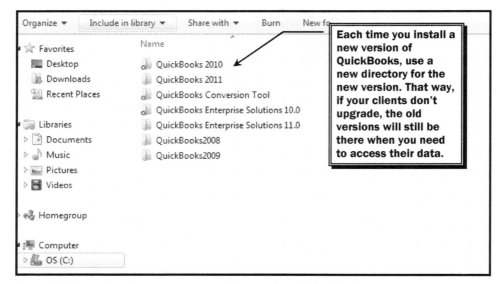

Figure 8-1 Windows Explorer showing separate directories for each QuickBooks version

Release Levels of QuickBooks

Although Intuit releases a new version of QuickBooks each year, there are small "patches" they make as they find problems in the software throughout the life of each version.

Each patch is released to users via the Internet. The *Update QuickBooks* screen (under the *File* menu on older versions, but under the *Help* menu in QuickBooks 2006 and later versions) is where you go to download, install, and configure your QuickBooks updates. Each patch increases the ***Release Level*** of the QuickBooks application. To see what release level of the software you have, type **Ctrl+1 (or F2)** while QuickBooks is running.

Figure 8-2 Press F2 to see which version and release level of QuickBooks you have.

To patch your software with the latest *maintenance release*, follow the steps in this example:

1.   From the *Help* menu (*File* menu in versions before 2006), select **Update QuickBooks**.

2.   In the *Update QuickBooks* screen, click on the *Options* tab (see Figure 8-3).

3.   In this screen you can configure QuickBooks to automatically update itself whenever new patches are released by Intuit. You can also "share downloads" with other users on the network. You should set the "share downloads" setting if you have several users on different computers accessing the same data file. That way, you'll be sure to keep everyone on the network up to date on the latest QuickBooks patches.

4.   The "Download Location" is the path to the folder where downloaded QuickBooks updates are stored before they are installed. If you share downloads, this path will change to the directory where your QuickBooks data file is stored.

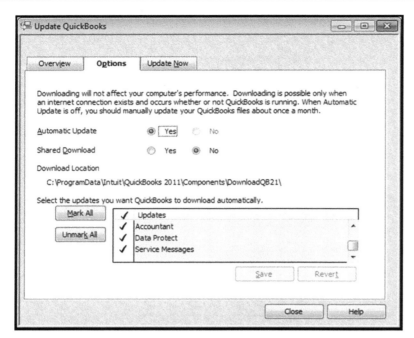

Figure 8-3 Update QuickBooks options screen

5.   To update QuickBooks, click the *Update Now* tab, and then click **Get Updates**.

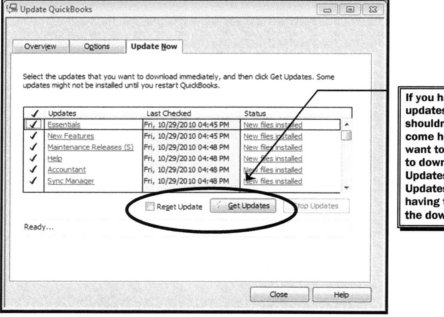

If you have automatic updates set, you shouldn't need to come here, but if you want to force updates to download, click Get Updates. Click Reset Updates if you're having trouble with the downloads.

Figure 8-4 Update QuickBooks options screen

6.   If you're having trouble getting the updates to download or install, try clicking **Reset Update** and then click **Get Updates** again. The download may take 10 minutes or more depending on your Internet connection speed.

7.   In some cases, it may be necessary to manually download patches from the Internet by going directly to the QuickBooks support site at www.quickbooks.com/support/updates.html. Follow the instructions there to download and install patches.

> **Note:** You can provide upgrade assistance to your clients that are not connected to the Internet. Download the updates from the QuickBooks website and burn them onto a CD or memory stick before your next visit to the client site.

Upgrading Data Files from Previous Versions

QuickBooks is upward compatible. This means that you can create a company file in one version and that file will be usable in any future version of QuickBooks. However, the reverse is not true. That is, if you create a data file in version 2015 of QuickBooks, you won't be able to work with the file in version 2014 or earlier versions. Also, as discussed on page 358, occasionally, different releases of the same version cannot exchange files. The same applies to upgrading to QuickBooks Enterprise Solutions. That is, once you upgrade, you won't be able to open the data file with any of the QuickBooks editions.

The first time you open your company file after installing a new version of QuickBooks, you'll get the message shown in Figure 8-5.

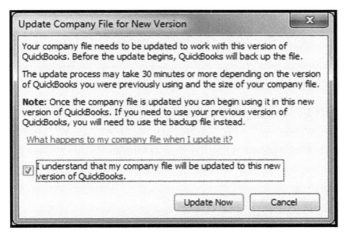

Figure 8-5 Update file message appears the first time you open a file with a new version of QuickBooks.

After you check the box and click **Update Now**, QuickBooks will convert your file to the new version, but it asks you to make a backup of the file before it converts. Make sure you store the backup file in a safe place. Also, you might want to name the file with the version that can open the file. For example, if you're upgrading from version 2014 to 2015, this backup file might be named "BeforeVer2015.QBB". That way, you'll know just by looking at the file name that version 2014 can open (restore) that backup file.

Maintenance Releases Effect on Data Files

Occasionally when a new maintenance release is installed, your data file must also be updated to work with the new release. This is an unfortunate necessity with many computer programs, but it is particularly unfortunate with QuickBooks files because it often causes Accountants to be unable to trade files with their clients. The problem occurs when you upgrade to a new release before your client (or vice versa), and that maintenance release changes the data file format. In these rare cases, after you install the new release, you will not be able to open the data file with earlier releases of the same version. Not to worry though, you will be warned by an onscreen message before applying the patch if it will result in incompatible data files.

Data File Compatibility Among QuickBooks Versions and Editions

QuickBooks Simple Start, Pro, and Premier (any edition) can use each other's files. This means that a file created in QuickBooks Pro can be used with the same "year version" of QuickBooks Simple Start, or with any of the Premier editions. However, since QuickBooks Simple Start does not have all the features that are available in the higher editions, you won't be able to access the advanced features in the Simple Start edition. That means, for example, that timesheets created in a company file using QuickBooks Pro or Premier won't be accessible when using the file with QuickBooks Simple Start.

> **Note:** As of the 2006 versions, QuickBooks Basic is no longer sold by Intuit. Simple Start is now the lowest priced QuickBooks product. It includes the ability to create invoices and estimates, write checks and accept credit cards.

QuickBooks Enterprise Solutions is essentially a different "version" in that you can upgrade files to Enterprise, but you cannot trade files back and forth between Enterprise and Premier, Pro, or Simple Start. So once you upgrade to Enterprise, you cannot use that data file with any of the other Editions (Simple Start, Pro, or Premier).

> **Note:** As there are many differences between the editions of QuickBooks it is recommended that you familiarize yourself with each version. QuickBooks Accountant allows you to **Toggle to Another Edition** so that you can compare the differences.

Upgrading to QuickBooks Enterprise Solutions

QuickBooks Enterprise Solutions provides larger companies with enhanced performance and features. If you have outgrown QuickBooks Premier by exceeding the file size recommendations (see page 678), or exceeding the limitations in lists, or if you need to have more than 5 users access the data file simultaneously, then you should consider upgrading to the Enterprise Solutions edition of QuickBooks. Enterprise Solutions also allows for more granular permissions levels. See page 393 for a more in-depth study of Enterprise Solutions.

Important: All of the features, workarounds, recommendations, and troubleshooting techniques in this book apply directly to the Enterprise Solutions product.

The key differences in the QuickBooks Enterprise Solutions product are:

- Supports up to 30 simultaneous users.
- Tracks 100,000+ Parts or Service Items (marketing materials state list limits at one million but testing has been limited).
- Tracks 100,000+ Names (Customers, Vendors, Employees, Other Names).
- Improved performance, especially with reports in multi-user environments.
- Better multi-user functionality (can do more without switching to single user).

- Better ability to configure user privileges (115+ different options) to allow some and prevent other activities on a user-by-user basis including view only access.
- Up to 15 custom fields in the item list, and up to 12 custom fields in customer, vendor and employee lists

For complete information on list sizes in Enterprise compared with the other editions of QuickBooks, see page 677.

Converting Data Files from Macintosh to Windows

A QuickBooks file on the Macintosh platform does not have the same file format as a Windows QuickBooks file, but there is some ability to convert files between the different platforms.

To convert a QuickBooks file on the Macintosh to Windows, you will need to be sure the process works on the versions you are using. Please check QuickBooks ProAdvisor Support.

> **Note:** If you are transferring files by CD or USB memory drive, you must create a file in QuickBooks for Mac using a media device that is formatted for Windows. See the Mac Help for more information about formatting a Windows disk.

The process of converting a file includes creating a backup file from QuickBooks for Mac and then restoring the file on a Windows computer with QuickBooks 2006 or higher. QuickBooks automatically converts the data to Windows format.

Follow the steps in this example to convert from Macintosh to Windows:

1. If necessary, upgrade to the latest version of QuickBooks for the Macintosh and open the company file.

2. If both computers do not have access to the same network, use a PC-formatted USB drive on the Macintosh, or use any one of several internet methods of transferring the company file backup.

3. From the *File* menu select **Create a file for QuickBooks Windows**. See Figure 8-6.

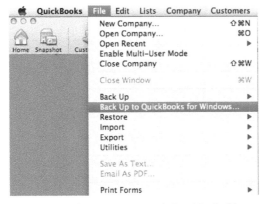

Figure 8-6 Backing up a Macintosh QuickBooks file to send to Windows

4. On the Enter Password window, enter a password for the file. Or choose to leave the field blank. This feature is available in QuickBooks 2011 and later, but not in older versions.

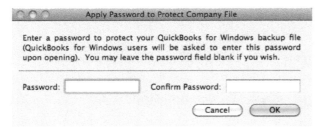

Figure 8-7 Enter Password

5.   Select the location for the backup and click **Save**. If possible, save the file to a location on the
network where you can access it from a Windows PC. This way, you won't have to use CDs
or USB drives.

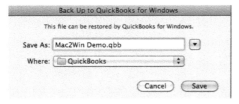

Figure 8-8 Saving the Mac file to a Windows disk or network location

6.   QuickBooks will create the backup, and if necessary, prompt you for a second (or third, or
more) diskette. The backup file will have a ".qbb" extension so that the Windows version of
QuickBooks can recognize it as a QuickBooks backup file.

Figure 8-9 Information screen about the .qbb file extension

7.   Take the backup to a Windows machine and launch QuickBooks for Windows.

8.   Select the *File* menu and then select **Open or Restore Company**.

9.   Select to **Restore a backup copy (.QBB)** as in Figure 8-10.

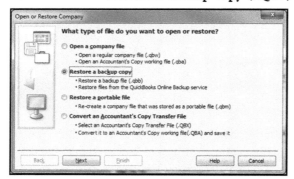

Figure 8-10 Restoring the Macintosh file to Windows

10.   Select **Local backup** on the next screen.

11.   Select the location of the backup file and select the file to be restored and click **Open**.

12.   QuickBooks converts the file from Macintosh to Windows format. The file will also require upgrading to the Windows version you are currently running. Enter **Yes** to confirm the upgrade.

Figure 8-11 Updating the file to the Windows version

13.   The file is now ready for use with QuickBooks for Windows.

Converting Data Files from Windows to Macintosh

Since there are fewer features in QuickBooks for the Mac, you don't want to make a habit of converting back and forth between Mac and Windows, because users may accidentally create data in the Windows version that cannot be accessed in the Macintosh version. If you are assisting a client in converting to QuickBooks for Mac, make sure they are aware of the differences in the two products. Many features available in the **Windows** product are not available in the **Mac** product.

> **Note:** Intuit also offers a conversion service from Windows to Mac. Search the QuickBooks website to find out more.

As a consultant, you may need to support clients who use Macintosh. For these clients, it may be necessary to convert their Mac file to Windows, work on the file in Windows, and then return a Mac file back to the client. This round trip is not a recommended practice because of the issues that can arise from this process.

In either of these situations, you can follow the steps below to convert a Windows file to a Macintosh file.

1.   With the file open in QuickBooks for Windows, select the *File* menu, then *Utilities*, and then select **Copy Company File for QuickBooks Mac**.

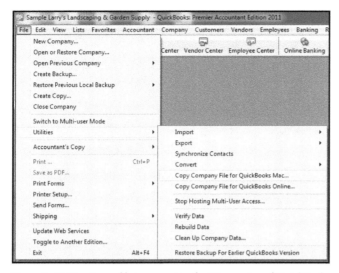

Figure 8-12 Creating a file to convert to the Mac version of QuickBooks

2.   Select the backup location (USB drive, or Network folder) and finish the backup process. The file will have a ".MAC.qbb" extension, and it will be configured for the Macintosh version of QuickBooks.

Figure 8-13 The exported file will have ".MAC.qbb" at the end of the file name.

3.   Copy this file onto the Mac's hard drive and open QuickBooks Pro for Mac.

4.   From the File menu, select **Restore** and then select **From a Disk**.

5.   Select the ".MAC.qbb" file you want to restore and then click **Open**.

6.   Then, if necessary, enter the name of the file to be restored and click **Save**.

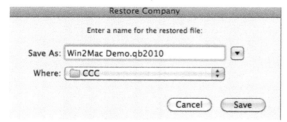

Figure 8-14 Naming the file to be restored

7.   When the file is opened, QuickBooks will show the name of the restored file.

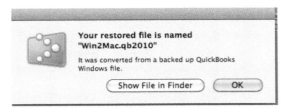

Figure 8-15 File name for the restored file

Data and Features Not Supported in QuickBooks for Mac

The features and data not converted to the Mac version are:

- Payroll and payroll items.
- Bank Feed aliases.
- Customized form templates as we know them in the PC version.
- Sales reps.
- Business planning.
- Progress Billing
- Price levels.
- Integration with third-party applications, including Microsoft Word, Outlook, and ACT!
- Sales order and back order tracking.
- Assembly items will be converted into non-inventory part items.
- Budgets created without an associated account.
- Transaction type "transfer" (will convert as journal entry).
- Expect that reconciliations will be incorrect, and will have to be adjusted.
- Transaction type "EFP payroll" (will convert as payroll liability check).
- Workers Comp Items.
- Fixed Asset Items.
- Multiple "ship to" addresses, preferred send method and payment information for Customers:Jobs.

Unsupported Reports in QuickBooks for Mac

The following preset reports are currently not supported by QuickBooks for Mac. You can, however, create many of these reports using the customization and filtering in QuickBooks for Mac.

- Profit & Loss Unclassified.
- Job Progress Invoices vs. Estimates.
- Open Purchase Orders By Job.
- Sales Tax Revenue Summary.
- Pending Builds.
- Income Tax Preparation.
- Profit & Loss Budget Performance.

- Balance Sheet by Class

Converting Quicken Files to QuickBooks

To convert a Quicken file, follow the steps in this example:

1. Open QuickBooks.

2. From the *File* menu, select *Utilities,* then *Convert,* and then *from Quicken*. If your client uses online banking in Quicken, click *View Help* to read more about converting online features from Quicken to QuickBooks. There are usually 3 files maintained for any given Quicken file. The extension for the conversion file will be **.qdf** or **.qdb**

3. Click *Convert* to bypass the notification.

4. Browse to the Quicken file and click *Open*.

5. QuickBooks will then convert the file, classifying all payees as Other Names. You should see a message similar to below concerning any issues with the conversion. Expect any accounts that have been deleted will have these types of issues.

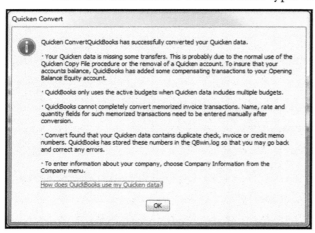

Figure 8-16 Quicken conversion message when complete

Warning

Converting Quicken files to QuickBooks works just fine, but quite often the results are not what you want. Quicken can be a single entry system, if used incorrectly. Since Quicken and QuickBooks work differently, you enter data somewhat differently in QuickBooks than you do in Quicken. In addition, QuickBooks has many features not available in Quicken such as Equity accounts, A/R and A/P accounts, and lists for customers, vendors, and employees. It is probably best to set up a completely new company file in QuickBooks using the ending balances in your Quicken accounts as the opening balances in your QuickBooks company file. At a minimum, if you decide to convert from Quicken to QuickBooks, carefully review the file after the conversion to see if the results are acceptable.

Converting Data Files from QuickBooks Desktop to QuickBooks Online

A QuickBooks Online data file is created in a true SAAS (Software as a Service) environment, and operates far differently than a Windows QuickBooks file. Intuit has provided the tools to convert from one platform to the other. However, this should not be viewed as a tool to convert from one platform to the other and back again. Converting back to the Desktop version can result in lost data.

Just as QuickBooks Desktop has several versions, QuickBooks Online has Simple Start, Online Essentials and Online Plus. In short, Simple Start only handles invoicing and cash transactions, Online Essentials adds online banking, sales tax, estimates and billing, phone and email support and 2 additional users. Online Plus can handle time tracking, budgeting and inventory, and adds 3 more users. Online Plus payroll uses Intuit Online Payroll integrated with Online Plus. With each progressive version, additional reports are available.

To convert a QuickBooks Desktop file to QuickBooks Online, you must have a new account with QuickBooks Online, with no data in it already, or willingness to write over it. There is a 30-day trial version. As part of their membership, QuickBooks ProAdvisors can request a free QuickBooks Online account. Each year, to keep this as a free account, the Pro Advisor must connect with QuickBooks Online customer service to verify continued membership in the Pro Advisor program in order to continue the free account. All QuickBooks Online versions allow for a free accountant user, to encourage clients to use their trusted advisors in setup, processing of data, and reporting.

Other considerations to moving to QuickBooks Online

1. Import of data file is limited to the first 30 days of an account being set up.
2. Limit on Desktop QBW file is 140 MB when converting
3. Only one company file allowed per account. You may, however, have multiple accounts
4. The only browser supported is Internet Explorer
5. Inventory transactions cannot be converted
6. Transfer takes time and the Desktop file must be in single user mode, or a backup for QuickBooks Online must be created.

Follow the steps in this example to convert from QuickBooks Desktop to QuickBooks Online:

1. With the file open in QuickBooks for Windows, select the *File* menu, then *Utilities*, and then select **Copy Company File for QuickBooks Online.**

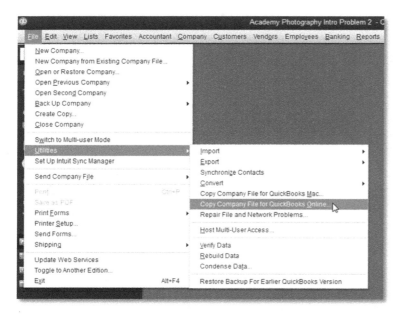

Figure 8-17 Creating a file to convert to QuickBooks Online

2.   If necessary, click **OK** to allow QuickBooks to close all open windows.

3.   Select the backup location and file name. QuickBooks will attempt to enter OE in the name before .QBW

Figure 8-18 The exported file will have ".OE.qbw" at the end of the file name

4.   Log on to QuickBooks Online. From the **Company** file menu, choose **More** and **Import QuickBooks Desktop Data**.

Figure 8-19 QuickBooks Online import menu option

5.   Type YES in the next screen

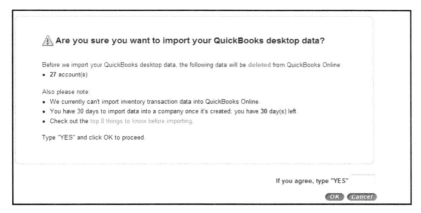

Figure 8-20 Importing QuickBooks Desktop data

6.   In the next screen, click on the **Install** button to install Active X to convert data. This takes only seconds. Then choose **All Data** for conversion, in Option 4, and click on the **Import Data** button.

Figure 8-21 Installing Active X

7.   Next, click on the **Browse** button to locate the backup you made in Steps1-3.

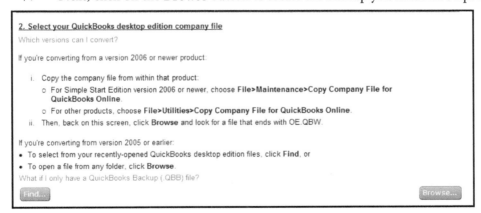

Figure 8-22 Choosing QuickBooks Online file created to convert

8.   Choose the data you want to convert – **Lists Only** or **All Data**

Figure 8-23 Choice of data to convert, creating archive and importing data

9.   Click on **Create Archive** button. This should not take a long time, considering file limitations for upload.

10.   Click on **Import Data.** See Figure 8-24 for upload screen.

Figure 8-24 Upload screen for conversion to QuickBooks Online

Figure 8-25 Completion of conversion

Expect a wait time to be able to log into the file. This is not an automatic process – the file must be converted by the QuickBooks Online team, and your client will receive a notice when the file is ready. Consultants should plan on two visits for conversion: one for uploading file and one for checking data and finishing setup.

Converting Data Files from QuickBooks Online to QuickBooks for Windows

Because QuickBooks Online is not as feature-rich as QuickBooks Windows version, there may be a need to move a client from QuickBooks Online to a hosted QuickBooks Desktop environment, or move the file back to the client's desktop. The conversion process is much easier, though not cleaner, to convert back.

1.   Log into QuickBooks Online, and under the **Company** menu, choose **More** and **Export Data.**

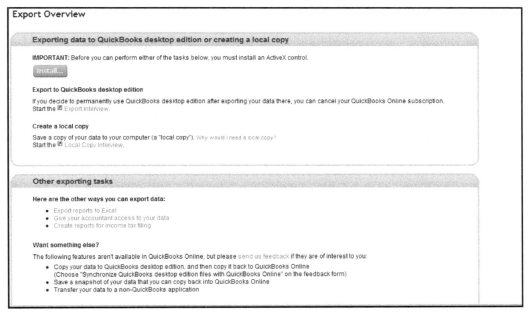

Figure 8-26 Options to export data from QuickBooks Online

2.   Click on Install to allow installation of an Active X control.

3.   Click on Export interview. You can choose to export only lists, or lists and transactions. You will also be asked what version of QuickBooks Windows will be used with the exported data file. Options will be offered for the type of business, and there is a list of details provided for export transactions and lists. See below for issues related to conversion. The last screen before requesting a backup is related to special issues your client may have with the conversion. You must check each item that you understand before clicking **Next.**

Figure 8-27 QuickBooks Online export questionnaire

4.   Now wait for notification on the home page for Things To Do. You should be able to download within 24 hours and restore the backup to QuickBooks for Windows.

Figure 8-28 Notice to Download Exported File

The process of downloading the file and allowing QuickBooks Online to convert the data may take many hours, depending on the internet speed and size of the data file.

Missing Functionality in QuickBooks Online

Because these products are so very different in how they are created, there are some definite differences in reporting and functionality in QuickBooks Online that most consultants have become accustomed to having in QuickBooks Accountant's Edition, which most consultants use. The "available anytime, anywhere" and instant availability of new features advantages of QuickBooks Online must be weighed against the missing features in QuickBooks Online:

- Accounts cannot be deactivated. Deleting accounts only makes them greyed out, and unable to user, but still visible.

- Some transactions cannot be deleted or changed, especially if an account is accidently deleted.

- Customized reporting is limiting in comparison to QuickBooks Desktop, but continues to improve with time.

- Bank and Credit Card reconciliations do not show uncleared transactions.

- Sales Reps can be listed on Invoices, but there is no list.

- Business planning is missing

- Progress Billing not available

- Price levels.

- Integration with many third-party applications, including Microsoft Word, Outlook, and ACT!

- Sales order and back order tracking.

- Assembly items and Group items not available

- Budgets created without an associated account.

- Fixed Asset Items.

- Multiple "ship to" addresses, preferred send method and payment information for Customers:Jobs.

- Multicurrency not supported.

- No .iif import capabilities

- Limited Custom Fields – and only available on Invoices

- Payroll job costing

- Pending Transactions

- Balance Sheet by Class

Converted Data Issues

Converting to QuickBooks Online from QuickBooks for Windows:

- Data not converted:
- Payroll transactions convert as journal entries
- Finance charges
- Pay sales tax and sales tax items
- Received items
- Item price levels
- Print mail labels and forms functions
- Customer, Vendor Types
- Online Bill Pay
- QuickBooks Credit Cards
- Tax Support
- All inactive list items imported as active list items
- Purchase and price details on items
- Item Type
- Memorized reports and memorized transactions
- Purchase Orders

- Users
- Some Vendor Contact Data
- Budgets
-
- Converting to QuickBooks for Windows from QuickBooks Online
- Data not Converted
- Will not convert to Nonprofit or Retail Industry Versions
- All items download as Services, and cannot be changed
- Chart of Account Detail Type
- Limitation on lines and number of characters in Chart of Accounts, Customer and Vendor Names and Lines of Addresses limited to 3
- Vendor Notes
- User and Location lists
- Recurring transactions
- Terms list
- Budgets
- Location and customer fields on invoices
- Estimates
- Company Name on Address for Checks
- Any transactions with two or more lines for Accounts Receivable or Accounts Payable become multiple journal entries
- Markup

Summary

In this chapter, you learned about the different versions and editions of QuickBooks and how to update and convert files from version to version. You learned:

- How to upgrade QuickBooks as new versions are released by Intuit (page 357)
- How to install several versions of QuickBooks on the same computer (page 357)
- How patches can be downloaded and installed to update QuickBooks (page 358)
- How to upgrade data files from one version to the next (page 361)
- When you should consider upgrading to QuickBooks Enterprise Solutions (page 362)
- Converting data files from the Macintosh version to the Windows version (page 363)
- Converting data files from the Windows version to the Macintosh version (page 365)
- Converting data files from Quicken (page 368)
- Converting data files from QuickBooks for Windows to QuickBooks Online (page 369)
- Converting data files from QuickBooks Online to QuickBooks for Windows (page 373)

Chapter 9
Networking QuickBooks

Objectives

In this chapter, you'll learn about installing and configuring QuickBooks in a networked environment. You'll learn:

- Installing QuickBooks in a Multi-User Environment (page 377)
- Software and Hardware Requirements for Multi-User Environments (page 378)
- Setup Procedures for QuickBooks Multi-User Access (page 379)
- What is the QuickBooks Database Server and how to configure it (page 380)
- Setup for sharing QuickBooks files on a server (page 383)
- Configuring the network for shared updates (page 386)
- How to verify proper multi-user setup in "recommended mode" (page 387)
- How to troubleshoot slow multi-user performance (page 389)
- How to resolve a "floating host" and when to use the "alternate setup" (page 390)

> **Note:**
> For purposes of this chapter, references to QuickBooks represent that year's version of QuickBooks Pro and Premier as well as QuickBooks Enterprise Solutions, unless noted differently. For example, QuickBooks 2015 would refer to QuickBooks Pro 2015 and Premier 2015 as well as to QuickBooks Enterprise Solutions 15.0.

Installation Options in a Multi-User Environment

QuickBooks 2006 and above use a new database which requires a different multi-user installation and setup as compared to earlier versions. For QuickBooks 2005 and prior, you set up multi-user access to the QuickBooks company file by simply installing QuickBooks on each workstation in your local area network and placing the QuickBooks company file (.QBW) in a folder accessible to all of the workstations. This shared folder could be on one of the workstations (peer-to-peer) or on a server (client-server).

With QuickBooks 2006 (only), you need to install QuickBooks on the computer where the data file physically resides, even if that computer is the server and no one intends to ever use QuickBooks on the server.

Starting with QuickBooks 2007 and later, there are two separate parts of the QuickBooks application that can be installed independently or together—the database server and the client application. You do not have to install the QuickBooks client application on the server unless QuickBooks will be used on the server computer to access QuickBooks data. Instead, you can simply install the QuickBooks database server only as described below. However, The Sleeter

Group recommends that you install the QuickBooks client application on the server anyway because it will give you convenient access to the client's QuickBooks data when you are working onsite or when you use desktop sharing software or Remote Desktop Services to access the client's server.

Another important reason to install the QuickBooks client application on the server is for data maintenance purposes. For example, it is highly recommended that when running *Rebuild*, it be done at the local machine where the QuickBooks company file resides. Also, for performing version upgrades on QuickBooks company files, it should be done at the local machine where the file resides.

Network Environment Description

You use QuickBooks in a network environment (i.e. with multiple users) if you:

- Have a client-server network where the server runs Microsoft Windows 2003 Server or Microsoft Windows 2008 Server, or have a peer-to-peer network with all peers running Windows XP or above.

- Store QuickBooks company file(s) on the server in a shared folder. Alternatively, you can store the data in a shared folder on one of the workstations. Note that you should locate the QuickBooks data (and database server software) on the computer with the most available RAM and processing capability.

- Install QuickBooks on two or more workstations, in order to open a QuickBooks company file on multiple workstations simultaneously.

Requirements

Verify that you have the following:

- Multiple QuickBooks licenses – You must have at least one license for each QuickBooks user in the network. You may install the database server on additional computers (the data servers) above the number of license(s) you purchased without need to purchase a separate license for that computer.

- QuickBooks Pro, Premier, or Enterprise Solutions.

- On the server computer (the computer on which the data files will be stored), Windows 2003 Server (or Small Business Server 2003) and Windows 2008 Server (or Small Business Server 2008) are supported; Windows 2000 Server is no longer supported on current QuickBooks versions.

- On each workstation, Windows XP Pro with Service Pack 2 (or higher) is strongly recommended. Windows XP Home edition can be configured to work, but are not recommended for a network environment and may take extra configuration time and efforts not discussed in this chapter. Windows 2000 (workstation) is no longer supported on current QuickBooks versions.

Setting Up QuickBooks for Multi-User Access

The recommended local area network setup configuration for QuickBooks 2007 and above is shown in Figure 9-1.

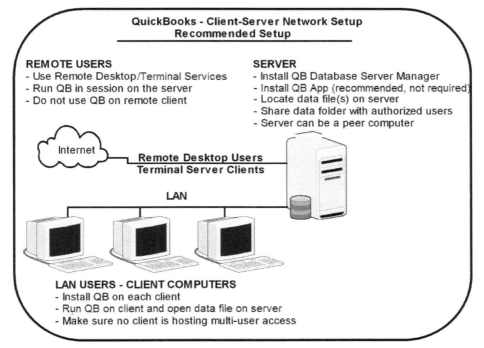

Figure 9-1 Recommended Setup for QuickBooks 2007 and above on a Local Area Network

Installing in a Multi-User Environment

Perform the steps in this exampleto setup QuickBooks in a Multi-User Environment:

1. Install all Windows updates on the server and the workstations. This is a general recommendation, but it's worth confirming because many problems can be attributed to down-rev operating systems.

> **Tip:** Have the client or the client's technology consultant install all Windows updates before you begin the QuickBooks installation engagement. Downloading and installing these updates can be very time consuming, especially when you download updates on multiple computers at the same time using the same Internet connection.

2. Install QuickBooks on each computer, starting with the server. If you're using a peer-to-peer environment, select the fastest computer to act as the server. The installation will first prompt you to choose between server and client installation. For the server installation, select **I'll be using QuickBooks on this computer, AND I'll be storing our company file here so it can be shared over our network** and click **Next** as shown in Figure 9-2; for each client installation, select **I'll be using QuickBooks on this computer** instead (choose that even if there are more than one).

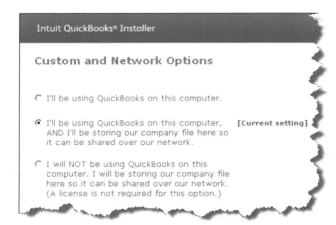

Figure 9-2 QuickBooks installation client/server selection window

Another way to interpret the *Network Options* window is that it provides the choice of whether to install **only** the QuickBooks application, **both** the QuickBooks application and the database server, or **only** the database server.

If your technology professional insists on not having the QuickBooks application installed on the server, you can select to install *Database Server Only* (the third option), but you will not be able to run QuickBooks on the server computer if this option is selected.

The QuickBooks Database Server

Whether you select to install the full QuickBooks application and the Database Server or to install the Database Server only, QuickBooks installs a program called the QuickBooks Database Server Manager. This program runs on the server and interacts with the QuickBooks database server "service." The database server service runs in the background and starts automatically at boot time, even if no users are logged in.

Verifying that the Database Service is Running

To verify or modify the database server installation, you can access it in the *Services* applet inside *Administrative Tools* in the server computer's Control Panel. This tool allows you to start, stop, or restart the Database Manager service or configure its setting to start automatically upon server boot-up.

Each QuickBooks version has its own database manager. Verify that the appropriate service(s) is running for the appropriate version(s) you are running. The filename will be "QuickBooks DB##" where ## is your version of QuickBooks Pro or Premier year or the version of Enterprise plus 10. For example, the file that corresponds with QuickBooks Enterprise 15 or QuickBooks Premier 2015 is QuickBooksDB25.

You can verify if a service is running by opening the Control Panel, selecting Administrative Tools and then selecting Services. In the example in Figure 9-3, each database manager for all of the available versions are running (started).

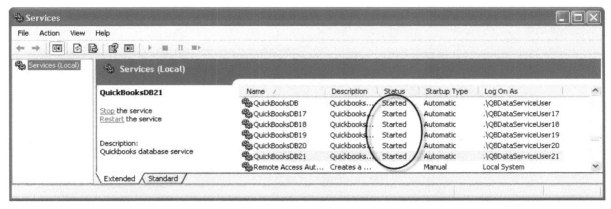

Figure 9-3 Services applet

The QuickBooks database service must be started on the server computer (i.e., the computer where the QuickBooks company file resides) in order for QuickBooks to operate in multi-user mode. If necessary, right-click on the service name and select *Start*. An easier way to start/stop the database service is to use the functions inside of the QuickBooks program itself. There are a few ways to start/stop the service. The first is to open a company file and switch to multi-user mode by selecting *Switch to Multi-user Mode* from the *File* menu (see Figure 9-4).

Figure 9-4 Switching to Multi-user Mode

If the service is not already started, it will be started automatically when QuickBooks switches to Multi-user mode. The other way to start and stop the database service is to select *File > Utilities > Stop Hosting* (or *Host*) *Multi-user Access…* as shown in Figure 9-5.

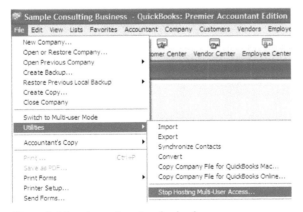

Figure 9-5 Starting or Stopping the database server

Note the two separate concepts:

1. **Hosting Multi-user Access** – When this feature is activated, it means this computer will act as the *host* of QuickBooks company files (databases) stored on this computer. It provides access to the files from other computers on the network, regardless of whether they are accessing the files in single- or multi-user mode. The key is that the database service on this computer will act as the server (or *host*) for anyone on the network that needs to access QuickBooks files on this computer.

2. **Multi-user mode** – Multi-user mode is something that each user can turn on or off within their QuickBooks client. In order for more than one QuickBooks client to have the same data file open, all must be in multi-user mode.

Configuring the Database Server Manager

In QuickBooks 2007 and above, you can modify the settings of the QuickBooks Database Server Manager by launching it (*Start > All Programs > QuickBooks* folder > *QuickBooks Database Server Manager*), or by right clicking its icon in the Windows System Tray and selecting **Open QuickBooks Database Server Manager** (Figure 9-6).

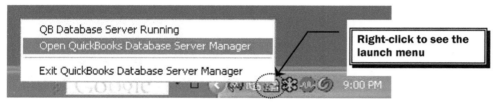

Figure 9-6 Database Server Manager in Windows System Tray

The Database Server Manager is shown in Figure 9-7.

Figure 9-7 QuickBooks Database Server Manager

On the *Scan Folders* tab, you should add every folder that contains QuickBooks company files. When you add a folder into the *Scan Folders* tab, the QuickBooks Database Server Manager will ensure that all files in that folder are available (hosted) to all clients on the network. This means that every interaction with data files in these folders (reading from or writing to the file) will be performed by the database server, and not the client software.

From the user's perspective, this all happens behind the scenes, but as a consultant you should understand that the data files are "locked" by the database server, and cannot be accessed directly by ANY other software. When a QuickBooks client on the network or an add-on application that uses the QuickBooks SDK needs to read or write data, these requests go " through" the database server to do so. See Figure 9-8 for a visual representation of how add-ons and QuickBooks client software interacts with the database server to read and write to the QuickBooks company file(s).

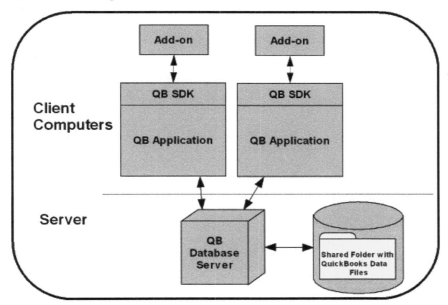

Figure 9-8 QB Database Server read/write process

Sharing QuickBooks Company Files on the Server

> **Note:** All steps below apply to QuickBooks 2006 and above and to QuickBooks Enterprise version 6 and above.

To provide access to all users on the network, you'll need to put the QuickBooks company files (QBW, ND, TLG) in a shared folder on the server computer. This shared folder (or folders) should be added to the "scan folders" as discussed above.

Setting up an Windows Security Group

> **Note:** This section applies when QuickBooks company files stored on Windows Server 2003 and 2008 (or Small Business Server 2003 and 2008).

Although not required, it is recommended to set up a Windows Security Group to facilitate ease-of-administration in your Windows network. For example, set up an Active Directory

Security Group called *QBAccess* (or another name that connotes QuickBooks access) and add each authorized user to that group. You'll need administrative rights to the server to set up this Security Group. By setting up a Security Group in the server, you can easily authorize or restrict users on the network from making changes to files in shared folders.

To create a Security Group, launch the *Active Directory Users and Computers* applet in the *Administrative Tools* folder in Control Panel on the server. Then create a new *Group* object and make it *Security* type (Figure 9-9). Follow the steps in the new object wizard to create the group.

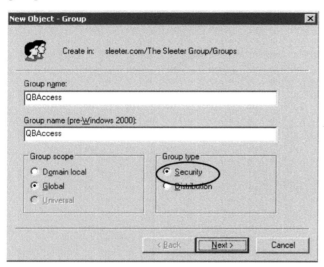

Figure 9-9 Creating an Active Directory Security Group

After the group is created, you can assign users into the Security Group (Figure 9-10).

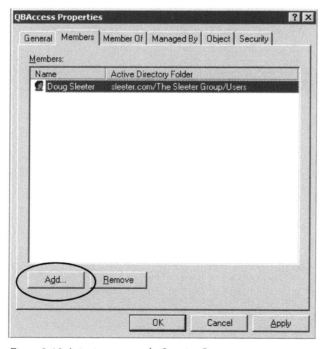

Figure 9-10 Assigning users to the Security Group

When creating a Security Group designed for users with QuickBooks access, ensure to add the appropriate QuickBooks database service user to ensure the database manager operates correctly. Upon installation, the QuickBooks database service automatically creates a unique username on the server for the specific purpose of running the database server. That username is different for each QuickBooks version. The name is "QBDataServiceUser##, where ## is the QuickBooks version year or the Enterprise version number plus 10. For example the file for QuickBooks Premier 2015 or Enterprise 15 would be QBDataServiceUser25.

Next, create the folder(s) on the server where you'll store your data files and assign access rights to that folder. Follow the steps in this example:

1. Create a folder where you'll store the QuickBooks company files

2. Right-click the folder and select **Sharing and Security…**

3. Select **Share this folder**, then click **Permissions** (Figure 9-11)

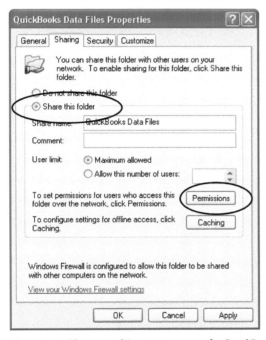

Figure 9-11 Sharing and Permissions screen for QuickBooks data folder

4. In the *Permissions* window, click **Add** to give your security group access to the folder.

5. In the *Select Users, Computers, or Groups* window, enter the Security Group name (see Figure 9-12) and click **OK.**

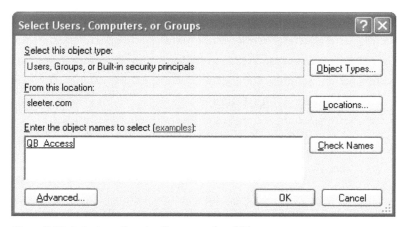

Figure 9-12 Assigning a Security Group to a data folder

6. In the *Permissions* window, click the *Allow* box for *Full Control, Change* and *Read* (see Figure 9-13) and click **OK** to save your changes.

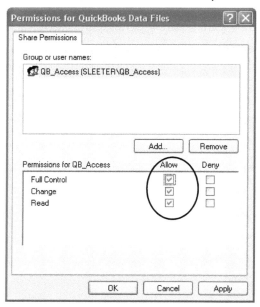

Figure 9-13 Assigning security to a folder

Sharing Maintenance Releases from Server

To keep all the QuickBooks clients synchronized with the latest QuickBooks maintenance releases, you can configure the server machine to download updates automatically and share the updates with the other QuickBooks clients on the network.

Perform the steps below **on the server** to configure the shared download:

1. From the *Help* menu, select **Update QuickBooks…** and click the **Options** tab.

2. Set the **Automatic Update** and **Shared Download** options to **Yes** (Figure 9-14). These settings ensure that updates are downloaded as they become available and all client computers get notified as new updates are available.

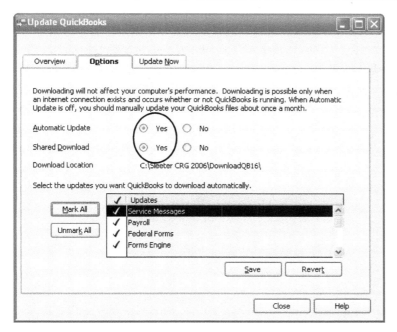

Figure 9-14 Update QuickBooks window

3. On client computers, you would access Update QuickBooks window and set the **Automatic Update** option to **No** and **Shared Download** to **Yes**.

Now that you've configured the update options, each client on the network can download the updates from the server instead of having to download from the Internet. Under normal circumstances you'll receive a message each time there is a new update ready for installation.

If necessary, you can manually update clients by selecting the *Update Now* tab in the *Update QuickBooks* window and clicking on **Get Updates.** QuickBooks will then download the maintenance releases from the server computer and install them into the QuickBooks program located on the client computer. Repeat this process on each client computer on the network.

> **Alternative Download Option:**
> Depending on circumstances, at times QuickBooks will not allow users to download updates from the Internet and/or access downloaded updates shared from the server. This problem may be related to firewall settings or some other connectivity issue.
>
> If connection problems persist, try to download a true "manual update" from the QuickBooks support site at
> http://support.quickbooks.intuit.com/support/productupdates.aspx.
> The downloaded executable file (.exe) can then be run at each computer. This method provides better control over the update process and ensures that every workstation in the network is on the same QuickBooks release.

Verifying Proper Multi-User Hosting Setup

As discussed before, there must be a "host" for the QuickBooks company file in order for QuickBooks to work in multi-user mode. In the recommended setup, you are setting up the server computer to "host" or "serve" data to other client machines on the network. This step is critical for the server to provide high-performance hosting of data files. To verify you have set up the server correctly, follow the steps in this example:

1. On the server with QuickBooks running, press **F2** and check the bottom section of the *Product Information* screen. The *Local Server Information* will show the server's computer name in the *Server Name* field surrounded by the prefix "QB" and the QuickBooks version (see Figure 9-15).

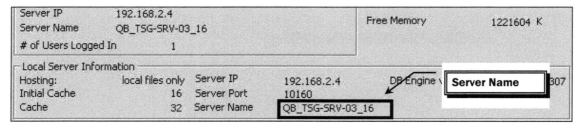

Figure 9-15 Product Information screen - Server hosting multi-user access

2. On each client computer, open the data file located on the server. Press **F2** and verify that all of the fields are empty in the *Local Server Information* section (see Figure 9-16). This ensures that the server is acting as the host of the data file and that none of the clients are acting as the host of the data file, a phenomenon known as having a "floating host" (see page 390).

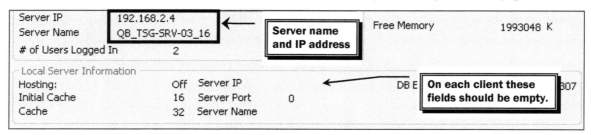

Figure 9-16 Product Information screen - QB client using file from the server

3. If any of the client workstations reports that it is the "server" of the data file or, if the lower portion of the screen shown in Figure 9-16 says "Hosting: Local Files only", you should stop the multi-user hosting function on that client. To do so, from the *File* menu, select *Utilities*, and then select **Stop Hosting Multi-User Access**.

Setting Up Users in the Company File

Another important part of setting up QuickBooks in a multi-user environment is to set up *users* of the file. You must setup users in each company file. When you create a data file, QuickBooks creates an *administrator* (called *Admin*). You should first set up a password for the *Admin* and then restrict access to that password to the owner of the company or the person in the office who will supervise the use of QuickBooks. *Admin* can add users to the file and give each user privileges (or permissions) to access various areas of the data file. For security purposes, it is best not to use *Admin* for regular QuickBooks work. It is a good practice for the administrator to log into QuickBooks using a separate username when using the file to enter transactions and run reports. The administrator should only log in using the *Admin* username when he or she needs to perform some action that is restricted to the administrator—like changing company preferences and maintaining users.

Unless *Admin* is the only username on the user list, QuickBooks prompts to enter a username and password each time someone opens the company data file. The access rights granted to users by the administrator determine what functions of QuickBooks they can access. For example, you can allow a user to have access to Accounts Receivable, Accounts Payable and Checking Account functions, but not Payroll or "sensitive activities" like online banking or entering Journal Entries. For a complete description of each privilege, click the *Help* button on the user setup screens. QuickBooks Enterprise Solutions allows for much more sophisticated user permission settings (refer to page 396). Companies who need more granular control over what users can access should consider upgrading to QuickBooks Enterprise Solutions.

After setting up user names and access rights (privileges) for each user of the QuickBooks company file, you are ready to begin using QuickBooks in a multi-user environment.

Troubleshooting Slow Multi-user Performance

If experiencing slow network or multi-user performance with QuickBooks, the simple solution may be to upgrade to QuickBooks Enterprise Solutions or at least the Enterprise Solutions Database Manager. This section may help you identify the issue.

If you're running QuickBooks Pro or Premier, the database engine is "tuned" to a maximum of 5 concurrent users and an associated level of database transaction handling. Even though a QuickBooks Pro or Premier company file is limited to 5 simultaneous users in multi-user mode in any given file, this database engine tuning speaks to the total number of users and data files being served by the file server (and database transactions being performed), not to the number of users in a single data file. The file server, where the database engine resides, typically hosts the QuickBooks company files. When the engine in use on the server is QuickBooks Pro or Premier, that file server is expecting to serve up to 5 concurrent users and their associated data files and no more.

However, in a large network, this becomes a problem because there could be a larger number of users (users with QuickBooks properly installed and licensed on their workstation), and all may be accessing files stored on a central file server. If the number of concurrent QuickBooks users exceeds 5 (regardless of whether they are all working on the same data file), the database server will get bogged down and may start disconnecting users from their sessions. The problems may not be seen in some networks, where users are working largely in single-user mode, but where multi-user access is required on the network, the thresholds are easily reached. The QuickBooks Enterprise Solutions edition of the database server is tuned to handle a larger number of concurrent users and database transactions.

When a network has a potential number of concurrent users greater than 5, and where multiple data files are located on a central file server, our recommendation is to use the

Enterprise Solutions database server rather than using the engine that ships with QuickBooks Pro or Premier. The Enterprise Solutions database server is compatible with QuickBooks Pro and Premier data files, and it significantly improves file server performance. For QuickBooks Pro/Premier users on larger networks, this means that they should plan the additional expense of a multi-user Enterprise Solutions license for the file server. The workstations can continue to operate with QuickBooks Pro/Premier versions.

"Floating Host" and "Alternate Multi-User Setup"

If QuickBooks is not installed on the server, or if the hosting options are improperly set on the server and/or client computers, your installation may be using a "floating host." With this configuration, the host of the QuickBooks company file will be the first client that opens the QuickBooks company file and (a) enters multi-user mode, or (b) selects the *Start Hosting Multi-User Access* option. Therefore, since the host of the data files could be different each day (depending on which computer opens the data file first), the setup is referred to as a "floating host" setup. The documentation also refers to this setup as the "alternate multi-user setup." The proper setup we described before is referred to as the "recommended multi-user setup."

Many configurations could cause a floating host condition, but all have the following characteristics:

- QuickBooks company files located on a shared network drive, and not "hosted" by QuickBooks installed on that computer
- One or more clients using are hosting multi-user access to the data file(s)

The main problems with a floating host are:

- Possible data loss if the current host of the data file is shut down while others are entering data
- Slow performance because each client must first "talk to" the host computer in order to read or write data to/from the file

Correcting a Floating Host Situation

Version 2006 users are most likely to have the floating host problem, but in version 2007 and above, it is theoretically possible that the problem will exist if the main server does not properly start up the database server, if it somehow gets turned off, or if it is running but clients are unable to communicate with it. It's quite unlikely to occur, but these procedures should correct the problem if it occurs.

In order to correct the floating host condition on your network, you will need to do the following:

Identify which computer should be the "host" for your data files and move the files to that computer. You should put your data files in a folder and share that folder with other users on the network. See the section beginning on page 383 for specifics.

1. On each client computer (all workstations that will not be the host of the data files), open each data file that has ever been opened by this client and deactivate multi-user hosting by selecting the **File** menu, then **Utilities**, and then select **Stop Hosting Multi-User Access...** (see Figure 9-17).

    If you don't see **Stop Hosting Multi-User Access...**, and instead see a menu item that says **Host Multi-User Access...**, then hosting is already disabled and you can skip this step and move to the next workstation.

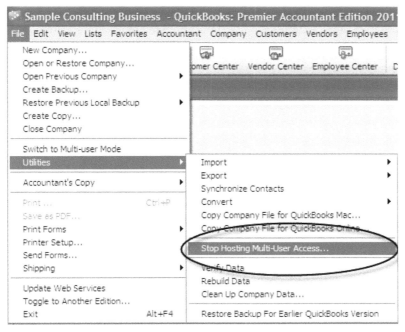

Figure 9-17 Deactivating Multi-User Hosting

Legitimate Uses of Alternate Setup

Although it is highly recommended that you use the "recommended setup", there are environments in which you won't be able to comply with its requirements. There are some environments in which there are legitimate uses of the "alternate setup" mode of multi-user installation. For example:

*   The QuickBooks company files are stored on a Novell Netware Server.
*   The QuickBooks company files are managed on a SAN (Storage Area Network).
*   The QuickBooks company files reside on a Windows Server that, by company policy, cannot have any other software installed on it, or is otherwise out of the control of the QuickBooks administrator.

In these cases, you should consider one of the following options:

*   Consider locating the QuickBooks company files on one of the network clients (the fastest computer with the most memory), and stopping hosting mode on all other clients on the network as discussed above.

- If you must store the QuickBooks company file(s) on the server, then consider designating one of the clients (the fastest computer with the most memory) as the "host". This is slightly different from the first case in that the data files will be on the server, and all other clients on the network will "go through" the designated host to access the data file. If you choose this approach, you must ensure that this host computer is always turned on before any of the other clients access the data file. That way, the database server on this "host" will serve the data files to the other users on the network.

The alternate network setup for QuickBooks 2006 and later is shown in Figure 9-18.

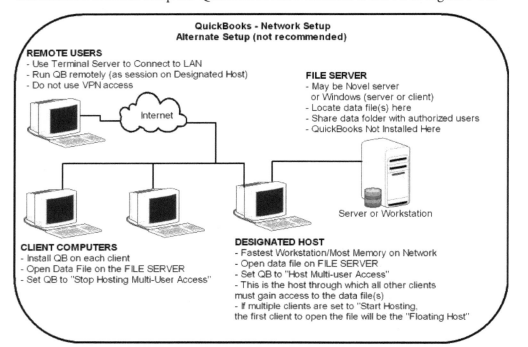

Figure 9-18 Alternate Setup for QuickBooks on a network

Summary

In this chapter, you learned about installing and configuring QuickBooks in a networked environment. You learned:

- Installing QuickBooks in a Multi-User Environment (page 377)
- Software and Hardware Requirements for Multi-User Environments (page 378)
- Setup Procedures for QuickBooks Multi-User Access (page 379)
- What is the QuickBooks Database Server and how to configure it (page 380)
- Setup for sharing QuickBooks files on a server (page 383)
- Configuring the network for shared updates (page 386)
- How to verify proper multi-user setup in "recommended mode" (page 387)
- How to troubleshoot slow multi-user performance (page 389)
- How to resolve a "floating host" and when to use the "alternate setup" (page 390)

Chapter 10
Enterprise Solutions

Objectives

In this chapter, you will learn about the features and benefits of QuickBooks Enterprise Solutions and how to work with them. You will become familiar with the key differences between Enterprise Solutions and other QuickBooks editions. You will learn the following about Enterprise Solutions:

- What is Enterprise Solutions (page 393)
- When to upgrade and what companies are a good fit (page 394)
- What are the List and User capacities (page 395)
- How to set up user access permissions (page 396)
- Track inventory in multiple locations (page 405)
- Reporting with QuickBooks Enterprise Solutions (page 405)
- Improved multi-user performance (page 407)
- Support for remote access using Remote Desktop Services (page 409)
- Fixed Asset Manager (page 410)
- Employee Organizer (page 410)
- The Enterprise Solutions Full Service Plan (page 410)
- Intuit Enterprise Online Applications (page 410)
- Linux support (page 411)

What Is Enterprise Solutions

QuickBooks is known as accounting software for small businesses. However, the emergence of a higher edition of QuickBooks—Enterprise Solutions—gives growing and larger companies another option before having to consider pricier mid-market applications.

QuickBooks Enterprise Solutions is the biggest, fastest, most robust and most secure edition of the Intuit QuickBooks financial software family. It is the biggest because it can support up to 30 simultaneous users (see page 396). It is fastest because it has been optimized to perform faster than lower editions of QuickBooks (Pro, and Premier), even with the increased number of concurrent users. It is most robust because it can handle much larger data files with little or no adverse effect. And it is more secure because it includes much greater "granularity" in user access permissions, allowing for more detailed, better structured user security (see page 396).

One of the greatest assets of Enterprise Solutions is the user interface. It has the familiar look and feel as other QuickBooks editions, making it very easy for most users to switch to

Enterprise Solutions. For users familiar with QuickBooks, the upgrade to Enterprise Solutions poses little or no learning curve because it appears the same as the QuickBooks editions that they already know.

In addition, an added benefit of Enterprise Solutions is the functionality to consolidate financial reports from different QuickBooks companies, all from inside Enterprise Solutions (see page 405) and virtually unlimited reporting capabilities via ODBC-compliant applications (see page 405). Also, just like QuickBooks Premier, Enterprise Solutions comes in industry-specific editions, offering terminology and reporting conducive to different industries. Enterprise Solutions includes a 12- month full-service plan, including no-cost software upgrades and unlimited dedicated technical support (see page 410).

QuickBooks Enterprise Solutions is designed for growing businesses, including those with several locations. It includes all the features of QuickBooks Pro and Premier Editions, plus:

- The capacity to track hundreds of thousands of inventory items, customers, and vendors
- Higher number of simultaneous users
- Consolidated reporting
- Open access to data using ODBC-compliant applications
- Unlimited support and product upgrades while under the Full Service Plan

Best Practices for Enterprise Solutions

There are several Best Practices you should keep in mind when considering and choosing QuickBooks Enterprise Solutions.

When to Upgrade

Growing companies currently using QuickBooks Pro and Premier may be starting to stretch their current product. For those users, moving to a new larger non-QuickBooks application can be very costly; for example, licensing, implementation, ongoing maintenance, and training costs on new software can be very high. For these users, Enterprise Solutions offers an easier way to support business growth while staying with the familiar QuickBooks interface, keeping the ease-of-use that QuickBooks is known for, while meeting the more complex demands of a larger business. And for businesses not on the QuickBooks platform, Enterprise Solutions offers an affordable option (compared to alternative mid-market applications) that is easy to use and cost-effective to maintain.

There are also situations when the features and functionality of QuickBooks Premier may suffice for some entities. However, if the number of users needed by an entity is three or more, it may make more monetary sense to choose Enterprise Solutions, even though QuickBooks Premier does support up to five users. Over a period of two years or more, because of the included upgrade protection under the Full Service Plan (see page 410), the total cost of ownership of Enterprise Solutions is lower when comparing to the cost of keeping up with QuickBooks Premier upgrades. And as an added benefit, the user gets the advantage of increased performance knowing they are on the highest platform of QuickBooks financial software. Essentially, the software is prepared to grow with them.

Enterprise Solution is a good fit for a company using QuickBooks Pro or Premier that needs more advanced user permissions. Users do not lose their familiar QuickBooks interface, but behind the scenes, the permissions are more detailed, giving management the ability to allow and restrict functions with much greater level of detail. Most growing and larger firms need that higher level of access permissions, because most such firms need the separation of duties that a good internal control system dictates.

Who Should Use Enterprise Solutions

Enterprise Solutions is designed for larger small and mid-size businesses. As a general guide, this includes companies with 20 or more employees and revenues of over $1 million. Generally, Enterprise Solutions is a good fit for companies in any of the following situations:

- Currently using QuickBooks Pro or Premier and stretching their software limits; for example, needing to add more Customer, Vendor, and Item information than QuickBooks Pro or Premier allow
- Having a QuickBooks data files larger than 100-150MB
- Needing more than 5 users in QuickBooks Premier or needing more than 3 users in QuickBooks Pro
- Having employees with specialized functions, such as companies with multiple separate departments that have different functional roles
- Having to access QuickBooks from multiple locations
- Looking for an alternative to accounting and business management software solutions that cost tens of thousands of dollars

Even though it may be designed for larger or growing firms, it is not exclusively for them. Some companies using the Enterprise Solutions platform do not require the added user capacity, but choose to implement it just because of the enhanced operability (faster, able to handle larger data files) or more secure access permissions.

List Capacity

Enterprise Solutions offers the most capacity of any QuickBooks financial product. From a technical standpoint, it allows you to add up to one million Names (Customers, Vendors, Employees, and Other Names combined) and up to one million Items (Inventory, Non-inventory, Service Items, etc.). However, testing at these levels has never really been done. Performance degradation may occur as your lists approach these sizeable thresholds. From a more practical and performance standpoint, Enterprise Solutions gives businesses room to grow with the capacity to add and track perhaps a hundred thousand Customers and Vendors, about 250 Employees (if you use QuickBooks Payroll), and around a hundred thousand Items. In general, The Sleeter Group recommends keeping list sizes under control, even when technical specifications allow for extremely large data sets.

Enterprise Solutions now has the ability to define more custom fields and to capture, track, and report on unique customer, vendor, and item information. For example, set custom fields to accept certain formats such as date, phone number, or select from a user-defined drop-down list to reduce data input errors. And you can use advanced filtering and sorting to run reports on the custom field information. The maximum number of custom fields for items is 15, while the maximum number of custom fields for vendors, customers and employees is 12 each. All custom fields can be defined as available in list entries, transactions, or both.

User Capacity

Enterprise Solutions breaks the user limit of QuickBooks Pro (3-users) and Premier (5-users). You can purchase from 1 to 30 users with Enterprise Solutions. Refer to the following table for user capacity in current and legacy versions of Enterprise Solutions:

ES 9.0 To Es 5.0	30-users
ES 7.0 and ES 8.0	20-users
ES 6.0	15-users
ES 5.0 and prior	10-users

Table 10-1 User capacity in current and legacy versions

User Permissions

Enterprise Solutions is designed for more complex user access permissions, to match the more complex functions of larger organizations. These advanced permissions enable companies to apply more granular user permissions to activities within all areas of QuickBooks. With Enterprise Solutions, companies can give employees access to the information and activities they need to do their jobs, without compromising data to accidental or intentional misuse. You can allow or restrict users' access to individual areas, functions, activities, lists, reports and, as an example, even different bank accounts (see Figure 10-1).

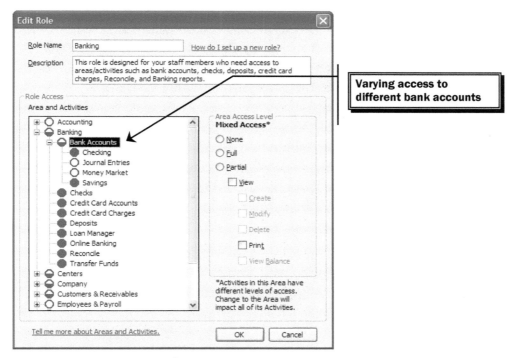

Figure 10-1 Assigning Access to Bank Accounts

Within each activity area, users can be granted access to *View, Create, Modify, Delete,* and *Print* (see Figure 10-2). Many experts observe how this function of access permissions in Enterprise Solutions is similar to that of much more complex, larger, more costly accounting software systems.

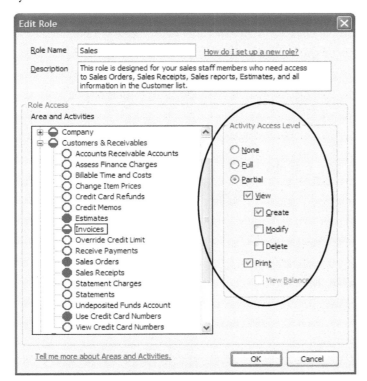

Figure 10-2 Example of Activity Access Levels

Users and Roles

Enterprise Solutions enables permission controls on over 115 individual activities, compared to 10 broad-area activities in QuickBooks Pro and Premier. Another important difference between Enterprise Solutions and lower editions of QuickBooks is that permissions are function or role-based, not user-based. *Users* are people who access the company file. *Roles* are permission sets that can be created or modified, then assigned to *Users*. *Roles* allow flexibility and offer customization of access levels for different users in a company. You create *Users* and assign *Roles* to them, thus connecting users to the corresponding permissions. This method proves much more efficient in the assignment of user rights by being able to quickly assign similar function-based permissions to multiple users without having to do it individually for each user as you would in QuickBooks Pro and Premier.

This use of *Roles* makes it more efficient to set up and maintain permissions, especially when there are a large number of users (which Enterprise Solutions is designed for). You can assign *Users* to multiple *Roles* and individual *Roles* to multiple *Users*. This increased granularity of control gives you the flexibility to customize access levels for each user.

Predefined User Roles

There are 13 predefined user *Roles*. You can modify these or design and add your own to the company's needs. Even better, you can duplicate a predefined *Role* and modify it to the company's needs, thus preserving the original predefined *Roles* that come with the program, essentially using the predefined *Roles* as *Role* templates. Each predefined *Role* template comes with a complete set of permissions designed for that function.

Predefined Roles include: **Accountant, Accounts Payable, Accounts Receivable, Banking, Finance, Full Access, Inventory, Payroll Manager, Payroll Processor, Purchasing, Sales, Time Tracking**, and **View-Only**. Table 10-2 below describes each of the predefined roles and how they are designed. Familiarize yourself with these roles and refer to them when designing user permissions in Enterprise Solutions.

Accountant	Designed for bookkeeping or accounting staff; access to areas/activities such as Journal Entries, Chart of Accounts, Setting Closing Date & Password, Accountant & Taxes and Company & Financial reports.
Accounts Payable	Designed for Accounts Payable staff members; access to areas/activities such as entering and paying bills, Purchase Orders, and Vendors & Payables reports.
Accounts Receivable	Designed for Accounts Receivable staff members; access to areas/activities such as Invoices, Receive Payments, Statements, Credit Memos, and Customers & Receivables reports.
Banking	Designed for staff members who need access to areas/activities such as Bank Accounts, Checks, Deposits, Credit Card Charges, Reconciling, and Banking reports.
Finance	Designed for finance staff members who need to be able to view most financial data; access to areas/activities such as Planning & Budgeting, Bank

	Accounts, Asset, Liability, and Equity Accounts, and Company & Financial reports.
Full Access	Designed for staff members who need full access to the company file with the exception of access to Company Information, Company Preferences, Archive & Condense, importing and exporting data, and setting file Closing Date & Password.
Inventory	Designed for staff members who work with inventory; access to areas/activities such as Adjusting Quantities on Hand, Build Assemblies, Item Receipts, and Inventory reports.
Payroll Manager	Designed for a Payroll Manager who needs full access to payroll functions such as the Employee Organizer, Paychecks, Employee and Paycheck information, and Payroll Adjustments.
Payroll Processor	Designed for staff members who process Paychecks and Payroll Liabilities; it does not allow access to the Employee Organizer.
Purchasing	Designed for purchasing staff members who need access to Purchase Orders and Purchases reports.
Sales	Designed for sales staff members who need access to Sales Orders, Sales Receipts, Invoices, Sales reports, Estimates, and the Customer list.
Time Tracking	Designed for staff members who need to work with Time Tracking functions such as importing and exporting Timer data, Single Time Activity tracking, Time reports, and the Weekly Time Sheet.
View-Only	Designed for view-only access to most areas of the company file; creating, modifying, deleting, and printing are not allowed.

Table 10-2 Predefined Roles

The Payroll *roles* ensure that no payroll holes remain open. Even if a user has access to a check register, the payroll data will be obfuscated unless the user also has access to one of the payroll roles. Additionally, if a user does not have access to payroll, the user can be prevented from accessing the payroll & compensation information in the Employee Center.

There are two more special *Roles*: **Admin** and **External Accountant**. Neither role can be deleted, edited, or duplicated. **Admin** is the QuickBooks administrator role; it provides full access to all areas of the company file. There are few functions that are restricted to this role, such as access to maintaining *Users and Roles*. **External Accountant** provides full access to all areas of QuickBooks except sensitive customer data, such as credit card numbers. Using the **External Accountant** role, you can use the Client Data Review tool (see page 337) to efficiently separate the changes you make in the data file from the changes your client makes, thus maximizing the functionality of QuickBooks Accountant.

How Permissions Transfer From Lower Editions of QuickBooks

User permissions from lower editions (QuickBooks Pro or Premier) or older versions of QuickBooks are structured based on *Users* and not on *Roles*. However, permissions are preserved when upgrading to Enterprise Solutions. Users will end up with the same access rights that they had in the previous edition/version. After the upgrade, a custom *Role* is automatically created for each user. For example, if a user named Anna had "Purchases and Accounts Payable" permission in the lower edition of QuickBooks, a new *Role* called "Anna's role" will be automatically created in Enterprise Solutions by the upgrade, and that *Role* will be made up of the same access to areas and activities that Anna had under "Purchases and Accounts Payable" in the previous edition/version.

For the sake of consistency, it is appropriate to eliminate these automatic user-based *Roles* after an upgrade and replace them with corresponding function-based *Roles* either from the *Predefined Roles* or from custom-made, position-based *Roles*.

Setting Up Users and Roles

In the following exercise, you will create a new *Role* for Estimators in a company and assign it to a user. We will use an existing *Role* as a template and modify it to our needs. To set up the new *Role*, follow the steps in this example:

1.   From the *Company* menu, select **Users**, then select **Set Up Users and Roles...**

2.   Click on the **Role List** tab.

3.   You will see the *Users and Roles* window (see Figure 10-3).

Figure 10-3 Users and Roles Window

4.   Scroll down on the *Roles* list and select the **Sales Role** and click **Duplicate...**

5.   In the *Duplicate Role* window, enter **Estimating** in the *Role Name* field.

6.   Change the *Description* as appropriate for this role; for example, enter **This role is for estimators, with no access to Sales Orders and Invoices**.

7.   Click on the **Customers & Receivables** area and select None from the *Activity Access Level* list.

8.   Expand the Customers & Receivables area and select Estimates.

9.   In the *Activity Access Level* list, check the *Create* and *Modify* boxes.

10.   Verify that your screen matches Figure 10-4 and click **OK.**

Figure 10-4 Duplicate Role Window

To assign the new role to a user, follow the steps in this example:

1.   On the *Users and Roles* window, click on the **User List** tab.

2.   Select **Darryl** and click **Edit.**

3.   Select any already *Assigned Roles* (right-hand list) and click **Remove.**

4.   Select the new **Estimating** role from the *Available Roles* (left-hand list) and click **Add.**

5.   Verify that your screen matches Figure 10-5 and click **OK**; ignore any warnings about QuickBooks having detected that this user does not have a password.

Figure 10-5 Edit User Window

Viewing User Permissions

The *Permissions Access by Users* report offers a high level view of existing permissions. This gives you a comprehensive view of which permissions individual users are assigned to, and what permissions each role has. You can view the report by *Users* or by *Roles*.

To generate a *Permissions Report by User*, follow the steps in this example:

1.   From the *Company* menu, select **Users**, then select **Set Up Users and Roles...**

2.   You will see the *Users and Roles* window (see Figure 10-6).

Figure 10-6 Users and Roles window

3.   From the *Users and Roles* window, click **View Permissions.**

4.   If you want to display a report showing permissions for all *Users*, in the *View Permissions* window checkmark each desired *User* and click **Display** (see Figure 10-7).

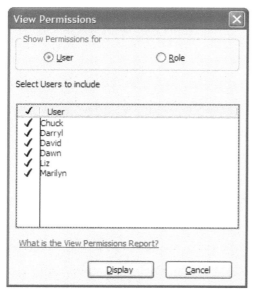

Figure 10-7 View Permissions window showing Users

5.   You will see the *Permissions Access by Users* report (see Figure 10-8).

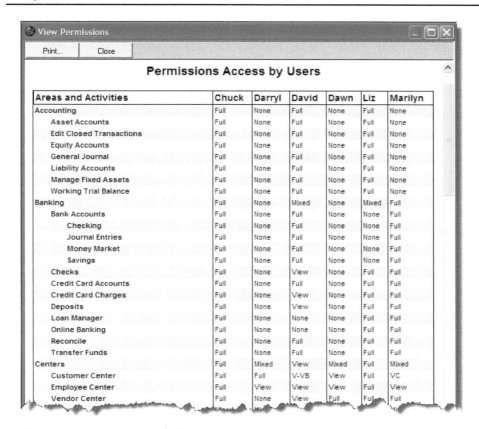

Figure 10-8 Permissions Report by Users

To generate a *Permissions Report by Role*, follow the steps in this example:

1. From the *Users and Roles* window, click **View Permissions** and select the **Show Permissions for *Role*** radio button.

2. If you want to display a report showing permissions for all *Roles*, in the *View Permissions* window checkmark each desired *Role* and click **Display** (see Figure 10-9).

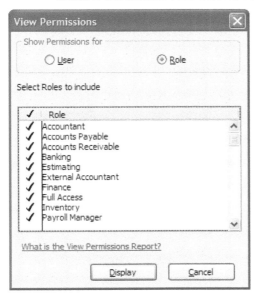

Figure 10-9 View Permissions window showing Roles

3.   You will see the *Permissions Access by Roles* report (see Figure 10-10).

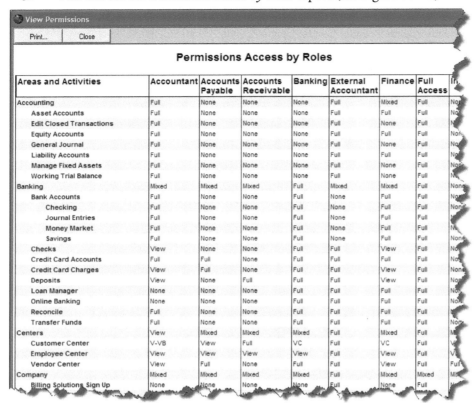

Areas and Activities	Accountant	Accounts Payable	Accounts Receivable	Banking	External Accountant	Finance	Full Access	
Accounting	Full	None	None	None	Full	Mixed	Full	No
Asset Accounts	Full	None	None	None	Full	Full	Full	No
Edit Closed Transactions	Full	None	None	None	Full	None	Full	N
Equity Accounts	Full	None	None	None	Full	Full	Full	Non
General Journal	Full	None	None	None	Full	None	Full	No
Liability Accounts	Full	None	None	None	Full	Full	Full	N
Manage Fixed Assets	Full	None	None	None	Full	None	Full	Nco
Working Trial Balance	Full	None	None	None	Full	None	Full	N
Banking	Mixed	Mixed	Mixed	Full	Mixed	Mixed	Full	None
Bank Accounts	Full	None	None	Full	None	Full	Full	N
Checking	Full	None	None	Full	None	Full	Full	Non
Journal Entries	Full	None	None	Full	None	Full	Full	
Money Market	Full	None	None	Full	None	Full	Full	N
Savings	Full	None	None	Full	None	Full	Full	None
Checks	View	None	None	Full	Full	View	Full	No
Credit Card Accounts	Full	Full	None	Full	Full	Full	Full	No
Credit Card Charges	View	Full	None	Full	Full	View	Full	None
Deposits	View	None	Full	Full	Full	View	Full	No
Loan Manager	None	None	None	Full	Full	Full	Full	No
Online Banking	None	None	None	Full	Full	Full	Full	No
Reconcile	Full	None	None	Full	Full	Full	Full	
Transfer Funds	Full	None	None	Full	Full	Full	Full	No
Centers	View	Mixed	Mixed	Mixed	Full	Mixed	Full	M
Customer Center	V-VB	View	Full	VC	Full	VC	Full	V
Employee Center	View	View	View	View	Full	View	Full	V
Vendor Center	View	Full	None	Full	Full	View	Full	Full
Company	Mixed	Mixed	Mixed	Mixed	Full	Mixed	Mixed	M
Billing Solutions Sign Up	None	None	None	None	Full	None	Full	

Figure 10-10 Permissions Report by Roles

Viewing Users

Enterprise Solutions has a tool for viewing what users are currently logged on to the company file. To access it, from the *Company* menu select **Users** then select **View Users...** (see Figure 10-11)

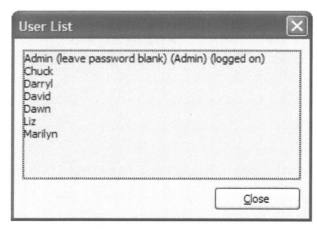

Figure 10-11 User List Window

Multi-Location Inventory

You can accurately track quantity and value of inventory items held in multiple locations with the Advanced Inventory function in QuickBooks Enterprise Solutions. For more about Inventory features in QuickBooks Enterprise Solutions, see 528.

Reporting

QuickBooks Enterprise Solutions has the ability to meet the needs of growing businesses, including more complicated accounting and reporting needs. It comes with over 120 standard, pre-defined reports and the flexibility to customize them and build new reports, as in QuickBooks Pro and Premier. And like QuickBooks Premier, Enterprise Solutions is available in industry-specific editions, each with additional industry-specific features and pre-defined reports. Enterprise Solutions Accountant includes all the reports from each of the Enterprise Solutions industry-specific editions.

Combined Financial Statements

If a company operates multiple entities, Enterprise Solutions can save time and errors by consolidating financial reports in one step. A *Combined Report* is a report that combines (i.e., consolidates) data from different QuickBooks company files and brings it together into one report. The data needs to be from a common time period. When you choose a report and the QuickBooks company files to draw from, Enterprise Solutions creates a Microsoft Excel spreadsheet with a column for each entity and a column that totals them all.

This is useful for parent companies and headquarters offices that want to pull together data from subsidiaries, divisions, or branches. Five financial reports are available for combining: **Balance Sheet Standard, Balance Sheet Summary, Profit & Loss Standard, Statement of Cash Flows, Trial Balance, Profit & Loss by Class, and Sales by Customer Summary.**

To be practical and useful for each of the above except for the Sales by Customer Summary report, the different QuickBooks company files should have the same or similar Chart of Accounts. Otherwise, accounts that are not in common will show zero dollars in the columns for each company that does not have the same accounts.

To create combined financial statements, follow the steps in this example:

Select Combine Reports From Multiple Companies from the *Reports* menu.

1. QuickBooks displays the Combine Reports From Multiple Companies window.

2. Click Add Files…

3. Browse for and select other QuickBooks company files you want to combine with the one already open.

4. Check the report(s) you want to combine from the **Select reports for combining** list.

5.   Select the appropriate **date range** and **report basis** (Accrual or Cash) and enter the desired **company name** to be shown on report header(s); an example of what the window would look like appears in Figure 10-12.

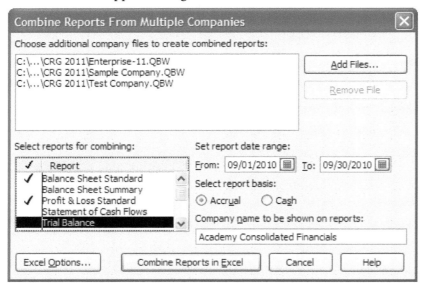

Figure 10-12 Combine Reports From Multiple Companies window

6.   Click **Combine Reports in Excel** and Enterprise Solutions will automatically open each company file sequentially and export the desired financial statements into Excel

QuickBooks Statement Writer

With the built-in QuickBooks Statement Writer you can create customized financial statements. It works directly within Microsoft Excel and provides design flexibility and real-time link to Enterprise Solutions data. You can choose predefined customizable financial statement templates or design your own. Some of the included functionalities allow you to roll-up multiple accounts into a single line, budget versus actual reporting, inserting columns and rows to show variances between columns (such as for different periods), and the ability to add subtotal rows. Also, even though it's inside Microsoft Excel, you can zoom directly from an amount in the custom financial statement to its source in Enterprise Solutions. QuickBooks Statement Writer's new features allow you to build financial statements on a per-class or per-job basis, or as a combination of classes, and you can set any date range for statements, including 4-week months or 13-week quarters. For more information on the QuickBooks Statement Writer, see page 601.

QODBC

With Enterprise Solutions, the included read-only ODBC driver software, called QODBC, allows the retrieval of QuickBooks data from outside QuickBooks with ODBC-compliant applications, such as Microsoft Excel or Access and Crystal Reports, to analyze and report data in multiple ways.

To configure QODBC, you must first download and install the ODBC Driver: from the *File* menu, select *Utilities* and then select *Set up ODBC* to download and install it. An in-depth explanation of how to configure and utilize QODBC is beyond the scope of this writing. For more information on QODBC, refer to the FLEXquarters.com, the developer of the ODBC driver, or CLEARIFY.com which is managed by the foremost expert on ODBC solutions, Chuck Vigeant.

Custom Reporting

A ODBC-based tool in QuickBooks Enterprise Solutions 11.0 and later is the Custom Reporting function. As opposed to SDK-based reporting (such as QODBC above), this tool access the QuickBooks SQL database directly, therefore it provides much faster access to the underlying QuickBooks data.

To access Custom Reporting, you must first set up an ODBC connection to your company file: from the *File* menu, select *Utilities* and then select *Custom Reporting…*, or from the *Reports* menu, select *Custom Reporting…* You will then follow the on-screen steps shown in Figure 10-13 to set up the ODBC connection.

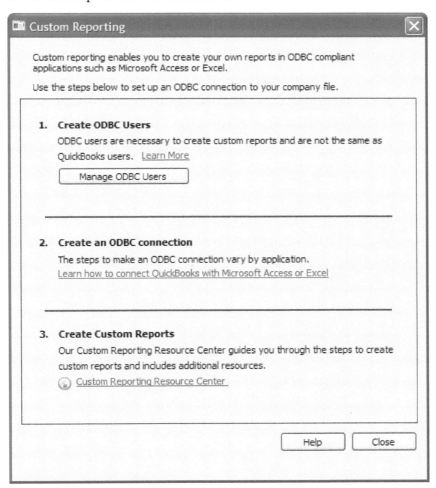

Figure 10-13 Custom Reporting window

It is important to understand that, even though this new tool provides direct access to the underlying QuickBooks data, it does not show the actual, raw database tables. Instead, it shows what are called "views", which give you a window to the raw QuickBooks data. A view is a dynamic stored query of the actual physical database table; it looks like a table, but in fact only fills up with data when you invoke its use. The reason for using views instead of the database directly is that the view contains only a subset of the actual table data and is organized in a way to make it easier for you to get what you want. It allows you to create reports without having to know the definition of every field in every database table.

A main advantage of the new Custom Reporting is that data access is as fast as it can be; data retrieval does not have to go through several layers like SDK-based tools do (such as QODBC). For more information on Custom Reporting, refer to CLEARIFY.com which is managed by the foremost expert on ODBC solutions, Chuck Vigeant.

Improved Multi-User Functionality

Enterprise Solutions operates faster than QuickBooks Pro/Premier, because its database server is optimized for larger multi-user access. The QuickBooks Pro/Premier database server is optimized or tuned for a maximum of only 5-users, versus up to 30-users for the Enterprise Solutions database server.

These improvements also provide some functional advantages. In Enterprise Solutions, you can do more activities in multi-user mode that require single-user mode in QuickBooks Pro/Premier. For example, you can delete list entries (Customers, Vendors, Items, and more) while in multi-user mode; QuickBooks Pro/Premier require single-user mode for deleting list entries. And because of this delayed write functionality, you can recover deleted entries before they get removed for good.

Recovering Deleted List Entries

If you are in multi-user mode, you can recover a list entry that has been marked for deletion. To "undelete" a list entry, simply open the list view to include inactive records and you will see the deleted record marked with a red X as in Figure 10-14. Click on the red X and the record will come back to normal, it will be "undeleted." Here we're using the example of a deleted record in the Items list, but the concept works the same with the Customers list, Vendors list, and most other lists, as long as you are in multi-user mode.

Figure 10-14 Item List showing a deleted record

The X looks just like the X noting when a record is inactive, except it is colored red. Records marked for deletion are actually removed from the QuickBooks company file as soon as Enterprise Solutions finds itself in single-user mode or when all users exit the company file.

Records marked for deletion allow themselves to be edited just like any other record. Also, if a record was marked for deletion inadvertently or by mistake and you try to use it in a transaction, such as using a marked-for-deletion Item in an Invoice, you will see a prompt as in Figure 10-15 from where you can Undelete the record. This is similar behavior as when attempting to use a record that has been marked inactive.

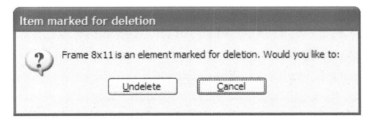

Figure 10-15 Attempting to use a record marked for deletion

Access from Multiple Locations—Remote Desktop Services

QuickBooks Enterprise Solutions is recommended for companies that need to access a single QuickBooks company file remotely or from multiple locations. It has the ability to connect remote workers through Microsoft Remote Desktop Services (RDS) software, formerly known as Terminal Services (TS). RDS enables the running of multiple independent Windows sessions concurrently from a single Windows Server computer.

The appropriate number of Enterprise Solutions purchased licenses is required for the total number of Enterprise Solutions users, including each user accessing via RDS or TS. For example, a company can have five users running Enterprise Solutions over the local area network at the main office and another five users running Enterprise Solutions remotely via RDS or TS, all from a single server. In this example, the company would need a 10-user license of Enterprise Solutions.

Microsoft Remote Desktop Services software is included with Windows Server 2008 and Windows Server 2003 (then called Terminal Services). The appropriate number of Remote Desktop or Terminal Server purchased licenses must be in place for proper use. When Enterprise Solutions is used only from RDS or TS, it has to be installed only once on the server computer; other computers would access Enterprise Solutions without having the program installed directly on their hard drives. In this scenario, the program resides on the server and all processing is done at the server, dramatically reducing network traffic.

Fixed Asset Manager

Fixed Asset Manager is the module for managing fixed assets from acquisition to disposition. It is the same module included with QuickBooks Accountant and it is included in all editions of Enterprise Solutions. To use the Fixed Asset Manager, users first enter assets into the Fixed Asset List, including information such as the asset's description, purchase date, purchase cost, depreciation method, and useful life. Then, using the Fixed Asset Manager, you can automate the calculations for depreciation and automatically create entries in QuickBooks to record the depreciation. Also, data from the Fixed Asset Manager can be transferred directly into any of several tax preparation programs.

For more information about the Fixed Asset Manager, see page 664.

Intuit Enterprise Online Applications

Enterprise Solutions makes available web-based business applications that integrate seamlessly with QuickBooks. Intuit Field Service Management ES (powered by Corrigo) is one of them. An in-depth detailed discussion of online applications is beyond the scope of this writing.

To access the Enterprise Online applications, click on the *Online Solutions* menu (just to the left of the Window menu) and select the individual online applications desired. This will launch a web browser where the user would log in to the online application.

Field Service Management ES

Intuit Field Service Management ES is designed for the contractor industry, specifically those with field service technicians, such as HVAC, irrigation, electrical, mechanical, and plumbing, just to name a few. It gives the dispatcher a dashboard-like view of information, including each technician's work orders, location, and status (see Figure 10-16) and the ability to drag and drop work orders between technicians. The application can track what each technician is working on, the status, arrival time, travel time, and hours clocked.

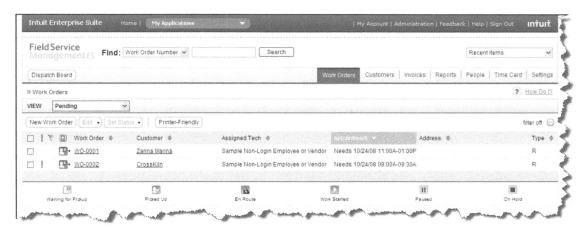

Figure 10-16 Field Service Management ES Work Orders view

Field Service Management ES also offers the ability to use cell phones and PDAs instead of a clipboard. This means that information and scheduling can be immediately dispatched to technicians, increasing efficiency and workers' productivity. Speaking of efficiency, the application integrates with Google Maps to track the workers and minimize travel time.

The parts list is synchronized with Enterprise Solutions. Field service technicians carry with them the parts catalog in their mobile device (cell phone or PDA), so that when they close a work order, they can find and add parts to the invoice right on their mobile device. Technicians also have the ability to receive payments in their mobile device through QuickBooks Merchant Services, reducing or eliminating invoicing and receiving payments steps in the office.

Field Service Management ES allows the capturing of staff's hours directly from the field, as it has a time card add-on function on the technician's mobile device that allows for their clocking in and out, reducing manual data entry and time cards. Timesheets are then uploaded to Enterprise Solutions for payroll processing.

Field Service Management ES offers another add-on function to track service contracts. For example, it can automatically create work orders for preventive maintenance customers and schedule them together with the rest of the work orders.

Basically, the purpose of Field Service Management ES is to answer who is doing what and where for contractor businesses.

Linux support

Technology professionals who choose Linux open source software as their server platform can run the Enterprise Solutions Database Server on their Linux server. The QuickBooks company file is stored on a Linux server and Enterprise solutions runs on Windows desktop clients to access that data. With Enterprise Solutions, you can utilize the server operating system of your choice to meet the needs of different technology environments.

As more QuickBooks companies adopt Linux, Intuit realized that Linux proponents needed an option. To address this, Intuit launched Linux support with Enterprise Solutions 7.0 R8 and it is available in versions 8.0 through 14.0. There are many different versions of Linux in the market; they are referred to as "distributions" instead of versions. The distribution officially supported for Enterprise Solutions 12.0 is *Fedora*. Enterprise Solutions will also work in other Linux distributions, even though they are not in the officially supported list; those include *CentOS, Debian, Mandriva, Novell Open Workgroup Small Business Edition, OpenSUSE,* and *Ubuntu.*

No matter which Linux distribution being used, all Linux systems require Samba software, a utility that enables Windows-based clients to connect to Linux-based servers. For more information on how to configure the Linux Database Server Manager, refer to Intuit's Linux Installation Guide on the Enterprise Solutions website at http://enterprisesuite.intuit.com/support/setup/ . The website also has links to the necessary downloads for the Linux Database Server Manager.

It's important to reiterate that Enterprise Solutions supports Linux servers, not desktops. Specifically, Enterprise Solutions supports running the QuickBooks Linux Database Server Manager only and not the QuickBooks application on a Linux machine.

Summary

In this chapter, you learned about the features QuickBooks Enterprise Solutions and the key differences between Enterprise Solutions and other QuickBooks editions.

- What is Enterprise Solutions (page 393)
- When to upgrade and what companies are a good fit (page 394)
- What are the List and User capacities (page 395)
- How to set up user access permissions (page 396)
- Track inventory in multiple locations (page 405)
- Reporting with QuickBooks Enterprise Solutions (page 405)
- Improved multi-user performance (page 407)
- Support for remote access using Remote Desktop Services (page 409)
- Fixed Asset Manager (page 410)
- Employee Organizer (page 410)
- The Enterprise Solutions Full Service Plan (page 410)
- The Intuit Enterprise Online Applications (page 410)
- Linux support (page 411)

Chapter 11
Special Payroll Topics

Objectives

This chapter covers the following special topics for handling payroll:

Mid-Year Payroll Setup

> **Note:**
> It is highly recommended that you use December 31 as your payroll Start Date, making this section unnecessary.

After you finish setting up your Payroll items and your employees in a new file, you may need to set up the year-to-date information for each employee, depending on your payroll start date.

The **payroll start date** is the date that you begin entering paychecks using QuickBooks for payroll. For example, if today is March 31, but you're setting up QuickBooks as of December 31, your QuickBooks start date is December 31. If you use QuickBooks payroll to enter all of the paychecks from January 1 through March 31, then your payroll start date is also December 31. On the other hand, if you don't plan to use QuickBooks to calculate the paychecks from January through March but instead you plan to just enter summaries of the payroll, then your payroll start date is March 31.

If your payroll Start Date is in the middle of the calendar year, you'll need to enter the detail of how much you paid to each employee so far this year. This detail must include the specifics of each Payroll item for each employee. Also, you'll need to enter the detail of the payroll tax payments you've made so far this year.

This information is necessary so that QuickBooks can:

- Print year-to-date figures correctly on paychecks.
- Include activity for the entire calendar year on W-2s.
- Include all year-to-date information on payroll reports.
- Correctly report year-to-date payroll information on payroll tax returns such as Forms 941 and 940.
- Stop accruing or withholding taxes at the proper time after compensation limits are reached.

In the following example, assume you're setting up in the middle of the calendar year. We'll use January 31 for the payroll start date so you'll need to enter year-to-date information for the January payroll.

Also assume you have already set up the rest of your QuickBooks file, including the balance of your payroll liabilities and your year-to-date payroll expenses. Also, assume you have already completed all the steps in payroll setup (for more on the standard steps to set up payroll, see *QuickBooks Complete 2015* by Douglas Sleeter). This means your financial statements are already up to date, but now you need to bring the Payroll items up to date.

Please note that since we already set up the account balances in the company setup, we don't want our year-to-date payroll figures to double those entries in the general ledger. For this reason, the Payroll Setup Interview only sets up your year-to-date balances for payroll items, and not the accounts to which they point.

As you enter setup amounts in this section, consider whether you want to enter detailed information for each employee as one lump sum for the whole year-to-date (this is not recommended due to the quarterly totals needed for the Form 940 at the end of the year), in total by quarter, or month, or as individual paychecks. If you enter each paycheck, your reports will be more detailed, but it will take longer during the setup phase. In this example, we will enter the total payroll for the year-to-date paychecks at January 31 even though Academy Glass does semi-monthly payroll.

Set up Year-to-Date Amounts

To set up year-to-date amounts, follow the steps in this example:

1. From the *Employees* menu, select **Payroll Setup**. The Payroll Setup Interview (Figure 11-1) shows the progress in setting up. Click **Continue**.

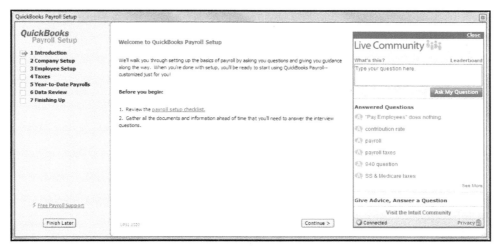

Figure 11-1 The Payroll Setup wizard

2.   Click **Yes** in the screen in Figure 11-2 and then click **Continue**.

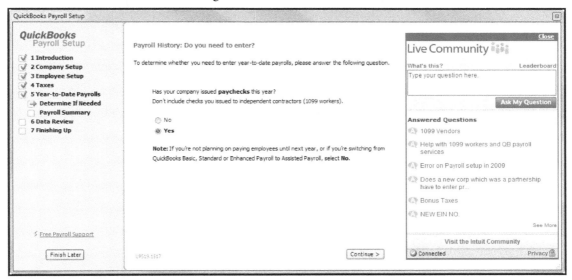

Figure 11-2 Payroll History: Do you need to enter?

3.   A new pop up window will appear to provide a spreadsheet look and feel for entering historical payroll data. Our example assumes Kati Reynolds was the only employee that earned any money previously this year. Choose **Kati Reynolds** from the *You're entering paychecks for* field.

4.   Click on the **arrow** next to January to expand that month.

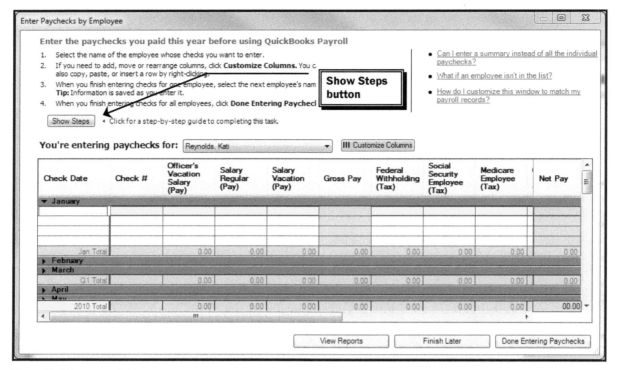

Figure 11-3 Enter payroll history

5.   Click on the **Customize Columns** button. The *Customize Columns* dialog box opens.

6.   It is possible to add additional columns to the spreadsheet as needed for entering historical information (Figure 11-4). When finished, click *OK*.

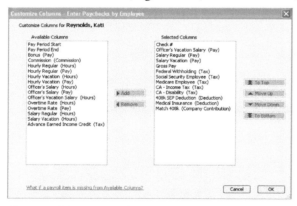

Figure 11-4 Customize Columns

7.   Click on **Show Steps** button on the Enter Paychecks by Employees window (see Figure 11-3) to see each step explained as shown in Figure 11-5. Click on any of the steps to remove the balloons.

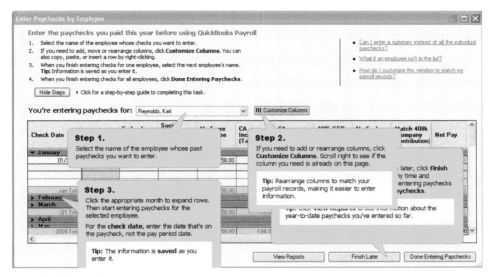

Figure 11-5 Show Steps

8.   Enter Paycheck information as shown in Figure 11-6 .

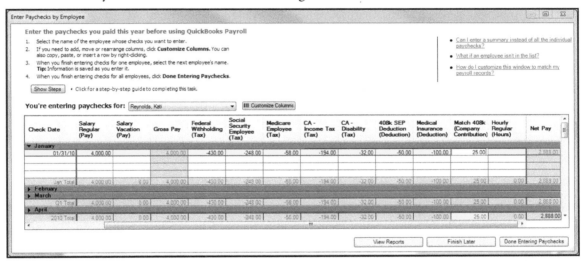

Figure 11-6 Entering Year To Date Information for Katie Reynolds

9.   The employer payroll taxes are calculated automatically.

10.   Click on the **View Reports** button in the Enter Paychecks by Employee window to review the data entry screen in Figure 11-7. When finished, close the browser window.

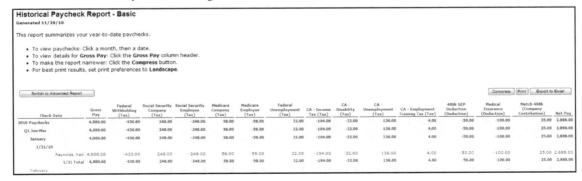

Figure 11-7 Review Earnings for Kati Reynolds

11.   Click on Done Entering Paychecks.

Enter YTD Payroll Tax Payments

After entering the year-to-date information for each employee, you also need to tell
QuickBooks which payroll taxes have already been paid. The payments should be entered by
quarter. Here is an example of the steps.

1.   Enter the data shown in the Enter payroll tax payments you've made window (see Figure
11-8).

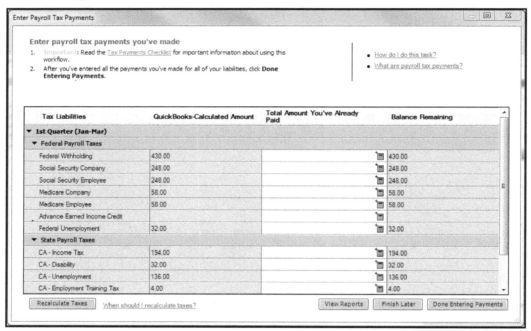

Figure 11-8 Enter payments for each item

2.   If multiple payments were made during the quarter, click on the calculator to the right of the
amount you have paid column (see Figure 11-9) and then click **Save**.

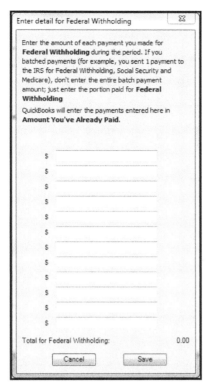

Figure 11-9 Enter payments for each item

3. Once all payment amounts have been entered (see Figure 11-10), click **Done Entering Payments**.

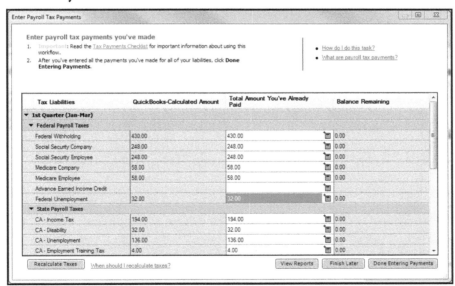

Figure 11-10 Review tax payments for each item

4. A message will appear to confirm that you have entered the tax payments accurately (see Figure 11-11). Click **Continue** to proceed.

Figure 11-11 Payment Confirmation window

5.   Click *Edit* to advance to the *Non-tax payments* screen as shown in Figure 11-12

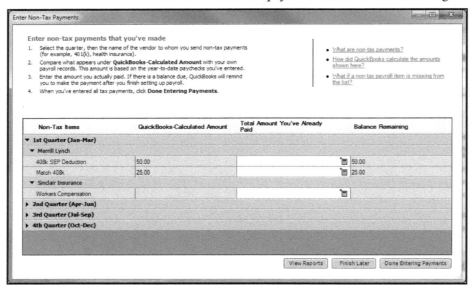

Figure 11-12 Review your non-tax payments window

6.   Enter the data shown Figure 11-13 in and then click **Done Entering Payments**.

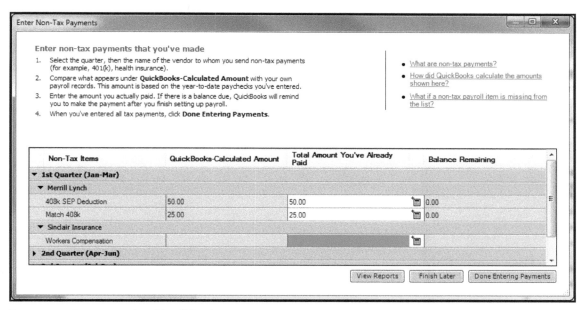

Figure 11-13 Payments made to Merrill Lynch

7.   If you have other payees or other time periods, you can enter them on the screen as shown above.

8.   On the ***Payroll Summary*** screen (see Figure 11-14), click **Continue**.

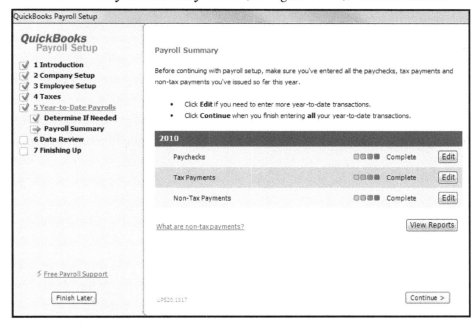

Figure 11-14 Paychecks, Tax Payments, and Non-Tax Payments are all complete

9.   Review your payroll data (see Figure 11-15). Choose **Yes**.

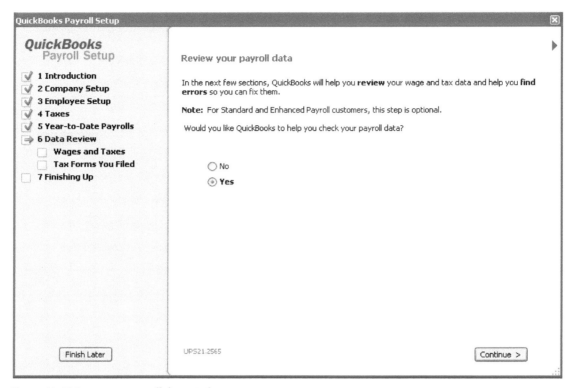

Figure 11-15 Review your payroll data window.

10.   Click *Continue* to advance to the *Wages and Taxes*. Click on **Continue**.

11.   Click Continue on the Wages and Taxes screen (see Figure 11-16).

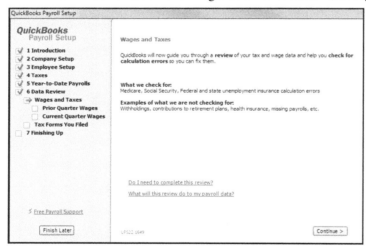

Figure 11-16 Wages and Taxes window

12.   If there are any variances, you'll see the screen shown in Figure 11-17. Click **View Errors**.

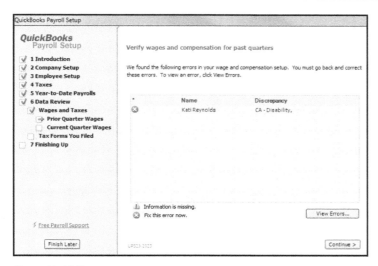

Figure 11-17 Errors screen.

13.   Review the errors. Click **Continue**.

Figure 11-18 Review errors screen.

14.   Close the error report by clicking on the "X" in the upper right corner. Click on **Continue**.
        The fix warnings screen will appear (see Figure 11-19), for our purposes, select **Ignore**
        Warnings. Based on the warnings in your own data, you should handle them appropriately.

Figure 11-19 Fix Warnings.

15.   Reconcile the payroll forms as shown in Figure 11-20. Click **Continue**.

Figure 11-20 Reconcile your payroll tax forms to your payroll data

16. In our example, only January payroll has been entered so the quarterly returns are not due
     yet. Choose **Yes** as shown in Figure 11-21. Click **Next**.

Figure 11-21 Yes, because the forms are not due yet

17. You've now finished the mid-year payroll setup. Click **Finish**.

Figure 11-22 You've reconciled your payroll tax forms screen.

18.   To finish and exit the *Payroll Setup Interview*, click **Go to the Payroll Center**.

Proofing Your Payroll Setup

Now that you've completed the payroll setup, check the accuracy of your setup by comparing QuickBooks reports with the reports from your accountant or payroll service. QuickBooks has a Payroll Checkup feature that helps you check your payroll setup by scanning your payroll data for any discrepancies.

When you change the taxability of a payroll item, enter year-to date information, or subscribe to one of the Payroll services, a prompt appears recommending that you run the Payroll Checkup to verify new or modified entries against your current payroll setup.

Run Payroll Checkup

To run the payroll checkup, follow the steps in this example:

1.   Select the **Employees** menu, then select **My Payroll Service**, and then select **Run Payroll Checkup**.

Figure 11-23 Selecting the Run Payroll Checkup utility

2.   Click **Continue** on the screen in Figure 11-24 to begin the checkup.

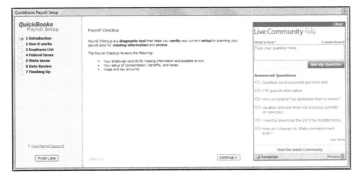

Figure 11-24 The Payroll Checkup screen

3.   The checkup process will take you through a series of screens showing warnings. For this example, you can ignore all of them by clicking **Continue** or **Finish**.

4.   You will finally reach the screen shown in Figure 11-25. Click **Finish**.

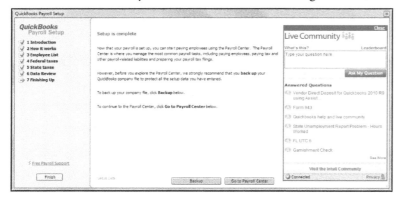

Figure 11-25 Set Up Is Complete screen

Verify Payroll Reports

After you successfully complete the payroll checkup, you'll also need to check your figures to make sure you recorded the correct opening balance numbers. Follow the steps in this example:

1.   Create a *Payroll Summary* report. Select the **Reports** menu, select **Employees & Payroll**, and then select **Payroll Summary** (see Figure 11-26).

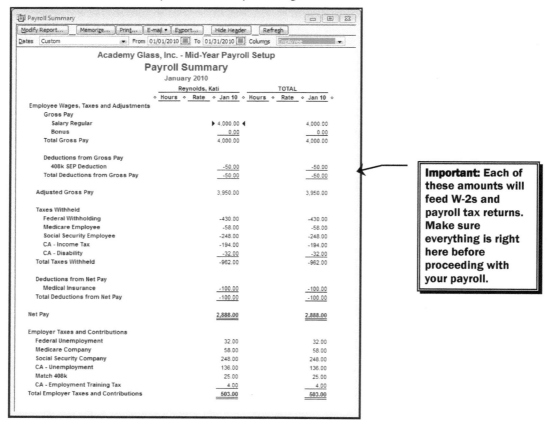

Figure 11-26 The Payroll Summary for January

Notice that the totals for each payroll item for your employees show on this report. Compare this with your other payroll records to make sure the figures match.

Correcting Errors in Employee YTD Amounts

If you find errors with the year-to-date amounts for any employee, follow the steps in this example to correct them:

1. Display the **Employee Center**, then click the *Transactions* tab, and then click **Year-to-Date Adjustments** (see Figure 11-27).

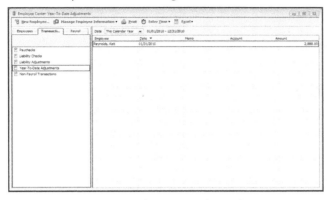

Figure 11-27 Year-to-Date Adjustments in the Employee Center

2. You can see all the adjustments (by employee) on this screen. Double-click on the top item in the list (see Figure 11-27) to display the transaction.

3. Make whatever corrections needed on the YTD Adjustments screen shown in Figure 11-28 and then click **OK** to save your changes. All amounts you entered in the *Payroll Setup Interview* can be modified here.

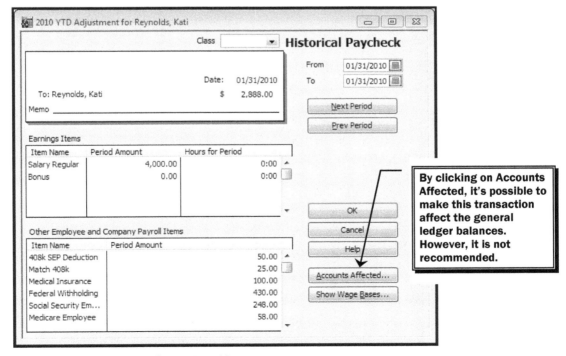

Figure 11-28 YTD Adjustment for Kati Reynolds

If you click the *Accounts Affected* button in Figure 11-28, you can change this transaction to also affect the general ledger account balances according to how the payroll items are connected to each account. In general you do NOT want to affect accounts when entering year-to-date payroll transactions because the general ledger balances would have been entered as part of the account set up.

> **Note:**
> On the adjustment in Figure 11-28, enter all amounts as positive numbers even if they are withholding amounts. For example, although federal withholding reduces the gross pay, you enter it as a positive number in this adjustment. When QuickBooks calculates net pay, it takes into account that some Items are withheld and others are added to the Earnings items.
>
> **Tip:**
> The best way to handle affecting accounts is to enter a journal entry with the year-to-date balances. That ensures your General Ledger accounts are accurate. Then, on all year-to-date adjustments, select *Do not affect accounts*. This ensures that all your Payroll items are accurate.

Verifying YTD Liability Payments

1. Next, create a *Payroll Liability Balances* report. Select the **Reports** menu, select **Employees & Payroll**, and then select **Payroll Liability Balances** (see Figure 11-29). Set the date for January through March.

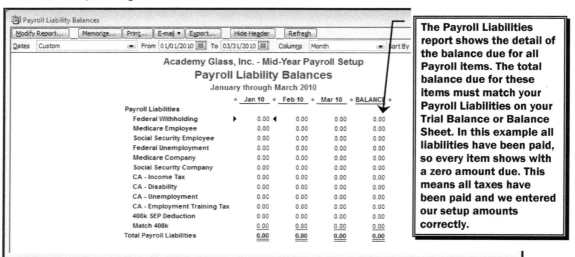

Figure 11-29 The Payroll Liability Balances report.

The *Payroll Liability Balances* report (see Figure 11-29) shows a separate column for each month and the total balance due for each Payroll item. Notice that you entered one set of historical paychecks dated in January, and then entered the payments made.

Correcting YTD Liability Payments

If you want to correct the year-to-date tax payment data, follow the steps in this example:

1.   Display the **Employee Center**, then click the *Transactions* tab, and then click **Liability Adjustments** (see Figure 11-30).

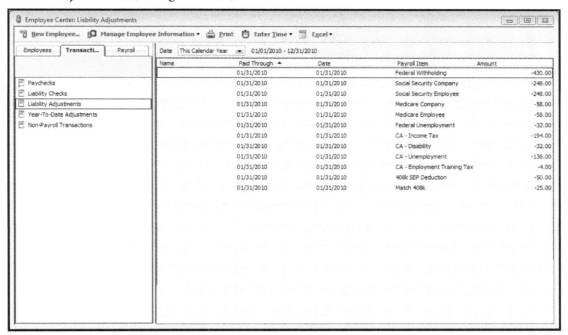

Figure 11-30 Liability Adjustments for Academy Glass

2.   You can see all the adjustments (by payroll item) on this screen. Double-click on each *item* in the list (see Figure 11-30) with a March 31 date to display and edit its transaction.

3.   Then set the dates for the *Payment* and *For Period Ending* fields to 1/31/10 as shown in Figure 11-31.

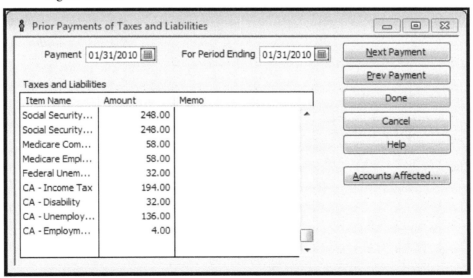

Figure 11-31 Prior Payments of Taxes window

> **Note:**
> The *For Period Ending* field is very important. QuickBooks uses this date to specify that this adjustment is for taxes owed as of the period ending date. For example, if you enter an adjustment representing a tax payment you made on 1/31 for tax you owed as of 12/31 the previous year, enter 12/31. In this example we're setting up a mid-year payroll, so we're entering the tax payments for the payroll paid during January.

4.   Click **Done** to record your changes. Any other errors you made during the year-to-date setup can be fixed on this screen so there is no need to go back to the *Payroll Setup Interview*.

Verifying the Trial Balance

You should also make sure your payroll records match with your *Trial Balance* report.

The numbers on this report show the differences between the amounts on the Employee YTD adjustment and the Prior Payments adjustment. They should be exactly what you owe for each Payroll item as of your payroll start date.

1.   Next, create a trial balance for your payroll setup date. Select the **Reports** menu, select **Accountant & Taxes**, and then select **Trial Balance** (see Figure 11-32).

2.   Set the *From date* and the *To date* fields to "01/31/2009" and press the *Tab* key.

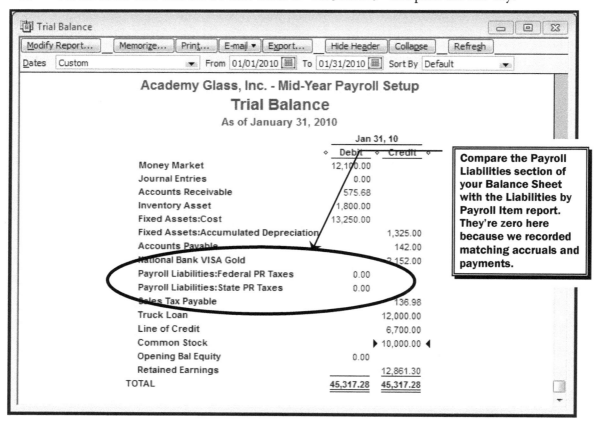

Figure 11-32 The trial balance.

3.   Check to see that the payroll liabilities on the *Trial Balance* match with the total liabilities shown on the *Payroll Liabilities* report. The amounts are zero on the Balance Sheet because you recorded equal amounts of accruals and payments for January.

After correctly setting up your QuickBooks payroll, the total liabilities on these two reports should match exactly.

This completes the process of setting up your payroll using a mid-year payroll start date.

Deciding on a Payroll Method

There are multiple considerations to take into account when choosing a payroll solution for the client. The following may not be all-inclusive, but will provide a map to follow when working with clients to provide the best solution for both client and consultant.

- Who will handle the payroll processing?
- Does the Client need or want additional services to be provided by the payroll service?
- Is job costing or project time costing important?
- Do customers get billed based on hours worked?
- Where are the employees? Multiple locations or just one?
- How many states do the employees work in?
- Are there special needs reporting, i.e. Certified Payroll?
- Who will have access to payroll and QuickBooks records?
- Do employees need direct deposit or debit cards?

It is important to consider the various payroll methods including those not related to QuickBooks solutions. The table below shows several options available to end user clients and to accountants as payroll providers.

Name	Prepared By	Add-ons	Online	Embedded in Software	After the Fact	Typical Cost
ADP	Either	401K, Health, Worker's Com, Debit Cards	Yes	No	No	$39/ Payroll
Paychex	Either	401K, Health, Worker's Com	Yes	No	No	$39/ Payroll
Intuit Online	Either	Worker's Comp, 401K, Health Debit Card	Yes	No, but easy to Import	No	$10.99-$42.99/ Month
SurePrep	Either	No	Yes	No	No	$60/ Month
QuickBooks Accountant's Enhanced Payroll	Accountant	Worker's Comp, 401K	No	Yes	Yes	$274-374/ Year

QuickBooks Basic Payroll	Either	No	No	Yes	No	$124-249/ Year
QuickBooks Enhanced	Either	Worker's Comp, 401K	No	Yes	No	$274-374/ Year
QuickBooks Assisted	Either	Worker's Comp, 401K	No	Yes	No	$69-120/ Month

Table 11-1 Payroll Solutions and pricing as of the publication date

Cost of these services range all the way from $10.99 per month for 5 employees to several hundred dollars per month. All of these services are readily available to end users with the exception of QuickBooks Accountant's Enhanced Payroll, and all have programs for Accountant that either provide for referral fees or the ability to resell and supervise the payroll service. Be aware that pricing may change and that the world of payroll changes quite frequently, as it is a very competitive market. All of these solutions will track vacation, sick and PTO and provide multiple payroll reports for management use.

When to use Intuit Online Payroll

Intuit Online Payroll for Small Business and Intuit Online Payroll for Accountants is essentially the same product. The difference is in pricing and the use of a console with marketing, resources and client tax reminders. Additionally, with the Accountant subscription, clients who process their own payroll will see a "branded" website with the accountant's logo. Pricing can go as low as $10.99 per client with 50 or more companies processing payroll under the accountant, so this is definitely a revenue source for the consultant to review.

QuickBooks for Windows has a one-click feature (see Figure 11-33) for downloading. Other software, such as QuickBooks Online can download Intuit Online Payroll using .iif import.

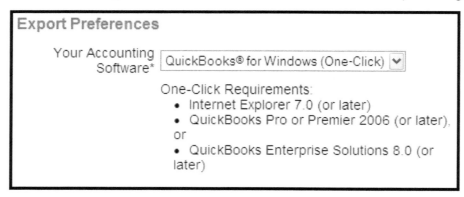

Figure 11-33 One-Click Export Option for Intuit Online Payroll

Intuit Online Payroll (IOP) can be used with any company up to 250 employees. The ideal company to use IOP is one that does not need job costing done inside QuickBooks, and either uses Enterprise to monitor permissions, or is small enough that only the owner and persons with permitted access to HR records also have permissions to access the checking account. IOP downloads as journal entries, with all the detail pointing to the correct accounts, as set up below by choosing Export Preferences under the Setup Menu (see Figure 11-34). Options also allow for how checks are going to be printed.

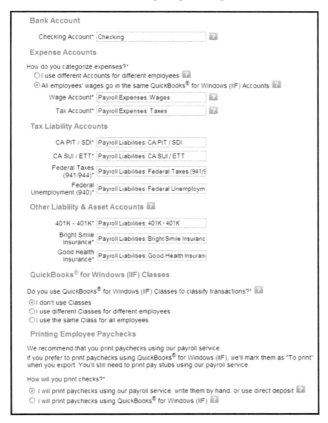

Figure 11-34 Intuit Online Payroll Export and Printing Options

IOP is also a terrific solution when the accountant does the payroll, or when the client travels or is location in different offices during the year. IOP handles payroll for all states, most of them with tax payments done electronically. Since all employees can have electronic access to their paystubs online, when direct deposit is the choice, organization-wide, there is little need for printed paper at all.

When to use Intuit Integrated Payroll

QuickBooks Basic, Enhanced, Assisted, and Enhanced Payroll for Accountants are all payroll solutions that are fully integrated with the QuickBooks data file and cannot be performed outside the product.

- **Basic** – this solution can be used when the accountant is onsite processing payroll or quarterlies, or reports for this are provided for the accountant. This is a subscription for processing payroll, using tax tables for correct calculation, and for processing Federal Forms, with reports provided for processing state forms.

- **Enhanced** – this solutions can be used when the client will be processing both Federal and State payroll forms using QuickBooks, as well as processing payroll. See Figure 11-35 for the differences, per the Intuit website for payroll sign-up.
- **Enhanced Payroll for Accountants** (EPA) is the same solution as Enhanced, but allows for 50 company EINs to be used, so processing can be done by the accountant for up to 50 companies with the same payroll subscription.

Exclusive to Enhanced Payroll:		
Conveniently file tax forms and pay payroll taxes electronically with E-File & Pay[1]	✓	✗
Automatically fills in the latest federal and most state payroll tax forms for you - just print, sign, and mail	✓	✗
Track workers' compensation[1]	✓	✗
Easily Pay Employees		
Create paychecks in just a few clicks: calculate earnings, payroll taxes and deductions	✓	✓
Print paychecks yourself, or use convenient Direct Deposit (additional fees apply)	✓	✓
Run customizable reports anytime to see how payroll affects your bottom line	✓	✓
Efficiently Pay Payroll Taxes and File Tax Forms		
Instantly calculates federal and state payroll taxes	✓	✓
Easily share data with your accountant	✓	✓
Automatically updates the latest federal and state payroll tax rates in QuickBooks	✓	✓
Integrates Seamlessly with QuickBooks		
Works within QuickBooks so there's no double data entry	✓	✓
Help When You Need It		
Contact our payroll specialists or use our 24/7 knowledge base to get answers anytime[3]	✓	✓

Figure 11-35 Differences in Enhanced and Basic Payroll Subscriptions

- **Assisted** – this solution works the best for most clients processing their own payroll. Once the payroll is processed, the client will "send" the data electronically to Intuit, with a PIN, from inside the data file, and Intuit will handle all tax payments and filings and post to the accounts in QuickBooks designated during the setup of the payroll service.

Questions to consider in final choices

There are several questions you should considering when choosing a payroll service. The recommended plan of action for determining your payroll solutions approach is to first determine if you will provide payroll. Second, make a checklist of what the client's needs are and determine the best solution considering all factors.

Do I, as an accountant, want to resell payroll as a service?

This first issue to consider is whether the consultant wants to resell the service. This is a big step. You should ask yourself the following:

- Do I know the payroll laws of my state?
- What are the limitations of what I will offer?
- Do I want to process payroll for my clients or do I want to train them to process and continue the relationship as a consultant?
- Can I price this payroll to ensure both my success and my clients' happiness with the service?

If you are reselling the service, you should consider QuickBooks Enhanced Payroll for Accountants, for desktop use and Intuit Online Payroll for Accountants. You will want an offering that will allow you the least effort in getting the information into QuickBooks. If you are the keeper of the data file, EPA will work. If the client is the keeper of the data file, IOP will probably be the better choice.

Alternative options to allow for accountant preparation, is to allow the client to sign up for the payroll service, but use the accountant for preparation, or as trusted advisor.

Intuit Online Payroll for Accountants

If you are fairly familiar with the laws of your state, consideration should be given to offering payroll service to your clients. In recent years, due to online technologies, offering payroll has become easier and profitable for consultants to offer. Intuit online payroll can be a completely electronic solution, providing employee view to paystubs, direct deposit, and electronic paying and filing of federal and state forms (most states are covered). With these solutions, the payroll processor can run payroll from anywhere in the world with high speed internet access.

Additionally, IOP (Intuit Online Payroll) can accrue for retirement and handle deductions for garnishments, reimbursements, and track holiday and vacation and sick pay. In recent years, the ability to use Pay-As-You-Go Worker's Comp and a small business 401K package, makes this product competitive with the larger payroll solutions.

IOP for Accountants offers a client login that is a white screen, with no Intuit branding, at www.managepayroll.com. This allows the accountant to offer branded payroll services.

Figure 11-36 Client login for IOP for Accountants

With accountant pricing as low as $10.99 for 5 employees, with unlimited payroll processing per month, the accountant can offer services competitive with other payroll services, with the added comfort to clients, of having a trusted advisor available. Billing for IOP for Accountants is done from Intuit by ACH monthly, so the accountant can determine pricing, and level of service to provide.

Features of Intuit Online Payroll for Accountants:

Unbranded client login

All emails and account withdrawals only reference "payroll"

Preferences for client access for: payroll only, payroll processing and employee setup, and full access to all features

Household and small business employers for up to 250 employees/contractors

Online access for employees, contractors and client owners

Direct Deposit for both employees and contractors at no additional cost

Vacation and Sick Pay Tracking

Time Tracking via clock in and out, or timesheet tracking, with approval capabilities

Email reminders to client, client and accountant, or accountant only for both payroll and tax payments and filings. Email reminders to client come from accountant email

Competitive choices for Worker's Comp Pay-as-you-go to allow for easier cash flow for clients, and elimination of lump-sum premiums

401K options at low pricing for administration

1099 electronic processing

Download to QuickBooks Online, QuickBooks for the MAC and QuickBooks for Windows (One-click import also available for QB for Windows)

Marketing for the Accountant, including customizable email, PowerPoint, flash demo for accountant website, test drive. Also available are printed brochures to customize with logo and branding, and sample engagement letters

List of resources for all states

Very easy to sell to existing clients

While the advantages far outweigh disadvantages for IOP, those items should be mentioned here:

Some W2 box options are not available, moving expenses among them.

A few states are not available for electronic paying and filing, but all forms are provided for printout.

There is only one reimbursements account, and only two fields for "other earnings

No job costing at this time

Payroll cannot be edited, but must be deleted and processed again

The process for handling payroll:

1. Payroll Setup, about a 15-minute process with 5 employees or less, with proper information available to begin: payroll year-to-date, if any, employee exemptions and status, pay rates, deductions, and taxes paid year to date. Processing payroll itself normally takes 5 minutes or less.

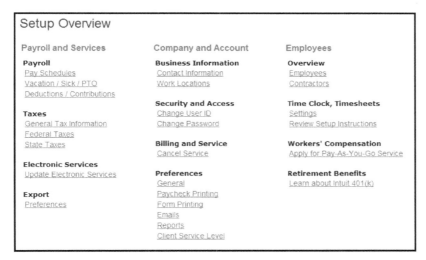

Figure 11-37 Intuit Online Payroll Setup Screen

2.   Email received by client and/or accountant:

```
From: Accountant Name [mailto:noreply@managepayroll.com]
Sent: Monday, November 15, 2010 7:11 AM
To: Accountant
Subject: Payday Reminder for Academy Glass


Dear Accountant Name:

This is your reminder that paychecks for direct deposit on 11/19/2010 must be approved and the money must be available in your
bank account by 5:00pm PT on 11/17/2010 for the pay period 11/07/2010-11/13/2010.

Employer:
    Timeless Skin Spa

Employees:
    Kati Reynolds
    James Smith
    Jim Moen
    Robert Black

To calculate your payroll and generate paystubs, go to https://www.managepayroll.com/elink?a=payday&d (if you cannot click on
this link, copy it and paste it into your browser's location box).
```

Figure 11-38 Email reminder to Process Payroll

3.   Process Payroll, with approved timecards, or fill in time

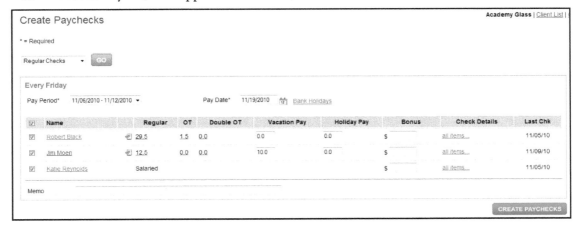

Figure 11-39 Create Paychecks with Approved Time

4.   Approve Payroll

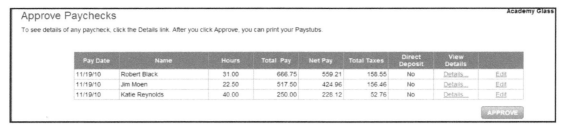

Figure 11-40 Approve Paychecks

5.   Balance of processes: View and Print, Modify Check Numbers (if NOT Direct Deposit), and Send Email, all of which can be done screen by screen, but are shown here all in one screen

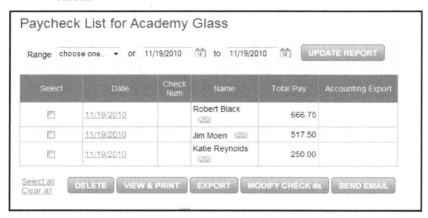

Figure 11-41 Paycheck list with processing choices

6.   If checks need to be printed, IOP brings up a .pdf which can be printed on blank check stock, or preprinted QuickBooks checks.

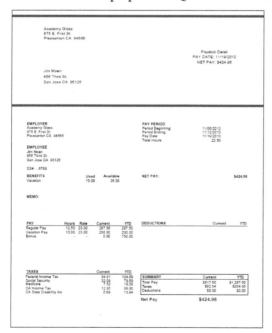

Figure 11-42 Printed paycheck

The process is simple enough that clients can be taught in one payroll lesson, with hands on.

Emails for employees for timecards setup. Emails from the same source send out email reminders for approver setup, pay approval and entering timecards. Emails are also sent to employees when paychecks are ready to view after payroll processing. It is a good idea to use personal emails for employees to allow access and notification should the employee leave the company.

```
From: PaycheckRecords.com [mailto:noreply@paycheckrecords.com]
Sent: Monday, November 08, 2010 6:31 PM
To: Jim Moen
Subject: View Paystubs and Enter Your Hours Online

Dear Jim Moen:

Your employer, Academy Glass, has set up access for you at PaycheckRecords.com. You can view and print your own pay stubs, and you'll get email notifications when you have a
new paystub. You can also enter your timesheets online. Just log in and enter your hours. At the end of the pay period, click Turn In. That's it.

If you haven't clicked Turn In by the last day of the pay period, we'll send you an email reminder.

Your temporary user ID is:

Derek62934

Your temporary password is:

58wnXHt3

You will need this information the first time you log in.

1. Go to www.paycheckrecords.com

2. Log in with the information above

To ensure the security of your account, we will then prompt you to verify some personal information and reset your password.

To view paystubs, click the Paystubs tab.

To enter your hours worked, click the Timesheet tab. If you make a mistake and click Turn In too early, you can always click the link at the bottom of your timesheet to
update it.

We hope you enjoy the convenience of online paystubs and timesheets!

Sincerely,

Paycheck Records
```

Figure 11-43 Invitation to Paycheck Records for Employee

All payroll and tax payments can be imported to QuickBooks – all versions except Simple Start. The accountant will set this up before the first payroll is processed, based on the chart of accounts. Additionally, import can be done in QuickBooks for Windows with one-click, but this is not recommended unless client is computer savvy, as updates are issued, and client is required to install updates.

Some Best Practices ideas for reselling payroll that successful practices have proposed are listed below. These practices differ from traditional payroll practices of clients calling in hours and accountant delivering checks or mailing. Following some, or all, of these best practices will ensure a profitable payroll practice.

- Flat Rate Offering, or Schedule of Fees provided to client
- Engagement Letter Signed, including client permission for accountant to pay payroll taxes on client's behalf, and client responsibility for available funds
- Payment to accountant as a contractor through the payroll service – auto-debit monthly
- Client processes payroll, with training provided by accountant
- Additional fees apply if accountant is also processes payroll, in addition to providing the payroll service
- If Accountant does process payroll, delivery of checks should be extra, or .pdf of checks provided for client to print
- Providing tax payment and tax filing, although electronic, provides client level of comfort knowing the accountant, as trusted advisor, is watching over the payroll process

- If client has no access, and is owner of QuickBooks file, accountant should provide payroll and payroll tax imports, and email notifications of withdrawals for taxes

Job Costing and Time Tracking

The integrated payroll solutions, Basic, Enhanced or Assisted, are the best solutions for eliminating duplicate job costing and time tracking data entry as well as for all the additional taxes to be job costed as payroll is done. This option allows either using time sheets or entering payroll hours directly on the paycheck.

Payroll preferences should be reviewed before beginning payroll for job costing. Job Costing should be checked, as well as Assign one class per Earning Item, as seen in Figure 11-44. This will allow for full job costing to both class and job per earnings item, and will permit the costing of payroll taxes to all jobs listed on the paycheck as well.

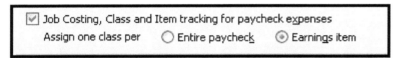

Figure 11-44 Job Costing Preferences

If time tracking is needed for billing purposes and employees are paid directly from those time cards, with client billing AND payroll is driven from the time sheets, then Basic and Enhanced are better options than IOP. Both Customer/Job and Payroll Item can be entered in the time sheet, as illustrated below in Figure 11-45.

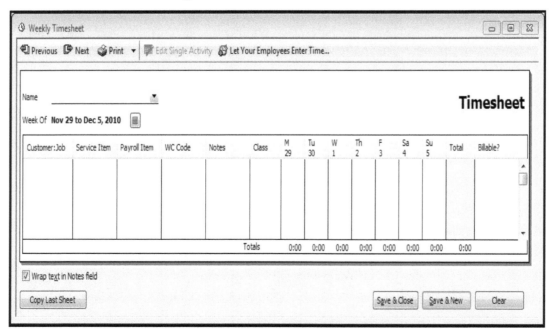

Figure 11-45 QuickBooks Time Sheet

Worker's Comp Issues

It is important to consider worker's comp issues when deciding which payroll solution is best for your client. QuickBooks Basic Payroll will not job cost or track worker's comp, but

QuickBooks Enhanced will. If it is important to track this for contractors or those that do project costing, Enhanced would be the best product.

If the client is looking for a worker's comp solution that does not require reporting at all, QuickBooks Assisted and Enhanced Payroll provides a great solution. XacpPAY© by Hartford provides a "pay as you go" product, sharing information with carrier after each payroll. ACH deductions are made following each payroll, eliminating large down payments, most audit adjustments and audit reporting. Also available in IOP, through Intego Insurance, a variety of worker's comp insurance options are available with a variety of carriers.

Where are the employees located?

If employees work in the same locations all the time, but there are multiple work sites, the accountant should be involved in setting up and training for payroll, even if the client processes the payroll. Assisted payroll is probably the best solution for this if there are states involved that Intuit Online Payroll does not support with electronic payment, as the processing will be cumbersome for the client. If the accountant is doing the payroll, the costs of handling this type of payroll would be prohibitive compared to using Assisted Payroll.

Also consider if employees use direct deposit. Processing payroll in multiple places, even if it's in the same city, can be more complicated when payroll checks must be printed, signed, and handed out.

- Processing payroll in one place, but live checks delivered to multiple locations can be done either with IOP or Enhanced or Basic, but time to deliver or mail checks should be considered in choosing which payroll solution to use.
- Accountant-prepared payroll using IOP with live checks can be delivered electronically using .pdf files. See Figure 11-46. These can be password protected, and printed at the additional locations with QuickBooks-compatible checks, as long as there is a signer at that location.

QuickBooks may not be the best answer for payroll needs if your clients' employees are located in multiple jurisdictions. Sports teams, with players in multiple states on the same payroll, or construction companies working in several states under Federal contracts, are not best suited to handling payroll with any of the Intuit solutions.

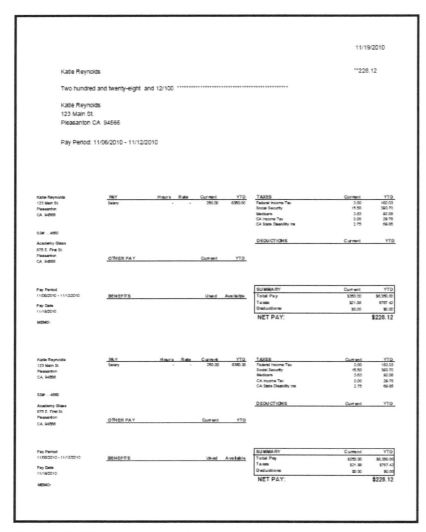

Figure 11-46 PDF format for payroll check using Intuit Online Payroll

Special Needs Reporting

While all payroll services provide multiple reporting options for clients, the integrated solutions are by far the best – custom reporting, such as Certified Payroll, can be created with payroll done inside QuickBooks using Basic or Enhanced. Because the transactions are created in the software, custom reporting needs can almost always be met. Additionally, if there are special needs like AIA reporting and Certificated payroll, looking at additional add-ons that can provide this formatting with the payroll transactions, would be a value-added service to provide to your clients.

Worker's Compensation

Depending on the state in which you pay wages, you'll have different needs for tracking worker's compensation. Some states require employers to obtain private worker's compensation insurance, and other states have a labor tax. Usually the employer pays 100% of the worker's compensation insurance premiums, but the labor tax is sometimes shared between the employer and the employee.

QuickBooks Enhanced and Assisted payroll services provide the functionality that tracks job-costs, and accrues worker's compensation premiums as each paycheck is recorded.

This section presents methods of tracking worker's compensation for three different types of businesses.

To Accrue or not to Accrue...

Many businesses don't need to provide full job costing of payroll expenses. In this case, it's best not to accrue worker's compensation premiums because the benefit is not worth the extra setup and complication. Also, there is an extra cost for the Assisted or Enhanced Payroll service that you may not need if you don't need the ability to print state quarterly reports and you don't plan to job-cost and accrue worker's compensation premiums.

On the other hand, many businesses must provide full job costing of payroll including worker's compensation. The third method shows how those businesses can track worker's compensation by accruing it with each paycheck.

Method 1: All Employees Work Under A Single Rate; No Job Costing

If each employee in your company works under only one rate and you do not need to track job costs, no special setup is necessary. Be sure that the regular, overtime, and double time wages are recorded to separate payroll items. Create a Payroll Summary report and set the date range to agree with your worker's compensation coverage period. Use the gross wage amounts to complete your worker's compensation report, including any adjustments necessary to exclude the overtime and double time excess, and then calculate and pay the premiums.

Method 2: Employees Have More Than One Rate; No Job Costing

If some of your employees earn wages in more than one worker's compensation category, use the following steps to calculate worker's compensation. This method does not accrue worker's compensation, but instead gives a method for breaking out wages by worker's compensation categories so that you can determine the wages subject to each category. This method does not address overtime, so it is less than perfect, but if overtime is not involved and if no job costing is required, it serves as a simple but effective way of tracking wages for your worker's compensation reporting.

1. Create separate hourly and/or salary Wage Items for each worker's compensation rate.

Example Wage Item names:

- Admin – Rate 1
- Framer – Rate 2
- Photographer – Rate 3
- Technician – Rate 4

2.   On paychecks and timesheets use the appropriate wage item to pay each employee according
      to the category in which they worked (see Figure 11-47). The wages paid in each category
      will then be tracked separately.

Earnings				
Item Name	Rate	Hours	Customer:Job	Service Item
5475 - Painting	15.00	12.00		24 Paint
5646 - Carpentry	25.00	16.00		25 Cleanup
5188 - Plumbing	25.00	8.00		14 Plumbing

Figure 11-47 Paycheck Detail – hours allocated to worker's compensation rates.

3.   Create a Payroll Summary report for a breakdown of wages by rate. Filter this report for all
      gross pay items, and then select total only. If you track sick, vacation, and overtime hours in
      QuickBooks, you will have at least four wage items for each rate. In this case, customize the
      report using **Modify Report** and filter for selected payroll items to create a separate report
      for each rate. Memorize each report for future use (See Figure 11-48 and Figure 11-49).

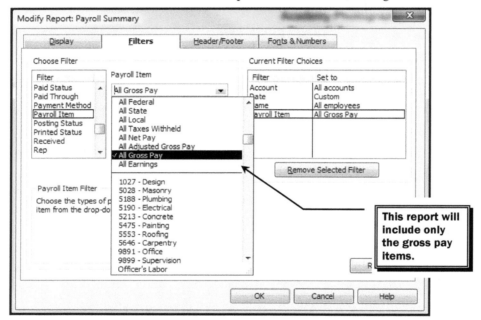

Figure 11-48 Filter Screen. Filtered for all Gross Pay Payroll Items.

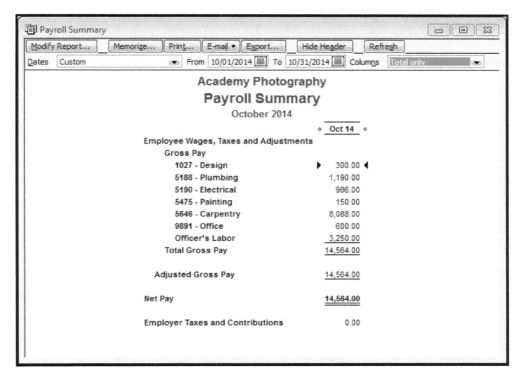

Figure 11-49 Payroll Summary Report – Filtered for All Gross Pay items.

Method 3: Worker's Compensation – Assisted and Enhanced

If you require detailed job costing and handling of overtime, it is best to accrue worker's compensation using the QuickBooks Assisted or Enhanced Payroll service.

Note that you must set up Workers Compensation before you run payroll, or your workers compensation reports will be incorrect or incomplete. There is no way to enter "year-to-date" information for your workers compensation premiums.

Therefore, if you start using the feature in the middle of your insurance year, in order to get the full picture of your workers compensation obligations for your insurance year, you will have to combine the information QuickBooks tracks with the information you tracked outside of QuickBooks before you started using the feature.

Overview of Worker's Compensation in Assisted and Enhanced Payroll Services

The first step in using the Worker's Compensation feature is to use the Workers Compensation Setup wizard. This wizard helps you assign default workers compensation codes to employees, decide whether you want to exclude overtime premiums from workers compensation premium calculations, and enter an experience modification factor, if you have one.

Then, as paychecks are created, QuickBooks accrues workers compensation premiums for each earnings item that has a worker's compensation code assigned to it. If you assigned a default code to an employee in the workers compensation setup, QuickBooks automatically assigns that code to the employee's earnings items on their paychecks.

To see how much workers compensation accrues on each paycheck, look for Workers Compensation in the Company Summary portion of the Preview Paycheck window.

The Worker's Compensation Summary report displays the accrued workers compensation premiums.

Also, with this method, you must use the Pay Liabilities window to create a payroll liability payment when you pay worker's compensation premiums.

The setup process below assumes you have already subscribed to the Assisted or Enhanced Payroll service.

Worker's Compensation Setup

To active Worker's Compensation tracking, follow the steps in this example:

1. Select the **Edit** menu and then select **Preferences**.

2. In the *Preferences* window, click **Payroll & Employees** in the list on the left.

3. Click the Company Preferences tab.

4. Click the **Worker's Compensation** button in the right hand section of the preferences window (Figure 11-50).

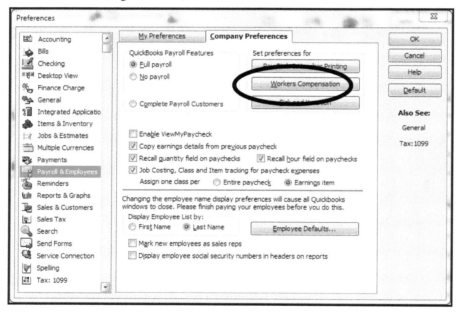

Figure 11-50 Payroll & Employees preferences

5. Click **Track Workers Comp** and set the other fields as shown in Figure 11-51. Then click **OK**.

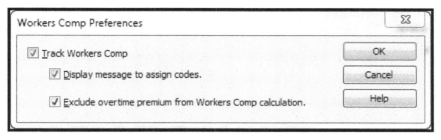

Figure 11-51 Worker's Comp Preferences

6.   Click **OK** to close the *Preferences* window.

7.   From the *Employees* menu, select **Workers Compensation** and then select **Set Up Workers Comp** (see Figure 11-52).

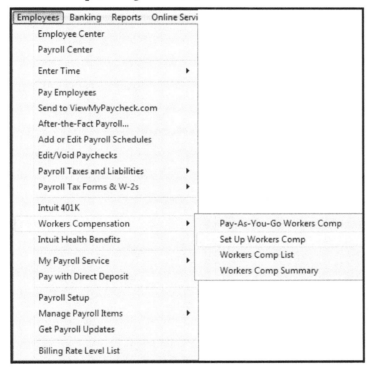

Figure 11-52 Selecting the Workers Comp setup wizard

> **Labor Tax Note:** If your state charges a labor tax and the employee pays a portion of this tax, create two Other Tax Items following the steps detailed in this section. Name the first item "Labor Tax Employer" and the second item "Labor Tax Employee." For the "Labor Tax Employee" item, select "Tax is paid by the employee." The two items are otherwise identical.

8.   The *Workers Compensation Setup* wizard is shown in Figure 11-53. Click **Next**.

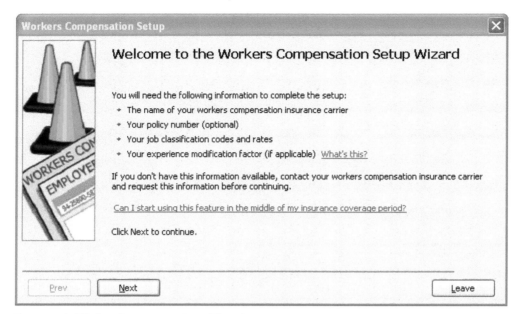

Figure 11-53 Workers Compensation Setup Wizard

9.   Enter your vendor and account number as shown in Figure 11-54 and then click **Next**.

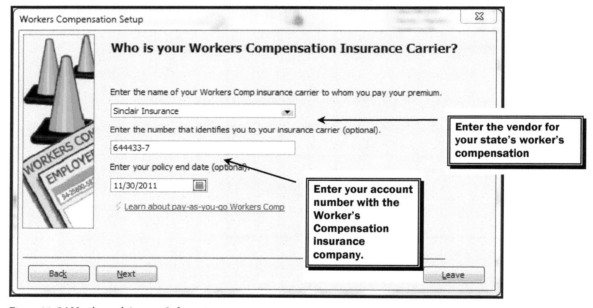

Figure 11-54 Vendor and Account Information

10.   Select **Add New** from the *Workers Comp Code* drop-down menu on Mike Mazuki's line.

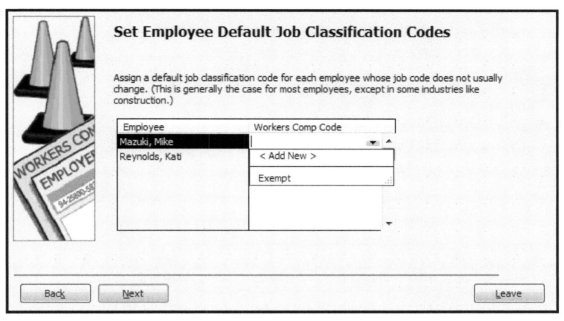

Figure 11-55 Tax Tracking Type

11.   Set up the Workers Comp code as shown in Figure 11-56 and then click **OK**.

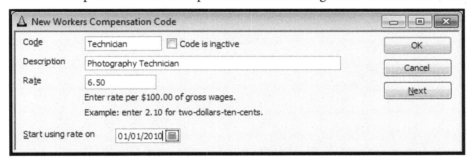

Figure 11-56 Workers Comp code for Mike Mazuki

12.   Select **Add New** from the *Workers Comp Code* drop-down menu on Kati Reynolds' line.

13.   Set up the Workers Comp code as shown in Figure 11-57 and then click **OK**.

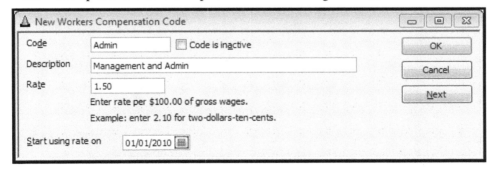

Figure 11-57 Workers Comp code for Kati Reynolds

14.   The Workers Compensation Setup wizard shows your progress (see Figure 11-58). Click **Next**.

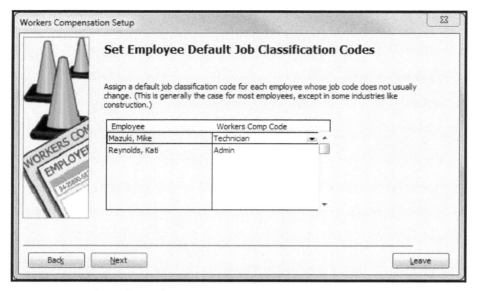

Figure 11-58 Employee Job Classifications

15.   On the *Enter your Experience Modification Factor* window (Figure 11-59), click **No** and then click **Next**.

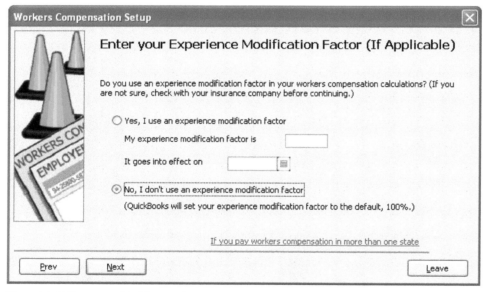

Figure 11-59 Experience Modification Factor screen

Experience Modification Factor: Some insurance companies assign you an experience modification factor to use when you calculate your workers compensation premiums. This rate is based on your company's record of workers compensation claims. The better your track record, the lower your rate (or at least the fewer increases), which sometimes results in a discount on your workers compensation premiums. The more claims you have, the higher your rate, which sometimes results in a higher premium.

If you use the Workers Compensation feature in QuickBooks and your insurer has asked you to use an experience modification rate in your workers compensation calculations, QuickBooks needs this information to provide you with accurate and complete workers calculations and compensation reports. If you are not sure whether you are supposed to use one or not, contact your workers compensation insurance company.

You initially enter your experience modification factor as part of the Workers Compensation Setup wizard. If the rate for your experience modification factor changes later, you can update it from the Workers Comp Code list.

16.   Click **Yes** in the *Overtime Payments* screen (Figure 11-60) and then click **Next**.

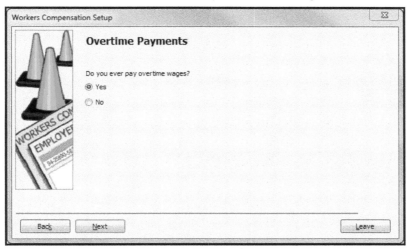

Figure 11-60 Overtime Payments screen.

17.   On the *Overtime Premiums and Workers Compensation Calculations* screen (Figure 11-61), make sure that **No** is selected and click **Next**.

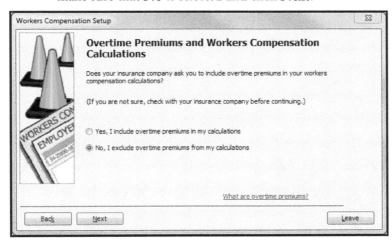

Figure 11-61 Overtime Premiums and Workers Compensation Calculations screen

18.   If you already have overtime items, you won't see the screen in Figure 11-62 and you can skip this step. Select **Time-and-a-half** and then click **Next**. This creates a payroll item called Overtime Rate in your Payroll Item list.

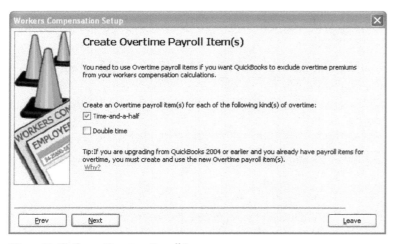

Figure 11-62 Create Overtime Payroll Items screen.

19.   Leave the default payroll item name and click **Next**.

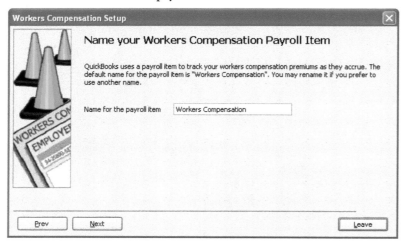

Figure 11-63 Naming the Workers Compensation Payroll Item

20.   In the next screen (Figure 11-64), you can see and review all the choices you made during
       the setup wizard. If anything is not correct, you can click Prev to back up to the appropriate
       screen, make the fix, and return to this last screen. Click **Finish**.

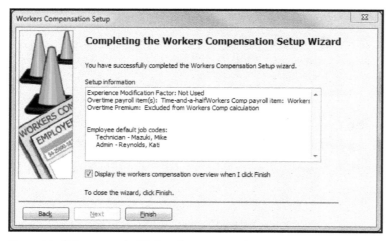

Figure 11-64 Reviewing the Workers Compensation Setup

21. QuickBooks displays help text for workers compensation. Review the help and then close the help screen.

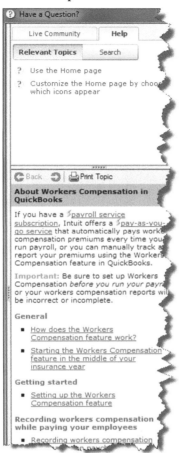

Figure 11-65 Onscreen help for workers compensation

Edit Worker's Comp Payroll item

After completing the workers compensation setup wizard, there are a few more steps to completing and customizing your workers compensation setup. The first is to edit the Workers Compensation item that was set up by the setup wizard.

1. Display the Payroll Items list, and double-click on the Workers Compensation item.

2. To track workers compensation by job in the P&L by Job report (and other reports), click **Track Expenses by Job** (Figure 11-66) and then click **Next**.

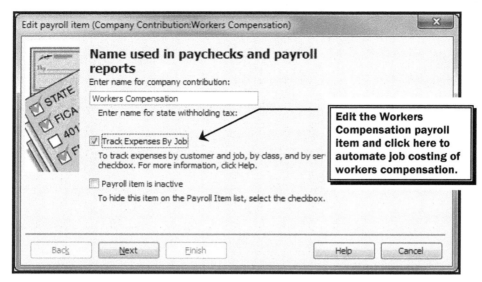

Figure 11-66 Editing the Workers Compensation Payroll Item

3.   Edit the *Liability account* and the *Expense account* to connect to the correct accounts in your chart of accounts. Note that you can only assign one expense account for each workers comp payroll item. If you need to separate expenses, you must create multiple workers comp items.

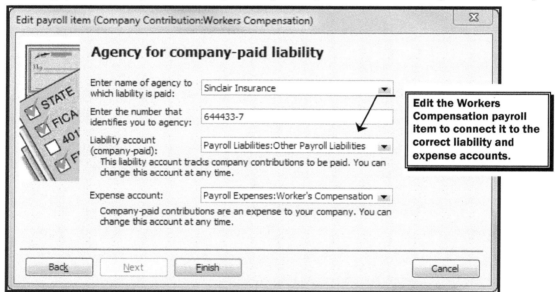

Figure 11-67 Editing the Workers Compensation Payroll Item to set liability and expense accounts

4.   Click **Finish**.

Modifying Worker's Compensation Defaults in Employee Records

To set the default workers compensation code for each employee, edit each employee as follows:

1.   From the Employee Center, double-click the employee's name to edit the employee record. Then select **Workers Compensation** from the *Change Tabs* menu, and select the primary workers comp code.

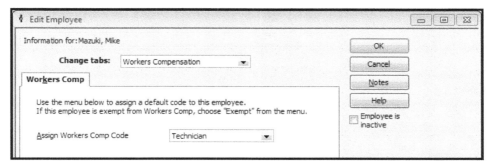

Figure 11-68 Selecting the default workers compensation code for this employee

Even if an employee works in different categories, this will set the default code, and you can override the default as you enter timesheets or directly.

2.   Click **OK** to accept the default changes and close the *Edit Employee* window.

Workers Comp Codes on Timesheets

For hourly employees, enter timesheets with Workers Comp codes.

1.   Display Mike Mazuki's timesheets for the first two weeks in January 2010 and assign WC codes as shown in Figure 11-69 and Figure 11-70.

2.   The data file already contains timesheet data for Mike Mazuki using the default **Technician** workers comp code in the WC Code column. Modify the timesheet data and add the **Admin** WC Code in the appropriate the columns as shown in Figure 11-69 and Figure 11-70.

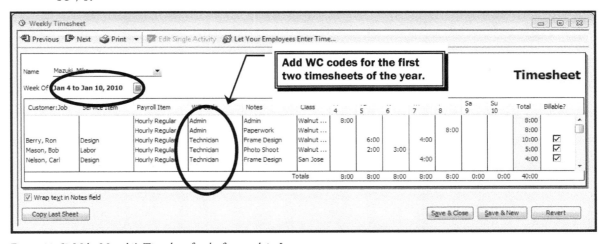

Figure 11-69 Mike Mazuki's Timesheet for the first week in January

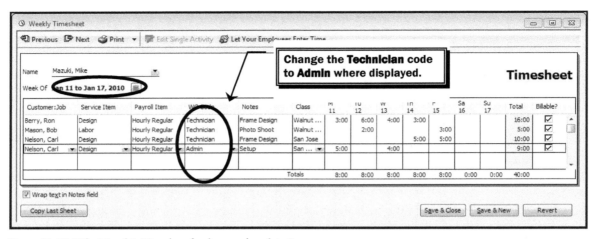

Figure 11-70 Mike Mazuki's Timesheet for the second week in January

Workers Comp Item on Paychecks

When you create paychecks, the workers compensation calculations are automatically added to the *Company Summary* section of each paycheck. Follow the steps in this example:

1.   Create Paychecks normally, using timesheet information available.

2.   At the *Review and Create Paychecks* step, click on name of each employee to review their paycheck detail (see Figure 11-71).

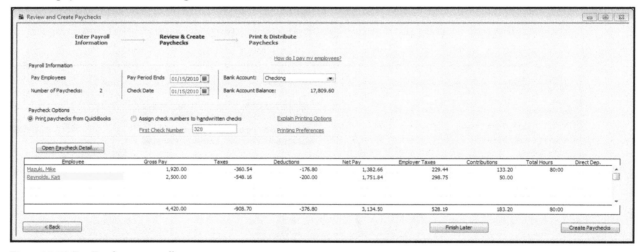

Figure 11-71 Pay Employees normally

3.   Click **Mike Mazuki** to review his paycheck detail. QuickBooks will multiply gross wages by the Worker's Compensation rate to accrue and job cost worker's compensation expense for this paycheck (see Figure 11-72). Click **OK** to return to the *Review and Create Paychecks* window.

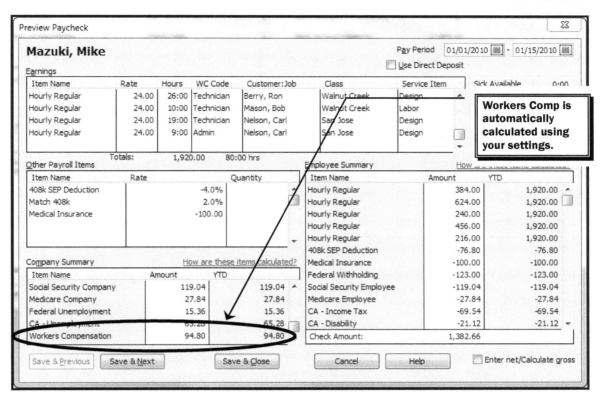

Figure 11-72 QuickBooks accrues worker's compensation expense based on your settings

4. Click **Kati Reynolds** to review her paycheck detail (see Figure 11-73). Click **OK** to return to the *Review and Create Paychecks* window.

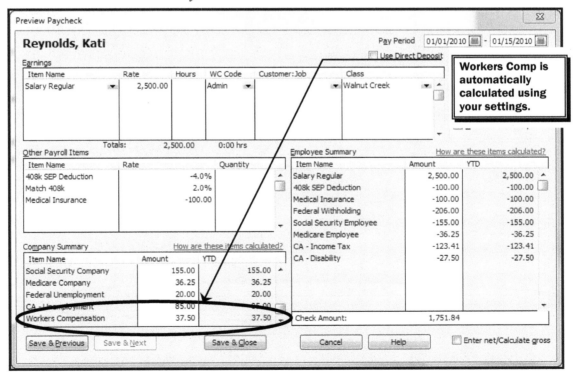

Figure 11-73 Kati Reynolds' paycheck with Workers Compensation calculated.

5.   Click Create Paychecks.

Paying Worker's Compensation Premiums

After you've entered your paychecks, QuickBooks will show your worker's compensation premiums as liabilities in the Pay Liabilities screen. To pay the liabilities, follow the steps in this example:

1.   Click **Pay Liabilities** in the *Employees* section on the home page.

2.   Enter the dates of coverage in the "From" and "Through" fields of the date range screen. Academy Photography files a worker's compensation report at the end of each calendar quarter. Click **OK**.

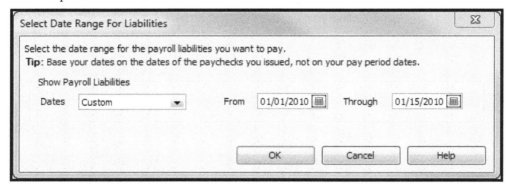

Figure 11-74 Payroll Liabilities Date Range

3.   Select the **Worker's Compensation** payroll item (see Figure 11-75) and click **Create**.

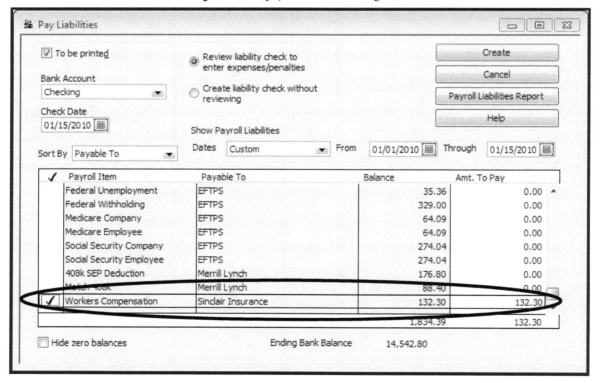

Figure 11-75 Pay worker's compensation premiums using the Pay Liabilities screen

4.   QuickBooks creates a check for the amount due (see Figure 11-76).

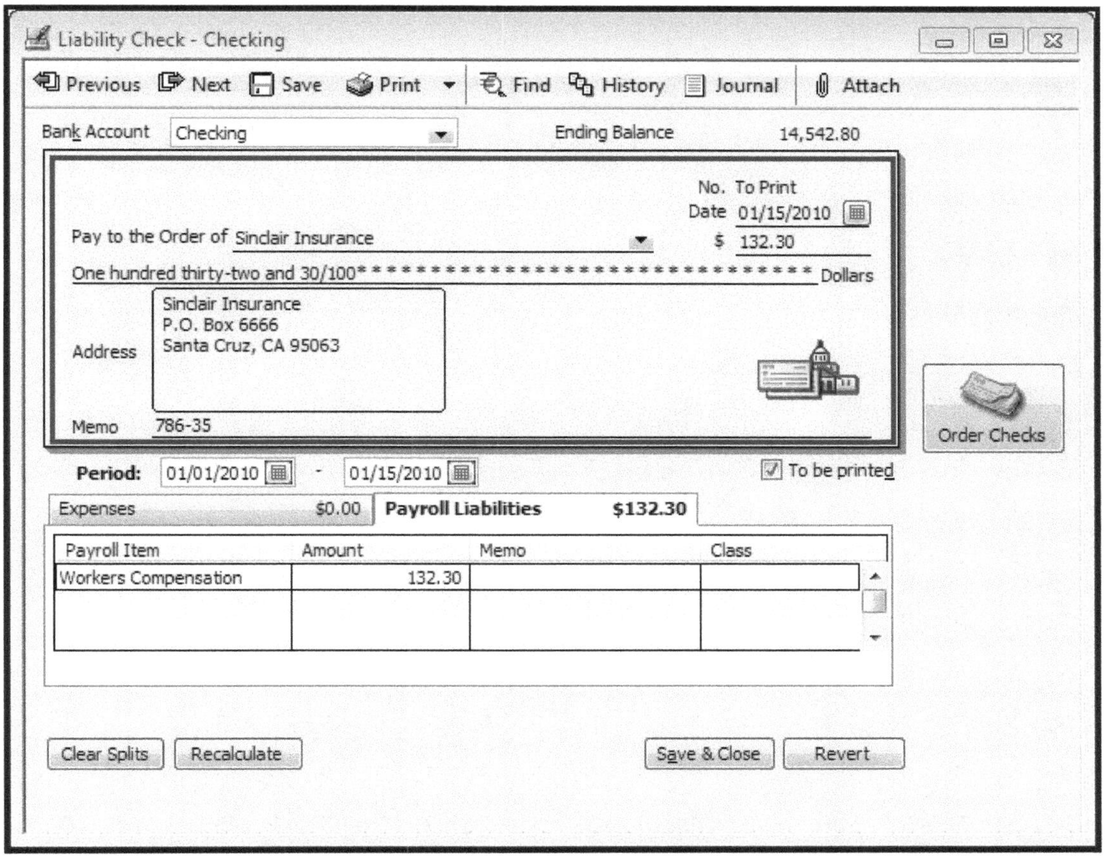

Figure 11-76 Liability Check for worker's compensation

Adjusting Workers Compensation Payments

Occasionally, you may need to adjust the amount to agree with the worker's compensation report. For example, Academy Photography received a miscellaneous credit of $10 to be applied to the payment. To record this adjustment, follow the steps in this example:

> **Note:** Do not use this method to apply overpayments from prior periods or estimated pre-payments. Instead refer to "Processing Pre-payments" on page 461.

1.   On the payroll liability check, click the Expenses tab and enter the credit amount as a negative number (see Figure 11-77).

2.   Code the adjustment to the Insurance:Work Comp expense account (see Figure 11-77).

3.   Click **Recalculate** to adjust the net amount of the check. If the adjustment is significant, you may want to split the adjustment up by job so that adjustment is allocated to each job.

4.   Click **Save & Close**, and then **OK** to record the transaction.

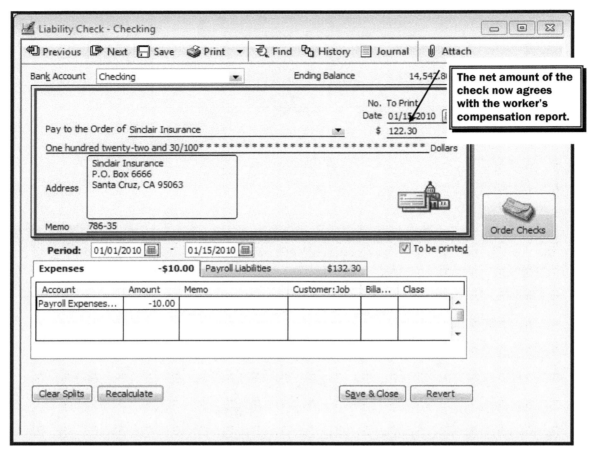

Figure 11-77 Liability Check Edit Screen

Workers Compensation Reports

There are several reports available for workers compensation. To create these reports, follow
the steps in this example:

1.   From the *Reports* menu, select **Employees & Payroll** and then select **Workers Comp
     Summary**. Then set the date range to view your report.

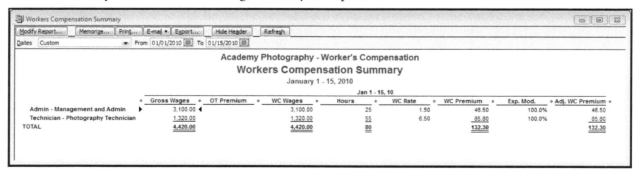

Figure 11-78 Workers Compensation Summary Report

2.   To view the Worker's Compensation by Job summary, select the *Reports* menu, select
     Employees & Payroll and then select **Workers Comp by Job Summary**. Then set the date
     range to view your report.

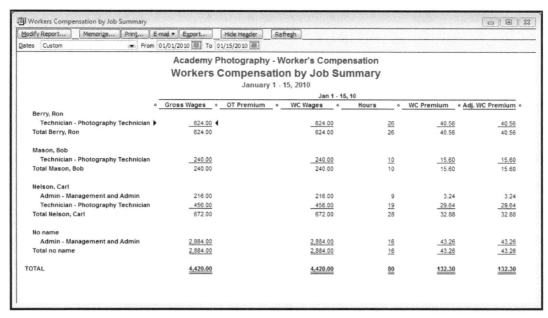

Figure 11-79 Workers Compensation by Job Summary Report

Processing Prepayments of Worker's Compensation

Some insurers require companies to pay an estimated premium at the beginning of the coverage period to be applied to the actual, calculated premium when filing the report.

To handle this situation, follow the steps in this example:

1. Code the prepayment check to an *Other Current Asset* account called **Prepaid Insurance**.

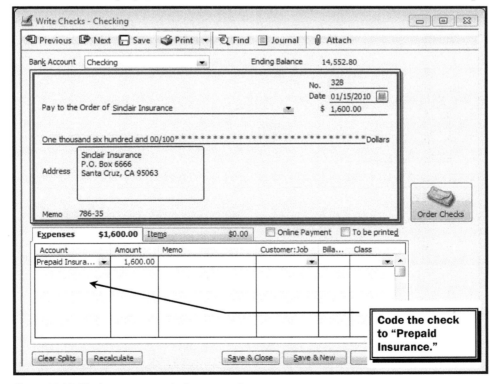

Figure 11-80 Check to pre-pay worker's compensation

2.   Edit the Workers Compensation Payroll item so that the Liability account field points to
      Prepaid Insurance instead of a liability account.

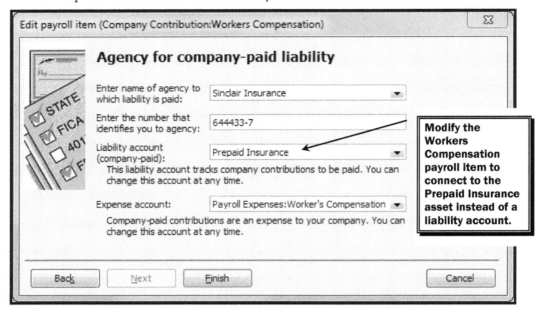

Figure 11-81 Liability Check Edit Screen

3.   Use the worker's compensation setup as described in Method 3 above.

4.   With the payroll item set to an Asset account, you will no longer need to use Pay Liabilities
      to clear the accruals because the accruals will now reduce the Prepaid Insurance account (see
      Figure 11-82).

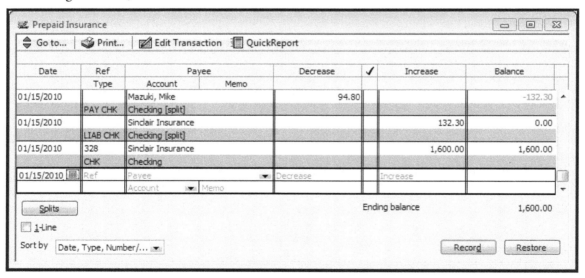

Figure 11-82 Prepaid Insurance account register

5.   Occasionally, you can *adjust* the Prepaid Insurance account to match the insurance
      company's records using a journal entry.

Employee Reimbursements

Employee Expenses

There are several ways to track, record and repay your employees for their expenses. Depending on the volume of expense transactions your employees have, you might choose different methods.

Whenever an employee of your company spends their personal money (either cash or charges on their personal credit card) on a business expense, and the company reimburses them for the expenses, the employee (including the owner) should submit an **expense report** including appropriate receipts to the company. The expense report should summarize all the expenses along with all the information necessary for the bookkeeper to categorize those expenses. The company treats the employee expense report as a Bill.

Employee Expense Reports – Reimburse through Pay Bills

1. First, set up a vendor record for the employee. In your vendor list, create a record with the employee's name and append a "- V" after the employee's name to distinguish it from the employee's record (see Figure 11-83). Set the *Print on Check as* field to the payee name without the "-V".

> **Note:**
> Consider entering the vendor name as last name, first name then the –V to be consistent with other individuals who are on the vendor list. The "Print on check as" would then be first name last name without the –V.

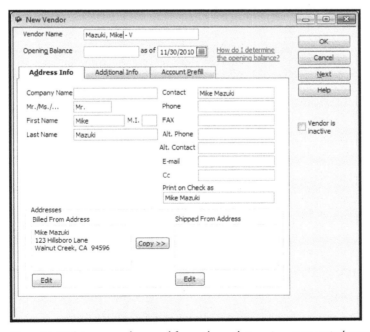

Figure 11-83 Set up a vendor record for employees that receive expense reimbursements.

2.   Enter a Bill to that vendor for the detailed expenses and pay the Bill normally. This keeps the expenses outside of the Payroll system, which simplifies the process of tracking employee expenses and reimbursements.

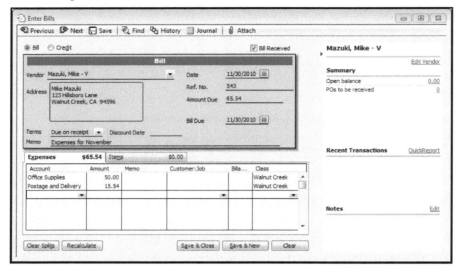

Figure 11-84 Use Bills to record information from employee expense reports

Employees Using a Company Credit Card

If the employee uses a company credit card, you'll need to enter each credit card charge in the credit card liability account. In this case, you won't have to reimburse the employee, however you should still require the employee to submit a report and related receipts for all expenditures.

> **Tip:** It is strongly recommended that you don't mix personal and business expenses in the same credit card account.

Issuing Advances for Expenses

If you issue advance checks to your employees before they incur **business expenses**, create a check to the employee (not a payroll check) and code it to Employee Advances (Other Current Asset). See Figure 11-85.

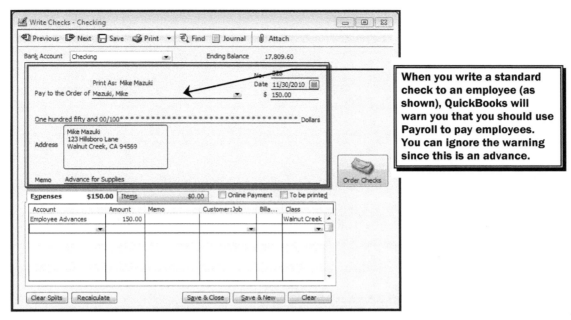

Figure 11-85 Use Write Checks to record employee advances.

When the employee submits an expense report, enter a journal entry detailing the expenses and offsetting to the Employee Advances account. Make sure to enter the employee's name in the name field on the Employee Advances line in the journal entry.

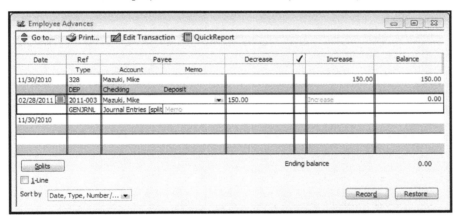

Figure 11-86 Employee Advances asset account register

This register (Figure 11-86) details all the expenses the employee used the advance for, and if the total advance is equal to the total expenses on the expense report, you won't need to withhold anything from the employee's paycheck to repay the company. If the employee owes the company money after taking into account the expense report, you can use the *Advance Repay* Payroll Item on the next payroll check.

Mileage Reimbursements

If you reimburse your employees for mileage or per diem expenses, it's best to handle the reimbursement as a vendor payment and require expense reports from your employees.

Enter the expense report as a Bill, just like every other bill. In the expense section of the bill, code all the expense totals for each expense shown on the report. Then, pay the Bill normally. This creates a separate check that does not involve payroll.

You can also use the Vehicle Mileage Tracker to record mileage, pass mileage through to invoices, and print mileage reports by vehicle.

Fringe Benefits

Fringe benefits are taxable benefits not paid in cash to employees. An example is a company car driven by an employee. The best way to track fringe benefits is by adding two Payroll Items. One is an **Addition** to gross pay with the W-2 tracking set to Fringe Benefits.

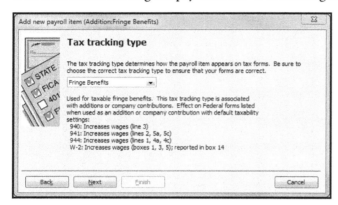

Figure 11-87 Addition item – Adds to gross pay, with tax tracking set to Fringe benefits.

The other is a **Deduction** from net pay (using the same account as the Addition Item) as shown in Figure 11-88. Use both of these Items on paychecks for employees who get this fringe benefit. The combination of these two Items makes QuickBooks track the benefit, increase taxable income, automatically increase the tax withholdings, and correctly accumulate data for the W-2.

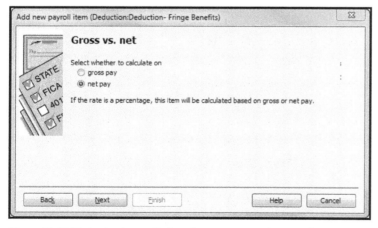

Figure 11-88 Deduction item – Deducts from net pay, with tax tracking set to none

These two Payroll Items should be added to each paycheck. This ensures that the benefit is taxed on each paycheck during the year and that the W-2 accurately reflects the benefit.

You can also record Fridge Benefits by directly adjusting the W-2, but the change will not affect any Payroll Reports and will be difficult to audit.

Adjust W-2s to Report Shareholder's Health Insurance

When S-Corp shareholders (those who own more than 2% of the company shares) are covered by the company health insurance plan (or long-term care plan), the IRS specifies that the benefit is reported in box 14 on their W-2. The easiest way to handle this in QuickBooks payroll is to create one single zero-dollar paycheck at the end of the year to record the total benefit amount onto the W-2.

> Note that S-Corp Medical health premiums increase taxable wages (Federal and State) and are subject to federal and state income tax. Therefore, the shareholders might prefer to have the health insurance premium added to each paycheck throughout the year so that they pay the taxes with each paycheck instead of having a lump of taxes due at the end of the year, but since the amount of tax is usually relatively small, we prefer doing a single adjustment (zero-dollar paycheck) at the end of each year, before the W-2s are prepared. You have to trick QuickBooks into making this adjustment, so this article explains the steps.

Making the Adjustment

To create your adjustment, you'll need to create two payroll items and a zero-dollar paycheck for each shareholder.

First, create a **company contribution** payroll item in the payroll item list. In the Liability and Expense Account fields, select the same account because we want this item to debit and credit the same account when we use it on paychecks. It's best to use the account you use to track your health insurance premium expenses.

Figure 11-89 Edit payroll item window

The tax tracking type determines how this item will affect the W-2, so it's critical that this is set to **SCorp Pd Med Premium**.

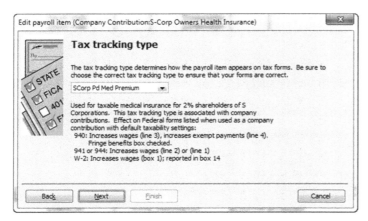

Figure 11-90 Tax Tracking in the Edit Payroll Item window

Leave the default checkmarks on the **Taxes** screen. These settings mean that the amount of health insurance premiums you add to paychecks are subject to Federal and State income taxes, but not Federal Unemployment, Medicare, or Social Security taxes.

Next, create an addition item. This is needed to trick QuickBooks into creating the zero-dollar paycheck. Normally, if you try to create a paycheck no earnings items but with other items that affect taxes, QuickBooks will calculate and deduct taxes, which results in a negative net check. However, QuickBooks won't let you create a paycheck with negative net pay.

So we need a trick. Our trick is to create an Addition payroll item that will act as a clearing item, similar to the one above. This item will be used to cover the employee paid taxes calculated on paycheck so that the end result is a net amount of zero.

Creating the Adjustment using a Paycheck

Create a zero-dollar paycheck for each shareholder as shown below. Make sure the date of the paycheck is within the year you want to affect. Clear out the earnings section of the paycheck and use the two items we created above in the Other Payroll Items section of the paycheck. Note that the S-Corp Adj Clearing item is added on one line, but then subtracted out on the next line. This is the trick that lets QuickBooks create this zero-dollar paycheck.

Note that you may have to override the taxes to zero. Make sure the net pay is zero, and confirm that the Company Summary section shows the correct information.

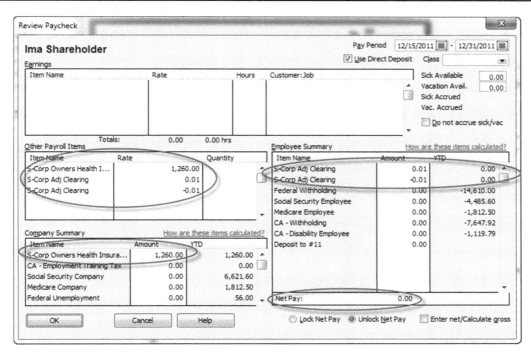

Figure 11-91Review Paycheck window

After you record this paycheck, preview the W-2 and verify that Box 1 and 16 increased by the amount of your health insurance adjustment. Also, verify that box 14 has SCorp MP followed by the correct amount.

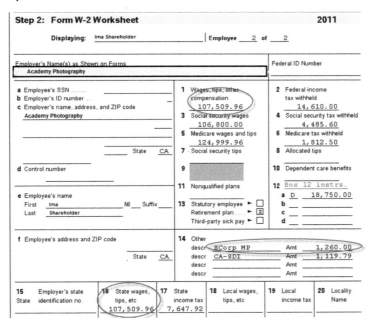

Note: If you use Assisted Payroll or ViewmyPaycheck, you must **send** the paycheck to the payroll service or to ViewmyPaycheck. See the help screens if you need help sending paychecks to the service.

Garnishments

To create Garnishment Payroll Items, follow the steps in this example:

1. Display the Payroll Item List and create a new item.

2. Use the *Custom Setup* to create a Deduction item, and enter the payee and account information. Then click **Next**.

3. Type **Garnishment** in *Enter name for deduction* field and click **Next**.

4. Select *Other Payroll Liabilities* in the Liability account field as shown in Figure 11-92. Click **Next**.

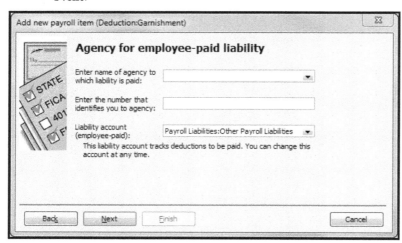

Figure 11-92 Liability account field

5. On the Tax tracking type screen, select **None**. Then click **Next**.

    Since garnishments do not reduce your taxable income, make sure you set the tax tracking type to **None**.

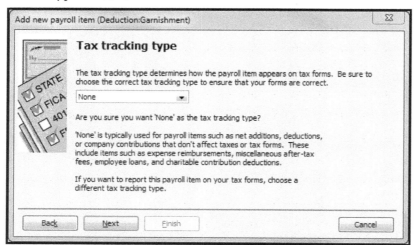

Figure 11-93 Set the tax tracking type on garnishments to None

6. On the Taxes screen, leave all of the items unchecked. Click **Next**.

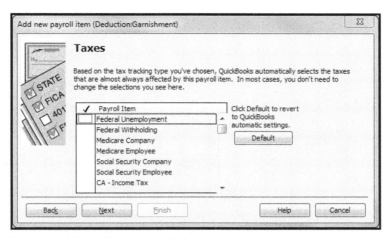

Figure 11-94 Leave all items unchecked.

7. On the Calculate Based on quantity screen, leave the **Neither** box checked and click **Next**.

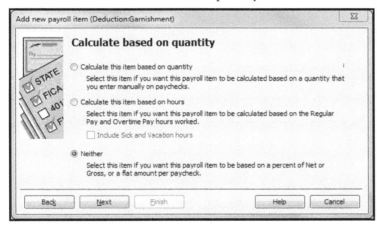

Figure 11-95 Leave Neither box checked.

8. On the Gross vs. Net screen, select **Net Pay** and click **Next**.

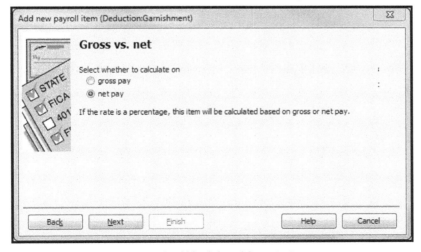

Figure 11-96 Garnishment items should be deducted from Net Pay.

9. Click **Finish** to save the new garnishment item.

Troubleshooting Payroll

Proofing the Payroll Liabilities Report

To proof the Payroll Liabilities report, compare the figures on this report with the Payroll Liability Accounts on the Balance Sheet.

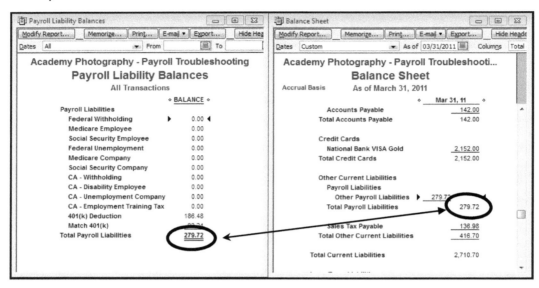

Figure 11-97 Payroll Liability/Balance Sheet Comparison

Under normal circumstances, the figures on these two reports will not agree as they do in Figure 11-97 because QuickBooks uses the date through which payroll liabilities were accrued to generate the Payroll Liabilities report. As in any accounting program, QuickBooks uses the transaction date to calculate the Balance Sheet. For example, if Academy Photography pays the first quarter's 401(k) liability on April 15, the Payroll Liabilities report will reflect the change as of March 31 (the date through which payroll liabilities were accrued) and the Balance Sheet will reflect the change on April 15, the date the check is written (see Figure 11-98).

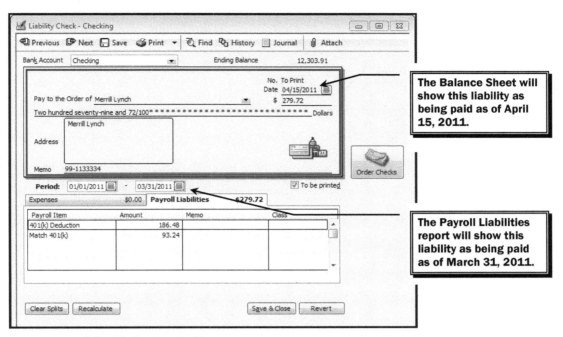

The Balance Sheet will show this liability as being paid as of April 15, 2011.

The Payroll Liabilities report will show this liability as being paid as of March 31, 2011.

Figure 11-98 Liability Check to Pay 410(k)

After creating the liability check shown in Figure 11-98, the total on the Payroll Liabilities report is now $279.72 less than the Balance Sheet.

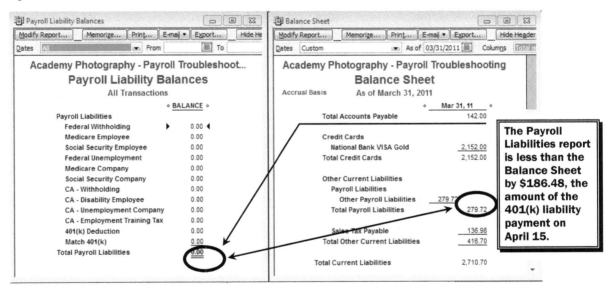

The Payroll Liabilities report is less than the Balance Sheet by $186.48, the amount of the 401(k) liability payment on April 15.

Figure 11-99 Payroll Liabilities/Balance Sheet Comparison

To reconcile the two reports, you'll need to modify the Payroll Liabilities report so that it calculates based on the same criteria as the Balance Sheet. Follow the steps in this example:

1. Click **Modify Report** on the Payroll Liabilities report.

2. Click the *Filters* Tab and then click the *Paid Through* filter on the right (see Figure 11-100).

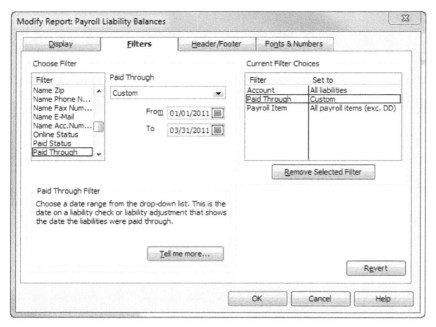

Figure 11-101

Figure 11-100 Modify Report window

3. Notice that the default filters for this report specify the "Paid Through" date. But there is no filtering for the date of the transaction. This means that a Payroll Liabilities report dated 03/31/2011 will exclude all transactions (regardless of their transaction date) that involve payroll liabilities paid through 3/31/2011. Since the check was written on 4/15/2011, the liability still shows on the 3/31/2011 Balance Sheet, but it doesn't show on the Payroll Liabilities report.

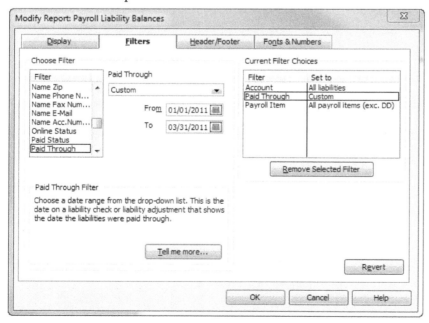

Figure 11-101 The Paid Through filter is causing the discrepancy.

4. Delete the Paid Through filter by clicking **Remove Selected Filter**.

5.   Scroll up in the *Filter* field and select **Date**.

6.   On the Date filter set the *From* and *To* fields to "01/1/2011" through "3/31/2011."

This causes the report to show only those transactions involving payroll liabilities with a transaction date between 01/01/2011 and 03/31/2011.

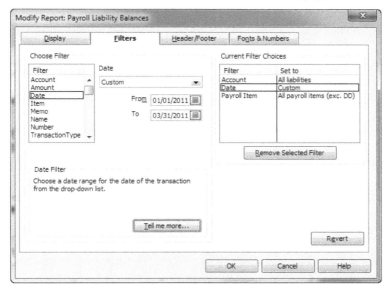

Figure 11-102 The Date Filter with the correct settings

7.   Now the filter is for the ***transaction*** date. This means the report will show only those transactions that were created as of 3/31/11.

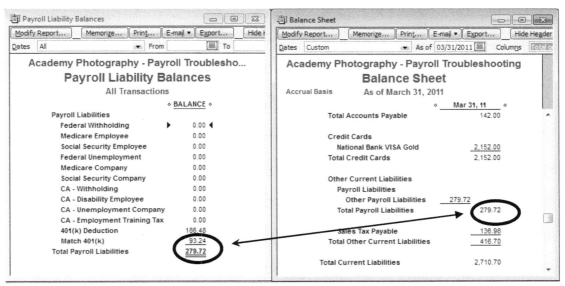

Figure 11-103 Payroll Liabilities Report/Balance Sheet Reconciliation

8.   If the two reports still do not agree check the following:

Check the "paid-through" date on payroll liability checks. The date should always be set to the last day of the payroll accrual period, usually the last day of the previous month. In the Pay Liabilities screen, QuickBooks will default to this date so if you pay payroll taxes on a weekly basis, change the **Show Liabilities as of** date to the week-ending date.

Confirm that the Payroll Items are linked to the correct liability accounts. To see if the Item is linked to the correct liability account, edit the Payroll Item and check the account in the Account field. If the account type is a liability account other than the "Payroll Liabilities" account (or a subaccount of "Payroll Liabilities"), QuickBooks will show the liability item in the Payroll Liabilities report but will not group the liability with other payroll liabilities on the Balance Sheet.

The client may have used a Check to pay payroll liabilities. See page 477 for more information.

The client may have used a Journal Entry to adjust Payroll Liability Accounts. See page 484 for more information.

The user may have entered a payroll liability adjustment with the setting "Do Not Affect Accounts." Search by transaction type for all liability adjustments and click **Accounts Affected** on each to confirm that they are set to affect liability and expense accounts.

> **Note**
> In some rare cases, it is appropriate to enter a liability adjustment and select "Do not affect accounts." Examples include when setting up payroll in the middle of a year and when a journal entry was used to adjust payroll. See page 484.

Proofing Payroll Records - Validating W-2s

At the end of the year, the best way to proof your payroll records is to run the following reports and perform the following checks.

Create these reports.

- Payroll Summary (Year-to-Date)
- Payroll Liability Balances (End of Year)
- Profit & Loss (Year-to-Date)
- Balance Sheet (End of Year)

Perform the following checks.

1. Compare each of the figures on the Payroll Summary by Employee with the W-2s. If they don't match, check the Payroll Items. The most common problems in this area are when Addition or Deduction Items are not marked correctly in the Taxes screen as shown below.

> **Important:** Even though you can change a payroll item's taxability on the screen below, it won't affect previously recorded transactions. For example, if you already have paychecks that use the 401k Employee item, if that item's **Taxes** screen is set up wrong, the changes you make to the item won't change the paychecks. If you want those transactions to affect taxes differently, you should delete all paychecks and recreate them. Be careful though, recreating paychecks might result in different net pay amounts, different liability accruals, and different payroll tax returns.

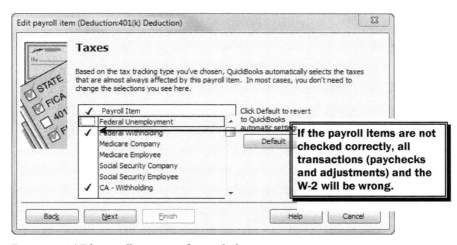

Figure 11-104 Edit payroll item to verify tax calculations

2. Compare the **total gross wages** on the **Payroll Summary by Employee** report with the **total gross wages** on the **Profit & Loss** report. If they don't match, check the Payroll Items. The most common problem occurs when the Gross Pay Payroll Item is not associated with the correct expense account.

3. Compare the Payroll Liabilities by Item report with the Balance Sheet. Compare the totals of the federal and state liabilities on the two reports. If they don't match, check for tax deposits that were made without using Pay Liabilities. Also check for adjustments made using the Adjust Liabilities function that did not affect accounts. Also, check for journal entries to payroll accounts (a no-no).

Correcting Common Payroll Errors

Problem 1: When a Check was used to Pay Payroll Liabilities

If you attempt to use a Check to pay payroll liabilities, QuickBooks displays the message in Figure 11-105 so that you would use the more appropriate method of paying payroll liabilities through the *Pay Payroll Liabilities* window.

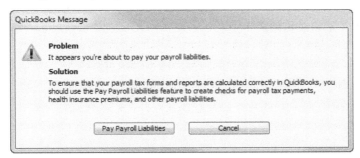

Figure 11-105 QuickBooks Message to use the Pay Payroll Liabilities window

However, you are able to override this message by clicking Cancel and using a Check to pay payroll liabilities (although not recommended). When a Check was used to pay payroll liabilities, the Payroll Liabilities report and the amounts that show in the Pay Liabilities screen will not agree to the Balance Sheet. To locate checks that were used to pay payroll liabilities create a Custom Transaction Detail Report, filtered for transaction type Check and all payroll liability accounts. Change the date range to "all." If a check was used to pay payroll liabilities, you have two options:

Use Pay Liabilities to create a Payroll Liability Payment (LIAB CHK) to duplicate the Check (CHK). Use the same date and check number as the original check. Once you have confirmed that the payroll liability check is exactly the same as the original check, including cleared status, delete the original check.

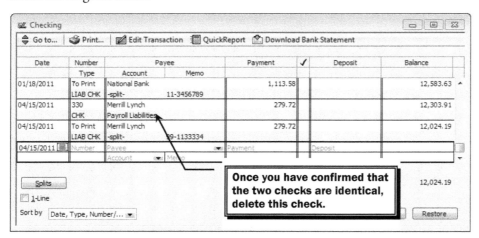

Figure 11-106 Check Register with Liability Check and Check

> **Note**
> If the original check (CHK) had been cleared on a previous bank reconciliation, you will need to clear the Liability Payment (LIAB CHK) through the Bank Reconciliation feature. Open the Bank Reconciliation screen for the account. Subtract $279.72 (the amount of the Liability Payment) to the amount in the *Beginning Balance* field. This will be your *Ending Balance*. Enter the date of the last bank reconciliation in the *Statement Date* field. Then click **Continue**. Locate and clear the Liability Payment. The difference field should show 0.00. Click **Reconcile Now** and print a Reconciliation Detail report for your records.

If the client used numerous checks to pay payroll liabilities, you can use a single Liability Adjustment to adjust the amount of each payroll item as shown in Figure 11-107 (but be very careful when doing this due to the various dates and how that will affect the payroll liability reports). Enter a negative amount to decrease the liability. Select "Do not Affect Accounts," so that your changes will not affect the Balance Sheet. Assuming the client coded the checks to the correct payroll liability accounts, the Balance Sheet will be accurate. If the client did not post the original check to the correct accounts, edit the check's account postings.

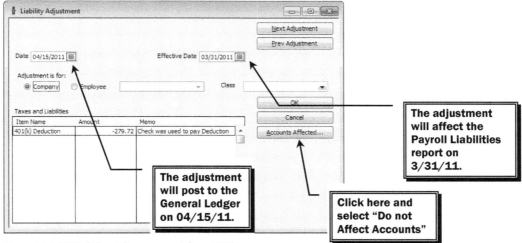

Figure 11-107 Liability Adjustment to Adjust 401(k)

Problem 2: Combining 940 and 941 Federal Tax Deposits on the Same Liability Check

If the client created a check for the 940 and 941 federal tax deposits on the same Pay Liabilities screen, QuickBooks might create a single check for both. It does this if the Federal Unemployment, Federal Withholding and FICA Payroll Items include the same vendor (e.g. the company's bank). Assuming that the client did *not* submit the composite check to the bank, perform the steps in this example to correct the problem:

1. Open each Liability Check and write down all information that shows on the screen, including the date of the Liability Check, the paid through date, the check number and the cleared status.

2. Delete the Liability Check and re-pay the payroll liabilities using two separate Pay Liabilities screens.

3. Open the bank account register and confirm that the check numbers and cleared status are the same as the deleted Liability Checks.

> **Note**
> Do not manually clear the Check in the account register. Instead, clear the Liability Check using the Bank Reconciliation feature. See the note on page 478 for more information.

Follow the steps in this example to avoid this problem in the future:

1. Create a separate vendor name for the Federal Unemployment Payroll Item as shown in Figure 11-108. Name the vendor "National Bank (940)."

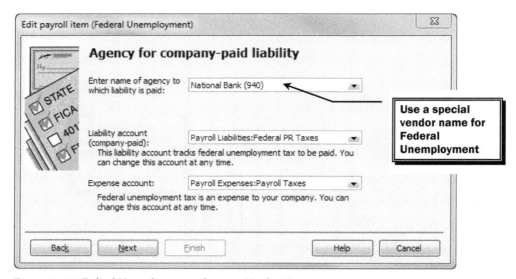

Figure 11-108 Federal Unemployment with unique Vendor Name

2.   Open the Pay Liabilities screen and notice that the National Bank (940) Vendor shows on the Federal Unemployment line.

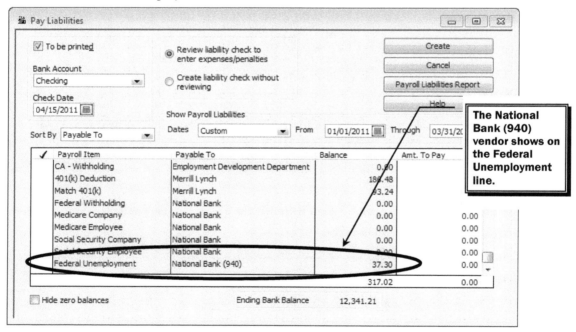

Figure 11-109 The Pay Liabilities screen

3.   Now when you select all 941 Payroll Items *and* the Federal Unemployment Payroll Items on the same Pay Liabilities screen, QuickBooks creates separate checks as shown in Figure 11-110.

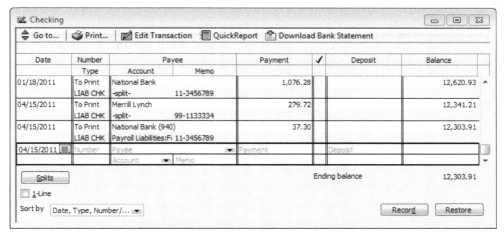

Figure 11-110 QuickBooks creates separate checks for the 941 and 940 deposits.

Problem 3: Overriding Amounts on the Pay Liabilities Screen

Note:
This example is used to demonstrate how overriding amounts on liability payments can be done. It is not meant to imply that you should do this, but instead how to deal with it when it occurs.

The Pay Liabilities screen allows you to adjust the "Amount Paid" column. Notice in Figure 11-111 that the user edited the Merrill Lynch payment and increased the amount of the payment to $100.00.

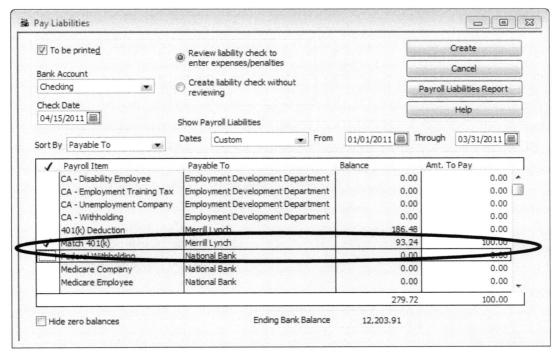

Figure 11-111 Pay Liabilities with Adjustment in the Amount to Pay Column

To correct the problem, perform the following steps:

1.   Use the Payroll Liabilities report to determine the adjustment amount necessary to reduce the balance to zero, or to the correct amount.

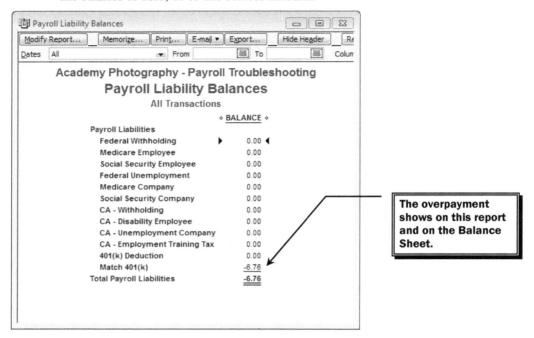

Figure 11-112 Payroll Liabilities Report with FUTA Overstatement.

2.   Double-click on the incorrect amount to see all transactions involved.

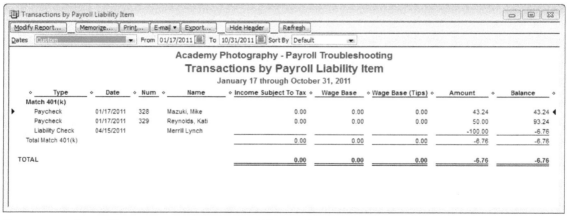

Figure 11-113 Custom Transaction Detail Report Filtered for Payroll Liability Checks.

3.   Locate the Payroll Liability Check that you need to correct (i.e., the liability check on which the client overrode the amount on the Pay Liabilities screen). Double-click to view the check.

4.   On the Payroll Liabilities tab, adjust the amount of each Payroll Item to match what *should* have been paid (see Figure 11-114).

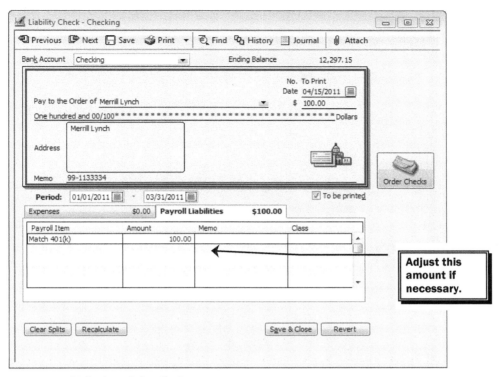

Figure 11-114 Edit the Liability Check.

5. If the check has already been printed and sent, you cannot change the total of the check, so you must make your adjustment on the *Expenses* tab.

6. Click on the *Expenses* tab of the liability check.

7. On the Expense tab, enter an adjustment coded to **Payroll Tax Expense** to bring the check's net total back to its original amount. If you expect to receive a refund of this overpayment, you can code the refunded amount (on the deposit) to the same account used on this adjustment (in this case Payroll Tax Expense). You could also use the Payroll Liability account for this adjustment.

8. Click **Save & Close** to record the adjusted Liability Check.

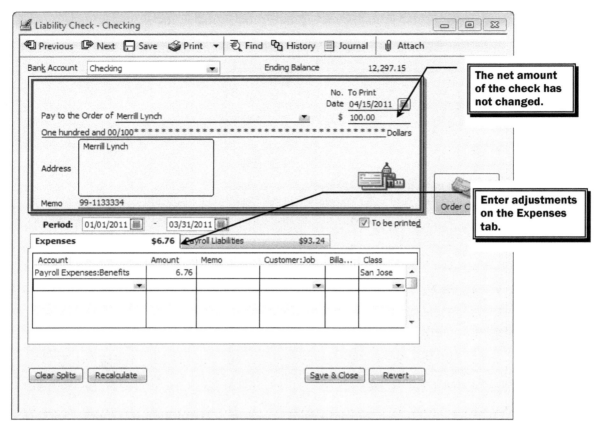

Figure 11-115 Liability Check Showing with Adjustment on Expenses tab

Problem 4: When a Journal Entry Was Used to Adjust Payroll Accounts

There is only one time when using journal entries for payroll accounts is recommended –
during the setup process. After setup, you should always adjust payroll accounts using other
methods described in this chapter instead of using journal entries. The reason for this is that
journal entries do not affect Payroll Items, and therefore adjusting payroll liabilities with
journal entries will create a discrepancy between the Payroll Liabilities reports and the other
account-based reports such as the Balance Sheet.

Perform the steps in this example to find and correct problems caused by journal entries to
payroll accounts:

1.   Create a Custom Transaction Detail Report.

2.   Click on the *Filters* tab.

3.   Filter by **Account** for selected accounts and select all of the payroll liability accounts.

4.   Change the **Date** range to "all."

5.   Filter by **Transaction Type** for "Journal."

6.   If you find journal entries on the report, create a **Payroll Liability Adjustment** that matches
the effect of the journal entry, but uses payroll items.

7. In the Liability Adjustment select **Do not Affect Accounts** so the adjustment will not affect the General Ledger. This adjustment brings the payroll items into balance with the account balances that were adjusted by the journal entry.

8. Make sure that the adjustment date is the same as the journal entry date, and that the effective date is set to the end of the payroll accrual period you are adjusting.

> **Note**
>
> If you adjust payroll items using a Payroll Liability adjustment, the adjustment may affect the W-2s for the company's employees as well as the amounts of tax deposits. Make sure the amounts on the journal entry are accurate and that they reflect actual payroll activity for the company before making the adjustment. If the journal entry amounts are inaccurate, delete the journal entry and enter the correct amounts using a liability adjustment, or several liability adjustments. In this case, set the liability adjustments to affect liability and expense accounts.

Problem 5: When Payroll Items Were Set Up Incorrectly

If one of your Payroll Items is calculating incorrectly or is posting to the wrong account, it may have been set up incorrectly. To troubleshoot a payroll item, follow the steps in this example:

1. Create a Payroll Item listing report and review the report to ensure that all payroll items post to the correct accounts. Correct any errors by double-clicking on the payroll item and editing the account(s) to which it posts.

2. Create a **QuickReport** on the Payroll Item. This shows all transactions that use that Item.

3. If you find an erroneous calculation, double-click on the line that has the problem. This displays the transaction in question.

4. Make the necessary adjustment on the original transaction, if possible.

5. If all the amounts are calculating incorrectly, check the Payroll Item setup. For example, if the Payroll Item is a deduction that is a percent of gross wages, it should be entered as 5%, not .05. Also, check the Taxes screen to make sure the correct items are selected.

When Paychecks Won't Calculate Correctly

There are several possible causes for paychecks not calculating correctly.

- Make sure each employee is set up with the **correct filing status** and other withholding information.
- Check to see that the Salary or Hourly Wage Payroll Items are being used correctly. If the employee is paid a fixed annual amount, edit the employee record in the employee list. In the employee's **Payroll and Compensation Info** screen, verify that the **rate** for the **Salary Item** is the annual salary (not the monthly or weekly amount).
- If the amount paid depends on how many hours the employee works, use an Hourly Wage Payroll Item. On the employee's **Payroll and Compensation Info** screen, enter the hourly rate for regular work first. If the employee has more than one rate (for example, one for regular work and one for overtime), create separate items for each.

- Verify that you have properly set up overtime items in the payroll item list. From the Payroll Item list, double-click an item to verify whether it's been set up to track overtime correctly (Figure 11-116).

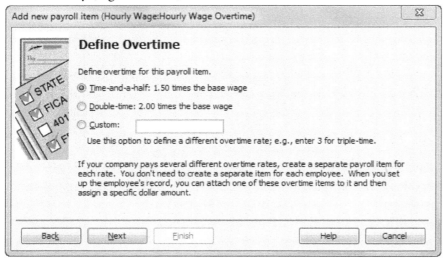

Figure 11-116 Overtime item

- Check the **Pay Period** field on the employee's **Payroll and Compensation Info** screen. Make sure it is set for how often you pay the employee.

- Additions or Deductions are not set up correctly. If the Addition or Deduction is a **percentage of gross or net pay**, use a **%** sign in the **Amount or %** field in the Item setup. For example, enter two percent as 2%, not 0.20.

- Payroll Items that are percentages of gross pay are entered in the **wrong order** on the **Payroll Info** tab or on the Paycheck. For Payroll Items that are a percentage of gross pay, the gross pay used in the calculation depends on the order of the Payroll Items on the paycheck.

- The **tax amounts** on paychecks will most likely *not* match amounts in **printed** wage-bracket **tax tables**. If your QuickBooks tax table is up to date for the federal government and your state, don't worry. QuickBooks is **more accurate** than printed wage-bracket tables. It calculates the taxes using formulas approved by the tax authorities. For federal income tax withholding, QuickBooks rounds to the nearest dollar, as authorized by federal tax authorities.

Using Zero-Dollar Checks to Record Payroll Costs by Job and Class

If you use an outside payroll service (or software other than QuickBooks) to process your payroll, using zero-dollar checks may be the easiest way to job cost payroll expenses.

One advantage to this method is that it does not require you to subscribe to any of the QuickBooks payroll services and it does not cost anything to implement. In fact, you can completely turn off the payroll option in the *Preferences* window and you'll never see any warnings about downloading tax tables or setting up your payroll. However, this method only *approximates* the payroll costs for jobs and classes, meaning that the amount of payroll expense allocated to each job and class will be based on the average hourly payroll expense of putting one person on any given job.

1. Using a journal entry, enter the totals for your payroll into the general ledger just as you normally do when using a payroll service. This entry should credit the bank account for net pay, and debit the gross wages, payroll taxes, and other accounts as necessary (see Figure 11-117).

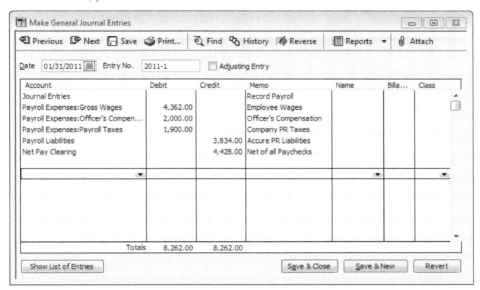

Figure 11-117 Journal entry to record payroll from payroll service reports

2. Compute the average cost incurred to place one person on any given job for one hour. To calculate this amount, you should look at your total payroll expenses for a given period (e.g. last quarter) including payroll taxes and worker's compensation, subtract all payroll expenses are not job costed (e.g., officer salaries), and then divide by the total number of hours all employees worked on all jobs during the period. For the purposes of this section, we will assume the average hourly expense to be $18.00.

3. Create a Bank account called **Payroll Service Clearing**. This will be a clearing account used to record the zero-dollar checks for the payroll job costing.

4. Create an Expense account called **Payroll Job Costs**.

> **Note:** If you have long-term contracts whereby you capture job costs on the balance sheet in an asset account, you should use an Other Current Asset instead of an expense for Payroll Job Costs. Then, continue with the setup and transactions shown in this method.

5. Edit each existing "Service" Item in your Item list, making them two-sided Items. Enter "Payroll Costs for Jobs and Classes" in the Description on Purchase Transactions field, enter "18.00" in the Cost field, and enter "Payroll Job Costs" in the Expense Account field (see Figure 11-118). Then click **OK** to save your changes.

> **Note:**
> This change to your Service Items will have no effect on their use in Sales Receipts or Invoices.

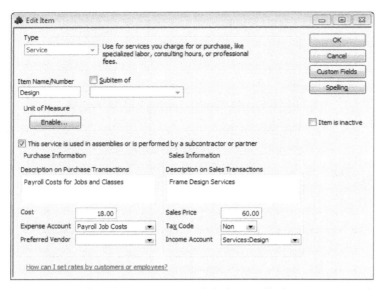

Figure 11-118 Edit each service item to include the Payroll Job Costs account and average cost per hour

6.   Create an **Other Name** record (not an Employee record) for each employee.

7.   Enter daily time sheet information for each employee using the **Other Name** record you just created. On each timesheet, include the Service Item, the name of the job on which the employee worked, and the class (if applicable).

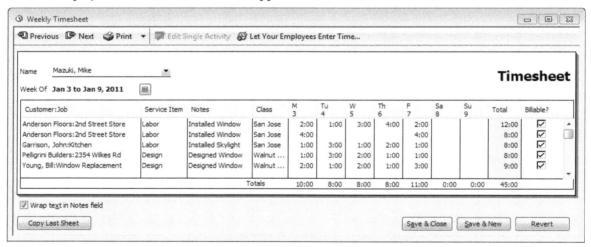

Figure 11-119 Detailed timesheets with jobs and classes

8.   Open the *Write Checks* window and select **Payroll Service Clearing** from the **Account** drop-down menu.

9.   Enter the employee's name (Other Name) on the *Pay to the Order of* field of the Check (see Figure 11-120). Then press TAB.

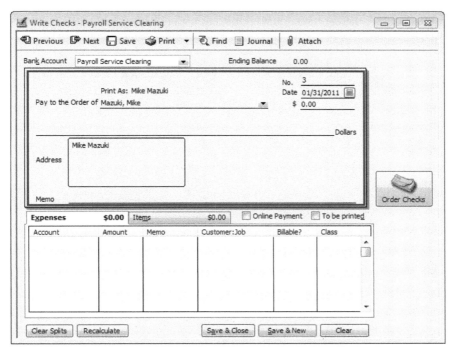

Figure 11-120 Write Checks window with employee's Other Name in the Pay to the Order of field

10.   QuickBooks will notify you that the name you entered has time sheet data in the file and ask if you want to use this information when creating this check (see Figure 11-121). Click **Yes**.

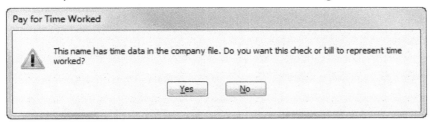

Figure 11-121 Pay for Time Worked window

11.   Enter the date range in the *Start Date* and *End Date* fields. Then click **OK**.

Select the period for which you want to job cost payroll expenses. If you use this method monthly, enter the beginning and ending date of the month. If you use this method quarterly, enter the beginning and ending date for the quarter.

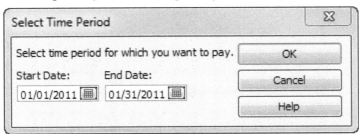

Figure 11-122 Select Time Period window

12.   QuickBooks will then import the timesheet information into the Items tab of the Check, multiplying the number of hours the employee worked by the average cost per hour to place the employee on any given job (see Figure 11-123).

Expenses	$0.00	Items	$3,330.00	☐ Online Payment	☐ To be printed		

Item	Description	Qty	Cost	Amount	Customer:Job	Bi...	Class
Labor	Payroll Costs for Jobs and Classes	4	18.00	72.00	Anderson Floors:2nd Street Store	☐	San Jose
Labor	Payroll Costs for Jobs and Classes	2	18.00	36.00	Anderson Floors:2nd Street Store	☐	San Jose
Labor	Payroll Costs for Jobs and Classes	1	18.00	18.00	Garrison, John:Kitchen	☐	San Jose
Design	Payroll Costs for Jobs and Classes	1	18.00	18.00	Pelligrini Builders:2354 Wilkes Rd	☐	Walnut Creek
Design	Payroll Costs for Jobs and Classes	2	18.00	36.00	Young, Bill:Window Replacement	☐	Walnut Creek
Labor	Payroll Costs for Jobs and Classes	1	18.00	18.00	Anderson Floors:2nd Street Store	☐	San Jose
Labor	Payroll Costs for Jobs and Classes	3	18.00	54.00	Garrison, John:Kitchen	☐	San Jose
Design	Payroll Costs for Jobs and Classes	3	18.00	54.00	Pelligrini Builders:2354 Wilkes Rd	☐	Walnut Creek
Design	Payroll Costs for Jobs and Classes	1	18.00	18.00	Young, Bill:Window Replacement	☐	Walnut Creek
Labor	Payroll Costs for Jobs and Classes	3	18.00	54.00	Anderson Floors:2nd Street Store	☐	San Jose
Labor	Payroll Costs for Jobs and Classes	1	18.00	18.00	Garrison, John:Kitchen	☐	San Jose
Design	Payroll Costs for Jobs and Classes	2	18.00	36.00	Pelligrini Builders:2354 Wilkes Rd	☐	Walnut Creek
Design	Payroll Costs for Jobs and Classes	2	18.00	36.00	Young, Bill:Window Replacement	☐	Walnut Creek
Labor	Payroll Costs for Jobs and Classes	4	18.00	72.00	Anderson Floors:2nd Street Store	☐	San Jose
Labor	Payroll Costs for Jobs and Classes	2	18.00	36.00	Garrison, John:Kitchen	☐	San Jose
Design	Payroll Costs for Jobs and Classes	1	18.00	18.00	Pelligrini Builders:2354 Wilkes Rd	☐	Walnut Creek
Design	Payroll Costs for Jobs and Classes	1	18.00	18.00	Young, Bill:Window Replacement	☐	Walnut Creek

Figure 11-123 The Items tab of the Write Checks window with imported time data

13.   Click the *Expenses* tab and then enter **Payroll Costs** in the *Account* field and the amount of the check as a negative number in the *Amount* field (see Figure 11-124).

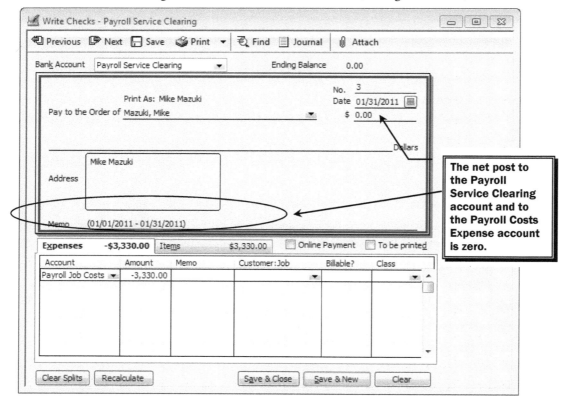

Figure 11-124 Use the Expenses tab to zero the amount of the Check

14.   Click **Save & Close** to record the zero-dollar check.

Since you already used a General Journal Entry to update the General Ledger for payroll expenses, payroll liabilities, and bank accounts, it is very important that this check not increase the balance in the **Payroll Job Costs** expense account. If it did, it would overstate expenses for the period. You must therefore zero-out the amount of the check as shown in Figure 11-124.

> **The accounting behind the scenes:**
> Essentially, this method uses a Check as a zero-dollar journal entry that feeds the job cost and class reports. The Items tab (Figure 11-123) increases (debits) the balance in the **Payroll Job Costs** expense account by $3330.00, allocating the amount over each job and class on which Mike Mazuki worked for the period. The *Expenses* tab (Figure 11-124) decreases (credits) the balance in the **Payroll Job Costs** expense account but does not affect job or class information. The job cost and class reports will therefore show the expenses by job and class, but the net effect on the General Ledger (e.g., the Profit & Loss Standard report) will be zero.

15.   Review the **Profit & Loss by Job** report to confirm that payroll expenses now show for specific jobs (see Figure 11-125). Be sure to include the date of the Zero Check created above (01/31/2011) in your report.

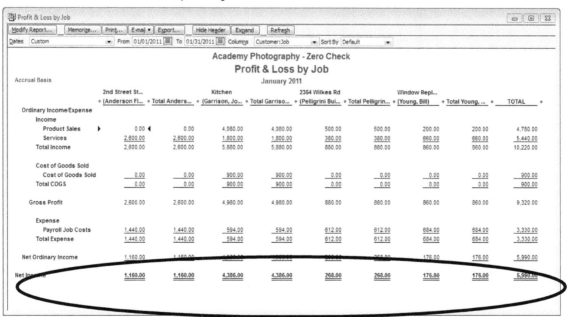

Figure 11-125 Profit & Loss by Job

16.   However, the **Profit & Loss Standard** report (and the general ledger as a whole) does not show any balance in the **Payroll Job Costs** account because you zeroed this account out when you recorded the check (see Figure 11-126).

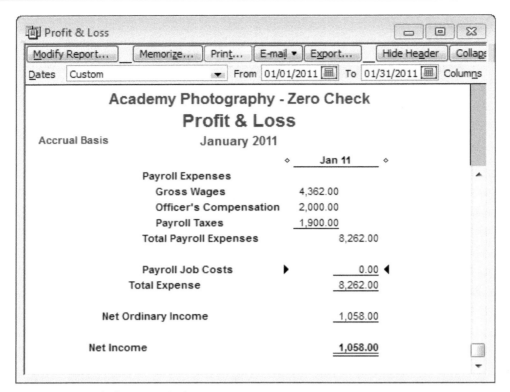

Figure 11-126 Profit & Loss Standard report

After-the-fact Payroll

Accounting professionals who provide payroll services often need to capture payroll information in QuickBooks, after the paychecks have been written by a different payroll system (i.e., not QuickBooks payroll). For example, you may use a payroll solution other than QuickBooks to process payroll, or you may use a separate QuickBooks file, or you may need to input payroll information using reports from the client's third party payroll provider. Regardless of the reasons, the After-the-fact payroll feature provides a flexible method of recording payroll transactions into QuickBooks so that all of the QuickBooks payroll reports work in addition to the general ledger reports.

The After-the-fact Payroll feature uses downloaded tax tables from Intuit, but the window shown below allows you to over-ride or round the calculated amounts. By calculating the withholdings, the After-the-fact Payroll feature helps confirm the data accuracy as you enter the paycheck amounts for each employee. This is especially important if the client calculates payroll manually.

The After-the-fact Payroll window also allows you to edit the order of the columns and to add or remove columns. For example, you may want to reorganize the columns to match the way the third party payroll data or report is organized.

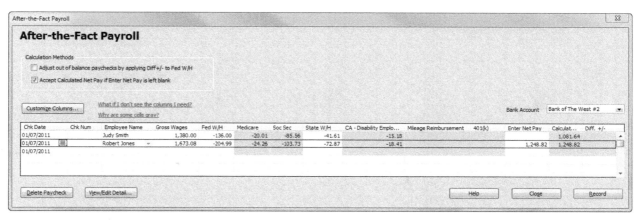

Figure 11-127 After-the-fact Payroll Window

Adjusting Payroll

If you want to adjust your Payroll Liability accounts without affecting Payroll Items, you can do so by using a journal entry. However, this is almost never a good way to make adjustments. In general, if you need to adjust any amounts in Payroll, it's best to adjust it in one of the following ways:

- If possible, make an adjustment on the employee's next paycheck. For example, if an employee did not receive the full amount of their bonus, add the adjustment to the employee's next paycheck. If the employee wants the amount now, create a check coded to Due from Employee, and then add the bonus to the employee's next paycheck. Enter a Deduction Item coded to Due from Employee to reduce the net amount of the paycheck.

  Making adjustments on future paychecks is the preferred method because it affects Employees, Items and Accounts, without the risk of creating discrepancies between payroll reports and actual payroll activity.

- As long as you have not distributed the paycheck: if you have not printed the paycheck, you may edit the original paycheck and then print. If the check was already printed, you should void and recreate the paycheck.

- Edit the Setup Year to Date amounts transactions. This might be necessary if your setup numbers were wrong.

- Use the Adjust Liabilities screen. This allows you to adjust Payroll Items (and optionally Accounts) and affect Employee records. Be careful with this approach because these adjustments affect W-2s.

Adjusting Liabilities Directly

If you've determined that an adjustment is needed and that you can't adjust your Payroll Items on future paychecks or liability payments, you'll need to adjust your Payroll Items directly.

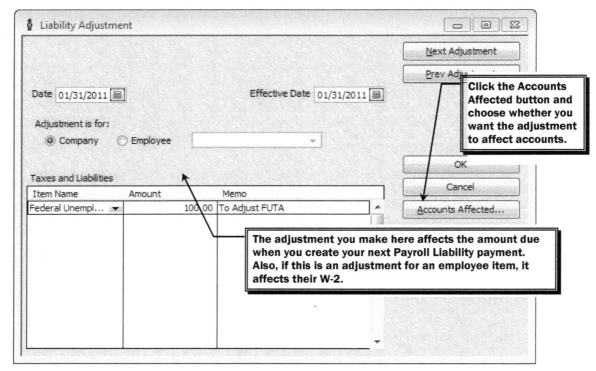

Figure 11-128 Directly adjusting a payroll liability amount

Enter a positive or negative number and it will adjust the year-to-date balance for that Payroll Item. If this adjustment affects any of your employee's year-to-date figures, enter the employee's name. The adjustment you make here affects the amount due when you create your next Payroll Liability payment. Also, if you enter an employee, it affects their W-2.

Adjusting for Incorrect Payroll Tax Deposits

What happens if the payroll taxes were **deposited incorrectly**? For example, when an incorrect tax deposit was made before recording anything in QuickBooks, or when someone used *Write Checks* instead of *Pay Liabilities* to record the payments.

In this case, you'll need to use the *Pay Liabilities* function to correctly record the tax deposit, and then adjust the amount of the tax deposit to match the check that was actually written. Also, if you already have CHK transactions recorded in QuickBooks, you'll need to replace those CHK transactions with LIAB CHK transactions.

> These steps are also appropriate when entering tax payments that were written **before** you started using QuickBooks Payroll.

1.   Start by recording the correct deposit as calculated by QuickBooks.

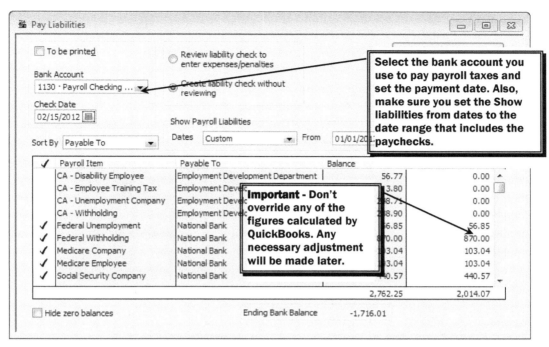

Figure 11-129 Paying the payroll liabilities calculated by QuickBooks.

2.   To adjust the amount of the check, click the expenses tab and enter the adjustment. This ensures the payroll items will no longer have an unpaid balance. The small adjustment is made to an expense account.

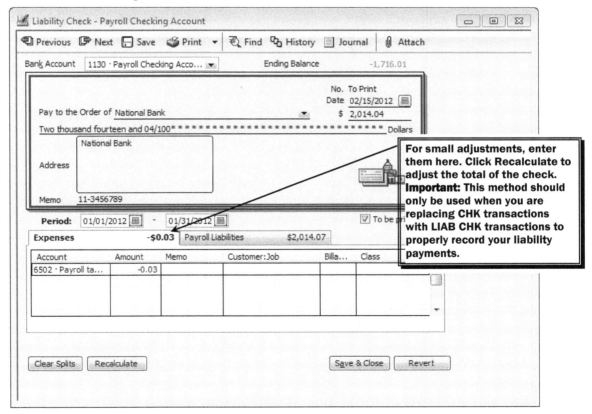

Figure 11-130 Adjusting liability payments (for small amounts) when liabilities were previously paid

3.   Next, if **Write Checks** (CHK transactions) had been used to enter the liability payments, you'll need to delete those transactions since the last step created liability payments (LIAB CHK transactions).

Tracking an Owner's or Partner's Time

In some businesses, owners and partners do not receive paychecks, but they still need to track their time activity, record the labor costs to specific jobs, and then pass the time through to their customers' Invoices.

To track an owner or partner's time for billing purposes, follow the steps in this example:

1.   Display the *Other Names* list by selecting the **Lists** menu and then selecting **Other Names List**.

2.   Select **New** from the **Other Names** menu at the bottom of the *Other Names List* window.

3.   Create an *Other Name* record for Vern Black, the owner of Academy Photography as shown in Figure 11-131.

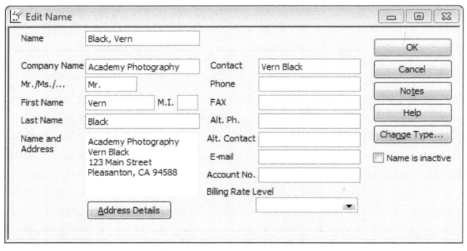

Figure 11-131 Other Name record for owner Vern Black

4.   Click **OK** to save Vern Black's record, and then close the *Other Names* list.

5.   Open the *Weekly Timesheet* window and enter the timesheet activity for Vern Black as shown in Figure 11-132.

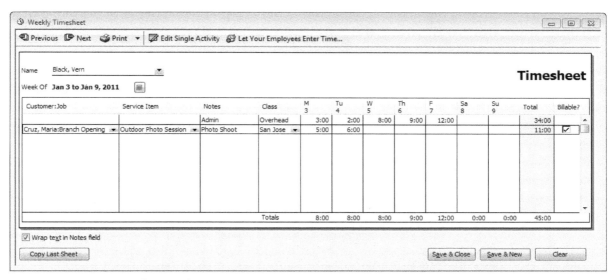

Figure 11-132 Time activity for Vern Black

6.   Click **Save & Close** to record the timesheet activity.

7.   To pass this time through to an Invoice for the customer, open the *Create Invoices* window and enter the Job *Cruz, Maria:Brack Opening* in the **Customer:Job** field. Click **OK** when QuickBooks displays the *Billable Time/Costs* window.

8.   The Choose Billable Time and Costs window opens. Click **Select All** and then click **OK** to transfer the timesheet information through to the Customer's Invoice (see Figure 11-133).

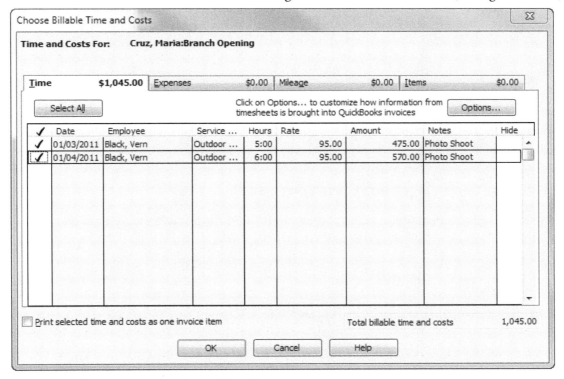

Figure 11-133 Time activity for Jim Moen and Vern Black

9.   Click **Save & Close** to record the Invoice.

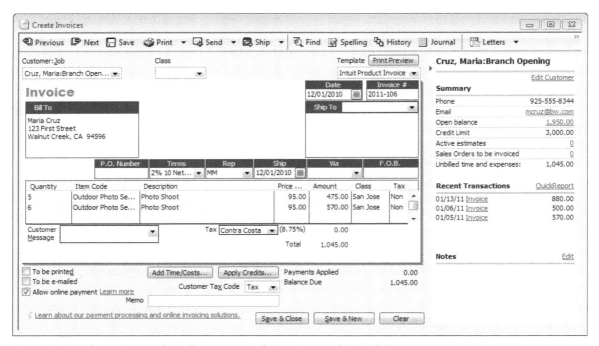

Figure 11-134 The Invoice now shows the time activity for Jim Moen and Vern Black.

Recording Costs for the Owner's Time

Usually you will not "pay" the owner for their time because owners generally take a "draw" (a check coded to Owner's Drawing) instead of getting paid through payroll. Therefore, the timesheet information for Vern Black will not get recorded as labor costs on Bill Young's Window Replacement Job.

Suppose you do want the "costs" for Vern Black's time to be reflected on your Job Cost reports. For example, you may want the costs to show on reports so you can accurately measure the true costs on the job even though your actual finanical records will not show any cost for the owner's time. The next section shows how you can pass Vern Black's timesheet information onto a zero-dollar check so that your job cost reports will show the costs.

Using Zero-Dollar Checks for Job Costing

If you want to track the <u>costs</u> of owners or partners on the P&L by Job Reports, you can use zero-dollar checks to record these expenses.

To allocate the costs of owner or partner time to jobs on the P&L by Job report, follow the steps in this example:

1.   Create a new **Expense** account called **Job Costs Allocated**.

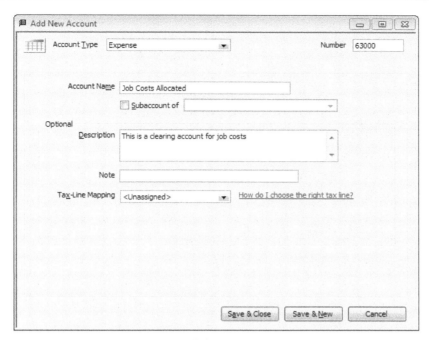

Figure 11-135 New Expense Account called Job Costs Allocated

2. From the *List* menu select **Item List**.

3. Edit the **Outdoor Photo Session** Service Item, making it a two-sided Item that tracks both the expense and income accounts associated with the item. Click the box next to **This service is used in assemblies or is performed by a subcontractor or partner** (see Figure 11-136).

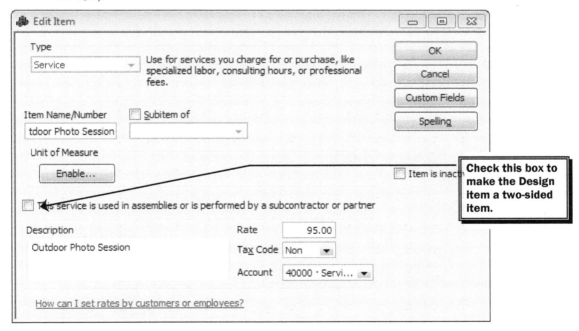

Figure 11-136 One-sided Design service item

4. Enter *Job Costs Allocated* in the *Description on Purchase Transactions* field, *40.00* in the *Cost* field, and select Job Costs Allocated in the *Expense Account* field (see Figure 11-137).

5. Click **OK** to save your changes.

> **Note:**
> This change to your Service Items will have no effect on their use in Sales Receipts or Invoices.

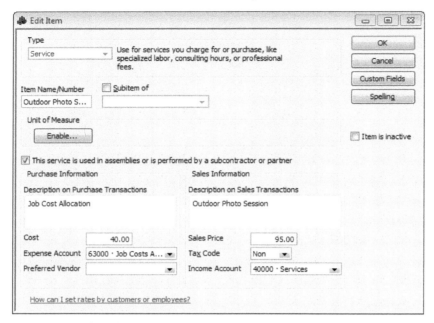

Figure 11-137 Edit each service item to include the Job Cost Payroll account and average cost per hour.

6.   On the Account Change screen (see Figure 11-138), click **Yes**. Since this is the first time you have entered an expense account into each of your service Items QuickBooks will not record any changes to the General Ledger.

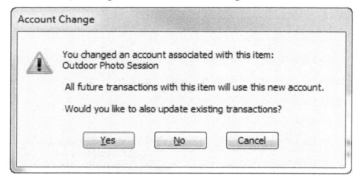

Figure 11-138 Account Change window

7.   Now make the same change to other Service items, making them two-sided items with Job Costs Allocated as the Expense account.

> **Note:**
> Do not edit Service Items for labor performed by outside contractors (e.g., subcontracted labor).

Now that you've set up the account and items to track job costs for your owners and partners, follow the steps in this example to record the transactions:

1.   Open the *Write Checks* screen and select the **Journal Entries** bank account in the *Bank Account* field.

2.   Enter **2007-1** in the *No.* field.

3.   Enter *1/31/2007* in the Date field. Press **TAB**.

4.   Select **Black, Vern** in the *Pay to the Order of* field and press **TAB** (see Figure 11-139).

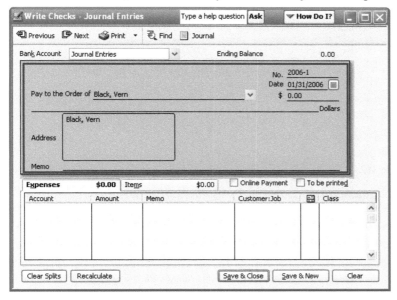

Figure 11-139 Write Checks screen with employee's Other Name in the Pay to the Order of field

5.   QuickBooks will notify you that the name you entered has time sheet data in the file and ask if you want to use this information when creating this check (see Figure 11-140). Click **Yes**.

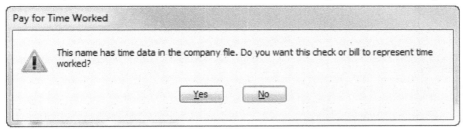

Figure 11-140 Pay for Time Worked window

> **Note**
> If you do not see the *Pay for Time Worked* message window, it probably means that the name you selected in the *Pay to the Order of* field does not have any timesheet information recorded; or, the timesheet information has already been allocated to a previous check or bill.

6.   Enter *01/01/2011* in the *Start Date* field and *01/31/2011* in the *End Date* field (see Figure 11-141). Then click **OK**.

Select the period for which you want to job cost payroll expenses. If you use this method monthly, enter the beginning and ending date of the month. If you use this method quarterly, enter the beginning and ending date for the quarter.

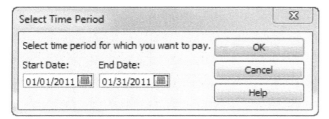

Figure 11-141 Select Time Period window

7.   QuickBooks will then transfer the timesheet information onto the *Items* Tab of the check, multiplying the number of hours worked by the average cost per hour (see Figure 11-142).

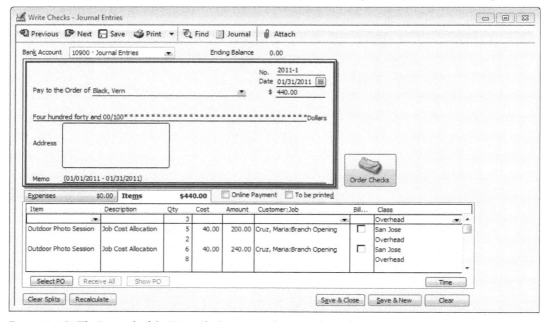

Figure 11-142 The Items tab of the Write Checks screen with imported time data

8.   Click the **Expenses** Tab, enter *Job Costs Allocated* in the *Account* field and the amount of the check as a negative number in the *Amount* field (see Figure 11-143).

9.   Click **Save & Close** to record the Check. It is very important that this check *not* increase the balance in the *Job Costs Allocated* expense account. If you do, you will overstate expenses for the period. You must therefore zero-out the amount of the check.

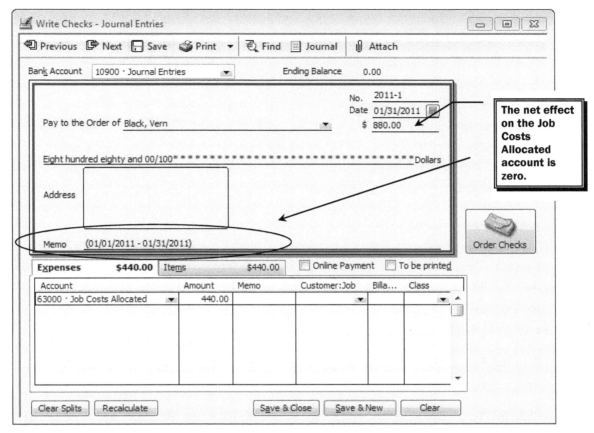

Figure 11-143 Use the Expenses tab to zero the amount of the Check.

The Accounting Behind the Scenes
Essentially, this method uses a Check as a zero-dollar journal entry that feeds the job cost reports. The Items Tab (Figure 11-142) increases (debits) the balance in the Job Costs Allocated Expense account by $440.00, allocating the amount over each job and class on which Vern Black worked for the period. The Expenses Tab (Figure 11-143) decreases (credits) the balance in the Job Costs Allocated Expense account but does not affect job or class information. The job cost reports will therefore show the expenses, but the net effect on the General Ledger (e.g. the Profit & Loss report) is zero.

Review the Profit & Loss by Job report to confirm that payroll expenses display for specific jobs (Figure 11-144).

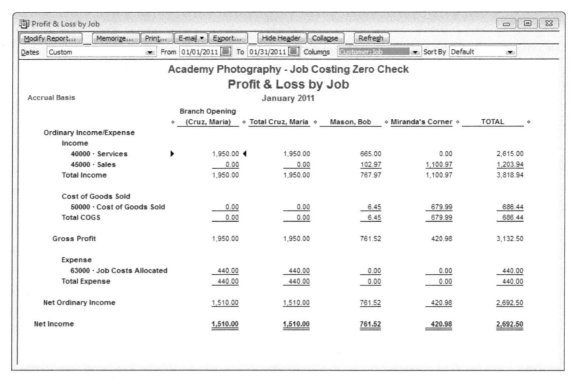

Figure 11-144 Profit & Loss by Job

Summary

In this chapter, you learned about the following special topics for handling payroll:

- Mid-Year Payroll Setup (page 413)
- Deciding on a Payroll Method (page431)
- Intuit Online Payroll for Accountants (page
- Track Worker's Compensation (page 442)
- Track Employee Expenses and Reimbursements (page 463)
- Handle Fringe Benefits in QuickBooks Payroll (page 466)
- Handle Garnishments in QuickBooks Payroll (page 467)
- Troubleshoot Problems in QuickBooks Payroll (page 472)
- Proof Payroll Records in QuickBooks (page 476)
- Use Zero-Dollar checks to record job cost when using a payroll service (page 486)
- After-the-fact Payroll (page 492)
- Adjusting Payroll (page 492)
- Tracking Owner's or Partner's Time (page 496)

Chapter 12
Inventory

Objectives

Many businesses have to manage inventory, but many don't understand how to use the inventory features in QuickBooks properly. This can be a critical issue because inventory often represents the largest asset that a business owns.

This chapter assumes that you have a basic understanding of important QuickBooks features such as the *item list, invoices* and *bills.*

After completing this chapter you should be able to:

- Understand how inventory costs flow through QuickBooks
- Properly set up an item list to manage inventory
- Understand how to use QuickBooks Inventory in a manufacturing environment
- Understand the additional inventory features found in QuickBooks Enterprise and Advanced Inventory

What Is Inventory

The simplest explanation is that you will be using QuickBooks to keep track of the *quantity on hand* that you have in stock of the items that you buy and sell, or that you use as a part of something you are building.

Let's imagine that you have an inventory item. You purchase it, and it has a cost. You may hold on to this item for a while, and eventually you will sell it. You might also use it as a part to build another inventory item that you will eventually sell. You need to know if you have any of the items on hand so you can sell it, or use it to build an assembly (for more on Inventory Assemblies, see page 523). The key point is that you are tracking both the quantity and the cost of the item.

In QuickBooks you will use two special kinds of items the *item list* – an *inventory part* item and possibly and *inventory assembly* item. The basic elements of these items are a *name,* a *description,* a *cost* and a *quantity on hand.*

As you use these special items in your purchase, adjustment and sales transactions, QuickBooks will track the cost and quantity for you.

Tracking Inventory with QuickBooks

Activating the Inventory Function

To be able to use inventory you have to enable the *Inventory* preference. Select *Edit* from the main menu, then *Preferences*. Click on the *Items & Inventory* preference and select the *Company Preferences* tab. Once you check the box for *Inventory and purchase orders are active* you will be able to work with *inventory part* and *inventory assembly* items.

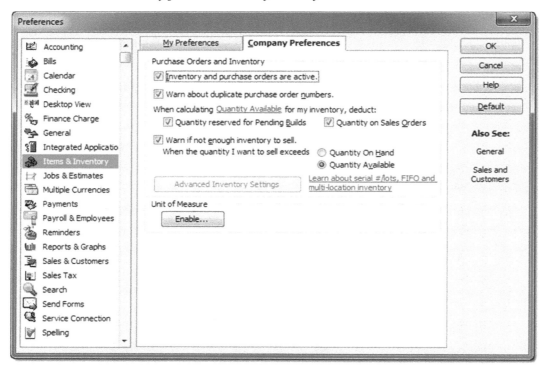

Figure 12-1 Inventory Preferences

Items and Why You Use Them

The Item List is one of the core features of QuickBooks. This is how you connect many of your basic QuickBooks functions with your Chart of Accounts, by using items in purchases, bills, invoices and many other transactions.

There are 11 different *types* of items that you can create in the item list, but only two have a *quantity* associated with them – the *inventory part* and *inventory assembly*. We'll focus our attention on these two item types, although other types may have related functions.

> An *inventory assembly* item is treated just like an *inventory part*, so any time we refer to an *inventory part* the information also applies to an *inventory assembly*. Note, though, that the *inventory assembly* item type is not available in QuickBooks Pro.

When you use **inventory part** Items to track inventory, QuickBooks handles all the accounting for you automatically, depending upon how you set them up in the Item list.

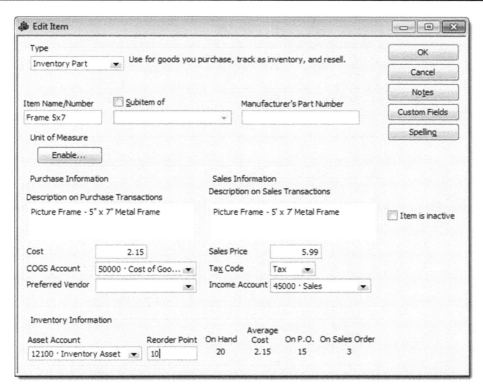

Figure 12-2 Editing an Item

Let's review the different fields in the *Edit Item* window:

- **Type:** Use this to select the type of item – using *Inventory Part* for items you wish to use to manage inventory.

- **Item Name/Number:** Every item must have an identifying name, which must be unique.

- **Subitem of:** You can create a hierarchy of names, with a master part and then "subitems" of that part. For example, you can create an item "Frame", and then create another item "5X7" that is a subitem of "Frame". You can also create another item "4X6" that is also a subitem of "Frame." This allows you to organize your item list into logical groupings. You will see these subitems noted with a colon (:) separating the parts of the name, such as "Frame:5X7". However, be careful. When you add a "Frame"5X7" item to an invoice, it will show on the <u>printed</u> form just as "5X7", without the fully qualified name.

- **Manufacturer's Part Number:** If you use a different name for an item than the manufacturer of an item, you can enter the name that the manufacturer uses in this field. This is useful in *purchase order* transactions, as you can add the *manufacturer's part number* field as a column. Note, though, that you can only specify one *manufacturer's part number* per item.

- **Unit of Measure:** Depending on which edition of QuickBooks you are using, you may be able to specify a *unit of measure* for this item.

- **Description on Purchase Transactions:** This will be the description of the item as it shows in purchase transactions.

- **Cost:** This is generally considered to be the *last purchase cost* for the item, although that doesn't have to be the case. Usually (depending on various preference settings) when you receive an item, the *unit purchase cost* is saved to this field. However, you can edit the field directly, or choose to not have it updated when the item is received. This is <u>not</u> an accounting value – it is not used (in most cases) for any financial transactions directly.

- **COGS Account:** When you sell an item the *average cost* of the item will be posted to this account.

- **Preferred Vendor:** You can choose one vendor from the *Vendor List* as the primary vendor for this item.

- **Description on Sales Transactions:** This will be the description of the item as it shows in sales transactions.

- **Sales Price:** This is the standard price that you sell this item for in sales transactions.

- **Tax Code:** Usually this is either *Tax* or *Non*, to control if the item is to be marked as taxable in sales transactions.

- **Income Account:** When you sell an item, the selling price for the item is posted to this account.

- **Asset Account:** This is the *inventory asset* account to be used for this item. If you receive the item, the received value is added to this account. If you sell the item, the average cost of the item is removed from this account.

- **Reorder Point:** You can specify a "minimum stocking level" for this item. If the *quantity on hand* falls below this point, the item will be flagged in the *Inventory Stock Status by Item* report, and listed in the *Reminders* window.

- **On Hand:** This is the quantity on hand for this item, the sum of all of the receipt and consumption transactions in the QuickBooks company file. This represents ALL transactions in the file without regards to the current date. Note that you can only edit this value in this window if you are adding a new item.

- **Average Cost:** This will be discussed in more detail later. This is the calculated cost of the item based on all receipt and value adjustment transactions. It cannot be directly edited, although you can set it in this window if you are adding a new item.

- **On P.O.:** This is the quantity of the item on open purchase orders.

- **On Sales Order:** This is the quantity of the item on open sales orders.

- **Item is Inactive:** Once you start to use an item in transactions you cannot delete it. You can, however, mark it as "inactive", and it will hide this item from many reports and forms. <u>Do not</u> do this if you have a *quantity on hand* for the item.

When you are creating a NEW item the *inventory information* section will have some different fields. In this case only you can enter the *on hand* value. QuickBooks will then take the *cost* value and multiply that by the *on hand* value to create a *total value*, and an *inventory value adjustment* transaction will be entered with those values using the *as of* date shown here. This is used to calculate the starting *average cost* for the item. It is generally best to <u>not</u> enter an *on hand* quantity this way – you should use receipt or other transactions. This inventory adjustment will post the value to the specified *asset account* and will make a balancing entry to the *opening balance equity* account.

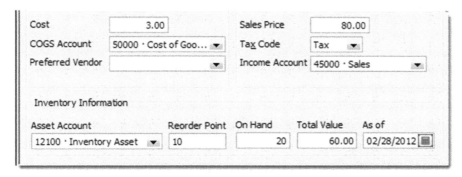

Figure 12-3 Inventory Information in the Edit Item window

Non-Inventory Parts

QuickBooks also provides a *non-inventory part* item in the item list. The idea here is that this is an inventory item that you are buying and selling, but you don't want to track the quantity on hand.

In general, it is best to focus your inventory control efforts on the key items that you have. Track quantities for items that represent a high value. Don't worry about tracking quantities that represent a low value. Use the 80/20 rule, which says that 80% of the value of your inventory is represented by only 20% of the items. Control quantities of those items representing the 80% of your inventory.

For the bulk of your items, which probably represent only 20% of the value, you can use *non-inventory parts*. Quantities aren't tracked. The items are expensed when you buy them, rather than when you sell them. You may perform an annual inventory count to see how many of these items that you have, and make a journal entry to adjust your expense and inventory asset accounts.

Perpetual Inventory

QuickBooks keeps a **perpetual** inventory, meaning that every purchase and every sale of inventory immediately updates all your account balances and reports. *Perpetual Inventory* in QuickBooks keeps a continuous record of increases, decreases, and balance on hand of inventory items.

When QuickBooks calculates the cost of inventory, it uses the *average cost* method. This divides the cost of inventory by the number of units in stock. It is most appropriate when prices paid for inventory do not vary significantly over time, and when inventory turnover is high (i.e., products sell through quickly). QuickBooks calculates the cost of inventory using this method.

Cost Fields in QuickBooks

If you are using QuickBooks to manage your inventory, you need to understand how QuickBooks deals with the **cost** of inventory items.

If you look at an *inventory part* item, you will see that there are two **cost** fields, *Cost* and *Average Cost*.

The **cost** field is a "reference" field. That is, it doesn't have any direct bearing on the *valuation* of your inventory, the cost of your inventory in your inventory asset account. The *cost* field is often referred to as the "last purchased cost", although that isn't always accurate. If you purchase an item and receive a bill for it, the cost that you receive the item at will usually be stored in this field. However, that is optional, and you also can edit this cost directly in this window. This value doesn't have a direct effect on your inventory valuation.

The **average cost** field is the field that is used in the calculation of the value of your inventory. This is calculated by QuickBooks based on the cost of receipt (and adjustment) transactions. You cannot directly edit this in the *Edit Item* window.

Inventory Valuation

QuickBooks values your inventory using an **average costing** calculation, as opposed to other types you may be familiar with, such as LIFO, FIFO, or specific costing. If you need another costing method, you will have to use a third party add-on program that manages inventory outside of QuickBooks, or purchase the additional *Advanced Inventory* option that is available for QuickBooks Enterprise (for more in Advance Inventory, see page 538).

When you use an inventory item on a purchase form (e.g., a Bill), QuickBooks increases (Debits) the Inventory Asset account for the *actual* cost of the inventory purchase. At the same time, it recalculates the **average cost** of this item as of that date.

When you use an inventory item in a sales transaction, QuickBooks increases (debits) the Cost of Goods Sold account and decreases (credits) Inventory Asset for the average cost of the items. This is in addition to recording income and accounts receivable

Each time you sell inventory items, the average cost per unit is multiplied by the number of units sold. Then this amount is deducted from the **inventory asset** account and added to the **cost of goods sold** account.

This can be a complicated subject – let's look at a simple example.

If you start with an item with no quantity, no value, and receive a quantity of 10 at $1.00 each, you will see that the **cost** is $1.00, and the **average cost** is also $1.00. You have $10.00 of inventory in your inventory asset account.

If you then receive another 10 items, but at a unit cost of $2.00, you will usually see the **cost** value set to be $2.00. However, the **average cost** of your inventory will show as $1.50. You started with 10 items and a value of $10.00, you added another 10 items at a value of $20.00, so you have 20 items with a value of $30.00. That gives you an **average cost** of $1.50.

If you sell one of these items in an invoice, the COGS account is incremented by the average cost of the item at the time of the sale.

An important issue to note is that if you sell all of your inventory, and then continue to sell the item so that you go to a negative quantity, the costing calculation runs into problems. QuickBooks can't accurately account for a negative balance, and you can see some very odd figures show up in the average cost field, and your inventory valuation reports. Once you bring the balances back to positive these figures should resolve themselves, but it is always a good idea to <u>not</u> allow inventory balances to go negative.

Adjusting Inventory

QuickBooks automatically adjusts inventory each time you purchase or sell Inventory Items. However, it may be necessary to manually adjust inventory after a physical count of your inventory, or in case of an increase or decrease in the value of your inventory on hand. For example, you might decrease the value of your inventory if it has lost value due to new technology trends.

To adjust inventory select the *Vendors* menu, then *Inventory Activities,* and then **Adjust Quantity/Value on Hand**. You can also find this in the *Inventory Activities* icon in the *Home Page*, or in the *Activities* button at the bottom of the *Item List.*

There are three types of adjustment transactions – *Quantity, Total Value* and *Quantity and Total Value.*

> If you are using the Advanced Inventory option in QuickBooks Enterprise there are additional inventory adjustment types, as explained later.

Adjusting the Quantity of Inventory On Hand

This is used only if you want to change the quantity on hand for a specific item. Select a *Quantity* adjustment type.

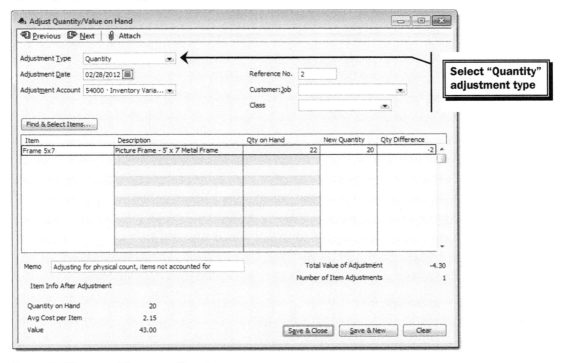

Figure 12-4 Inventory Adjustment - Quantity

Notice that QuickBooks calculates the quantity difference (-2) in the *Qty Difference* column. Also, notice that QuickBooks automatically calculates the *Total Value of Adjustment* in the bottom right corner. QuickBooks uses the *average cost* of the item on the date of the transaction.

This adjustment will post to the *inventory asset* account for the selected item, with a balancing posting to the *adjustment account* that you select. This does <u>not</u> change the *average cost* of the item. You are increasing or decreasing the *inventory asset* balance by the adjustment value shown.

Adjusting the Value of Inventory On Hand

This is used only if you want to change the value (average cost) for a specific item. Select a *Total Value* adjustment type.

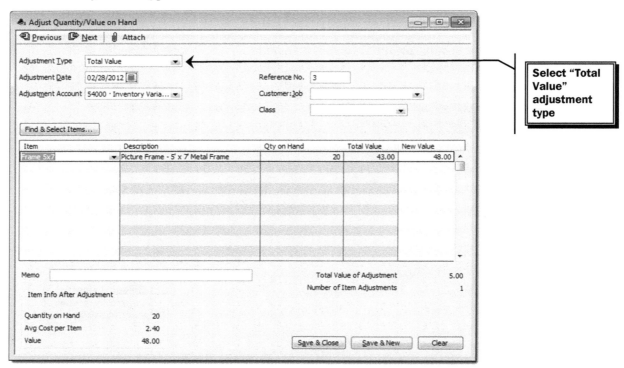

Figure 12-5 Inventory Adjustment - Total Value

At the start of this transaction this item had an *average cost* of $2.15. With a quantity on hand of 20, the value of this item is $43.00. We have adjusted the value to be $48.00 – this changes the *average cost* of the items on hand to be $2.40 since we have not changed the quantity. The difference between these valuations is $5.00 (as shown in the window), and this is added to the item's *inventory asset* account with a balancing posting to the selected adjustment account.

It is rare to use this kind of transaction.

Adjusting the Quantity *and* the Value

QuickBooks also provides you with an inventory adjustment type where you can adjust both the quantity and the value. Again, this is rarely used.

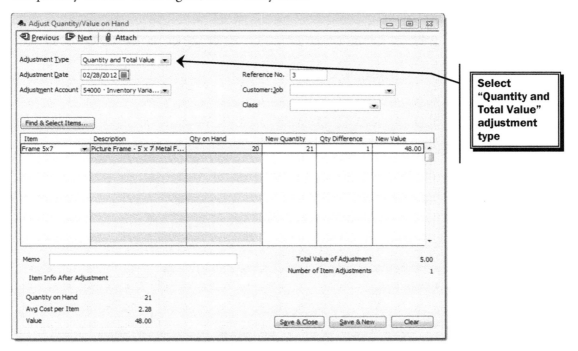

Figure 12-6 Inventory Adjustment - Quantity and Total Value

Basic Inventory Reports

QuickBooks provides several reports for inventory analysis. Note that many of the inventory reports are <u>not</u> as customizable as you may be used to with other QuickBooks reports.

For daily management of inventory, use the **Stock Status by Item** report, the **Stock Status by Vendor** report, or the **Inventory Valuation Summary** report. These reports give a quick overview of inventory counts and inventory values.

For detailed research about transactions involving Inventory, use the **Inventory Item QuickReport** or the **Inventory Valuation Detail** report.

There are a number of other valuable reports that can be used to evaluate or manage your inventory, as we will list below.

Inventory reports can be found in the *Reports* menu in the *Inventory* section. However, this doesn't include all reports. You can find a more comprehensive listing by opening the *Item List* and clicking on the *Reports* button at the bottom.

Inventory Item QuickReport

The **Inventory Item QuickReport** is useful for seeing all transactions involving an Inventory Item. You will find this by selecting an individual item in the *Item List* and either right clicking on it or clicking the *Reports* button at the bottom of the list, and selecting the *QuickReport*.

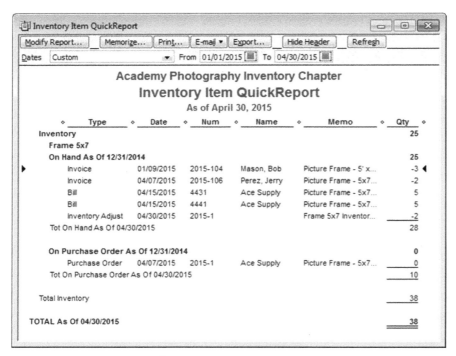

Figure 12-7 Inventory Item QuickReport

Inventory Stock Status by Item

The **Inventory Stock Status by Item** report is useful for getting a quick snapshot of each inventory part, and the number of units on hand and on order. In addition, this report gives you information about your inventory turnover, showing a column for sales per week.

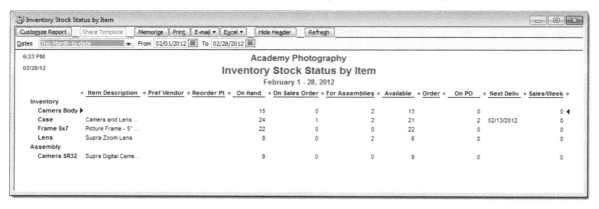

Figure 12-8 Inventory Stock Status by Item report

This report can be used to highlight an interesting optional feature of QuickBooks Premier and Enterprise – *Available Inventory*. We've discussed the *quantity on hand* value for an *inventory part* and *inventory assembly*. "Available" inventory is the *quantity on hand* minus the quantity that is "promised" in *sales order* and *pending build* transactions (*pending builds* will be discussed in more detail later).

If you sell an inventory part in an invoice, that reduces the *quantity on hand*. If you consume a component part when building an *inventory assembly*, that also reduces the *quantity on hand* for the item. However, a *sales order* and *pending build* are not "posting" transactions, so they don't reduce the *quantity on hand*. These are just "promises" or potential uses of those components.

If you look at the "Case" item in Figure 12-8, you will see that there are 24 "on hand". There is another that is included in an open sales order, and two that are included in a pending build for some assembly. That leaves you with 21 that are "available" – items that as of the report ending date are not committed to something.

The quantity on *purchase orders* is not included, as those are to be received at some future date, not the date of the report (QuickBooks ignores the "delivery date" of the purchase order).

This is an optional feature. You must enable it in your *Items & Inventory* preferences. Note that if you enable this you can set QuickBooks to warn you if the quantity you want to sell exceeds the *quantity available* instead of the *quantity on hand*.

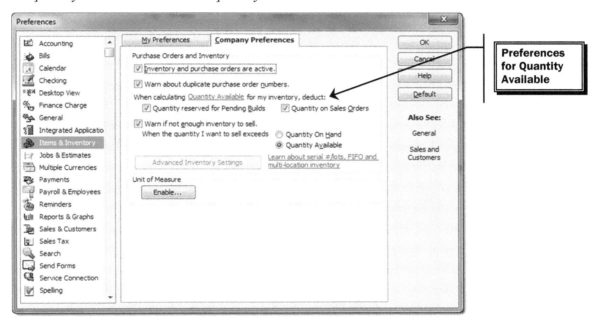

Figure 12-9 Preferences to enable the Quantity Available feature

Inventory Stock Status by Vendor

The **Inventory Stock Status by Vendor** report gives you information about your inventory parts, including how many are on hand, and how many are on order. This report is sorted by the *Preferred Vendor* field in the item. Other than this, it is the same as the *Inventory Stock Status by Item* report.

Inventory Valuation Summary

The **Inventory Valuation Summary** report gives you information about the value of your inventory Items on a certain date. This report shows each item in inventory, the quantity on-hand, the average cost, and the retail value of each item.

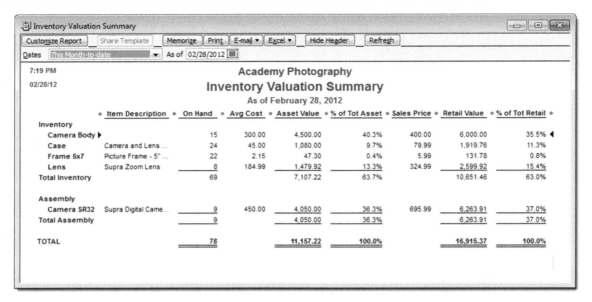

Figure 12-10 Inventory Valuation Summary report

Inventory Valuation Detail

The *Inventory Valuation Detail* report is useful in examining the transactions that affect the asset value of an item in a given period of time. Note the *Asset Value* column on the right, which gives you a running balance by date.

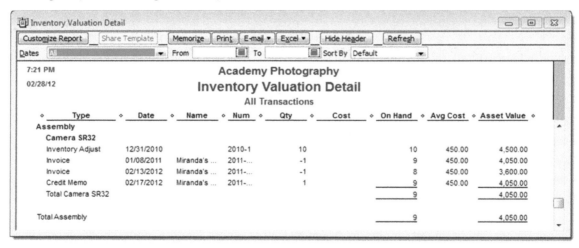

Figure 12-11 Inventory Valuation Detail report

Physical Inventory Worksheet

Many businesses will conduct a periodic count of the items that they have on hand, to compare to their business records. The **Physical Inventory Worksheet** is used to help with this task.

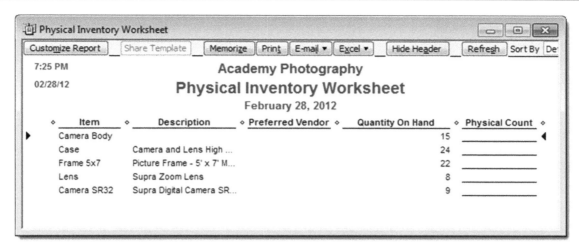

Figure 12-12 Physical Inventory report

Other Inventory Reports

There are a number of additional reports and graphs that you can find by clicking on the *Reports* button at the bottom of the item list. These reports are not limited to *inventory part* and *inventory assembly* items.

- **Item Price List**: This lists the *sales price* for each item. This won't incorporate "custom prices" from *price level list* records.

- **Item List**: This is a simple listing of the items in the item list, including basic information on the items.

- **Sales by Item (Summary and Detail)**: These reports list the items that have been sold, including the price and COGS values.

- **Open Sales Orders (by Item and by Customer):** These list items that are included in open sales orders. To see the item details you may need to modify the reports.

- **Purchase by Vendor /Item (Summary and Detail):** A set of reports that list the items you have purchased, sorted either by vendor or by item. You can see a summary or a listing of every purchase transaction in detail.

- **Open Purchase Orders (Summary, Detail or by Job):** These list the items that are on purchase orders that have not been received. You may have to modify the reports to see the item details.

- **Item Profitability:** This report lists the items sold in the selected period, and lists the "actual cost" and "actual revenue". You can double click on the cost or revenue for an item to see a detailed *Item Actual Detail* report.

- **Item Estimates vs. Actuals:** This will be used to compare costs of items involved in estimates, comparing them to the actual invoice, if you are using progress invoicing.

- **Sales Graph:** This provides you with a visual representation of sales by item, by customer, or by sales rep. It includes both a bar chart and a pie chart.

Inventory Center

Intuit has added an **Inventory Center** to the program, bringing many inventory related features together in one "center" as has been done with customers, vendors and so forth.

Note that the Inventory Center is not available in QuickBooks Pro

If you work with QuickBooks you are familiar with the *item list*. This is a simple list of your items, with some buttons at the bottom to access certain activities. You can modify the display to see different columns, but if you want to see details about the item you have to edit it, or go to a report somewhere.

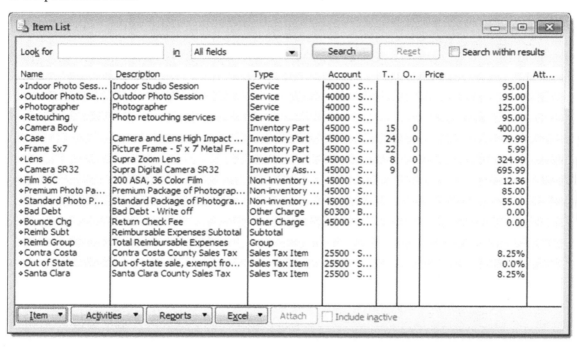

Figure 12-13 Item List, available in all editions

The *Inventory Center is focused just on inventory part and inventory assembly items, those items where you are tracking a quantity on hand. This can be accessed from the Vendors menu, under Inventory Activities.*

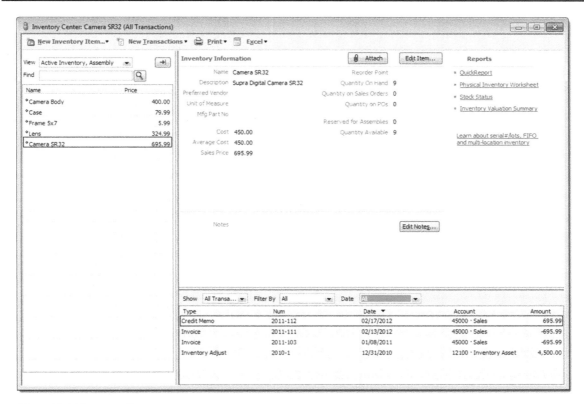

Figure 12-14 Inventory Center

On the left you see a list of your *inventory part* and *inventory assembly* items. Excluding the other item types lets you focus on inventory functions.

You can modify this list to add different columns (just as in the *item list*) by right clicking on the columns headings and selecting **Customize Columns**.

There are filters at the top of the list that let you filter what is shown in the listing. The *Custom Filter* option lets you select for key words in item name, custom fields, and notes.

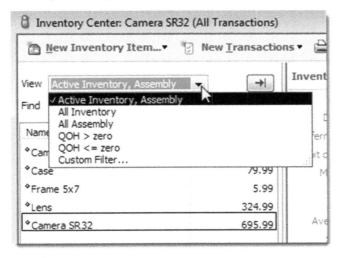

Figure 12-15 Filter options for the items in the Inventory Center

The top center of the *Inventory Center* window shows you basic information about the item, so that you don't have to edit the item to see inside.

At the right you see a list of the most commonly used reports, so that you don't have to search for them in another menu or take up space in your icon bar or favorites list.

At the bottom of the window is a filterable list of transactions that include the selected item, which is very convenient.

QuickBooks for Manufacturing

There is a definite lack of documentation on how to use QuickBooks in a manufacturing business in the information that Intuit provides. Although there is a *Manufacturing and Wholesale* edition, there aren't many features that are unique to manufacturing.

There are many "types" of manufacturing businesses, each has unique requirements. QuickBooks is a better fit for "assembly" manufacturers, those that are making assembled items based on discrete components. Once you start getting into more specialized manufacturing, such as chemical or other process industries, QuickBooks becomes less useful.

Starting with the Basics – Inventory Assembly Items

The basic element for a manufacturing firm using QuickBooks is the *inventory assembly* item. This is essentially the same as an *inventory part,* but it also includes a list of *components* that are used to create this part. This list of components is called a *bill of materials* or *BOM.*

> It is important to note that the *inventory assembly* item type is only available in Premier and Enterprise. It is not supported in QuickBooks Pro.

The basic process to get started with assembling items is:

- Create the items that are components of your assembly.
- Create the inventory assembly and assign it the parts you will use to build that assembly.
- "Build" or assemble your inventory assemblies.

Create the Items

QuickBooks Premier and Enterprise provides us with 11 different item *types,* of which 5 can be used as *component* items in an *inventory assembly.* Each item type has its own characteristics and uses, as we'll explain below.

QuickBooks won't allow you to use a *subtotal, discount, payment, sales tax, sales tax group* or *group* item as a component.

Inventory Part

This is the most obvious, and basic kind of item you can add to an *inventory assembly.* An *inventory part* is an item that you are buying and stocking, where you want to track the quantity you have on hand. These will be parts that have significant value that you want to track, and you want to make sure that you have enough on hand to build your assembly.

Using *inventory part* items provides you with some advantages and some disadvantages in QuickBooks. An advantage – you can track how many you have on hand, and see them in a variety of QuickBooks management reports. A disadvantage – you must have a positive inventory balance of the inventory part components before you can build an inventory assembly – if you don't have the component parts, you can't build the assembly.

When you purchase these items, the cost of the item is saved in the *inventory asset* account. When you *build* the assembly, the value of the *inventory part* items will be moved out of the component inventory asset account and moved into the assembly inventory asset account.

Inventory Assembly

QuickBooks allows you to use an *inventory assembly* as a component in another *inventory assembly*. This can be referred to as a "sub-assembly", although QuickBooks doesn't use that term.

An *inventory assembly* component item is treated the same as an *inventory part* – you must have an adequate supply of the assembly component to be able to build the higher level assembly. Costs are handled the same way here as they are with the *inventory part* components.

Using "sub-assemblies" this way provides you with the ability to break down your complicated products into simpler, more manageable groupings. In general it is best if you can keep a list of components down to one printed page (or less), so that you can easily see what is included in the assembly. By using sub-assemblies you can simply a complicated **Bill of Materials**. In addition, QuickBooks Premier **limits you to 100 component items in a Bill of Material**, so for complicated assemblies in Premier you <u>must</u> use sub-assemblies. Note that Enterprise has a limit of 500 component items.

Using sub-assemblies does create more work in some cases, since QuickBooks won't print or process a "multiple level" assembly item all at once.

Non-Inventory Part

Sometimes there are parts that you use in your building process that don't represent a large portion of the value of your inventory, or of the assembly itself. These are parts that you don't worry about tracking quantity – you buy them in bulk and just order more when you see that the "bin" is getting low. They could be things like small washers, screws, and so forth. These are often good candidates to be *non-inventory parts*.

When you buy a non-inventory part it is "expensed" right away, rather than capitalized. It is important that you set these items up in the correct way. Make sure that you check the box titled "This item is used in assemblies…"

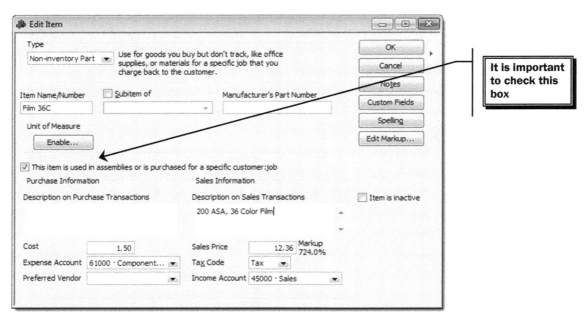

Figure 12-16 Edit Item window for a Non-inventory Part

When you check this box you make this a "two-sided" item, with separate expense and sales accounts.

When you purchase this item the "cost" of the purchase is posted to the expense account. When you build an assembly that uses this item the "cost" is removed from the expense account and included in the inventory asset account of the assembly.

You would use these kinds of parts when the cost of an individual item is very small, so that you don't worry about tracking the balance on hand of the parts. If you lose some during processing (drop them on the floor, etc.) the loss has already been expensed. However, if the items are hard to come by or take a long time to acquire, you may still consider using them as an *inventory part* item.

Service and Other Charge Items

You can add both *service* and *other charge* items as components to an *inventory assembly*. There isn't a large difference between the two, other than being able to specify a unit of measure for *service* items but not for *other charge* items. With either item type, make it a "two sided" item by clicking the "used in assemblies" box, as described for *non-inventory part* items

You can use these items to add non-material costs to an assembly. It makes sense to use *service* items for outside processing charges, labor and the like. Use *other charge* items for setup costs.

If you have some work done on an assembly by an outside processor, such as deburring or coating, add this cost to the assembly item using one of these items. When you pay the vendor for the outside processing the cost goes to your expense account. When you build the item, the cost is "capitalized", removed from the expense account and added to the inventory asset for the assembly.

You can also use this to "burden" your assembly with your own payroll costs in the same way, using a *service* item that points to your payroll expense account.

Create the Inventory Assemblies

An *inventory assembly* item has all of the same characteristics of an *inventory* part. You have a *cost*, the three *accounts* (income, COGS and asset), descriptions and so forth. The primary difference from an *inventory part* is that you can assign a component list, a *bill of materials* (or "BOM"). This is a list of all of the parts that you would use to create this assembly.

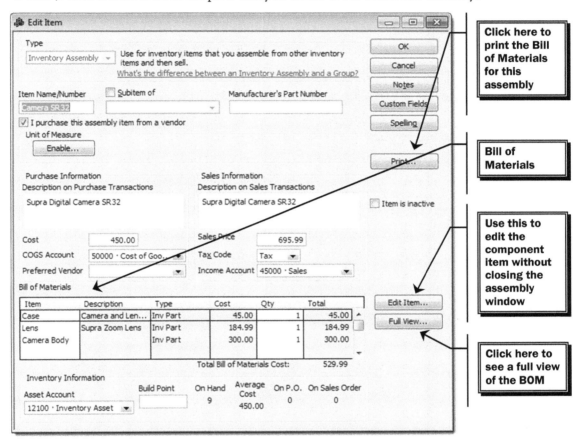

Figure 12-17 Creating an Inventory Assembly item

For each component you can specify the *item* to use and the *quantity* to use. You would also specify a *unit of measure* if that feature is enabled.

Note that you cannot enter a negative quantity, or a quantity of zero.

You can delete components by using Ctrl+Del, and insert a blank line to add a new component by using Ctrl+Ins. <u>Do not</u> leave a blank line in the component list, by either inserting a line without adding a new component, or by erasing the *item* field. Blank lines will sometimes cause the program to crash when issuing a build transaction.

At the bottom of the *Edit Item* window you will see a field for *build point*. This differs from an *inventory part* which will have a *reorder point*. While the concept is the same, QuickBooks treats these differently. Both can generate *reminders* when your quantity on hand falls below the specified point. However, the *Stock Status by Item* report will only place a checkmark by *inventory parts* that have a quantity on hand less than the *reorder point. Inventory assembly* items will not be marked this way on this report.

At the right side of the *Edit Item* window you will see a *Print* button, which can be used to print the bill of materials. This report does not have a template or *modify* button, so you cannot change its appearance.

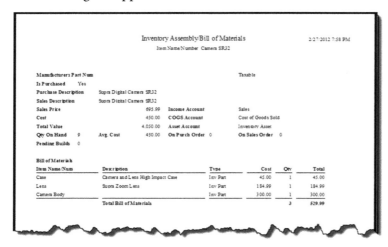

Figure 12-18 A Printed Bill of Materials

Build the Assemblies

Now that you have defined the parts and assemblies, we can build the assembly. From the *Activities* button at the bottom of the item list, click **Build Assemblies (you can also select this from the Inventory Activities icon on the Home Page, or by selecting Vendors in the menu and then Inventory Activities)**. In the *Build Assemblies* dialog you will select the assembly to build, specify the date you want to build this on, and enter the number to build.

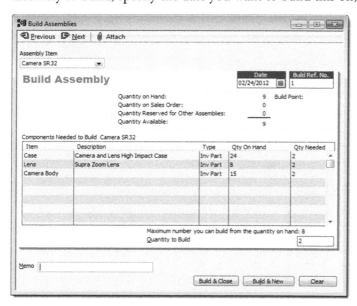

Figure 12-19 Building an Assembly

When you click either of the *build* buttons, the program will save this build transaction (if possible). Two things happen now:

1.   QuickBooks will remove the *quantity needed* amount of each of the component items from the quantity on hand.

2.   QuickBooks will increase the quantity of the inventory assembly item by the *quantity to build*.

Essentially we are moving the cost of the inventory part assets into the inventory assembly asset. The transaction will use the *average cost* of the component items, as of the transaction date, and add that to the cost of the assembly item (this will be discussed in more detail below).

A few comments on what happens here:

- Note the *maximum number you can build…* value. QuickBooks won't let you build an assembly if you don't have enough parts on hand to build it. This value shows you how many you can build with the parts that you have, as of the date of the transaction.

- If you enter a *quantity to build* that is higher than that *maximum number*, QuickBooks will mark the "build" as *Pending*. This means that it hasn't been built, it is waiting to be built. There are reports that list the *pending* builds.

- When you enter the *quantity to build* much of the information in this dialog will not be updated <u>until</u> you move the cursor to another field, such as the date or memo. This can be confusing at first. When you move the cursor off that field the *qty needed* is updated, and the *pending* stamp could be displayed.

The *Date* field is very important. This is the date that the *build* transaction takes place. The *quantity on hand* for the component parts is based on your inventory status as of this date. Sometimes people get frustrated – they look at an inventory report and it says you have enough, but this dialog says you don't! The issue is usually the dates – if the report is dated after a PO is received, but your build is dated earlier, you might not have had those parts on this date. Adjust the date in either your report, or the build.

As you might expect, the same issue relates to the assemblies you build – they are only available on or after the build date, not before.

Inventory Assembly Cost, Average Cost and Total BOM Cost

When you look at the *Edit Item* window for an *inventory assembly* item you will see three *cost* values shown: *Cost, Total Bill of Materials Cost* and *Average Cost*. How do these relate, and how are they used?

The *average cost* of the assembly is a value maintained by QuickBooks based on purchases, builds and inventory adjustments. Just like an *inventory part*, if you purchase this *inventory assembly* the billed cost will be incorporated in the average cost. *Inventory value* adjustments will also update the average cost. The difference for an *inventory assembly* is that when you *build* the assembly, the *average cost* of the component items, as of the build transaction date, will be added up and used to update the assembly average cost.

The *cost* value can be updated by directly editing it, or by a purchase transaction if you allow that to update the assembly.

If you look at the bottom of the Bill of Materials you will see a value that is unique to the *inventory assembly* item, the **Total Bill of Materials Cost**. This <u>should</u> represent the current cost to manufacture this assembly, but this value could be misleading.

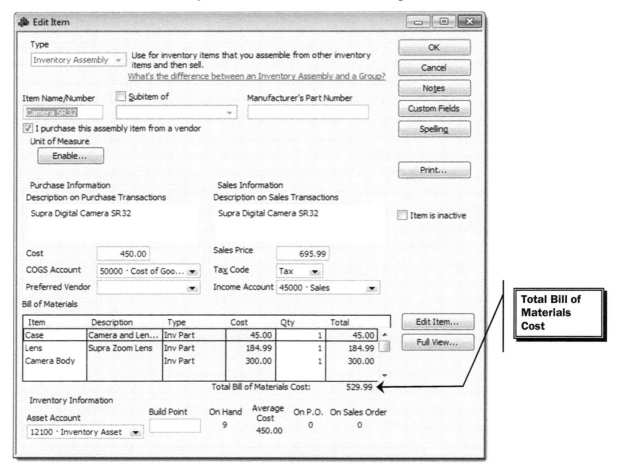

Figure 12-20 Cost fields of an Inventory Assembly

Looking at the Bill of Materials, you see that each component has a *cost* listed. The *cost* value shown in the Bill of Materials is the *cost* value for that component, not the *average cost*. This is clear for an *inventory part* item, but what about *non-inventory, service* and *other charge* items? This is one of the reasons that you want to check the box in those items that says that this item is used in an assembly – because then you have a *cost* field to provide the value for the Bill of Materials. So the *Total Bill of Materials Cost* shown here is the sum of the *cost* fields of the items multiplied by the quantity for each item.

Logically you would think that this would be the *current cost to build this assembly*, which would be a valuable managerial number. It doesn't represent the actual cost to build as will be used in financial transactions because the actual cost is based on the *average cost* of components, not the *cost*. Assuming that your *cost* values for components is the latest purchased cost, the *Total Bill of Materials* cost should be what it would cost you to build this assembly if you had to purchase all new parts.

The problem with this is that the **figures that are shown here are misleading**. As you build an assembly, the *total bill of materials cost* is not used anywhere. Most importantly, it isn't used to update the *cost* field for the assembly. If you <u>buy</u> the assembly, the *cost* is updated with the purchase cost. But if you <u>build</u> the assembly, *cost* is not changed.

This becomes more important if you are using *inventory assembly* items as components in the BOM. Since the *cost* of the sub-assembly is not updated when you build it, the *cost* shows in the higher level assembly BOM does not reflect any real value. So the higher level *Total Bill of Material Cost* value is inaccurate, possibly even misleading.

Why is this important? Most companies will want to base their selling price on the cost of manufacturing their item. It is important that you have accurate information to make these decisions. It is common to want to update prices based on the **current cost of acquisition**. That is, you want the BOM cost to reflect the *last purchase cost* of the components, not necessarily the *average cost*. If you are updating the *cost* field when you purchase your parts then you have this information in the database for components.

Pending Builds

Build transactions can be marked as "pending", which is essentially putting them on hold until you actually want to build the assembly. This is a transaction that does not adjust the quantity on hand of the assembly or the component items.

You can mark a build transaction as "pending" when the *Build Assemblies* window is open by selecting *Edit* and then **Mark Build as Pending**. A "Pending" stamp shows on the transaction.

In addition, if you try to create a *build* transaction for a quantity of assemblies that cannot be built on the transaction date, due to a shortage of components, QuickBooks will ask you if you want to save the transaction as "pending". You cannot save a *build* transaction if you have a component shortage unless it is marked as "pending".

QuickBooks has a *Pending Builds* report (in *Reports/Inventory*) that will list all pending builds.

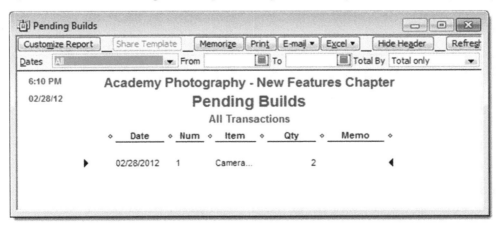

Figure 12-21 Pending Builds report

In addition, the *Inventory Stock Status by Item* report will add a column "For Assemblies" which will list all of the components that are listed in "pending" build transactions. This reduces the "available" inventory. This only shows if you have checked the *Quantity reserved for Pending Builds* option in the *Items & Inventory* preferences.

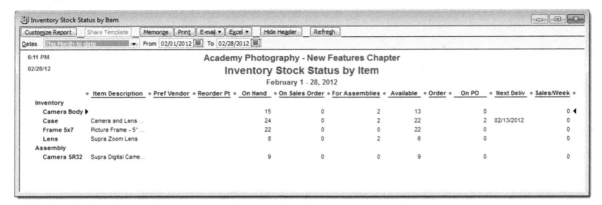

Figure 12-22 Inventory Stock Status by Item showing Available Inventory

Enterprise Features

QuickBooks Enterprise has a number of inventory features that are not found in QuickBooks Pro or Premier.

Inventory Menu

There is an *Inventory* menu added to the menu bar starting with Enterprise V12.0. This, along with the *Inventory Center*, helps to gather the many inventory-related functions and reports into a single location so they are easy to find.

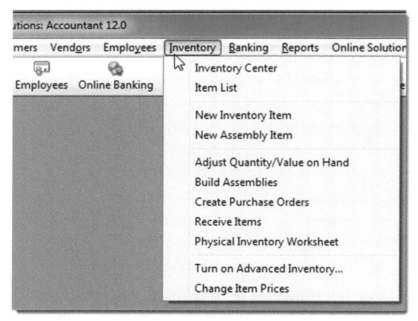

Figure 12-23 Inventory Menu

Price Level Lists

QuickBooks allows you to have 750 *price level list* records, up from 100 allowed in Pro and Premier

Inventory Assembly Items

You can have 500 component items in the Bill of Materials an *inventory assembly* item with QuickBooks Enterprise. Premier has a limit of 100 items.

Inventory Center

With Enterprise the *Inventory Center* supports one additional feature – the ability to associate an image with items. You can drag an image and drop it on to the image portion of the display.

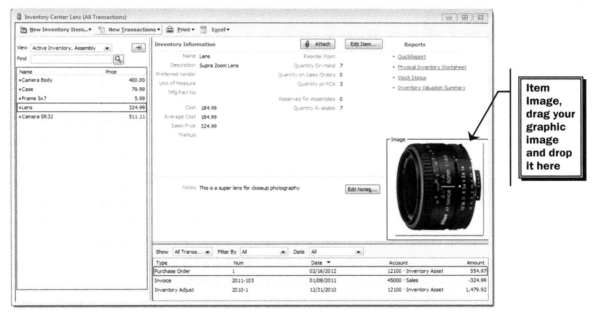

This has limited value (as of Enterprise 15) because this is the only place that this image can be seen. You cannot add it to reports, nor can you add it to invoices or other sales transactions.

Item images are stored in the *images* folder that is found in the folder where the QBW file is located. This is the same folder where logo graphic images are stored for sales form templates.

Additional Build Assembly Features in Enterprise

Enterprise provides a great deal more flexibility when you issue a *Build Assembly* transaction. You have the ability to change the quantities of individual items, and you can add or delete component items from the BOM.

Here is the *Build Assemblies* window from Premier:

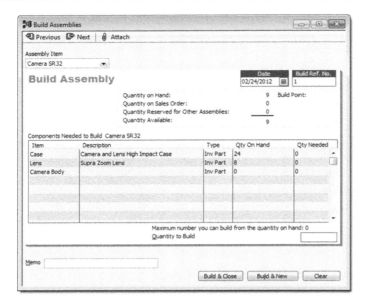

Figure 12-24 Build Assemblies window from Premier

Now, compare this to the same window in Enterprise:

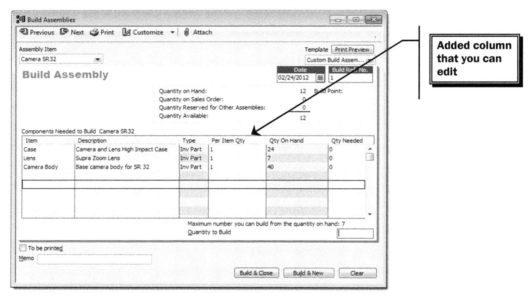

Figure 12-25 Build Assemblies window in Enterprise

There is an added column, *Per Item Qty*. This allows you to change the quantity used of a
component. You can increase (or decrease) the quantity. Note that you cannot change the
quantity to zero, QuickBooks will not allow that.

In addition, you can delete a component entirely by selecting it and pressing *Ctrl+Del*, or you
can add another component by clicking on a blank line and adding the information.

Changes you make here are not saved back to the BOM as defined in the inventory assembly
record in the item list. Changes here are only saved as a part of the "build" when you issue it.

This is a very useful feature when you have assemblies that you modify or customize to fit a
particular order.

Another difference is that you can print a *build assembly* report for this particular build by clicking the *print* button at the top of the window. You also have the ability to edit the template for this report (form) just as you can edit sales transaction templates.

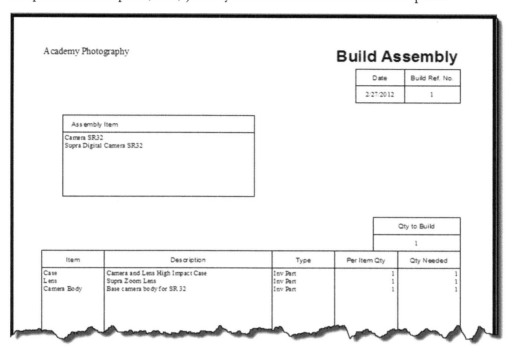

Figure 12-26 Build Assembly report from Enterprise

Customization options are very limited, however.

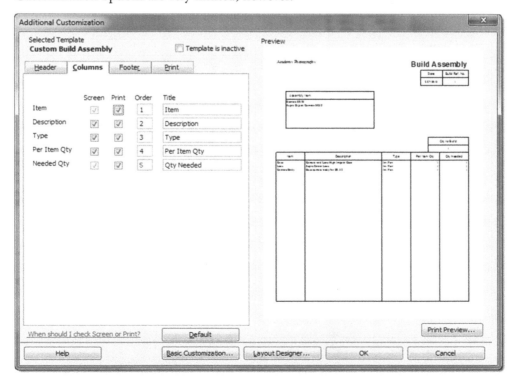

Figure 12-27 Customizing the Build Assembly report

Enhanced Inventory Receiving

If you work with inventory in QuickBooks you are probably aware of the hassle of receiving inventory and the related billing – you can't disconnect the receipt from the bill. There are a number of problems that come up because of this, and the workarounds are a hassle. Intuit introduced a new option in QuickBooks Enterprise Solutions 2012 that is intended to address this, *Enhanced Inventory Receiving* (or EIR). Essentially, with this enabled QuickBooks splits the *item receipt* from the *bill*, making two transactions.

It is important that you understand this before you use it, because once you select this option you can't change your mind, as the option cannot be turned off.

In addition, the initial versions of this new feature can create new problems in certain situations. To keep up to date on the issues that you may run into with this feature, see the QuickBooks and Beyond blog at http://www.sleeter.com/blog/tag/enhanced-inventory-receiving/

Problems with Item Receipts

In QuickBooks an item receipt and the bill for that item receipt are **one transaction**. You can't separate them. You must have a one-to-one ratio of bill and item receipt (since it gets wrapped up into one transaction). This creates a number of different problems depending on your situation. Each of these has a workaround, but workarounds are not the best way to operate your business.

Here are a few of the problems you can run into with the standard method of receiving items in QuickBooks:

- You may need to pay for items you have received before you actually receive the items. Entering a receipt with the accurate *billing date* increases your inventory before it should.

- If you enter an item receipt, and later you enter the bill, most people will change the transaction date to be the bill date so that the accounting transaction for the bill is accurate. **This changes the item receipt to that same date**. This can have far reaching consequences such as changing COGS calculations and possibly even turning *inventory assembly build* transactions into pending builds.

- What if you receive a bill from your vendor that covers several different item receipts, on different days? QuickBooks doesn't provide you with a simple way to deal with this, as there must be a one-to-one relationship between bills and receipts.

- What if you receive multiple bills from your vendor for one item receipt? QuickBooks again doesn't provide you with a simple way to deal with this, as there must be a one-to-one relationship between bills and receipts.

- In many businesses proper procedures will separate the *inventory receiving* department from the *accounts payable* department. QuickBooks makes this a single transaction, so you can't make that separation.

To solve these problems, Intuit has introduced an optional feature, *Enhanced Inventory Receiving*, which is **available only in QuickBooks Enterprise Solutions V12.0 or later.**

This separates the item receipt from the bill, which should resolve each of the problems that are list above. When the item is received, the expected value of that is posted into an *inventory offset account*. Later, when you enter the bill, that offset account is adjusted. Dates for the bill do not change the date of the receipt.

Potential Problems

There are a number of concerns about this feature, as it is implemented at this time. These problems exist in the first releases of Enterprise 12.0. Some of these issues may be resolved by Intuit in subsequent releases.

- **You can't turn this off once selected**. If you enable this feature and don't like the results, you can't go back other than to restore an old backup file.
- **This creates many more transactions** than before. You used to have a single bill transaction, now you have a separate bill and item receipt. That doubles the number of transactions for this activity.
- **This can change prior period financials**. You may find that when you enable this feature that there are some changes in your financials based on rounding differences when the records are split. In many cases the differences are small, but these can show up in all prior financial periods.
- **This might interfere with some third party add-ons**. This is unlikely to be an issue for most situations, but if you have an add-on product that works with receipts/bills, it might not work properly after this change.

Inventory balances may change. In some testing with early versions there were indications that the quantity on hand for some items may have changed during the conversion. This has not been fully explored at this time.

Linking problems may lead to errors. If you start with a purchase order, then enter an item receipt, and later enter the bill for this, the bill is linked to the purchase order. If you had a partial receipt of the item, you may not notice this when entering the bill, as from there you only see the original purchase order (the full amount).

The Inventory Offset Account might not be accurate. EIR applies to inventory parts and inventory assemblies. But if you use other item types in the Items tab of a bill, these items incorrectly adjust the inventory offset account.

If an Item Receipt is in a different period than a bill, incorrect adjustments may occur. If you receive an item, close that period, then enter the bill in the next period, AND the bill changes the received cost, EIR will go back to the original item receipt and change the amount posted to the inventory offset account. This can change your balance sheet in that closed period.

Some of these issues may be resolved in a later release, but this points out why you should be cautious in using this feature.

Working with EIR

To turn this feature on, go to the *Items & Inventory preferences* and click the **Enable** button under *Enhanced Inventory Receiving*.

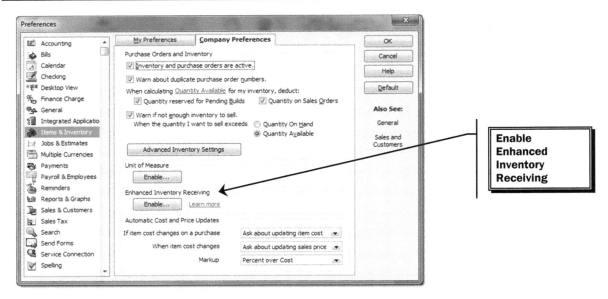

Figure 12-28 Enhanced Inventory Receiving Preference

When you enable this preference QuickBooks will make a backup copy of your file and then it will go through the entire company file, changing all *Bill* transactions for inventory items into two transactions, an *Item Receipt* and a *Bill.* The program will display a summary of the changes. You may find that there are some changes to item costs due to rounding errors in this conversion, with the differences being posted to a new account, *Inventory Offset.*

There are a number of screens and processes that are going to be changed.

In an *Item Receipt* you see that the *Expenses* tab is no longer found.

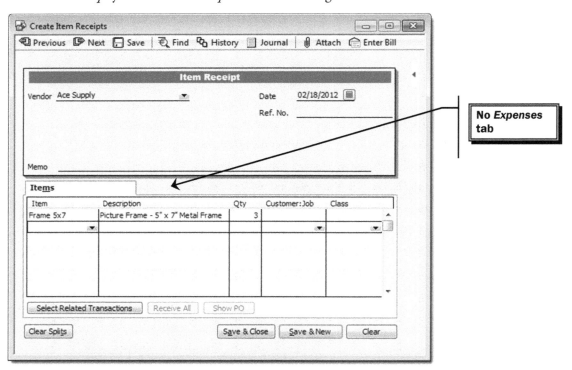

Figure 12-29 Item Receipt with EIR enabled

Enhanced Inventory Receiving will create a new *Other Current Liability* account in your Chart of Accounts called **Inventory Offset Account**. When you enter an item receipt for an inventory part or inventory assembly QuickBooks will debit *Inventory Asset* and credit *Inventory Offset Account*.

When you enter an *Item Receipt* QuickBooks will debit the *Inventory Offset Account* and credit *Accounts Payable*.

Automatic Cost/Price Update

Enterprise V 12.0 added a significant change in how costs and prices are updated when you receive a purchased item, *Automatic Cost and Price Updates*.

Prior to this, options for automatic updates of costs and prices have been limited. If you receive an inventory part and the cost changes, you are asked if you want to update the *cost* field. You can turn this question off, but that applies to ALL items. If you change the *cost*, the *sales price* is not updated. This confuses people, because there is a *markup* preference – but that isn't used here (only for new items).

Now we have (in Enterprise) greater control over how costs are updated, as well as the ability to update prices at the same time. Note that this applies only to *inventory part* and *inventory assembly* items.

Looking at the *Items & Inventory* preferences you will see a number of options relating to cost and price updates.

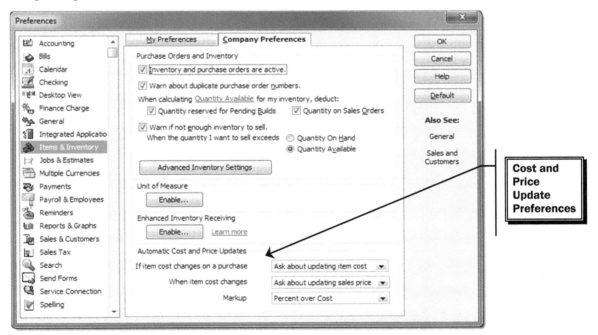

When you create a purchase order, or receive an item in an item receipt or bill, and the expected or received cost is different than the cost value for the item (not the average cost), QuickBooks will look at the preference setting for If item cost changes on a purchase. There are three options:

Always update item cost: The item cost will always be updated if there is a change, without asking.

Never update item cost: The item cost will not be updated if there is a change, and you won't be asked.

Ask about updating item cost: If the cost is different, a window will open asking you what to do.

Next, if the cost is updated in the item based on the preferences above (and possibly your responses), QuickBooks will look at the When item cost changes preference to see what should be done with the sales price. Again, there are three options, always update, never update, and ask.

Finally, if the sales price is updated then the Markup preference controls how the sales price is updated. There can be a percent over cost or an amount over cost. The markup value is stored in the item record. Do you want the price to be updated by (for example) 10%, or $10.00?

On top of all this, you will find a similar set of preferences in the Edit Item window for each item. This provides the same options, and you can use them to override the general preference settings (as well as to set the markup value.

These are set by clicking the Edit Markup button.

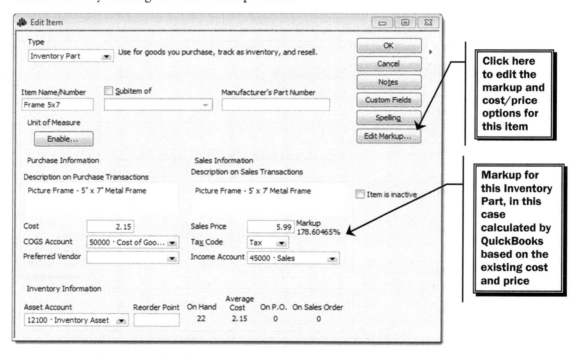

Figure 12-30 Markup options in the Edit Item window

In the *Edit Markup* window you can change the *cost, sales price* and *markup* values. You can override the default preferences for the *type of markup* and the settings on what to do if the cost changes.

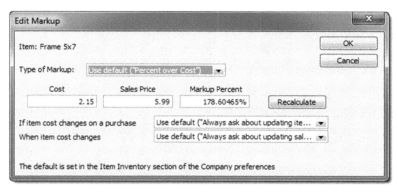

Figure 12-31 Edit Markup window to set cost/price update preferences per item

So how does this work? If you create a purchase order, item receipt, bill, credit card charge or check for an item and change the cost, QuickBooks looks at the preferences. If either of the preferences (*if item cost changes* or *when item cost changes*) is set to "ask", then the *Item's Cost Changed* window opens. This is tricky – if EITHER of the preferences is set to ask, the window opens. If you say "never ask" for item cost, but "ask" for the price setting, the window still opens.

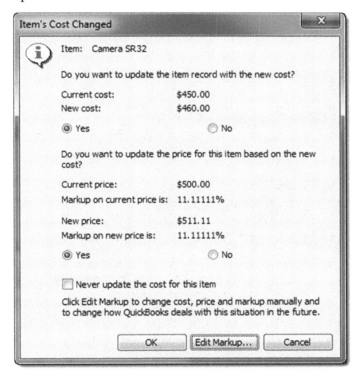

Figure 12-32 Popup window to update cost and price if received cost changes

The default settings in this window will depend on your preference settings, both global preference and per-item preference.

Note that there is an *Edit Markup* button, which opens the same *Edit Markup* window we saw above. Also note that there is a box for *Never update the cost for this item*, to turn updates off for this one item.

This can be a confusing setup, and there isn't a good way to audit all items. It also can place a lot of control in the receiving clerk's hands. However, the flexibility is very helpful. And this is the first time that we have had the ability to have sales prices fluctuate with received costs.

Advanced Inventory (Enterprise add-on)

Advanced Inventory is a feature that is available only in QuickBooks Enterprise V11.0 and later. There is an additional subscription fee.

If you are currently enrolled in the Intuit ProAdvisor program you are provided with a subscription to this feature, although it may only be valid for the most current year of QuickBooks. This allows you to support clients using the feature.

Since this is available as an annual subscription that means that there are several issues to take into account before starting to use this:

- If you don't renew the subscription then you lose access to all of the features.
- This is only available for the most current year of QuickBooks Enterprise, so you must update to the latest release every year.

This is not a third-party add-on product, it was developed by Intuit, and it is fully integrated with the standard QuickBooks user interface.

To enable this feature select *Edit* then *Preferences* and go to the *Items & Inventory* preference. In the *Company Preferences* tab, click the **Advanced Inventory Settings** button.

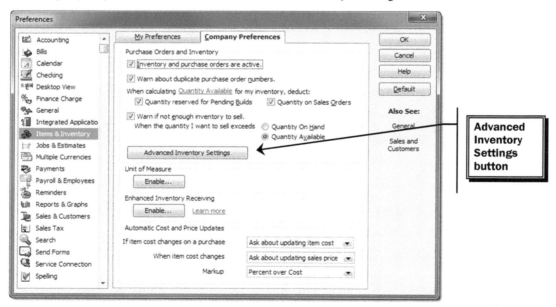

Figure 12-33 Advanced Inventory Settings in Items & Inventory Preferences

This will open a window that allows you to enable each of the features that Advanced Inventory supports, as well as setting specific parameters for each.

In QuickBooks Enterprise V11.0 and later only the *Multiple Inventory Sites* feature was available. *Lot Numbers, Serial Numbers* and *FIFO Costing* were added in QuickBooks Enterprise V12.0

Note that you cannot enable both *Lot Numbers* and *Serial Numbers* in the same company file.

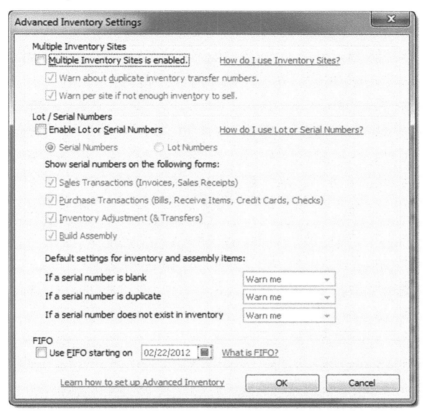

Figure 12-34 Advanced Inventory Settings window

Combining and Switching Features

You can select any combination of these features, <u>other than</u> Lot Numbers and Serial Numbers. You can have only one of those two options.

You can also turn the features on and off as you wish. However, it is not recommended that you do that often. Changing to and from FIFO costing will change your financial statements. Turning Lot Numbers or Serial Numbers on, then off, then on again may leave you with some orphaned or incorrect data in the database.

One special case – you might not be able to **switch** between Lot Tracking and Serial Numbers. Moving from one to the other may give you this error message:

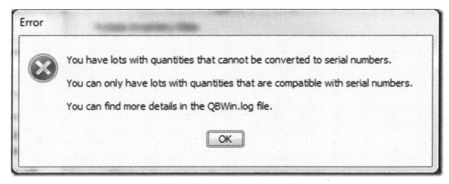

Figure 12-35 Warning if you change from Lots to Serial Numbers

Multiple Inventory Sites

This feature allows you to track how much inventory (number of units and related dollar value) you have at multiple "sites" that you can identify. You are limited to 200 "sites".

With this feature you can:

- Set site-specific reorder points so you know when to replenish inventory at each site.
- Purchase items for a specific site.
- Transfer items between sites.
- Build assemblies using parts from different sites.
- Run site-specific reports.

When you first enable this feature you will be asked to create a site to contain all of the items used up to this point. All of your current inventory will start off at this site, all past transactions will be associated with this site. You should create a site that represents your most commonly used main location.

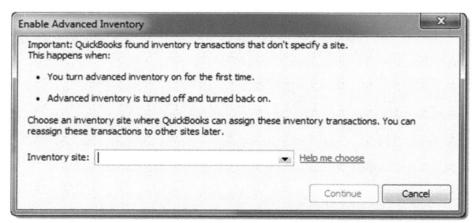

Figure 12-36 Enabling Inventory Sites

You can edit the *site list* by selecting *Lists* and then **Inventory Site List**. In this example the "Main Warehouse" is the site that was created when the feature was enabled. "Drop Ship" is a site that QuickBooks automatically creates for use in purchase orders.

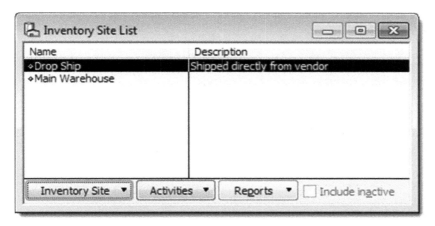

Figure 12-37 Inventory Site List

The *inventory site* record has a number of fields. However, at this time the majority of this information is not available in any QuickBooks report, nor is it available in any of the QuickBooks programming interfaces.

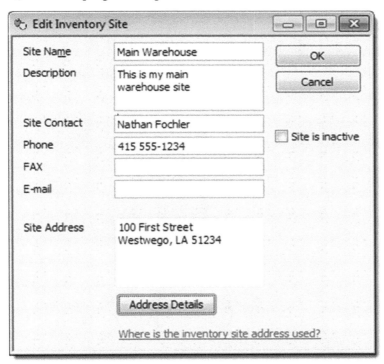

Figure 12-38 Inventory Site information

Now that you have enabled *inventory sites*, any transaction that affects the quantity on hand of an inventory part or assembly will now include a *site* column or field. You cannot save one of these transactions without specifying a site.

For example, in an *item receipt* or *bill*:

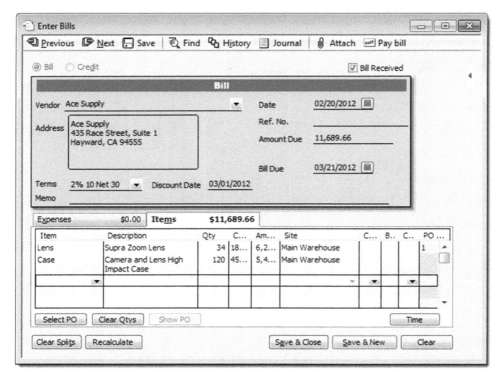

Figure 12-39 Bill with Inventory Sites

As well as an *invoice*:

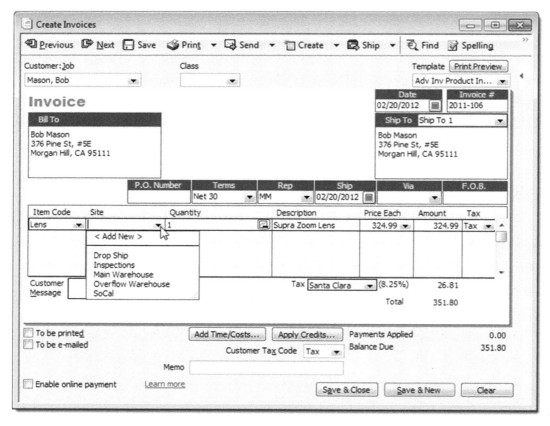

Figure 12-40 Invoice with Inventory Sites

If the transaction is a "non-posting" transaction (like a sales order) you aren't <u>required</u> to enter the site information. However, if you turn that sales order into an invoice you cannot save it until site information is entered.

Inventory Adjustments now require you to select a site for the adjustment. This is <u>not</u> used to transfer items from one site to another. Note that the balance for the site is shown in the lower left of this window.

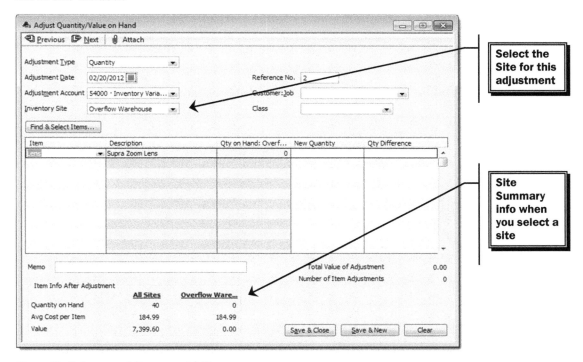

Figure 12-41 Inventory Adjustment with Sites

If you wish to move items from one site to another you would use the **transfer inventory** transaction (found in the *Inventory* menu, or in the *Activities* button at the bottom of the *Site List*.

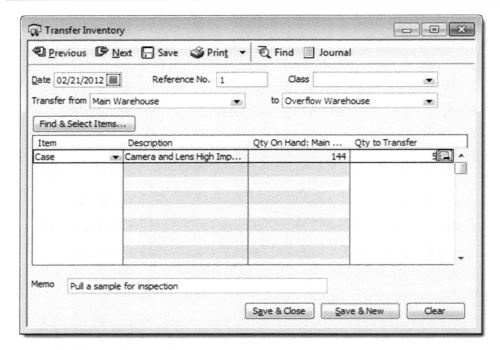

Figure 12-42 Transfer Inventory between sites

If you click the *availability* graph icon in the *Qty to Transfer* column you get a detailed display of information about this transfer.

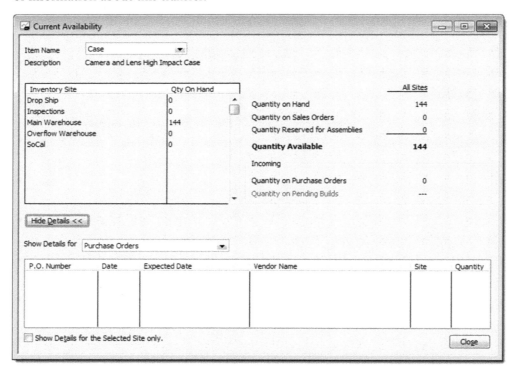

Figure 12-43 Current Availability when using Sites

Every site has a separate *reorder point* for each item. You can edit this through the *Set Reorder Points* window, which you can find by selecting *Inventory* and then *Set Reorder Points*.

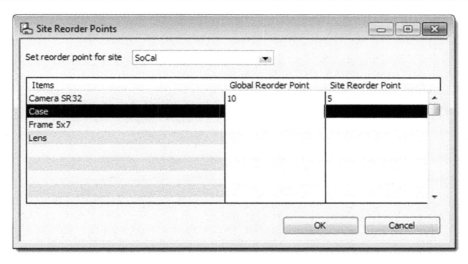

Figure 12-44 Reorder Points for items by Site

Site Reports

Several reports are available specifically for site information:

- Inventory Site Listing
- Quantity On Hand By Site
- Inventory Stock Status By Site
- Pending Builds By Site
- Inventory Valuation Summary By Site
- Inventory Sales By Site
- Physical Inventory Worksheet

These reports include a "site" dropdown choice at the top of the report window.

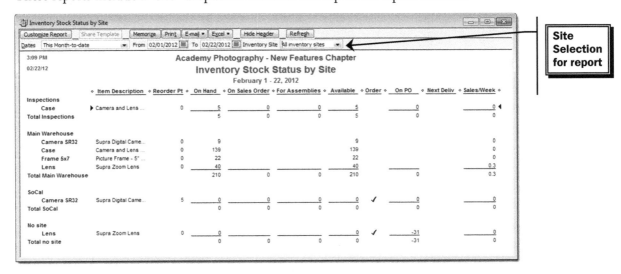

FIFO costing

As has been discussed earlier, QuickBooks calculates an *average cost* for inventory items, which is used for all costing. Many businesses find that this is not sufficient and would rather have

FIFO (First In, First Out) costing. This is one of the options in QuickBooks Enterprise with Advanced Inventory.

FIFO costing is a simple concept, but complicated to implement. You buy an item at a cost and keep track of *how many* you bought *at that cost*. This creates "cost lots" of a given number of items and their cost, at a particular date. When you sell an item, the program finds the oldest "cost lot" that has some items left, and uses those first.

You can enable this feature by checking the "Use FIFO" box at the bottom of the *Advanced Inventory Settings* window. You must enter a "starting" date. QuickBooks will use average costing up until that date, and then move all existing inventory into a "cost lot" on that date using the average cost as of that date. All transactions after that date are reconfigured to use FIFO cost lots.

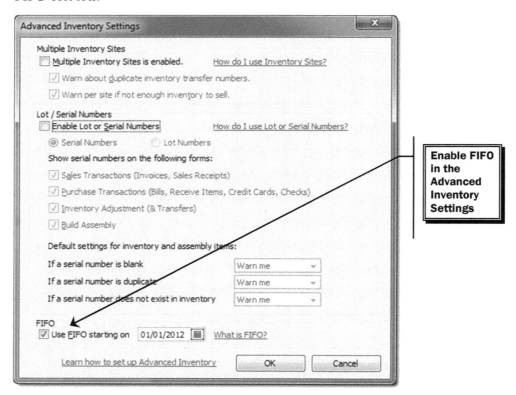

Figure 12-45 FIFO Settings

Do not select a starting date that is in a closed period, as the conversion to FIFO costing could affect your COGS values.

Inventory Costing Example

Let's run through a very simple example to show how this works, and how it changes costing in QuickBooks.

This is a simple example just to illustrate the difference of the two costing methods. This won't cover all of the situations and issues that might come up. Let's start with an item, a "stapler", where you have a zero balance on hand. We'll enter four transactions:

1. A bill (item receipt) for 5 units at $5.00 each on 9/1/2011

2. A second bill (item receipt) for 5 units at $8.00 each on 9/2/2011

3. An invoice for 4 units on 9/3/2011

4. Another invoice for 4 units on 9/4/2011

We have added $65 to our inventory asset account through the purchases – the key will be how much we have left at the end of the sales.

If we perform these steps in QuickBooks when **using average costing** (the default mode), you can see that the average cost of the item is shown as $6.50. Note that the total value remaining in this case is $13.00 (two items at $6.50 each). The total posted to COGS is 8 units at $6.50 each, or $52.00.

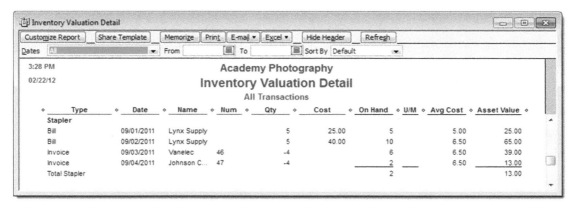

Figure 12-46 Inventory Valuation using Average Costing

Now, let's take a look at the results if we had performed the same transactions with FIFO costing enabled.

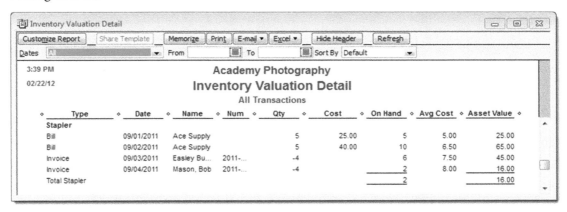

Figure 12-47 Inventory Valuation using FIFO Costing

You can see a number of differences here. The key to look at is the *Asset Value* column. You can see that when we are done, we have $16.00 left in the inventory asset account, with $49.00 being posted to COGS. How was this calculated?

- The first sale consumed four of the items at $5.00 each ($20.00 to COGS).

- The second sale consumed one item at $5.00 and three items at $8.00 ($29.00 to COGS).

There is an *avg cost* column showing in the report. That is the new average cost based on what remains in inventory. In this case, 2 items and a total asset value of $16.00. This is <u>not</u> a financial figure, it is just a value to give you some idea as to what the average cost is at any point of time.

This is a very simple example – what is important to note here is that when we are done, each of the costing methods post different values to COGS, and leave you with different values remaining in the inventory asset account. However, if we had sold those last two remaining items (bringing inventory asset to zero in this case), the <u>total</u> amount posted to COGS would have been identical.

Using this option doesn't create any additional work for you. You aren't going to pick the "cost lots" to consume – all that happens behind the scenes.

FIFO Cost Lot History by Item

Intuit introduced FIFO Costing as an option in Enterprise V12 last year, if you purchased the additional Advanced Inventory feature. With Enterprise V13 a new **FIFO Cost Lot History by Item** report has been added to support this feature.

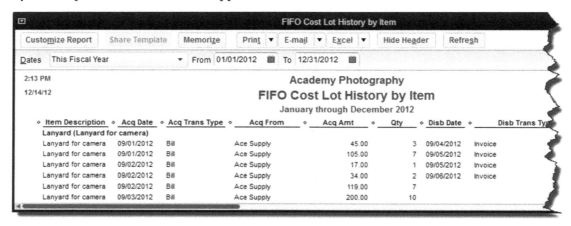

Figure 48 FIFO Cost Lot History Report

This is the only report in QuickBooks that lets us take a peek into FIFO Cost Lots. If you look at it carefully you can see that it details the transactions that occurred per lot, on the **consumption** side of things. This report, as presented, can be confusing until you understand how it is presenting information.

The Acq columns ("Acquisition") will include purchases, inventory adjustments and customer returns.

The Disb columns ("Disbursement") show disbursements that are matched with these acquisitions. There isn't going to be a one-to-one relationship.

A very nice feature is that if you QuickZoom on a line the program will open **both** of the transactions involved in the line (if there are two). That is useful.

Looking at this report line by line:

- We consumed 3 from a lot, using $45.00 in value.
- We consumed 7 from a lot using $105.00 in value. We can infer that this is the same cost lot as above, since the price per unit is the same ($15.00).
- We consumed 1 from a lot for $17.00. This must be another lot as the unit value is different.
- We consumed 2 from a lot for $34.00 – that lot that has a $17.00 unit cost.

Now the records start to look different, as they don't include *disbursement* information. These represent the *remaining cost lots* that have not been consumed.

- There is a lot of 7 for $119.00 – that is the remaining quantity of the $17.00 cost lot.
- There is a lot of 10 at $200.00, which is a $20.00 cost lot.

Barcode Scanning

Inventory management using Barcode scanners and printers has been a key element of many businesses for a long time. There are a number of very good QuickBooks add-on products that provide support for barcodes, but Intuit has ignored this opportunity until this year.

What Intuit is providing is a simple way to print bar codes, and some aid in using them to get your data into QuickBooks. This is a very basic implementation of barcode scanning and printing.

Enabling Barcode Support

Select the *Barcodes* tab in the *Advanced Inventory Settings* window. Check the Enable barcode scanning button to turn this feature on.

This will create a *barcode number* field in the Item List. You can enter your own values there, or you can use the *Barcode Wizard* to assign values.

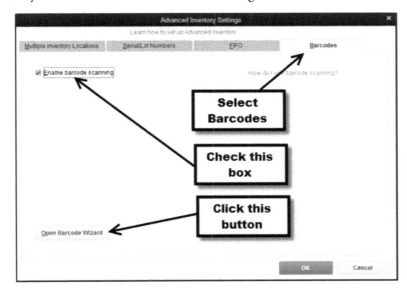

Figure 49 Enabling Barcodes

The *barcode wizard* will take you through the steps to create values in the *barcode number* field.

550 Inventory – Advanced Inventory (Enterprise add-on)

The first step in creating the *barcode number* value is to select the source value that will be used.

Figure 50 Barcode Wizard - Selecting Value

The options here are:

- **I don't currently track barcodes in QuickBooks:** QuickBooks will generate a barcode value for you.
- **Copy barcodes from the Item Name field:** QuickBooks will use the current item name as the barcode value.
- **Copy barcodes from Manufacturer's Part Number: QuickBooks will use the manufacturer's part number as the barcode value.**
- **Copy Barcodes from Purchase Information: QuickBooks will use the** purchase description, or if it is a single sided part just the description.
- **Copy barcodes from 'custom field':** If you have been playing with barcodes in a third party product already, this may be the option for you. You will see a listing for each of the custom fields that you may have in your item list.

In some cases there isn't a proper *source value* for the barcode number, QuickBooks will create an **auto-generated barcode number. You will see an auto-generated value when:**

- You select the *I don't currently track barcodes* option.
- If you select ANY OTHER option, and for some reason the value in that field doesn't meet the QuickBooks criteria for a value.

After you have selected the source field to use, the barcode setup wizard will ask you which item types to create barcodes for. You may just select *inventory part* items, or you could create them for all items.

Inventory – Advanced Inventory (Enterprise add-on)

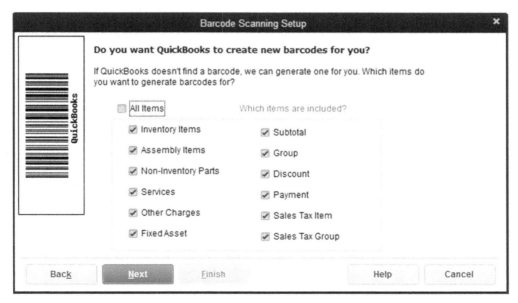

Figure 51 Barcode Wizard - Select Item Types

The barcodes aren't generated until you actually close the Preferences window.

Now you will see the barcode number field in the item record:

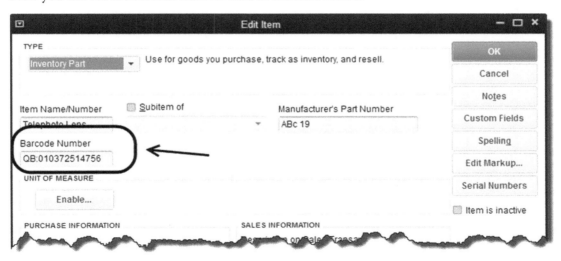

Figure 52 Barcode Number in Item Record

Note that you CAN edit the barcode number in the Edit Item window. However, the barcode number must be unique for each item. You will not be allowed to change it to a value used by another item.

You can customize the columns in the Item List to show both the *barcode number* and a graphic image of the barcode value.

Figure 53 Item List with Barcodes

QuickBooks Barcode Format

If you use the *barcode wizard* to create barcodes, the source values must meet certain criteria. If they don't then QuickBooks will create an auto-generated value.

The main criteria are:

- The value **must have at least 6 characters, and be no more than 30 characters long.**
- The value must consist entirely of digits, letters and any of the following special characters: space, minus, plus, period, colon or forward slash (/).
- The value must be unique – that is, only one item can use this value.

When QuickBooks prints or displays a barcode it will use the **Code 128** symbology, which is a commonly used format. It allows upper and lower case letters, digits, and a fairly reasonable selection of special characters. You do not have a choice in the printed format. While QuickBooks **prints** using Code 128, you should be able to **scan** values from any other barcode symbology that your scanner can accommodate.

Other Ways to Enter Barcodes

You can add your own barcode data directly to the barcode field by using the *Add/Edit Multiple List Entries* feature – the barcode field can be added to the item display. This only works for service, inventory part, inventory assembly and non-inventory part items.

Figure 54 Add/Edit Multiple List Entries with Barcodes

Barcode Scanners and QuickBooks

Selecting an appropriate barcode scanner that works with QuickBooks (and uses the special features we'll describe below) can be tricky. We recommend that you purchase one scanner to try, from a source that lets you return it if you find it doesn't work.

The scanner needs to be a USB scanner that you plug directly into your computer. This scanner must be seen by Windows as a "secondary keyboard". Note that some scanners that meet this requirement still might not work.

Current scanners that work with the QuickBooks Point of Sale should work, as do many scanners from Wasp Technologies. You can also get low cost no-name USB scanners through sources like Amazon.

Printing Barcodes

There are very few places where you can actually print a barcode image in QuickBooks:

- Item Listing report (found in the *reports* dropdown at the bottom of the *item list*).
- Physical Inventory Worksheet report (found in the *Reports/Inventory* menu)
- Item Barcode report (found in the *Reports/Inventory* menu)
- Print Labels (found in the *File/Print Forms/Labels* menu)

Figure 55 Item Barcodes report

Your options for printing labels are very limited. Select *File* then *Print Forms* and then Labels. This option has been available in the past, usually to print customer or vendor labels. This has been updated to add item barcodes.

Figure 56 Barcode Label options

Data Entry

There are a number of transaction windows in QuickBooks that are barcode-enabled. These transactions will recognize that you have scanned a barcode image and will perform in a unique fashion. Note that if you do NOT see these actions then QuickBooks is not recognizing your barcode scanner properly.

If you have a barcode-enabled transaction window open and you scan a barcode, the program will look to see if that scanned item is already entered in the form. If it is not, then the program will add the item to the form – regardless of the field that your cursor is on at the time. If the item already exists in the form, it will increment the quantity by one.

This feature is enabled in:

- Purchase Orders
- Bills
- Bill Credits
- Item Receipts
- Sales Orders
- Estimates
- Invoices
- Sales Receipt
- Credit Memos
- Checks
- Credit Card Charges
- Credit Card Credits

For transactions like Checks, where you have a separate tab for items and expenses, you don't even have to be on the correct tab to start, the program will switch you to the right place.

Here are some other barcode-enabled windows:

- Inventory Center: Scanning the code will take you to the item in the list.
- Item List: Same as the Inventory Center.
- New/Edit Item Window: Enters the barcode in the barcode field.
- Add/Edit Multiple Lists: Enters the barcode in the barcode field.
- The Search window – the program will recognize this as a barcode and search for all related records.

Another nice feature of barcode support is how it works if you have enabled serial number tracking. If you add an item to an order, and then scan serial number values that exist for that item, each time you scan a serial number the quantity of that item will be incremented and the serial number will be added to the appropriate field.

Note that you cannot PRINT serial number barcodes from QuickBooks.

Receiving Items

Barcode scanning is also enabled when receiving items from a purchase order. When you enter a receipt or a bill you can click on the **Select PO** button to open a window that lists open purchase orders (or, select the Vendor in the receipt/bill and you will be asked if you want to use open PO's). If the barcode feature is enabled you will see a new checkbox – **I am scanning items.**

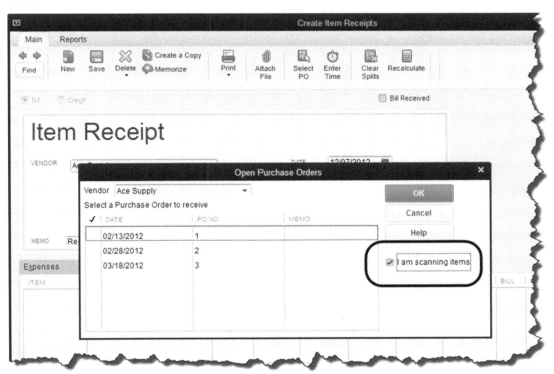

Figure 57 Receiving Items with Barcodes

If you select a purchase order and check this box you will see that the qty column in the bill or item receipt has been replaced by two columns, **Rcv'd Qty** and **PO Qty**. The Rcv'd Qty column starts off blank, and as you scan items with the barcode scanner the count will increment.

After you have scanned all of the received items, click the Compare To PO button. If there are any times where the *Rcv'd Qty* is not equal to the *PO Qty*, that quantity will be highlighted in red.

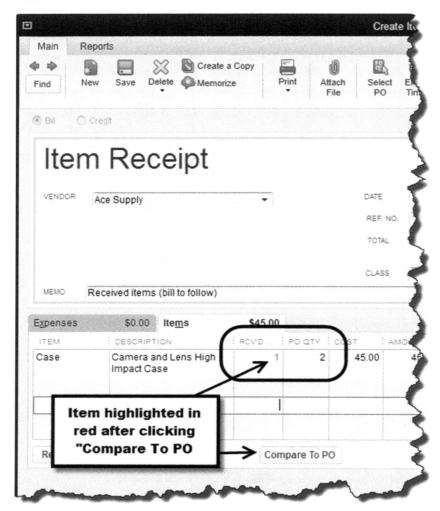

Figure 58 Receiving with Barcodes

Bin Location Tracking

Intuit introduced the multiple inventory site feature in QuickBooks Enterprise V11, as a part of the optional Advanced Inventory feature. This allowed you to create up to 200 Inventory Sites to hold your QuickBooks inventory. This year they are expanding this feature to add a second level, **Locations** within Inventory Sites, which is something that many people have been asking for.

The general concept of inventory sites was that you would define a small number of places where you could hold your inventory – along the lines of multiple warehouses or store locations. Intuit wasn't talking about specific "bins" or places within the warehouse, they were thinking on a larger scale. Given this approach, in Enterprise V11 and V12 they limited the number of inventory sites to 200. That works for large scale "sites", but it doesn't fit all situations. If you have a warehouse with a lot of unique bin locations then the initial release Advanced Inventory didn't work well for you.

In QuickBooks Enterprise Solutions V13 **we now have the ability to define** locations **within those sites.** In addition, the limit in this list is **now capped at 1,000,000 entries**, which should be more widely acceptable.

Note that Intuit isn't always consistent as to how they reference this feature. In some places it will refer to a "location", in other places to a "bin". As new revisions of the program come out it looks like they are moving towards using "bin".

Enabling QuickBooks Bin Locations for Inventory Sites

This feature is only available in QuickBooks Enterprise with the optional Advanced Inventory subscription. In your *Preferences* select *Items & Inventory* and click the **Advanced Inventory Settings** button.

If you have not enabled Multiple Inventory Sites already, you will need to check that box. This will open the Enable Multiple Inventory Sites window, where you can create an inventory site for your current inventory. All of your items on hand will be moved to this inventory site.

Figure 59 Specify Initial Site

Now that you have an inventory site created (or, if you already had this set up) you can enable the new location feature by checking the **Track Locations within Inventory Sites** box.

QuickBooks doesn't ask you for a name for the starting bin location, instead it will place everything in a bin location named **Unassigned**.

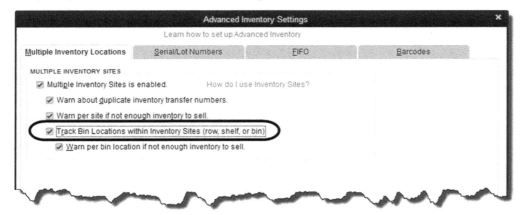

Figure 60 Enable Bin Locations

Bin Locations are essentially "sub-sites", similar to what you have with items and sub-items.

Figure 61 Bin Locations under Inventory Sites

You can add new inventory sites and locations to the Inventory Site List (found in the *Lists* menu). Here's a window to add a new inventory site.

Figure 62 Inventory Site

If you wish to add a location within a given site you will use the same window – check the **is a bin within site** *box* and select the *inventory site* that holds this bin.

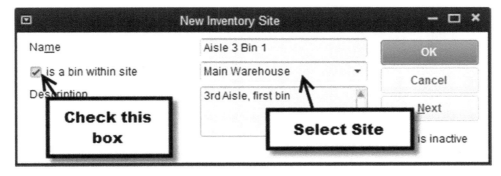

Figure 63 Creating a Bin

Now that we have it set up, whenever you have a transaction where items are received, sold, adjusted or built you have the option to specify both the inventory site and the bin location.

When you enable this feature you have a new option in the *Add/Edit Multiple List Entries* feature for inventory sites, and you can specify if a record is a location (bin) within a site. The organization of this is a bit confusing, however. If you have a main "site" then the *site name* shows in the *site name* column. If you have a bin within that site then the *location name* shows in the *site name* column, and the *site name* shows in the *is a location within this site* column.

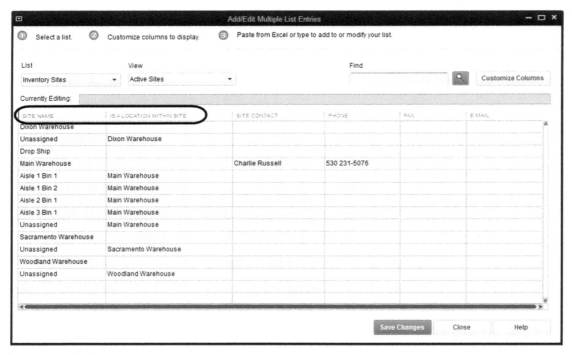

Figure 64 Add/Edit Multiple List Entries with location information

Receiving Items

As you would expect, when you are receiving items you can specify a site and location.

Figure 65 Item Receipt with site and bin

If you select the dropdown list with the *Print* icon you will see a new option, a *sorted stock list.*

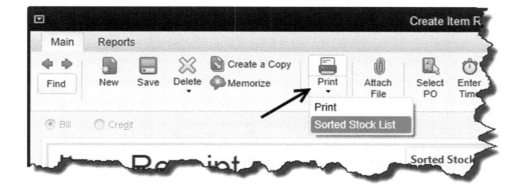

Figure 66 Item Receipt Print Sorted Stock List

This is a "receiving" report that will sort your receipts by site and bin within site.

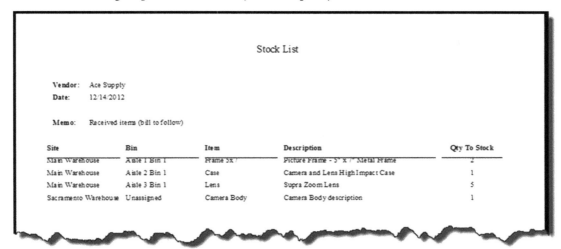

Figure 67 Sorted Stock List

Sales Forms

Similar to what we see in the item receipt, you can get a *sorted pick list* for a *sales order* transaction that will print a picking list for the items in the sales order, sorted by site and bin.

Default Bin Locations in Sales and Receipts

You can specify a *default bin location* to use for an item in sales and purchasing transactions for each item. You will find a *bins* tab in the *inventory center*. This will list the site/bins that have a quantity on hand for the selected item. You can check the one you want to use as the default for both purchasing and sales transactions.

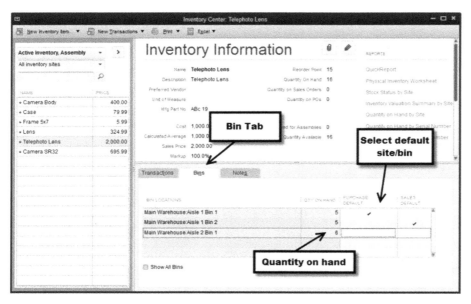

Figure 68 Inventory Center - Default Bin

New Bin/Location Reports

There are a number of new reports, as well as modifications to existing reports

- Inventory Site Listing: This report now includes the locations along with the sites. The formatting isn't the easiest to work with as far as how it displays site/location names.

- Inventory Site List: This report is formatted in an indented fashion that makes it easier to see site and location information, but it cannot be modified. It is hard to find – it isn't in the *Reports* menu. You will find it by selecting *Lists* and then selecting the *Inventory Site List*. In the bottom of the list select the *Inventory Site* button and select Print List.

- **Items by Bin Location:** This is a new report, which shows the quantity you have on hand at each bin. You can use this to get a list of the serial numbers you have at each location.

Several other reports have been modified to allow you to include information by location. In these reports you will see an *Inventory Site* dropdown list at the top of the report. You can use this to select all sites, a particular site, locations, and more.

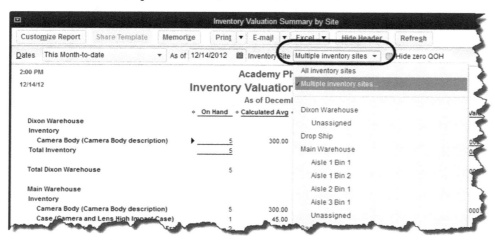

Figure 69 Inventory Site option in Inventory reports

If you select *multiple inventory sites* a window opens that lets you select specific sites or specific locations (not both). You can also hide the bin location information.

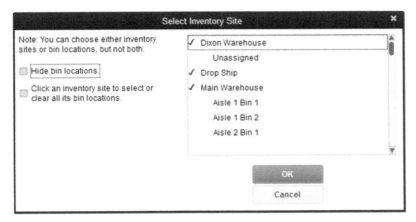

Figure 70 Select Inventory Site in Inventory Reports

This option is available in:

* Inventory Stock Status by Site
Inventory Valuation Summary by Site

Quantity on Hand by Location

Lot Tracking

Lot tracking is basically tracking the quantity you have of items purchased (or manufactured) in "Lots", or groups of some sort. This is used in many different industries (and is <u>required</u> by regulation in some) and it has been a missing feature in QuickBooks inventory. Intuit added this starting with Enterprise V12.0 with Advanced Inventory.

You can enable this feature by checking the **Enable Lot or Serial Numbers** box in the *Advanced Inventory Settings* window, and selecting **Lot Numbers**.

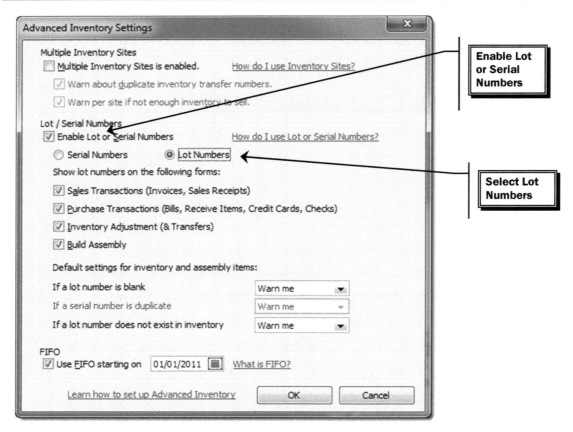

Figure 12-71 Enabling Lot Numbers in Advanced Inventory Settings

You can only select Lot Numbers <u>or</u> Serial Numbers, you cannot combine both.

This feature does not impact the financial aspects of inventory transactions, so no conversion takes place. You can turn the feature on or off as you wish. Note, however, that if you turn it on, enter some lot numbers, turn it off, then come back later and turn it back on, it is not clear what happens with existing lot number records in the database. We don't recommend that you do this. However, it is nice to know that you can turn it off if you don't like it.

When you receive an inventory part (or assembly) you can enter a *Lot Number* in the last column. You will have one lot number per receipt of an item. Lot numbers can be up to 40 characters long, and must not have any spaces. If you enter something like "Lot 55" you will get a warning that you can only enter one lot number per line – some logic from the Serial tracking feature has crept in here (it is taking the space as a break between two ID's).

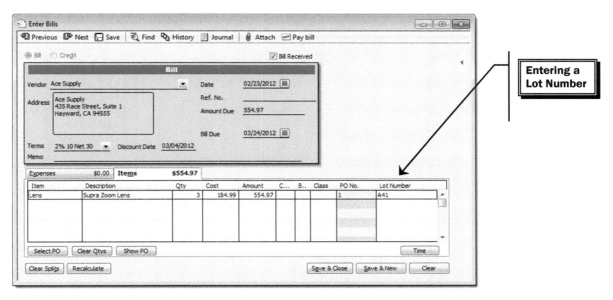

Figure 12-72 Entering Lot Numbers in a Bill

When I sell an item, I can pick a lot number to work with. Note that if I pick a lot number that lot must have enough items to fulfill the quantity I requested. Looking at the sample below if I enter a quantity of 13 I cannot pick a lot, as none is large enough.

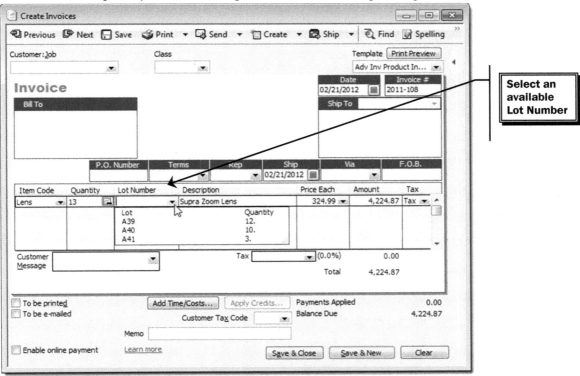

Figure 12-73 Entering a Lot Number in an Invoice

I would have to enter this item twice on the invoice, selecting a different lot on each line.

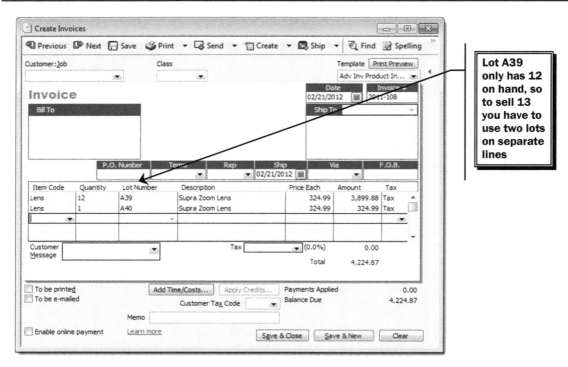

Figure 12-74 Selling items from multiple Lots

You can still buy or sell the item without a lot number. You may get a warning (depending on your preference settings) but you won't be stopped.

Note that you can set the warning preferences on an item-by-item basis, which is good. You may have some items that you won't be controlling by lots. Click the *Lot Numbers* button in the *Edit Item* window.

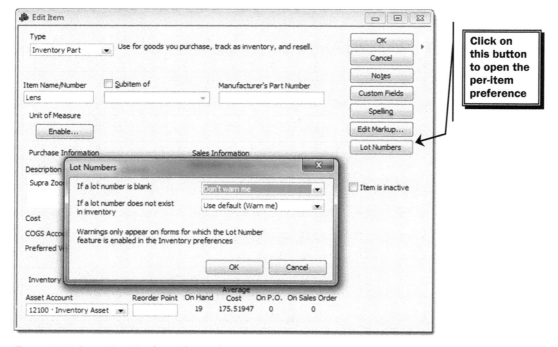

Figure 12-75 Setting Lot Number preferences by item

Adjust Quantity/Value on Hand has a new adjustment type, *Lot Number*. You can use this to adjust the quantity in a particular lot. This doesn't change the *quantity on hand*, just the quantity in the lot. So there are no adjustments to your chart of account. Changing this here does <u>not</u> change the original receipt transaction, just the quantity in the lot.

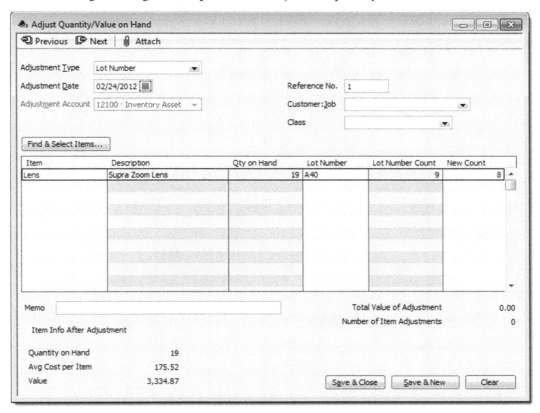

Figure 12-76 Lot Number type of Inventory Adjustment

The quantities in the lots aren't forced to be equal to the item's quantity on hand. Lots are not a financial transaction. The program is just providing this as an additional item of information. The total quantity of the lots does not have to match the total quantity on hand.

Lot Tracking Reports

There are two reports that have been added to manage Lot Numbers, *Transaction List by Lot Number* and *Lot Numbers in Stock*.

When you select the *Transaction List by Lot Number* report you must select a specific item and a specific lot number. This will list all transactions that affect that lot.

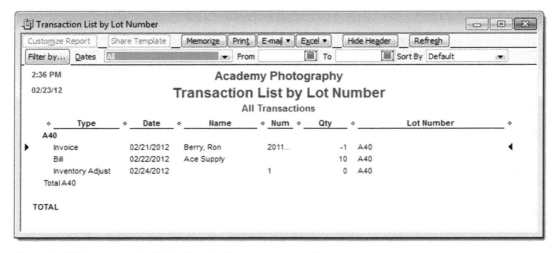

Figure 12-77 Transaction List by Lot Number for a given item and lot

The *Lot Numbers in Stock* report is simple, it just lists the lot numbers for each item and includes no information about quantities.

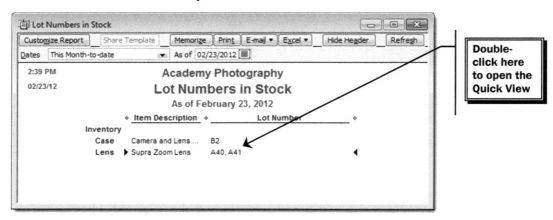

Figure 12-78 Lot Numbers in Stock Report

You can click on any individual item in this report to get a Quick View, but this cannot be printed.

Figure 12-79 Quick View of Lots and their quantity

If you select an item in the *Inventory Center* you will see that there are two links on the right, under "Recall Information". The term "Recall" implies that you need to locate all transactions for an item that may have a product recall.

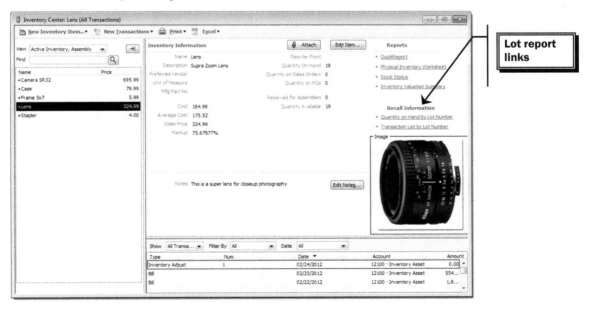

Figure 12-80 Inventory Center with Lot "Recall" information

The option for the *Quantity on Hand by Lot Number* will open the same Quick View as you get from the *Lot Numbers in Stock* report.

Serial Tracking

Serial number tracking is a key requirement for many inventory based businesses. Until now, if you wanted this feature in QuickBooks you had to use an expensive third party add-on product that would move inventory functions entirely outside of the QuickBooks company file. Intuit added this starting with Enterprise V12.0 with Advanced Inventory.

You can enable this feature by checking the **Enable Lot or Serial Numbers** box in the *Advanced Inventory Settings* window, and selecting **Lot Numbers**.

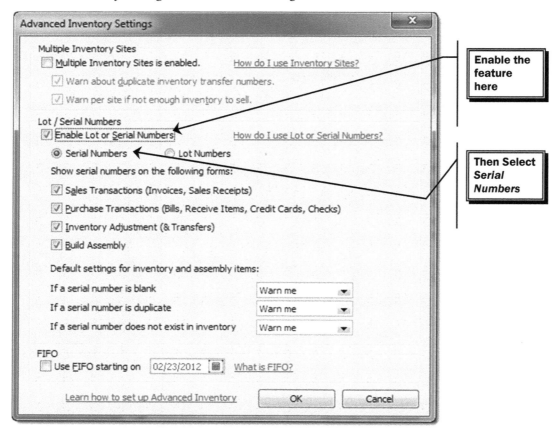

Figure 12-81 Advanced Inventory settings for Serial Numbers

You can only select Lot Numbers <u>or</u> Serial Numbers, you cannot combine both.

This feature does not impact the financial aspects of inventory transactions, so no conversion takes place. You can turn the feature on or off as you wish. Note, however, that if you turn it on, enter some serial numbers, turn it off, then come back later and turn it back on, it is not clear what happens with existing serial number records in the database. We don't recommend that you do this. However, it is nice to know that you can turn it off if you don't like it.

Note that you can turn off the warnings for serial numbers for any individual item by editing the item and clicking on the **Serial Numbers** button.

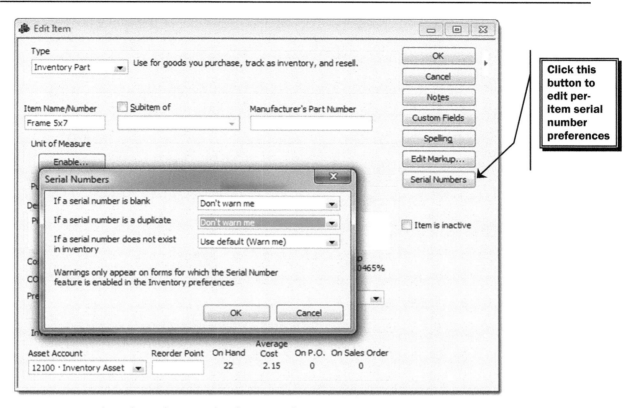

Figure 12-82 Serial Number Preferences in the Edit Item window

If I receive an inventory part (or assembly) I can enter a *Serial Number* for each of the items in the last column.

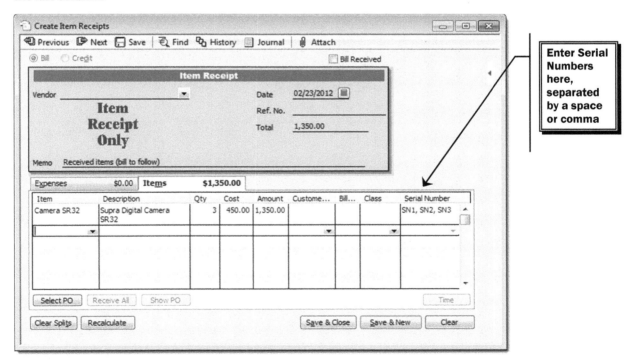

Figure 12-83 Serial Numbers in the Item Receipt window

Serial numbers can be up to 40 characters long, and must not have any spaces. You can enter them all in line here, separating each serial number from the others by either a space or a comma.

You must enter the same number of serial numbers as the *quantity* for the line, or you can leave the serial number field empty.

When you are entering serial numbers here you will see a small down-arrow next to the field. Click on this and you will see a dropdown menu with the option *Quick View for Serial Numbers*. This opens a window that you can use to easily enter your serial numbers line by line.

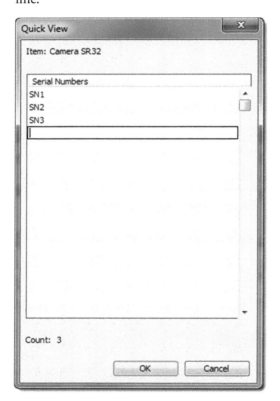

Figure 12-84 Serial Number QuickView to add multiple serial numbers

When I sell the item, I can select the serial numbers for the order. If you just start typing in a serial number the program will show you the list that matches. Or, you can click on one of the other options for selecting serial numbers.

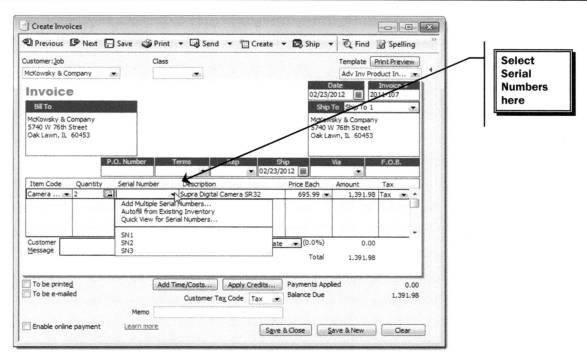

Figure 12-85 Selecting Serial Numbers in an Invoice

Add Multiple Serial Numbers will open a window that lets you easily locate and select serial numbers. There is a nice filter feature at the top, where you can limit the list that is displayed to include serial numbers that start with, end with or contain a particular value.

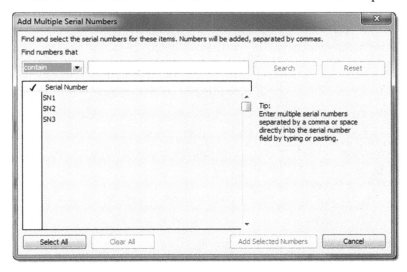

Figure 12-86 Selecting Multiple Serial Numbers

Autofill from Existing Inventory is easy to understand – select this, QuickBooks will select the serial numbers to match what you enter for the quantity to sell.

Quick View for Serial Numbers opens a Quick View window like what we saw above in the item receipt. This will let you *add* new serial numbers that don't already exist, which isn't a good feature if you are trying to control how serial numbers are managed. A key issue in managing serialized inventory is to have the proper control over who can create serial numbers, so the ability for the order entry clerk to add serial numbers here breaks this control process.

Adjusting Inventory

Adjust Quantity/Value on Hand has a new adjustment type, *Serial Number*. You can use this to add or remove serial numbers. This doesn't change the *quantity on hand*.

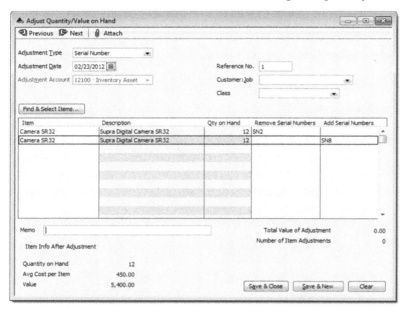

Figure 12-87 Serial Number inventory adjustment

The quantity of serial numbers is not forced to be equal to the item's quantity on hand. There is no financial control here – you can have more serial numbers, or less, than the quantity of items on hand.

Serial Number Reports

There are two reports that have been added to manage Serial Numbers, *Transaction List by Serial Number* and *Lot Numbers in Stock*.

When you select the *Transaction List by Serial Number* report you must select a specific item and a specific serial number. This will list all transactions that use that serial number. This report is for "SN1", although the report doesn't include that information.

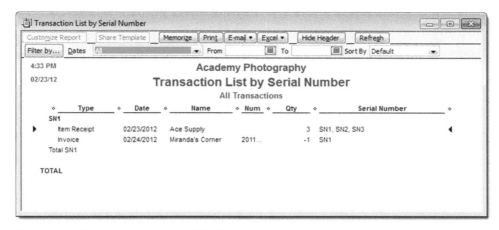

Figure 12-88 Transaction List by Serial Number report

The *Serial Numbers in Stock* report is a simple report, it just lists the serial numbers for each item. No quantities.

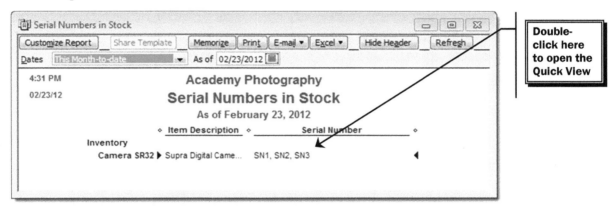

Figure 12-89 Serial Numbers in Stock Report

You can click on any individual item in this report to get a Quick View, but this cannot be printed.

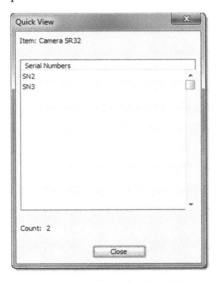

Figure 12-90 Serial Number Quick View

If you select an item in the *Inventory Center* you will see that there are two links for reports on the right. The option for *Quantity on Hand by Serial Number* will open the same Quick View as shown above.

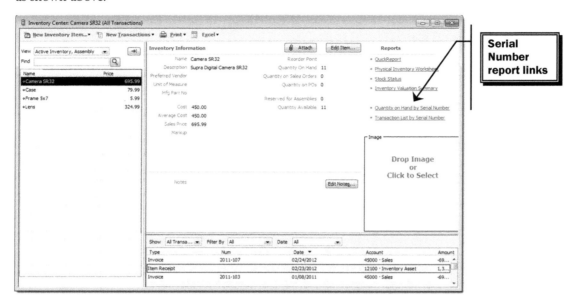

Figure 12-91 Serial Number report links in Inventory Center

A number of other reports can be modified to add the serial number as a column. I'm not sure how widespread this is. One useful report is the *Sales by Customer Detail* – as I show here with the serial number added.

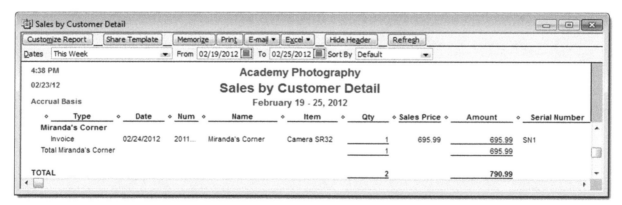

Figure 12-92 Sales by Customer Detail Report modified to add a Serial Number column

Chapter 13
Reports and Graphs

Objectives

After completing this chapter, you should be able to:

- Describe the principles of report customization, understand what you can and cannot do with QuickBooks reports (page 577)
- Understanding QuickBooks Cash Basis Reports (page 580)
- Memorize and group reports (page 595)
- Process and print multiple reports in batches (page 597)
- Use the QuickBooks Statement Writer(page 600)

QuickBooks reports allow you to get the information you need to make critical business decisions. In this chapter, you'll learn how to create a variety of reports to help you manage your business. Every report in QuickBooks gives you immediate, up-to-date information about your company's performance.

There are literally hundreds of reports available in QuickBooks. These allow you to manipulate the numbers so that you can look at your data in any way you wish. In addition to the built-in reports, you can *modify* reports to include or exclude whatever data you want. To control the look of your reports, you can customize the formatting of headers, footers, fonts, or columns.

When you get a report looking just the way you want, you can *memorize* it so that you can quickly create it again later.

Principles of Report Customization

To make your reports show only the information you want, you can **modify** (i.e., *customize*) the reports. All reports can be modified and filtered in some way, so familiarize yourself with Figure 13-1 and Figure 13-2 and learn how they affect different reports.

Use the **Modify Report** button on any report to add or delete columns, and change several other formats of the report.

Changing the Report Display

When you click **Modify Report** QuickBooks defaults to the Display tab of the Modify report screen (see Figure 13-1). Use this tab to change the date of the report, the reporting basis, the columns that show on the report and the way the report sorts or totals.

Depending on the type of report you are modifying, this screen will show a selection of columns to add or remove or will show sub-columns for period comparison and percentages as

shown below – summary reports (see Figure 13-1). List reports include a column selection
menu and sort options only.

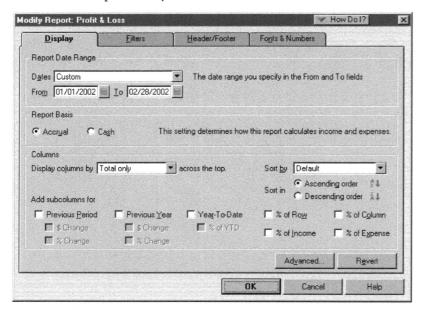

Figure 13-1 The Display tab of the Modify Report: Profit & Loss screen

Click **Advanced** to show additional options as shown in Figure 13-2 and Figure 13-3. As with
the Display tab, the options are different for summary and detail reports. List reports do not
have an **Advanced** button.

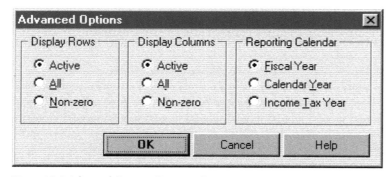

Figure 13-2 Advanced Option - Summary Reports

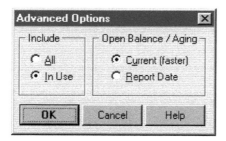

Figure 13-3 Advanced Options - Detail Reports

Changing the Information Included on the Report

Use the **Filters** tab on the Modify Report screen to narrow the contents of reports so that you can analyze specific areas of your business. On the Filters tab, you can choose specific accounts, dates, names, or Items to include on the report. The more filters you add to a report, the less information it will show, allowing you to review the information you need without having to scan through hundreds, or even thousands, of transactions. Figure 13-4 shows the standard filtering for a Profit & Loss report. Notice that the report includes all income and expense accounts. The report is also filtered using a custom date. You can change the date by selecting Date from the filter list, by modifying the date fields on the Display tab, or by changing the date fields that show in the report.

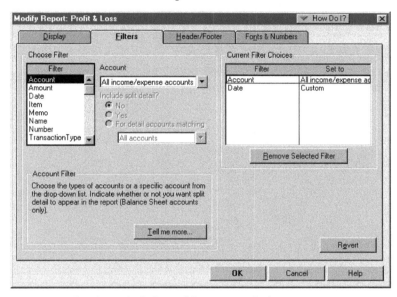

Figure 13-4 The Filters tab of The Modify Report: Profit & Loss screen

Changing the Header and Footer Information

Click the Header/Footer tab to change the header and footer information for the report. This tab allows you to change the title of the report as well as the subtitle. It also allows you to show or conceal the time, date and basis of the report. Changes made to this tab will not affect the information that QuickBooks includes in the report.

Changing Fonts and Numbers

Click the Fonts & Numbers tab to change the size and style of the text as well as the way numbers are displayed. This tab allows you to show negative numbers in parentheses or with a trailing minus. It also allows you to show negative numbers in a bright red color. You can also use this tab to remove the decimals from numbers – causing the amounts to round to the nearest dollar, or to divide the amounts by 1,000, for larger companies that show amounts in thousands.

Other than rounding to the nearest dollar, or thousands of dollars, this tab has no effect on the information that QuickBooks includes in the report.

What you Cannot Do with QuickBooks Reports

QuickBooks reports are powerful, and extremely customizable, however there are a few things that you cannot accomplish with the built-in QuickBooks reports. The list below gives you a few examples of report limitations. Consider this list as you think through the design of your clients' data files.

What You Cannot Do with QuickBooks Reports

- **Filter by more than one name type on the same report.** For example, if you need to filter a report to show all of the purchases from a specific **Vendor** that were used for a specific **Job**, QuickBooks will not allow you to filter by both the vendor name and the job name on the same report.
- You cannot change the **indentations** of non-collapsed reports.
- **You cannot collapse sub-account and sub-items for more than one level.** For example, if you have a three tiered account structure (e.g., Office Equipment:Computers:Printers) QuickBooks will allow you to collapse the report to show either all subaccounts or no subaccounts.
- **You cannot change the labels of any line except for accounts.** For example, QuickBooks refers to total cash as Total Checking/Savings. You cannot change the wording to Total Cash using the Modify Report screen.

In previous editions, we have included the *Balance Sheet by Class* in the list of reports that are not possible. With QuickBooks 2011 and later, there is a new report called *Balance Sheet by Class*. However, we feel this report should be called "Listing of Selected Assets, Liabilities, and Equity Account Balances, By Class."

Understanding QuickBooks Cash Basis Reports

One of the best features of QuickBooks is that it does not lock you in to the Cash or Accrual Basis. This means you can use accrual basis reports throughout the year for management information, and use cash basis reports for preparing your taxes. This doesn't mean QuickBooks keeps two sets of books; it just means that, in order to present a cash basis financial statement, it does its best to convert from Accrual to Cash Basis. However, you may find that the cash basis balance sheet has any number of troubling numbers on it, so it's important to understand exactly what QuickBooks does and doesn't do when it converts from Accrual to cash.

In general, QuickBooks removes unreceived income and unpaid expenses from your reports. It also adds income and expenses from last year that were received or paid during the current year. However, as discussed below, there are several nuances that usually cause the cash basis reports to be inaccurate. This section starts with the basics of how to create QuickBooks cash basis reports, and then discuss several areas where you may have trouble. If you want to skip to the problem areas, here is a list of them:

- How Cash Basis Reports are calculated (see page 581).
- Limitations of QuickBooks Cash Basis Reports (see page 583).

- Troubleshooting Out-of-Balance Cash Basis Balance Sheets (see page 583).
- Proofing A/R and A/P on Cash Basis Reports (see page 584).
- Tricks for Completing the Cash Basis Conversion for Financial Statement Presentation (see page 586).
- How Partially Paid Invoices and Bills affect Cash Basis Reports (see page 589).

Reporting Preferences for Cash Basis

You can use the preferences to change the default basis for QuickBooks reports. To change the preferences, follow the steps in this example:

1.   Select the *Edit* menu and then select **Preferences**.

2.   Scroll down and click on **Reports & Graphs**. Then click the **Company Preferences** tab.

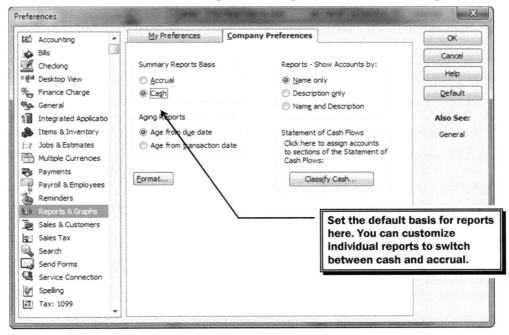

Figure 13-5 Set the default for summary reports to Cash or Accrual.

How Cash Basis Reports are Calculated

On the cash basis P&L report, QuickBooks omits from income the total of all open invoices using Items associated with income (or expense) accounts and it adds to income the total receipts against invoices dated in prior years.

Similarly, on a Cash Basis Balance Sheet, QuickBooks reduces Accounts Receivable by the total of all Open Invoices that use Items associated with income (or expense) accounts.

The same thing happens with unpaid bills except that expenses and Accounts Payable are involved. That is, all unpaid bills will be removed from the cash basis Balance Sheet and P&L as long as the coding on the bill is to an expense (or income) account.

Normally, you wouldn't expect to find a balance in A/R or A/P on a cash basis balance sheet. However, if you do find a balance in **A/R or A/P on a Cash Basis Balance Sheet**, it's probably due to one of the following situations.

> **Note**
> If the cash basis Balance sheet shows balances in A/R or A/P, determining the cause of the balance as described below may not solve the problem. You may need to manually adjust the balance in A/R or A/P. See *Completing the Cash Basis Conversion* on page 586 for more information.

- Check the *open* invoices and unapplied **credit memos**. Do they include an **item** that **points to a balance sheet account**? When an invoice or credit memo includes an Item that is associated with a balance sheet account, that transaction will affect A/R on both the accrual and cash basis balance sheet (i.e. A/R will have a balance even on the cash basis). To fix this, see the section on completing the cash basis conversion on page 586.

- Check the **open invoices** and unapplied **credit memos**. Do they include an **Inventory Part**? If so, the "average cost" of the inventory item is left as a debit in A/R, with an offsetting credit to Inventory Asset.

- If **A/R** has a **negative** balance, it is probably due to unapplied payments. An unapplied payment is an *open* transaction that involves both A/R and another balance sheet account (usually Undeposited funds), so this transaction will not be removed from the cash basis A/R balance. Create an Open Invoices report and look for negative numbers. If you find both positive and negative numbers on this report, use the Receive Payments screen to apply the payments to your open invoices. If there are no Invoices to which you can appropriately apply the payments, see the section on completing the cash basis conversion on page 586.

- Check the unpaid **bills** and **bill credits**. If they include an item that is associated with a **balance sheet account**, they won't be removed on the cash basis reports. For example, if the client enters a bill for a loan at the bank or a credit card that is tracked as a liability account in QuickBooks, the bill will credit A/P and debit the liability account. Since the bill is connected to a balance sheet account, the transaction affects both A/P and the offsetting balance sheet account (loan payable or credit card payable) on the cash basis Balance Sheet.

- If **A/P** has a **negative** balance, it is probably due to a Check coded to Accounts Payable (e.g., a prepayment to a vendor coded to Accounts Payable) or to an overpayment made to a vendor using the Pay Bills screen. Create an Unpaid Bills report and look for negative numbers. If you find negative numbers on this report, use the Pay Bills screen to apply the prepayments (Checks) or overpayments (Bill Payments) to your unpaid bills. If there are no bills to which you can appropriately apply these debits to A/P, see the section on completing the cash basis conversion on page 586.

- Check for journal entries that hit A/R or A/P accounts. If Accounts Receivable or Accounts Payable is on the top line of the Journal Entry and the offset is to one or more income or expense accounts, QuickBooks removes (i.e. ignores) the journal entry on the cash basis Balance Sheet. To quickly solve this problem, enter the "Journal Entries" bank account on the top line of the journal entry as described on page 89.

Limitations of QuickBooks Cash Basis Reports

There are several things that QuickBooks does not do when calculating the cash basis Balance Sheet.

- **Unpaid Payroll Taxes** – There is no removal of unpaid payroll taxes from the cash basis Balance Sheet, or from the cash basis P&L.
- **Prepaids** – QuickBooks does not consider any balance sheet accounts for prepaid expenses, customer prepayments, retainers, etc. when calculating the cash basis Balance Sheet.
- **Credit Card Liabilities** – If bills are entered for the Credit Card liabilities, the corresponding Accounts Payable amount will remain on the cash basis Balance Sheet until the bill is paid.
- **Sales Tax Payable** – QuickBooks uses the settings in the Sales Tax Preferences screen (Edit>Preferences>Sales Tax, Company Preferences) to determine the amount of Sales Tax payable on the Sales Tax Liability reports. However, on the cash basis Balance Sheet, QuickBooks reduces the balance in sales tax payable for unreceived sales tax (i.e. Sales Tax on open invoices).

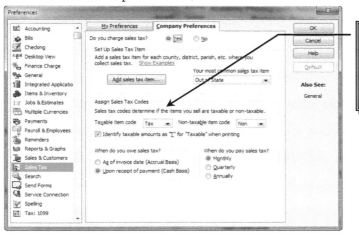

Figure 13-6 Sales Tax Preferences

Troubleshooting Out-of-Balance Balance Sheets

If the cash basis Balance Sheet is out of balance (i.e., if total **Assets** does not equal total **Liabilities and Equity**, the problem could be caused by using customer discounts instead of credit memos. There is a bug in QuickBooks (all editions, all years) that causes the cash basis Balance Sheet to be out of balance if discount transactions are coded to balance sheet accounts.

For example, if an invoice was paid, or partially paid using a discount transaction and the other side (the Debit) was coded to a balance sheet account (e.g. Customer Prepayments or Retainers), it will cause the cash basis Balance Sheet to be out of balance.

Unfortunately, QuickBooks doesn't provide an easy way to search for discount transactions, so you'll have to use the Find command, filtered for all Payment transactions. The resulting find report will show the transactions "Type" column, and you can look for Discount transactions in the report. If you see any coded to balance sheet accounts, those are the problem transactions.

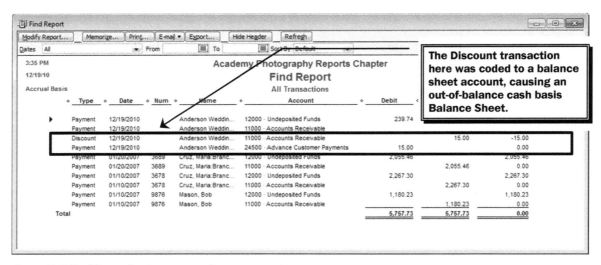

Figure 13-7 Find Report showing customer discount transactions

To fix the problem, delete the discount transaction(s) and create customer Credit Memo(s) instead.

Proofing A/R and A/P on the Cash Basis Balance Sheet

To proof the balances of A/R and A/P on the Cash Basis Balance Sheet, use QuickZoom to display the transactions behind the numbers on the Balance Sheet.

1. Create a Cash Basis Balance Sheet. Select the *Reports* menu, choose **Company & Financial**, and then choose **Balance Sheet Standard**.

   If your preferences are set to default to Accrual Basis reports, click **Modify Report** on the Balance Sheet report and select **Cash Basis**. Then click **OK**.

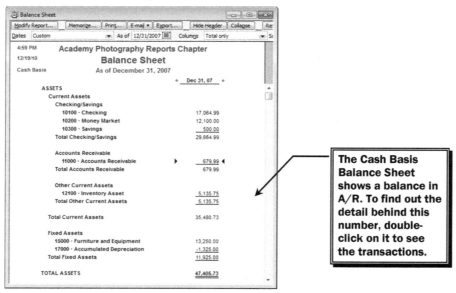

Figure 13-8 A Cash-Basis Balance Sheet with A/R

2.   The Cash Basis Balance Sheet above has a balance in Accounts Receivable. To see why, double-click on the A/R balance to see the transactions behind it.

3.   Set the date range on the Transactions by Account Report to clear the From date and leave the To date set to the end of the period you are evaluating.

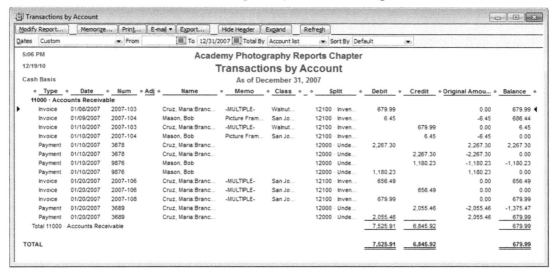

Figure 13-9 Transactions behind the A/R account from the Cash-Basis Balance Sheet

4.   The Transactions by Account report shows all transactions dated through the *To date* that use Accounts Receivable. However, we only want to see the open transactions, and we only want to see those transactions that were open as of the report date.

5.   Click **Modify Report** and then click the advanced button. Then select "Report Date" in the Open Balance/Aging section and click OK. This setting tells QuickBooks to only consider invoices that were *open* as of the date on the report, as opposed to just looking for whether they were ever paid (possibly after the report date).

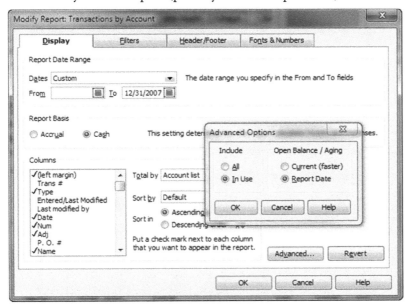

Figure 13-10 Setting the Open Balance/Aging option to "Report Date"

6.   Click the **Filters** tab.

7.   Filter the Transactions by Account report to only include transactions with a **Paid Status** of **Open**.

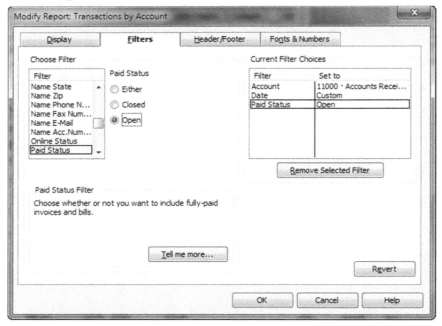

Figure 13-11 Filter the transactions report to include only "open transactions."

Now, the Transactions by Account Report shows that a single transaction is causing the Cash Basis Balance Sheet to show a balance in A/R. In this case, it's an open invoice with an Inventory sale, so the average cost of that inventory remains in A/R. The offsetting amount is a credit in the Inventory Asset account representing the reduction in inventory for the items on the invoice.

As you can see, all open transactions in the A/R account that use other balance sheet accounts, remain on the cash basis Balance Sheet.

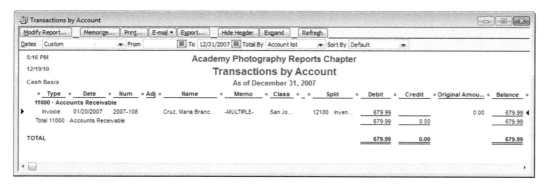

Figure 13-12 The filtered transaction report. Includes a single transaction with a paid status of "open."

Completing the Cash Basis Conversion

Although QuickBooks does a great job of removing invoices and bills when you create a cash basis report, it does not reverse any accruals you make for prepaid expenses or unearned income. As shown in Figure 13-8 it also does not reverse any A/R or A/P amounts that offset to balance sheet accounts other than Sales Tax Payable. In order to create a true cash basis Balance Sheet, you may need to enter journal entries to reverse accruals for prepaid income and expenses. There are two options:

Option 1: When There is No Need to Preserve Accrual Basis Year-End Reports

Using the totals from the filtered "Transactions by Account" report as shown in Figure 13-12, create a journal entry to adjust the balance in A/R. In the example above, the balance of $600 in Accounts Receivable came from an Invoice with a $600 reduction in Inventory for the sale of an Inventory Part Item. To complete the cash basis conversion, create a Journal Entry like the one shown in Figure 13-13.

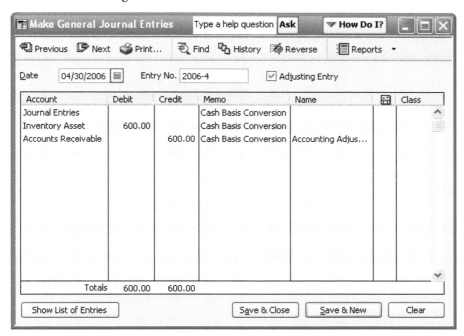

Figure 13-13 Journal Entry to complete the cash basis conversion

1.   Do the same for A/P as necessary, using a separate Journal Entry.

Important
You **must not** use Accounts Receivable or Accounts Payable on the top line of these journal entries when the offset to AR or AP involves one or more income or expense accounts. If you do, the transaction will be considered "open" and therefore it will not change the cash basis reports. Instead, use the workaround of putting the Journal Entries bank account on the top line of the journal entry (see *Using a Bank Account to Track Journal Entries* on page 89).
Also, you must enter a customer name in the **name** field on the A/R line of the journal entry, and you must use a vendor name on the A/P line. To keep things simple, create separate names for these adjustments. For example, use "Accounting Adjustments – C" for A/R adjustments and "Accounting Adjustments – V" for A/P adjustments.

---

2.   If necessary, create additional journal entries to debit accrued income or credit accrued expenses that are not associated with A/R or A/P.

3.   Enter reversing entries as of the first day of the following reporting period. Depending on
     how many journal entries you created, it might be fastest to memorize each entry from steps
     1-3, and reverse the debits and credits.

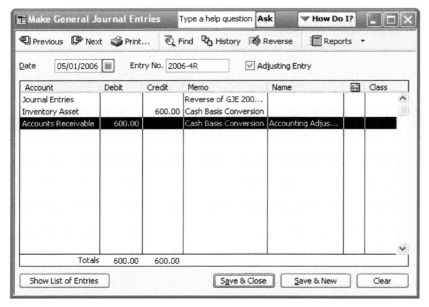

Figure 13-14 Entry to reverse the cash basis conversion

> **Note**
> QuickBooks 2002 and above (Premier and Enterprise) include a "Reverse" button on the
> journal entry screen. The reverse button creates a separate journal entry transaction with
> the debits and credits inverted. The default date for the reversing entry is the first day of
> the month after the date of the original journal entry. For example, if you enter a journal
> entry dated July 8, 2002 and click the "Reverse" button, QuickBooks creates a reversing
> entry dated August 1, 2002. You have the option of viewing and making changes to the
> reversing entry before saving.

4.   Lock the file. If it won't cause too many restrictions, lock the file as of the date of your
     reversing entries (i.e. the first day of the next reporting period). In any case, lock the file as of
     the last day of the prior reporting period to preserve your cash basis conversion. For more
     information on locking the data file, see page 100.

Option 2: Preserves Accrual Basis Year-End Reports

Some accountants prefer to complete the cash basis conversion outside of QuickBooks (e.g.
using a spreadsheet) to preserve Accrual Basis Year-End Reports. **Be careful with this
approach**, as it does not create auditable "entries" in the books. Document everything you
change and keep your notes. If you want a complete, auditable cash basis file in QuickBooks
but want to leave the accrual basis reports intact, use the following method.

1.   Create a backup of the data file.

2.   Restore the backup file you just created and give the restored file a slightly different name
     (e.g. Academy Glass – 200X Cash). Make sure to store this file in a separate folder on your
     client's hard drive so that your client will not accidentally use this file to process transactions.

Make sure the file name refers to the financial reporting year. The cash basis file will be for reporting purposes only.

3. Using the total from the filtered "Transactions by Account" report as shown in Figure 13-12, create a journal entry to adjust the balance in the A/R account. Do the same for A/P as necessary, using a separate journal entry.

> **Important**
>
> You **must not** use Accounts Receivable or Accounts Payable on the top line of these journal entries if the offset to AR or AP involves on ore more incomes or expense accounts See the note on page 587 for more information.

4. If necessary, create additional journal entries to debit accrued income or credit accrued expenses that are not associated with A/R or A/P.

5. Lock the file as of the last day of the prior reporting period.

Cash Basis Reporting for Partially Paid Invoices and Bills

If your client's data file includes partially paid invoices or bills, QuickBooks applies part of the income to cash basis reports by allocating the payment evenly across all split detail. For example, the Invoice in Figure 13-15 increases income in two different income accounts.

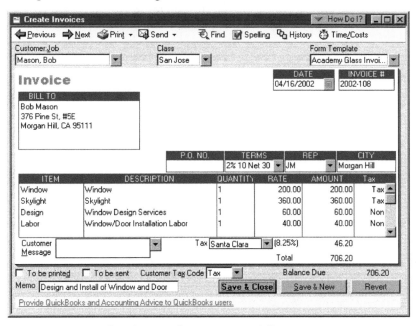

Figure 13-15 Invoice for Bob Mason that increases two different income accounts

The Part Items (Window and 104-Slider) credit an income account called "Product Sales" in the amount of $560 and the Service Items (Design and Labor) credit an income account called "Services" in the amount of $100. See Figure 13-16.

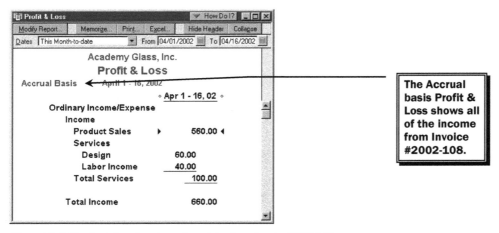

Figure 13-16 Profit & Loss showing only activity from Invoice 2002-108

If Bob Mason pays *half* the balance of the Invoice, the Cash basis Profit & Loss will show an increase to Product Sales for $280 ($560/2) and an increase to Services for $50 ($100/2). See Figure 13-17.

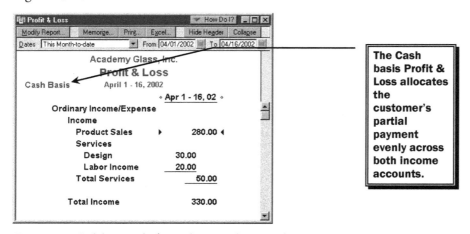

Figure 13-17 Cash basis Profit & Loss showing only activity from Invoice 2002-108

> **Note**
> When you set up a new QuickBooks data file for your client, you need to enter each open Invoice into the file separately. Many of these open Invoices may be partially paid. To properly setup the data file you will need to enter each partially paid Invoice using its *original* detail and totals and then enter a payment from the customer for the partial payment. Code the payment to Undeposited Funds and then enter a zero-dollar deposit into the Journal Entries account. Select the transaction in the Payments to Deposit screen (which clears undeposited funds), and enter an offsetting negative amount coded to Opening Balance Equity. If you enter just the unpaid balance of the Invoice, QuickBooks will not be able to accurately calculate the Cash Basis Profit & Loss or Cash or Cash basis Sales reports. The same applies to partially paid bills. When you create a Bill Payment for the partial payment of the bill, use the Journal Entries bank account to pay the bill. Then enter a Journal Entry to debit Journal Entries (to clear the balance) and credit Opening Balance Equity.

Displaying Debit and Credit Columns in Reports

QuickBooks Accountant uses Debit and Credit columns on almost every transaction detail report. However, when you use your client's edition of QuickBooks the default columns are Amount and Balance. Perform the steps in this example to remove these columns and replace them with Debit and Credit columns.

1. Open the detail report and then click **Modify Report**. See Figure 13-18 below.

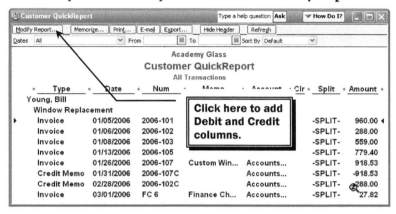

Figure 13-18 QuickReport for Bill Young: Window Replacement with Amount column

2. On the *Display* tab, deselect **Amount** and select **Debit** and **Credit**. Then, click **OK**.

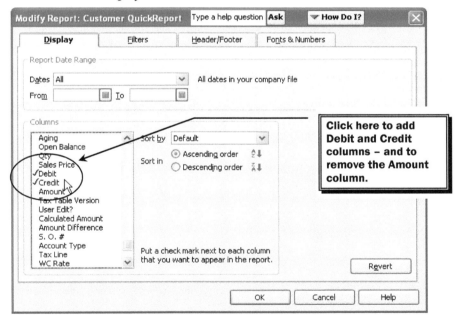

Figure 13-19 Modify Report Window - Debit and Credit Column Selections

3. QuickBooks shows the amounts on the report as Debits and Credits as shown in Figure 13-20. Memorize the report for future use.

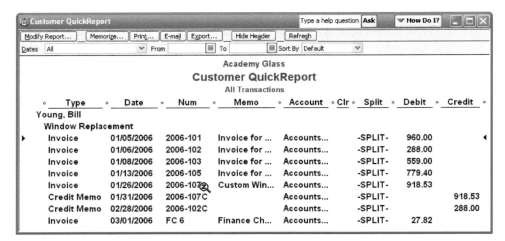

Figure 13-20 QuickReport with Debit and Credit Columns

Transaction History Report

Many transactions in QuickBooks are linked to other transactions. For example, when you apply a customer Payment or Credit Memo to an Invoice, QuickBooks links the payment and/or Credit Memo to the Invoice in the database. This link causes reduces (or zeros) the Invoice's open balance.

The ability to see these links between transactions is essential, especially when you are troubleshooting problems with the data file. For example, if Invoices show on the Open Invoice report but the client assures you the Invoices are paid, you will need to follow the links between the Invoices and the payments to research the problem.

QuickBooks refers to these links as the "Transaction History." Perform the steps in this example to view the Transaction History (links):

1. Open the transaction. In this example we will open a Bill from Ingram Micro as shown in Figure 13-21 below.

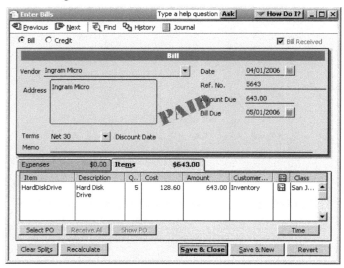

Figure 13-21 Paid Bill from Ingram Micro

2.   Click the **History** button at the top of the Bill. Alternatively, select the **Reports** menu, and then select **Transaction History**. QuickBooks displays the window shown in Figure 13-22 below.

Some windows will not have a *History* button, so using the *Reports* menu is the only way to show the Transaction History (links).

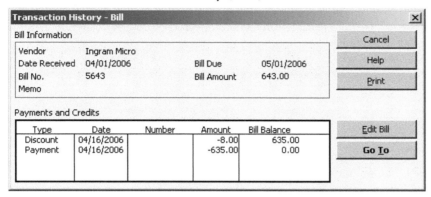

Figure 13-22 Transaction History for a Bill

3.   Click **Print** to view the transaction History in a report format as shown in Figure 13-23 below.

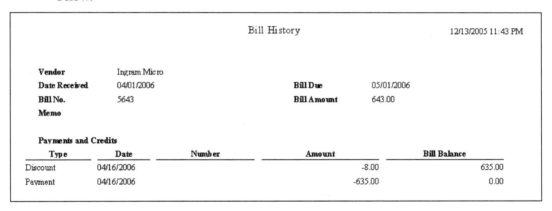

Figure 13-23 Transaction History report for a Bill

4.   You can use the window shown in Figure 13-22 to access the transactions to which the Bill is linked. If you are troubleshooting a problem with the Accounts Payable sub-ledger, you can edit the payments or discount, as necessary, and then save your changes. Editing the linked transactions will not break the link.

> **Note**
> At times, you may need to break the link between two transactions. You can break the link by deleting and re-entering the linked transactions. If the transaction is linked to an Invoice or Bill, you can change the customer or vendor name (respectively) to break the link.
>
> **Tip**
> A Bill or Invoice may have a very complicated payment and/or credit history. In other words, the Bill or Invoice may be linked to numerous payments and credits. You can create a Transaction History report to show the vendor or customer the payment and credit history, as necessary to resolve disputes or conflicts.

Transaction Journal Report

Every posting transaction in QuickBooks posts Debits and Credits to the General Ledger. However, in QuickBooks the accounts may not show on the transaction window. For example, an Invoice debits and credits several different accounts on the General Ledger, but you see only Items, not the accounts.

QuickBooks refers to these Debits and Credits as the "Transaction Journal." Perform the steps in this example to create a Transaction Journal report.

1. Open the *saved* transaction. This example uses a saved Invoice for Bill Young's Window Replacement job as shown in Figure 13-24 below.

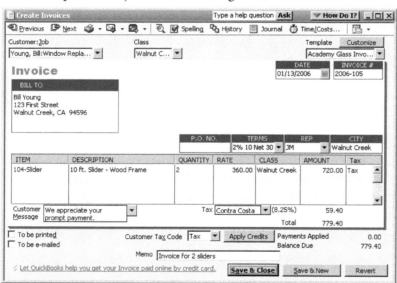

Figure 13-24 Transaction for Bill Young's Window Replacement Job

2. Click the **Journal** button. Alternatively, press Ctrl+Y, or select the **Reports** menu and then select **Transaction Journal**. QuickBooks creates the report shown in Figure 13-25 below. Some windows do not have a *Journal* button. Using the *Reports* menu is the only way to create a Transaction Journal for these types of transactions. Notice that the simple, one line Invoice posts several Debits and Credits to the General Ledger. The 104-Slider is an Inventory Item, so QuickBooks posts a credit to Inventory Asset and a Debit to Cost of

Goods Sold as part of the Transaction Journal. The transaction also accrues Sales Tax, so the Transaction Journal posts a credit to Sales Tax Payable.

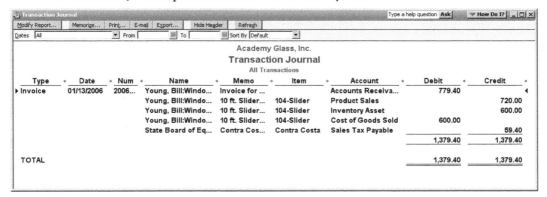

Figure 13-25 Transaction Journal for Bill Young's Invoice

Memorizing Reports

After you have modified a report, you can *memorize* the format and filtering so that you don't have to perform all of the modification steps the next time you want to view the report.

> **Note:**
> Memorizing a report does not memorize the data on the report, only the format, dates, and filtering.

If you enter specific dates, QuickBooks will use those dates the next time you bring up the report. However, if you select a *relative* date range in the *Dates* field (e.g., Last Fiscal Quarter, Last Year, or This Year to Date) before memorizing a report, QuickBooks will use the relative dates the next time you create the report.

For example, if you memorize a report with the *Dates* field set to **Last Fiscal Quarter**, that report will always use dates for the fiscal quarter prior to the current date (see Figure 13-26).

Figure 13-26 The Dates field showing a relative date range

Follow the steps in this example:

1.   With the *Sales of Services to Walnut Creek Customers* report displayed, click **Memorize** at the top of the report.

2.   In the *Memorize Report* window, the name for the report is automatically filled in. QuickBooks uses the report title as the default name for the memorized report (see Figure 13-27). The name can be modified if desired.

Figure 13-27 Memorize Report window

3.   Click the Checkbox next to **Save in Memorized Report Group:** and select **Customers** from the drop-down list as shown in Figure 13-27.

You can group your reports into similar types when you memorize them. This allows you to run several reports in a group by selecting them in the *Process Multiple Reports* window.

4.   Click **OK** and close the report.

Viewing Memorized Reports

The next time you want to see this report follow the steps in this example:

1.   From the *Report Center*, click on the **Memorized** link in the *Reports* title bar.

Notice that QuickBooks displays the reports in groups according to how you memorized them.

2.   Select the report you just memorized and click **Display.** Alternatively, double-click on the report in the list (see Figure 13-28).

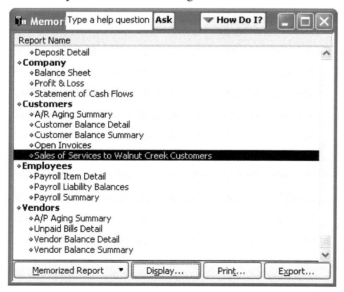

Figure 13-28 Memorized Report List window

3.   Close all open report windows.

Processing Multiple Reports

QuickBooks allows you to combine several reports into a group, so that you can later display and/or print the reports in the group as a batch. Report Groups are available in all editions of QuickBooks. QuickBooks Enterprise Solutions edition includes Condensed Financial Statements that allow you to create reports from multiple companies. For more on Condensed Financial Statements, see page 405.

Report Groups

As you can see in the Memorized Report list shown in Figure 13-28, you can have as many reports as you want in a group by memorizing the report and assigning it to the group. If you want to reassign a report to another group, click on the diamond to the left of the report in the Memorized Reports list and drag the mouse up or down until the report appears under the desired group. If you drag it to where it is no longer below a group name, it will not belong to any group.

Processing Multiple Reports

QuickBooks allows you to print reports as a batch. You may want to use this feature to print a series of monthly reports for your files (e.g., monthly Profit and Loss and Balance Sheet reports). Since we cannot process multiple reports from the Report Center, in this example, we will begin with the *Reports* menu.

> Note:
> See the *New Features* chapter starting on page 54 for more about *Send Multiple Reports* and *Commented Reports*.

1. From the **Reports** menu select **Process Multiple Reports** (see Figure 13-29).

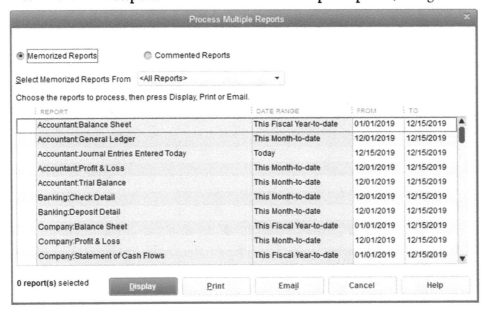

Figure 13-29 Process Multiple Reports window

> **Note:**
> Click in the column to the left of the report you want to include when you print or display your reports. Select the *From* and *To* date ranges of the report you wish to print in the columns on the right. Your date ranges will not match the ones displayed in Figure 13-29 and Figure 13-30. If you print the same group of reports on a regular basis, create a new Report Group in the *Memorize Reports List* window to combine the reports under a single group. Then you can select the group name in the *Select Memorized Reports From* field.

2.   Select **Customers** from the *Select Memorized Reports From* drop-down list (see Figure 13-30).

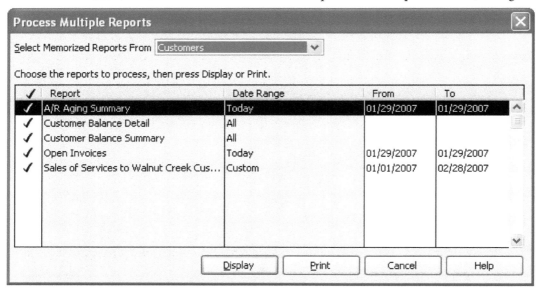

Figure 13-30 Customers Report Group

3.   If you do not want to display or print all the reports in the group, uncheck (√) the left column to deselect the reports you want to omit. Click **Display** to show the reports on the window (see Figure 13-31) or click **Print** to print all the reports.

> If your *Home* page is maximized, make sure to **Restore Down** (⬚) the window so that your reports will display in the cascade style shown in Figure 13-31.

4.   Close all open report windows. Click **No** if QuickBooks prompts you to memorize the reports.

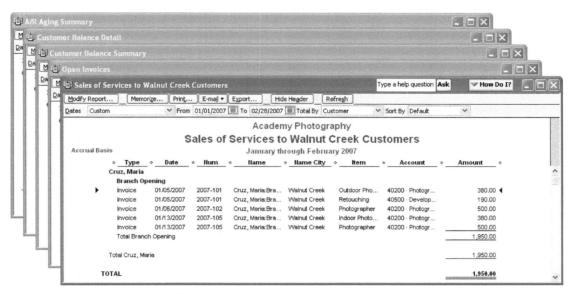

Figure 13-31 All of the reports in the Customer report group

Printing Reports

Every report in QuickBooks is printable. When you print reports, QuickBooks allows you to specify the orientation (landscape or portrait) and page-count characteristics for the reports.

1.   Create a Profit & Loss by Job report dated *01/01/2007* to *01/31/2007*.

2.   To print the report, click **Print** at the top of the window.

> **Another Way:**
> To print a report, press CTRL+P or select the **File** menu and then select **Print Report**.

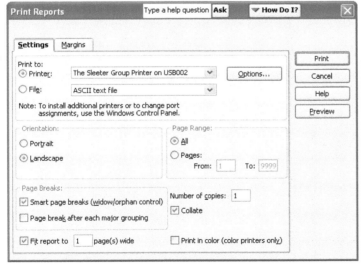

Figure 13-32 Print Report window

3.   The **Print Reports** window displays. Your settings will be different than the settings shown in Figure 13-32.

4.   QuickBooks normally selects your default printer, but you can select another printer from the *Printer* drop-down list.

5.   Select **Landscape** in the *Orientation* section.

The Portrait setting makes the print appear from left to right across the 8½-inch dimension of the page ("straight up"), while the Landscape setting makes the print appear across the 11-inch dimension of the page ("sideways").

6.   Confirm that the **Smart page breaks (widow/orphan control)** setting is selected (see Figure 13-33). This setting keeps related data from splitting across two pages.

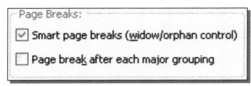

Figure 13-33 Page Breaks setting

Using **Smart page breaks**, you can control (to some extent) where page breaks occur on reports so that your pages don't break in inappropriate places. Using **Page break after each major grouping**, you can have QuickBooks break the pages after each major grouping of accounts. For example, in the Profit & Loss report, all Income and Cost of Goods Sold accounts will be on the first page (or pages), and all the Expense accounts will begin on a new page. In other reports, like the Customer Balance Detail and Vendor Balance Detail reports, this setting will cause each Customer and Vendor to begin on a new page, respectively.

7.   Select **Fit report to 1 pages wide** (see Figure 13-34). When you select this option, QuickBooks reduces the font size of the report so the width of all columns does not exceed 8½" (in portrait mode) or 11" (in landscape mode).

Figure 13-34 Select Fit report to 1 page(s) wide

Before you print any report, it's a good idea to preview the report to make sure it will print the way you want.

8.   Click the **Preview** button on the *Print Reports* window.

9.   If everything looks right, click **Print** to print the report.

10.   Close all open report windows.

> **Note:**
> QuickBooks saves the setting on the *Print Reports* window for memorized reports.

QuickBooks Statement Writer

If you need to present proper financial statements from QuickBooks data, you've most likely been frustrated for years by the extra steps you've needed to go through to get the job done. Intuit has made several ill-fated attempts to resolve the problem, but in general, creating GAAP financial statements from QuickBooks data has been painful, expensive, and complicated. There are several third-party solutions that take data out of QuickBooks to create proper financial statements, and those solutions work fine, but the extra hassle of exporting/importing is not ideal. The good news is that in versions 2010 and later of QuickBooks, I think we finally have a workable solution.

The solution is QuickBooks Statement Writer (QSW). QSW is a vastly-improved offering that allows accounting professionals to prepare GAAP-compliant financial statements as well as a wide range of management reports. It uses Microsoft® Excel as the platform for creating and customizing financials so you can design exactly what you want and then save "templates" for future reports for the same client, or for other clients.

QSW is implemented as a set of macros in Excel that links directly into the QuickBooks data. This means you can refresh the data directly into your formatted reports as opposed to exporting and then reformatting each month.

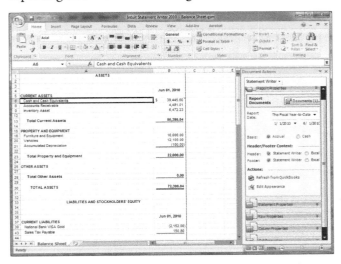

Figure 13-35 QuickBooks Statement Writer Connects QuickBooks Data with Microsoft Excel

You can use QSW to create financial reports for your clients and to create a report that not only includes the client financial report, but also other materials you enter or scan. Once you've finalized the reports, you can create one pdf that contains multiple reports and documents such as disclosures or accountant's notes.

The QuickBooks Statement Writer provides several built-in functions that streamline report customization and formatting. For example, there is a feature that allows you to combine several rows of a report into a single row. This lets you do things like combine separate cash accounts into one line on the financial statement and allow you to rename that line to "Cash and Cash Equivalents".

Features of the QuickBooks Statement Writer include:

- Create customized financial statements in Excel from QuickBooks data adding all the additional features and reporting flexibility available in Excel.

- Create statements from scratch, or use the pre-defined templates. Templates come in a variety of formats for Balance Sheets, Income Statements, Cash Flow Statements, Budget to Actual Statements, and multiple supporting statement documents.

- Refresh reports with current QuickBooks data without leaving the QSW tool.

- Combine multiple QuickBooks account lines into one line on financial statements without changing the QuickBooks chart of accounts.

- Add rows or columns of detail using QuickBooks data and Excel functionality.

- Drill down to QuickBooks data and modify QuickBooks transactions within the QSW tool.

- Automatically include new accounts on reports if and when they are added to the chart of accounts.

Working With the QuickBooks Statement Writer

Once you launch the Statement Writer tool from QuickBooks, Excel will launch along with the QSW macros that tech Excel how to build and manage your reports. Inside Excel, you'll see the QSW Document Actions pane that provides specific options used to customize reports. To expand the menu options available click on the drop-down arrow next to the each action (row) name. These QSW specific document actions are only available when you launch QSW from within QuickBooks.

Report Properties

The Report Properties pane allows you to modify the reporting period, change the basis of the report, and add extra pages, documents and attachments (see Figure 13-36).

Figure 13-36 Report Properties within the Statement Writer

Statement Properties

The Statement Properties pane allows you to modify the title and add job and class filtering to the report (see Figure 13-37).

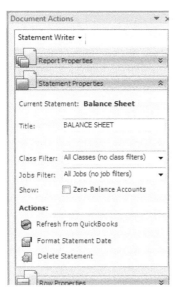

Figure 13-37 Statement Properties

Row Properties

Use Row Properties (see Figure 13-38) to manage the data in a single or in multiple rows. Row Properties activities allow you to change the label or accounts shown on a specific row.

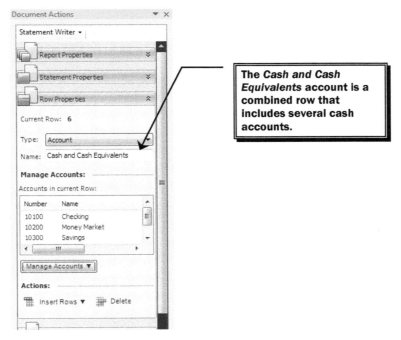

Figure 13-38 Row Properties

The row properties pane includes a "Manage Accounts" drop-down that controls rows in the statement including:

- Combining rows together (roll-up), splitting out previously combined rows, adding new rows or deleting rows in a statement.

- Link for "Show all Accounts" will display all accounts. Accounts in red indicate they are new or missing from the current statement.

When you want to add multiple accounts into a single row on a report, you can select the accounts from the window shown in Figure 13-39.

Figure 13-39 Row Properties Accounts List

Column Properties

With Column Properties, you can add a new column as shown in Figure 13-40.

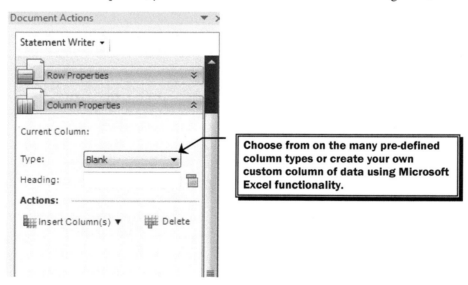

Figure 13-40 Column Properties

Use column properties to control the type of data in a column including:

- Data types: Accounts, Normal, % of Budget, % of the Whole, QuickBooks Data and Variance (see).
- Multiple choices for date type, such as Current / Prior Period, Specific Month, Specific Quarter.
- Option to select the number of years of data to display.

- Option to select a specific class or all classes for reporting.

You can create custom columns that perform math calculations on other data in the report as shown in Figure 13-41.

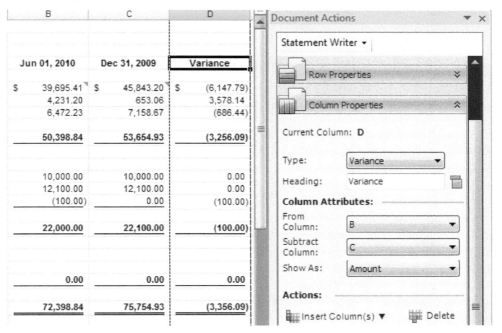

Figure 13-41 Column Properties to control the type of data displayed in a single column

Preferences

The QSW preferences allow you to add your specific preparer information to your statements including the accounting firm information, name, address, etc., and other defaults such as headers/footers, number formatting, and where data is to be stored on the network.

Using QSW in a Networked and/or Multi-User Environment

According to Intuit's support site, QuickBooks Statement Writer (QSW) statement files (.qsm) and their associated "appearance files" (.qss) can be stored on a server or network drive. However, it is not possible to open and work with the files while they are located on the server, unless you modify security policies on the server. Because Intuit doesn't recommend that, the files should be local when working with them. This means you need to copy the QSW files to your local drive before working with them, and, when finished, copy them back to the server.

Another important consideration for accounting firms planning to have multiple staff members working with financial statements is the multi-user issue. Keep in mind that while QSW can be used while QuickBooks is in multi-user mode, it is not possible to have more than one user access the same QSW file at the same time.

The Net of it...

When you add up all the features of QSW and then add power of Excel to fill in virtually any missing functionality, the QuickBooks Statement Writer should be the only tool you'll need for creating GAAP financial statements from QuickBooks data. With the direct link to the

QuickBooks file, you'll most likely find a dramatic reduction in the time it takes you to create, format and publish client financial statements. The networking and multi-user issues may cause your firm to struggle with some type of workaround or staff training for how to implement best practices in managing data files, but if you can get over that hump, this tool is a great value.

Financial Statement Designer

QuickBooks Accountant 2008 and earlier and QuickBooks Enterprise 8 and earlier includes an add-on program called the Financial Statement Designer. It was replaced with the QuickBooks Statement Writer in the 2009 edition. For more on the QuickBooks Statement Writer, see page 600.

The Financial Statement Designer provides a large selection of customizable financial statements "templates" that you can customize to meet your needs. It includes templates for balance sheets, income statements, statements of cash flows, as well as compilation and review letters. With this program you can create a standard set of financial statements that comply with Generally Accepted Accounting Principles (GAAP).

To launch the Financial Statement Designer, select the **Reports** menu and then select **Financial Statement Designer**.

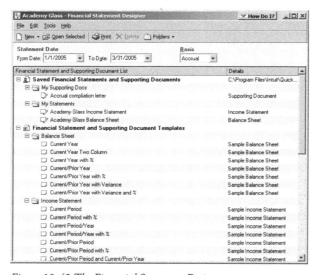

Figure 13-42 The Financial Statement Designer

The designer interacts directly with your QuickBooks data so that you zoom back to transaction data, make changes, and then return to your reports in the designer.

For complete details and instructions on using the designer, consult the Help system from within the Financial Statement Designer program.

Customization Features

You can use the Financial Statement Designer to design your statement layouts by starting with one of the 20 built-in financial statement layouts provided, or you can start from scratch, essentially starting with a blank spreadsheet-like screen to which you add labels, accounts, and columns of numbers. The Financial Statement Editor allows you to control the appearance of the columns, rows, and individual cells on the statement. You can insert or delete columns to show or hide prior period balances, variances, or percentages and it allows you to "filter" data so you can include, exclude, or consolidate accounts, classes, customers, or jobs into summary numbers.

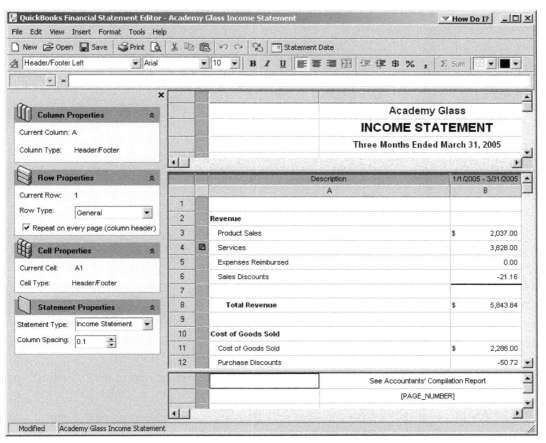

Figure 13-43 Customizing your Financial Statements

Supporting Documents

The integrated word processor can be used to create your supporting documents. It includes several standard compilation, review, and audit engagement letters, or you can create a letter from scratch. You can include variable information in your letters such as the client address information, accounting firm address information, statement dates and accounting basis of the reports.

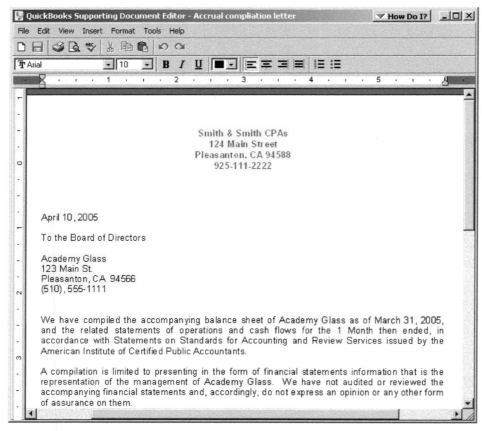

Figure 13-44 Integrated Word Processor

Printing Financial Statements in Batches

When you're finished designing your financial statements and supporting documents, you can print the whole set in whatever order you specify. You also can save the reports to PDF Files and then email them to your client. In subsequent periods, you only need to update the dates, and all of the formats and print order are preserved.

Converting Financial Statement Designer Documents

The QuickBooks Statement Writer included with QuickBooks 2009 and later replaces the Financial Statement Designer reporting tool used in prior versions of QuickBooks. However, your previously created Financial Statement Designer documents can be converted and used with the new QuickBooks Statement Writer.

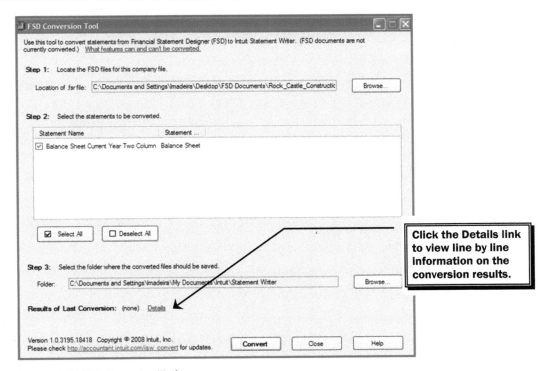

Figure 13-45 FSD Conversion Tool

What features can be converted from FSD to QSW?

- You can only convert balance, income statements and supporting documents.

- Inactive Accounts are not used in QSW and are not converted.

- Formatting is not converted. You must use the QSW Appearance features to apply formats to the converted statement.

- If you renamed a total row in FSD, it will not be converted.

- Most rollups convert correctly. However, if you have changed an account name and number, it will not be included in a rollup. Inactive Accounts are not included in rollups.

- If you see #NAME or #REF in the converted file, something did not convert correctly. Try recreating the contents of the cell that contains the invalid name or reference.

Advanced Reporting

Intuit offers an **Advanced Reporting** feature in QuickBooks Enterprise Solutions. Although more flexible than reporting with standard QuickBooks Desktop, it is also somewhat complicated to use. It will copy your database into a separate data store and let you generate all kinds of reports and graphs.

For more on the Advanced Reporting feature, see page 54.

Summary

Summary of Key Points

In this chapter, you learned about QuickBooks reports. There are literally thousands of reports that you can generate from QuickBooks by modifying the standard reports. You should now be familiar with how to use QuickBooks to do all of the following:

- Describe the principles of report customization, understand what you can and cannot do with QuickBooks reports (page 577)
- Understanding QuickBooks Cash Basis Reports (page 580)
- Memorize and group reports (page 595)
- Process and print multiple reports in batches (page 597)
- Use the QuickBooks Statement Writer(page 600)

Chapter 14
QuickBooks Add-ons

Objectives

After completing this chapter, you should be able to:

- What are the benefits of using Third Party Add-on Products (page 611)
- How to evaluate Add-ons (page 612)
- What are the limitations from the Intuit SDK (page 612)
- Best practices for implementing QuickBooks Add-ons (page 613)
- Installing Add-ons and Connecting to QuickBooks (page 615)

Why use Add-on Products

QuickBooks, as versatile it is, cannot do absolutely everything, nor can it satisfy all business needs for all types of industries. End users in a variety of industries often keep some detailed industry-specific information outside of their QuickBooks Financial Solutions product, and then re-enter summary or detail information into QuickBooks for the purposes of preparing financials. In addition, they may need specific reports or functions that QuickBooks by itself does not provide.

Third party add-ons are software programs developed by companies independent of Intuit. These programs perform a variety of functions on their own, but also have the added feature of integrating with QuickBooks. Many of these programs perform functions that are considered vital in certain industries or business areas, while eliminating the need for the end user to change to a custom or industry-specific accounting package. This allows the end user to track more data and produce better reporting than QuickBooks alone provides, while staying with the familiar, comfortable and user-friendly QuickBooks program.

A perfect example of an area where add-ons are needed is in Human Resource Administration. Since QuickBooks is primarily a financial and accounting product, its features are naturally somewhat limited in the area of Human Resource Administration. For example, tracking employee evaluations, or employee scheduling, or health insurance benefit plan enrollment, or 401k plan administration, or any of countless other needs in the human resources area, something outside of QuickBooks has to be used.

The developers make use of the Software Development Kit (SDK) for QuickBooks desktop development, which is provided at no charge to them by Intuit. The ideology of the SDK is "Never Enter Data Twice" (NED2) and to facilitate the sharing of information both ways behind the scenes between QuickBooks and the add-on product.

Note: The SDK is only available for Windows versions of QuickBooks. There is no programming interface available for QuickBooks for Mac.

When an add-on is used properly, it expands the power of QuickBooks without creating extra work.

Life Before QuickBooks Add-ons

Prior to the release of the SDK, IIF (Intuit Interchange Format) files were used to import lists (and, to a limited extent, transactions) into QuickBooks. IIF files are specially formatted tab-delimited text files that can be opened and edited in Excel. Although the IIF method still can be used today, it is not recommended by Intuit for other than the most basic of list imports (and do not forget that QuickBooks also has an Excel list import function for customers, vendors, and items) by the most expert of users.

Here are some of the limitations of the IIF method:

- Import files are very difficult to create properly, especially for files containing transactions as opposed to just lists
- No error checking or log file after the import
- No safeguards against duplicate imports of transactions
- No safeguards against accidental overwriting of previously existing list entries
- Can create unintended odd list entries in QuickBooks, such as a new bank account or new service item
- Two-way sharing of information is not possible using IIF files
- The integration is not seamless; it requires separate file preparation, single-user mode, and being signed in as the Admin user in QuickBooks

For more about IIF files, see 298.

SDK Limitations

Keep in mind that the add-ons are developed independently and are not affiliated with Intuit in any other way. This means that Intuit does not recommend, guarantee, troubleshoot or provide any support whatsoever with regards to these applications. For issues regarding installation, use, and integration, the user must deal solely with the developer.

These product surprises may also include compatibility with your computer's operating system or network settings. In addition, it is very important to assess how easy the add-on is to use, and how well it is documented. Even the most powerful add-on will have limited usefulness if it is not user-friendly or if there is a poor or non-existent *Help* menu or manual. It is advisable to discuss the type and amount of technical support that comes with the add-on and at what price. Often there is an annual cost for technical support, with different levels at different prices (e.g. phone support, e-mail support, etc.).

SDK design limitations also exist. For example, a computer with more than one country's version of QuickBooks installed on it may cause a 3rd party add-on not to work. This is because the SDK used by the add-on is "confused" as to which version of the SDK it should communicate with. In this situation, it is best to keep each country's version of QuickBooks on a separate machine.

Another constraint of the SDK is that it does not support all QuickBooks fields and transactions. For example, add-on applications cannot access the details of payroll transactions, and cannot create paycheck transactions. The following limitations are among those that currently exist in the SDK:

- Customers' multiple Ship To addresses cannot be accessed
- Online banking is not available (by design due to the sensitive nature of the information)
- Accessing payroll information is not available

A further complication to evaluating add-on products is that Intuit has suspended their testing/certification program for SDK programs. Thie Intuit Marketplace doesn't include newly developed products and information is no longer being updated. We recommend looking for add-on products outside the Intuit Marketplace.

Custom Add-on Developers

After all the searching, you may not find a ready-made solution that solves your problem. If that is the case, locating a custom developer might be in order.

Add-ons Best Practices

There are several "best practices" that should be used anytime you are testing, installing or using a 3rd party add-on.

Testing Best Practices

Any add-on, no matter how reputable, must be tested out to assess its applicability and compatibility with a particular situation. Be sure to back up the QuickBooks data file on external media prior to initiating the installation and integration of the add-on. Be aware that in addition to the QuickBooks data file and any related QuickBooks files (such as the *.tlg and *.nd files and the Images directory), there may be a separate database for the add-on program. It is important to know the precise name and location of this database file.

Furthermore, ensure that any 3rd party database file is adequately and regularly (i.e. daily) backed up and that anyone accessing this database file has sufficient network security privileges to do so. The database for the 3rd party add-on can be just as valuable to the end-user as the QuickBooks data file, so treat both with respect and care.

User Names and Permissions Best Practices

Most add-on products will have their own sets of user names and associated permissions, so you should not assume that a QuickBooks user's name and permission level will automatically carry over to the 3rd party add-on. These user names and permission levels must be independently created in the new software.

One useful practice is to create a user in QuickBooks named after the 3rd party add-on (e.g. "Fishbowl" in the case of Fishbowl Inventory). This user name should have permission access all areas of QuickBooks, and when the add-on connects to QuickBooks it should "log in" to QuickBooks under this user name. With this practice, the audit trail in QuickBooks will identify all transactions that have been entered and/or modified by the add-on application.

The steps for creating the special user in QuickBooks are as follows (note that user setup in Enterprise Solutions varies from this example a bit):

1.   Select Company, then Set Up Users and Passwords, then Set Up Users.

2.   Click Add User.

3.   Enter the new user name that matches the 3rd party add-on (e.g. *Fishbowl*). See Figure 14-1

Figure 14-1 Set up user password and access window

4.   Enter and confirm the password for this new user.

5.   Click **Next**.

6.   In the *Access for User* window, check **All areas of QuickBooks** (see Figure 14-2).

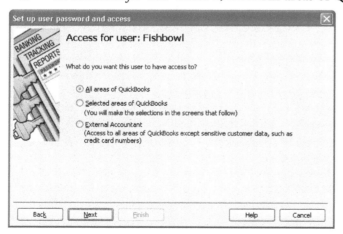

Figure 14-2 Set up user Password and Access - All Areas

7.   Click **Next**.

8.   In the Warning window, click **Yes** to confirm access to all areas (see Figure 14-3).

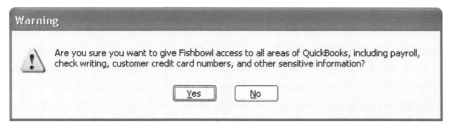

Figure 14-3 Permissions Warning

9.   The final window will show a matrix of areas and access levels, showing only Y's and n/a's. Click **Finish** (see Figure 14-4).

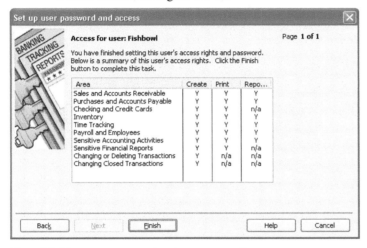

Figure 14-4 Set up user password and access - access for user

Client Server Best Practices

Often, the 3rd party add-on will have a Server component and a Client component (as is the case with QuickBooks). The installation instructions of each individual software package should be followed, however, in general it's best to install the Server software on the network server where the 3rd party data (and the QuickBooks data file) resides. The Client software for the add-on is installed on each workstation as is the case with the QuickBooks client software. Each Client will connect to the Server through the network. To provide the best performance, the connection between the add-on and QuickBooks should occur between the add-on's Server component and QuickBooks on the server computer instead of through a network connection. Check the documentation from the add-on developer for specific setup recommendations.

Installing Add-ons and Connecting to QuickBooks

There is no "one size fits all" methodology for 3rd party add-on installations and integrations with QuickBooks data. Each product has its own installation and integration instructions, however these are some general guidelines for connecting with QuickBooks.

Connecting to QuickBooks

There will generally be two procedures to connecting the 3rd party add-on with QuickBooks initially. One procedure will be on the QuickBooks side, while the other procedure will be on the 3rd party add-on side. Depending on the add-on, the user will at some point be prompted in QuickBooks to enable the integrated application to access the data file.

After installing the add-on product, follow instructions within the new software for linking this product with a particular QuickBooks data file.

In this example, we use Fishbowl Inventory (see Figure 14-5).

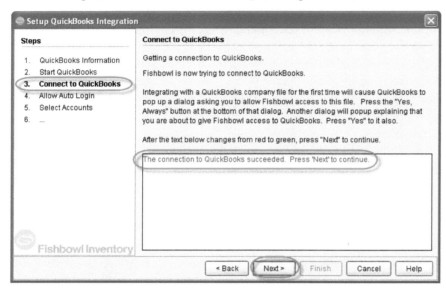

Figure 14-5 Setup QuickBooks Integration screen in Fishbowl

1.   Initiate the QuickBooks connection within the 3rd party application.

2.   In Fishbowl, there are on-screen instructions (see Figure 14-6) for both the add-on and the QuickBooks side of the initial setup.

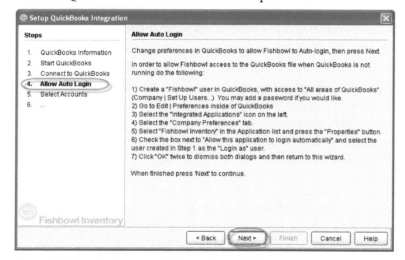

Figure 14-6 Auto Login screen with instructions in Fishbowl

3.   Make sure QuickBooks is running in the desired data file. The *QuickBooks – Application with No Certificate* dialog box appears (See Figure 14-7).

4.   Choose **Yes, always; allow access even if QuickBooks is not running**, or other option appropriate to your 3rd party add-on.

5.   Click the **Continue** button.

Figure 14-7 Message about new add-on software attempting to access data file

6.   A *Confirm to Proceed* window appears. Choose **Yes**.

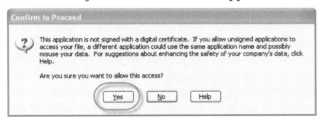

Figure 14-8 Confirm to Proceed window in QuickBooks

7.   QuickBooks will display the *Access Confirmation* screen. Select **Done**:

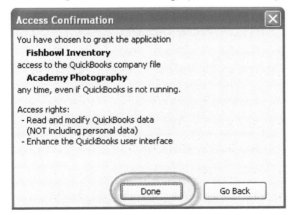

Figure 14-9 Access Confirmation screen in QuickBooks

You can find information on the installed 3rd party programs that have access to the current QuickBooks data file in QuickBooks.

1.   Select **Edit**, then **Preferences**, then **Integrated Applications**, then **Company Preferences**. You must be signed into QuickBooks as the Admin user (see Figure 14-10).

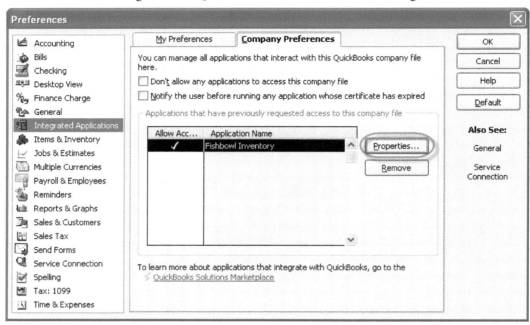

Figure 14-10 Integrated Applications Company Preferences window in QuickBooks

2.   Highlight the application name and select **Properties** in the *Company Preferences* window. The *Access Rights* information for that 3rd party add-on information is displayed. Ensure that the *Allow this application to login automatically* is checked. Choose the newly-created user in the drop-down menu under *Login as* (in this case, choose user named **Fishbowl**). Select **OK**:

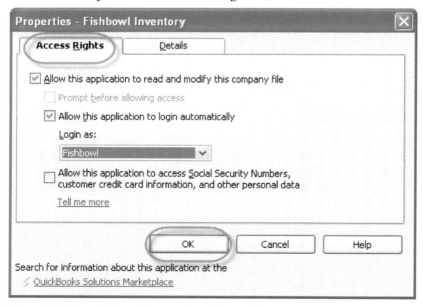

Figure 14-11 Access Rights information for 3rd party add-on

3.   The *Details* tab contains information about the first time and the last time the 3rd party add-on accessed this particular data file.

In the 3rd party add-on, there will often be additional screens to finalize the initial link and set up the properties of future integrations (such as how often the "talking to QuickBooks" is done, if it is done automatically or manually, etc.).

1.   In Fishbowl, the initial integration involves choosing accounts and importing lists. Continue choosing the appropriate option until the initial integration is complete (see Figure 14-12 and Figure 14-13).

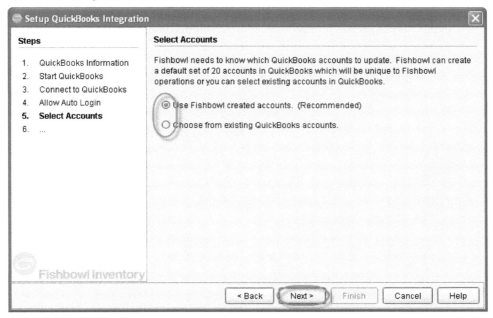

Figure 14-12 Select Accounts for initial integration between Fishbowl and QuickBooks

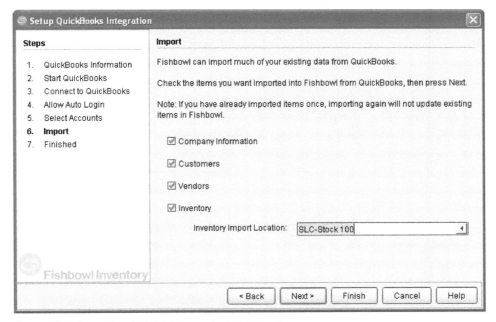

Figure 14-13 Import lists for initial integration in Fishbowl

2.   The initial integration has been completed and an *Import* window appears with the results. Select **OK**.

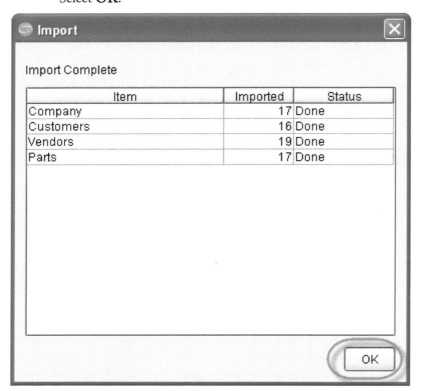

Figure 14-14 Import log from Fishbowl

One can look in QuickBooks to see the effects of the initial integration. The Item List in QuickBooks includes the Fishbowl items following the Fishbowl initial integration (see Figure 14-15).

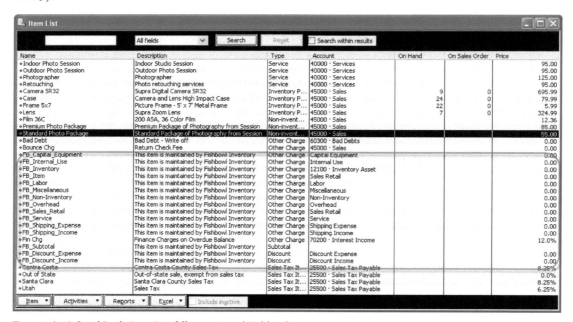

Figure 14-15 QuickBooks Item List following initial Fishbowl integration

You should verify that both QuickBooks and the 3rd party add-contain the correct list and the company information to confirm they were brought over properly (see Figure 14-16).

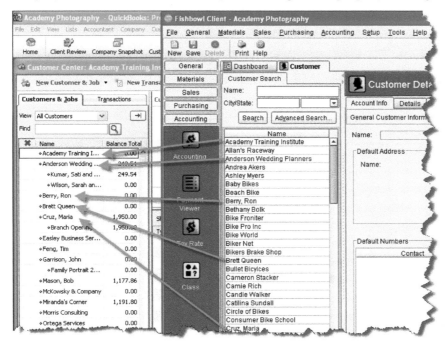

Figure 14-16 Comparison of Academy Photography customer lists in both QuickBooks and Fishbowl

Subsequent integrations between QuickBooks and the add-on will be performed either automatically (at a frequency chosen in the add-on integration properties) or manually, depending on what is offered by the add-on and what is desired in the end user environment.

In Fishbowl, for example, choosing the *Accounting* tab will allow the user to choose when to Export the data to QuickBooks using the *Export* button (see Figure 14-17 and Figure 14-18).

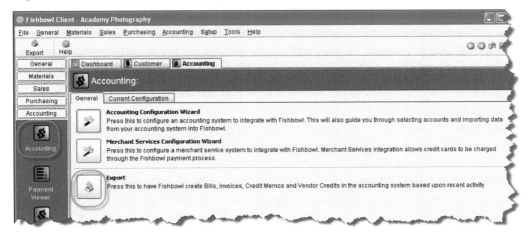

Figure 14-17 Export screen in Fishbowl

Figure 14-18 Export screen from Fishbowl

Once the export function is completed, the *Audit Trail* report in QuickBooks shows the transactions brought over during the export, and the user is clearly the user name created specifically for the 3rd party integration.

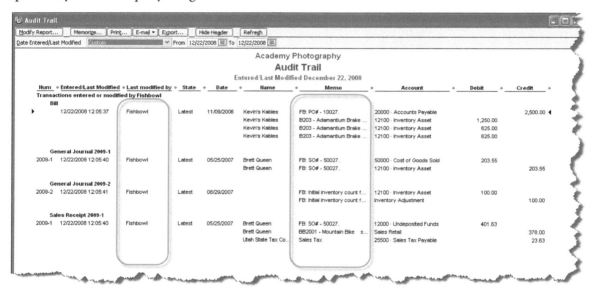

Figure 14-19 Audit Trail in QuickBooks after export from Fishbowl

There will be variations in the procedure for creating a QuickBooks connection in different 3rd party add-ons. Although we have used Fishbowl Inventory in these examples, you will find similarities and differences with other add-ons. Keep in mind that these examples are specific to Fishbowl Inventory, which has comprehensive and helpful instructions.

Having one or more well-researched, useful add-ons to make available to your clients can help give you an edge over other consultants, as you are offering more tools to your clients that help enhance QuickBooks and their overall business management systems. Just be aware that if there is a problem with the add-on or with the integration, it could reflect poorly on you. Conversely, if you know your add-ons and are prepared, you can come out a hero.

What is the QuickBooks API?

In recent years Intuit introduced a new programming interface for developers of QuickBooks add-on products. The name of this new interface, and its capabilities, have changed dramatically over the past few years. This has led to much confusion for developers, ProAdvisors and consumers.

When the new interface was first released it was intended to work with both QuickBooks desktop versions and QuickBooks Online. For desktop versions, the Intuit Sync Manager"application would be installed, and this application would copy your desktop database to an Intuit server "in the Cloud". The add-on application would communicate with this Cloud database, and Intuit Sync Manager would keep it synchronized with the desktop database.

A separate marketplace was created to list products that used the new interface, the Intuit App Center (http://apps.intuit.com/).

Near the end of 2013 Intuit recognized that this approach wasn't working smoothly for QuickBooks desktop products. Intuit Sync Manager was a complicated program to maintain, and many desktop users didn't want to have their data replicated in the Cloud. Intuit decided that they would focus their attention on QuickBooks Online, and renamed the new interface the QuickBooks API. They returned the focus for desktop add-on products to the SDK, and no longer allow new products to be developed for the desktop using the new interface.

Any existing products that used the QuickBooks API interface for desktop versions of QuickBooks are still supported, but no new applications will be allowed to use this approach (although some exceptions may be allowed).

Confusing? Yes, it is, but in the long run this will work out for the best. QuickBooks Online add-ons will use the cloud based QuickBooks API, QuickBooks desktop add-ons will use the established SDK. The only question will be how much support will Intuit provide to SDK developers.

Summary

In this chapter, you learned about the following topics:

- What are the benefits of using Third Party Add-on Products (page 611)
- How to evaluate Add-ons (page 612)
- What are the limitations from the Intuit SDK (page 612)
- Best practices for implementing QuickBooks Add-ons (page 613)
- Installing Add-ons and Connecting to QuickBooks (page 615)

Chapter 15
Sales Tax

Objectives

After completing this chapter, you should be able to:

- Activate Sales Tax and set Sales Tax Preferences (page 625)
- Use Sales Tax Items on Sales Forms (page 629)
- Set up Sales Tax Items (page 629)
- Use Sales Tax Codes on Sales Forms (page 631)
- Set up Sales Tax Codes (page 632)
- Assign Sales Tax Codes to Items (page 633)
- Assign Sales Tax Codes to Customers (page 634)
- Use QuickBooks reports to assist in preparing your sales tax return (page 637)
- Adjust Sales Tax Payable (page 638)
- Pay Sales Tax (page 641)
- Set up and use Sales Tax Groups (page 642)
- Categorize Revenue by Sales Tax Code (page 644)
- Solve problems in Sales Tax (page 645)
- Sales Tax and Cash Basis (page 653)

If you sell products and certain types of services, chances are you will need to collect and remit sales tax. In many states, aside from the state tax, each county or city may impose an additional tax that businesses are required to track and report.

If you sell non-taxable goods and services, or if you sell to customers that are exempt from paying sales tax, your state will probably require a breakdown of non-taxable sales and the reason sales tax was not imposed.

These differing conditions may not apply in all jurisdictions, but QuickBooks allows you to track sales tax for all of these different situations.

If you are not familiar with the sales tax rates or reporting requirements in your area, consult your state agency, your local QuickBooks advisor, or accountant for guidance.

Setting up Sales Tax

Activating Sales Tax and Setting Preferences

You must set up your **Sales Tax Preferences** before using the Sales Tax feature in QuickBooks.

Click the Manage Sales Tax button on the Home Page.

1.   The Manage Sales Tax dialog box will appear (see Figure 15-1).

2.   Click the **Sales Tax Preferences…** button in the *Get Started* section.

Alternatively, you could select Preferences from the Edit menu, then select the Sales Tax Company preferences.

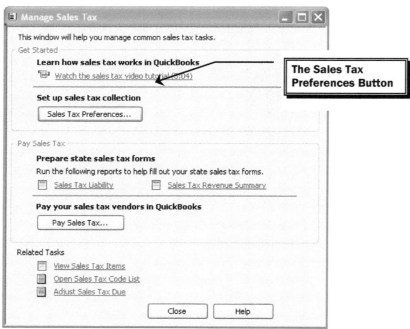

Figure 15-1 The Manage Sales Tax Dialog Box

3.   The Sales Tax Company Preferences dialog box appears.

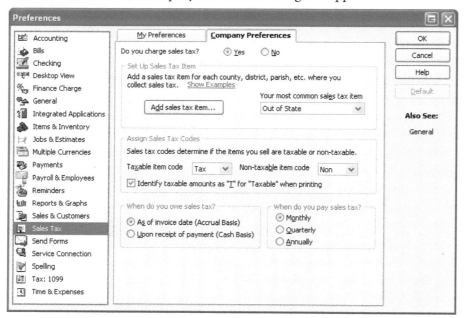

Figure 15-2 Sales Tax Company Preferences

4.   Leave **Yes** selected in the *Do You Charge Sales Tax* section (see Figure 15-3).

Do you charge sales tax?   ◉ <u>Y</u>es   ○ <u>N</u>o

Figure 15-3 Use these options to turn on Sales Tax tracking

> **Note:**
> In your practice file, Sales Tax is already activated. However, if you setup your own data file you will need to activate it by clicking **Yes** either in the Sales Tax Preferences, as shown in Figure 15-3, or when prompted in the EasyStep Interview.

5.   In the *Set Up Sales Tax Items* section, notice *Out of State* is selected in the *Most common sales tax* field. Change this field to **Contra Costa** (see Figure 15-4).

> **Note:**
> The sales tax item listed in the *Most common sales tax* field becomes the default sales tax item on new customer records, and on Sales receipts and Invoices.

Set Up Sales Tax Item

Add a sales tax item for each county, district, parish, etc. where you collect sales tax.   Show Examples

Add sales tax item...   Your most common sa<u>l</u>es tax item

Contra Costa

Figure 15-4 Select the most common Sales Tax Item you use on sales forms

6.   In the *Assign Sales Tax Codes* section, **Tax** is the default code in the *Taxable item code* field and **Non** is the default for the *Non-Taxable item code* field (see Figure 15-5).

The codes you enter here will become the default codes when you set up new Customers and Items. You can supply the appropriate *Sales Tax Code* on exempt customer records and non-taxable Items. For more information about *Sales Tax Codes,* see page 631.

7.   The *Mark taxable amounts with "T" when printing* box is checked (see Figure 15-5).

When you use taxable items on sales forms (e.g., Inventory Parts marked taxable in the Item setup), QuickBooks will print a **T** on that line of the invoice, sales receipt, or credit memo. It is usually best to leave this box checked to clearly distinguish which items are subject to sales tax on printed forms.

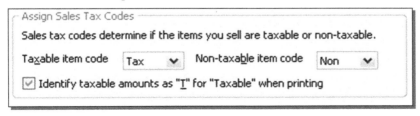

Assign Sales Tax Codes

Sales tax codes determine if the items you sell are taxable or non-taxable.

Ta<u>x</u>able item code   Tax   Non-taxa<u>b</u>le item code   Non

☑ Identify taxable amounts as "<u>T</u>" for "Taxable" when printing

Figure 15-5 Select the Default Sales Tax Codes

8.   In the When do you owe sales tax section, leave **As of invoice date (Accrual Basis)** selected
      as shown in Figure 15-6.

      With *As of Invoice date* selected in this section, sales tax reports will show that you owe sales
      tax for all taxable sales, including unpaid amounts from your open Invoices.

      If you select **Upon receipt of payment (Cash Basis)**, the reports will reflect sales tax only
      from sales on which payments have been received. Check your state sales tax rules and set
      this *Sales Tax Preference* accordingly.

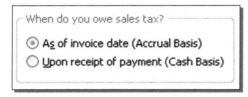

Figure 15-6 Owe Sales Tax on Accrual or Cash Basis

9.   In the ***When do you pay sales tax?*** section, **Monthly** is already selected (see Figure 15-7).

      Many states require you to pay sales tax monthly. However, if your company pays its sales
      tax quarterly or annually, select the appropriate option on this portion of the window.

      This setting controls the default date for the *Show sales tax due through* field of the *Pay Sales
      Tax* window. If you select **Monthly**, the default date will be the end of last month. If you
      select **Quarterly** or **Annually**, the default date will be the end of last calendar quarter or year
      respectively.

Figure 15-7 Pay Sales Tax section

10.   Click **OK** to save your changes.

11.   If you made changes on the preference screen before clicking **OK**, QuickBooks may display
      the *Updating Sales Tax* window (see Figure 15-8).

      When you turn on *Sales Tax Tracking*, QuickBooks provides the option to automatically
      enter the **Tax** *Sales Tax Code* in existing customer records and Inventory and Non-inventory
      Part Items. If the majority of your customers and items are taxable, it is best to leave both of
      these boxes checked. If necessary, you can edit customer records and Items. See *Editing the
      Sales Tax Codes on Items and Customers* on page 633 for more information.

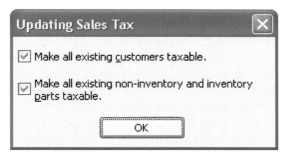

Figure 15-8 Updating Sales Tax window

12.   Click **OK** on the *Updating Sales Tax* window.

Sales Tax Items

Sales Tax Items are used on sales forms to calculate the amount of sales tax due on each sale.

Using Sales Tax Items on Sales Forms

On sales forms, Sales Tax is calculated at the bottom of the form, separately from the rest of the Items on the form. To see this, display Invoice 2010-104 (*Customer* menu→ *Create Invoice*→ **Previous** button). See Figure 15-9. Close the window after reviewing the form.

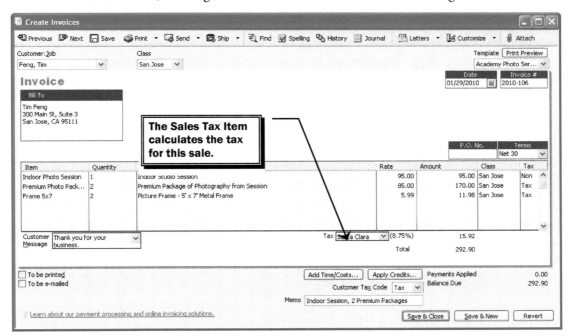

Figure 15-9 Invoice using the Santa Clara Sales Tax Item

Setting Up Sales Tax Items

To set up your Sales Tax Items, follow the steps in this example:

1. Select the *Lists* menu and then select **Item List**. Alternatively, click the **Items & Services** icon on the *Home* page.

2. To add a new Item, select the **Item** button at the bottom of the *Item list* and then select **New**.

3. Select **Sales Tax Item** in the *Type* drop-down list and press **Tab**.

4. Enter the *Tax Name*, *Description*, *Tax Rate*, and *Tax Agency*, as shown in Figure 15-10. This item will track all sales activity (taxable and nontaxable) for Alameda County and will charge each customer 8.75% in sales tax. The sales taxes collected using the *Alameda Sales Tax Item* will increase the amount due to the *State Board of Equalization*.

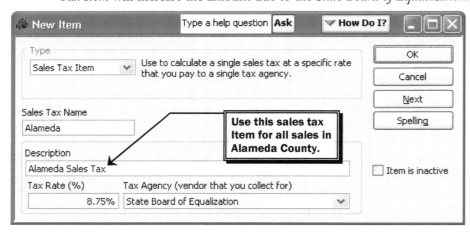

Figure 15-10 Setting up a Sales Tax item

5. Click **OK** to save the Item.

> **The accounting behind the scenes:**
> **Sales Tax Items** automatically calculate the sales tax on each sales form by applying the sales tax rate to all taxable items on that sale. QuickBooks increases (credits) Sales Tax Payable for the amount of sales tax on the sale. Also, QuickBooks tracks the amount due by *Tax Agency* in the **Sales Tax Liability** report and in the *Pay Sales Tax* window.

Figure 15-11 includes three additional *Sales Tax Items* for tracking sales in *Contra Costa* and *Santa Clara* counties as well as *Out of State* sales.

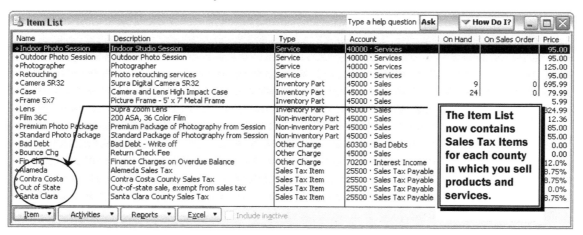

Figure 15-11 Item list

> **Note:**
> If you remit sales tax to **only one agency** (e.g., California's State Board of Equalization) but you collect sales tax in several different counties or cities, create a separate *Sales Tax Item* for each taxable location in which you sell products. This allows you to track different sales tax rates for each locale.
>
> **Note:**
> If you pay sales tax to **more than one agency,** you should use *Sales Tax Group*s to combine several different Sales Tax Items into a group tax rate. See page 642 for more information.

Sales Tax Codes

Sales Tax Codes are an additional classification for calculating and reporting sales tax. A Sales Tax Code is assigned to each product or service item, as well as to each customer.

Sales Tax Codes serve two purposes. First, Sales Tax Codes indicate whether a specific product or service is taxable or non-taxable. Secondly, Sales Tax Codes categorize revenue based on the reason you charged or did not charge sales tax.

If your sales tax agency requires reporting for different types of exempt sales, you may wish to create several non-taxable Sales Tax Codes for each type of non-taxable sale (e.g., **RSR** for non-taxable resellers).

Using Sales Tax Codes on Sales Forms

If you use a taxable *Sales Tax Code* in the *Customer Tax Code* field on sales forms, QuickBooks will charge sales tax (see Figure 15-12). If you use a non-taxable *Sales Tax Code*, QuickBooks will not charge sales tax unless you override the sales tax code (to a taxable code) on one of the lines in the body of the form.

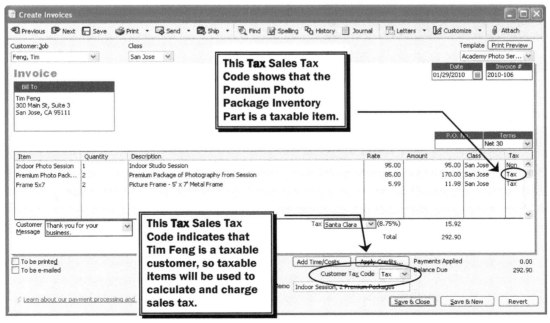

Figure 15-12 Invoice with taxable items

When you set up a customer record, the *Sales Tax Code* you enter in the customer record becomes the default in the *Customer Tax Code* field on sales forms (see Figure 15-12).

Similarly, when you set up Items, the *Sales Tax Code* you enter in the Item record becomes the default Tax Code in the body of sales forms (Figure 15-17).

You can override the *Sales Tax Code* at the bottom of sales forms (by using the *Customer Tax Code* drop-down list), or on each line in the body of the Invoice.

For more information on using Sales Tax Codes to categorize revenue, see page 644.

Setting up Sales Tax Codes

To set up a Sales Tax Code, follow the steps in this example:

1.   From the *Lists* menu select **Sales Tax Code List**. QuickBooks displays the Sales Tax Code List window (see Figure 15-13).

Figure 15-13 Sales Tax Code List

2.   To add a new one, you would select **New** from the *Sales Tax Code* button at the bottom of the list. To edit a Sale Tax Code, double-click it in the list.

3.   Double-click the first Tax Code (**Tax**) in the list.

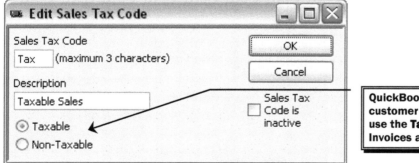

Figure 15-14 Edit Sales Tax Code window

4.   Each *Sales Tax Code* has a taxable or non-taxable status (see Figure 15-14).

5.   Click **Cancel**. For this example, you will not create a new Tax Code.

6.   Close the Sales Tax Code List window.

Editing the Sales Tax Codes on Items and Customers

Assigning Sales Tax Codes to Items

To assign a default Sales Tax Code to an Item, follow the steps in this example:

1. From the *Reports* menu, select **List** and then select **Item Listing**.

2. To make the report more useful for viewing the Sales Tax Code on each Item, click **Modify Report** and remove all columns except **Item**, **Description**, **Type**, and **Sales Tax Code** as shown in Figure 15-15. You will need to scroll down to deselect additional items.

3. Select **Type** from the *Sort by* drop-down list.

4. Click **OK** when finished.

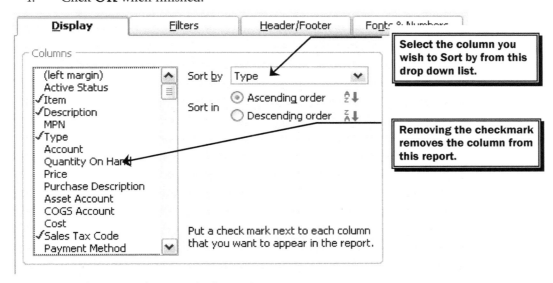

Figure 15-15 Changing Display settings for the Item Listing

5. Move your cursor over the *Sales Tax Code* column header. Your cursor will appear as a hand. Click and drag the column so that it appears immediately to the right of the **Item** column (see Figure 15-16).

Figure 15-16 Item Listing showing Sales Tax Codes for each Item

To edit the *Sales Tax Code* for an Item in the list, double-click the Item name.

6.   Double-click on the Item.

7.   Leave the *Tax Code* field set to Non as shown in Figure 15-17.

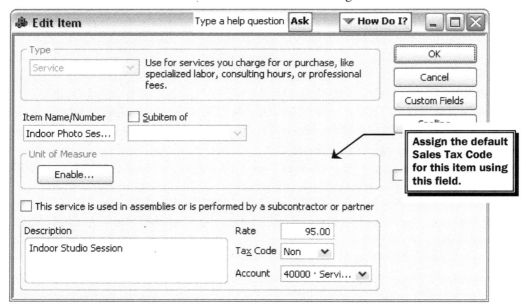

Figure 15-17 Edit the Sales Tax Code on each Item as necessary

8.   Click **OK** to close the *Edit Item* window.

Assigning Sales Tax Codes to Customers

To view and edit Sales Tax Codes on customer records, follow the steps in this example:

1.   From the *Reports* menu, select **List** and then select **Customer Contact List**.

2.   To make the report more useful for viewing the Sales Tax Code for each Customer, click
      Modify Report. Scroll down the list to select **Sales Tax Code, Tax item,** and **Resale Num**
      from the *Columns* section (see Figure 15-18). Remove all other check marks except
      Customer. Click **OK** when finished.

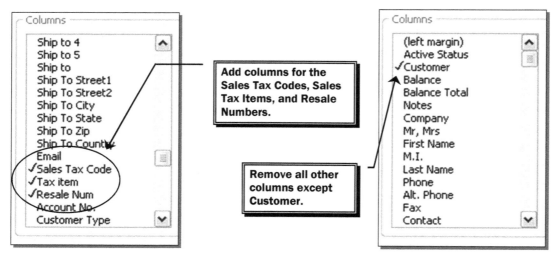

Figure 15-18 Modify Report window for the Customer Contact list

3.   To the right of the *Sales Tax Code* column header, click and drag the diamond to widen the column to view the data. Your cursor will be replaced with a cross symbol and a dotted line will indicate the column edge. Repeat this step for the *Tax Item* column and the *Resale Num* column if needed (see Figure 15-19).

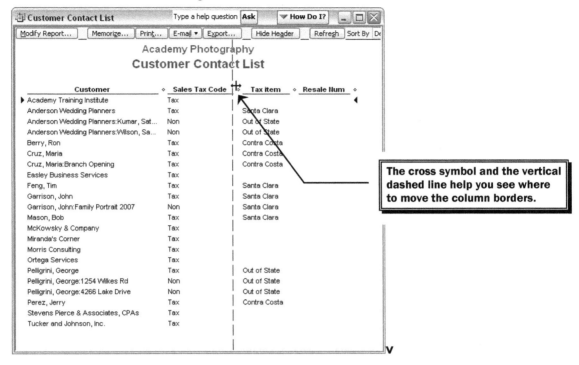

Figure 15-19 Customer Contact List with Sales Tax Code and Tax item columns

To edit the sales tax information for a customer, double-click the customer name in the report.

4.   Double-click on **Berry, Ron** in the Customer Contact report.

5.   Click the **Additional Information** tab to edit the *Tax Code, Tax Item,* and *Resale Number* as necessary (see Figure 15-20).

6.   Click **OK** when finished. Then close the *Customer Contact List* report and the *Item Listing* report by clicking the close box in the upper right corner of the report.

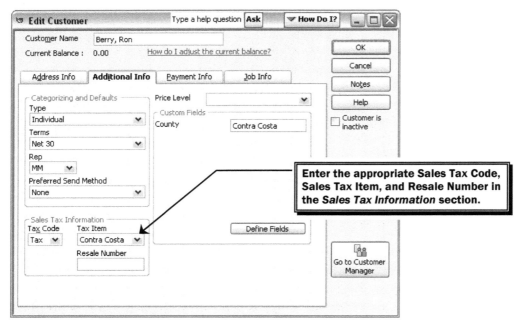

Figure 15-20 Editing the Sales Tax Information for customers

> **Did you know?**
> Jobs follow the sales tax status of their parent Customer, so no sales tax information is
> shown on the Additional Info tab of a Job record. Jobs show on reports with a colon (:)
> after the customer name. For example, Branch Opening is a job belonging to Maria Cruz
> in Figure 15-19.
>
> **Tip:**
> If the customer is not subject to sales tax, select **Non** and enter the customer's resale or
> other exemption number in the *Resale Number* field. While this is helpful for you when
> you review your records, your state may require you to retain written proof of this status.
> Consult your sales tax agency or accountant for more detailed information.

Calculating Sales Tax on Sales Forms

When you properly set up your QuickBooks items, Customers, Sales Tax Codes, and
Preferences, QuickBooks automatically calculates and tracks sales tax on each sale.

As illustrated in Figure 15-21 and detailed in the steps above, each line on a sale shows a
separate Item that is taxed according to the combination of how the Item, Tax Code, and
Customer is set up. When you set up Items, you indicate which Sales Tax Code normally
applies to that item. In addition, when you set up a customer record, you indicate the Sales
Tax Item and Sales Tax Code to be used for that customer.

Then, when you create a sale (Invoice or Sales Receipt), the Customer Tax Code and the Sales
Tax Item are taken from the customer's record and filled into the Customer Tax Code and Tax
fields on the form. The Customer Tax Code overrides the Tax Code on each line item. If
necessary, you can override the Tax Code on each line of the sales form or at the bottom of the
form. The Tax Item, which can also be overridden, determines the rate to charge on the sum
of all taxable line items on the sale.

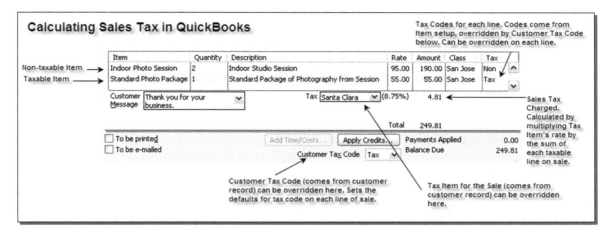

Figure 15-21 Calculating Sales Tax in QuickBooks

QuickBooks and Your Sales Tax Return

Academy Photography files its sales tax return to a single vendor called the State Board of Equalization. In this example, we will run reports for the first quarter of 2010.

The Sales Tax Liability Report

The *Sales Tax Liability* report provides you with the information you need to prepare your sales tax return, including a breakdown of sales and sales tax collected by county and sales tax agency.

1. If necessary, open the Manage Sales Tax dialog box.

2. Click the **Sales Tax Liability** link under the *Pay Sales Tax* section (see Figure 15-22).

    You can also open the *Sales Tax Liability* report by selecting *Vendors & Payables* from the *Reports* menu and then selecting *Sales Tax Liability*.

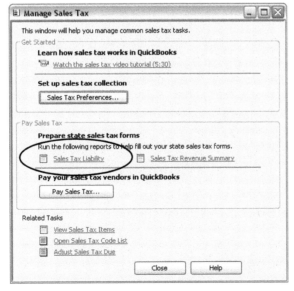

Figure 15-22 The Sales Tax Liability link in the Manage Sales Tax dialog box

3.   Set date fields and then press **Tab** (see Figure 15-23).

> **Tip:**
> If you file sales taxes quarterly, be sure to choose the *Quarterly* option in *Pay Sales Tax* section of the *Sales Tax* Preferences. Your reports will default to the last calendar quarter automatically. Similarly, for *Month* or *Annual* choices they will default to those period dates as well.

4.   You should print this report for your records. Keep the report open for now.

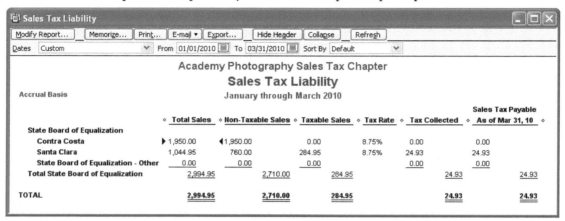

Figure 15-23 Sales Tax Liability report

The *Sales Tax Liability* report shows total sales in each county and shows the taxable sales separately from the nontaxable sales. In addition, you can see the tax rates and tax collected in each county.

The *Tax Collected* column shows how much tax you have collected on sales for the period. If you have made any sales tax payments for this period or owe tax from prior periods, the *Sales Tax Payable* column will reflect these activities.

To see the detail of transactions that comprise the *Sales Tax Liability* report, double-click on any dollar amount in the report.

The **State Board of Equalization – Other** line on the report shows any adjustments to the Sales Tax Payable account that you make using a *General Journal Entry* or the *Sales Tax Adjustment* window (see Figure 15-24). This line is zero because there are no sales tax adjustments recorded for this period.

Recording Discounts, Penalties, Interest and Rounding

The amount of sales tax you owe on the sales tax return will often not match the amount accrued in QuickBooks. This could be caused by several factors:

- Some sales tax agencies require you to round sales tax to the nearest dollar when preparing the return.
- Many sales tax agencies offer discounts for timely filing.

- Many sales tax agencies charge interest and penalties for filing late. Though interest and penalties are often paid separately, many agencies provide an option for including them with the return.

While you are preparing your sales tax return, you may need to create a *Sales Tax Adjustment.* If so, create the adjustment *before* you record the sales tax payment so that QuickBooks will show the correct amount to pay. For example, Academy Photography's sales tax payment for the first quarter of 2010 will be rounded to the nearest dollar with an adjustment of $0.07, changing the amount owed from $24.93 (see Figure 15-23) to $25.00.

1.   From the *Vendors* menu, select **Sales Tax** and then select **Adjust Sales Tax Due**.

      You could also click the **Adjust Sales Tax** link in the *Manage Sales Tax* dialog box.

2.   This opens the *Sales Tax Adjustment* window shown in Figure 15-24.

3.   Enter the date in the *Adjustment Date* field and press **Tab**.

      In the *Adjustment Date* field, enter the last day of the month for which you are filing your sales tax returns and making sales tax payments.

Figure 15-24 Sales Tax Adjustment window

4.   Select a general class in the *Class* field and press **Tab**.

      Make sure you assign a class to your adjustments. Otherwise, the adjustment will show in the *Unclassified* column on the Profit & Loss by Class report. If the adjustment is related to a specific class (e.g., tax paid on the purchase of a resale item for a specific location), you can enter the appropriate class in this field. If your adjustment to sales tax affects more than one class, you should enter separate adjustments for each class that is affected. As an alternative, you can make this adjustment using a *General Journal Entry*, which will allow you to designate multiple classes on a single adjustment.

5.   Enter a tracking number in the *Entry No.* field and press **Tab**.

When you record an adjustment to sales tax on the *Sales Tax Adjustment* window, QuickBooks creates a General Journal Entry transaction. Therefore, QuickBooks enters this number sequentially using the same numbering sequence as the General Journal Entry window.

6. Select the sales tax vendor from the *Sales Tax Vendor* drop-down list and press **Tab**.

    This is the agency to which you pay sales tax. If you file sales tax returns to more than one agency, you should enter a separate Sales Tax Adjustment for each sales tax return you file.

7. Select the **Miscellaneous** account from the *Adjustment Account* drop-down list.

    If you are adjusting your sale tax to record a timely filing discount, select an appropriate account such as *Other Income* or *Sales Tax Discount*. If you are recording Interest, choose *Interest Expense* or *Fines & Penalties* for late filing fees.

8. Select **Increase Sales Tax By** in the *Adjustment* section.

    Since you are rounding up to the nearest dollar, you need to increase the amount of sales tax you owe. If you are recording interest or penalties, select **Increase Sales Tax By** in this section. If you are recording timely filing discounts, select **Reduce Sales Tax By**.

9. Enter *0.07* in the *Amount* field and then press **Tab**.

10. Enter Sales Tax Rounding Adjustment in the Memo field.

11. Click **OK** to record the adjustment.

The Sales Tax Liability report now shows the adjustment in the *State Board of Equalization – Other* row (see Figure 15-25). The total in the *Sales Tax Payable* column now agrees to the total sales tax due on the return.

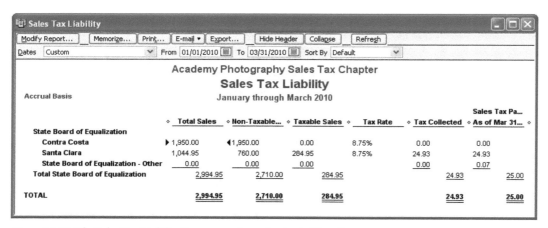

Figure 15-25 The Sales Tax Liability Report now shows the timely filing discount.

12. Close the report by clicking the X in the upper right corner of the report.

> **The accounting behind the scenes:**
> If the adjustment reduces (debits) Sales Tax Payable, QuickBooks will credit the account you enter in the *Adjustment Account* field. If the adjustment increases (credits) Sales Tax Payable, QuickBooks will debit the account you enter in the *Adjustment Account* field.

Paying Sales Tax

After you prepare your sales tax return and make necessary adjustments for discounts, interest, penalties, or rounding, create a sales tax payment for the amount you owe.

When you pay your sales tax, do not use the *Write Checks* window because the payment will not affect the *Sales Tax Items*. It also will not show properly on the Sales Tax Liability reports. To correctly pay your sales tax liability, use the **Pay Sales Tax** window.

1. From the *Home* page, select the **Manage Sales Tax** icon, if necessary.

2. Click the **Pay Sales Tax...** button in the center of the *Manage Sales Tax* dialog box.

   Alternatively, from the *Vendors* menu, select **Sales Tax** and then select **Pay Sales Tax**.

3. The *Pay Sales Tax* window displays. In the *Pay From Account* field, **Checking** already displays so press **Tab**.

   This field allows you to select the account from which you wish to pay your sales tax.

4. Enter *the check date* in the *Check Date* field and press **Tab**.

   This field is the date of *when* you are paying the sales tax.

5. Enter the desired date in the *Show sales tax due through* field and press **Tab**.

   Enter the last day of the sales tax reporting period in this field. For example, if you are filing your sales tax return for the first quarter, enter the last day of March in this field.

6. Enter a check number in the *Starting Check No* field and press **Tab**.

   QuickBooks automatically enters the next check number sequentially. Since the last check written on the Checking account was #6007, QuickBooks entered **6008** in this field.

7. Click in the **Pay** column (see Figure 15-26) on all the lines that have a balance.

   The last line shows the rounding adjustment you recorded using the Sales Tax Adjustment window.

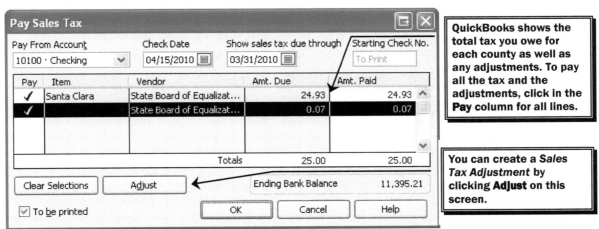

Figure 15-26 Pay Sales Tax window

8.   QuickBooks now shows a total in the Sales Tax Payment. Click **OK** to record the Sales Tax Payment.

After you record the sales tax payment, QuickBooks will create a special type of check called a Sales Tax Payment (TAXPMT) in your checking account for the total tax due to each sales tax agency (Vendor).

> **Important:**
> QuickBooks allows you to adjust the amounts in the *Amt. Paid* column. However, if you do you will retain an incorrect (overstated) balance in Sales Tax Payable for the period. If you need to change the amount of sales tax due, use a Sales Tax Adjustment, as shown in Figure 15-24. To quickly access the Sales Tax Adjustment window, click **Adjust** on the Pay Sales Tax window (see Figure 15-26).

Advanced Sales Tax Topics

Sales Tax Groups

In many states, multiple sales taxes must be collected and paid to separate agencies. In this case, you should use Sales Tax Groups to combine individual Sales Tax Items into a total tax.

Sales Tax Group Items allow you to combine multiple Sales Tax Items together so that each city, district, county, and state tax is tracked separately, while only the combined rate of all the Sales Tax Items shows on sales forms.

For example, if the county charges sales tax at a rate of 4% and the state charges sales tax at a rate of 4.25%, the combined rate collected from the customer would be 8.25%.

Setting up Sales Tax Group Items

1.   Create separate Sales Tax Items for the county and the state, as shown in Figure 15-27 and Figure 15-28.

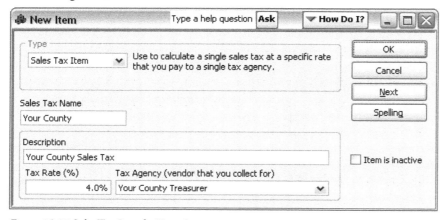

Figure 15-27 Sales Tax Item for Your County

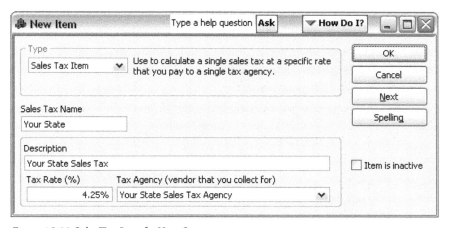

Figure 15-28 Sales Tax Item for Your State

2.   With the Item list displayed, select the **Item** menu and select **New**.

3.   Select **Sales Tax Group** from the *Type* drop-down list.

4.   Using Figure 15-29 for reference, enter the *Group Name/Number* and *Description* and then select the county and state Sales Tax Items in the *Tax Item* field at the bottom of the window.

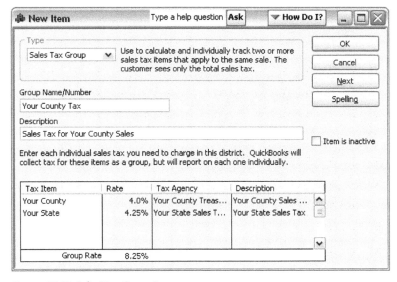

Figure 15-29 Sales Tax Group Item

5.   Click **OK** to save the *Sales Tax Group* Item.

Notice in Figure 15-29 that the combined rate of these two Sales Tax Items is 8.25%. This rate will appear on Invoices and Sales Receipts when you use this *Sales Tax Group* Item. On each sale, QuickBooks will allocate 4.0% to the county item and 4.25% to the state item. When you pay sales tax, QuickBooks will create separate checks to the county agency and the state agency for the appropriate amounts.

Categorizing Revenue Based on Sales Tax Codes

QuickBooks provides a breakdown of revenue by Sales Tax Code on the **Sales Tax Revenue Summary** report (see Figure 15-30). To display the report, select **Vendors & Payables** from the *Reports* menu and then select **Sales Tax Revenue Summary**.

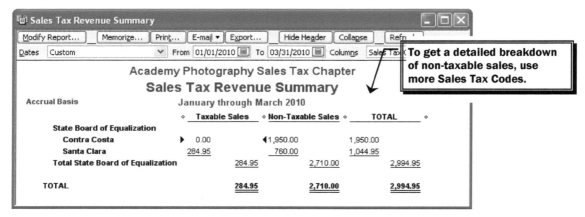

Figure 15-30 Sales Tax Revenue Summary with QuickBooks default Sales Tax Codes

If your sales tax agency requires a detailed breakdown of tax exempt sales, use Sales Tax Codes to produce the information you need. Use Sales Tax Codes to categorize your sales by the reason you charged, or did not charge, sales tax.

If you create separate Sales Tax Code for each type of non-taxable customer, like government agencies, not-for-profit organizations, or resellers, your Sales Tax Code list will look similar to the one in Figure 15-31. To display the list, select **Sales Tax Code List** from the *List* menu.

Figure 15-31 Sales Tax Code List

Then, when you use these Sales Tax Codes on sales forms according to why you charge or do not charge sales tax, QuickBooks will show a separate column for each Sales Tax Code in the *Sales Tax Revenue Summary* report (see Figure 15-32). To display the report, select **Vendors & Payables** from the *Reports* menu and then select **Sales Tax Revenue Summary**.

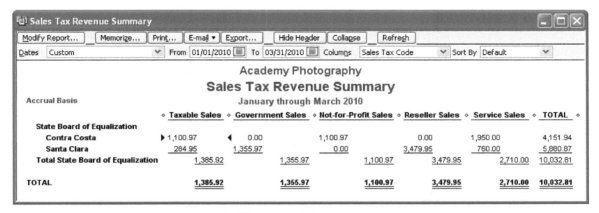

Figure 15-32 Sales Tax Revenue Summary with additional Sales Tax Codes

To view each individual sale, double-click on any amount in the **Sales Tax Revenue Summary** report. This will display a **Transaction Detail** report showing each transaction affecting that Sales Tax Code.

Sales Tax Problem Solving

Proofing Sales Tax Reports

To prepare your sales tax return, you must first validate the numbers on the Sales Tax Liability and Sales Tax Revenue Summary reports. The following sections will help you confirm the accuracy of information on sales tax reports and will provide steps for making necessary corrections.

Does the total of the Sales Tax Payable column on the Sales Tax Liability report match the Sales Tax Payable figure on the Balance Sheet?

If not, make sure that the reporting basis is the same on both reports. For example, if you accrue sales tax *Upon Receipt of Payment* make sure to use a cash basis Balance Sheet. If the two amounts still do not match the data file may be corrupted. Run **Verify Data** to check the data integrity. For more information on repairing corrupted data files see page 210.

Does Total Sales on sales tax reports agree to the total income on the Profit and Loss?

If not there may be several causes:

Items Used On Sales Forms That Post To Non-Income Accounts

QuickBooks calculates the sales columns on the sales tax reports from the total of each Invoice, Sales Receipt, and Credit Memo (net of sales tax) regardless of the type of item used. Since some items may point to non-income accounts (e.g. an item to record prepayments that posts to unearned income) the total sales on the Sales Tax Liability and Sales Tax Revenue Summary reports will not agree to total income on the Profit & Loss. To correct this problem, filter the Sales Tax Liability and Sales Tax Revenue Summary reports by account for *All Ordinary Income Accounts*. Then memorize the report for future use.

Discounts Taken on Bills

If you take discounts on bills by clicking **Set Discounts** in the Pay Bills screen, QuickBooks increases Income but does not increase sales on the Sales Tax Liability and Sales Tax Revenue Summary reports. You will need to reduce this amount for Total Income on the Profit & Loss by the amount of discounts taken before attempting to reconcile the two reports.

Transactions Other Than Sales Forms Affect Income Accounts

Only sales forms (Invoices, Sales Receipts or Credit Memos) will affect the sales amounts on the Sales Tax Liability and Sales Tax Revenue Summary reports. Using the Search command, search by *Transaction Type* for all transactions other than Invoices, Sales Receipts and Credit Memos, by *Account* for *All Ordinary Income Accounts*, and by *Date* for the current fiscal period. If QuickBooks finds any transactions you will need to reverse their effect on Income before the two reports will reconcile.

Are Some Lines on the Sales Tax Liability Report Missing a Sales Tax Item?

If so there may be several causes:

When Write Checks or Pay Bills Was Used to Pay Sales Tax

For example, assume the client paid their sales taxes for March using a Check instead of a Sales Tax Payment. The Check amount was $886.00. Notice that the Sales Tax Liability report shown in Figure 15-33 includes a negative amount for State Board of Equalization in the amount of $886.00.

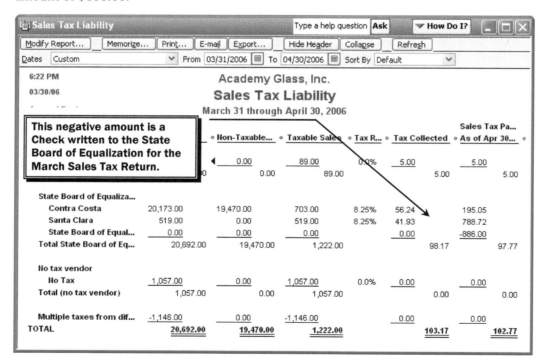

Figure 15-33 Sales Tax Liability Report showing negative amounts

If you have QuickBooks Accountant, a quick way to fix this type of problem is to use the Client Data Review tool.

1. Click **Client Review** in the toolbar, or select **Client Data Review** from the Accountant menu.

2. Scroll down in the Client Data Review screen to the Sale Tax section and click on Fix Incorrectly Recorded Sales Tax.

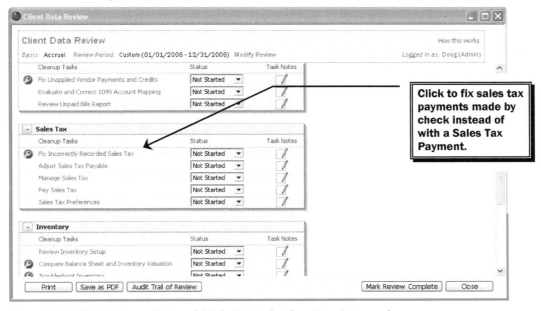

Figure 15-34 Click Fix Incorrectly Recorded Sales Tax in the Client Data Review tool.

3. Set the dates in the client data review so that is searches for the transactions within the date range of the problem transaction.

4. The screen in Figure 15-35 shows a list of checks coded to Sales Tax Payable.

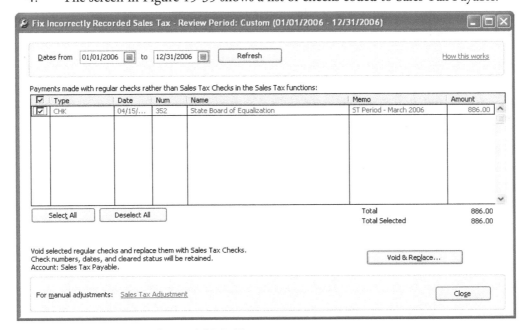

Figure 15-35 The Fix Incorrectly Recorded Sales Tax screen.

5.   Click to select the incorrectly recorded sales tax payment and press **Void & Replace**.

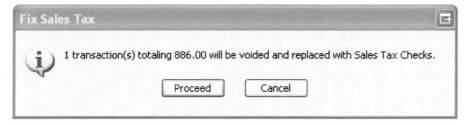

Figure 15-36 The check will be voided and new Sales Tax Payment will be created.

6.   You can see in the check register that QuickBooks has voided the original check, and
      replaced it with a TAXPMT for the same amount, and with the same check number.

Date	Number	Payee	Payment	✓	Deposit	Balance
	Type	Account Memo				
04/10/2006	343	Ace Glass	350.00			12,809.83
	CHK	Cost of Goods Solc				
04/15/2006	352	State Board of Equalization	0.00	✓		12,809.83
	CHK	Sales Tax Payable VOID: ST Period - M				
04/15/2006	352	State Board of Equalization	886.00			11,923.83
	TAXPMT	-split- Replaces check #3				
04/15/2006	To Print	Ace Glass	200.00			11,723.83
	BILLPMT	Accounts Payable Acct# 43-234				

Ending balance   5,046.31

Figure 15-37 The Voided CHK and the replacement TAXPMT for the sales tax payment

If you do not have the Account Edition (and therefore you do not have the Client Data
Review Tool), perform the steps in this exampleto locate the Check and correct the problem.

1.   To find the incorrectly recorded Check, double-click the negative number on the report.
      You will need to perform Steps 2-7 for all Checks displayed on the transaction report.

> **Note**
> If a Bill shows when you drill-down, confirm that the Bill has been paid. If the Bill has not
> been paid, simply delete the Bill. Use caution if the Bill is dated in a closed period. If the
> Bill has been paid, follow Steps 2-6 regarding the **Bill Payment** that is linked to the Bill.
> Then delete the Bill. If Journal Entries show when you double-click, see *Adjusting Sales
> Tax by Item* on page 651.

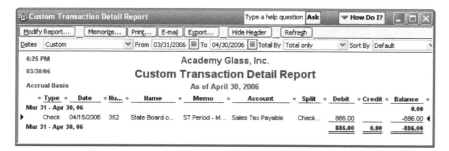

Figure 15-38 QuickBooks creates this report when you drill-down on the negative number.

2.   Note the date, payee, amount, number and cleared status of the Check. Then delete the Check.

3.   Select the *Vendors* menu, choose **Sales Tax** and then chose **Pay Sales Tax**.

4.   Set the *Check Date* field to the date of the original Check and the *Show sales tax due through* field to the last day of the sales tax report period for which the client made a payment. For example, since the client paid sales taxes for March 20015 using a Check dated 04/15/2015, enter *03/31/2015* in the *Show sales tax due through* field and enter *04/15/2015* in the *Check Date* field. Then, enter the number for the client's Check in the *Starting Check No.* field.

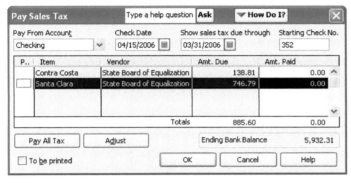

Figure 15-39 Pay Sales Tax screen showing the negative amount

5.   The total sales tax for the period does not agree to the amount of the Check because the client rounded Sales Tax up to the nearest dollar. This created a $0.40 discrepancy. Create a Sales Tax Adjustment to eliminate the discrepancy. Click **Adjust** on the Pay Sales Tax screen and enter the adjustment shown in Figure 15-40. Other possible reasons for a discrepancy include the recording of discounts, penalties, or interest.

Enter the date through which Sales Taxes were paid, not the date of the Check. You want this adjustment to show on the Sales Tax Liability report for 03/01/2006 – 03/31/2006.

Figure 15-40Sales Tax Adjustment for Rounding

> **Note**
> The amount of sales tax the client paid using a Check should agree to the sales tax return. If it does not, adjust the amount in the Pay Sales Tax screen to agree to the client's Check – *not* to the Sales Tax Return. Doing so will leave a balance in the Pay Sales Tax Window for the difference. Have the client create an additional Sales Tax Payment (TAXPMT) transaction to settle the difference with the sales tax agency.

6.   Select the taxes to pay, netting them against any adjustments and record the Tax Payment. The amount should agree to the client's check you deleted in Step 2 above.

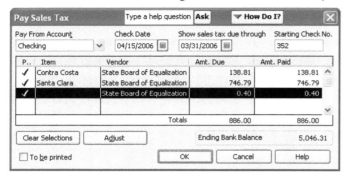

Figure 15-41 The amount of sales tax now agrees to the client's Check.

7.   If the Check used to pay sales tax had a *cleared* status (i.e. the Check was reconciled), open the bank account register, select the Sales Tax Payment (TAXPMT) and click the Check column to manually clear the Tax Payment.

> **Note**
> You must clear the Tax Payment using the Bank Reconciliation feature. Open the Bank Reconciliation screen for the account. Add $886.00 (the amount of the Tax Payment) to the amount in the *Beginning Balance* field. This will be your *Ending Balance.* Enter the date of the last bank reconciliation in the *Statement Date* field. Then click **Continue.** Locate and clear the Tax Payment. The difference field should show 0.00. Click **Reconcile Now** and print a Reconciliation Detail report for your records.

Sales Tax Adjustments Directly in the Sales Tax Register or with a Journal Entry

If a journal entry was used to adjust Sales Tax Payable, or if an entry was made directly in the Sales Tax Payable register, QuickBooks will not know where the amount should go on the sales tax reports, and it won't know what to put on the voucher for the sales tax payment. The issue here is that there is no *sales tax item* or *sales tax code* associated with the adjustment, and those are critical to the way QuickBooks tracks sales tax accruals and payments.

There are only two situations when a journal entry should be used to adjust sales tax:

1.   During setup when you're entering the balance due in excess of the amounts shown on the open invoices from before the start date.

2.   To record adjustments for rounding, discounts, penalties, and use tax accruals. Note that the *Adjust Sales Tax* form creates a journal entry and it should be used for these types of adjustments only.

To address the problem when a journal entry was made for Sales Tax Payable, follow the steps in this example:

1.   Confirm that the amount is not an adjustment for rounding, discounts penalties, interest, use tax or other amounts that appear on the sales tax return (e.g. sales tax paid on resale merchandise). Inspect the Journal Entry and review the memo information to determine the reason for the adjustment.

2. If you conclude that it is adjusting for a customer return, you should void the journal entry and record the customer return using a credit memo with full detail of what was returned, and the sales tax credit will be calculated automatically for you.

3. If the adjustment was for something other than a customer return, you may want to replace the journal entry with a full adjustment of sales tax by item. For more information, see *Adjusting Sales Tax by Item* on page 651.

Adjusting Sales Tax by Item

For all adjustments to sales tax other than for recording discounts, interest, penalties and rounding, you'll need to adjust Sales Tax Payable in a way that causes both the Sales Tax Payable account *and* the Sales Tax Items to reflect the change. In this case, do not use a Sales Tax Adjustment, a journal entry or a register transaction to adjust Sales Tax Payable. If you do, the Sales Tax Liability report, and the Pay Sales Tax screen *may* show a positive or negative offset on a separate line called with no Sales Tax Item.

In this example, let's assume that the Contra Costa tax item liability should be $340.31 and Santa Clara should be $444.18. Both are overstated by $2,500.00 (see Figure 15-42).

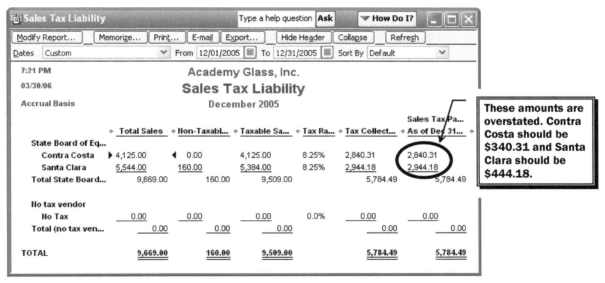

Figure 15-42 Sales Tax Liability report

To create an adjustment that affects each sales tax item individually, use a Sales Receipt or Credit Memo to adjust sales tax as follows:

1. Create an Other Current Asset account called *Adjustment Clearing*.

2. Create a taxable Sales Tax Code called *ADJ*.

3. Create a Customer called *Accounting Adjustments* that uses the ADJ tax code.

4. Create an Other Charge Item called *Adjustment Clearing* that posts to the *Adjustment Clearing* Other Current Asset account and uses the ADJ tax code.

5. Create a Sales Tax Item called *No Tax* with a 0% rate.

6.   Create a Credit Memo and enter the *ADJ* code at the bottom and the *No Tax* Item in the *Tax* field at the bottom of the Credit Memo (see Figure 15-43).

7.   In the body of the Credit Memo, enter the Sales Tax Item (or Items) that needs to be credited. In the Amount column, enter the total amount of the debit that applies to that item (see Figure 15-43).

> **Note**
> If you need to credit Sales Tax Payable, perform Steps 1-5 above but use a Sales Receipt instead of a Credit Memo.

8.   Using the *Adjustment Clearing* Item, enter an offset amount to bring the Credit Memo balance to zero (see Figure 15-43).

> **Note**
> If the offset to Sales Tax Payable is an ordinary income account, use an Item that points to the appropriate income account instead of the *Adjustment Clearing* Item. Also, use a non-taxable Sales Tax Code called ADJ to record this line of the Invoice.

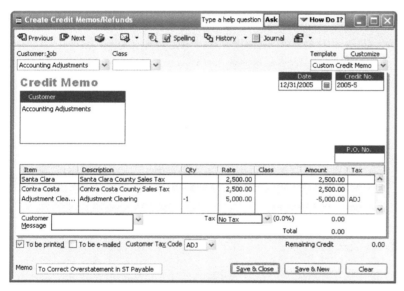

Figure 15-43 Credit Memo to Adjust Sales Tax by Item

9.   Click **Save & Close** to record the adjustment.

10.   The Sales Tax Liability report will show 5,000 additional non-taxable sales, but since it's in a separate section of the report, you can ignore it when prepare the sales tax return. Although this is not ideal, the only other way to accomplish this adjustment would be to edit each transaction that erroneously charged tax.

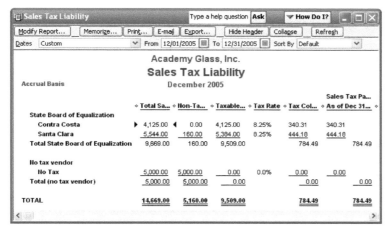

Figure 15-44 Sales Tax Liability Report

11.   The Pay Sales Tax screen (and Sales Tax Liability Report) now shows the correct liability amounts for both Santa Clara and Contra Costa (see Figure 15-45).

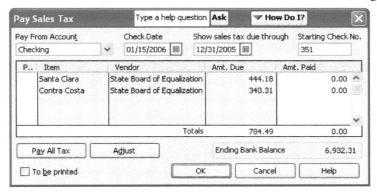

Figure 15-45 Each Sales Tax Item shows the correct amount.

12.   Enter a journal entry to clear the balance in the Adjustment Clearing account, using the appropriate account(s) as an offset. Note that in some cases, this may involve refunding overcharged taxes to customer.

Sales Tax and Cash Basis

There are two separate settings for cash basis in QuickBooks. One is a setting for financial reports (Edit>Preferences>Reports & Graphs>Company Settings), and the other is specifically for sales tax reports (Edit>Preferences>Sales Tax>Company Preferences). Depending on how you have those settings, you may find discrepancies between the balance in Sales Tax Payable on the Balance Sheet (or other financial reports) compared with the Sales Tax Liability reports.

For example, if you have the reports set to Accrual Basis, but you have the Sales Tax set to *Upon Receipt of Payment*, then the Balance Sheet will most likely show a higher amount due in Sales Tax Payable than shows on the Sales Tax Liability reports. This is because the Sales Tax Liability reports will remove any unpaid invoices from the balance due, while the accrual Balance Sheet will include them. For this situation, to verify that the file is correct, make sure you compare the cash basis balance sheet with the cash basis Sales Tax reports.

Summary

Sales tax tracking is automatic and runs smoothly if you set up and operate QuickBooks correctly.

If your QuickBooks file was not set up correctly, or if the Sales Tax feature has not been properly used in the past, you will probably have to diagnose and repair the problems before sales tax will operate correctly for the future. It is very important that your setup and data entry procedures are accurate in order to keep the sales tax feature working smoothly.

In this chapter, you learned that QuickBooks allows you to track sales tax that you collect from your customers. You should now be familiar with how to use QuickBooks to do all of the following:

- Activate Sales Tax and set Sales Tax Preferences (page 625)
- Use Sales Tax Items on Sales Forms (page 629)
- Set up Sales Tax Items (page 629)
- Use Sales Tax Codes on Sales Forms (page 631)
- Set up Sales Tax Codes (page 632)
- Assign Sales Tax Codes to Items (page 633)
- Assign Sales Tax Codes to Customers (page 634)
- Use QuickBooks reports to assist in preparing your sales tax return (page 637)
- Adjust Sales Tax Payable (page 638)
- Pay Sales Tax (page 641)
- Set up and use Sales Tax Groups (page 642)
- Categorize Revenue by Sales Tax Code (page 644)
- Solve problems in Sales Tax (page 645)
- Sales Tax and Cash Basis (page 653)

Chapter 16 Adjustments and Year-End Procedures

Objectives

After completing this chapter, you should be able to:

- Process 1099 forms for vendors (page 655)
- Edit, void, and delete transactions (page 657)
- Track fixed assets (page 662)
- Memorize and schedule transactions to be automatically entered (page 666)
- Close the year and enter special transactions for sole proprietorships and partnerships (page 670)

In this chapter, you will learn how to process 1099s, edit and void transactions in current and closed periods, and you'll learn how to use journal entries and zero-dollar checks to adjust balances and close the year. You will also learn how to track your fixed assets, memorize transactions, and use the closing date in QuickBooks.

Processing 1099s

At the end of each year, you must prepare and send an IRS Form 1099 to each of your eligible vendors and to the IRS. Form 1099 must be sent to your vendors by the last day of January following the applicable year.

Form 1099-MISC is used to report payments made to vendors who performed business-related services for your company. Typically, the term *services* includes work by independent contractors, professional services, rent payments, commissions, and so on. Before preparing 1099-forms, you should have a clear understanding of which vendors should receive them, as well as what types of payments are eligible for reporting on Form 1099. For IRS instructions on this topic, you may visit the IRS forms and publication site and search for 1099 instructions at http://www.irs.gov/formspubs/index.html.

> **Note:**
> QuickBooks is only capable of preparing 1099-MISC. If you need to prepare other types of 1099s (e.g. 1099-INT, 1099-DIV), you will need to do so outside of QuickBooks.
>
> IRS regulations require that if you file 250 or more 1099 forms of any type, you must submit them electronically or magnetically. Electronic payment (e-payment) of 1099-MISC forms is only possible with QuickBooks Enhanced Payroll Service.

When set up properly, QuickBooks automatically tracks the details of your payments to 1099 vendors. Each time you make a payment to a 1099 vendor and use an account designated as a 1099-related expense, QuickBooks automatically adds the payment to the vendor's 1099.

At the end of the year, you can view your 1099-related payments by creating a **1099 Detail** report. After verifying that the report includes the right vendors and covers the right accounts, you can print 1099s directly onto preprinted 1099 forms.

> **Note:**
> Intuit no longer offers a free one-time download of the current tax tables as it did in times past. To download new tax tables and payroll forms, you will need to subscribe to a QuickBooks payroll service. Accurate tax tables are required to print data correctly on forms in the years following the release date of your QuickBooks version.

The 1099 Wizard

QuickBooks uses the **1099 and 1096 Wizard** to help create accurate 1099 and 1096 forms. Once activated, the wizard will allow users to go through four steps to process these forms:

1.   Review and edit 1099 vendors.

2.   Setup account mapping preferences for 1099s.

3.   Run a summary report to review 1099 data.

4.   Print 1099 and 1096 forms.

To activate the QuickBooks **1099 and 1096 Wizard**, follow the steps in this example:

1.   Select **Print 1099s/1096** from the *Vendors* menu.

2.   QuickBooks displays the **1099 and 1096 Wizard** window (see Figure 16-1). We will use the 4-Step process above to create and print 1099 and 1096 forms.

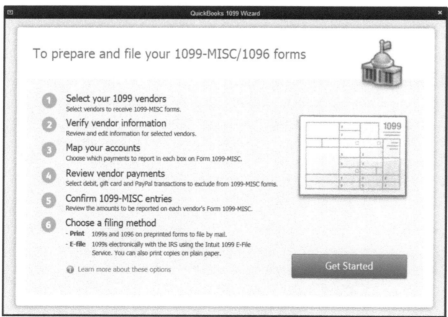

Figure 16-1 QuickBooks 1099 and 1096 Wizard

Editing 1099 Information in Vendor Records

In this first step, verify your 1099 Vendors. You can edit each 1099 vendor to confirm or update that you have their complete name, address, and identification number (e.g., social security number or federal employer identification number). Vendors are required by law to provide you with this information and it is best to collect this data when you first engage the vendor. Require the vendor to complete a W-9 Form before they begin services so that their information is on file. You can download W-9 forms in a PDF version from the IRS at http://www.irs.gov/formspubs/index.html. The IRS may reject 1099s that you submit if the taxpayer ID is incorrect.

To review and edit the 1099 vendors, follow the steps in this example:

1. QuickBooks will display the *Select your 1099 vendors* window showing the selected 1099 vendors (see Figure 16-2). Review the *Create Form 1099-MISC* column to verify that all vendors eligible for 1099s are checked. Click **Continue**.

Figure 16-2 Verify your 1099 vendors

2. The Verify your 1099 vendors' information window appears. You can edit any vendor information. (see Figure 16-3). Double click on the address information to see multiple lines. The address information is particularly important if the forms are mailed, however, the correct address is also required for e-filing. Click **Continue**.

Figure 16-3 Verify your 1099 vendors' information window

3.   The *Map vendor payment accounts* window appears. Check **Report all payments in Box 7**
      (see Figure 16-4).

      Account mapping allows you to select the QuickBooks accounts you use to track 1099
      vendor payments and the threshold amount you will report to the IRS. Since this is a
      company-wide preference, only the Administrator can modify the 1099 mapping
      preferences.

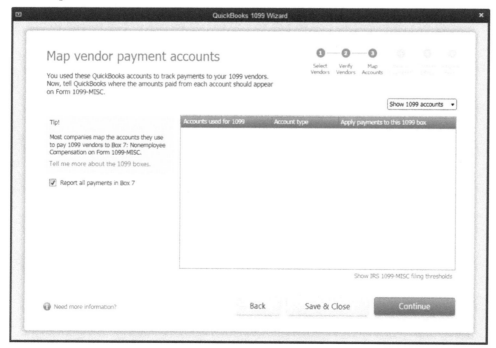

Figure 16-4 The Map vendor payment accounts window – your screen may vary

> **Note:**
> If you're uncertain which box to map an account to, talk with your accountant or QuickBooks Pro Advisor.
>
> Also, when Items are used to track purchases, these Items correspond to an account in the Chart of Accounts list. Therefore, when you use Items to track payments to 1099 vendors, make sure the proper 1099 accounts are used when creating new Items.

4. Click **Continue** on the remainder of the *QuickBooks 1099 Wizard* windows after reviewing the options and confirming the information. Click **Save & Close** on the final window without filing.

Editing, Voiding, and Deleting Transactions

Unlike many other accounting programs, QuickBooks allows you to change any transaction at any time as long as you have sufficient privileges. However, you should almost never change transactions dated in closed accounting periods, or transactions that have been reconciled with a bank statement.

> **Key Term:**
> For the purposes of this discussion, a *Closed Accounting Period* is a period for which you've already issued financial statements and/or filed tax returns.

When you change or delete a transaction, QuickBooks updates the General Ledger with your change, as of the date of the modified or deleted transaction. Therefore, if you modify or delete transactions in a closed accounting period, your QuickBooks financial statements will change for that period, causing discrepancies between your QuickBooks reports and your tax return.

In QuickBooks, the *Closing Date* field is used to lock your data file to prevent users from making changes on or before a specified date. See page 100 for information about setting the Closing Date in QuickBooks.

> **Tip:**
> Using the *Closing Date*, a period can be closed even if there is not a tax return for the period. For example, you can close the books through January 31, 2007, even though your last tax return was dated December 31, 2006. If management makes decisions based on *printed* financial information dated January 31, 2007, any changes to QuickBooks information dated before January 31, 2007 will cause the reports in QuickBooks to disagree with the printed reports. Also, many companies submit financial information to third parties (e.g., banks) during their tax year on a monthly or quarterly basis.

Some companies close their books monthly, but other companies only close the books quarterly or annually. Make sure you know how often your company closes periods before you make changes to transactions that might affect closed periods.

> **Tip:**
> At the very least, you should lock the file at the end of each fiscal and/or calendar year. You may also choose to lock the file monthly, after you perform bank reconciliations and adjusting entries for the month.

Editing Transactions

From time to time, you may need to modify transactions to correct posting errors. To edit (or modify) a transaction in QuickBooks, change the data directly on the form. For example, if you forgot to add a charge for an Outdoor Photo Shoot to Invoice 2007-106 and you have not already sent the invoice to your customer or client, you will need to add a line for the photo session on the previously created invoice.

To edit an existing transaction, follow the steps in this example:

1.   Navigate to the required invoice (see Figure 16-5).

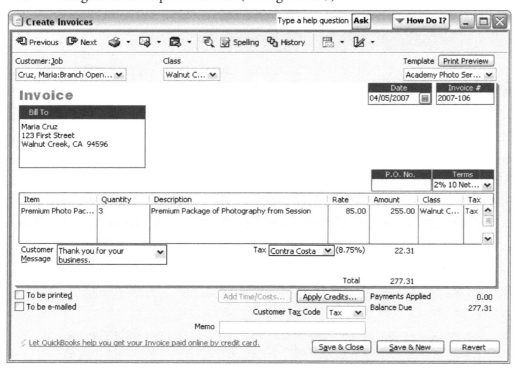

Figure 16-5 Edit the transaction on the Create Invoices form

2.   Click on the second line in the main body of the invoice and enter the corrected item in the *Item* column (see Figure 16-6).

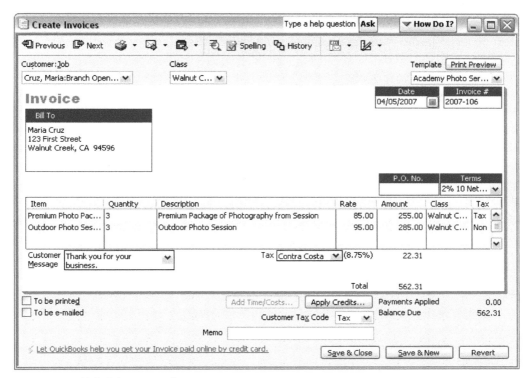

Figure 16-6 Add the labor Item to the Invoice.

3.   Click **Save & Close** to save the Invoice.

4.   On the *Recording Transaction* dialog box, click **Yes**. This message confirms that you really want to change the transaction (see Figure 16-7).

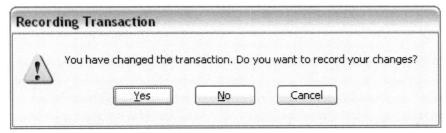

Figure 16-7 Recording Transaction window

> **Note:**
> Do not use this method of changing transactions if you have already sent the Invoice to the customer. In this case, you will need to create a new Invoice with the separate charge. Also, you should never change transactions dated in a closed accounting period.

Voiding and Deleting Transactions

Voiding and deleting transactions both have the same effect on the General Ledger – the effect is to zero out the debits and the credits specified by the transaction.

There is one significant difference between voiding and deleting. When you void a transaction, QuickBooks keeps a record of the date, number, and detail of the transaction. When you delete a transaction, QuickBooks removes it completely from your file.

The *Audit Trail* feature of QuickBooks tracks changes and deletions of transactions. The Audit Trail report lists each accounting transaction and every addition, deletion, or modification that affects that transaction. For more information about the *Audit Trail*, see the QuickBooks Onscreen Help.

In addition to the audit trail, QuickBooks has a *Voided/Deleted Transactions* report that lists all voided and deleted transactions. This report is very useful when you have a number of users in a file and transactions seem to disappear, since the report shows the time, date and user name of the changes or deletions.

In general, voiding is better than deleting transactions. In either case, make sure you keep a record of voided and deleted transactions. The record should include the date of the voided or deleted transaction and the reason for it.

To **delete** a transaction:

1. Select the transaction you wish to delete; it may be displayed in a register or form.
2. Select the **Edit** menu and then select **Delete** (or press **Ctrl+D**).
3. On the *Delete Transaction* window, click **OK.**

To **void** a transaction:

1. Select the transaction in a register or display it in the form.
2. Select the **Edit** menu and then select **Void** (or right-click on the transaction and select **Void** from the shortcut menu).
3. Click the **Record** button at the bottom of the window.
4. If you attempt to close the window without recording the transaction, the *Recording Transaction* window displays. If this is the case, click **Yes** to record the transaction.

> **Note:**
> Proper accounting procedures do not allow you to simply delete transactions at will. However, in some cases it is perfectly fine to use the **Delete** command. For example, it is acceptable to delete a check that you have not printed. On the other hand, if you have already printed the check, you should **Void** the check instead of deleting it. That way, you will have a record of the voided check and keep the numbering sequence intact in the register.

Tracking Fixed Assets

When you purchase office equipment, buildings, computers, vehicles, or other assets that have useful lives of more than one year, you'll want to add them to your Balance Sheet and record the depreciation of the assets periodically. Check with your accountant if you need help deciding which purchases should be added to a fixed asset account.

To track your asset values, create a separate fixed asset account for each grouping of assets you want to track on the Balance Sheet. Several accounts, such as *Furniture and Equipment, Vehicles, and Accumulated Depreciation* are created with the default Chart of Accounts.

Figure 16-8 Fixed Assets and Accumulated Depreciation Accounts

---

The accounting behind the scenes

As you purchase fixed assets, code the purchases to the appropriate Fixed Asset account. This increases (debits) the fixed asset account and decreases (credits) the checking account (assuming you used a check).

When you record depreciation, the entry will increase (debit) the *Depreciation Expense* account and increase (credit) the *Accumulated Depreciation* account. The *Accumulated Depreciation* account is known as a "contra" account because it normally carries a credit balance (i.e., a negative balance) given that asset accounts typically have debit balances.

Key Term:

A *Contra Account* is an account that carries a balance that is opposite from the normal balance for that account type. For example, an asset that carries a credit balance is a contra asset account since assets normally carries a debit balance. Also, an income account that carries a debit balance (e.g., Sales Discounts) is a contra income account since income accounts normally carries a credit balance.

To see the Net Book Value of Fixed Assets for *Furniture and Equipment* on the Balance Sheet, select **Company & Financial** from the *Reports* menu and then select **Balance Sheet Standard**. Enter the date in the *As of* field and press **Tab**. You will now be able to view the *Cost, Accumulated Depreciation*, and NBV of the Company's Furniture and Equipment Fixed Assets (see Figure 16-9).

Key Term:

Net Book Value (NBV) is the book value of your Fixed Asset at any point in time. Calculate NBV by subtracting the amount of use of the asset (accumulated depreciation) from the original purchase price to determine the value of the remaining useful life. As you can see in Figure 16-9, the original cost of Furniture and Equipment is $13,250. The accumulated depreciation to date is $1,325. Therefore, the Net Book Value of *Furniture and Equipment* is $11,925.

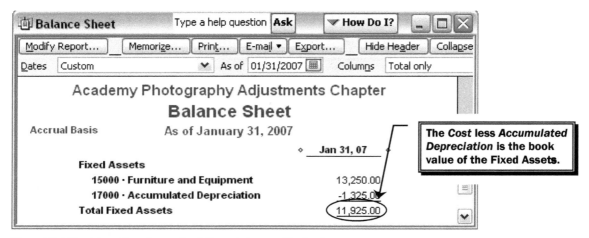

Figure 16-9 Fixed Asset Cost, Accumulated Depreciation, and book value

Another way to track your asset values would be to create three accounts for each group of assets. A control (or master) account and two subaccounts.

See Figure 16-10 for an example of how this could look in your *Chart of Accounts*.

The control account must be a Fixed Asset type of account in the *Chart of Accounts*. Each control account will have two subaccounts: a *Cost* account and an *Accumulated Depreciation* account.

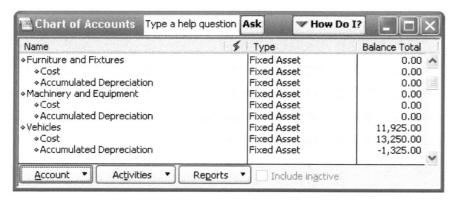

Figure 16-10 Another Way to Set-up Fixed Assets in the Chart of Accounts

> **Note:**
> Alphabetically, the subaccount *Accumulated Depreciation* precedes the subaccount *Cost*. Therefore, QuickBooks automatically places *Accumulated Depreciation* above *Cost* when you create the accounts. However, the preferred format for financial statements lists *Accumulated Depreciation* (the contra account) below *Cost* (the asset account). To reorder the accounts to match the preferred format, open the Chart of Accounts list. Then, click the diamond next to the *Accumulated Depreciation* subaccount and drag it below the *Cost* subaccount.

Using the Fixed Asset List

If you have QuickBooks Pro, Premier or Enterprise, you can track detailed information about your company's Fixed Assets. You can set up detailed information about each asset using the

Fixed Asset Item List. Then, if your accountant uses QuickBooks Accountant, he or she can use the Fixed Asset Manager to individually calculate and track depreciation on each asset.

> **Accounting Tip:**
> Conduct a physical inventory of fixed assets annually to assure proper tracking and reporting. Your accountant may currently maintain this list for your company. QuickBooks can track the original cost for each Fixed Asset and the related depreciation for each asset of the company.

To set up your assets in the *Fixed Asset Item List*, follow the steps in this example:

1.   Select the **Lists** menu and then select **Fixed Asset Item List**.

2.   Select the **Item** menu at the bottom of the *Fixed Assed Item List* window and then select **New** (or press CTRL+N). See Figure 16-11.

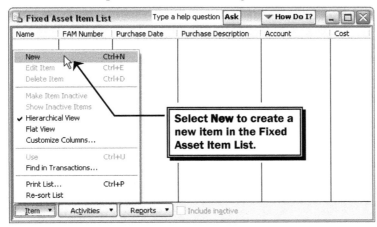

Figure 16-11 Fixed Asset Item List

3.   Complete the information for the delivery truck (see Figure 16-12).

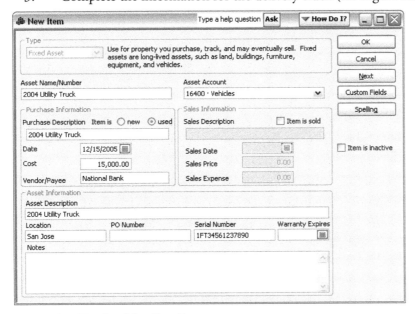

Figure 16-12 New Fixed Asset Item Entry

4.   Press **OK** to save the fixed asset record.

> **Important:**
> There is no accounting entry made when you set up a fixed asset in the *Fixed Asset Item List*. This is why you must enter the opening balances for your fixed asset accounts in addition to setting them up in the *Fixed Asset Item List.*

Calculating and Recording Depreciation

If your accountant has QuickBooks Accountant, he or she can use the Fixed Asset Manager to calculate and enter depreciation into your company file. You can find out more about the Fixed Asset Manager on page 410.

If you prefer to calculate the depreciation yourself, rather than relying on your Accountant, you can select **Planning & Budgeting** from the *Company* menu, select **Decision Tools**, and then finally select **Depreciate Your Assets**. Follow the onscreen wizard to calculate the annual depreciation for each of your fixed assets.

Otherwise, to record depreciation each month using the straight-line method, determine the total annual depreciation, divide that amount by 12, and then record the depreciation expense each month using a journal entry.

1.   Select **Make General Journal Entries** from the *Company* menu.

2.   Create a General Journal such as shown in Figure 16-13.

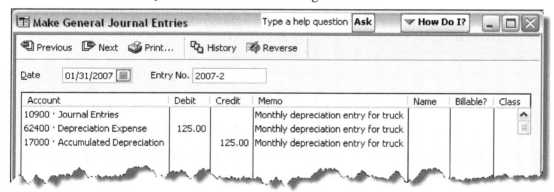

Figure 16-13 Monthly Depreciation Entry for 2004 Truck

Memorized Transactions

If you frequently enter the same transaction (or similar ones), you can memorize and schedule the entry of the transaction. For example, if you want QuickBooks to automatically enter the depreciation journal entry each month, you can memorize the transaction and then schedule it to be automatically entered.

Memorizing a Journal Entry

In this example, we will memorize the depreciation on a truck:

1.   Before saving the General Journal Entry, select **Memorize General Journal** from the *Edit* menu (or press CTRL+M).

2.   Enter *2004 Truck Depreciation* in the *Name* field.

      Use names that you will recognize so that you can easily find this transaction in the **Memorized Transaction** list.

3.   Set the fields as shown in Figure 16-14 to indicate when and how often you want the transaction entered and then click **OK**.

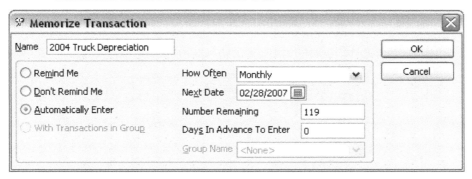

Figure 16-14 2004 Truck Depreciation memorized information

4.   Select **Save & Close** to record the Journal Entry. If QuickBooks displays a dialog box regarding *Tracking Fixed Assets on Journal Entries*, click **OK**.

5.   Close all your open windows by clicking the close box in the upper right corner.

> **Did You Know?**
> You can memorize *most* transactions in QuickBooks. Just display the transaction, then select **Memorize [Transaction Name]** from the *Edit* menu, or right click on the transaction and select **Memorize [Transaction Name]**. You can also press CTRL+M. The Memorized Transaction List contains all the transactions that you have memorized. To display this list, select **Memorized Transaction List** from the *List* menu.

Now, every time you launch QuickBooks, it checks your *Memorized Transaction* list for transactions that need to be entered automatically. If the system date is on or after the date in the *Next Date* field (minus the number in the *Days In Advance To Enter* field), QuickBooks will ask you if you want to enter the memorized transaction (see Figure 16-15).

When you launch QuickBooks and the scheduled transaction is due to be entered, the message in Figure 16-15 will display. If you click **Now**, QuickBooks will automatically enter that transaction as a General Journal entry.

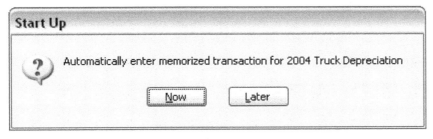

Figure 16-15 Memorized transaction reminder on Start Up

We do not want to enter the transaction into the General Journal now, so do not re-launch QuickBooks. If you have re-launched QuickBooks and this dialog box displays, click the **Later** button, and then click **OK** when a warning appears so the transaction will not be recorded.

Deleting, Rescheduling, and Editing Memorized Transactions

Rescheduling or Renaming Memorized Transactions

To edit the schedule or name of a memorized transaction, follow the steps in this example:

1. Select the **Memorized Transaction List** from the *Lists* menu, or press CTRL+T.

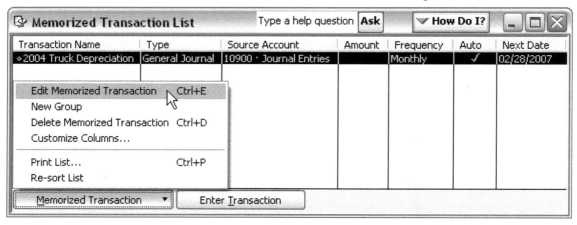

Figure 16-16 Memorized Transaction List

2. Select the 2004 Truck Depreciation transaction in the *Memorized Transaction List*. Select **Edit Memorized Transaction** from the *Memorized Transaction* drop-down list or press CTRL+E (see Figure 16-16).

3. The *Schedule Memorized Transaction* window displays (see Figure 16-17). This window allows you to reschedule or rename the transaction, but it does not allow you to edit the actual transaction. Click **Cancel** and close all open windows.

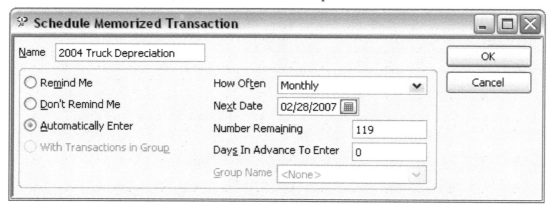

Figure 16-17 Schedule Memorized Transaction window

Editing Memorized Transactions

In addition to editing the schedule or other attributes of a memorized transaction, sometimes it is necessary to edit the actual contents of the transaction such as the items, prices, or coding.

To edit the contents of a memorized transaction, follow the steps in this example:

1. Select the **Memorized Transaction List** from the *Lists* menu, or press CTRL+T.

2. To edit the 2004 Truck Depreciation memorized transaction, double-click it in the **Memorized Transaction List**.

    This displays a new transaction (see Figure 16-18) with the contents of the memorized transaction. You can change anything on the transaction and then rememorize it. In this case we will add the **San Jose** class.

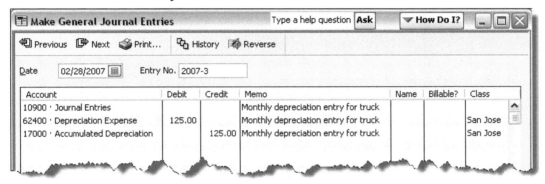

Figure 16-18 Edit the transaction as necessary

3. To rememorize the transaction, select **Memorize General Journal** from the *Edit* menu, or press CTRL+M.

4. To save your edited transaction in the *Memorized Transaction* list click **Replace** (see Figure 16-19).

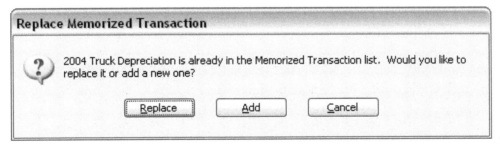

Figure 16-19 Replace Memorized Transaction message

5. Click **Clear** to erase the contents of the Journal Entry and then click **Save & Close**. This will save the changes to the memorized transaction without entering the transaction in the General Journal.

Deleting Memorized Transactions

To delete a memorized transaction, follow the steps in this example:

1. Select the **Memorized Transaction List** from the *Lists* menu, or press CTRL+T.

2. **2004 Truck Depreciation** is already selected because it is the first and only Memorized Transaction on the list.

3. Select **Delete Memorized Transaction** from the *Memorized Transaction* drop-down list, or press CTRL+D (see Figure 16-20).

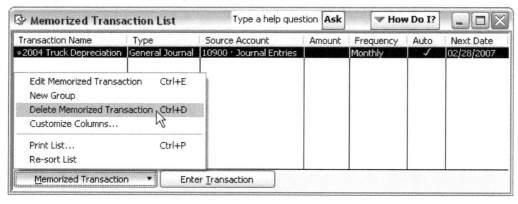

Figure 16-20 Deleting Memorized Transaction option

4. For now, click **Cancel** on the *Delete Memorized Transaction* dialog box so the memorized transaction will not be deleted (see Figure 16-21).

Figure 16-21 Delete Memorized Transaction

5. Close all open windows.

Closing the Year

At the end of each year, accounting principles dictate that you must enter an adjusting entry to transfer net income or loss into the Retained Earnings (or Owners Equity) account. This entry is known as the *closing entry*.

However, in QuickBooks **you do not need to make this entry**. QuickBooks does it for you, automatically. When you create a Balance Sheet, QuickBooks calculates the balance in Retained Earnings by adding together the total net income for all prior years. At the end of your company's fiscal year, QuickBooks automatically transfers the net income into Retained Earnings.

On the left side of the example in Table 16-1, notice that the Balance Sheet for 12/31/2013 shows net income for the year is $100,000.00. The right side shows the same Balance Sheet, but for the next day (January 1, 2015). Since January is in a new year, last year's net income has been automatically transferred to the Retained Earnings account.

Equity on Dec 31, 2015		Equity on Jan 1, 2016	
Opening Bal Equity	0.00	Opening Bal Equity	0.00
Preferred Stock	50,000.00	Preferred Stock	50,000.00
Common Stock	75,000.00	Common Stock	75,000.00
Retained Earnings	100,000.00	Retained Earnings	200,000.00
Net Income	100,000.00	Net Income	0.00
Total Equity	325,000.00	Total Equity	325,000.00

Table 16-1 Example of QuickBooks closing entry

There are two advantages to QuickBooks automatically closing the year for you. First, you do not have to create the year-end entry, which can be time-consuming. Second, the details of your income and expenses are not erased each year, as some programs require.

Closing the Accounting Period

The following is a list of actions you should take at the end of each accounting period. Perform these steps as often as you close your company's books. Many companies close monthly or quarterly, while some close yearly. No matter when you close, these steps are to help you create proper reports that incorporate year-end transactions. These entries may be non-cash entries such as depreciation, prepaid expense allocations, and adjustments to equity to properly reflect the closing of the year.

At the end of the year (or period), consider doing some or all of the following:

1. Enter depreciation entries.

2. Reconcile cash, credit card, and loan accounts with the period-end statements.

3. If your business has inventory, perform a physical inventory on the last day of the year. Following the inventory count, enter an Inventory Adjustment transaction in QuickBooks if necessary.

4. If you are on the accrual basis of accounting, prepare General Journal Entries to accrue expenses and revenues. Ask your accountant for help with these entries.

5. If your business is a partnership, enter a General Journal Entry to distribute net income for the year to each of the partner's capital accounts. If your business is a sole proprietorship, enter a General Journal Entry closing *Owners Draw* into *Owners Equity*. See the section below for more information.

6. Run reports for the year and verify their accuracy. Enter adjusting entries as necessary and rerun the reports.

7. Print and file the following reports as of your closing date: General Ledger, Balance Sheet Standard, Statement of Cash Flows, Trial Balance, Inventory Valuation Summary, and Profit & Loss Standard for the year.

8.   Back up your data file on a special backup drive, network server, or CD ROM. The year-end backup should be permanent and stored in a safe place.

9.   Set the closing date to the last day of the period and set a closing date password to prevent transactions in the closed period from being changed. See page 100 for details on setting the closing date.

10.   Consider using the Cleanup Data File utility. This will condense (reduce) the size of your data file, but will probably not be necessary every year. Data file cleanup is an involved process that should be done by your accountant or QuickBooks consultant.

> **Note:**
> *The Cleanup Data File* utility is only covered in the Sleeter Group's *Consultant's Reference Guide*. For additional information on condensing, consult the QuickBooks onscreen help.

Recording Closing Entries for Sole Proprietorships and Partnerships

> **Note:**
> **Do not enter the transactions in this section.** However, do familiarize yourself with these issues, so that you can properly close the year in a sole proprietorship or partnership company.

Sole proprietorships have the following accounts in the Equity section of the *Chart of Accounts* (see Figure 16-22).

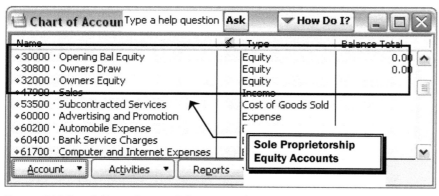

Figure 16-22 Sample Equity Section - Sole Proprietorships

Partnerships have the following accounts (or similar accounts) in the Equity section of the *Chart of Accounts* (see Figure 16-23). Although this list of accounts has a *Retained Earnings* account, it will be cleared out at the end of each year to keep it from accumulating a balance.

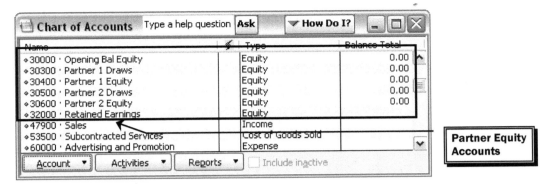

Figure 16-23 Sample Equity section - Partnerships

Throughout the year, as owners put money into and take money out of the business, you will add transactions that increase and decrease the appropriate equity accounts. In a sole proprietorship, you will use the *Owners Equity* and *Owners Draw* accounts. In a partnership, you will use the Equity and Draws accounts for each partner.

To record owners' investments in the company, enter a deposit transaction in your *Checking* account (or the account to which you make deposits), and enter *Owners Equity* in the *From Account* field (see Figure 16-24).

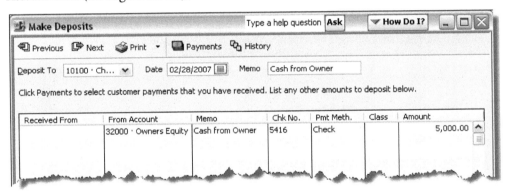

Figure 16-24 Record owner's investments in the Make Deposits window

To record owner's withdrawals from the company, enter a check transaction in the *Checking* account (or the account from which the owner draws money), and enter **Owners Draw** in the *Account* field (see Figure 16-25).

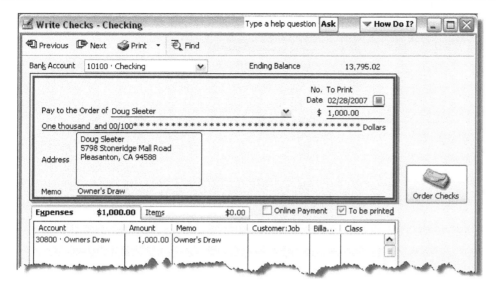

Figure 16-25 Record owner's withdrawals as a check transaction

Closing Sole Proprietorship Draw Accounts

At the end of each year, you will create a General Journal Entry to zero out the *Owners Draw* account and close it into *Owners Equity* (see Figure 16-26).

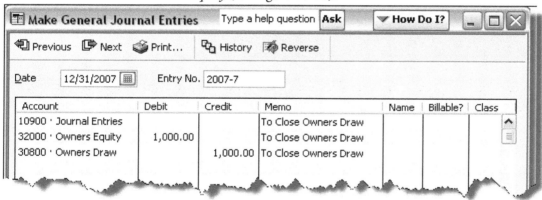

Figure 16-26 General Journal Entry to close Owners Draw

To find the amounts for this journal entry, create a **Trial Balance** report for the end of the year. Use the balance in the *Owners Draw* account for a General Journal Entry to close the account. For example, if your **Trial Balance** shows a *debit* balance of $5000.00 in *Owners Draw*, enter $**5000.00** in the *credit* column on the *Owners Draw* line of this General Journal Entry. Then enter a debit to the *Owners Equity* account to make the entry balance.

Closing Partnership Draws Accounts

To close the *Partners Draws* accounts into each *Partners Equity* account, use a General Journal Entry like the one shown in Figure 16-27. Use the same process explained above to get the numbers from the year-end Trial Balance.

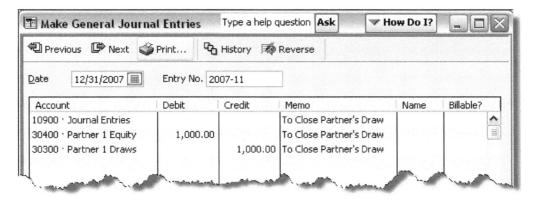

Figure 16-27 General Journal Entry to close partner's draws accounts

Distributing Net Income to Partners

With partnerships, you need to use a General Journal Entry to distribute the profits of the company into each of the partner's profit accounts. After making all adjusting entries, create a *Profit & Loss* report for the year. Use the *Net Income* figure at the bottom of the *Profit & Loss* report to create the General Journal Entry, in Figure 16-28. In this example, assume net income for the year is $50,000 and that there are two equal partners in the business.

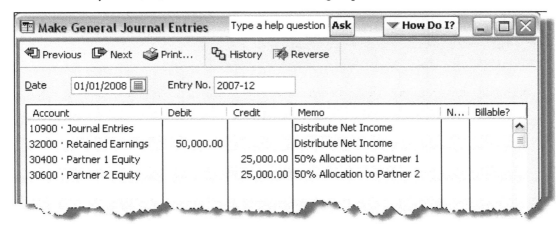

Figure 16-28 Use a General Journal entry to distribute partner's profits

Note that the General Journal Entry in Figure 16-28 debits *Retained Earnings*. That is because QuickBooks automatically closes net income into Retained Earnings each year. This is the entry you'll make each year to zero out the balance in *Retained Earnings* and distribute the net income to the partners.

Also, note that the General Journal Entry is dated January 1. That is because there is no after-closing Balance Sheet in QuickBooks. The December 31st Balance Sheet should show undistributed net income for the year. If the General Journal Entry were made on December 31, you would never be able to see a proper (before closing) December 31st Balance Sheet. Therefore, to preserve the December 31st before-closing Balance Sheet, use January 1st for this closing entry. If you want to see an after-closing Balance Sheet, use January 1st for that Balance Sheet.

> **Tip:**
> To preserve the after-closing date Balance Sheet, it is best to change the date on all
> normal business transactions that occur on January 1st to January 2nd. Use January 1st
> exclusively for the previous year's closing entries.

Summary

In this chapter, you learned how to use QuickBooks to do the following:

- Process 1099 forms for vendors (page 655)
- Edit, void, and delete transactions (page 657)
- Track fixed assets (page 662)
- Memorize and schedule transactions to be automatically entered (page 666)
- Close the year and enter special transactions for sole proprietorships and partnerships (page 670).

Chapter 17
Appendix

QuickBooks Limitations

Technical Limitations

The maximum number of transactions QuickBooks can handle is 2 billion. In other words, the number of transactions is limited more by your system's disk space and memory than by QuickBooks.

The maximum number of items in QuickBooks lists is shown in Table A-1. Note that for Items and Names in Enterprise the limit we list is a "practical" limit. That is, you can have more records than we list, but performance will be severely degraded (and the possibility of file corruption is greatly increased).

List Name	Pro, Premier	Enterprise	Macintosh
Chart of Accounts	10,000	10,000	10,000
Items – including inventory items	14,500	100,000	16,000
Fixed Asset Items	10,000	10,000	NA
Name Lists Combined – Combined total of Customers, Vendors, Employees, and Other Names	14,500	100,000	16,000
Single Name List (Customers, Vendors, Employees, or Other Name)	10,000	100,000	16,000
Sales Reps	14,500	29,000	NA
Sales Tax Codes	10,000	10,000	NA
Price Levels	100	750	NA
Per-Item Price Levels (Premier/Enterprise only)	100	750	NA
Billing Rate Levels (Premier Contractor, Professional	100	100	NA

Services, Accountant and Enterprise only)			
Memorized Transactions	14,500	29,000	30,000
Memorized Reports	14,500	29,000	??
Payroll Items	10,000	10,000	NA
Classes	10,000	10,000	10,000
Job Types (Pro only)	10,000	10,000	10,000
Vendor Types	10,000	10,000	10,000
Customer Types	10,000	10,000	10,000
A/R Terms and A/P Terms added together	10,000	10,000	10,000
Payment Methods	10,000	10,000	10,000
Shipping Methods	10,000	10,000	??
Customer Messages	10,000	10,000	10,000
To Do Items	10,000	10,000	??
Custom Fields (for customers, vendors, employees)	7 per list, 15 aggregate	12 per list, 30 aggregate	7 per list, 15 aggregate
Custom Fields (for items)	5	15	5
Form Templates	14,500	14,500	??

Table A-1 QuickBooks Maximums

Practical Limitations

The typical QuickBooks customer is a small business with 20 or fewer employees and annual revenue of less than 2 million dollars. Generally, we like to keep only a few years of detailed transactions in a data file before starting a completely new file. This depends on how much the file grows, but generally, a new file will need to be built every few years.

Data File Size

In general, The Sleeter Group recommends keeping data file sizes to within the following limits. For Simple Start, Pro and Premier editions (through QuickBooks 2006), keeping the file size to 100MB or less. For Enterprise Solutions, the file should not be much larger than 250 MB. For version 2007 and above, Premier files should not exceed 200MB and Enterprise files should not exceed 300MB.

Recommended Data File Size Maximums		
QuickBooks Editions	Pro, or Premier	Enterprise Solutions
Through version 2006	100MB or smaller	250MB or smaller
Version 2007 and later	200MB or smaller	350MB or smaller

Table A-2 Recommended Data File Size Maximums

These file size recommendations are general guidelines, based on several factors, but there is no specific maximum file size, and your system will not come to a crashing halt if you exceed these recommended sizes. As the data file grows, the overall performance of the software declines, and the risk of data corruption increases.

The rate of growth of a QuickBooks data file varies from company to company. There is no average or typical data file size, since every business tracks information differently in QuickBooks. How quickly a data file grows depends on the number of transactions, the amount of information entered per transaction, and the number of links per transaction.

For example, in QuickBooks 2005 and below, someone who enters 500, 1-line invoices per month might find that their data file is smaller than another person who enters 100, 5-line invoices per month. Also, someone who usually receives five separate payments per invoice would have a larger file than someone who typically receives only one payment per invoice.

To find out how big a data file is, open the company file and press *F2 (or Ctrl+1)*.

If you need to estimate the growth of a company file and project the size into the future, with QuickBooks 2005 and below, you can calculate the average number of monthly transactions and then apply this formula. If a company enters 100 transactions per month, on average, the data file will grow by around 200K per month (100 *2K = 200K), or 2.4MB per year (200K *12=2.4MB). In QuickBooks 2006 and higher, the growth calculation is not as predictable, but in general, the formula above will give an approximation of the growth. Note that in QuickBooks 2006 and higher, a brand new (essentially blank) data file will be approximately 6MB compared with approximately 700kb for the earlier versions.

If the annual data file size is less than 30-50 MB, QuickBooks should be quite suitable for the company. If the growth is much more than that, you should consider using QuickBooks Enterprise Solutions. If you think your data file size will exceed the recommended maximums, perhaps there are ways you could restructure either the level of detail in transactions, or maybe you could enter summarized information instead of each individual transaction as they occur.

Keep in mind that the combination of an Invoice, Payment, and Deposit are three separate transactions. Multiply the average number or monthly transactions by 2K (2 kilobytes) to determine how much the data file will grow each month.

> **Important:** The 2K multiplier does not include list information, which will also grow as new names are added to the data file. Don't forget to include list sizes when projecting the growth of the data file. See Table A-1 for maximum list sizes.

The upper limit on how large a QuickBooks data file can grow without causing noticeable performance degradation varies depending on the computer you're using. Make sure you have at least the following hardware for QuickBooks.

Minimum Hardware Requirements for QuickBooks 2015 Editions

	Pro	Premier	Enterprise
Processor Pentium II (or Similar AMD)	At Least 2.0 GHz Processor	At Least 2 GHz Processor, 2.4 recommended	At Least 2 GHz for each client and server, 2.4 recommended
RAM	At Least 1 GB (2 GB for Windows 8 64 bit)	At Least 1 GB for single user (2 GB for Windows 8 64 bit), at least 2 GB for multiple users	At Least 1GB for client and for server (more recommended for both as file size increases)
Hard Disk Space Available	2.5 GB	2.5 GB	2.5 GB for each client and server
Internet Access	All online features and services require Internet access.	All online features and services require Internet access.	All online features and services require Internet access
CD-ROM	4x CD-ROM Drive for CD installation	4x CD-ROM Drive for CD installation	4x CD-ROM Drive for CD installation
Monitor	1024x768, only the default DPI setting is supported (96 dpi/100%)	1024x768, only the default DPI setting is supported (96 dpi/100%)	1024x768, only the default DPI setting is supported (96 dpi/100%)
Operating System	Windows Vista (SP 1 or later) Windows 7 Windows 8 Windows Server 2012 Windows Small Business Server 2011, 2008	Windows Vista (SP 1 or later) Windows 7 Windows 8 Windows Server 2012 Windows Small Business Server 2011, 2008	Windows Vista (SP 1 or later) Windows 7 Windows 8 Windows Server 2012 Windows Small Business Server 2011, 2008

	Windows Server 2008, 2008 R2, 2003 (SP2)	Windows Server 2008, 2008 R2, 2003 (SP2)	Windows Server 2008, 2008 R2, 2003 (SP2)

Table A-3 Minimum Hardware Requirements

For Linux configuration, see the Enterprise Chapter

In addition to the hardware requirements above, some features require other software. For example, the Write Letters function requires Microsoft Word 2000 or above. In general, you'll want to have the following software installed on the computer.

Minimum Software Recommendations for QuickBooks 2015 Editions

Office	Microsoft Office (2003 or later) Note that some features will not work with 64 bit versions of Office. See this KB article for details: http://support.quickbooks.intuit.com/support/Articles/INF24382
PDF tools	Adobe Acrobat 5.0 or higher
Internet Explorer	10 (R3 and later), 9, 8 and 7

Table A-4 Companion Software Recommendations

Troubleshooting Slow Performance

If performance becomes an issue or you decide you do not want to keep detailed transactions for prior years, you can condense a QuickBooks data file using the Clean Up Data utility. Before you condense a data file, please read the section beginning on page 317.

If you find that QuickBooks is getting slow when entering or recording transactions, you might want to check the following:

Is the Hard Disk Almost Full?

If your hard disk gets too full, you'll begin to notice that your whole system tends to run slower.

A general rule for maintaining your hard disk performance is to keep at least 11% of the size of the hard drive free. So, a 200GB hard drive should always have at least 2GB free.

Delete any unneeded data files, and uninstall unused programs. Make sure you always use the Add/Remove Programs control panel to remove programs from your computer. NEVER delete a program from the Windows Explorer as this will cause problems in your Windows registry.

Is the Audit Trail Active?

In QuickBooks 2006 and higher, the Audit Trail is always on, so there is no way to change this preference. In earlier versions, you can disable the Audit Trail (not recommended). See page 103 for a discussion of the Audit Trail and how to turn it off in earlier versions.

Is Automatically Recall Last Transaction for This Name Active?

From the **Edit** menu choose **Preferences**. Choose **General** from the left area of the Preferences window. If the *Automatically recall last transaction for this name* option is selected, you can increase performance slightly by turning it off. This option requires QuickBooks to search backward for the last transaction using the payee name. If the register contains a large number of transactions, this can slow data entry.

Are Several Reports Open?

If you have reports open and the *Reports & Graphs* preference is set to refresh automatically, the open reports automatically recalculate each time you add new transactions.

To improve the performance, either close all open reports, and/or turn off the refresh automatically preference in the *Reports & Graphs* preferences.

Is the Data File Too Large?

If your data file is too large, performance will suffer. Generally, you should keep QuickBooks data files under 150MB or so. This is not an actual limit, but a general guideline for keeping things working smoothly and performance is a big part of that. If the file is nearing the 150MB range, you may want to condense the file or set up a new file. For a discussion of condensing, see page 317.

Use F2 to Check Details of Your Software

If you need to know details about your QuickBooks version, or about the size of your company file, press **F2**. This is particularly useful if you need to know how large the data file is, how many transactions are in the file, or what release level of QuickBooks you are running.

1.   Launch QuickBooks and open your company file.

2.   Press **F2**.

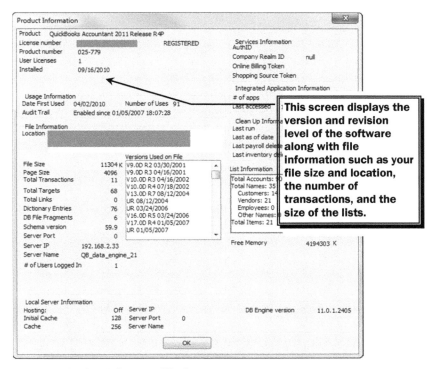

Figure 17-1 Product Information Window

Keyboard Shortcuts

Date Shortcuts			More Options		
When cursor is in a date field, this key	**Causes the date to become...**		**When editing a transaction, this key**	**Results:**	
y	First day of displayed calendar year		Tab	Move the cursor to the next field.	
r	Last day of displayed calendar year		Shift + Tab	Move the cursor to the previous editable field	
m	First day of displayed month		Return (or Enter)	Record the transaction (when black border is highlighting OK, Next, or Prev button)	
h	Last day of displayed month		Esc	Cancel editing and close the current window	
t	Today		F2 or Ctrl + 1	Display information about QuickBooks and your company file details	
w	First day of displayed week		Ctrl + a	Open the Chart of Accounts	
k	Last day of displayed week		Ctrl + d	Delete selected transaction or list Item	

+	Next day
-	Previous day

Form Fields and Registers

When a form field is selected	Results:
Ctrl + Del	Delete a line from a detail area
Ctrl + Ins	Insert a new line in a detail area
Ctrl + z	**Undo** last change
Space Bar	Select or unselect a checkbox
Page Up	Scroll register view or reports 1 page up
Page Down	Scroll register view or reports 1 page down
Home, Home, Home	Go to the top of a register (first transaction)
End, End, End	Go to the bottom of a register (last transaction)

Ctrl + e	Edit transaction or list item
Ctrl + f	Find a transaction
Ctrl + g	Go to the other account register affected by this transaction
Ctrl + h	Get the history (A/R or A/P) for the currently selected transaction
Ctrl + i	Create Invoice
Ctrl + j	Display Customer Center
Ctrl + m	Memorize a transaction
Ctrl + n	New transaction (Bill, Check, Deposit, List Item, Invoice)
Ctrl + r	Go to the register associated with the current transaction.
Ctrl + t	Display Memorized Transaction List
Ctrl + y	Display transaction journal
Ctrl + w	Display write check window

For more keyboard shortcuts, see the QuickBooks and Beyond article on Keyboard Shortcuts at http://www.sleeter.com/blog/2012/07/quickbooks-keyboard-shortcuts/.

Index

CPSIA information can be obtained
at www.ICGtesting.com
Printed in the USA
LVHW072333100419
613768LV00027B/823/P

9 781942 417